William Amos has for several years been the editorial director of five county magazines, following a decade as a columnist with the *Liverpool Daily Post*. He is also the author of *Literary Liverpool* (1971), and has spent nearly ten years researching for *The Originals*. He lives in the Lake District.

THE ORIGINALS

Who's Really Who in Fiction

WILLIAM AMOS

SPHERE BOOKS LIMITED

Sphere Books Limited, 27 Wrights Lane, London W8 5TZ
First published in Great Britain in 1985 by Jonathan Cape Ltd
Copyright © 1985 by William Amos
Published by Sphere Books 1987

Illustrations are reproduced by kind permission of the following:
BBC Hulton Picture Library (nos 1, 6, 7, 8, 9, 10, 12–17);
Jonathan Cape Ltd (nos 3, 12–17); Ann Chisholm (no 11);
The Times, London (nos 2, 5)

TRADE
MARK

Printed and bound in Great Britain by
Cox & Wyman Ltd, Reading

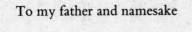
To my father and namesake

CONTENTS

FOREWORD

In five minutes, I jotted down the names of thirty characters and their originals. That was when the idea for this book first came to me. How many more might I round up, I wondered, if I really applied myself to it? Ten years later the total was 3,000. Now I had too many examples. Those of lesser interest had to be shown the door. Others easily looked up elsewhere were likewise excluded – Dryden's legion of counterparts got their marching orders, as did the army of Burns originals, although a few who might be considered conspicuous by their absence were retained.

The selection made, the next task was to impose some kind of order. Characters are arranged alphabetically, surnames first (for those who have them). Russian characters are in most instances to be found under their first names – surnames are rarely used in that country, and I have felt it wrong to enter them under their patronymics. Thus, Nastasya Filipovna is listed as Nastasya Filipovna, not Filipovna, Nastasya. (Two obvious exceptions to this general rule are the Karamazovs and the Karenins.)

Wherever possible I have tried to indicate the strength of the identification and the extent to which the character is based on the model – whether the identification is admitted by the author or assumed; whether the character is wholly or partly inspired by the original; or whether the model is a prototype whose example, rather than personal acquaintance, has suggested him to the author. Writers both add to and subtract from their models in developing fictitious counterparts. For example, Barry Gifford and Lawrence Lee, the authors of *Jack's Book: Jack Kerouac in the Lives and Words of his Friends* (1979), reveal in consuming detail how many models used by Kerouac are usually only part of the characters they have inspired, and in real life might have acted quite differently from them.

Because real-life models appear under other names not only in novels and plays but also in essays and poetry, my net has been cast wide to embrace the whole of literature.

The outcome is a book containing facts previously unpublished and information to be found in no other single source. Like all works of reference, however, it is indebted to others which have ploughed allied fields. Although I have not relied solely, for example, on Richard Ellmann's definitive study of Joyce for my *Ulysses* entries or on George D. Painter's exhaustive account of Proust for *A la recherche du temps perdu*, without such biographies the hill to be climbed would have been much steeper. A bibliography of major works consulted is given for easy reference at the end of the book, thus enabling me to avoid tiresome repetition in the main body of the text, where references are confined to those of particular significance for readers wishing to explore further.

W.D.A.

INTRODUCTION:
ORIGINAL SINS

When an author denies his characters have real-life originals, don't believe him. Tolstoy, Dickens and Maugham; Meredith, Wells and Waugh . . . all were less than honest.

Tolstoy's use of relatives as models was obvious to his family, yet he noted how sorry he would be should anyone think he intended to depict any real person. In denying his use of Leigh Hunt as 'Harold Skimpole', Dickens added deviousness to duplicity, privately revelling in his portrait's accuracy, publicly disavowing all resemblance and averting his victim's wrath by publishing favourable profiles elsewhere. Maugham denied basing a character on Hugh Walpole, only to admit the identification once his model was dead.

Adroitly, Meredith deflected the protest of another agonised original: 'This is too bad of you', a young friend cried, 'Willoughby is me!' 'No, my dear fellow, he is all of us.'

Wells's disingenuous preface to one of his novels ('If a character in a book should have the luck to seem like a real human being that is no excuse for imagining an "original"') fooled no one: the models were all too recognisable, and publisher after publisher declined to handle *Apropos of Dolores* through fear of libel. Evelyn Waugh sought to persuade Cyril Connolly that he was not in *Unconditional Surrender* by blaming the identification on idiots ignorant of the processes of the imagination . . . But 'Everard Spruce' is indisputably Connolly all the same.

And so it goes on. Agatha Christie claimed all her characters were pure fiction, despite the presence of her second husband and Sir Leonard Woolley's wife in *Murder in Mesopotamia*; and although Graham Greene has said he finds it impossible to write about real people, several are to be found variously disguised in his novels.

Perhaps it is egotism that prompts some authors to prefer readers to think all characters are created solely from the imagination, forged only on the anvil of the writer's genius — an attitude dismissed by

Maugham as self-deception. But although most authors use models from life, few do so without transmuting them, often beyond recognition. Though there would have been no 'Lord Jim' without Augustine Podmore Williams, the imagination of Conrad swiftly transformed Williams into another character altogether. Forster, Huxley, Isherwood, Mauriac, Moravia and Powell – all have described their use of real people; and all have echoed the emphasis placed by Charlotte Brontë on reality's role in *suggesting*, never dictating events and characters.

Compton-Burnett found acquaintances too flat for the purposes of her novels; they had to be exaggerated. Maugham felt that a character borrowed from life without further development was never completely convincing. Joyce Cary considered real-life models too complex for his requirements, just as Huxley found it necessary to simplify the people he used. Anthony Powell and Graham Greene have both expressed their belief that real-life models, undeveloped, can successfully be used only as minor characters . . . which may be the reason why the novels of Gilbert Cannan are no longer read: it was his practice virtually to transcribe all his models onto the page, with little modification. Lawrence credited him with having the memory of a lawyer, and the outcome was not so much fiction as faction.

If unadorned, drawn-from-life portrayal succeeds only with walking-on parts, and models for major characters are transformed into the author's own creation after the first couple of paragraphs, are originals really necessary? Listen long enough to writers and you might conclude that their models are inconsequential to the point of irrelevance. Certainly, the readers' guessing games which originals inspire are for authors a great irritant.

For Proust, they were particularly vexing. His habit of combining several people's traits in a single character meant that as many as half-a-dozen different identifications could be partially correct, but none could be entirely right – a situation as exasperating for readers as it must have been exhausting for Proust, trying to explain his artistry. Balzac complained of the impertinence of more than seventy women who claimed to be his 'Foedora'. Goethe had to travel incognito to avoid being pestered by people wishing to know who was the real 'Charlotte'. Auden viewed attempts to identify Shakespeare's 'Dark Lady' as little more than idle curiosity – were they to succeed, he contended, they would in no way illuminate the sonnets. William Cooper – with the publication of one of his novels postponed through risk of libel – wished people would concentrate on reading him instead of trying to spot originals. And Evelyn Waugh castigated asses who treated fiction as a gossip column.

Ironically, the angriest outbursts have tended to come from authors whose readers' speculations were right. Fuelling their ire is an understandable horror of litigation. In 1910 a libel action established that where there was evidence that some people might reasonably believe a plaintiff was the person referred to, it was immaterial that the writer never intended to refer to him. The minefield thus created for authors has prompted Graham Greene to recall a firm of solicitors who in the 1930s specialised in cross-checking characters' names with entries in the London telephone directory. The rarer the name, the greater the risk — hence Greene's use of Jones, Brown and Smith in *The Comedians*.

Happily, these hazards have been reduced by the Defamation Act of 1952. No longer can the innocent novelist be so easily convicted of libelling a person unknown to him; but publishers must establish either that the words were not defamatory or that no reference to the plaintiff was intended and no circumstances were known by which he or she might be thought to be referred to. They are also required to withdraw offending material, and this, coupled with the cost of establishing innocence, means that unintentional defamation is still best avoided — witness the case of Sir Nigel Fisher, MP. In 1980 he accepted an apology and his legal costs in settlement of a High Court action over a fictional reference to an MP of the same name in an educational text-book — a mishap which also cost the authors a substantial donation to a charity of the MP's choice.

Same-name trouble has long been a pitfall for writers. Hawthorne was bedevilled by it, 'Judge Pyncheon' in *The House of the Seven Gables* turning out to have a number of namesakes. Thackeray's *Catherine* — about a notorious eighteenth-century murderess, Catherine Hayes — fell foul of the Irish prima donna, Catherine Hayes. Changing his name to 'Lewis Seymour', a reader sued George Moore for writing *Lewis Seymour and Some Women*; he lost his case. A four-year delay in the publication of a now long-forgotten novel, *Eustace Conway* (1834), meant that its villain, 'Captain Marryat', a name unknown at the time of writing, now had a celebrated namesake in Captain Marryat, author of *Peter Simple*. Marryat promptly proposed a duel which *Eustace Conway*'s unfortunate creator had to decline, being in holy orders. Understandable though that was, Larry Niven's choice of 'Naomi Mitchison' as the name of the principal character in *The Patchwork Girl* (1980) verges on the incredible: one wonders how both author and publisher managed to remain unaware of the existence of Naomi Mitchison, writer. When a character follows a profession, it is advisable to check that there is nobody of the same name doing the same job. Tom Sharpe doubtless thought he was safe with his television personality Cuthbert Cuthbertson in *Porterhouse Blue* (1974) ... until Cuthbert Cuthbertson, BBC television producer, took legal action.

But in striving to concoct improbable names, novelists can never win: reality always outstrips them. Lucius Quintus Cincinnatus Lamar, Miss Bullock Fetherstonhaugh, Unity Valkyrie Mitford, Tryphena Sparks, Ada Nemesis Cooper ... these are the names of real-life originals, not characters. And as Evelyn Waugh remarked, what novelist could have invented the name Asquith?

However unlikely the name you have devised, somebody, somewhere, will be signing his cheques with it. Sue Townsend's *The Secret Diary of Adrian Mole* (1982) cast an unwelcome spotlight on Adrian Mole, a lecturer at a North London polytechnic. Indeed, names don't even have to match for an author to be in trouble. In 1891 a West African trader, James Pinnock, was awarded £200 damages against the publishers Chapman and Hall when he alleged he had been portrayed as 'James Peacock', a West African trader who owed his fortune to sharp practice. Forty years later, the syllabic similarity between 'Q. C. Savory' and J. B. Priestley, together with other factors suggesting Priestley, caused Graham Greene's *Stamboul Train* to be withdrawn for reprinting.

It has been Isherwood's practice to obtain written declarations from his originals that they will not sue, and this precaution is now often insisted upon by publishers sensing possible trouble. For as Angela Thirkell's publisher once cautioned her, the stock, prefatory 'all characters are imaginary' disclaimer is worthless, cutting no ice either with public or with lawyers. ('All the characters in *Changing Places* and *Small World* are figments of the imagination', David Lodge tells me. 'It says so in the prefatory note at the beginning of each book, so it must be true ... ').

Such is now the cost of defending a libel action that if you fancy you might be identified with a character in a novel about to be published you need only intimate that you might sue and that can be enough to stop publication, whether the character is modelled upon you or not. In 1983, Sheila MacLeod's seventh novel ~~002~~ about the break-up of a show-business marriage ~~002~~ encountered this problem when publishers refused to handle it without clearance from her ex-husband, a well known singer/actor. He would not sign an undertaking not to sue, so *Axioms* remained in limbo until a less inhibited house brought it out in 1984. Other publishers had not been persuaded by MacLeod's insistence that her novel's show-business husband bore no relation to her own ex-spouse, nor were they moved by her protest at the absurdity of authors having to obtain clearance for publication from their fictitious characters. Similarly, publishers tend not to share Evelyn Waugh's view that no offence will be taken by an original, however closely portrayed, provided he is presented as being attractive to women.

Oh for the days, as Anthony Burgess has remarked, when instead of seeking money for their petty injuries, originals would settle the matter more healthily with fisticuffs; or authors would respond, as did Hemingway, by offering to knock a protesting model down a few times, or perhaps once, depending upon his ability to get up again. Some forty years later, however, Hemingway was more circumspect, declining an invitation to describe his technique for transmuting real life into fiction lest it serve as a handbook for libel lawyers.

Traduced originals, Hemingway had come to realise, could be on to a good thing. By 1981, nobody was left in any doubt of it: a Wyoming jury awarded a baton-twirling Miss America contestant libel damages totalling $26,500,000 (more than £10 million) against a US magazine publisher. She claimed her friends thought a sexually adventurous, baton-twirling Miss America aspirant in a story was based on her. The publisher's decision to appeal was as predictable as his protest that if checks had to be made to ensure no fictional character resembled a real person, no further fiction would be published in America.

Less consideration is accorded originals who are merely exploited rather than misrepresented. When he learned of the success of *King Solomon's Mines*, the Swazi warrior who was the inspiration of 'Umslopogaas' hinted in vain that a share of the profits would be more acceptable than the hunting knife Rider Haggard gave him. Similarly, the original of the romantic doctor in Maugham's 'The Happy Man' complained that Maugham and several other writers had profited handsomely from his story . . . but what was in it for him?

The spectacle of models on the make should not blind us, however, to the pain of being fictionalised. It is difficult not to feel sorry for the devastated Hugh Walpole, whose last years were blighted by Maugham's portrayal of him as Alroy Kear in *Cakes and Ale*.

'Kear' might have been modified had Maugham's novel appeared in the nineteenth-century heyday of serial publication. This allowed authors to make amends to offended originals, and the models themselves to influence the subsequent development of the characters they inspired. The minuscule Mrs Jane Seymour Hill, London chiropodist and hairdresser, much distressed by her portrayal as 'Miss Mowcher' in Dickens's *David Copperfield*, promptly charged the author with heartless caricature of her deformities, causing him to reintroduce her more favourably in later instalments.

Far from taking offence, other originals have delighted in their portrayal. Alexander Woollcott was so tickled by his representation as the impossible 'Sheridan Whiteside' in Moss Hart and George S. Kaufman's *The Man Who Came to Dinner* that he toured with the play in the role he had inspired. Similarly diverted by the notion of being portrayed on the stage, the London drama critic of *The Times*, A. B. Walkley, allowed the actor playing 'Trotter' in Shaw's *Fanny's First Play* to study him closely before deciding on make-up.

Originals have also been known to graduate from models to become their authors' accomplices. Richmal Crompton's 'William' drafted the occasional story for his sister when her inspiration waned; Sapper's 'Bulldog Drummond' took over at his creator's typewriter when Sapper died, as did the original of 'Albert Campion' upon the demise of Margery Allingham.

This incestuous, literary self-cloning is but an extension of the fundamental fact that most characters in fiction are to some degree a projection of aspects of their creators. But writers contemplating suing anyone for suggesting self-portrayal should ponder the experience of Stephen Vizinczey. In 1971 he took legal action against a German magazine which had identified him with the hero of his *In Praise of Older Women*. He was awarded derisory damages of one halfpenny 002 without costs, which virtually bankrupted him.

We should not be surprised by authors' denials of their originals. Fiction, after all, is licensed lie-telling. 'When I was a little boy', Isaac Bashevis Singer has remarked, 'they called me a liar but now that I am grown up they call me a writer.'

And when an aggrieved original protests, mendacity can be kinder than the brutal honesty of George Eliot. Apologising to a clergyman who had recognised himself in *Scenes of Clerical Life*, she explained that she had thought he was dead.

As one approaches the present day, identifiable models become increasingly thin on the ground: not because they are no longer used, but because no writer is going to risk a libel action while they are still around. William Burroughs admits to basing 'Hamburger Mary' in *Nova Express* on a scientologist from Portland, Oregon, but he's not saying who. Anita Brookner tells me she prefers to keep her sources to herself, and who can blame her? 'I fear all the people in *Not a Penny More, Not a Penny Less* are still very much alive (crooks included)', says Jeffrey Archer, lips consequently sealed. And while I could put names to Cliff Lewis in John Osborne's *Look Back in Anger,* Dolores Ryan in Jacqueline Susann's *Dolores* or Artemisa and Helena in Gore Vidal's *Two Sisters,* for the time being it is prudent not to . . .

Libel, however, is not the only reason for authors' reluctance to admit to drawing characters from life. For some, originals are an embarrassment. Their models have served their purpose: they have given the creative wheel a shove, but now it has left them far behind and the author in the driving seat is loth to acknowledge them. It is a curious stance. A chef might present a confection as all his own work, but he would never claim it owed nothing to the ingredients.

'A novelist who puts real people into his books will simplify and change them to the point where they have lost touch with their originals', says A. N. Wilson, complaining that this does not stop posterity from believing that Princess Maria Bolkonskaya 'is' Tolstoy's mother or that Lady Diana Cooper 'is' Mrs Algernon Stitch.

That belief is held because the originals are recognisable in those characters. Princess Maria and Mrs Stitch may well have attributes not to be found in their models. One expects writers to transform, exaggerate, embellish and otherwise develop their characters. That is their business. But so long as the initial inspiration for those characters remains identifiable, identified they will be.

Martin Amis claims that only minor writers use real people for major characters. Exit, limping, Dickens, Tolstoy, Proust . . . and not a few notable writers of our own time, I fancy. But to discover who is really who in the novels of today we will have to await the authors' embalmment in biographies and the publication of their correspondence. A letter from the critic Mary Furness to Martin Amis about Mary in *Other People,* perhaps? Or a note from Amis to Clive James about Nicholas Crane in *Brilliant Creatures*?

There are those who contend that the identification of originals has less to do with literature than with vulgar curiosity. But just as a wall owes much to the builder's choice of bricks, so literature cannot be divorced from its raw materials ~~002~~ people. Through their personalities and predicaments, their eccentricities and exploits, the people thronging the pages of this book have inspired both characters and plots. However loftily their contribution is dismissed, one fact is indisputable: without them, those characters and plots would never have been created.

A

'A', in the essays of William Hazlitt. Sooner or later, Mozart's *Don Giovanni* would have been performed in England anyway; that this was sooner rather than later was due to William Ayrton (1777–1858), who was Hazlitt's 'A'. The son of a vicar-choral of St Paul's Cathedral, and son-in-law of the composer Samuel Arnold, he went abroad in 1816 to recruit singers for Italian opera at the King's Theatre in London. There, in the following year, he was responsible for England's first production of *Don Giovanni*. So successful was his season that his career as a musical director must have seemed assured. But he was less adept at directing people, and disputes within his fractious company forced him to resign. When he again took the post of musical director, in 1821, opposition from a hostile committee compelled him to resign a second time. Devoting the rest of his life to writing, he became the leading music critic of his day, with friends including the essayist Charles Lamb and George Hogarth (see Wickfield, Agnes).

ABBOTT, Jerusha ('Judy'), in Jean Webster's *Daddy-Long-Legs* (1912). Adelaide Crapsey (1878–1914) wrote but one small volume of verse, published in the year after her death, but for that she is still remembered. It was edited by her friend, the New York writer Jean Webster, who is believed to have modelled Judy Abbott upon her. A year later, Webster herself was dead.

ABERCROMBIE, Sir Ambrose, in Evelyn Waugh's *The Loved One: An Anglo-American Tragedy* (1948), according to Sheridan Morley's *Tales from the Hollywood Raj* (1983), is the England cricketer turned Hollywood film actor, Sir C. Aubrey Smith (1863–1948), who died the day before filming of *The Forsyte Saga* was due to start. In this he was to have played Old Jolyon, a role he had long coveted. Epitomising Britain, he was in 1937 described by the *New York Times* as 'the Bank of England, the cliffs of Dover, the rock of Gibraltar and several super-dreadnoughts rolled into one'. See also Hinsley, Sir Francis.

ACHILLES, in Hilda Doolittle's *Helen in Egypt* (1961), represents D.H. Lawrence (see Rampion, Mark), who prior to 1918 was among Hilda Doolittle's intimates — so much so that he has been among those credited with the paternity of her daughter, Perdita, although Cecil Gray (see Sharpe, James) was more probably the father. Doolittle laments her rejection by Lawrence in her poem 'The Poet'.

ACTAEON, in Ben Jonson's *Cynthia's Revels* (1601), is Robert Devereux, Second Earl of Essex (1567–1601). A favourite of Elizabeth I, he incurred her displeasure by his lack of success in opposing rebels in Ireland and by conspiring to compel her to dismiss his political enemies. He was beheaded for treason.

ADAMS, Dr Henry, in Ernest Hemingway's 'Indian Camp' (*In Our Time*, 1925), is the author's father, Dr Clarence Edmonds Hemingway, a general practitioner from Oak Park, Illinois. In poor health and financial difficulties, he committed suicide with a revolver in 1928. Thirty-three years later, his son chose a shot-gun.

ADAMS, Parson, in Henry Fielding's *Joseph Andrews* (1742). So absent-minded was the Revd William Young (1702–57) that he was reputed once to have written a letter to himself, and while an army chaplain to have strolled, Aeschylus in hand, into the lines of the enemy, who obligingly directed him back to his regiment. From Gillingham, in Dorset, he collaborated with Fielding in translating Aristophanes' *Plutus*. When it was suggested to him that he was Parson Adams, he is said to have threatened to knock his 'accuser' down. He was one of the witnesses to the assignment of the novel's copyright, sold for £183 11s.

ADLER, Irene, in Sir Arthur Conan Doyle's 'A Scandal in Bohemia' (1891; *The Adventures of Sherlock Holmes*, 1892), has two suggested prototypes, in Ludmilla Hubel and Lola Montez. Hubel, an Austrian actress, was mistress and subsequently wife of the Austro-Hungarian emperor's nephew, Archduke John Salvator of Tuscany, with whom she disappeared in 1891 when the ship taking them to a new life in South America was presumed to have sunk.

Montez was the Irish-born American adventuress and dancer Marie Dolores Eliza Rosanna Gilbert (1818–61). As mistress of the elderly King Ludwig of Bavaria she found herself in virtual control of the country, from which she was banished after the King was compelled to abdicate. After further escapades, including fleeing, a fugitive from a charge of bigamy, from England to Spain, she settled in San Francisco, devoting her remaining years to caring for outcast women.

ADRIAN, in Mary Shelley's *The Last Man* (1826). For students of science fiction, the appeal of *The Last Man* is its pioneering role as the second novel of that genre. For those more interested in the author's husband, it presents in Adrian a portrait of Percy Bysshe Shelley. See Glowry, Scythrop.

AG, in Ernest Hemingway's 'A Very Short Story' (*In Our Time*, 1925), is Agnes H. von Kurowski (see Barkley, Catherine). In later editions, Hemingway prudently changed the character's name to Luz.

AGATE, in George Moore's 'Lui et elles' (*Memoirs of My Dead Life*, 1921), is Mrs Pearl Craigie (see Theale, Milly), with whom Moore collaborated as a playwright, becoming infatuated with her ... and not a little resentful when she discarded him in favour of Lord Curzon (see Derringham, John).

AGATHA, Aunt, in P.G. Wodehouse's Bertie Wooster stories (1915–74), is the author's aunt, Mary Deane (1845–1940), sister of Louisa (see Travers, Dahlia Portarlington) and a novelist and poet of despotic temperament.

AGATHA MIKHAILOVNA, in Leo Tolstoy's *Anna Karenina* (1873–7). Seduced by the author while she was employed in his aunt's house, Agatha Mikhailovna Trubetskaya was dismissed when her mistress discovered the liaison. She subsequently obtained a post with Tolstoy's sister Marya, raising her children. Such was her devotion to animals that she supplied mice with milk, spiders with flies and could not bring herself to tread on a cockroach or to eat meat. The Tolstoy children called her 'the dogs' governess' because she supervised the kennels. Reprimanded for using a new dressing-gown (hand-made by her mistress) for the accouchement of one of her bitches, she replied: 'Come now, little countess, do you really

think a dressing-gown is worth more than one of God's creatures?'
She habitually knitted a stocking as she walked.

AGNES, in Henrik Ibsen's *Brand* (1866), is in part Thea Bruun,
sister of Christopher Bruun (see Brand). Ibsen met her when she was
living near Rome in 1864, her mother having taken her to Italy to
alleviate her tuberculosis. She died after returning to her native
Norway a few months later.

AGNÈS, in Molière's *L'École des femmes* (1664), is supposedly
part-inspired by the actress Armande Béjart (1645–1700), who
married Molière in 1662. Sister of Molière's dramatic collaborator
and putative mistress, Madeleine Béjart, she has been described as a
talented, vivacious *ingénue*. The marriage was not a happy one, and
following her husband's death she married Guérin Estriché. She
retired from the stage in 1694.

A.H., in Alexander Pope's 'Bathos, the art of sinking in Poetry'
(*Miscellanies*, 1727–8) and *The Dunciad* (1728), is Aaron Hill
(1685–1750), dramatist, miscellaneous writer, and floater of
schemes to supply wood from Scotland for naval shipbuilding, to
colonise what later became Georgia, to extract oil from beechmast
and to manufacture potash – all unsuccessful.

AHAB, Captain, in Herman Melville's *Moby-Dick* (1851), has as
prototype Owen Chase, first mate of the whaler *Essex*, which in
1820 was sunk in the Pacific by a sperm whale. For ninety-one days,
Chase and four other survivors drifted in an open boat. Three died,
and on Chase's suggestion he and his companion ate the last man to
perish before they were picked up by a ship from London, bound for
Chile. Chase recorded his adventure in *Narrative of the Most Extraordinary and Distressing Ship Wreck of the Whaleship Essex*.

AHEARN, in Irwin Shaw's *The Young Lions* (1948). Critics welcomed this as an outstanding novel of the Second World War and it
has gone into many editions. But the novelist Ernest Hemingway
(1898–1961) – according to his biographer, Carlos Baker –
thought it a disgraceful, ignoble book, written by a coward who had
never fired a shot in anger. He took the American war correspondent, Ahearn, to be a caricature of himself, and saw his younger
brother, the journalist and wartime documentary film-maker
Leicester Hemingway (1915–   ), in Private Leroy Keane, an

obnoxious communications clerk striving to live up to the image of an elder brother who had been a hero of the First World War. While Shaw might have had Hemingway in mind as Ahearn's prototype – though there *were* other American war correspondents – Hemingway's identification of Keane as his brother suggests paranoia.

AIGLEMONT, Julie d', in Honoré de Balzac's *La Femme de trente ans* (1831–4), is George Sand (see Maupin, Camille). Princess Cristina Belgiojoso (see Foedora) has also been suggested as a prototype.

AILEEN, Lady, in Frances Hodgson Burnett's *The Captain's Youngest* (1894; published in the United States as *Piccino*), is part-inspired by Helena, Comtesse de Noailles (*d.* 1908), an Englishwoman whose mother was a member of the Baring banking family. In 1849, at the age of twenty-five, she married Antonin, second son of Juste de Noailles, Prince-Duc de Poix; they separated three years later. Her eccentricities included refusing to travel when the wind was in the east; having red glass in her windows for health reasons; wearing a fur hat in bed; hanging a string of onions by her bedroom door to repel infection; eating all her meals behind a screen; and keeping a cow tethered by every ground-floor window so that its beneficent breath could infuse each room. In 1865 she bought and adopted the child model Maria Pasqua (see Piccino), subsequently recounting the story of the adoption to Burnett, who had made her acquaintance in the South of France. Maria's life is chronicled in Magdalen Goffin's *Maria Pasqua* (1979).

AIMÉ, in Marcel Proust's *A la recherche du temps perdu* (1913–27). Remember the story of the two men who opened a sandwich bar and were so proud of their range that they offered £10,000 to anyone ordering a sandwich they could not supply? It wasn't long before the partner behind the counter rushed, panic-stricken, into the back room where his colleague was buttering bread. Somebody had ordered an elephant sandwich. 'Leave this to me,' said the back-room partner, making his way to the counter. 'Elephant sandwiches, sir? Certainly. How many thousand do you require? What? You expect us to cut up our elephant just for *one* sandwich . . . !' Stay with me: we are now arriving at the Proust connection. Aimé is principally inspired by Olivier Dabescat, a Basque who was appointed head waiter at the Ritz Hotel, Paris, upon its opening in 1898. For Dabescat, nothing was too much trouble: even the diets of guests' exotic pets were catered for, with live pigeons and rabbits.

And to satisfy an American's whim, Dabescat duly served elephant's feet, without so much as a blink, I suspect, of his monocled eyelid. Not for him the conservationist conscience of the sandwich-bar proprietor; he arranged for a zoo elephant to be slaughtered.

AIRCASTLE, Mr, in Samuel Foote's *The Cozeners* (1774), is the Irish classical scholar and poet Usher Gahagan, who in 1749 went to the scaffold for coinage offences. While in Newgate Prison awaiting execution, he translated Pope's *Messiah* and *Temple of Fame* into Latin verse, dedicating the published result to the prime minister, in the forlorn hope of a pardon.

ALBERT, in Johann Wolfgang von Goethe's *The Sorrows of Young Werther* (1774), is Johann Christian Kestner (1741—1800), a Wetzlar lawyer and friend of the author. He married Charlotte Buff (see Charlotte).

ALBRECHT, Grand Duke, in Thomas Mann's *Royal Highness* (1909), is modelled on the author's elder brother, Heinrich Mann (see Settembrini). Heinrich and Albrecht parted their hair in precisely the same way and both suffered from neurasthenia, which Heinrich described as 'my profession and my fate'. The portrait is both affectionate and prescient: Albrecht abdicates in favour of his young brother, just as Heinrich was in time eclipsed by young Thomas.

ALCONLEIGH, Lord, in Nancy Mitford's *The Pursuit of Love* (1945) and *Love in a Cold Climate* (1949), is the author's father, David Bertram Ogilvy Freeman-Mitford, Second Baron Redesdale (1878—1958). His sporting proclivities included hunting his children with a bloodhound, enlivening his time in a London office (before he came into his inheritance) by hunting rats with a mongoose, and hiring a chub-fuddler to further his campaign against coarse fish. Prior to 1939, he shared the pro-Nazi enthusiasm of his daughter Unity (see Malmains, Eugenia), declaring Hitler to be 'a right-thinking man of irreproachable sincerity and honesty' and an example the Germans could be 'proud to follow'.

ALCYON, in Edmund Spenser's *Colin Clouts Come Home Againe* (1595) and *Daphnaïda* (1591), is the poet and translator Sir Arthur Gorges (d. 1625). Also a navigator, in 1597 he commanded Raleigh's flagship on the Islands voyage. *Daphnaïda* is an elegy on the death of his wife, Lady Douglas.

ALDEN, Roberta, in Theodore Dreiser's *An American Tragedy* (1925), is Grace 'Billie' Brown, a secretary in a New York factory who in 1906, at the age of eighteen, was seduced and murdered by her employer's social-climbing nephew (see Griffiths, Clyde).

ALDINGTON, Lord and Lady, in Ford Madox Ford's *The New Humpty-Dumpty* (1912, written under the pseudonym Daniel Chaucer), are supposedly Arthur Marwood, with whom Ford founded the *English Review*, and Ford's mistress, the feminist novelist Violet Hunt. See Tietjens, Christopher and Nesbit, Norah.

ALDWINKLE, Mrs, in Aldous Huxley's *Those Barren Leaves* (1925), owes her egotism and life-style to Lady Ottoline Morrell (see Roddice, Hermione and Wimbush, Priscilla). Her forceful patronage was sometimes resented by those she strove to influence and assist. 'Why must you always use your *will* so much, why can't you let things be, without always grasping and trying to know and to dominate?' asked D.H. Lawrence. Huxley was an undergraduate when he first made her acquaintance, writing home, 'Lady Ottoline . . . is a quite incredible creature – arty beyond the dreams of avarice . . . She is intelligent, but her affectation is overwhelming.'

ALEXANDRA, in Muriel Spark's *The Abbess of Crewe* (1974), represents Richard Nixon (see Monckton, President Richard) in this satire on the Watergate scandal. Researching the novel's background, the author asked Harold Macmillan if he had bugged anyone. He replied that he would never be such a fool as to bug himself (as Nixon had done), and recalled an overseas visit during which he had been invited to go out into the open, where his hosts thought he might talk with less restraint. But he remained on his guard, he told Spark, because he was aware that even the trees were bugged. Thus, the poplars in her book's Avenue of Meditation became similarly equipped.

AL FAY, Baydr, in Harold Robbins's *The Pirate* (1974), has as prototype Adnan Khashoggi, a Saudi Arabian entrepreneur whose accoutrements have included a private Boeing jet, a £22 million yacht and an English wife who, after their divorce in 1974, sued him for $2540 million – a world-record matrimonial claim. In 1975, during investigation of the Lockheed international bribes scandal, it emerged that in seven years Khashoggi received $106 million commission from the aircraft corporation. In 1979, he sued the US aircraft manufacturer Northrop Corporation for more than £100 million to cover an alleged defaulted commission on sales of fighter planes to Saudi Arabia.

ALICE, in Lewis Carroll's *Alice's Adventures in Wonderland* (1865) and *Through the Looking-Glass* (1872). 'I have had scores of child-friends since your time,' the author wrote to Alice Pleasance Liddell after her marriage, 'but they have been quite a different thing.' Yet when she wrote asking him to be godfather to one of her sons, he did not reply: she had grown up, and when his young friends matured he tended to lose interest. Alice Liddell was born in 1852, the daughter of Henry George Liddell, an Oxford double first who was co-author of Liddell and Scott's *Greek Lexicon*, became head of Westminster School in 1846 and in 1855 was appointed Dean of Christ Church, Oxford, where Carroll (Charles Lutwidge Dodgson) was a mathematics lecturer. It was as a pioneer amateur photographer that Dodgson made the acquaintance of the Liddell children, conceiving an affection for Alice in particular. Mrs Liddell, however, became uneasy about his relationship with her daughter and discouraged his attentions, destroying all his early letters to Alice ... who in 1928 sold the original manuscript of *Alice in Wonderland* for £15,400. As a girl, she had drawing lessons at Oxford from Ruskin (see Herbert, Mr) and loved and was loved by Prince Leopold, youngest son of Queen Victoria and fourth in line of succession, but his marriage to a commoner was out of the question. (Ironically, recent genealogical research has shown Alice to have been Queen Elizabeth II's fourth cousin twice removed.) In 1880 she married Reginald Gervis Hargreaves (1852–1926), son of a wealthy calico printer of Accrington, Lancashire, and a student of Dodgson from 1872 to 1878. They had three sons (one named after Leopold), two of whom were killed in the First World War. Alice died in 1934 and was buried in Hampshire, at the parish church of Lyndhurst. Several candidates have been suggested as John Tenniel's model for the illustrations of *Alice*. Dodgson chose Mary Hilton Probert (née Badcock), daughter of a canon of Ripon. Spotting her portrait in a photographer's shop window, he sent a copy to the artist, but he later complained that Tenniel refused to use models, the illustrator declaring 'he no more needed one than I should a multiplication table.' Tenniel has been said to have used instead Kate Blaker (née Lemon), daughter of Mark

Lemon, editor of *Punch*. Tenniel gave Kate a first edition of *Alice's Adventures in Wonderland*; Dodgson presented Mary with a first edition of *Through the Looking-Glass*. Alice Theodora Fox (née Raikes, *b.* 1862) is credited with inspiring the notion of 'Looking-Glass Country'. A distant cousin of Dodgson and eldest daughter of Henry Cecil Raikes, MP, who became Postmaster General, she is said to have given the author the idea for *Through the Looking-Glass* in the course of a conversation about mirror images.

ALICE, in A.A. Milne's *When We Were Very Young* (1924) and *Now We Are Six* (1927), was in real life named Olive and was nanny to the author's son (see Christopher Robin). When her charge left home for boarding school in 1929, she became Mrs Alfred Brockwell. Her husband was not, however, one of the Buckingham Palace guard, as Milne's verses suggest. A former soldier, he was at the time of his marriage a Post Office engineer also serving in the Territorial Army – he was later awarded the British Empire Medal and the Imperial Service Medal. In retirement, the couple lived in the Sussex village of Three Oaks.

ALISSA, in André Gide's *La Porte étroite* (1909), is in part the author's wife, Madeleine. Somewhat puritanical, she found her chances of earthly love blighted by her husband's homosexuality.

ALLEN, Charles Wrexell, in the American novelist Winston Churchill's *The Celebrity* (1898). The outstanding New York newspaper reporter of his day, Richard Harding Davis (1864–1916) is Churchill's 'celebrity'. His coverage of six wars made him a household name, and to this he added the talents of a prolific novelist, short-story writer and dramatist – he wrote twenty-five plays. How did he find the time? Perhaps the answer is that he was a compulsive writer: as managing editor of *Harper's Weekly*, he roamed the world sending back 'letters' for publication and eventual collection in five books.

ALLWORTHY, Squire, in Henry Fielding's *Tom Jones* (1749), is the author's benefactor, Ralph Allen (1694–1764) of Prior Park, Bath. Of obscure origin, he became deputy postmaster of Bath and made his fortune by devising, in 1720, a system of cross-posts for England and Wales, establishing daily horse mails to the larger towns. This gave him an average annual income of £12,000, and he amassed further wealth by quarrying Combe Down for Bath free-

stone, a material predominant in the rebuilding of the city. He is said
to have given Fielding £200 before he even met him; after the
author's death he helped to educate Fielding's children; and in his
will he left £100 each to Fielding's widow and surviving members of
her family. His philanthropy prompted Pope's lines in the *Epilogue to
the Satires of Horace*: 'Let humble Allen with an awkward shame/Do
good by stealth, and blush to find it fame.'

ALMAYER, in Joseph Conrad's *Almayer's Folly* (1895) and *An
Outcast of the Islands* (1896), is William Charles Olmeyer
(1848–1900). Born in Java, of Dutch extraction, he was a trader in
Berau, Borneo, when the author first met him in 1887. Olmeyer had
taken charge of the trading station in 1870, having been sent there by
a relative by marriage, Captain William Lingard (see Lingard, Tom).
Noted for his grandiose ideas, he spent part of his time in the
hinterland, prospecting for gold. His wife, 'Mrs Almayer' in
Conrad's novels, was a Eurasian who bore him eleven children; she
died in 1892.

ALMOND, Julia. See Starling, Julia.

ALPHA THE MORALIST, in Czesław Miłosz's *The Captive
Mind* (1953), is the Polish allegorical novelist Jerzy Andrzejewski
(1909–83), author of *Ashes and Diamonds* (1948).

ALTHEA, in Richard Lovelace's 'To Althea from Prison' (*c.*1642),
is supposedly Lucy Sacheverell, to whom the poet was betrothed.
Also suggested as his 'Lucasta', she is said to have married another,
supposing Lovelace to have died from wounds at Dunkirk.

ALVAN, in George Meredith's *The Tragic Comedians* (1880).
Though wealthy and addicted to good living, the pioneer German
socialist Ferdinand Lassalle (1825–64) was indefatigable in his prosecution of unfashionable causes. He is Meredith's Alvan in this novel,
which is based on his love for Helene von Dönniges (see von
Rüdiger, Clotilde), who gave way to parental pressure and abandoned her plans to marry him. Learning that he had been supplanted
by Count Racowitza of Walachia, Lassalle fought a duel with his
rival, sustaining wounds from which he died.

AMANDA, in the *Spring* (1728) of James Thomson's *The Seasons*
(1726–30), is Elizabeth Young, a Scot whom Thomson wished to

marry. Her mother forbade the match, fearing that her daughter would be reduced to singing the poet's ballads in the streets, and Miss Young married an admiral instead.

AMARINTH, Esme, in Robert Hichens's *The Green Carnation* (1894), is the dramatist, poet and wit Oscar Wilde (1854–1900). Originally published anonymously, with dialogue sufficiently Wildean to prompt Wilde to deny authorship, *The Green Carnation* owes its title to Wilde's habit of wearing a flower dyed thus. In publicising Wilde's relationship with a peer (Lord Alfred Douglas – see Hastings, Lord Reggie), the book strengthened the Marquess of Queensberry's resolve to ruin the playwright who had taken up with his son.

AMARYLLIS, in Edmund Spenser's *Colin Clouts Come Home Againe* (1595). A link spanning nearly four centuries connects Amaryllis with Britain's royal family today. She is Alice, daughter of Sir John Spencer of Althorp, Northants, with whose family Spenser claimed relationship and which in 1981 provided Britain's heir to the throne with a bride, Lady Diana Spencer. As Countess-Dowager of Derby, Alice inspired Milton's 'Arcades' (?1633). Following the death of her husband, the Fifth Earl, she in 1600 became the third wife of the First Viscount Brackley. She died in 1637.

AMAZON, the, in Rémy de Gourmont's *Lettres à l'Amazone* (1921), is Natalie Clifford Barney (see Flossie), who managed to entice the lupus-disfigured author out of his self-imposed seclusion and into society again. She owed her 'Amazon' sobriquet to her practice of riding bowler-hatted each morning in the Bois de Boulogne.

AMAZONS. See Blackett, Nancy and Peggy.

AMBIENT, Mark, in Henry James's 'The Author of *Beltraffio*' (1884), has as prototype John Addington Symonds (see Opalstein). James's story was inspired by gossip that Symonds's writings were hated by his wife.

AMBROSE, in Christopher Isherwood's *Down There on a Visit* (1962), is Francis Turville-Petre (*d.* 1942), a syphilitic, homosexual English archaeologist who was among Isherwood's Berlin contemporaries. In 1933 he leased a Greek island upon which he was joined by Isherwood and the author's boyfriend of that time. He died in Egypt.

AMBROSE, Helen, in Virginia Woolf's *The Voyage Out* (1915), is the author's sister, Vanessa Bell (née Stephen, 1879–1961), a noted artist of the Bloomsbury Group. She had a child by Duncan Grant (see Forbes, Duncan), married Clive Bell (see Bell, Jonathan), was the lover of Roger Fry (see Whitby, Martin), and was regarded by the author as perfection personified, the epitome of naturalness.

AMELIA, in Henry Fielding's *Amelia* (1752), is Charlotte Fielding (née Cradock, *d.* 1744), a Salisbury beauty who in 1734 became the author's first wife. The novel's overturning of a chaise, with the scarring of the heroine's nose, is based on a real-life incident. Fielding's 'glowing language', wrote Lady Bute, daughter of his friend Lady Mary Wortley, 'did not do more than justice to the amiable qualities of the original, or to her beauty, although this had suffered a little from the accident related in the novel – a frightful overturn, which destroyed the gristle of her nose.'

ANCIENT MARINER, the, in Samuel Taylor Coleridge's *The Rime of the Ancient Mariner* (1798). It has been suggested that the Ancient Mariner was prompted by Fletcher Christian, the Manx acting-mate who led the mutiny on the *Bounty* in 1789. When the remains of the *Bounty* were discovered off Pitcairn Island in 1957, Patrick O'Donovan wrote of Christian in the *Observer*: 'There is a persistent story that he escaped to England with gold taken from the *Bounty*, that he was recognised in Plymouth by a surviving mutineer, that he made his way to the Lake District, even that he was the inspiration of the Ancient Mariner.'

ANDERSON, Esker, in John Ehrlichman's *The Company* (1976), is Lyndon Baines Johnson (1908–73), President of the United States from 1963 to 1969.

ANDRÉE, in Marcel Proust's *A la recherche du temps perdu* (1913–27), is part-inspired by Anna Agostinelli, common-law wife of Alfred Agostinelli (see Simonet, Albertine).

ANGEL, in Evelyn Waugh's *The Ordeal of Gilbert Pinfold* (1957), was inspired by Dr Stephen Black (1912–   ), a physician, author, filmwriter, broadcaster and hypnotist from Horsham who in 1953 conducted a BBC radio interview with Waugh. Suffering from hallucinations believed to have been caused by his excessive use of pain-killing drugs for rheumatism, Waugh later became convinced that Black was persecuting him through the use of long-range telepathy. It was upon this experience that he based his novel.

ANGEL, Elise, in John Cowper Powys's *After My Fashion* (written 1920, published 1980), is Isadora Duncan (1878–1927), pioneer of free love and free dance (as opposed to classical ballet). Among her lovers were the millionaire Paris Singer and the stage designer Gordon Craig (see Mann, Charles), by each of whom she had a child (both infants subsequently drowned). She married the eccentric Russian poet Yesenin, and died when her scarf caught in the wheel of a car and strangled her. Powys met her in New York and felt her to be the first woman of undoubted genius to perceive any value in himself.

ANGEL, Ib, in 'Copenhagen Season' (*Last Tales*, 1957) by Isak Dinesen (the pseudonym of Karen Blixen), is the author's father, the Danish writer and MP Wilhelm Dinesen (1845–95). His death by his own hand was partly attributed to lingering sorrow over the death of Countess Agnes Frijs (see von Galen, Adelaide).

ANGEL, Mrs, in Malcolm Muggeridge's *In a Valley of this Restless Mind* (1938), is Rosie Potter, daughter of a chairman of the Great Western Railway, sister of Beatrice Webb (see Bailey, Altiora; see also Brett, Mrs Daniel), and aunt of the author's wife.

ANGELUS, Dr Cyril, in James Bridie's *Dr Angelus* (1947), has as prototype Dr Edward William Pritchard (1825–65), a Glasgow physician who in 1865 was convicted of the murder of his wife and mother-in-law. He was also suspected of killing a housemaid who had been his mistress. Fellow citizens regarded him as a pillar of rectitude – a reputation he carefully cultivated – until his trial revealed the ruthlessness of which he was capable when his own interests were threatened.

ANN, in Lettice Cooper's *Black Bethlehem* (1947), is Eileen Orwell (see Waterlow, Rosemary), a wartime colleague of the author at the Ministry of Food in London; she prepared recipes and scripts for BBC 'Kitchen Front' broadcasts.

ANNA, in the sonnets of Charles Lamb, is Ann Simmons, a neighbour with whom he fell in love during his adolescence in Widford, Hertfordshire. She married John Thomas Bartram, moving to London where her husband was a silversmith and pawn-broker with premises near Leicester Square, and bearing him a son and three daughters, one of whom married the distinguished surgeon William Coulson (1802—77).

ANNA, in Gertrude Stein's 'The Good Anna' (*Three Lives*, 1933), is Lena Lebender, a German who kept house for the author and her brother during their turn-of-the-century student days in Baltimore.

ANNE, in Simone de Beauvoir's *Quand prime le spirituel* (1979), is the author's schoolfellow Elizabeth ('Zaza') Mabille, who thought her bourgeois parents would never consent to her marrying the fellow-student she loved, and later succumbed to a disease believed to be meningitis.

ANNETTE, in the early lyrics of Johann Wolfgang von Goethe, is Anna Katharina Schönkopf, with whom the writer fell in love when dining at the house of her father, a Leipzig wine merchant.

ANNIE, in Jack Kerouac's *The Subterraneans* (1958), is Luanne Henderson. See Marylou.

ANNUNZIATA, in Hans Christian Andersen's *The Improvisatore* (1835). 'There was not a piece of furniture in their apartment that had not been thrown by the father at the daughter's head, in the course of the moral and artistic training he bestowed upon her,' said the actress Fanny Kemble, quoting a friend who had known the model for Annunziata as a 'wild and wayward but wonderful girl'. She was the mezzo-soprano Maria Felicita Malibran (née Garcia, 1808—36), a celebrated opera singer heard by Andersen in Naples on several occasions. Kemble's informant, the French consul in New York, said that as a girl Malibran 'would fly into passions of rage, in which she would set her teeth in the sleeve of her silk gown and rend great pieces out of the thick texture as if it were muslin . . . She then would fall rigid on the floor, without motion, breath, pulse, or colour, though not fainting, in a sort of catalepsy of rage'. Pauline Viardot (see Natalya Petrovna) was her sister. No wonder the father threw furniture. On stage, Malibran over-acted and played the fool, pinching tenors' bottoms in love scenes; yet she was a dedicated singer, forever schooling and aiming her voice at fresh challenges. At twenty-eight, appearing in Manchester and suffering from the after effects of a bad fall from a horse, she insisted on giving an encore, collapsed, and died a few days later. Accounts of her performance suggest an exciting, 'over the top' quality, remarks Rupert Christiansen in *Prima Donna* (1984). 'Like Judy Garland,' says Christiansen, 'she seems to have communicated a sense of danger, a sense of someone pushing her own resources beyond all reasonable limits and who was prepared to risk failure in the attempt.'

ANSELL, in E.M. Forster's *The Longest Journey* (1907), is supposedly an amalgam of Alfred Richard Ainsworth (1879–1959), a classics scholar and philosopher who joined the Board of Education, retiring in 1940 as Deputy Secretary, and Professor H.O. Meredith (1878–1964), one of Forster's lovers and a potent early influence. A brilliant undergraduate, Meredith failed to fulfil his early promise. After lecturing at Manchester University he became Professor of Economics at Queen's University, Belfast. He was thrice married. With Forster, both Ainsworth and Meredith were members of the Cambridge Conversazione Society (The Apostles).

ANSTRUTHERS, Sir Nigel, in Frances Hodgson Burnett's *The Shuttle* (1907), is the author's husband and business manager Dr Stephen Townesend (1859–1914). He qualified at St Bartholomew's Hospital and later became a Fellow of the Royal College of Surgeons, but he was primarily interested in acting – a career he had wanted to follow in opposition to the wishes of his father, rector of St Michael's, Burleigh Street, in the Strand. He subsequently became a novelist. Ten years Burnett's junior, he married her in 1900. They soon separated. As an animal lover, he criticised the Archbishop of York for unveiling a window to the memory of a hunting man, and died from pneumonia after rising from his sick-bed in defence of a fox being hunted in his grounds. His story is told in Ann Thwaite's *Waiting for the Party: the Life of Frances Hodgson Burnett 1849–1924* (1974).

ANTEKIRTT, Dr (Mathias Sandorf), in Jules Verne's *Mathias Sandorf* (1885), is part-inspired by Louis Salvator (1847–1915), Archduke of Tuscany, noted traveller, prolific writer and owner of a Minorca estate.

ANTICANT, Dr Pessimist, in Anthony Trollope's *The Warden* (1855), is a caricature of Thomas Carlyle (1795–1881), historian, essayist and student of German literature.

ANTIJACK, Mr Anyside, in Thomas Love Peacock's *Melincourt* (1817), is the English statesman George Canning (1770–1827), founder of *The Anti-Jacobin*, a periodical opposed to what he considered subversive philosophical and political principles.

ANTONIO, in Ernest Hemingway's *The Fifth Column* (1938), is Pepe Quintanilla, Loyalist head of counter-espionage in the Spanish Civil War.

ANZOLETTO, in George Sand's *Consuelo* (1842–3), is Alfred de Musset. See Laurent.

APE, Mrs Melrose, in Evelyn Waugh's *Vile Bodies* (1930), has as prototype the American gospeller Aimée Semple McPherson (1890–1944), who made a million dollars with her message but was discredited when discovered in a compromising situation with one of her workers. She claimed she had been kidnapped.

APOLLINAX, Mr, in T.S. Eliot's 'Mr Apollinax' (written 1915; *Prufrock and Other Observations*, 1917). In 1914, Bertrand Russell (see Mattheson, Sir Joshua) was a visiting professor at Harvard. He found Eliot to be his most civilised student, though lacking in vitality. Mr Apollinax is Eliot's view of Russell at that time.

APPEL, Milton, in Philip Roth's *The Anatomy Lesson* (1984). Interviewing Roth in the *Sunday Times* in 1984, Ian Hamilton commented that reviewers had confidently identified Appel as the literary critic Irving Howe (1920–   ), noted for his contributions to the *New York Times Book Review*. 'Milton Appel is not in this book because I was once demolished in print by Irving Howe,' Roth replied. 'Milton Appel is in this book because half of being a writer is being indignant. And being *right*. If you only knew how *right* we are. Show me a writer who isn't furious about being misrepresented, misread, or unread, and who isn't sure he's right.'

APPIUS, in Alexander Pope's *Essay on Criticism* (1711), is the short-tempered critic and unsuccessful playwright John Dennis (1657–1734), author of the tragedy *Appius and Virginia* (1709) and inventor of a thunder effect for the theatre. Dennis replied with a published response deriding the deformity of Pope, a four foot six hunchback. At the time of the signing of the Treaty of Utrecht, he is reputed to have asked the Duke of Marlborough to insert a clause to protect him from French vengeance. Marlborough replied that although the French might regard himself as an even greater enemy, *he* was not seeking any such protection.

APPLEYARD, Ronnie, in Kingsley Amis's *I Want It Now* (1968). Cheerfully admitting that Appleyard has been taken to be the television broadcaster David Frost (1939–), the author denies the identification: 'Neither Jake Richardson nor Roger Micheldene nor any of my other characters have "originals" in real life. The only time I have based characters on real people was in *I Like It Here* (1958). Here Harry Banyon and his wife and adopted son are "based on" Harold Tyrrell and his wife Lucia and their adopted son. Nothing since.' Harold *who*? Was this, I asked, a leg-pull? 'No,' Amis replied. 'As you will now be finding out, the truth is very often trivial and dull.'

APSLEY, Major Basil and Lady Daphne, in D.H. Lawrence's 'The Ladybird' (*The Ladybird*, 1923), were suggested by the Hon. Herbert and Lady Cynthia Asquith (see Pervin, Maurice and Isabel). Like Asquith, Apsley returns from the war, wounded both physically and mentally; like Lady Cynthia, Lady Daphne is an impoverished aristocrat.

ARAMIS, in Alexandre Dumas's *The Three Musketeers* (1844), is Henri d'Aramitz, squire and patron of the living of Aramitz (now Aramits) in the province of Béarn. He joined the King's Musketeers in 1640.

ARANGO, General Tereso, in Alberto Moravia's *The Fancy Dress Party* (1941), is the Italian dictator Benito Mussolini (1883–1945), who failed to recognise himself in the portrait but was quick to prohibit a reprint when the caricature was pointed out to him. He was executed by Italian partisans, his body hung upside down from a petrol pump in Milan beside that of his mistress, Clara Petacci. 'Serve him right!' declared the charlady of Harold Nicolson (see Chilleywater, the Hon. Harold) on seeing a newspaper photograph of this spectacle. 'A gentleman like that driving about in a car with a lady not his wife!'

ARBUTHNOT, Sandy, in John Buchan's *Greenmantle* (1916), *The Three Hostages* (1924) and *The Courts of the Morning* (1929). Ask the real Sandy Arbuthnot to stand up, and two larger-than-life figures of the past would rise. But Arbuthnot is not a composite. He is possibly the only instance of a character changing models, beginning his career based on one man and later adopting the appearance and personality of another. In *Greenmantle* the model is the Hon. Aubrey Herbert (1880–1923), second son of the Fourth Earl of Carnarvon. An accomplished linguist, he often cultivated the appearance of a tramp, travelling widely in Korea, China and the Balkans – Albania twice offered him its throne. Short-sightedness did not stop him climbing the pinnacles of colleges at Oxford, where he took a first in Modern History and was regarded as the worst-dressed undergraduate. So that his myopia should not bar him from the army, he joined the British Expeditionary Force in 1914 by subterfuge. In the uniform of an officer of the Irish Guards, he mingled with them as they emerged from Wellington Barracks. Friends smuggled him on board the unit's troopship, subsequently introducing him to the colonel, who reluctantly accepted him. Wounded in the retreat from Mons, he was captured (armed with an alpenstock), rescued by the French and transferred to intelligence work in the Middle East – on a mission to Mesopotamia, he was led blindfold through the Turkish lines to negotiate with Khalil Pasha. Years earlier, Herbert had blindfolded himself to learn typing without vision, in anticipation of the total loss of sight which overtook him in 1922 while he was addressing Parliament – since 1911, he had been an unorthodox, negotiated-peace-supporting Tory MP. To recover his sight, he followed the advice of his old Balliol tutor and had his teeth removed (it was popularly believed that teeth and sight were inter-related). As a result, he died from blood poisoning. His daughter, Laura, became the second wife of Evelyn Waugh (see Blow, Christopher). In *The Courts of the Morning*, T.E. Lawrence (see Ransom, Michael) becomes Arbuthnot's model. Curiously, life anticipated art: Herbert and Lawrence were together involved in 1916 in an unsuccessful mission to relieve Kut-al-Amara. What did Herbert think of the man who replaced him as Buchan's inspiration? He found Lawrence 'attractive but walking in his own halo . . . an odd gnome, half cad – with a touch of genius'. It was with Buchan's assistance that Lawrence re-enlisted in the RAF after becoming disillusioned with life in the Tank Corps.

ARCATI, Madame, in Noël Coward's *Blithe Spirit* (1941), is the novelist and playwright Clemence Dane (pseudonym of Winifred

Ashton, *d.* 1965). An extrovert whose enthusiasms included painting, sculpting and pottery, she was cherished for her innocent use of
the *double entendre* – to a friend inquiring after the health of her
goldfish last seen wilting in a pool without shade, she replied, 'Oh,
they're all right now! They've got a vast erection covered with
everlasting pea!' It was after she had expressed an interest in acting
that Coward created Madame Arcati for her, with a view to her
playing the part which subsequently became the 'property' of Margaret Rutherford.

ARCHER, Isabel, in Henry James's *The Portrait of a Lady* (1881).
As his biographer Leon Edel records, in 1865 James visited the White
Mountains, New Hampshire, in the company of two young veter-
ans of the Civil War. There the three danced attendance on 'Minny'
Temple (see Theale, Milly). *The Portrait of a Lady* echoes this
situation, with Isabel – modelled upon 'Minny' – receiving the
attentions of a trio of admirers.

ARCHER, Mr, in W.M. Thackeray's *The History of Pendennis*
(1848–50), is Tom Hill. See Pry, Paul.

ARCHER, Bishop Timothy, in Philip K. Dick's *The Trans-
migration of Timothy Archer* (1982), has as prototype James Albert
Pike (1913–69), Episcopalian Bishop of California from 1958 to
1966. Accused of heresy when he disputed the doctrine of the Trinity
and denied the Virgin Birth, he subsequently claimed that his son,
who had committed suicide, had visited him at a seance. Formerly a
lawyer, he achieved popularity in the 1950s with his Sunday television programme, *The Dean Pike Show*. Critics regarded him as a
prophet of the devil, and he – seldom out of controversy – styled
himself 'God's maverick'. His showmanship (for his cathedral, he
commissioned a stained-glass window portraying the astronaut
John H. Glenn), his alcoholism and his divorce from his wife of
twenty-five years and subsequent remarriage further estranged him
from his Church. He died from a fall sustained while wandering in
the Judaean wilderness – he and his second wife had become lost
after taking a wrong turning and had driven into the desert.

ARDAN, Michel, in Jules Verne's *From the Earth to the Moon* (1864)
and *Around the Moon* (1870), is the French photographer-balloonist
'Nadar' (Gaspard Félix Tournachon, 1820–1910). The founder of a
Society for Aerial Locomotion, he led a company of balloonists

during the siege of Paris in 1870—1, took the first successful photograph from a balloon in 1858 and, at another extreme, photographed the sewers of Paris by electric light. He also pioneered the photo-interview and, as a caricaturist, established the *Revue comique* in 1849.

ARGYLE, James, in D.H. Lawrence's *Aaron's Rod* (1922), is the writer Norman Douglas (1868—1952). 'Such tosh I never read,' he remarked of the caricature. Subsequently, conveniently forgetting his own use of thinly disguised acquaintances in his novel *South Wind*, Douglas attacked Lawrence for 'personality mongering', describing it as 'not only bad literature but bad breeding.'

ARMADO, Don Adriano de, in William Shakespeare's *Love's Labour's Lost* (1598), has a suggested model in the explorer and poet Sir Walter Raleigh (?1552—1618), a leading member of the intellectual group known as the School of Night, to which the play makes reference.

ARNHEIM, Dr Paul, in Robert Musil's *The Man Without Qualities* (1930—43), is Walther Rathenau (1867—1922), German industrialist, statesman, philosopher and writer. In 1915 he became president of AEG, a firm founded by his father. He was his country's Foreign Minister, and it was as a dedicated seeker of an enduring peace after the First World War that he was assassinated by nationalist extremists.

ARNOLD, in Philip Larkin's 'Self's the Man' (*The Whitsun Weddings*, 1964), is the late Arthur Wood, a colleague of the author at the Brynmor Jones Library, Hull University.

ARNOLD, in Heinrich Mann's *Zwischen den Rassen* (1907), is the author's brother, the novelist Thomas Mann (1875—1955).

ARNOUX, Madame, in Gustave Flaubert's *L'Éducation sentimentale* (1869), is Élisa Foucault Schlesinger (1810—88), with whom Flaubert fell in love when he was fifteen, she twenty-six. Ostensibly at that time the wife of Maurice Schlesinger, a music publisher Flaubert and his parents met on holiday at Trouville, she was in fact still married to Émile Judéa, who had presented her to Schlesinger in exchange for financial assistance extricating him from a scrape he had got into through dishonesty. Only after Judéa's death in 1840 were the couple able to marry. Despite Schlesinger's subsequent blatant unfaithfulness, she did not become Flaubert's mistress. As she remained on a pedestal throughout the author's life, it may be surmised that she never disillusioned him by allowing him to possess her. She ended her days in the Illenau lunatic asylum.

ARROWBY, Adam, in Iris Murdoch's *The Sea, The Sea* (1978), is the author's father, Wills John Hughes Murdoch, who after serving in the Irish cavalry in the First World War became a senior Whitehall civil servant. Murdoch divulged Adam Arrowby's identity in an interview when the novel won the Booker Prize, describing her father as 'a quiet bookish man and somehow the gentlest being I have ever encountered.'

ARTAGNAN, d', in Alexandre Dumas's *The Three Musketeers* (1844), was born Charles de Batz-Castelmore in 1623 and took the name Sieur of Artagnan, a property in the Basses-Pyrénées, from his mother's family of Montesquiou. He came from wealthy bourgeois stock and in 1640 left Gascony for Paris, where he served with distinction under Louis XIV and Mazarin, in 1667 becoming *capitaine lieutenant* of the First Company of King's Musketeers. Subsequently governor of Lille, he was killed by a stray bullet at the siege of Maastricht in 1673.

ARTHEZ, Daniel d', in Honoré de Balzac's *Illusions perdues* (1835–43) and *Secrets de la Princesse de Cadignan* (1839), is believed to be an amalgam of the French novelist, poet and dramatist Alfred de Vigny (1797–1863) and the author's magistrate friend, Jean Thomassy.

ARTHUR, in D.H. Lawrence's *Kangaroo* (1923), is Stanley Hocking, a son of the Hocking family who farmed at Tregerthen Farm, near Zennor, during Lawrence's Cornish sojourn in 1916–17. Stanley Hocking subsequently moved to London. Lawrence's view of Cornish people in general was that none had had a new thought in 1300 years.

ARTHUR, George, in Thomas Hughes's *Tom Brown's Schooldays* (1857), is supposedly Arthur Penrhyn Stanley (1815–81), Dean of Westminster and author of a *Life of Dr Arnold* (1841). Stanley, however, left Rugby School in 1834 – the year of Hughes's arrival. But as a boy Stanley certainly resembled George Arthur, both physically and mentally, and it is possible that Hughes took his portrait from a profile supplied by his own elder brother, George, who also attended Rugby School — though with such lack of academic success that the headmaster asked his parents to remove him.

ARTHUR, Sir, in Ford Madox Ford's *The Marsden Case* (1923), is the Rt Hon. Arthur James Balfour (see Evesham). Sir Arthur has Balfour's demeanour and, like Balfour, involves himself in a long-running affair — Balfour lived with a woman to whom he was not married.

A.S., in Charles Lamb's 'Oxford in the Vacation' (1820; *Essays of Elia*, 1823), is Anne Benson Procter (née Skeeper, 1799–1888), literary hostess, acid wit, and from 1824 wife of the writer and lawyer Bryan Waller Procter ('Barry Cornwall' — 'Never, boy, wed a wit,' began his poem 'Advice on Marriage'). Thackeray, Dickens and Carlyle were among her friends, and she is the dedicatee of *Eōthen*, by A.W. Kinglake, who studied law with her husband.

ASCHENBACH, Gustav von. See von Aschenbach, Gustav.

ASHBURNHAM, Edward and Leonora, in Ford Madox Ford's *The Good Soldier* (1915), are respectively an amalgam of King Edward VII (1841–1910) and Arthur Marwood (see Tietjens, Christopher); and of the author's wife (see Macdonald, Countess), Arthur Marwood's wife Caroline — daughter of a farmer and racehorse-owner from Bridlington, Yorkshire — and Violet Hunt (see Nesbit, Norah).

ASHBURTON, Mary, in Henry Longfellow's *Hyperion* (1839), has as prototype the author's second wife, Frances Appleton (*d*. 1861), whom he married in 1843. Daughter of a cotton-mill owner, she was a founder of the Massachusetts city of Lowell and sister of the poet Thomas G. Appleton (1812–84). She died from burns when her dress accidentally caught fire.

ASHLEY, (Lady) Brett, in Ernest Hemingway's *The Sun Also Rises* (1926; published in England as *Fiesta*), is Duff, Lady Twysden (née Smurthwaite, 1896–1938). In 1917 she married Sir Roger Thomas Twysden, Bt, who divorced her in 1926 — a year after Hemingway first encountered her in Paris. The daughter of a

Yorkshireman – her father lived at Prior House, Richmond – she was the mother of the eleventh baronet.

ASHMEADE, Sandy, in Christopher Isherwood's *Prater Violet* (1945), is a composite of the author's Repton School contemporary, the playwright Sir Basil Bartlett (1905–   ), and the film director Robert Stevenson (1905–   ), associate producer of *Little Friend* (1933) for which Isherwood wrote the screenplay. Stevenson's subsequent films have included *King Solomon's Mines, Tom Brown's Schooldays, Jane Eyre, Kidnapped* and *Mary Poppins*.

ASHMORE, the Revd Dr, in Edith Wharton's *The Age of Innocence* (1920), is the Boston-born Episcopal clergyman, the Revd Dr E.A. Washburn (1819–81), rector of Calvary Church, New York, from 1865 to 1881, and father of the author's closest childhood friend.

ASHTON, Frank, in Frank Hardy's *Power Without Glory* (1950), is the London-born Australian Labour Party politician Frank Anstey (1865–1940). Arriving in Australia as a stowaway, he entered politics from the Seamen's Union, becoming a government minister.

ASHTON, Lucy, in Sir Walter Scott's *The Bride of Lammermoor* (1819), is Janet Dalrymple (d. 1669), eldest daughter of Sir James Dalrymple, First Viscount of Stair (1619–95). One popular tradition has it that she stabbed her husband to death on their wedding night and died shortly afterwards, insane; another, that her husband was murdered on his wedding night by her true love, whose suit had been prohibited by her parents. In fact, she was engaged to the impecunious Archibald, Third Lord Rutherfurd (d. 1685), but was talked out of this by her bible-quoting mother's invocation of Numbers 30:5. She died a month after her marriage to her mother's choice, David Dunbar, heir of Sir David Dunbar, of Baldoon. Her husband subsequently married a daughter of the Seventh Earl of Eglintoun and died in Edinburgh in 1682, after falling from his horse.

ASHTON, Rafe, in Hilda Doolittle's *Bid Me to Live* (1960), is the author's husband, the poet, novelist, critic and biographer Richard Aldington (1892–1962), who left her for Dorothy Yorke (see Carter, Bella). He subsequently had a ten-year liaison with Brigit

Patmore (see Browning, Clariss) and then married her daughter-in-law.

ASPASIA, in Leonard Woolf's *The Wise Virgins* (1914), is the author's wife, the novelist and critic Virginia Woolf (1882—1941). Daughter of Sir Leslie Stephen (see Ramsay, Mr) and sister of Vanessa Bell (see Ambrose, Helen), she drowned herself following intermittent mental illness.

ASRA, in the poems of Samuel Taylor Coleridge, is Sara Hutchinson (1775—1835), sister-in-law of William Wordsworth (see Paperstamp, Peter Paypaul) and the object of Coleridge's hopeless passion.

ASSHETON, Ralph, in Violet Hunt's *Sooner or Later* (1904), is Oswald Crawfurd (*d*. 1909), a British consular official whose appointments included the governorship of Singapore. Also a novelist and prolific miscellaneous writer, he became chairman of the publishers Chapman and Hall and is reputed to have given the author syphilis. He was fifty-six, she twenty-eight, when they first met in 1890. Their affair lasted from 1892 to 1898, but when Crawfurd's wife died in 1899 he did not marry Hunt. In 1902 he married another.

ASSISTANT COMMISSIONER, the, in Graham Greene's *It's a Battlefield* (1934). Greene himself discloses the part-inspiration for this character in his introduction to the 1970 edition of the novel. It is his uncle, Sir (William) Graham Greene (1857—1950), Permanent Secretary to the Admiralty from 1911 to 1917.

ASTARTE, in Lord Byron's *Manfred* (1817), is the poet's half-sister, Augusta Leigh (1783—1851), with whom he is reputed to have had an incestuous relationship.

ASTRAEA, in Alexander Pope's *Imitations of Horace* (1733), is the poet, playwright and novelist Mrs Aphra Behn (1640—89), whose nickname was 'The Divine Astraea' and whose *Oroonoko, or the Royal Slave* (*c.*1658) is credited with being the first English philosophical novel to discuss abstract subjects. Charles II employed her as a spy in the Netherlands. When she reported that the Dutch fleet proposed to sail up the Thames, setting fire to English ships in harbour, nobody believed her ... until it happened.

ASTRÉE, in Honoré d'Urfé's *L'Astrée* (1607–27), is Diana of Châteaumorand, a wealthy heiress who was for twenty-two years the author's sister-in-law. After his brother left her to become a priest, the novelist married her himself. The union, handicapped by Diana's infertility and habit of sharing table and bed with her dogs, did not last. They separated, d'Urfé retiring to Piedmont, where he wrote *L'Astrée*. As the author's sister-in-law, Diana is represented as Astrée; after her divorce from his brother, she is represented as another character, Diane.

ATABALIPA, in John Milton's *Paradise Lost* (1667), is Atahualpa (*d.* 1533), ruler of Quito and subsequently Inca of Peru. Captured by Spaniards, he was – as an idolator – sentenced to death by burning. But upon professing Christianity, he was permitted to expire by strangulation, his execution being followed by cremation.

ATALL, Sir Positive, in Thomas Shadwell's *The Sullen Lovers, or The Impertinents* (1668), is the dramatist Sir Robert Howard (1626–98), knighted for his courage in battle at Newbury, imprisoned in Windsor Castle during the Commonwealth and later auditor of the exchequer. Dryden, who married Howard's sister, helped him in his writing of *The Indian Queen*.

ATHELRED, in Robert Louis Stevenson's 'Talk and Talkers' (*Memories and Portraits*, 1887), is the author's friend and companion on *An Inland Voyage* (1878), Sir Walter Simpson (1843–98), whose father, Sir James Young Simpson, was in 1866 knighted for his pioneering use of chloroform as an anaesthetic.

ATHOS, in Alexandre Dumas's *The Three Musketeers* (1844), is Armand de Sillègue, seigneur of Athos and Autevielle in the Basses-Pyrénées. A King's Musketeer, he died in 1643 – his death certificate implying that his demise was the outcome of a duel.

ATKINS, J.L., in Dylan Thomas and John Davenport's *The Death of the King's Canary* (written 1940, published 1976), is T.S. Eliot (see Horty, Mr). Bereft of inspiration, Davenport was as a young man advised by Eliot to write nothing for a decade. Acting on this, he afterwards blamed Eliot for his own failure ever to write poetry again.

ATOSSA, in Alexander Pope's 'On the Characters of Women' (*Moral Essays*, 1731–5), is Sarah Churchill (née Jennings), Duchess of Marlborough (1660–1744), favourite of Queen Anne until the monarch tired of her domineering nature. Rumour had it that Pope accepted a £1000 bribe from the Duchess to suppress publication. This may explain why the Atossa portrait and two others were withheld until the work's 1751 edition. Atossa, according to Herodotus, was a follower of Sappho . . . just as the Duchess was a friend of Lady Mary Wortley Montagu, Pope's 'Sappho'.

ATTICUS, in Alexander Pope's *Cytherea, or poems upon Love and Intrigue* (1723) and *Epistle to Dr Arbuthnot* (1735), is the essayist Joseph Addison (1672–1719), who had outraged Pope by declaring his translation of Homer's *Iliad* to be less faithful than that by Thomas Tickell.

AUBREY, Cordelia, in Rebecca West's *The Fountain Overflows* (1957) and *This Real Night* (1984), is believed to be an unsympathetic portrait of the author's eldest sister, Dr Letitia Fairfield (*d.* 1978), who was London County Council's Senior Medical Officer from 1911 to 1948. If this is the case, it was with some gall that the author dedicated *The Fountain Overflows* to her.

AUSTIN, N.E., in C.P. Snow's *The Search* (1934), is a caricature of the atomic physicist Lord Rutherford (1871–1937) . . . 'but of course with nothing like Rutherford's power or depth', says Snow in John Halperin's *C.P. Snow: An Oral Biography* (1983).

AVDIEV, in Vladimir Dudintsev's *Not By Bread Alone* (1956), is supposedly the Russian geneticist and academician Trofim Denisovich Lysenko (1898–1976).

AVELLANOS, Don José, in Joseph Conrad's *Nostromo* (1904), is Santiago Pérez Triana, a Colombian diplomat introduced to the author by R.B. Cunninghame Graham (see Gould, Charles; Hushabye, Hector).

AVERY, Helen, in F. Scott Fitzgerald's 'Magnetism' (1928; *The Stories of F. Scott Fitzgerald*, 1951). The author's flirtation with Lois Moran (see Hoyt, Rosemary) prompted his wife to set fire to the furniture in their suite at the Ambassador Hotel. Or so he told Sheilah Graham, who in *The Real Scott Fitzgerald* (1976) concludes that as Moran — supposedly the model for Helen Avery — later visited the Fitzgeralds, the writer's Hollywood fling with her in 1927 was not consummated.

AYESHA, in H. Rider Haggard's *She* (1887) and *Ayesha: The Return of She* (1905). According to D.S. Higgins's *Rider Haggard: the Great Storyteller* (1981), Ayesha was inspired by the author's 'unattainable woman', Mary Elizabeth Archer (née Jackson, 1854–1909), a wealthy Yorkshire farmer's daughter whom Haggard met and fell in love with at a dance in Richmond, at the age of nineteen. Seeking his fortune in Africa, by the time he was twenty-one Haggard was Recorder of the Assizes Court of Transvaal and looking forward to returning home to Elizabeth . . . until she wrote that she had married another. The news so unsettled him that he gave up his career, tried ostrich farming unsuccessfully and then returned home, where he read for the Bar, married . . . and was Elizabeth's lifelong support after her husband absconded with her inheritance to Africa (where he died from syphilis, and where their son was ultimately to become Governor of Uganda). Prospering from his novels, Haggard bought for Elizabeth as her home the Red House, in Aldeburgh, Suffolk (subsequently the residence of the composer Benjamin Britten). There she lived until her death from the disease that had killed her husband.

AZIZ, Dr, in E.M. Forster's *A Passage to India* (1924), is Syed Ross Masood (1890–1937), a Punjabi who was the author's Latin pupil in 1913, and with whom Forster fell in love. Although this was not reciprocated, the two remained friends, Forster staying with Masood during his first visit to the East. In 1929, Masood became Vice-Chancellor of Aligarh University (founded in 1920 by his grandfather, the Indian reformer Sir Syed Ahmed Khan). Resigning when he became the victim of political infighting, he ended his dispirited days as Bhopal's Minister of Education.

B

'B', in E.E. Cummings's *The Enormous Room* (1922), is William Slater Brown, the author's fellow-prisoner in a French concentration camp. Both had joined an American ambulance unit in France in 1917. Brown's letters home were felt by French censors to suggest incipient mutiny, so he was arrested. Cummings, deemed guilty by association with Brown – and refusing to say he hated the Germans – was interned with him. Brown later became an intimate of Hart Crane (see Smith, Henry Martin).

BADGERY, Lord, in Aldous Huxley's 'The Tillotson Banquet' (1921; *Mortal Coils*, 1922). Until this story appeared, the Huxleys and the Sitwells had dined together on Thursday nights, as John Pearson records in *Façades: Edith, Osbert and Sacheverell Sitwell* (1978). But so clinically and mercilessly was Osbert Sitwell delineated as Badgery that the portrait caused a rift in the friendship – few people, after all, would relish being reminded of their 'heavy waxen mask' of a face, 'little lustreless pig's eyes' and 'pale thick lips', quite apart from being otherwise held up to ridicule. For Sitwell's retaliation, see Erasmus, William. See also Whittlebot, Gob.

BAGOT, Aubrey, in George Bernard Shaw's *Too True to be Good* (1931), is part-inspired by the actor Robert Loraine (1876–1935), whom Shaw treated like a son and who, as an aviator, flew the Irish Sea as early as 1910. Awarded the DSO and the MC in the First World War, he was recovering from wounds in hospital when he proudly told Shaw how he had bombed a small town.

BAGSHAW, the Revd Boom, in A.S.M. Hutchinson's *If Winter Comes* (1921), is the Revd Basil Bourchier, priest of St Jude's, Hampstead, and a cousin of the actor-manager, Arthur Bourchier.

Something of a showman, he was noted for histrionics in the pulpit, for the theatricality of his services and for his contributions to the popular press. His friends included Lord Northcliffe (see Tilbury, Lord).

BAGSHAW, Lindsay ('Books-do-furnish-a-room'), in Anthony Powell's *A Dance to the Music of Time* sequence (1951–75). The critic Hilary Spurling – author of the *Handbook to Anthony Powell's Music of Time* – has suggested that Bagshaw is part-inspired by the journalist and author Malcolm Muggeridge (1903–), as he was in his mid-thirties when Powell first came to know him. In his four-volume autobiography, *To Keep the Ball Rolling* (1976–82), Powell discloses that Bagshaw owes his knowledge of London pubs to Bobby Roberts (see Fotheringham) and his journalistic versatility to a theatre critic of the *Financial Times* (unnamed).

BAILEY, Oscar and Altiora, in H.G. Wells's *The New Machiavelli* (1911). When a woman's wedding ring is inscribed PBP – *pro bono publico* – she becomes a sitting target for the first novelist to spot it. So it was that the social reformers Sidney (1859–1947) and Beatrice Webb (1858–1943) became Oscar and Altiora. Describing marriage as 'the waste-paper basket of the emotions', Beatrice found Sidney physically repulsive and for two years resisted his courtship. 'His tiny tadpole body, unhealthy skin, lack of manner, cockney pronunciation, poverty, are all against him,' she noted. Meanwhile, frustration brought Sidney out in spots. Assuring her that together they could change the world, he wooed her with a draft pamphlet on the municipal inspection of factories, having decided, correctly, that this was the way to her heart. She finally accepted him – for 'reason, not love', she emphasised – and laid down terms for their partnership with the caution, 'I am doing more for you than I would for any other man because you are a Socialist and I am a Socialist.' After their engagement she returned a full-length photograph he had sent. It was 'hideous', she said – 'let me have your head only ... it is the head only that I am marrying.' Their honeymoon was spent studying Irish trade unions, and this marriage of minds went on to become instrumental in founding the London School of Economics, the *New Statesman* and the Fabian Society.

BAKER, Julius, in George Bernard Shaw's *Misalliance* (1910), has as prototype Horace George Rayner (*b.* 1879), who in 1907 walked into the office of William Whiteley, the pioneer London department-store owner, and claimed to be his bastard son. When his request for money was rejected he drew a gun, threatening suicide. Whiteley called for the police, whereupon Rayner shot him, inflicting wounds from which he died. Rayner's suicide attempt, however, merely disfigured his face. He was sentenced to death, but then reprieved and given penal servitude for life.

BALCAIRN, the Earl of, in Evelyn Waugh's *Vile Bodies* (1930), is supposedly part-inspired by Patrick Balfour, Baron Kinross (1904–77), an Oxford contemporary of the author and subsequently a fellow-journalist in Ethiopia. He was also a gossip columnist of the *Daily Sketch*.

BALIOL, Mrs Martha Bethune, in Sir Walter Scott's *Chronicles of the Canongate* (1827). W.S. Crockett's *The Scott Originals* (1912) identifies this original as Anne Murray Keith (*d.* 1818), daughter of the British minister in Vienna and a noted Edinburgh hostess at the George Square flat which she shared with her cousin, Anne, Countess of Balcarres. She also appears as Mrs Sydney Hume in Mrs A. Gillespie Smyth's *Probation*.

BALLADINO, Antonio, in Ben Jonson's *The Case is Altered* (written 1599, published 1609), is the dramatist and poet Anthony Munday (1553–1633), who in 1588 translated the romance *Palladino of England*.

BALTIMORE, Scott, in Pierre Rey's *The Greek* (1974). Among the identifications of originals and prototypes in popular fiction of the 1960s and 1970s made by John Sutherland in *Best Sellers* (1981) is that of John F. Kennedy (1917–63), President of the United States from 1960 to 1963, as Scott Baltimore.

BANFORD, Jill, in D.H. Lawrence's 'The Fox' (1922; *The Lady-bird*, 1923), is Cecily Lambert who, with her cousin, Violet Monk, tenant-farmed Grimsbury Farm, Long Lane, Hermitage, Berkshire. Complaining that it was execrable taste to belittle her for no fault of her own, while accepting her hospitality, Cecily Lambert declared that it was her cousin who was possessive and jealous.

BANJO, in Moss Hart and George S. Kaufman's *The Man Who Came to Dinner* (1939), is Arthur ('Harpo') Marx (1888–1964), mute musician member of the Marx Brothers film comedy team. The identification is made in Scott Meredith's *George S. Kaufman and the Algonquin Table* (1974), which records that Harpo himself appeared on stage in the role, speaking his first lines for twenty-five years.

BANKES, Mr, in Virginia Woolf's *To the Lighthouse* (1927). Woolf's biographer, Quentin Bell, suggests an original in Walter Headlam (1866–1908), Greek scholar and Fellow of King's College, Cambridge. He had the reputation of being a flirt, and he was also rumoured to have a penchant for little girls.

BARBAN, Tommy, in F. Scott Fitzgerald's *Tender is the Night* (1934), is primarily Édouard Jozan (1899–   ), a French aviator with whom the author's wife had an affair at St Raphaël in 1925. Fitzgerald claimed he had challenged Jozan to a duel, each firing a shot which missed, but Ernest Hemingway recalled Fitzgerald telling him several versions of the incident. Questioned by Nancy Milford, Jozan (who subsequently had a distinguished career in the French navy, retiring in 1959 with the rank of admiral) made no mention of a duel and said the affair had not been consummated.

BARBARA, in Hugh Kingsmill's *The Will to Love* (written under the name Hugh Lunn, 1913), is part-inspired by the novelist and playwright Enid Bagnold (1889–1981), a colleague of the author on the magazines *Hearth & Home* and *Modern Society*, edited by Frank Harris (see Parker, Ralph), to whom Miss Bagnold lost her virginity. '"Sex", said Frank Harris, "is the gateway to life." So I went through the gateway in an upper room of the Café Royal', she recorded in her autobiography.

BARBARA S——, in Charles Lamb's essay of that title (1825; *Last Essays of Elia*, 1833), is the actress and comedienne Frances Maria 'Fanny' Kelly (1790–1882), who made her Drury Lane début in 1797 and in 1840 built her own theatre – the Royalty, in Dean Street – under the patronage of the Duke of Devonshire. Lamb proposed to her, unsuccessfully.

BARFLEUR, in Theodore Dreiser's *A Traveller at Forty* (1913), is Grant Richards (1872–1948), monocled, twice-bankrupted, man-of-the-world publisher. He was reputedly the first in his profession to quote unfavourable comments in his books' advertising. His autobiography, George Bernard Shaw suggested, should be entitled

'The Tragedy of a Publisher who Allowed Himself to Fall in Love with Literature'.

BARKLEY, Catherine, in Ernest Hemingway's *A Farewell to Arms* (1929), is part-inspired by the author's first wife, Hadley Richardson, of St Louis, who was seven years his senior. They married in 1921 and divorced in 1927. Also discernible is Agnes H. von Kurowski (*b.* 1892), an American Red Cross nurse with whom the author fell in love in 1918, when she tended his wounds at a Milan military hospital. Born in Germantown, Pennsylvania, she, too, was seven years Hemingway's senior and, as Michael S. Reynolds remarks in *Hemingway's First War* (1976), was noted for her beauty. In 1927 she became directress of the Haitian General Hospital, Port au Prince, and in the following year in Haiti she met and married an auditor, Howard Preston Garner, from whom she was divorced in 1931.

BARNABAS, Savvy, in George Bernard Shaw's *Back to Methuse-lah* (1921), was admitted by Shaw to be a latterday Margot Tennant (see Dodo). The caricature justified itself, he said, by annoying Asquith, her husband.

BARNARD, in Christopher Isherwood's *Lions and Shadows* (1938), is John Layard, an anthropologist and former pupil of the American psychologist Homer Lane. A contemporary of Isherwood in Berlin, he was an influence on the poetry of Auden (see Weston, Hugh), in the 1930s. Isherwood's memoirs, *Christopher and His Kind* (1977), tell how in 1929 Layard attempted suicide by shooting himself through the mouth. Upon finding himself still alive, though seriously injured, he took a taxi to Auden's abode and asked him to complete the job. Instead, Auden summoned an ambulance.

BARNES, Lett, in Hilda Doolittle's *Bid Me To Live* (1960), is Ezra Pound, to whom Doolittle was engaged. See Lowndes, George.

BARNETT, Jim, in Mary McCarthy's 'Portrait of the Intellectual as a Yale Man' (*The Company She Keeps*, 1942). The boyish appearance and some of the career features of the journalist and author John Chamberlain (1903–) are to be found in Jim Barnett. 'He knew that I didn't know him very well, and that therefore in the story he was just a kind of good-looking clothes-hanger', McCarthy said in a *Paris Review* interview in 1962. Chamberlain was books editor of

Harper's Magazine from 1939 to 1947 and editor of *Life* from 1945 to 1950. 'Since my own identification with the Left in those days was purely out of a depression-induced pessimism . . . I have never been able to see myself in Jim Barnett's shoes', Chamberlain wrote in 'The Novels of Mary McCarthy' (*The Creative Present*, 1963). 'I thought socialism was a stomach appeal, and said so. Where Jim Barnett "sold out", I merely recovered my optimism — or maybe it was my nerve.'

BARRACE, Miss, in Henry James's *The Ambassadors* (1903), is Henrietta Reubell (*b*. ?1849), an American whose Paris salon's *habitués* included James, Oscar Wilde and James McNeill Whistler. With her vivid red hair, expressive features and bejewelled fingers, she put Sir William Rothenstein in mind of Queen Elizabeth — if one could imagine the monarch with a parrot-shrill voice and an American accent.

BARTLEBY, in Herman Melville's 'Bartleby, the Scrivener. A Story of Wall Street' (1853), was possibly suggested by the author's friend, George J. Adler, a German philologist whose agoraphobia caused him to be sent to a New Jersey asylum shortly before this story's publication.

BARTLETT, Charlotte, in E.M. Forster's *A Room with a View* (1908), according to P.N. Furbank in *E.M. Forster: a Life* (2 vols, 1977–8), is the author's aunt, Mrs W.H. Forster (née Emily Nash), who was utterly dominated by her husband (see Failing, Mrs).

BARTON, Amos, in George Eliot's 'The Sad Fortunes of the Rev. Amos Barton' (*Scenes of Clerical Life*, 1858), is the Revd John Gwyther (*d*. 1873), who in 1841 suddenly left his parish, Chilvers Coton in Warwickshire, where he had been curate-in-charge for ten years. He was subsequently vicar of Fewston, in Yorkshire. Receiving a pained letter from Gwyther, regretting that she had seen fit to make 'public my private history', the author apologised, explaining that she had thought he was dead.

BASKERVILLES, the, in Sir Arthur Conan Doyle's *The Hound of the Baskervilles* (1902), have a number of putative prototypes. It has been suggested that they are the Vaughans of Hergest Court, reputed by local folklore to be haunted by the black dog of Hergest (Hereford and Worcester). The Vaughans were related to the Baskervilles of Clyro Court, Hay-on-Wye, and it was with Lady Dorothy Baskerville's consent that Doyle used her family's name, considering it more euphonious. Another account has it that Doyle took the name from a coachman who drove him round Devon while he researched the novel's setting. It has also been claimed that the Baskervilles were inspired by the Cabell family, who lived in Brook, on Dartmoor. They were said to have been plagued by a spectral hound, following Richard Cabell's murder of his wife, whose dog turned on and killed Cabell but was itself stabbed to death in the process. According to Charles Higham's *The Adventures of Conan Doyle* (1976), the author was told of this legend by a journalist, Fletcher Robinson, who had heard it from the novelist Max Pemberton, and who accompanied Doyle to Dartmoor and Brook Manor.

BASSET-CREWE, Cynthia, in Gilbert Cannan's *Peter Homunculus* (1909), is Sylvia Llewelyn Davies (1866–1910), daughter of the artist and novelist George Du Maurier. Upon her barrister husband's death from cancer, her five sons were adopted by J.M. Barrie (see Wilson, Murray), whose wife left him for Cannan.

BATES, Norman, in Robert Bloch's *Psycho* (1959). So horrific were the activities of Bates's prototype that Bloch toned them down, fearing readers would find them too revolting. And while Hitchcock's film of the book showed Bates wearing women's clothes, it stopped short of the original's admission that he also wore women's skins. His prototype was Ed Gein, a Wisconsin farmhand and handyman. In 1957, police investigating the disappearance of a Plainfield widow acted on information that Gein's van had been seen near the woman's hardware store. At Gein's farm they found her hanging by her heels in a shed. She had been decapitated and 'dressed like a deer'. Her heart was discovered in a coffee-can on a stove. Nine death masks were found in the house, where chairs were covered with women's skins. Gein had killed two women, taking the remains of thirteen more from their graves. He died in a Wisconsin mental institution in 1984, aged seventy-seven.

BATES, Proosian, in Rudyard Kipling's *Stalky and Co.* (1899), is Cormell Price (*d.* 1910), who was known by this nickname by boys of the United Services College in Westward Ho, which he founded in 1874, as headmaster. He was previously a Haileybury housemaster, and his sobriquet derived, illogically, from the fact that he had earlier been a tutor in Russia.

BATTIUS, Obed, in James Fenimore Cooper's *The Prairie* (1827), is Thomas Nuttall. See N, Mr.

BATTLE, Sarah, in Charles Lamb's 'Mrs Battle's Opinions on Whist' (1821; *Essays of Elia*, 1823), is supposedly Sarah Burney (1758—1832), daughter of a noted London bookseller, Thomas Payne, wife of Admiral James Burney, and sister-in-law of the novelist and diarist Fanny Burney. The Burneys first met the Lambs in 1803.

BATTLER, Ernest, in George Bernard Shaw's *Geneva* (1938). This play had hardly been written before it was overtaken by events. In casting Adolf Hitler (see Ui, Arturo) as Battler, Shaw presented him as a man of integrity. Ironically, there is something almost Shavian about the Führer's observation that to succeed a lie should be a whopper, which would be believed if it were repeated loudly enough and often enough — 'the great masses of the people . . . will more easily fall victims to a great lie than to a small one.' Acknowledging his portraits of Hitler and Mussolini (see Bombardone) to be idealised, Shaw said: 'Instead of making the worst of all the dictators, which only drives them out of the League [of Nations], I have made the best of them, and may even challenge them to live up to these portraits if they can.' His models proving contrary, Shaw tried to retrieve the situation by writing a new, updating conclusion for *Geneva* upon the outbreak of war. Once again, Hitler was ahead of him . . .

BAVOIL, Mme, in J-K Huysmans's *La Cathédrale* (1898) and *L'Oblat* (1903), is Julie Thibault (*d.* 1907), housekeeper and 'priestess' to Joseph-Antoine Boullan (see Johannès, Dr) and subsequently the author's housekeeper.

BAYER, in Christopher Isherwood's *Mr Norris Changes Trains* (1935), according to Isherwood's biographer, Brian Finney, is Willi Münzenberg, a Communist organiser in Berlin in the early 1930s.

BAYNES, Charlotte and Mrs, in W.M. Thackeray's *The Adventures of Philip* (1861—2). Charlotte is Isabella Shawe (see Sedley, Amelia). Mrs Baynes is Mrs Matthew Shawe, widow of Lt-Col. Matthew Shawe (*d.* 1825), who commanded the 84th Regiment of Foot in India. She became the author's mother-in-law after vigorously scheming to break his engagement to her daughter, relenting only when his impecuniousness seemed likely to be relieved by his appointment as Paris correspondent of *The Constitutional*.

BAYS, in Alexander Pope's *The Dunciad* (1728), is Lewis Theobald (1688–1744), littérateur, who had incensed Pope with his incisive criticism of the poet's editorship of Shakespeare; in the rewritten, 1743 edition of *The Dunciad*, Bays is the poet laureate and actor-dramatist Colley Cibber (1671–1757), who in playing Bayes in Villiers's *The Rehearsal* had ridiculed the farce *Three Hours After Marriage* (1717), for which Pope was known to have been partly responsible.

BAZAROV, Yevgeny Vasil'evich, in Ivan Turgenev's *Fathers and Sons* (1862) — otherwise known as *Fathers and Children* — is supposedly the novel's dedicatee, the Russian literary critic Vissarion Grigorevich Belinsky (1811–48), noted for the vigour with which he expressed his frequently changing views. Bazarov was also thought by contemporaries to suggest aspects of the radical literary critics Nikolay Gavrilovich Chernyshevsky (1828–89) and Nikolay Aleksandrovich Dobrolyubov (1836–61).

BAZHAKULOFF, in Norman Douglas's *South Wind* (1917), is part-inspired by Gregory Efimovich Rasputin (1871–1916), a Russian monk who achieved considerable influence at the court of Nicholas II in St Petersburg. When he began to interfere in politics he was assassinated by noblemen, who shot him after failing to despatch him with wine laced with a strong dose of potassium cyanide.

BEARD, Captain John, in Joseph Conrad's *Youth* (1902), is Captain Elijah Beard (b. 1824), to whom the author in 1881 became second mate on the barque 'Palestine', an elderly vessel destroyed when its cargo caught fire the following year.

BEATRICE, in Dante Alighieri's *Vita nuova* (c.1292) and *Divina commedia* (c.1300), is supposedly Beatrice Portinari (1266–90), whom Dante met when both were children. They were never more than nodding acquaintances. She married Simone de Bardi, c.1287.

BEAUCHAMP, Nevil, in George Meredith's *Beauchamp's Career* (1875), is Rear-Admiral Frederick Augustus Maxse (1833–1900), naval ADC to Lord Raglan during the siege of Sebastopol. Subsequently entering politics, he contested Southampton unsuccessfully in 1868, with Meredith in support, and, again unsuccessfully, Tower Hamlets in 1874. He was an uncompromising extremist, the fanatical fervour with which he advanced his views being matched by the frequency with which he changed them. Kitty Maxse (see Dalloway, Clarissa) was his daughter-in-law, and Meredith named his son, William Maxse Meredith, after him.

BEAUFORT, Julius, in Edith Wharton's *The Age of Innocence* (1920), is supposedly an amalgam of August Belmont (1816–90), the German-American New York banker, politician, art collector and turf patron, and the author's cousin, George Alfred Jones, who turned embezzler to maintain his mistress.

BEAVER, John, in Evelyn Waugh's *A Handful of Dust* (1934), is Sir John Heygate, Bt (1903–76), for whom Waugh's first wife, Evelyn Gardner, left him in 1930. The son of an Eton housemaster, Heygate was at that time working for the BBC, which he left on being cited as co-respondent in Waugh's divorce. In 1936, Heygate was in turn divorced from Waugh's former wife. He subsequently remarried, was divorced again, and married his third wife in 1951. Succeeding to his title in 1940 on the death of an uncle, he served as a Royal Artillery bombardier in the Second World War. In his later years, acute bouts of depression hastened his death. His Eton contemporaries included George Orwell (see 'O'), who appears in his *Decent Fellows* (1930) as a college praepostor. 'One realises one was the rather feeble villain in *A Handful of Dust*,' he wrote to Michael Davie, editor of Waugh's *Diaries*, in 1975. 'But much later on EW used to ask Tony Powell about me in a friendly manner.'

BEAVER, Mrs, *idem*, bears 'a suspicious resemblance' to Syrie Maugham (see Middleton, Constance), according to her biographer, Richard B. Fisher. Waugh's character is an interior decorator (as was Syrie) who considers that a house fire that harms nobody but housemaids is to be welcomed in providing work for her profession. Her girl employees, who pay her in order to learn her art, are occupied with menial tasks.

BEAVIS, Mr, in Aldous Huxley's *Eyeless in Gaza* (1936). According to Huxley's biographer, Sybille Bedford, it was from Frieda Lawrence's account of her first husband, Ernest Weekley (see Tressider, Dr Frederic), that Huxley derived the philological aspect of Beavis.

BECH, Henry, in John Updike's *Bech: A Book* (1970) and *Bech is Back* (1983). This Jewish-American writer is first encountered as having become a 'name' on the strength of a successful first novel and not much since — a novella, some journalism and a third book slaughtered by the critics. That has not stopped him from becoming a campus idol and a popular interviewee happy to take his ego for a walk ... and never mind the writing: sustained by such fringe activities, he no longer needs to write. It is a fate which has threatened many an American novelist. Capote, Bellow and Malamud come to mind, as does Updike himself, for Bech is in a sense his *alter ego*. Critics have been reminded of Norman Mailer (see Marker, Harvey), and not just because Bech is a Mailer look-alike. 'Look how much time Norman Mailer wastes', Updike remarked in 1984, 'on having to be Norman Mailer.'

BECK, Madame, in Charlotte Brontë's *Villette* (1853), is Mme Claire Zoë Heger, wife of Constantin Heger (see Emmanuel, Paul). The author's infatuation with Heger caused his wife subsequently to forbid her name to be mentioned in the household, a regimen unaltered by both the novelist's fame and her death. Charlotte, for her part, expressly forbade a French translation of *Villette*, but a pirated edition was on sale in Brussels by 1855.

BEDE, Adam, in George Eliot's *Adam Bede* (1859), is part-inspired by the author's father, Robert Evans (1773–1849), agent of Francis Parker Newdigate (see Wybrow, Captain Anthony), of Arbury Hall, Warwickshire. Evans was noted both for his strength of character and for his physique. He would carry single-handed a heavy ladder normally requiring three men to move it; and when, travelling on a coach, he was told by a woman sitting next to him that a burly sailor on her other side was making himself offensive, Evans changed places with her, took the sailor by the collar and forced him beneath the seat, holding him there for the rest of the journey. 'The character of Adam and one or two incidents connected with him were suggested by my father's early life,' said the author, 'but Adam is not my father any more than Dinah [see Morris, Dinah] is my aunt.'

BEDE, Seth, *idem*, according to Marghanita Laski, is the author's uncle, Samuel Evans (1777–1858), manager of a mill in Wirksworth, Derbyshire. Converted to Methodism in 1795, he in 1804 married Elizabeth Tomlinson (see Morris, Dinah), who bore him three children.

BEE-LIPS, in Ernest Hemingway's *To Have and Have Not* (1937), is Georgie Brooks, a lawyer and politician in Key West, Florida, whom Hemingway first met in 1928.

BEESWAX, Sir Timothy, in Anthony Trollope's *The Duke's Children* (1880), has a possible prototype in Benjamin Disraeli. See Daubeny, Mr.

BEEZLEY, Florence, in P.G. Wodehouse's *Tales of St Austin's* (1903), according to N.T.P. Murphy's *In Search of Blandings* (1981), is Dr Helen Marion Wodehouse. See Craye, Lady Florence.

BEGGS, Judge, in Zelda Fitzgerald's *Save Me the Waltz* (1932), according to Matthew J. Bruccoli's *Some Sort of Epic Grandeur: The Life of F. Scott Fitzgerald* (1982), is the author's father, Judge Anthony D. Sayre (*d.* 1931), of Alabama Supreme Court.

BELFIELD, in Fanny Burney's *Cecilia* (1782), is the author Percival Stockdale (1736−1811), who sailed with Byng's expedition to relieve Minorca in 1756 and returned to edit the *Critical Review* and the *Universal Magazine*. He was subsequently rector of Hinxworth, Hertfordshire (1780), and of Lesbury and Long Houghton, Northumberland (1783).

BELFIELD, Diana, in Henry James's 'Longstaff's Marriage' (1878; *The Madonna of the Future and Other Tales*, 1879). The author's biographer, Leon Edel, surmises that the original of Diana Belfield was Mary ('Minny') Temple, the story's Longstaff representing James himself. See Theale, Milly.

BELINDA, in Alexander Pope's *The Rape of the Lock* (1712−14). One snip with a pair of scissors gave Arabella Fermor (*d.* 1738) a place in literary history. The daughter of James Fermor, of Tusmore, in Oxfordshire, she in 1715 married Francis Perkins of Ufton Court, Reading. The poem was prompted by young Lord Petre's snipping-off of a lock of her hair − a liberty much resented and the cause of a feud between the Fermor and Petre families. Pope's mock-heroic verses were an attempt to dispel the tension, and were intended to make the warring families see the matter in its true perspective. In its original form, the poem was published with Miss Fermor's consent, but when it was later republished, somewhat expanded, she was incensed. Her sense of outrage, however, was later replaced by conceit, Mrs Perkins being not at all averse to recognition as the original of 'Belinda'.

BELL, Geoffrey, in Wyndham Lewis's *The Roaring Queen* (1936), is the literary critic and poet Gerald Gould (1885–1936), father of the artist Michael Ayrton. He was a life-long Socialist, associate editor of the *Daily Herald* from 1919 to 1922, and a pioneer supporter of women's suffrage.

BELL, Jonathan, in Wyndham Lewis's *The Apes of God* (1930), is the art critic and poet Clive Bell (1881–1964), husband of Vanessa Bell (see Ambrose, Helen).

BELL, Laura, in W.M. Thackeray's *The History of Pendennis* (1848–50), is Mrs William Henry Brookfield (see Castlewood, Lady), according to Gordon N. Ray's *The Buried Life: A Study of the Relation between Thackeray's Fiction and his Personal History* (1952).

BELLAIR, Lady, in Benjamin Disraeli's *Henrietta Temple* (1837), is supposedly Mary Monckton. See Hunter, Mrs Leo.

BELLARS, Pearl, in Aldous Huxley's *Limbo* (1920), is Mrs Humphry Ward. See Foxe, Mrs.

BELLGROVE, Dr, in Mervyn Peake's *Gormenghast* (1950), is suggested by the author's biographer, John Watney, to be George Robertson (1883–1956), headmaster of Eltham College during Peake's period there as a pupil (1923–9). Robertson left Eltham in 1926 to become head of George Watson's College in Edinburgh, of which he was an old boy. He retired in 1943.

BELLINGER, Lord, in Sir Arthur Conan Doyle's 'The Second Stain' (1903; *The Return of Sherlock Holmes*, 1905). The author's biographer, Charles Higham, finds Bellinger 'clearly suggestive of' the Third Marquess of Salisbury (1830–1903). Doyle was a friend of Balfour (see Holdhurst, Lord), who succeeded Salisbury as prime minister.

BELLONI, Sandra, in George Meredith's *Sandra Belloni* (originally *Emilia in England*, 1864), is Emilia Macirone, subsequently Lady Hornby. Her mother, the widow of a former ADC to Murat, was landlady of a prestigious boarding-house, The Limes, Weybridge, Surrey, where the author and his first wife took lodgings in 1850. Becoming a close friend of Mary Ellen Meredith (see Mount, Bella), Lady Hornby tried in vain to effect a reconciliation with Meredith.

BELNAVE, Marianna, in Jules Sandeau's *Marianna* (1839), is the author's lover, George Sand (see Maupin, Camille). The evolution of *Marianna* is described in Curtis Cate's *George Sand* (1975).

BENDICK, Catherine, in Dorothy L. Sayers's *Gaudy Night* (1935), is the novelist Doreen Wallace (1897–   ), an Oxford contemporary of Sayers. She married Rowland H. Rash, a farmer from Wortham, Suffolk, and in 1922 became a militant agitator for the abolition of tithes, as Janet Hitchman notes in *Such a Strange Lady: A Biography of Dorothy L. Sayers* (1975).

BENJAMIN, in Thomas Mann's trilogy *Joseph and his Brethren* (1933–43), is the author's brother Viktor Mann (1890–1949), according to Henry Hatfield's *Thomas Mann* (1951). Viktor began his career as an agronomist, later entering banking in Munich, and was the author of a history of the Mann family, published posthumously.

BENSON, Revd Thurston, in Elizabeth Gaskell's *Ruth* (1853). Such was the character and career of the Revd William Turner, as described in Winifred Gérin's biography of the author (1976), that it would have been remarkable had he not found his way into one of Gaskell's novels. It was to his household that the author was sent as a girl, following the death of her father – Turner's first wife was Gaskell's mother's cousin. A Newcastle Unitarian minister and schoolmaster, he organised relief during famines and strikes and pioneered popular education. Among those he helped was the young George Stephenson, later to achieve eminence as a railway pioneer. Turner retired to Manchester in 1843, to live with his unmarried daughter. Upon her death, when he was past ninety and nearly blind, he informed his old congregation that he would in future accept only £15 of the £30 pension they had granted him, as he needed but half the original sum for himself. When he died, aged ninety-five, the author's husband delivered the funeral sermon.

BERGMANN, Dr Friedrich, in Christopher Isherwood's *Prater Violet* (1945), is the Austrian-born film director Berthold Viertel (1885–1953), to whom the author was introduced in London in 1933 by Jean Ross (see Bowles, Sally). Subsequently working together, Isherwood and Viertel became friends and neighbours at the Californian resort of Santa Monica. Viertel's films included Garbo's *Queen Christina* and *Anna Christie* (her first talking role).

BERGOTTE, in Marcel Proust's *A la recherche du temps perdu* (1913–27), is primarily the writer Anatole France (Jacques Anatole Thibault, 1844–1924), who is also to be found in the character de Norpois. However, many others contributed to Bergotte, including the novelist Maurice Barrès (1862–1923); the novelist Paul Bourget (1852–1935); Marie-Alphonse Darlu (1849–1921), the author's philosophy lecturer at the Lycée Condorcet in the 1880s; the novelist Alphonse Daudet (1840–97), with whose son, Lucien, Proust had a homosexual relationship; the drama critic Jules Lemaître (1853–1914); Prince Edmond de Polignac (1822–1901), dilettante musician and composer and husband of Winnaretta Singer (see Vinaigrette), whom he married in 1893, jumping over a chair to prove he was still young enough for matrimony; Ernest Renan (1823–92), a Hebrew scholar and historian to whom Bergotte owes his nose; and John Ruskin (see Herbert, Mr), a profound influence on Proust.

BERMA, *idem*, is an amalgam of the actresses Sarah Bernhardt (1845–1923) and Réjane (Gabrielle-Charlotte Réju, 1857–1920). The character's name is possibly a corruption of that of another actress of the day, Marie Brema, known as La Brema.

BERNARD, in Virginia Woolf's *The Waves* (1931). Bernard can be observed taking shape in Woolf's diary references to the literary critic Sir Desmond MacCarthy (1877–1952). His talent was flawed by indolence, and he failed to fulfil his early promise. He married the daughter of Blanche Cornish (see Cravister, Mrs).

BERNERS, Isopel, in George Borrow's *Lavengro* (1851), has a suggested original in Elizabeth Jarvis, born in 1803 at Long Melford, in Suffolk, the illegitimate child of Elizabeth Jarvis (*d.* 1805). In Borrow's early draft of the novel, Isopel is referred to as 'your Bess', and is described as the illegitimate daughter of a mother of the same name.

BERNSTEIN, J., in Michael Sadleir's *Forlorn Sunset* (1947), is identified in Victor Neuburg's *The Batsford Companion to Popular Literature* (1983) as William Dugdale (1800–68), a fugitive London publisher of erotica, who died in prison.

BERTHEROY, in Émile Zola's *Paris* (1897–8), according to F.W.J. Hemmings's *Émile Zola* (1953), is the French chemist and politician Pierre Eugène Marcellin Berthelot (1827–1907).

BERTRAND, Archie, in Hugh Walpole's *John Cornelius* (1937). Portrayed as a cynical, arrogant pessimist who writes in a 'simple English style and tells the public about the little bit of life he has seen', Bertrand is identified by Walpole's biographer, Sir Rupert Hart-Davis, as the novelist, dramatist and short-story writer W. Somerset Maugham (1874–1965). Distressed by Maugham's caricature of himself (see Kear, Alroy), Walpole acknowledges Bertrand to be 'more delightful to read than any of his contemporaries' but adds that he 'does not give joy in retrospect.'

BEULIER, in Marcel Proust's *Jean Santeuil* (1952), is Marie-Alphonse Darlu. See Bergotte.

BEVILL, Thomas, (later Lord Grampound), in C.P. Snow's *The New Men* (1954) and *Homecomings* (1956), is Maurice Pascal Alers, First Baron Hankey of the Chart (1877–1963), who in 1939 was appointed Minister without Portfolio in the British War Cabinet. It was as a member of his wartime manpower committees that Snow came to know and revere him. Alers was a former Secretary of the Imperial War Cabinet (1917–18) and Secretary of the Cabinet (1919–38). Bevill's original was revealed in the *Sunday Telegraph* by Kenneth Rose, in a tribute to Snow upon his death in 1980.

BEYNON, Butcher, in Dylan Thomas's *Under Milk Wood* (1954), is Carl Eynon, butcher, of St Clears, Dyfed, four miles from Laugharne, the Welsh town which is the play's principal setting. Thomas would occasionally see him walking from his cold store to his shop, carrying a cleaver and accompanied by his dachshund, which in the play becomes a corgi.

BIDLAKE, John, in Aldous Huxley's *Point Counter Point* (1928). The artist Augustus John (1878–1961) is Bidlake's probable prototype. His models included Maria Nys, subsequently Huxley's wife. To name but two sources, George Woodcock's *Dawn and the Darkest Hour: A Study of Aldous Huxley* (1972) says 'John Bidlake is Augustus John spiked with Renoir', and Keith May's *Aldous Huxley* (1972) says 'It has been widely accepted since publication that John Bidlake is based on Augustus John.' What gives one pause for thought, however, is the fact that Sybille Bedford, author of the definitive two-volume Huxley biography, makes no such connection . . .

BIGELOW-MARTIN, Dr, in James Purdy's *Cabot Wright Begins* (1965). Did Purdy have in mind the author of *The Function of the Orgasm* in his creation of Bigelow-Martin? In *City of Words: American Fiction 1950–70* (1971), Tony Tanner remarks that Bigelow-Martin is 'one of those strange instructors and doctors, mixtures of charlatan and genius, who appear so frequently in novels by writers as different as Bellow, Barth and Burroughs, and perhaps owe something to the figure of Wilhelm Reich'. An Austrian who settled in America in 1939, Reich (1897–1957) was a psychiatrist specialising in sexuality. He championed the orgasm's importance to mental health and sought to identify libido with electrical energy which he recorded through electrodes positioned on the body. Often in dispute with others, he was expelled from the International Psychoanalytic Association in 1934 and at the time of his death was in prison, gaoled for contempt of court.

BIGGLES (James Bigglesworth), in W.E. Johns's 'Biggles' stories, commencing with 'The White Fokker' (*The Camels are Coming*, 1932). Now here's a curious, previously unknown sidelight on the Second World War. The daughter of Richmal Crompton's 'William' tells me that her father spent the war in Iceland with the RAF. From another source, I learn that the Air Officer Commanding Iceland at that time was Air Commodore Cecil George Wigglesworth (1893–1961), upon whom Biggles was modelled. They must have met, neither (I presume) knowing 'who' the other was. The identity of the man behind Biggles began to emerge in 1949, when Johns disclosed in the *Radio Times* that 'Bigglesworth' was not unlike the name of the officer who had been an inspiration for his hero. A check through the Air Force list would have revealed Wigglesworth soon enough, but Peter Berresford Ellis and Piers Williams tried a different tack in researching *By Jove, Biggles! The Life of Captain W.E.*

Johns (1981). They approached a sister of Johns's illustrator, Howard Leigh, and she promptly named Wigglesworth, with whom the author had served in the First World War. Like his brother — Air Marshall Sir Philip Wigglesworth — Air Commodore Wigglesworth was commissioned in the Royal Naval Air Service, subsequently transferring to the RAF. His second war is the story of an opportunity missed. Unaware that it had the combined might of Biggles and William tucked away in Iceland, the War Office neglected to exploit the situation. Imagine the havoc that pair could have caused had Britain allowed them to be captured . . .

BIGWIG, in Richard Adams's *Watership Down* (1972). 'Bigwig', the author tells me, 'was Captain Paddy Kavanagh, RASC, who was killed at Arnhem and lies in the Airborne Division cemetery at Oosterbeck, east of Arnhem. He was a most gallant officer.' Captain Kavanagh came from Ireland and as a civilian had been a journalist. His article on parachuting, 'How We Pushed Off — Into Nothing', appeared in a Sunday newspaper in 1944. 'At the time of his death', says Richard Adams, 'I should say that Paddy would have been about twenty-eight or twenty-nine.'

BILHAM, John Little, in Henry James's *The Ambassadors* (1903), is supposedly Jonathan Sturges (1864–1911), a Princeton graduate crippled by poliomyelitis. Born in New York, he was the author of a number of stories, a translator of Maupassant, and a friend of both James (to whom he suggested the plot of *The Ambassadors*) and Whistler (see Sibley, Joe).

BIRCH, Dr, in W.M. Thackeray's *Dr Birch and his Young Friends* (1849), is Dr John Russell (1787–1863), headmaster of Charterhouse from 1811 to 1832. Thackeray's Charterhouse schoolfellow, H.G. Liddell (see Alice), who detested Russell's regime, complained, 'We have to sit for hours hearing him hackering on to try if he can to beat into the heads of those at the bottom by constant reiterated repetition what we know perfectly well by once going over; which of course renders what we do very little.'

BIRDSEYE, Miss, in Henry James's *The Bostonians* (1886), has a putative prototype in Elizabeth Palmer Peabody (1804–94), bookseller sister-in-law of the writer Nathaniel Hawthorne and a noted social reformer. She worked as an assistant in the Temple School, Boston, run by Louisa M. Alcott's father, and in 1860 established

America's first kindergarten. Ten years later, she was instrumental in the opening of America's first public kindergarten, in Boston.

BIRKIN, Sir Hereward, in Henry Williamson's saga *A Chronicle of Ancient Sunlight* (1951–69). 'We like Henry so much but he will take it all so seriously', said Sir Oswald Mosley of Williamson, his loyal supporter. 'It' was the Fascist cause, which both Mosley and Williamson embraced. Mosley (see Webley, Everard) is Birkin. Williamson's association with him and his own declared admiration for Hitler caused the author to be interned, briefly, in 1939. In 1968, Williamson reflected, 'Mosley, who is still my great friend, had the idea for the welfare state two generations ahead. He cared for three million unemployed, he wanted to make the motor roads. He was told he couldn't get the money because the City of London would not allow the second Labour government to have the loan. So he said: Who rules? The City of London or the Parliament that's elected? Then he went into the streets and his reputation, of course, went down . . . '

BISWAS, Mohun, in V.S. Naipaul's *A House for Mr Biswas* (1961), is the author's father, Seepersad Naipaul (1906–53), an imaginative, crusading reporter on the *Trinidad Guardian* and author of *Gurudeva and Other Indian Tales* (1943). Acknowledging this, the novelist disclosed in *Finding the Centre* (1984) that not until after the publication of *Mr Biswas* did he discover that his father's career had been ruined by a breakdown. The success of *Mr Biswas* had prompted somebody to send him a newspaper cutting describing Naipaul senior's enforced sacrifice of a goat to the goddess Kali. Seepersad had earlier reported such a sacrifice, attacking it as a superstitious practice, had received a note in Hindi instructing him to perform the same sacrifice himself or die within the week, had given in, and had gone mad as a consequence. 'He looked in the mirror one day', V.S. Naipaul's mother told him, 'and couldn't see himself. And he began to scream.'

BLACKETT, Nancy and Peggy, in Arthur Ransome's *Swallows and Amazons* saga (1930–47), have putative prototypes in Georgina and Pauline Rawdon-Smith, who holidayed at Tent Lodge, Coniston, at the time Ransome drafted *Swallows and Amazons* in the vicinity. Pauline went on to become a sailing instructor and the inventor of a seat enabling handicapped sailors to change sides when tacking, as Christina Hardyment records in *Arthur Ransome and*

Captain Flint's Trunk (1984). Hardyment thinks it more likely, however, that the model for Nancy is Taqui Altounyan (see Walker, John).

BLACKHOUSE, Tommy, in Evelyn Waugh's *Officers and Gentlemen* (1955), is supposedly part-inspired by Major-General Sir Robert Laycock (1907–68), the novel's dedicatee and – as a briga-dier – the author's wartime commanding officer. In Crete, his equipment included a book of crossword puzzles. In North Africa, in 1941, he led an abortive attempt to kidnap Rommel at his Cyrenaican HQ.

BLACKTHORNE, John, in James Clavell's *Shōgun* (1975), has as prototype William Adams (*d.* 1620), an English navigator from Gillingham, Kent. Serving with a Dutch fleet, he was detained when his ship put in to the island of Kiushiu, Japan, in 1600. He remained in Japan for the rest of his life, becoming a favourite of the *shōgun* Iyeyasu (who presented him with a large estate) and marrying into the Japanese aristocracy – although he had a wife and family in Kent.

BLADE, Millicent, in Evelyn Waugh's 'On Guard' (1934; *Mr Loveday's Little Outing and Other Sad Stories*, 1936), is Lady Mary ('Maimie') Lygon (1910–82), daughter of the Seventh Earl Beau-champ. In 1939 she married Prince Vsevolode Joannovit Romanovsky-Pavlovsky, in Russia. The marriage was dissolved in 1956. Her friendship with the author is chronicled by Waugh's biographer, Christopher Sykes.

BLADES, Zulu, in Wyndham Lewis's *The Apes of God* (1930). Not everybody would have wished to be presented as quite such a lusting colonial, but according to Jeffrey Meyers, Lewis's biographer, Roy Campbell (see Grovell, Dick) enjoyed cutting a colourful figure and doubtless relished this portrait – a favourable one, by Lewis's standards, for Campbell was a staunch friend.

BLAINE, Leonard, in Margaret Truman's *Murder in the White House* (1980), has as probable prototype Dean Acheson (1893–1971), US Secretary of State from 1949 to 1953.

BLAIR, Senator Theodore, in James Reichley's *Hail to the Chief* (1960), is Senator Robert A. Taft (1889–1953). 'Just as triumph for Eisenhower meant failure for Taft in 1952, so victory for Lucas P.

Starbuck is the last defeat for Theodore Blair', comments Joseph Blotner in *The Modern American Political Novel* (1966).

BLAIR-KENNEDY, John, in Noël Coward's *South Sea Bubble* (1956). According to Robert Lorin Calder's *W. Somerset Maugham and The Quest for Freedom* (1972), this representation of a cynical novelist is part-inspired by W. Somerset Maugham. See Bertrand, Archie.

BLAKE, Harry, in Hugh Walpole's 'The Whistle' (*All Souls' Night*, 1933), is Harold Cheevers. See Christian, Charlie.

BLAKE, Royden, in John Cheever's 'A Miscellany of Characters That Will Not Appear' (*Some People, Places and Things That Will Not Appear in My Next Novel*, 1961). The novelist and critic Julian Barnes has suggested a prototype for Blake in the American writer John O'Hara (1905–70).

BLANCHE, Anthony, in Evelyn Waugh's *Brideshead Revisited* (1945), is an amalgam of Brian Howard (see Silk, Ambrose) and Sir Harold Acton (1904–   ), historian, novelist and an Oxford contemporary of the author. 'Most people delight in recognizing themselves in a book,' Acton remarks in his *Memoirs of an Aesthete* (1948). 'It helps to persuade them that they exist.'

BLANCOVE, Edward, in George Meredith's *Rhoda Fleming* (1865), is Edward Peacock, son of the novelist Thomas Love Peacock and brother-in-law of the author. Like his father, he worked in London's East India House.

BLANKTON, Carla, in Gore Vidal's *In a Yellow Wood* (1947), is Anaïs Nin. See Donegal, Marietta.

BLIGH, Betty, in Wyndham Lewis's *The Apes of God* (1930). Dora Carrington (see Morrison) was petite, Lytton Strachey, whom she loved, exceptionally tall. Thus, Lewis sends Strachey (Matthew Plunkett) to a psychiatrist, who advises him to select a lady of Lilliputian proportions . . . Carrington (Betty Bligh).

BLIMBER, Cornelia, in Charles Dickens's *Dombey and Son* (1847–8), is supposedly Louisa Menzies (née King, ?1827–94), eldest daughter of Joseph Charles King, at whose College School in

St John's Wood she taught Greek. Two of Dickens's children attended King's establishment, and Louisa Menzies contributed a story and a serial to Dickens's *Household Words* in 1854 and 1855, respectively.

BLISS, Judith, in Noël Coward's *Hay Fever* (1925), has as proto-type the American actress Laurette Taylor (1884–1946), wife of the dramatist Hartley Manners. She was celebrated for her title-role appearances in *Peg O' My Heart* and was a noted society hostess at her home in Riverside Drive, New York. Describing her as 'lovable, intolerant and entirely devoid of tact', Coward paid tribute in his autobiography, *Present Indicative* (1937), to her quick wit — 'she could pounce from a great height with all the swift accuracy of a pelican diving into the sea, seldom failing to spear some poor, wriggling fish, and disquieting considerably the other fish present ... I am only grateful to Fate that no guest of the Hartley Manners thought of writing *Hay Fever* before I did.'

BLOATER, Lillian, in Ronald Firbank's *The Flower Beneath the Foot* (1923). When Victoria Gellybore-Frinton (Vita Sackville-West) declares that hardly anyone 'is doing anything for English Letters', herself and Lillian Bloater excepted, Firbank's Lillian is Sackville-West's friend, Virginia Woolf (see Aspasia), identified by Brigid Brophy in her Firbank biography, *Prancing Novelist* (1973).

BLOCH, in Marcel Proust's *A la recherche du temps perdu* (1913–27), is supposedly an amalgam of René Blum (1878–1942), miscel-laneous writer and brother of the critic-turned-statesman Léon Blum, first Socialist prime minister of France; Léon Brunschvieg (1869–1944), philosopher and editor of the works of Pascal; the author's schoolfellow, Horace Finaly (1871–1945), brother of Marie Finaly (see Simonet, Albertine), a Jewish banker's son who became Director of the Bank of Paris and the Netherlands, and France's Minister of Finance; the French critic and poet, Fernand Gregh (1873–1960), founder of the *Humanisme* poetical movement; Abel Hermant (1862–1950), novelist, dramatist and journalist; and Pierre Quillard (1868–1912), poet, classical scholar and politician with a conversational penchant for applying high-flown, Homeric phrases to mundane matters.

BLOOD, Arthur, in Ford Madox Ford's *Mr Fleight* (1913), is Arthur Marwood. See Tietjens, Christopher.

BLOOM, Leopold, in James Joyce's *Ulysses* (1922). Joyce's Proustian practice of melding a variety of individuals into one character is particularly evident in Bloom. The author's biographer, Richard Ellmann, perceives a number of models: Charles Chance (see M'Coy, C.P.), who, like Bloom, had several occupations and whose wife, like Bloom's Molly, was a singer with a 'professional' name — 'Madame Marie Tallon', as opposed to Molly's 'Madame Marion Tweedy'; Alfred H. Hunter, a Dublin-Jewish cuckold — Joyce's brother, Stanislaus, said that the author spoke to him in 1906 of his plan to write *Ulysses*, portraying Hunter; Teodoro Mayer, founder in 1881 of the Trieste evening newspaper *Il piccolo della sera*, subsequently an Italian senator and, like Bloom, the son of a Hungarian pedlar; and the Italian novelist Italo Svevo (Ettore Schmitz, 1861–1928), whom Joyce taught English at the Berlitz School in Trieste, later taking him up as an elderly protégé — like Bloom, Svevo married a Gentile, changed his name (albeit only as a writer), was familiar with Jewish customs and shared Bloom's taste in food.

BLOOM, Molly, *idem*, is part-inspired by Nora Barnacle (*d.* 1951), who after nearly thirty years as the author's common-law wife married him in 1931, when she was forty-seven, their son twenty-six and their daughter twenty-three. The daughter of a Galway baker, she was a Dublin hotel chambermaid when she first met Joyce, in 1904. When Molly Bloom's soliloquy was praised to her as a masterly interpretation of feminine psychology, she replied irritably that Joyce didn't understand women at all. Also discerned in Molly Bloom are Amalia Popper (see Clery, Emma) and Signora Nicolas Santos, wife of a Trieste fruiterer and custodian of a complexion which kept her indoors all day, mixing her own beauty creams.

BLOUGRAM, Bishop, in Robert Browning's 'Bishop Blougram's Apology' (*Men and Women*, 1855), is Cardinal Nicholas Wiseman (1802–65), a persuasive exponent of his faith. His appointment in 1850 as cardinal and archbishop of Westminster — part of Pope Pius IX's plan for reviving a diocesan hierarchy in England — was widely resented as a sign of papal aspirations to territorial rule. The potentially explosive situation was defused by Wiseman's diplomacy, his reputation as one of the most gifted men of his day, and his pamphlet, 'Appeal to the English People'.

BLOW, Christopher, in Harold Acton's 'A Morning at Upshott's (*The Soul's Gymnasium*, 1982), is the novelist Evelyn Waugh (1903−66), who nearly forty years earlier had used Acton as a model (see Blanche, Anthony).

BLUEBEARD, in Charles Perrault's *Histoires et contes du temps passé* (1697), has a putative original in England's Henry VIII (1491−1547), notorious for his six wives, two of whom were beheaded. Brittany tradition, however, suggests a prototype in Gilles de Laval, Baron Retz (?1404−1440), a marshal of France and supporter of Joan of Arc, with whom he fought against the English at Orléans. A necromancer, he was executed for kidnapping and killing children. Unlike Bluebeard, he had only one wife, who left him. Another possible prototype is Comorre (or Conomor), a sixth-century Breton tyrant alleged by Alain Bouchard in *Grandes Croniques* (1531) to have murdered a number of wives.

BLUMENFELD, in P.G. Wodehouse's *The Inimitable Jeeves* (1923), is the American theatrical manager and producer, Abraham Lincoln Erlanger (1860−1930), who relied on a nephew to tell him whether or not the public would like a projected show.

BLUNTSCHLI, Captain, in George Bernard Shaw's *Arms and the Man* (1894). In Bluntschli and his rival, Sergius, Shaw presents two contrasting protagonists of Socialism: the diligent, low-profile, analytical Sidney Webb (see Bailey, Oscar), represented by Bluntschli; and the dramatic, bull-at-a-gate, R.B. Cunninghame Graham (see Hushabye, Hector), in the form of Sergius. Like Bluntschli, Webb was not one for the frontal assault when other methods might achieve the same ends; very much a man of action Cunninghame Graham led a charge against the police in Trafalgar Square.

BLUSTER, Sir Boreas, in Anthony Trollope's *Marion Fay* (1882). This Post Office chief is surely the author's Post Office superior, Sir Rowland Hill (see Hardlines, Sir Gregory), on the evidence of Trollope's uneasy relationship with his boss (see Buffle, Sir Raffle). Trollope had retired from the Post Office in 1870 and Hill had died in 1879, so the author was able to say what he liked about both.

BOANERGES, Bill, in George Bernard Shaw's *The Apple Cart* (1929). Noting that Shaw was 'assiduous in collecting human beings', his secretary, Blanche Patch, in *Thirty Years with GBS*

(1951), identifies Boanerges as the English politician John Burns (1858–1943), leader of the trade unionists' Progressive Party and of an 1889 dock strike. He was MP for Battersea (1892–1918), president of the Local Government Board (1905–14) and president of the Board of Trade (1914), resigning on the declaration of war.

BOBBE, Comrade, in Richard Aldington's *Death of a Hero* (1929). A 'sandy-haired, narrow-chested little man with spiteful blue eyes and a malevolent class hatred', Bobbe 'exercised his malevolence with comparative impunity by trading upon his working-class origin and his indigestion, of which he had been dying for 20 years.' His 'vanity and class consciousness made him yearn for affairs with upper-class women, although he was obviously a homosexual type.' Jaundiced though this portrait is – from a pen apparently itself dripping with malevolence – the sitter is clearly D.H. Lawrence (see Rampion, Mark). The reference to his penchant for upper-class women is presumably inspired by his friendship with Lady Cynthia Asquith and perhaps also by his affair with Frieda von Richthofen, which led to marriage. (For Lawrence's ambivalent sexuality, see Buryan, John Thomas and Crich, Gerald.) His long-standing 'indigestion' was consumption, of which he died in the year following this novel's publication. When Aldington showed him sections of *Death of a Hero* in manuscript, Lawrence warned: 'If you publish this, you'll lose what reputation you have – you're plainly on the way to an insane asylum.'

BOFFIN, in Charles Dickens's *Our Mutual Friend* (1864–5), is Henry Dodd, a philanthropic London dust-contractor who owned a vast dust-heap in Shepherdess Fields, Islington. Upon his daughter's marriage, he presented her with another of his dust-heaps, which she subsequently sold for £10,000. According to Dickens's biographer, F.G. Kitton, Dodd was addicted to the theatre, endowing several dramatic charities and establishing an unsuccessful drama college.

BOGNOR, Lord, in Harold Nicolson's *Some People* (1927), is supposedly the Rt Hon. Sir Percy Loraine, Twelfth Bart of Kirkharle (1880–1961), a career diplomat who was successively British Minister to Persia (1921–6), British Minister to Athens (1926–9, his staff including Alastair Graham – see Lennox, Hamish), High Commissioner for Egypt and the Sudan (1929–33), British Ambassador in Turkey (1933–9) and British Ambassador in Rome (1939–40). He dismissed *Some People* as 'a cad's book'.

BOGROV, Michael, in Arthur Koestler's *Darkness at Noon* (1940). When Pavel Dybenko (*d.* 1938) was rehabilitated in *Pravda* in 1964, Koestler confirmed that he had created Bogrov with Dybenko very much in mind. Joining the Communist Party in 1912, Dybenko led a mutiny on a Russian battleship in 1915 and during the Russian Revolution in 1917 led his fellow seamen in the battle against the old regime. He subsequently married one of Lenin's close associates, and became People's Commissar of the Navy Ministry. He was shot during a Stalinist purge, but upon his rehabilitation was described as a victim of Stalin's personality cult who had perished as a result of malicious slander.

BOHEMIA, the King of, in Sir Arthur Conan Doyle's 'A Scandal in Bohemia' (1891; *The Adventures of Sherlock Holmes*, 1892), has as prototype Edward, Prince of Wales (1841—1910), who in the year of the story's original publication was involved as a witness in the Tranby Croft affair in which Sir William Gordon-Cumming sued five men who had accused him of cheating at baccarat. Prince Edward was the eldest son of Queen Victoria, and became King Edward VII in 1901. The illustrator Sidney Paget's portrayal of the King of Bohemia was inspired by the appearance of the Prince of Wales's nephew, Wilhelm II of Germany.

BOHUN, Lord Horatio, in H.G. Wells's *The Holy Terror* (1939), is Sir Oswald Mosley (see Webley, Everard). As J.R. Hammond notes in *An H.G. Wells Companion* (1979), Bohun's party is a caricature of Mosley's Blackshirts.

BOK, Yakov Shepsovitchy, in Bernard Malamud's *The Fixer* (1966), has as prototype Mendel Beiliss, a Russian Jew employed in a brick factory, who in 1913 was tried in Kiev for the ritual murder of a Christian boy. He was acquitted.

BOLD, John, in Anthony Trollope's *The Warden* (1855), has a probable prototype in the Revd Robert Whiston, a mid-nineteenth-century headmaster of Rochester Cathedral Grammar School whose story is told in Ralph Arnold's *The Whiston Matter* (1961). He accused the cathedral's Dean and Chapter of violating their own statutes of 1545 in failing to educate and maintain twenty poor boys at the school, and failing to maintain four exhibitioners at universities. Whiston's widely reported legal battles with the cathedral authorities, who sacked and reinstated him twice, are believed to be the inspiration of Trollope's plot, although Whiston's rancorous litigious personality is not reflected in Bold. An accomplished propagandist, Whiston got a good press, and the Dean and Chapter a bad one. Trollope's assessment of the personalities involved would have been based on what he read in the newspapers.

BOLEYN, Dan, in Wyndham Lewis's *The Apes of God* (1930). As the author's biographer, Jeffrey Meyers, comments, it is an indication of the affection Lewis could inspire that Stephen Spender (see Savage, Stephen) could suffer this portrait of himself as an effeminate, moronic, would-be poet and remain his satirist's friend. Like Boleyn, he was an outstandingly handsome young man prone to nose-bleeds. Meyers's *The Enemy: a biography of Wyndham Lewis* (1980) notes that Spender confirms he was the model.

BOLKONSKAYA, Princess Lise, in Leo Tolstoy's *War and Peace* (1865–72), has been identified by the translator and biographer David Magarshack as Princess Louisa Volkonskaya, a pretty relative of the author, who in his early twenties was much enamoured of her.

BOLKONSKAYA, Princess Maria Nikolaevna, *idem*, according to Edward Crankshaw's *Tolstoy: The Making of a Novelist* (1974), is Maria Nikolaevna Tolstoy (née Volkonsky, 1790–1830), the author's mother, who died in childbirth when he was two. Five years older than her husband, she was a wealthy heiress whom Tolstoy's father had married for her money. Although devoted to her five children, she had a reputation for hardness, disliking any display of emotion.

BOLKONSKY, Prince Nikolai Andreevich, *idem*, is the author's maternal grandfather, Prince Nikolai Sergeevich Volkonsky (1753–1821), who suddenly abandoned a distinguished public career to retire to the family estate, where he devoted himself to wood-carving and land-drainage.

BOLOFF, Alexander, in Vadim Kozhevnikoff's *Sword and Shield* (1966), is supposedly Colonel Rudolf Abel (*d.* 1971), who from 1948 to 1957 directed the Soviet spy network in the United States from an artist's studio in Brooklyn. Betrayed by an assistant, he was gaoled for thirty years, but was in 1962 exchanged for the American airman Francis Gary Powers, whose U2 spy plane had been shot down over

Russia two years earlier. Abel died in Moscow from lung cancer, aged sixty-eight.

BOLTON, Anna, in Louis Bromfield's *What Became of Anna Bolton?* (1945). Staying with friends in the country, the society hostess Laura Corrigan (née Whitrock, 1879−1948) casually picked up an axe and displayed a remarkable aptitude for chopping wood. What her hosts did not know, because she kept her origins to herself, was that she was the daughter of a Wisconsin lumberjack. The model for Anna Bolton, she in 1916 became the wife of a Cleveland steel millionaire and determined to establish herself as a hostess. Arriving in London in 1921, she rented an imposing residence, hired the social secretary of the Marchioness of Londonderry and swiftly bought her way into society. She was an unabashed snob − Chips Channon (see Templeton, Elliott) remarked that she talked of royalty even when standing on her head (a posture to which she was much addicted). She was also compulsively generous. Her party-game prizes cost hundreds of pounds and she thought nothing of spending several thousand on an evening. Caught up in occupied France in the early 1940s, she behaved with conspicuous courage. Although a social-climbing joke, she was regarded with affection for her naivety, warm-heartedness, gaffes and malapropisms. Back from a Mediterranean cruise, she was asked if she had seen the Dardanelles. No, she said, but she'd had a letter of introduction to them.

BOMBARDONE, Bardo, in George Bernard Shaw's *Geneva* (1938), is Benito Mussolini. See Arango, General Tereso.

BOND, James, in Ian Fleming's James Bond novels and short stories (1953−66), is supposedly an amalgam of a number of men with whom the author served in British Naval Intelligence in the Second World War. They include Commander Dunstan Curtis (1910−83), who played a leading role in the raid on St Nazaire, commanded the naval element of a Royal Marines assault unit which captured enemy ciphers in a raid on Algiers, and was Deputy Secretary General of the Council of Europe from 1954 to 1960; Commander Wilfred Albert ('Bill') Dunderdale (1899−   ), a Russian-speaking veteran of First World War intelligence operations in the Black Sea, whose first wife was Dorothy Hyde (d. 1978), former wife of the writer Montgomery Hyde and an intelligence expert in the forgery of signatures and undetectable opening of diplomatic mail; and Lt-Commander Michael Mason (1900−82), a

Royal Navy boxing champion who was involved in an attempt to cut the Nazis' oil supply by blocking the Danube, was Commodore of the Royal Ocean Racing Club from 1937 to 1947, High Sheriff of Oxfordshire in 1951 and Hon. Director of the Royal Agricultural Society of England from 1950 to 1952. Dusko Popov (*d.* 1981), a Yugoslav-born double agent involved in a number of Fleming's assignments, may have helped to inspire the gambling scene in *Casino Royale* (1953) — in Portugal, allegedly watched by Fleming, he gambled with $50,000 given to him by the Germans to pass to a contact in London ... money he was committed to hand to his employer, the British Government. Fleming, however, said the *Casino Royale* scene was prompted by his own unsuccessful attempt to 'clean out' some gamblers he suspected of being Nazi agents in Portugal. Code-named 'Tricycle', Popov was the son of a wealthy family and was an accomplished sportsman and linguist. He claimed to have tipped off the FBI's director that Pearl Harbour was to be attacked, only to have his warning ignored — perhaps because of his playboy image. He died in southern France, aged sixty-nine. Another suggested prototype is Sidney Reilly (Sigmund Rosenblum, 1874–?1925), a British spy who vanished in Russia in the 1920s. Born in Poland, he began spying for Britain in 1897. His coups reputedly included the discovery of the order of battle of the German fleet on the eve of the First World War. His sexual prowess was legendary — he had eleven passports and a 'wife' to go with each. Hunting him in 1918, the Russians arrested eight women, each of whom believed she was married to Reilly. In 1925 he disappeared, believed caught and executed by the Russians after the discovery of his planned coup against the Bolsheviks. Fleming was aware of his career, but said Bond was 'not a Sidney Reilly'. Bond acquired his name from James Bond, author of *Birds of the West Indies*, a favourite book of Fleming at his Jamaican retreat, where the ornithological Bond was among his neighbours.

BONIFACE, Adora, in Carl Van Vechten's *Nigger Heaven* (1926), according to Bruce Kellner's *Carl Van Vechten and the Irreverent Decades* (1968), is the Harlem hostess A'lelia Walker, wealthy daughter of Mrs C.J. Walker (1867–1919) of Indianapolis, inventor of a commercially successful hair-straightening process for Negresses.

BONSEN, the Revd Bobugo, in Frederick Rolfe's *The Desire and Pursuit of the Whole* (1934), is Monsignor Robert Hugh Benson (1871–1914), a Roman Catholic priest in the Westminster archdiocese, author of the best-sellers *The Lord of the World* and *The Dawn of All* and brother of the writers A.C. and E.F. Benson. Robert Benson's account of his acquaintance with Rolfe is to be found in his novel *Initiation*, in which Benson is Sir Nevill Fanning and Rolfe is Enid.

BONZO, in William Gerhardie's *Of Mortal Love* (1936), is John Ferrar Holms (*d.* 1934), a remarkable athlete who as a teenager in the First World War won the Military Cross after single-handedly killing four Germans he had surprised having breakfast. In the ensuing mêlée, he despatched them by hammering them over their heads with a piece of iron. Taken prisoner at nineteen, he had Hugh Kingsmill (see Fisher, Max) for a companion in captivity. Friends considered him a man of great talents gone to waste, for he was never able to harness his latent writing ability and wandered the world in poverty. His last job was as chauffeur-paramour in Paris to the American heiress and art collector Peggy Guggenheim. He died aged thirty-seven, failing to recover from the anaesthetic for a wrist operation. Holms was identified as Bonzo by Philip Toynbee in the *Observer* on 21 January 1962, and an account of his life by Lance Sieveking appeared in the *Listener* on 31 January 1957.

BOON, George, in H.G. Wells's *Boon* (1915), is largely inspired by the American novelist Henry James (1843–1916). In response to Wells's claim that novels should be vehicles for propaganda, not art, James replied, 'It is art that *makes* life, makes interest, makes importance, and I know of no substitute whatever for the force and beauty of its process. If I were Boon I should say that any pretence of such a substitute is helpless and hopeless humbug; but I wouldn't be Boon for the world, and am only yours faithfully, Henry James.'

BOOT, William, in Evelyn Waugh's *Scoop* (1938). In 1974, when William Deedes (1913–   ) was about to become editor of the *Daily Telegraph*, the *Sunday Times* suggested he was at least in part the original of Boot – in 1935 he was sent by the *Morning Post* to cover the Italian invasion of Abyssinia and he shared a house with Waugh in Addis Ababa. Although Deedes has written of this experience, he has not claimed to be Boot and the identification is unlikely. Boot is surely largely a self-portrait of Waugh, the dilettante reporter late with his copy. Deedes at that time had four years' newspaper experience ... and was chosen for the Abyssinian assignment, he believed, because he was unmarried and therefore cheaper to insure.

BORDEREAU, Juliana and Tita, in Henry James's *The Aspern Papers* (1888). Juliana has as prototype Claire Clairmont (1798–1879), step-daughter of the atheist philosopher William Godwin, friend of Shelley, with whom her step-sister eloped, and mother of Lord Byron's daughter, Allegra. Living in Florence with her niece, she was in 1878 visited by an American who gained admission to her house with the intention of acquiring her priceless correspondence of the Shelley-Byron era. He failed in his mission (see Jarvis, Henry). Tita is supposedly part-inspired by the American novelist Constance Fenimore Woolson (1840–94), a great-niece of James Fenimore Cooper. She is believed to have cherished an affection for James (some years her junior) which he felt physically unable to return, and died after falling – or throwing herself – from her bedroom window in Venice.

BORGÉ, Isabelle, in F. Scott Fitzgerald's *This Side of Paradise* (1920), is identified by Fitzgerald's biographer, Arthur Mizener, as Ginevra King, daughter of a wealthy family from Lake Forest, Chicago. The author first met her when she was a student at Westover and he was at Princeton University. He later looked back on her as his first love. In 1918 she married another.

BOSINNEY, Philip, in John Galsworthy's *The Man of Property* (1906), is an amalgam of Edward Garnett (see Lea) and the architect Philip Speakman Webb (1831–1915). It was upon Garnett that the author modelled Bosinney's character, while Webb served as proto-type for the architect. On the advice of Garnett, his publisher's reader, Galsworthy rewrote his original draft in which Bosinney committed suicide because of financial worries – Garnett argued that it was inconceivable that a man of Bosinney's nature would kill himself because of a money problem. Webb was founder (with William Morris, in 1877) of the Society for the Protection of Ancient Buildings. One of his clients recalled that when he told Webb the sort of house he had in mind, he was treated to a lecture on the supreme importance of quality: 'I suppose I managed to excite his suspicion that as I was to live in the house, I, too, might have a view or two now and then, and might here and there want a voice which might be dissonant from his own, for he bid me to reflect that he was very despotic, that he would never make a concession he might think unwise to economy, nor please his client at the expense of his conscience.'

BOSS, in Alexander Zinoviev's *The Yawning Heights* (1979), is the Soviet dictator Joseph Stalin (1879—1953).

BOULBON, Dr du, in Marcel Proust's *A la recherche du temps perdu* (1913—27), is Dr Édouard Brissaud (1852—1909), a physician for whose *L'Hygiène des asthmatiques* Proust's father wrote a preface. A fashionable St Germain physician, Le Reboulet, has also been discerned in du Boulbon.

BOURGH, Lady Catherine de, in Jane Austen's *Pride and Prejudice* (1813), has a suggested model in Grizel, Second Countess Stanhope (1719—1811). Forceful and domineering, she brought up her granddaughter, the noted traveller Lady Hester Stanhope, following the death of Lady Hester's mother.

BOURIENNE, Mlle, in Leo Tolstoy's *War and Peace* (1865—72), has as prototype Louise Hénissienne, the French companion of the author's mother, to whom the Countess gave an estate and 75,000 roubles.

BOVARY, Charles and Emma, in Gustave Flaubert's *Madame Bovary* (1856), have as prototypes Eugène Delamare, a Rouen surgeon who studied under the author's father, and his wife, Delphine (née Conturier, 1822—48). A widower, Delamare married Delphine, the pretty daughter of a farmer, in 1839. She was much influenced by romantic novels, and finding that life with a middle-aged provincial physician could never match her ideals, she passed from ennui to nymphomania and debt, finally killing herself with arsenic. Her husband, too, committed suicide. Emma Bovary is also supposedly part-inspired by the author's mistress, the poet Louise Colet (1808—76), who once declared that the missing arms of the Venus de Milo had at last been discovered — in the sleeves of her dress.

BOWLES, Sally, in Christopher Isherwood's *Sally Bowles* (1937) and *Goodbye to Berlin* (1939). The daughter of a Scottish cotton merchant, Jean Ross (*d.* 1973) was brought up in Egypt but at seventeen rebelled against the leisured opulence of her home life and went to Berlin. There she worked as a cabaret singer, making up with her personality for what she lacked as a vocalist and becoming Isherwood's occasional flatmate and his model for Bowles. On returning to Britain she married Claud Cockburn (see Seymour,

Humphrey); their daughter Sarah Cockburn became a barrister and a novelist, writing under the name Sarah Caudwell. In Cheltenham, Jean Ross shared a house with Olive Mangeot (see Cheuret, Madame), and by interesting a film director in Isherwood's work she was instrumental in his involvement with Hollywood.

BOX-BENDER, Arthur, in Evelyn Waugh's *Men at Arms* (1952), is Brendan Bracken (see Mottram, Rex), according to Waugh's biographer, Christopher Sykes, who knew Bracken well.

BOXER, Tom, in W.M. Thackeray's *The History of Henry Esmond Esq.* (1852), is John Forster (see Podsnap). 'Has Forster in the *Examiner* attacked Thackeray's lectures on the English Humorists out of injudicious loyalty to Dickens?' asks Gordon N. Ray in *Buried Life: A Study of the Relation between Thackeray's Fiction and his Personal History* (1952). 'He figures as Tom Boxer who, because he is "Mr Congreve's man", falls foul in the *Observator* of a new comedy by Dick Steele.'

BOYLAN, Blazes, in James Joyce's *Ulysses* (1922), is part-inspired by Oliver St John Gogarty (see Mulligan, Buck). For the character's appearance and life-style, Joyce is also believed to have drawn on a Dublin post-office worker named Creech, and upon Ted Keogh, a Dublin horse-dealer, junk-shop proprietor and prize-fighter manager.

BOYLE, Sir Harry, in Charles Lever's *Charles O'Malley, the Irish Dragoon* (1840), is Sir Boyle Roche (1743–1807), an Irish politician noted for 'bulls' including 'Why should we do anything for posterity? What has posterity done for us?'

BOYTHORN, Lawrence, in Charles Dickens's *Bleak House* (1852–3), is Walter Savage Landor (1775–1864), a poet and miscellaneous writer noted for his irascibility, generosity, prejudices and penchant for domestic pets.

BRACEGIRDLE, Mary, in Aldous Huxley's *Crome Yellow* (1921). In a letter, Huxley records sleeping on the roof at Garsington — the home of Lady Ottoline Morrell — 'in company with an artistic young woman with short hair and purple pyjamas'. That description fits Dora Carrington (see Morrison), whom Huxley met at Garsington. In *Crome Yellow*, Ivor Lombard spends a night on the roof with

Mary Bracegirdle, whose personality echoes that of Carrington . . . whose relationship with Mark Gertler (see Loerke) was probably the inspiration of Anne Wimbush's liaison with Gombauld in *Crome Yellow*.

BRADDOCKS, Mr and Mrs Henry, in Ernest Hemingway's *The Sun Also Rises* (1926; published in England as *Fiesta*), are the novelist Ford Madox Ford (1873–1939), for whose *Transatlantic Review* Hemingway worked in Paris, and Ford's mistress, Stella Bowen. See Wannop, Valentine.

BRADLEY, in Frances Trollope's *The Blue Belles of England* (1842), is the painter Edwin Landseer (1802–73), a favourite artist of Queen Victoria. He is reputed to have suffered a mental breakdown in 1840 upon the rejection of his proposal of marriage to the recently widowed Duchess of Bedford.

BRADLEY, Dame Beatrice (formerly Mrs Beatrice Adela Lestrange Bradley), in Gladys Mitchell's detective novels (1929–84). Interviewed in 1979, Gladys Mitchell disclosed that Dame Beatrice was 'based on two women – a very wealthy old lady to whom my aunt was housekeeper, and the warden of my own hostel at college.' The author attended Goldsmiths' and University colleges, London. When she was a student, Goldsmiths' alone had at least eight women's hostels. I think it unlikely that the two colleges' records would show which hostel(s) Gladys Mitchell occupied, and even if this information were available there would probably be three or four wardens from which to choose. So if you *really* want to know who contributed the academic part of Dame Beatrice, the field is yours . . .

BRADLEY, Tommy and Helene, in Ernest Hemingway's *To Have and Have Not* (1937), according to Carlos Baker, are George Grant Mason, a Havana-based Pan American Airways official, and his wife, Jane, whom Hemingway first met on the liner *Ile de France* in 1931.

BRADSHAWE, in C.F. Hoffman's *Greyslaer* (1840), is part-inspired by Colonel Solomon P. Sharp. See Octavia.

BRADSTREET, Anne, in John Berryman's *Homage to Mistress Bradstreet* (1956), is part-inspired by the poet's first wife, Eileen

Simpson (née Mulligan), psychotherapist, novelist and short-story writer, although the work is primarily an ode to the colonial poet Anne Bradstreet (?1612–72). 'Her life was so intertwined with ours it was sometimes difficult for him [Berryman] to distinguish between her and himself, between her and me', remarks Simpson in *Poets in their Youth* (1982).

BRADWARDINE, the Baron of, in Sir Walter Scott's *Waverley* (1814), is believed to be the author's childhood friend and mentor, Alexander Stewart (*d.* 1795), of Invernahyle, a veteran of the battle of Prestonpans. After living in hiding on his estate, he was pardoned under the Act of Indemnity of 1747. Another suggested prototype is Alexander, Fourth Lord Forbes of Pitsligo (1678–1762), who at sixty-seven took part in the rebellion of 1745. As a consequence he lost his lands and for the rest of his life led a fugitive existence, often disguised as a beggar.

BRADWARDINE, the Baron of, in W.M. Thackeray's *The Book of Snobs* (1846–7). In their *Thackeray Dictionary* (1910), Isadore Gilbert Mudge and M. Earl Sears identify Bradwardine as the novelist Sir Walter Scott (1771–1832), appearing under the name of one of his own characters (see previous entry).

BRADY, Cecilia, in F. Scott Fitzgerald's *The Last Tycoon* (1941), brings together the youth of the author's daughter, Frances Scott ('Scottie') Fitzgerald (1921–), and Fitzgerald's one-time script-writing colleague Budd Schulberg (1914–), novelist son of a Hollywood film producer.

BRADY, Kid, in P.G. Wodehouse's *Psmith, Journalist* (1915), is modelled in part on the American boxer Kid McCoy (Norman Selby), winner of the world welterweight title in 1896, and ten times married (to eight women), serving eight years' penal servitude following the death of one of his spouses. In a rash moment, the author asked McCoy for a bout. The boxer accepted the challenge, but the contest never took place, much to Wodehouse's relief.

BRADY, Pat, in F. Scott Fitzgerald's *The Last Tycoon* (1941), has three suggested originals: the film producer Joseph L. Mankiewicz (1909–), noted for his predilection for rewriting others' work – including Fitzgerald's script for *Three Comrades*; Edgar J. Mannix (*d.* 1963), a Metro-Goldwyn-Mayer vice president addicted to practical jokes, who entered the film industry in 1916, joined MGM in 1925 and was so trusted by Clark Gable that the film-star refused to sign his first contract, saying he had shaken hands with Eddie Mannix and that was good enough for him; and Louis B. Mayer. See Brinkmeyer.

BRAGALDI, in Charlotte Barnes's *Octavia Bragaldi* (1837), is Jeroboam O. Beauchamp. See Octavia.

BRAILSFORD, Madge, in George Bernard Shaw's *Love Among the Artists* (1881). Margot Peters's *Bernard Shaw and the Actresses* (1980) identifies Brailsford as being part-inspired by the author's sister Lucinda Frances (1853–1920), who as a soprano appeared on the stage as Miss Lucy Carr Shaw, was noted for her beauty and wit and in her youth complained that her brother listened to all she said, and wrote down the good bits as his own. Both Oscar Wilde and his brother, Willie, were said to have fallen in love with her. In 1887 she married the tenor Charles Butterfield. They were divorced in 1909, and eleven years later she died from consumption.

BRAMBLE, Colonel, in André Maurois's *Les Silences du Colonel Bramble* (1918), is part-inspired by Dr George William James, a distinguished London psychiatrist who, as a Royal Army Medical Corps captain, served in the First World War with the author. Maurois was attached to the British Army as a liaison officer.

BRAND, in Henrik Ibsen's *Brand* (1866), is principally modelled upon Christopher Bruun, an uncompromising young Norwegian theological student whom Ibsen came to know in Rome in 1864. They became friends for life. Brand has also been taken to be the Danish philosopher Søren Kierkegaard (1813–55), who appears as a parrot in Hans Andersen's 'The Galoshes of Fortune'.

BRANDENFELD, Frieda, in Franz Kafka's 'The Judgement' (1916), is part-inspired by Felice Bauer. See Bürstner, Fräulein.

BRANDERHAM, Jabes, in Emily Brontë's *Wuthering Heights* (1847), is the Revd Jabez Bunting (1779–1858), superintendent of the Halifax circuit during the Luddite riots, pioneer advocate of the involvement of laymen in Wesleyan church management, president of the Theological Institute from 1834 to 1858, and four times president of the Methodist Conference. The author's father disapproved of Bunting, disliking his church 'politics' and finding him pompous and arrogant.

BRANDERS, Hans, in Reginald Turner's *Davray's Affairs* (1906). 'His eyes, which were the best part of his face, were given to troubling men and women alike. When they looked at women it was difficult to say whether they were being used for love-making, or for prying into the heart of the person on whom they gazed; and when they fell on men, especially men who had a good opinion of themselves, they seemed to be lighting, in kindly fashion, on a weak point.' That is Max Beerbohm (see Quin, Auberon) in the guise of Hans Branders. Sir Rupert Hart-Davis, editor of *Max Beerbohm: Letters to Reggie Turner* (1964), believes that Turner forewarned Beerbohm that he was to be in the novel, for there is a Beerbohm letter playfully proposing to take legal advice.

BRANDES, Easter, in J.G. Huneker's *Painted Veils* (1920). Elements of three opera singers are perceived in Brandes by the author's biographer, Arnold T. Schwab, who names Mary Garden (1874–1967), Sybil Sanderson (1865–1903) and Olive Fremstad (1871–1951) as the models. Garden, whose parents left Aberdeen to settle in Chicago, achieved overnight success as a stand-in and was noted for her unshakable composure. When Debussy chose her to create his Mélisande and fell in love with her, she deflected his advances by praising his wife. Though her lovers were numerous, she confessed herself incapable of passion and was an outspoken feminist — 'she talks too much', explained a man arrested in Chicago for trying to kill her. Sanderson, for whom Massenet wrote *Thaïs*, was a Californian engaged at one time to Randolph Hearst (see Stoyte, Mr); to thwart the romance, her parents sent her to Paris. Fremstad was the illegitimate adopted daughter of Scandinavian parents who settled in Minnesota. A temperamental performer who lived for her career, she left the stage in early middle age after differences with the manager of the New York Metropolitan Opera, spending the rest of her life as a recluse. She believed in doing her homework: before appearing as Salome, she acquired first-hand experience of the weight of a head on a plate by going to a morgue.

BRANDETSKI, Cyril and Simeon, in Ford Madox Ford's *The Simple Life Limited* (published under the pseudonym Daniel Chaucer, 1911). In *The Life in the Fiction of Ford Madox Ford* (1980), Thomas C. Moser discerns Sergei Stepniak (S.M. Kravchinsky; see

Laspara, Julius) in Cyril Brandetski; and Ford's friend and collaborator, the novelist Joseph Conrad (1857–1924), in Simeon. As Rebecca West has written, 'The relationship began beautifully, with Ford as guru instructing the grateful Polish disciple in the refinements of English prose, and it ended with Conrad and Jessie [his wife] going frantic in their efforts to get the Djinn back into the bottle' (*Sunday Telegraph*, 7 May 1972).

BRANGWEN, Gudrun, in D.H. Lawrence's *The Rainbow* (1915) and *Women in Love* (1920), is inspired partly by the New Zealand short-story writer Katherine Mansfield (1888–1923), whose second husband was John Middleton Murry (see Crich, Gerald), and partly by the author's wife's younger sister, Johanna ('Nusch') von Richthofen (1882–1971), who married first Max von Schreibershofen (*b.* 1864), and then Emil von Krug (1870–1944).

BRANGWEN, Ursula, *idem*. The more shabbily some women are treated, the greater is their devotion, or at least so it was with Louie Burrows (1888–1962), the primary model for Ursula. She was a student-teacher with Lawrence in Ilkeston and then in Nottingham, and he was engaged to her from December 1910 to February 1912, breaking it off on the pretext that a severe attack of pneumonia had changed him and that doctors had advised him not to marry, at least for some considerable time. Becoming headmistress of a succession of schools in Leicestershire, she was interested in spiritualism and in 1941 married Frederick Heath, a widowed boot- and shoe-manufacturer, after a medium assured her that his first wife wished it. On her death, she left 165 letters and postcards written to her by Lawrence, having for years carried the tenderest of them in a special pocket sewn into her corsets, and having thrice visited his grave, the last occasion being in 1950. Also to be seen in Ursula Brangwen are traces of Frieda Lawrence (see Somers, Harriet), with whom the author eloped three months after terminating his engagement to Miss Burrows.

BRANGWEN, Will, *idem*, is Alfred Burrows, a wood-carver and church organist from Cossall, Nottinghamshire, and the father of Louie Burrows (see Brangwen, Ursula).

BRAXTON, Stephen, in Max Beerbohm's 'Maltby and Braxton' (*Seven Men*, 1919), as Beerbohm himself confirmed, is in part William Butler Yeats (1865–1939), the Irish poet and dramatist.

BRÉAUTÉ, Hannibal (Babal) de, in Marcel Proust's *A la recherche du temps perdu* (1913—27), is an amalgam of Marquis Henri de Breteuil, friend of the Prince of Wales and husband of an American heiress, and Comte Louis de Turenne, noted for his unreliable investment tips and equally unfortunate dabbling in matchmaking.

BRENDAN, Gareth, in Harold Robbins's *Dreams Die First* (1977), has as prototype the American magazine publisher and gaming club entrepreneur Hugh Hefner (1926—   ), who founded *Playboy* in 1953 and in 1960 opened the first of his Playboy clubs.

BRENNBAUM, in Ezra Pound's *Hugh Selwyn Mauberley* (1920). Known as 'The Incomparable Max', Max Beerbohm (see Quin, Auberon) here becomes 'the impeccable' Brennbaum . . . and Pound elsewhere refers to 'the impeccable Beerbohm'. But Pound, presenting Brennbaum as a Jew, appears to have assumed that Beerbohm was Jewish, which he was not.

BRETHERTON, Miss, in Mrs Humphry Ward's *Miss Bretherton* (1884), is the American actress Mary Antoinette Anderson (1859—1940), who played Rosalind in the production of *As You Like It* which opened the Shakespeare Memorial Theatre at Stratford-upon-Avon. She retired in 1889, but in the First World War returned to the stage in a number of productions in aid of disabled servicemen. Witnessing one of these performances, Cynthia Asquith (see Pervin, Isabel) noted that it gave the lie to the legend that the actress owed her success merely to her beauty.

BRETT, Mr and Mrs Daniel, in Malcolm Muggeridge's *In a Valley of this Restless Mind* (1938), are Sidney and Beatrice Webb (see Bailey, Oscar and Altiora), as Muggeridge disclosed in an interview when the book was reissued in 1978. Beatrice was his wife's aunt. After a lifetime of social reforming and sexless marriage, said Muggeridge, she had commented on her 'naughty' sister Rosie (the book's near-nymphomaniac Mrs Angel), 'You know, Rosie was right.'

BRETTON, Dr John and Mrs Bretton, in Charlotte Brontë's *Villette* (1853). The author was normally loth to admit using real people for her characters. But when her publisher was slow to acknowledge receipt of the manuscript of *Villette* she confessed to Elizabeth Gaskell that she feared he might be offended by the similarity between the Brettons and himself and his mother. Bretton is George Murray Smith (1824–1901), of Smith & Elder (first established, as booksellers, in 1816). He founded the *Cornhill Magazine* (1859), the *Pall Mall Gazette* (1865), and the *Dictionary of National Biography* (1882). Mrs Bretton is his mother, Elizabeth Murray, the daughter of a glass manufacturer from Elgin, in Scotland. In 1820 she married George Smith, co-founder of Smith & Elder. Her son noted in 1900 that Mrs Bretton used several of his mother's expressions verbatim.

BRICHOT, in Marcel Proust's *A la recherche du temps perdu* (1913–27), is a composite of Victor Brochard, philosophy professor at the Sorbonne, Dreyfusard, author of a highly regarded work on the Greek sceptics and sufferer from incipient blindness attributed by the uncharitable to a venereal disease; and Joseph Reinach (1856–1921), politician, Dreyfusard, *Figaro* columnist and author of a seven-volume account of the Dreyfus affair.

BRICKNELL, Jim, in D.H. Lawrence's *Aaron's Rod* (1922). According to Harry T. Moore's *The Intelligent Heart: The Story of D.H. Lawrence* (1955), Bricknell is Captain James Robert White (1879–1946), son of a British field marshal and a veteran of the Boer War, in which he served in the Gordon Highlanders. In 1913 he was an organiser of the Irish Citizens' Army during the Dublin transport workers' strike. Following service with the Red Cross in France in 1914–15, he was in 1916 sentenced to three months' imprisonment for attempting to foment a miners' strike in Wales in an effort to secure a stay of execution for an Irish political prisoner.

BRIDAU, Joseph, in Honoré de Balzac's *Ursule Mirouët* (1841), *La Rabouilleuse* (1841–2), *Un Début dans la vie* (1842) and *Entre savants* (1845). Sometimes an author's slip of the pen removes any doubt as to his model for a character. In *Ursule Mirouët* Joseph Bridau paints Goethe's Mephistopheles. So did the artist Eugène Delacroix (1799–1863). Then, in *Entre savants*, Joseph momentarily becomes Eugène Bridau ...

BRIDEHEAD, Sue, in Thomas Hardy's *Jude the Obscure* (1896). According to Hardy's second wife, Sue Bridehead is modelled in part upon the Hon. Mrs Arthur Henniker-Major (née the Hon. Florence Ellen Hungerford Henniker, 1855–1923), a novelist with whom Hardy fell in love in the 1890s. Their friendship endured for thirty years, she impressed by his literary eminence, he much taken with her as a 'modern' woman and in awe of her background — a daughter of Monckton Milnes, First Baron Houghton (see Bulbul, Clarence), she was sister of Lord Crewe, a god-daughter of Florence Nightingale, and her husband became a major-general. There are also parallels between Sue Bridehead and the life of Hardy's cousin, Tryphena Sparks (1851–90), a schoolmistress to whom he is believed to have become engaged in 1867, although her brother maintained that Hardy was more attracted to his other sister, Martha. She became head of the girls' department of Plymouth Public Free School and in 1877 married Charles Gale, owner of the South Western Hotel in Topsham, Devon, bearing him four children.

BRIDGES, Dorothy, in Ernest Hemingway's *The Fifth Column* (1938). In Dorothy Bridges, the author all but transcribes Martha Gellhorn (see Maria) on to the page. They share the same looks, profession, cultured voice, academic background, domesticity, insistence on hygiene . . . and silver-fox cape.

BRIDGETTINA, in Elizabeth Hamilton's *The Memoirs of Modern Philosophers* (1800), is supposedly Mary Hays (?1763–1843), author of the six-volume *Female Biography: or Memoirs of illustrious and celebrated Women of all ages and countries* (1803). Her circle included William Godwin and Mary Wollstonecraft (see Marguerite), she was acquainted with Coleridge and Southey, and Lamb wrote: 'G— forbid I should/pass my days/with miss H-ys.'

BRIERS, Detective Chief Superintendent Frank, in C.P. Snow's *A Coat of Varnish* (1979), has as prototype Commander Ronald Harvey, head of the Murder Squad of London's Metropolitan Police and subsequently Adviser on Crime to the Chief Inspector of Constabulary, England and Wales.

BRIGGS, Stanley, in P.G. Wodehouse's *Not George Washington* (1907), is the actor-manager Sir Seymour Hicks (see Higgs). In 1906, notes N.T.P. Murphy's *In Search of Blandings* (1981), Hicks employed Wodehouse to write topical verses for the show *The Beauty of Bath*.

BRIGIT, in George Moore's *Ulick and Soracha* (1926), owes the description of her back to the author's sight of the naked hindquarters of Nancy Cunard (see Storm, Iris). A friend of the family since her childhood (and, some have suspected, her natural father), as an old man he pleaded with her to allow him to view her nude, from behind. It was shortly after she gratified this wish that the description of her back appeared in his next novel.

BRINKMEYER, in P.G. Wodehouse's *Laughing Gas* (1936), has as prototype Louis B. Mayer (1885–1957), scrap merchant turned cinema manager turned film distributor, who in 1924 formed the Metro-Goldwyn-Mayer film company with Sam Goldwyn (see Llewellyn, Ivor) and became its production chief. He was noted for his ability to feign anything from tears to a heart attack to secure a business advantage, although in dealing with clients of less sensitivity he favoured a right hook to the jaw.

BRISSENDEN, Russ, in Jack London's *Martin Eden* (1909), is supposedly the American poet George Sterling (1869–1926), who was much influenced by Bierce. Seventeen years after Brissenden's fictional suicide, Sterling killed himself in fact.

BRITLING, Mrs, in H.G. Wells's *Mr Britling Sees It Through* (1916), is identified in Lovat Dickson's *H.G. Wells – His Turbulent Life and Times* (1969) as the author's second wife, Amy Catherine Robbins. See Stanley, Ann Veronica.

BROADBENT, in George Bernard Shaw's *John Bull's Other Island* (1907), was taken by H.G. Wells (see Wilson, Hypo) to be a caricature of himself.

BROCK, Harry, in Garson Kanin's *Born Yesterday* (1946), is in part Harry Cohn (1891–1958), abrasive president and head of production of Columbia Pictures, who bought the play's film rights for a record one million dollars. Not noted for his interest in aesthetics, Cohn once said to a designer who had requested more money for the set of a love scene: 'Lemme tell you something. If in this whole ——— country when we show that scene there's one ——— person who'll be looking at your ——— wall . . . then we're in trouble.' He attracted extremes of affection and antipathy, and the Hollywood turn-out for his funeral prompted Red Skelton to remark: 'Well, it only proves what they always say – give the public something they want to see, and they'll come out for it.'

BROCK, Lord, in Anthony Trollope's *Can You Forgive Her?* (1864), *Phineas Finn* (1869), *Phineas Redux* (1874) and *The Prime Minister* (1876), is the British statesman Lord Palmerston (1784–1865), who was prime minister from 1855 to 1858 and again from 1859 to 1865. His career so closely paralleled Brock's, as John Halperin argues convincingly in *Trollope and Politics* (1977), that he is unmistakably Brock's model.

BROCKLEHURST, Revd Mr, in Charlotte Brontë's *Jane Eyre* (1847). Was the alleged model for Brocklehurst really the harsh zealot depicted? True, he did write, 'How dreadful is the wickedness of many children, who seem ripe at an early age for every act of sin which they are capable of performing . . .'. But there was another side to the Revd William Carus Wilson (1792–1859), vicar of Tunstall, Lancashire, who in 1823 founded Cowan Bridge School for the daughters of clergymen. The Brontë sisters attended this establishment, Maria (see Burns, Helen) and Elizabeth – Charlotte's elder sisters – dying after contracting consumption at the school and being sent home. Charlotte and Emily were subsequently removed from the school by their father. Charlotte's unhappy memory of the school and its 'black marble clergyman' contrasts, however, with the recollections of another pupil, Emma Jane Worboise: 'His works of love and mercy were manifold. He was thoroughly sincere and unostentatiously generous. A kinder man I never knew.' Editor of the penny papers the *Friendly Visitor* and the *Children's Friend*, Wilson founded five schools and was involved in the building of several churches. Single-handed, he conducted a mission to the British Army in India, and his preaching of temperance in Portsmouth was so potent that a local brewer promptly retired from his business.

BROGAN, Lewis, in Simone de Beauvoir's *The Mandarins* (1954). 'I've been in whorehouses all over the world and the woman there always closes the door, whether it's in Korea or India. But this woman flung the door open and called in the public and the Press', lamented the American novelist Nelson Algren (1909–81) the day before he died. Interviewed by W.J. Weatherby for the *Sunday Times*, he was recalling his affair with Simone de Beauvoir which led to his portrayal as Lewis Brogan. 'She gave me a disguise, another name, in *The Mandarins*, but in a later book . . . she tried to make our relationship into a great international literary affair, naming me and quoting from some of my letters . . . Hell, love letters should be private.'

BROMPTON, Sir Ralph, in Evelyn Waugh's *Unconditional Surrender* (1961). The author's biographer, Christopher Sykes, suggests that Waugh had Harold Nicolson (see Chilleywater, the Hon. Harold) 'occasionally in mind' when he created Sir Ralph, to whom pomposity and homosexuality come equally naturally.

BROOKES, Winsome, in Ronald Firbank's *Vainglory* (1915), is the poet Rupert Brooke (1887–1915), to whom Firbank thought himself superior as a writer.

BROWBOROUGH, in Anthony Trollope's *Phineas Redux* (1874), is Sir Henry Edwards. See Griffenbottom.

BROWN, Araminta, in Enid Bagnold's *National Velvet* (1935), has as model a butcher's wife from Rottingdean, the mother of Winnie Hilder (see Brown, Velvet).

BROWN, Arthur, in C.P. Snow's *The Light and the Dark* (1947), *The Masters* (1951), *The Affair* (1960) and *Last Things* (1970), is Sydney Grose (*d.* 1980, aged ninety-four), senior tutor and Fellow of Christ's College, Cambridge.

BROWN, Captain, in Elizabeth Gaskell's *Cranford* (1851–3), is supposedly Captain Henry Hill, a drummer-boy in the Peninsular War and a veteran of Waterloo. On half pay in the 1850s, he was adjutant of the Earl of Chester's Yeomanry, residing in King Street, Knutsford.

BROWN, Father, in G.K. Chesterton's 'Father Brown' stories (1911–35), is Monsignor John O'Connor (1871–1952), priest in charge for thirty-two years of St Cuthbert's Church, Bradford. Chesterton first met him in 1904, at the home of a mutual acquaintance near Keighley, when the author was lecturing in the West Riding of Yorkshire. Walking together on Ilkley Moor, they found themselves discussing detective stories and crime in general. Back at the home of their host, O'Connor chatted with two undergraduate guests about trends in music and painting. As the priest left the room, the students turned to Chesterton and remarked that while O'Connor's conversation on the arts was all that they might have expected, they felt that such a person, facing all the evil of the world, ought to know something of it and not just minister to the innocent and virtuous. 'This', O'Connor later recalled, 'struck Chesterton as

extremely ironic, coming on top of our recent wild talk, for he knew
that compared with my experience of the ways of the world, the two
undergraduates knew about as much about evil as two babies in the
same perambulator.'

BROWN, Father, in Ronald Firbank's *Inclinations* (1916), is Canon
John Gray (1866–1934). After a working-class childhood in
London's Bethnal Green, where he left school at thirteen, he became
a *fin de siècle* poet and a protégé of Oscar Wilde, who in 1893 financed
the publication of his collection of poems, *Silverpoints*. Entering the
Roman Catholic Church, he was ordained at the turn of the century
and became a priest in Edinburgh, in the parish first of St Patrick's
and then of St Peter's, Morningside. See also Gray, Dorian.

BROWN, Thomas Dunn, in Edgar Allan Poe's 'The Literati of
New York City' (1846), is the American poet Thomas Dunn English
(1819–1902). Stung by Poe's ridicule into publishing a scurrilous
reply, he was successfully sued for libel by the author.

BROWN, Tom, in Thomas Hughes's *Tom Brown's Schooldays*
(1857). Replying in 1895 to a correspondent who had asked if Tom
Brown was a real boy, the author said that he was 'at least 20 boys,
for I knew at least that number of Tom Browns at Rugby.' Contemporaries, however, took Brown to be largely a self-portrait,
although Thomas Seccombe, assistant editor of the *Dictionary of
National Biography* from 1891 to 1901, asserted in the *Encyclopaedia
Britannica* (13th edn) that Brown was primarily the author's brother,
George Hughes (see also Arthur, George), who wrote a notable
poem on the Oxford and Cambridge Boat Race of 1868.

BROWN, Velvet, in Enid Bagnold's *National Velvet* (1935), is a
composite of Winnie Hilder, a butcher's daughter from Rottingdean, who with her two sisters rode a lot and became a friend of the
author's daughter; Laurian Jones, the author's horse-mad daughter,
subsequently Comtesse Pierre d'Harcourt, author of the novel *Prince
Leopold and Anna*; and Jean Asquith, whose family rented a house
owned by Enid Bagnold's husband, Sir Roderick Jones.

BROWN, William, in Richmal Crompton's 'William' stories
(1919–70). Life for William's original did not quite match Crompton's schoolboy fantasy of killing a lion with his bare hands, but
service with the police in Rhodesia with big-game hunting on the

side was not a bad start. William was primarily inspired by the author's brother, John Lamburn, who was educated at Bury Grammar School, in Lancashire, and at Manchester University. His father, the Revd E.J.S. Lamburn, a master at Bury Grammar School from 1876 until his death in 1915, wanted him to enter the Church. Instead, John Lamburn went to Rhodesia. He later worked for a commercial firm in China, and in the Second World War served with the RAF in Iceland, under Air Commodore C.G. Wigglesworth (see Biggles). Spelling his name 'Lambourne', he was the author of a number of books on natural history and he also drafted some of the William stories, helping his sister out when her inspiration flagged. He died in 1972, aged seventy-nine. William was also modelled in part upon the author's nephew, Tom Disher.

BROWNE, Hector, in Viviane Ventura's *April Fool* (1983), is supposedly Victor Lownes (1928–   ), who until 1981 was managing director of the American-based Playboy Enterprises' four British casinos, having established Playboy's European operation in 1964. He was dismissed after the Gaming Board and police objected to renewal of the Playboy casinos' gaming licences. During his regime he was reputedly Britain's highest-paid executive. His loss-of-office compensation was reported to be £125,000 a year for three years, and he subsequently opened a new night club in Chicago and invested in other clubs in England.

BROWNING, Clariss, in D.H. Lawrence's *Aaron's Rod* (1922), according to Lawrence's biographer Harry T. Moore, among others, is Brigit Patmore (née Morrison-Scott, 1882–1965), Dublin-born wife of John Deighton Patmore (grandson of the poet, Coventry Patmore). She subsequently lived with Richard Aldington (see Ashton, Rafe), who left her for her daughter-in-law.

BRUCE, Janet, in Gertrude Stein's *Fernhurst* (1971), is Mary Gwinn. See Thornton, Helen.

BRUGA, Count, in Ben Hecht's *Count Bruga* (1926), is the American poet and novelist Max Bodenheim (1892–1954), who had a love-hate working relationship with Hecht, with whom he often collaborated as a writer. As a down-and-out literary bum, he became one of the sights of Chicago. He and his third wife were murdered when he tried to defend her from the approaches of a drunken young drop-out with whom they were living in New York.

BRUTUS, in Mercy Otis Warren's *The Adulateur* (1773), is the author's brother, James Otis (1725–83), a Boston lawyer who became an eloquent opponent of British colonialism. In an affray in 1769 with Customs commissioners who had accused him of treason, he sustained a sword wound to the head, an injury to which his subsequent insanity was attributed. He allegedly expressed the wish from time to time that he might be struck by lightning, and this wish was granted when he met his death in this way, at Andover, Massachusetts.

BUCK-AND-BALK, Lady, in Djuna Barnes's *The Ladies' Almanack* (1928). Romaine Brooks's biographer, Meryle Secrest, identifies the original of Buck-and-Balk as Marguerite Radclyffe Hall (1880–1943), a lesbian who dressed as a man, preferred to be addressed as 'John' and was cited as co-respondent by Sir Ernest Troubridge after she had seduced his wife (see Tilly-Tweed-in-Blood). Her novel, *The Well of Loneliness* (1928), is concerned with the difficulties besetting women of her kind.

BUCKET, Inspector, in Charles Dickens's *Bleak House* (1852–3), is primarily Inspector Charles Frederick Field, a pioneer Scotland Yard detective with whom Dickens spent some time gathering material for a *Household Words* article, 'On Duty with Inspector Field'.

BUCKTROUT, Baby, in Wyndham Lewis's *The Roaring Queen* (1936). The author's widow said that Bucktrout was Nancy Cunard (see Storm, Iris), with whom Lewis had an affair in Venice in 1922. His biographer, Jeffrey Meyers, notes that Cunard tried unsuccessfully to woo Lewis from right-wing politics. In a letter written shortly before her death she expressed her admiration for him as a painter and writer, though 'on the whole, he was half a SHIT'. For both halves, see Lypiatt, Casimir.

BUDD, Colonel, in Anthony Powell's *The Military Philosophers* (1968), according to Powell's memoirs, is Sir Alan Lascelles (1887–1981), assistant private secretary to George V and Edward VIII and private secretary to George VI and Elizabeth II.

BUDDEN, Octavius, in Charles Dickens's 'Mr Minns and his Cousin' (*Sketches by 'Boz'*, 1836), is John Porter Leigh, a Hackney coal and corn merchant who lived in Lea Bridge Road, Lower

Clapton, and was father of Marianne Leigh (see Dartle, Rosa). Dickens's first choice of name for Budden was Bagshaw, and this is how he appears in the first publication of the sketch, under the title 'A Dinner at Poplar Walk' (the *Monthly Magazine*, December 1833).

BUDDENBROOK FAMILY, in Thomas Mann's *Buddenbrooks* (1901). A number of the author's relatives went towards the making of the Buddenbrooks, as Nigel Hamilton notes in *The Brothers Mann* (1978). Betty Buddenbrook is the author's grandmother, Elizabeth Mann (née Marty, *d.* 1890), daughter of Johann Heinrich Marty (see Kröger, Lebrecht). Christian Buddenbrook is Thomas Mann's uncle, Friedrich Mann (*b.* 1847), whose partiality for drink and inaptitude for business caused him to be dismissed from the family firm. In 1913 he publicised his dislike of his *Buddenbrooks* portrait by taking advertising space in a Lübeck newspaper, urging readers to 'treat the book as it deserves' and remarking of his nephew that it was a sorry bird that defiled its own nest. Gerda Buddenbrook is the author's mother, Julia Mann (née Bruhns), the daughter of a Lübeck emigrant to South America who established an export company, sugar plantation and attendant mills in Brazil and married the daughter of a prosperous Portuguese planter. Unlike her husband, whom she married in 1869, Julia Mann encouraged her sons' literary aspirations. She died in 1923, aged seventy-seven. Old Buddenbrook is Thomas Mann's grandfather, Johann Siegmund Mann (*b.* 1797), a Lübeck grain merchant and Brazilian vice-consul. Thomas Buddenbrook is the author's father, Thomas Johann Heinrich Mann (1840—91), who at twenty-two, on the death of his father, became head of the family firm. He was later a Lübeck senator. Tony Buddenbrook is the author's twice-divorced aunt, Elizabeth Amalia Hippolite Mann (*b.* 1838), daughter of J.S. Mann. Her poetry was apparently as insufferable as her self-righteousness.

BUFFLE, Sir Raffle, in Anthony Trollope's *The Last Chronicle of Barset* (1867), is Trollope's Post Office chief, Sir Rowland Hill (see Hardlines, Sir Gregory). They disliked each other. Trollope's notorious rudeness and temper cannot have helped, while Hill — peeved by his subordinate's success as a writer — tried unsuccessfully to block the novelist's leave of absence to tour America. In a letter to the *Athenaeum*, Trollope referred to earning his bread by writing ... 'as though', sneered Hill, 'literature were his "profession".' 'Profession' or not, it earned Trollope nearly £70,000 in thirty-four years: rather more, one presumes, than he received from the Post Office.

BUFO, in Alexander Pope's *An Epistle to Dr Arbuthnot* (1735), has a suggested model in George Bubb Dodington (1691–1762), a politician who in 1761 became Baron Melcombe. A noted patron of men of letters, he is the 'Dodington' in Thomson's *Summer* (1727).

BUINOVSKY, Commander, in Alexander Solzhenitsyn's *One Day in the Life of Ivan Denisovich* (1962). According to David Burg and George Feifer's *Solzhenitsyn* (1972), Commander Buinovsky is Boris Burkovsky, a Russian naval commander. After serving as liaison officer to the United States naval mission during the Yalta Conference of 1945, he was arrested and sentenced to twenty-five years' imprisonment as an American spy. In the early 1950s he was a fellow inmate of the author at Ekibastuz camp for political prisoners. Subsequently rehabilitated, he was given command of the former cruiser *Aurora*, a floating museum moored in the Neva at Leningrad, where Solzhenitsyn met him again by chance in 1962.

BUK, Janko, in James A. Michener's *Poland* (1983), has as prototype the Polish Solidarity leader, Lech Walesa (1943–   ), winner of the 1983 Nobel peace prize. Leading militant farmers against the Minister of Agriculture and the Communist government, Buk becomes – like Walesa – an international figure, visiting the Pope and lunching with President Reagan.

BULAT, Władysław, in Tadeusz Konwicki's *A Minor Apocalypse* (1983). The critic Peter Kemp suggests (*Times Literary Supplement*, 25 November 1983) that Bulat is a scornful portrait of the Polish film director, Andrzej Wajda (1926–   ). In 1983 Wajda was sacked from his directorship of Warsaw's 'X' film unit, following government complaints of anti-state activity. Konwicki is himself a noted Polish film-maker.

BULBUL, Clarence, in W.M. Thackeray's 'Our Street' (1848; *Christmas Books,* 1857) and *The History of Pendennis* (1848–50), is Richard Monckton Milnes, First Baron Houghton (1809–85), poet, politician and a contemporary of Thackeray at Trinity College, Cambridge.

BULLER, in Alec Waugh's *The Loom of Youth* (1917), is the Sherborne School rugby coach and housemaster, G.M. Carey.

BULLINGTON, Viscount, in W.M. Thackeray's *The Luck of Barry Lyndon* (1844), has as prototype John Lyon, Tenth Earl of Strathmore (1769–1820), who disappeared for a number of years following the second marriage of his mother, the Countess of Strathmore (see Lyndon, Honoria, Countess of). He died the day after his own wedding.

BULPINGTON, Theodore, in H.G. Wells's *The Bulpington of Blup* (1932), is Ford Madox Ford (see Braddocks, Henry), who had enjoyed himself at Wells's expense with a less than complimentary portrait in *The New Humpty-Dumpty* (see Pett, Herbert).

BULWIG, in W.M. Thackeray's *Mr Yellowplush's Ajew* (1838), is Edward Bulwer-Lytton, First Baron Lytton (1803–73), prolific novelist, poet and dramatist.

BUMPPO, Natty, in James Fenimore Cooper's *The Pioneers* (1823) and *The Deerslayer* (1841), is the American frontiersman Daniel Boone (1734–1820), who in 1769–71 explored Kentucky, erecting in 1775 a fort at what became Boonesborough. Captured by Shawnee Indians in 1778, he escaped to warn the fort of an impending attack, which was repelled after a ten-day siege in which Boone played a leading role as one of the defenders. He also appears as 'Hawkeye' in Cooper's *The Last of the Mohicans* (1826) and as 'Pathfinder' in *The Pathfinder* (1840).

BUMPTIOUS, Serjeant, in R.S. Surtees's *Jorrocks's Jaunts and Jollities* (1838), according to Frederick Watson's *Robert Smith Surtees: A Critical Survey* (1933), is Serjeant C.C. Bompas. See Buzfuz, Serjeant.

BUNDLE, Joseph, in Osbert Sitwell's 'Alive – Alive Oh!' (*Dumb Animal*, 1930). The unspeakable art of original-spotting requires an ear for detail. Authors tend to give similar-sounding names to the people they are sending up. (Thus, in the hands of Clive James, the literary editor Claire Tomalin becomes Clara Tomahawk.) Bundle is an aural nudge. Who does he sound like? Run through the list of Georgian poets, of whom Bundle is an example. Ah, Edmund Blunden, of course! But don't just take my word for it. Cyril

Connolly has also remarked upon Bundle's similarity to Blunden (1896–1974), who out-lived and -wrote the Georgian label and was in 1966 elected Professor of Poetry at Oxford University ('What a bit of luck!' he said). An unassuming man whose life was coloured by his experience of the trenches in the First World War, he reflected in 1968 on the chore of receiving shoals of verse from would-be poets: 'As Oxford Professor the poor dears seem to think I'm a general authority – which I'm not. They expect answers to come out as if they were putting pennies into a machine. I don't really know what to tell some of them. As far as current writing goes, I know that young men want to get girls into bed – and I agree with them in principle. But we know enough about it. As far as poetry is concerned, I don't want to know any more. The best advice I can give to anyone who wants to publish poetry is simply to persist.'

BUNGAY, Mr, in W.M. Thackeray's *The History of Pendennis* (1848–50), is supposedly Henry Colburn (*d.* 1855), founder in 1814 of the *New Monthly Magazine* and first publisher of the diaries of Evelyn and Pepys. Disraeli's first novel also bore his imprint.

BUNTER, Alfred, in H.G. Wells's *Brynhild* (1937), is supposedly D.H. Lawrence (see Rampion, Mark). Like Lawrence, Bunter is a bearded, lower-middle-class, highly-sexed, imaginative writer. And his wife's name is Freda . . .

BUNTER, Billy, in Frank Richards's Greyfriars School stories (1908–65), owes his obese appearance to Lewis Ross Higgins (*d.* 1919), overweight editor of the comic *Chuckles* from 1914 until his death at thirty-four (he suffered from a glandular disorder), and an art critic for *Punch*. In the stories' earliest illustrations, Bunter was modelled on three brothers: Alan, Bruce and Alexander Mitchell. Their father, artist and novelist Hutton Mitchell, was Bunter's first illustrator, and the boys later recalled stuffing pillows into their trousers to achieve a satisfactory rotundity. They subsequently emigrated, Alan and Bruce settling in Montreal, and Alexander in Brisbane.

BUNTHORNE, Reginald, in W.S. Gilbert's libretto for *Patience* (1881), was taken by Dante Gabriel Rossetti (see Don Juan) to be a caricature of himself. Bunthorne was popularly identified, however, with Oscar Wilde (see Amarinth, Esme), D'Oyly Carte and Wilde's agent opportunistically sending him on a lecture tour of the United States in advance of the arrival of the new operetta.

BUNTING, Fred, in H.G. Wells's *The Sea Lady* (1902), is Hugh Popham, son of the author's neighbours at Sandgate, Kent, in 1899–1900. His daughter, Olivier, married Quentin Bell, Virginia Woolf's nephew.

BURGE, Joyce, in George Bernard Shaw's *Back to Methuselah* (1921). Shaw's stage directions ensured that Burge would mirror David Lloyd George (1863–1945) – 'a well-fed man turned fifty, with a broad forehead and grey hair which, his neck being short, falls almost to his collar.' In 1916 Lloyd George had ousted his fellow Liberal, Asquith (see Lubin), from the premiership of Britain. He remained as leader of the coalition government until the Conservatives returned to power in 1922. Burge's reference to his success with munitions echoes Lloyd George's revitalisation of Britain's ordnance factories.

BURLAP, Denis, in Aldous Huxley's *Point Counter Point* (1928), is the critic, novelist and poet John Middleton Murry (1889–1957), under whose editorship Huxley worked on the *Athenaeum*, joining the staff of that journal in 1919. Although Murry's first reaction to Burlap was to consider challenging Huxley to a duel, he swallowed his anger and in a letter to a friend attempted to shrug the matter off with the comment that his previous impression that Huxley had little notion of what he, Murry, was driving at was now confirmed. See also Crich, Gerald.

BURLEIGH, Cecil, in H.G. Wells's *Men Like Gods* (1923), is Arthur Balfour (see Evesham, Sir Arthur). Wells presents Burleigh as being 'intelligently receptive', echoing a phrase he had earlier used elsewhere to describe Balfour. The 'great Conservative leader ... tall, slender, grey-headed' was swiftly recognised as Balfour.

BURLY, in Robert Louis Stevenson's 'Talk and Talkers' (1882; *Memories and Portraits* 1887), is W.E. Henley. See Silver, Long John

BURNELL, Stanley, in Katherine Mansfield's *Prelude* (1918) and 'At the Bay' (*Bliss and Other Stories*, 1920). According to Antony Alpers, Mansfield's biographer, Stanley Burnell is the author's father, Sir Harold Beauchamp (1858–1938), a Wellington businessman who was chairman of the Bank of New Zealand and of Imperial Chemical Industries of New Zealand. Although he paid her an allowance to enable her to live in England and pursue a literary career, she called him 'the richest man in New Zealand and the meanest.'

BURNS, Helen, in Charlotte Brontë's *Jane Eyre* (1847), is the author's sister, Maria Brontë (1813–25), who died of consumption allegedly contracted while attending the Cowan Bridge School for the daughters of clergymen, in Lancashire.

BURNSIDE, Mr, in Howard Spring's *Hard Facts* (1944). According to Marion Howard Spring's *Howard* (1967), Mr Burnside is Canon Peter Green (1871–1961), rector of St Philip's, Salford, from 1911 to 1950, and a prolific author. In 1919 he refused the bishopric of Lincoln.

BÜRSTNER, Fräulein, in Franz Kafka's *The Trial* (1925), is part-inspired by Felice Bauer (d. 1960), a Berlin shorthand-typist whom the author first met in Prague in 1912, at the home of his friend, Max Brod. They were twice engaged, Kafka writing to her daily (sometimes two or three times a day) from Prague. In all, he addressed more than 250,000 words to her, and their relationship endured until 1917, when Kafka learned that he had tuberculosis. In 1919 Felice Bauer married a Berlin businessman, moving first to Switzerland and in 1936 to the United States. Her identification with several Kafka characters, all with the initials FB, is to be found in Kafka's *Letters to Felice* (Frankfurt 1968; London 1974).

BURY, Lady Caroline, in Graham Greene's *It's a Battlefield* (1934), is part-inspired by Lady Ottoline Morrell (see Roddice, Hermione). 'I was aware of Lady Ottoline Morrell's presence in the background of Lady Caroline', wrote the author in his introduction to the 1970 edition of the novel.

BURYAN, John Thomas, in D.H. Lawrence's *Kangaroo* (1923), is William Henry Hocking, a son of Lawrence's neighbour at Tregethern Farm, near Zennor, during the author's Cornish sojourn of 1916–17. When Lawrence sought a close physical relationship with him, Hocking shied away. He married a year after the Lawrences left Cornwall.

BUTCHER, Guy, in Wyndham Lewis's *Tarr* (1918), is Captain Guy Baker (*d.* 1918), a wealthy and womanising retired army officer who presented his collection of early Lewis drawings to the Victoria and Albert Museum. He died in an influenza epidemic.

BUTLER, Rhett, in Margaret Mitchell's *Gone with the Wind* (1936). The author's first husband, Berrien Kinnard ('Red') Upshaw, is in part the model for Butler. A Georgia University footballer, he was subsequently expelled from Annapolis Military Academy and became a bootlegger and merchant seaman. He married the author in 1929, deserted her, and returned briefly only — it is believed — to rape her. Aged forty-seven, and a down-and-out, he fell to his death from a flophouse in Galveston, Texas, a few months before the author was killed in a motoring accident in 1949. The genesis of *Gone with the Wind* is chronicled by Anne Edwards's *The Road to Tara: The Life of Margaret Mitchell* (1983).

BUTTERBOY, Donald, in Wyndham Lewis's *The Roaring Queen* (1936). Two candidates jostle for the dubious distinction of recognition as the model for Butterboy, winner of a 'Book of the Week' award and the hero of this novel. Walter Allen, in an introduction to the 1973 edition of *The Roaring Queen*, identified Butterboy as Brian Howard (see Silk, Ambrose). This was promptly challenged by Cyril Connolly: 'Brian Howard who published only one book — his poems in 1931 — could never have been a "Book of the Week" winner nor could he be described as a "queen" — the title, at that time, was more suitable for Godfrey Winn, then a novelist.' From the accounts of other contemporaries, however, it appears that Howard was very much an overt homosexual, his behaviour quite congruent with the novel's title. But Connolly's Winn suggestion is thought-provoking. Perhaps Lewis was having a go at both.

BUZFUZ, Serjeant, in Charles Dickens's *The Posthumous Papers of the Pickwick Club* (1836–7), is Serjeant C.C. Bompas, a London counsel of the 1830s noted for his pomposity.

BUZZARD, Justice, in Tobias Smollett's *Humphry Clinker* (1771), is supposedly Sir John Hawkins (1719–89), a Middlesex magistrate and author of a Life of Samuel Johnson, of whom he was an executor. Hawkins's principal work, *A General History of the Science and Practice of Music*, was published in 1776.

BYKOV, in Fyodor Dostoevsky's *Poor Folk* (1846), is supposedly the author's guardian and brother-in-law, Pyotr Karepin (*d.* 1850), chief manager of Count Golitsyn's estates, director of the office of Moscow's Governor-General and twenty-five years Dostoevsky's senior. The recipient of many begging letters from the author, in 1840 he married Dostoevsky's eldest sister, who was nearly thirty years his junior.

BYRON, Cashel, in George Bernard Shaw's *Cashel Byron's Profession* (1886), is an amalgam of Pakenham Beatty (see Erskine, Chichester) and the lightweight boxer Jack Burke (*d.* 1913), who was noted for his powers of endurance in long-fought contests. Burke's 7 hours 10 minutes' contest of 110 rounds with Andy Bowen in New Orleans in 1893 was finally declared 'no contest' when Bowen stumbled through exhaustion. In his declining years, Burke appeared with his wife in a vaudeville boxing act. Shaw's passion for boxing is entertainingly explored in Benny Green's *Shaw's Champions: G.B.S. and Prizefighting from Cashel Byron to Gene Tunney* (1978).

C

C, in Ronald Knox's *A Spiritual Aeneid* (1918). For forty years, those who knew the identity of C kept it to themselves, although it was the subject of speculation, reawakened with the publication of Evelyn Waugh's study of Knox, which preserved the model's anonymity. In 1959 it was suggested to Malcolm Muggeridge that C might be Harold Macmillan (1894–   ), at that time prime minister and subsequently the First Earl of Stockton. Muggeridge telephoned Waugh's mother-in-law. Taken off-guard by his direct question, she confirmed that C was indeed Macmillan — much to Waugh's annoyance. For Muggeridge followed this up with an item in the *New Statesman* suggesting the identity had been suppressed lest the Conservatives should find it electorally disadvantageous. Knox had been Macmillan's tutor, resigning in some dudgeon after his pupil's Nonconformist mother requested him not to discuss religion with her son.

CACOETHES, Reinhold, in Jack Kerouac's *The Dharma Bums* (1958), is the American poet, essayist, critic and translator Kenneth Rexroth (1905–82).

CADURCIS, Lord, in Benjamin Disraeli's *Venetia* (1837), is the poet Lord Byron (1788–1824). Disraeli was so imbued with the Byron legend that he engaged as a manservant the poet's gondolier, in whose arms Byron died at Missolonghi, and subsequently awarded the gondolier's widow a Civil List pension.

CADURCIS, Mrs, *idem*, is Mrs Catherine Byron (née Gordon, 1765–1811), mother of the poet. A Scots heiress whose excitability once caused her to bite a piece from a saucer, she displayed unswerving zeal in trying to ensure that her son did not emulate the ruinous career of his father.

CAËL, in Pierre Drieu la Rochelle's *Gilles* (1939), is the French Communist poet André Breton (1896–1966), one of the founders of the Surrealist movement.

CAESAR, Julius, in Georg Kaiser's *The Silver Lake* (1933), is Adolf Hitler (see Ui, Arturo). The caricature prompted the Führer's propaganda minister, Goebbels (see Gribbles), to ban the play the day after its opening in Leipzig.

CAIRN, in Jean Rhys's *Postures* (1928). If this portrait of Ernest Hemingway (see Ahearn) seems slight and distant, it is because Rhys did not know him personally. In Paris in the 1920s he impressed her — as she recalled in her old age — as 'a terribly gay man . . . always at the dances and the thing that struck me most was that he enjoyed himself so much. He *enjoyed* everything.'

CALDWELL, George, in John Updike's *The Centaur* (1963), is the author's father, Wesley R. Updike, a Pennsylvania mathematics teacher from New Jersey. When the author was criticised for presenting an exaggerated caricature, his father defended him: 'No, it's the truth. The kid got me right.'

CALHOUN, Ailie, in F. Scott Fitzgerald's 'The Last of the Belles' (1929; *Taps at Reveille*, 1935), is largely inspired by the author's wife, Zelda Sayre (see Diver, Nicole). The story is set at a time when airmen from Camp Taylor sought to impress her with aerobatics over her home. This activity became so prevalent that the flights over Judge Sayre's house had to be banned by the camp's commanding officer.

CALLAMAY, Mr, in Aldous Huxley's *Crome Yellow* (1921), is Herbert Henry Asquith. See Lubin, Henry Hopkins.

CALLUM, Dick, in Arthur Ransome's *Winter Holiday* (1933), *Coot Club* (1934), *Pigeon Post* (1936), *The Big Six* (1940), *The Picts and the Martyrs* (1943) and *Great Northern?* (1947), although largely a self-portrait of the author, is also supposedly part-inspired by Richard Farquhar Scott (1914–), son of Ransome's friend Ted Scott, editor of the *Manchester Guardian*, who drowned while sailing on Lake Windermere in 1932. Dick Scott subsequently entered the Foreign Office and was later Washington correspondent of the *Guardian* and chairman of the newspaper's trustees.

CALMAN, Miles, in F. Scott Fitzgerald's 'Crazy Sunday' (1932; *Taps at Reveille*, 1935), 'the only American-born director with both an interesting temperament and an artistic conscience', has been taken to be Irving Thalberg (see Stahr, Monroe). The story stemmed from a party at Thalberg's home, at which Fitzgerald (for neither the first nor the last time) made a fool of himself. Calman's talent and sensitivity fit Thalberg, but his weak, neurotic nature does not. Fitzgerald told Sheilah Graham that Calman was the film director King Vidor (1895–1982). This puzzled her because Calman was clearly Thalberg at least in part. In *The Real F. Scott Fitzgerald* (1976) she suspects that the author may have named Vidor because he regarded the director as a rival for her love. 'Most likely, Miles Calman was a compound of several of the Hollywood magnates, Thalberg among them,' she concludes, 'since Scott rarely used a single real-life prototype in his stories. It was his custom to blend the characteristics of several people, his own included, to make one character.'

CALVERT, Roy, in C.P. Snow's *Strangers and Brothers* (1940), *The Light and the Dark* (1947), *Time of Hope* (1949) and *The Masters* (1951), is Charles Allberry (?1911–43), a Fellow of Christ's College, Cambridge. An orientalist, he joined the RAF in the Second World War and was killed during a raid on Essen.

CAMBREMER, Dowager Marquise de, in Marcel Proust's *A la recherche du temps perdu* (1913–27), is Princesse Rachel Bassaraba de Brancovan (née Mussurus, 1847–1923), daughter of a Turkish ambassador to Britain, widow of Prince Gregoire de Brancovan of Romania and mother of the poet Anna de Noailles (1876–1933). A noted exponent of Chopin at the keyboard, she was also a patron of Enesco, Fauré and Paderewski, with whom she had an affair. Proust first met her in 1893.

CAMBREMER, Marquise de, *idem*, is part-inspired by the Comtesse d'Haussonville (née Pauline d'Harcourt). Daughter of the Duc d'Harcourt, she was reputed to have the smallest ears in Paris. She married Comte Gabriel Othenin d'Haussonville (see Guermantes, Basin, Duc de).

CAMILLE, in Jack Kerouac's *On the Road* (1957), is Carolyn Robinson, who as a Bennington College graduate reading fine arts at

Denver University had an affair with Neal Cassady (see Moriarty, Dean), becoming his second wife in 1947.

CAMPANATI, Carlo, in Anthony Burgess's *Earthly Powers* (1980). Destined to become Pope Gregory XVII, Campanati modernises the Roman Catholic Church in 1958 — like the reforming Pope John XXIII, who initiated the Vatican Council. Elements of both Pope John XXIII (Angelo Giuseppe Roncalli, 1881–1963) and Pope John Paul II (Karol Jozef Wojtyla, 1920–) have been discerned in Campanati.

CAMPBELL, Clementina, in H.G. Wells's *The World of William Clissold* (1926). Inspired by the author's advocacy of free love, the radical writer Odette Keun (*b.* 1887) wrote him a fan letter. A meeting was arranged at a hotel in Geneva. Keun turned out the light before admitting him to her room and they promptly retired to bed, neither having seen the other. That was in 1923, when Keun, born in Constantinople of Dutch parentage, was thirty-six and Wells fifty-eight. She lived with Wells for about ten years in Provence, where he built a dwelling for the liaison. Carved over the fireplace was 'Two Lovers Built This House' — a text parodied by P.G. Wodehouse in *The Code of the Woosters* (1938).

CAMPBELL, Howard, in Kurt Vonnegut's *Mother Night* (1961), makes anti-Semitic propaganda broadcasts for the Nazis. This has prompted Tony Tanner to suggest in *City of Words* (1971) that Campbell may have been based on Ezra Pound, who made similar broadcasts for the Fascists. Vonnegut tells me, however, that Howard Campbell 'was inspired by two people, neither one of them Ezra Pound. One was the Englishman "Lord Haw Haw", who became a funny and interesting and ultimately terrible radio propagandist for the Nazis. His name was Joyce, and he was hanged, I think. I used to listen to him on the radio, fascinated, and to speculate about what sort of American might have done what he did. The other inspiration was a scheming American who tried to recruit American prisoners of war for the German Army, for combat on the Russian front. I met him when I was a PW in Dresden, and my guess is that he was a German actor. Still, I played with the idea of his being what he claimed to be. So far as I know, there was no American turncoat on the order of England's Joyce. I knew about Pound, of course, but he wouldn't have been much use to me in *Mother Night*. I wanted my man to be fairly ordinary. Pound was off-scale for at least two reasons: he was cracked, and he was a world class artist. A third reason: Pound was a passionate anti-Semite. He was sincere in his anti-Semitism, as Campbell was not. This, in my opinion, made Campbell a more alarming war criminal than Lord Haw Haw or Pound.' The defence of William Joyce (1906–46) at his trial was that he was an American citizen, born in New York after his Irish father had become a naturalised American. In 1933, however, Joyce had represented himself as British and had obtained a British passport. The prosecution claimed this showed he owed allegiance to the Crown, and he was executed for high treason.

CAMPBELL, Jane, in Harold Nicolson's *Public Faces* (1932). Remembered by one of her BBC colleagues as the only member of the staff who brought a dog into the office and got away with it, Hilda Matheson (*d.* 1941) was in part the inspiration for Jane Campbell. Nicolson acknowledged two models for this character: Matheson, who in 1928 became the BBC's Head of Talks and who was among his wife's lovers; and Gertrude Bell (1868–1926), travel-ler, archaeologist, authority on Arabia and the first woman to obtain a first-class honours degree in modern history.

CAMPION, Albert, in twenty-one detective novels by Margery Allingham, commencing with *The Crime at Black Dudley* (1929), is modelled upon the author's husband, Philip Youngman Carter, artist and journalist, whom she married in 1927. After her death in 1966 he wrote two further novels featuring Campion. Carter's autobiography *All I Did Was This*, was published in 1983.

CAMPION, Luis, in F. Scott Fitzgerald's *Tender is the Night* (1934). Asked to define what his countrymen meant by 'a cad', Sir Charles Mendl, British Embassy press attaché in Paris from 1926 to 1940, pondered awhile before replying in exasperation, 'Oh, hang it, a cad is just someone who makes you go all crinkly-toes.' Small wonder that American expatriates relished his extreme Britishness. Fitzgerald portrays Campion as a homosexual, but Sir Charles was twice married; and his Britishness did not stop him from marrying an American, nor from retiring to Beverly Hills, California.

CANALIS, Constant-Cyr-Melchior, Baron de, in Honoré de Balzac's *Illusions perdues* (1837–43), *Mémoires de deux jeunes mariées* (1841) and *Modeste Mignon* (1844). To disguise their originals, authors sometimes go to such lengths to underline the differences between character and model that the smokescreen serves only to confirm readers' suspicions. Thus, Canalis is believed to be the French poet-statesman Alphonse-Marie-Louis de Prat de Lamartine (1790–1869) because of the care Balzac took to draw distinctions between the two.

CANNON, George, in Arnold Bennett's *The Roll-Call* (1918), is part-inspired by the architect A.E. Rickards (*d.* 1920), who was responsible for designing the Central Hall, Westminster. Bennett considered Rickards and H.G. Wells (see Wilson, Hypo) the two most interesting, provocative and stimulating men he had met.

CANTLEMERE, Lord, in Sir Arthur Conan Doyle's 'The Adventure of the Mazarin Stone' (1926; *The Case-book of Sherlock Holmes*, 1927), has as probable prototype the Third Marquess of Salisbury. See Bellinger, Lord.

CANTWELL, Colonel, in Ernest Hemingway's *Across the River and into the Trees* (1950), is inspired partly by Colonel (later General) Charles Trueman Lanham, who was commanding the American 22nd Regiment in Normandy in 1944 when Hemingway first met him and remained a friend for the rest of the novelist's life; and partly by Colonel Charles Sweeney, a mercenary when Hemingway first met him in Constantinople, in 1922, while reporting the war between Greece and Turkey, and struck up a friendship which endured nearly forty years.

CAPER, Mr, in *The Fall of British Tyranny* (1776), attributed to Joseph or John Leacock, is General John Burgoyne (?1722–92), an English soldier prominent in the American War of Independence.

CAPRARO, in Maxwell Anderson and Harold Hickerson's *Gods of the Lightning* (1928), has as prototype Bartolomeo Vanzetti. See Macready.

CARABAS, the Marquis of, in Benjamin Disraeli's *Vivian Grey* (1826–7), has two putative originals: the Earl of Clanricarde, and the publisher John Murray. Ulrick John de Burgh, Fourteenth Earl of Clanricarde (1802–74), was created First Marquis in 1825. He became British ambassador to St Petersburg, Postmaster-General and Lord Privy Seal, and married the daughter of George Canning (see Antijack, Mr Anyside). Murray (1778–1843) founded the

Quarterly Review and was a friend of Byron (see Cadurcis, Lord) and of Disraeli's father. Disraeli tried unsuccessfully to persuade him to launch a Canningite newspaper, and 'Carabas' is said to have cost the author Murray's friendship, although the publisher subsequently issued two of Disraeli's books.

CARAWAY, Lady Virginia, in W.J. Turner's *The Aesthetes* (1927), according to S.J. Darroch's *Ottoline* (1976), is Lady Ottoline Morrell. See Roddice, Hermione.

CARDAN, Mr, in Aldous Huxley's *Those Barren Leaves* (1925). As George Woodcock notes in *Dawn and the Darkest Hour: a study of Aldous Huxley* (1972), this novel was written when Huxley was seeing a lot of Norman Douglas (see Argyle, James), who was at that time living in Florence. A potent influence on Huxley, Douglas was a formidable debater, and it is this aspect of him that is supposedly reflected in Cardan.

CARDONA, Marie, in Albert Camus's *The Outsider* (1942), is Mme Christiane Davila, sister of Pierre Galindo (see Meursault). In 1936, she moved in to the Algiers house in which Camus and friends were living. A secretary with an Algiers car-sales firm, she typed most of the manuscripts of Camus, who called her 'La Terre'. She is believed to be the inspiration of his *Noces à Tipasa*. The character's name was that of the author's maternal grandmother.

CAREY, Revd William and Louise, in W. Somerset Maugham's *Of Human Bondage* (1915), are the author's uncle and aunt, the Revd Henry Macdonald Maugham (*d.* 1897), vicar of Whitstable, Kent, and his wife, Barbara Sophie Maugham (née von Scheidlin, *d.* 1892). As a child, the author was sent to live with this couple, spending several unhappy years at the vicarage.

CARFRY, in Edith Wharton's *The Age of Innocence* (1920), is Henry Leyden Stevens (1859–85), tubercular son of Mrs Paran Stevens (see Mingott, Mrs Manson). In 1882 his brief engagement to the author was terminated on the insistence of his socially ambitious mother.

CARGILL, the Revd Josiah, in Sir Walter Scott's *St Ronan's Well* (1823), is Dr Alexander Duncan (1708–95). The son of an Aberdeen weaver, he was minister of Smailholm, Roxburgh, when Scott lived there as a boy. Their acquaintanceship endured, Scott last visiting the scholarly recluse — author of a number of devotional and historical books — a few days before his death. Cargill's absent-minded studiousness may also have been suggested by the Revd Alexander Affleck, minister of Lyne and Megget, Roxburgh, from 1814 to 1845.

CARLETON, Amy, in Thomas Wolfe's *You Can't Go Home Again* (1940), is Emily Davies Vanderbilt, an American divorcee from whose attentions the author fled in Paris.

CARLTON, Beverly, in Moss Hart and George S. Kaufman's *The Man Who Came to Dinner* (1939). As a young man, the dramatist Noël Coward (1899—1973) was introduced to Alexander Woollcott (see Whiteside, Sheridan) by Kaufman's wife. He quickly became an object of Woollcott's admiration and propagandising . . . and the model for Beverly Carlton.

CARMICHAEL, A.A., in Evelyn Waugh's 'Charles Ryder's Schooldays' (written 1945, published 1982), is J.F. Roxburgh. See Fagan, Dr Augustus.

CARMICHAEL, Augustus, in Virginia Woolf's *To the Lighthouse* (1927), is suggested by Woolf's biographer, Quentin Bell, to be Joseph Wolstenholme, a talented Cambridge mathematician who left when he found his attitudes and opium-addiction incompatible with university life.

CARMODY, Frank, in Jack Kerouac's *The Subterraneans* (1958), is William S. Burroughs. See Dennison, Will.

CARNAL, Lady, in Michael Arlen's *Piracy* (1922), according to Anne Chisholm's *Nancy Cunard* (1979), is Emerald, Lady Cunard (1872—1948), mother of Nancy Cunard (see Storm, Iris). As Maude Burke, a Californian heiress, she in 1895 married Sir Bache Cunard, grandson of the founder of the Cunard steamship line, and became a noted hostess. Her lovers included the novelist George Moore (1852—1933) and the conductor Sir Thomas Beecham (1879—1961).

CARR, Leonard, in F. Tennyson Jesse's *A Pin to see the Peepshow* (1934), has as prototype Frederick Bywaters, who as a twenty-year-old ship's writer with the P & O Line was in 1923 hanged for the murder of his lover's husband (see Starling, Herbert and Julia).

CARSON, Henry, in Elizabeth Gaskell's *Mary Barton* (1848), owes the manner of his demise to the murder in 1831 of a cotton manufacturer's son, Thomas Ashton, of Hyde, Cheshire, who was in dispute with a trade union. Social reformers of his day considered him to be among the more enlightened employers.

CARTER, Bella, in Hilda Doolittle's *Bid Me to Live* (1960), is Dorothy ('Arabella') Yorke (*b.* 1892), an American interior decorator who worked in London and Paris and had affairs with the author's husband, Richard Aldington (see Ashton, Rafe), and with John Cournos (see Wimsey, Lord Peter).

CARTER, Captain Humphrey Cooper, in Wyndham Lewis's *Snooty Baronet* (1932), is Rupert Grayson (1897–   ), novelist and publisher son of the Liverpool shipbuilder Sir Henry Grayson.

CARTER, Nick, the American pulp fiction hero created by John R. Coryell in 'The Old Detective's Pupil' (1886), was probably based on Allan Pinkerton (1819–84), a Chicago ex-policeman who in 1850 founded America's first detective agency, in Chicago.

CARTERET, Charles, in Henry James's *The Tragic Muse* (1890), is Archibald Philip Primrose, Fifth Earl of Rosebery (1847–1929) and Prime Minister of Britain from 1894 to 1895.

CARTON, Sydney, in Charles Dickens's *A Tale of Two Cities* (1859), was in 1914 suggested by Sir Edward Clarke, KC, to have been modelled upon Gordon Allen, a barrister in the London chambers of Edwin James (see Stryver). After James was found guilty of malpractice and disbarred, Allen was discovered in his chambers on the verge of starvation. Fellow barristers rallied round, enabling him to emigrate to New Zealand, where he established a new practice in Wellington.

CARTWRIGHT, in D.H. Lawrence's *St Mawr* (1925), is Frederick Carter (*d.* 1967), an artist whose writings on St John's 'Revelation' inspired Lawrence to write *Apocalypse* (1930). Lawrence visited Carter in Pontesbury, Shropshire, in 1923–4, intrigued by the manuscript of his 'The Dragon of the Alchemists'. In 1932, Carter published *D.H. Lawrence and the Body Mystical*.

CARY, Jonquil, in F. Scott Fitzgerald's 'The Sensible Thing' (1924; *All the Sad Young Men*, 1926). This story mirrors the author's experience with his then fiancée, Zelda Sayre (see Diver, Nicole) — the tale's Jonquil Cary — who despaired of his ever earning enough to be able to marry and suggested ending their engagement. It was, as Fitzgerald acknowledged, 'about Zelda and me. All true.'

CASAMASSIMA, the Princess, in Henry James's *Roderick Hudson* (1876) and *The Princess Casamassima* (1886), is Elena Lowe, a Boston widow's daughter whom James first met in Rome in 1873. In the following year she married Gerald Perry, son of Sir William Perry, a retired British consul.

CASAUBON, the Revd Edward, in George Eliot's *Middlemarch* (1872), has three putative models: Dr Robert Herbert Brabant, Robert William Mackay and Mark Pattison. Brabant, a Devizes physician of independent means whose patients included the poets Samuel Taylor Coleridge and Thomas Moore, retired to devote himself to biblical study and engaged Eliot as his assistant, to work on German translation. Although he was nearly forty years her senior, Eliot's attachment to him was so resented by his wife that Eliot had to leave his household. His contemporary, the writer Eliza Lynn Linton, described him as 'a learned man who used up his literary energies in thought and desire to do rather than in actually doing . . . ever writing and re-writing, correcting and destroying, he never got further than the introductory chapter of a book which he intended to be epoch making and the final destroyer of superstition and theological dogma.' Mackay (1803–82), like Casaubon, married at forty-eight. He was the author of *The Progress of the Intellect, as Exemplified in the Religious Development of the Greeks and Hebrews*, on which Eliot wrote a notice in the *Westminster Review* in 1851. Pattison (1813–84), Rector of Lincoln College, Oxford, was the author of a work on the sixteenth-century French theologian Isaac Casaubon. Those who knew him found his popular identification with Eliot's Casaubon implausible. My sources include Walter Allen's *George Eliot* (1964) and Gordon S. Haight's *George Eliot* (1968).

CASBY, Flora. See Finching, Flora.

CASSELIS, David, in Robert Graves's *But It Still Goes On* (1930), represents the homosexual aspect of Siegfried Sassoon (see Victor,

Siegfried). In the First World War, Graves shared army quarters with Sassoon on Merseyside. After Sassoon had torn off his Military Cross ribbon and thrown it into the Mersey, he was court-martialled and sent to a military hospital near Edinburgh as a sufferer from shell-shock. Graves was detailed to escort him. Sassoon duly arrived at the hospital. Graves missed the train.

CASTELLI, in Charlotte Barnes's *Octavia Bragaldi* (1837), is Colonel Solomon P. Sharp. See Octavia.

CASTLEWOOD, Lady, in W.M. Thackeray's *The History of Henry Esmond Esq.* (1852), is Mrs William Henry Brookfield (née Jane Octavia Elton, 1821–96), youngest daughter of Sir Charles Abraham Elton, of Clevedon Court, Somerset. She was unhappily married to an undistinguished London clergyman (see Whitestock, Frank) who had been a promising Cambridge contemporary of the author. Thackeray was besotted with her and paid her frequent visits, much to Brookfield's discomfiture. She led the author to believe hers was a loveless marriage, and when in 1849 she became pregnant he was much distressed, racked by envy of her husband with whom he subsequently quarrelled.

CAT, Captain, in Dylan Thomas's *Under Milk Wood* (1954), is John Thomas, master of a collier which plied between Kidwelly, in Carmarthenshire, and Bideford, Devon. He retired to Laugharne, Carmarthenshire, where he was afflicted by blindness and gained a reputation for reminiscences as colourful as his actual maritime experience was prosaic.

CATHCART, Mr, in D.H. Lawrence's 'The Man Who Loved Islands' (1927; *The Woman Who Rode Away*, 1928). 'I was living on next to nothing on Capri . . . D.H. Lawrence came out to live there and he stayed six months', recalled Cathcart's original, the island-dwelling writer Sir Compton Mackenzie (1883–1972), in an interview shortly before he died with Godfrey Smith of the *Sunday Times*. 'He wrote a thing about me called "The Man Who Loved Islands" in which I finally committed suicide. I said I was going to injunct for it, but I changed my mind.' Instead, he contented himself with ticking-off Lawrence about a botanical slip. 'He had written too beautifully about flowers', noted Mackenzie in his memoirs, 'to be easily forgiven for covering a granite island in the Channel with cowslips; he should know that cowslips favour lime.'

CATON, L.S., in Kingsley Amis's *Lucky Jim* (1954), *That Uncertain Feeling* (1955), *Take a Girl Like You* (1960), *One Fat Englishman* (1963) and *The Anti-Death League* (1966), is the publisher Reginald Ashley Caton (1897–1971), founder of the Fortune Press, which issued Amis's first book, *Bright November*, and was also first to publish Philip Larkin (see Dixon, Jim). Reclusive and often dressed like a vagrant, Caton owned more than ninety houses in Brighton and left nearly £130,000.

CATSKILL, Rupert, in H.G. Wells's *Men Like Gods* (1923). 'One of the characters got out of my control, and began to speak and act in a way so like Mr Churchill that even I could see the resemblance', said Wells, tongue-in-cheek, after this novel's publication. 'I was shocked and alarmed. I had to stun the character and hustle it out of the way, but not before it made a long characteristic speech and started a war.' He was referring to Catskill, the novel's Secretary of State for War . . . a post held from 1919 to 1921 by Winston Churchill (1874–1965), Britain's prime minister for the war years and from 1951 to 1955.

CAVAILLON, in Sidonie-Gabrielle Colette's *La Vagabonde* (1910), is the French music-hall entertainer and film-star Maurice Chevalier (1888–1972), according to James Harding's *Maurice Chevalier* (1983).

CAVAN, Edward, in May Sarton's *Faithful are the Wounds* (1955), is Professor F.O. Matthiessen (1902–50), influential Harvard tutor in literature and author of studies of Theodore Dreiser, Henry James and T.S. Eliot. He committed suicide, leaving a note referring to acute depression.

CAVENDISH, Julie and Tony, in Edna Ferber and George S. Kaufman's *The Royal Family* (1927), are the American actress Ethel Barrymore (1879–1959) and her brother, the actor John Barrymore (1882–1942). So sympathetic did the authors feel their treatment of the Barrymores had been, that they contemplated asking the originals to fill the two roles when the play had its première. The Barrymores thought otherwise, Ethel declining to speak to the authors for several years.

CAWDOR, the Thane of, in William Shakespeare's *Macbeth* (1623), is believed to be modelled upon Robert Devereux, Second Earl of Essex. See Actaeon.

CÉLIMÈNE, in Molière's play *Le Misanthrope* (1666), is supposedly part-inspired by Armande Béjart (see Agnès), who took the role in the original production.

CENCI, Beatrice, in Percy Bysshe Shelley's *The Cenci* (1819), although based on a real-life person of that name — the daughter (*d.* 1599) of Count Francesco Cenci — is also part-inspired (according to Thomas Love Peacock) by Eliza O'Neill (see Fotheringay, Miss) and her performance as Bianca in Milman's *Fazzio*, which Shelley witnessed in 1818.

CERILLO, Juan, in Malcolm Lowry's *Under the Volcano* (1947), is Juan Fernando Márquez (also known as Fernando Atonalzin), who became a close friend of the author in 1937 during Lowry's Mexican sojourn, in Oaxaca. According to Lowry, Márquez/Atonalzin was a Zapotecan who, after studying chemistry at Mexico University, became a bank courier. He was shot dead in a drunken brawl at Villahermosa in 1939.

CH——, in Charles Lamb's 'The Superannuated Man' (1825; *Last Essays of Elia*, 1833), is John Chambers (*d.* 1872), son of a clergyman from Radway, Warwickshire, and a fellow clerk of the author at London's East India House. There, Chambers's arrival, on a white horse, was said to be so punctual that people set their watches by it. His recollections of Lamb were published posthumously in *Macmillan's Magazine* (1879).

CHAFFERY, Mr, in H.G. Wells's *Love and Mr Lewisham* (1900), supposedly owes his cheerfully expressed amorality to Alfred Williams. See Julip, Uncle John.

CHALABRE, Monsieur de, in Elizabeth Gaskell's 'My French Master' (1853), is one Rogier, a fugitive from the French Revolution who settled in Knutsford, Cheshire, and to sustain himself taught French and dancing. In his youth, the statesman William Pitt was one of Rogier's pupils. Many years later, the Frenchman confided to a friend that there was nothing in Pitt's dancing 'to indicate what a great man he would turn out'. Notorious for the absurdity of his notions, Rogier claimed that Gibraltar could be defended by pouring scalding buttermilk over invaders, and in an audience with Earl Grey advocated conquering enemies by dropping bombs on them from balloons. Tongue-in-cheek, the prime minister referred Rogier to the War Office, where the Secretary for War asked how the balloons were to be guided to their targets. 'Easily enough!' replied Rogier. 'Send up a thousand balloons, and some of them will be sure to do execution.'

CHALLENGER, Professor George Edward, in Sir Arthur Conan Doyle's *The Lost World* (1912), *The Poison Belt* (1913) and *The Land of Mist* (1926). 'Take your medicine, and if that does no good, swallow the cork. There's nothing better when you are sinking.' That was the advice given to a patient by Dr George Turnavine Budd (*d.* 1889), to whom Challenger owes some of his characteristics. The son of a Bristol physician noted for his pioneering work in the control of typhoid and scarlet fever, Budd was a fellow medical student of the author in Edinburgh and early distinguished himself by eloping with a Ward in Chancery and marrying her. A giant of a man, he was said to be too hot-tempered and contemptuous of rules to gain the Rugby International cap for which his physical prowess qualified him. In 1882, Doyle joined him in a Plymouth practice in which Budd did not hesitate forcefully to eject from his surgery any patient who irritated him. Something of a miracle-cure charlatan, he sought publicity by turning patients away. Upon his premature death, an autopsy revealed an abnormality of the brain. Also perceived in Challenger have been Sir Edwin Ray Lankester (1847–1929), a populariser of science noted for his short temper, who was Professor of Zoology and Comparative Anatomy of University College, London, from 1874 to 1890, Linacre Professor of Comparative Anatomy at Oxford from 1891 to 1898 and Director of Natural History at the British Museum from 1898 to 1907; William Rutherford (1839–99), Professor of Physiology at Edinburgh University, to whom Challenger is believed to owe something of his physique and voice; and George Bernard Shaw (see Quint, Peter), a suggested inspiration of Challenger's perverseness and insensitivity. The character's surname may have been suggested by the Challenger Expedition of 1872–6, an exercise in deep-sea exploration employing HMS *Challenger*. This corvette was also used by an expedition which collected zoological specimens analysed at Edinburgh University, which Doyle attended.

CHALLONER, Lady Joan, in Ouida's *Friendship* (1878). The obstacle to the author's attempted conquest of an Italian nobleman, the model for Lady Joan Challoner is Mrs Janet Ross (*d.* 1927), daughter of Lady Duff Gordon (see Ida, Princess). In 1860 she married Henry James Ross, a banker and archaeologist twenty years her senior, settling with him first in Egypt and then in Italy. In Florence in the 1870s she was the mistress of the Marchese Lotteria Lotharingo della Stufa (see Ioris, Prince), managing his estate — and her own husband — and thwarting Ouida's designs on della Stuffa. She published her memoirs in 1912. For her Meredith connection, see Jocelyn, Rose.

CHALMERS, Allen, in Christopher Isherwood's *All the Conspirators* (1928), and *Lions and Shadows* (1938), is the novelist Edward Upward (1903–), who attended Repton School with Isherwood, collaborated with him as a writer and was subsequently for eighteen years a member of the Communist Party and for twenty-nine years a master (with an aversion to beating) at Alleyn's Grammar School, Dulwich, retiring from teaching in 1961 and moving from London to the Isle of Wight. See Jonathan Fryer's biography of Isherwood (1977).

CHAMBERS, Sheriff Ned, in Sinclair Lewis and Dore Schary's *Storm in the West* (written 1943, published 1963), is Neville Chamberlain (1869–1940), Britain's prime minister from 1937 to 1940. His policy of appeasement towards Nazi Germany and Fascist Italy failed to avert the Second World War, for which Churchill (see Catskill, Rupert) replaced him as Britain's leader.

CHAMBOST-LÉVADÉ, Eric, in Roger Martin du Gard's *Le Lieutenant-Colonel de Maumort* (written 1941–58, published 1984), is the French philosopher and critic Paul Desjardins (1859–1940), who at his home in Pontigny, Burgundy, conducted an annual series of summerschools-cum-retreats from 1905 to 1939.

CHAMBOUVARD, in Émile Zola's *L'Oeuvre* (1885–6), is an amalgam of the painter Gustave Courbet (1819–77) and the sculptor Jean-Baptiste Clésinger (1814–83), son-in-law of George Sand (see Maupin, Camille). F. W. J. Hemmings's *Émile Zola* (1953) makes the identification.

CHANCEL, Walter, in Sinclair Lewis and Dore Schary's *Storm in the West* (written 1943, published 1963), is Sir Winston Churchill. See Catskill, Rupert.

CHANTELOUVE, M. and Mme Hyacinthe, in J-K Huys-
mans's *Là-bas* (1891). M. Chantelouve is in part the French novelist
and Catholic historian Charles Buet (*d.* 1897). Mme Hyacinthe is an
amalgam of Buet's wife and Berthe Courrière (1852–1915), daughter of a Lille financier, a model, the mistress of Jean-Baptiste
Clésinger (see Chambouvard), and subsequently the life-long companion of the Symbolist writer Rémy de Gourmont (1858–1915),
whom she first met in 1886. She was noted for her association with
the occult, and from the carpet-bag which accompanied her every-
where she would feed her dogs with wafers she declared to be
consecrated. She was certified insane and committed to asylums in
1890 and 1906. Also contributing to Mme Chantelouve, suggests
Huysmans's biographer, Robert Baldick, are Jeanne Jacquemin,
mistress of the Marseilles artist Auguste Lauzet; and Henriette
Maillat, black-magician and blackmailer, with whom Huysmans
had a brief affair in 1888. (Objecting to his wish to regulate the
relationship to a once-a-week visit, Henriette terminated the
romance by thanking him for his calendar-regulated affection,
regretting that this was not her measure – her heart took 'a larger
size of glove'; her lovers also included the essayist and dramatist
Joséphin Péladan).

CHARLES, Nora, in Dashiell Hammett's *The Thin Man* (1934), is
the American dramatist Lillian Hellman (1905–84), with whom
Hammett lived for the greater part of thirty years.

CHARLIE, in John le Carré's *The Little Drummer Girl* (1983). In
appearance, personality, background and politics, Charlie is the
author's half-sister, the actress Charlotte Cornwell. This she confirmed at the time of the novel's publication, although she said she
was the 'skeleton' for Charlie rather than the model. 'I think my
background, with its hopelessly mixed-up bourgeois values, gives
me a sense of what Charlie is about', she told Hugh McIlvanney of
the *Observer*. 'Charlie's upbringing has been strange, too, the sort
that encouraged her to flirt with far-out left-wing organisations as I
did.' The daughter of a fraudulent businessman who was gaoled
both in Britain and abroad and died owing more than £1 million, she
is – like Charlie – a pro-Palestinian political radical.

CHARLOTTE (Lotte), in Johann Wolfgang von Goethe's *The
Sorrows of Young Werther* (1774), is primarily Charlotte Buff
(1753–1828), daughter of the principal magistrate of Wetzlar.

Goethe met and fell in love with her in 1772, while pursuing his legal career by gaining experience of the Wetzlar-based imperial law courts. In 1773 she married his friend, Kestner (see Albert). Also contributing to Lotte (her dark eyes in particular) is Maximiliane Brentano (1756–95), daughter of the novelist Sophie von La Roche. She married a Frankfurt merchant, already the father of five children, who became suspicious of Goethe's attentions to his young wife and banned him from the house.

CHARLUS, Baron Palamède de, in Marcel Proust's *A la recherche du temps perdu* (1913–27). The shock of recognising himself as Charlus is reputed to have led to the death of the primary model, the poet and art critic Comte Robert de Montesquiou-Fezensac (1855–1921), who first met Proust in 1893. Describing himself as resembling a greyhound in a greatcoat, he wore make-up and was often accompanied by a gilt tortoise. His mistresses included Sarah Bernhardt (see Berma), until he conceived a passion for his male secretary. Also contributing to Charlus are Baron Jacques Doasan, who lost one of his boyfriends to Montesquiou and squandered his fortune on his love for an unresponsive Polish violinist; and the journalist and critic Jean Lorrain (Paul Duval, 1856–1906), with whom Proust fought a duel in which neither was injured.

CHASTELLER, Bathilde de, in Stendhal's *Lucien Leuwen* (written 1834–5, published 1894), is in part Matilde Dembowski. See de la Mole, Mathilde.

CHATSWORTH, in Christopher Isherwood's *Prater Violet* (1945), is an amalgam of the Hollywood film executives Chan Balcon and Victor Saville (1897–   ), according to Isherwood's biographer, Brian Finney.

CHATTERLEY, Sir Clifford and Lady, in D.H. Lawrence's *Lady Chatterley's Lover* (1928). In the late 1870s William Arkwright (1857–1925), of the textile manufacturing family of Sutton Scarsdale, Derbyshire, was rendered impotent by a riding accident. This has been recorded by the Lawrence biographer, Keith Sagar. Arkwright was subsequently unhappily married to Agnes Mary Summers-Cox, the couple living apart for much of the time, and their situation is believed to have suggested the Chatterleys' predicament to Lawrence. Another Lawrence biographer, Paul Delany, suggests the Chatterleys' circumstances may also have been part-

inspired by those of the Hon. Herbert and Lady Cynthia Asquith
(see Pervin, Maurice and Isabel). She, too, had married at twenty-
three a man six years her senior, was of Scots descent and had a
disabled husband who had lost an elder brother on the battlefield in
1916. Janice S. Robinson, biographer of Hilda Doolittle, believes
that, psychologically, Sir Clifford is modelled upon Richard Aldington (see Ashton, Rafe). A further ingredient, according to the
Sitwells' biographer, John Pearson, is Osbert Sitwell (see
Whittlebot, Gob), whom Lawrence met in 1927 while working on
the novel's third draft, in which he incorporated some of Sitwell's
characteristics and family circumstances. Robinson surmises that
Hilda Doolittle (see Masters, Miranda) is the model for Constance
Chatterley; but when the novel was adjudged not to be obscene
following a prosecution under the Obscene Publications Act the
author's sister, Mrs Emily King, said, 'He was asked who Lady
Chatterley was based on. He said "Partly Frieda" – that was his
German-born wife' (*Daily Express*, 3 November 1960). And Professor V.J.A. Kiparsky wrote from Berlin (*Sunday Times*, 6 November 1960) suggesting, by no means implausibly, that Lawrence had
taken both characters and plot from Ilya Ehrenburg's 'Fifth Pipe'
(*Thirteen Pipes*, 1923), in which the gamekeeper role is filled by a
dog-keeper.

CHAUMONT, the Marquis de, in Harold Nicolson's *Some People*
(1927). According to Philippe Julian and John Phillips's *Violet Trefusis* (1976), and James Lees-Milne's *Harold Nicolson* (1980–1), Chaumont's original is an amalgam of two of the author's lovers, Comte
Jean de Gaigneron – a friend of Marcel Proust (see Larti) – and
Pierre de Lacretelle, a French diplomat's journalist son who lost an
inherited fortune at the gaming tables of Monte Carlo. The author of
a study of Madame de Staël and an intimate of Jean Cocteau (see
Octave), he was tortured by the Gestapo in the Second World War.

CHEERYBLE, Ned (Edwin) **and Charles**, in Charles Dickens's
Nicholas Nickleby (1838–9). Most Dickens biographies note that the
originals of the almost too good to be true Cheeryble brothers were
two sons of a Scottish cattle dealer, William (?1769–1842) and
Daniel (?1780–1855) Grant. What they don't disclose is Daniel's fall
from grace. The brothers were Manchester merchants and Ramsbottom calico printers, and Dickens met them at a dinner party in
Manchester in 1838. They were noted as model employers (exemplified by Samuel Smile's *Self-help*, 1860 edn), and upon William's

death Dickens wrote from Niagara Falls to a friend, 'One of the noble hearts who sat for the Cheeryble Brothers is dead; if I had been in England I would certainly have gone into mourning for the loss of such a glorious life.' It was William's lot, as a magistrate, to read the Riot Act at Chatterton on 26 April 1826, after which troops opened fire on machine-breaking hand-loom weavers, killing a number variously reported as totalling six and ten. Daniel died thirty years after blighting the family name through his association with a woman whom he kept in Manchester and who in 1825 bore him a son, Daniel Grant Bretherton — a scandal which prompted William to withdraw from society, resigning from Bury Subscription Library. The brothers are buried, side by side, in the chancel of the church they built, St Andrew's, Ramsbottom.

CHELL, the Countess of, in Arnold Bennett's *Tales of the Five Towns* (1905), *The Grim Smile of the Five Towns* (1907) and *The Card* (1911). Imagine Bennett's discomfiture when, shortly after *The Card* appeared, he attended a dinner party and found himself seated next to his model for the countess: Millicent, Duchess of Sutherland (1867–1955), whom he had not previously met, for his Countess of Chell had been based solely on her reputation. Why, she asked him, had he ridiculed her? What she really took exception to, she said, was his suggestion that she was invariably late. She was, she claimed, a stickler for punctuality. Daughter of the Fourth Earl of Rosslyn and step-sister of the Countess of Warwick (see Homartyn, Lady), she was mayoress of Longton, Staffordshire, and President of the Potteries Cripples' Guild. Such was her involvement in many causes that she acquired the sobriquet 'Meddlesome Millie'. She was much concerned with infant mortality, lead poisoning among pottery workers and the incidence of phthisis in the Potteries. She also instituted educational reforms in rural Scotland and created one of the first Red Cross hospitals in France in the First World War. When this was overrun by the Germans, she used her acquaintance with the Kaiser to extricate the unit; in the Second World War, she bluffed her way out of occupied France. All this activity was perhaps a salve for an unhappy private life. She was married three times: to the Duke of Sutherland (*d.* 1913), who was already in love with a married relative; to a soldier partial to other women; and to a third husband who did not like women at all. Her second and third marriages were dissolved.

CHÉRI. See Peloux, Fred.

CHÉRIE, in Edmond de Goncourt's *Chérie* (1884), is the Russian diarist Marie Bashkirtseff (1860–84), who arrived in France with her mother when she was twelve and later became infatuated with the Duke of Hamilton, the statesman Cassagnac and a steeplechase rider whose neck she wished to be broken in preference to his marrying another woman. She told Goncourt that *Chérie* was full of platitudes. Shortly after its publication she died from consumption, her ambition to gain recognition as a painter only partly realised.

CHERRY-MARVEL, Mr, in Michael Arlen's *The Green Hat* (1924), is Harry Melvill. See Dearborn, Hugh.

CHESTER, Nicholas, in Rose Macaulay's *What Not: A Prophetic Comedy* (1918), is Gerald O'Donovan (*d.* 1942). After leaving the Catholic priesthood he married an Irish colonel's daughter and became a novelist and social worker – in 1910–11, he was a sub-warden at London's Toynbee Hall. The author first met him in 1918 while working in the Italian Section of the British Government's Department for Propaganda in Enemy Countries. O'Donovan was the Section's head, and they became lovers, their relationship continuing for the rest of his life.

CHEURET, M., Mme and Édouard, in Christopher Isherwood's *Lions and Shadows* (1938), are the concert violinist André Mangeot (1883–   ), to whom the author was secretary in the late 1920s, his wife Olive, and their son Sylvain. The Mangeots were divorced in 1931 when Olive tired of her husband's affairs – his passions included one for his former pupil, Rachel Monkhouse (see Marmaduke), to whom Isherwood had introduced him.

CHEVEREL, Sir Anthony, and Sir Christopher and Lady, in George Eliot's 'Mr Gilfil's Love Story' (*Scenes of Clerical Life*, 1858), have as prototypes respectively Sir Richard Newdigate (1644–1727), of Arbury Hall, Warwickshire, an English chief justice during Richard Cromwell's protectorate; Sir Roger Newdigate (1719–1806), antiquary, Member of Parliament and founder of Oxford's Newdigate Prize; and Sir Roger's second wife (née Hester Margaretta Mundy, 1737–1800), of Harefield, Middlesex, and Arbury Hall. The author's father was an estate manager for the Newdigate family.

CHÈVRE-FEUILLE, Jacques, in Zelda Fitzgerald's *Save Me The Waltz* (1932), is Édouard Jozan, according to the Fitzgerald biographer, Matthew J. Bruccoli. See Barban, Tommy.

CHEYNE, Romola, in V. Sackville-West's *The Edwardians* (1930), is Alice Keppel (*d.* 1947), daughter of Admiral Sir William Edmonstone. In 1891 she married Colonel George Keppel, but she is best known as the mistress of King Edward VII. She died aged seventy-eight.

CHHOKRAPUR, the Maharaja of, in J.R. Ackerley's *Hindoo Holiday* (1932), is the Maharaja Vishnwarath Singh Bahadur (1866–1932), an affable, homosexually-inclined eccentric obsessed with the Meaning of Life and the Nature of God. Ackerley was tutor to his son.

CHILLEYWATER, the Hon. Harold and Mrs, in Ronald Firbank's *The Flower Beneath the Foot* (1923), are the diplomat, biographer and critic, the Hon. Sir Harold Nicolson (1886–1968), who first met Firbank in Spain in 1905, and Nicolson's wife, the Hon. Victoria Sackville-West (see Orlando). In his boyhood, Nicolson was the model for the child in the illustrations of Hilaire Belloc's *The Bad Child's Book of Beasts* (1896).

CHILTERN, Lord, in Anthony Trollope's *Phineas Finn* (1869) and *Phineas Redux* (1874), was taken by the author's contemporaries to be Lord Hartington — Spencer Compton Cavendish (1833–1908), who in 1891 became Eighth Duke of Devonshire and was leader of the Liberal party 1875–80. Originals suggested a century later, however, are John Henry De la Poer Beresford, Fifth Marquess of Waterford (1844–95), and Thomas Pitt, Baron Camelford (1775–1804), who as a naval officer was flogged for disobeying orders and was noted for his equally merciless lashing of seamen under him; he was killed in a duel with a friend.

CHINNERY, in Gilbert Cannan's *Time and Eternity* (1919), is the chinless actor and dramatist Miles Malleson (1888–1969), who admired Cannan's profile and thought he might make a career in films. It was Malleson who in 1916 introduced Cannan to Gwen Wilson (see Day, Clara).

CHIPS, Mr (Arthur Chipping), in James Hilton's *Good-Bye, Mr Chips* (1934), is an amalgam of the author's father, John Hilton, who was for some thirty years headmaster of Chapel End Senior Boys' School, Walthamstow; and W.H. Balgarnie (*d.* 1951), classics master and a house master (1904–29) at the Leys School, Cambridge, which the author attended. When a stage version of the novel was first produced in London, Balgarnie was invited as a special guest and was allocated a box.

CHIRON, in Hilda Doolittle's *Helen in Egypt* (1961), is Havelock Ellis. See Jerry.

CHIRRUP, Mr and Mrs, in Charles Dickens's 'Nice Little Couple' (*Sketches of Young Couples*, 1840), are supposedly the London bookseller-turned-publisher William Hall (?1801–47) and his wife. It was Hall who made the proposal which resulted in Dickens writing *Pickwick Papers*.

CHITTERLOW, Harry, in H.G. Wells's *Kipps* (1905), is Sidney Bowkett (?1868–1937), a friend of the author's youth in Bromley, Kent. Bowkett subsequently became a playwright, his comedies enjoying transient success.

CHITTY, Mrs, in Osbert Sitwell's 'That Flesh is Heir To' (*Dumb-Animal*, 1930), is Violet Hammersley, a society beauty, London hostess and friend of Violet Trefusis (see Romanovitch, Princess 'Sasha'). She was among Sitwell's fellow passengers on a cruise during which many succumbed to an unidentified illness.

CHLOE, in Alexander Pope's *Moral Essays* (1731–5), is King George II's mistress, Henrietta, Countess of Suffolk (?1681–1767), daughter of Sir Henry Hobart, of Blickling, Norfolk. This portrait of Henrietta, together with two others, was withheld until the work's 1751 edition.

CHO-CHO-SAN, in John Luther Long's 'Madame Butterfly' (1898), Long and David Belasco's play of that name (1900) and Puccini's opera *Madama Butterfly* (1904–6), is Tsuru Yamamuri (1851–99), a Nagasaki geisha who attempted suicide when officialdom tried to part her from her son by a Scot, Thomas Blake Glover. After service with the East India Company, Glover had settled in

Nagasaki in 1859 as an arms dealer, later establishing a shipyard and coal mine. The geisha's son later joined his father.

CHOKE, General Cyrus, in Charles Dickens's *Martin Chuzzlewit* (1843–4), is supposedly General Edmund Pendleton Gaines (1777–1849), an irascible American soldier continuously at odds with his country's War Department. Promoted Brigadier-General after his defence of Fort Erie against the British in 1812, he lived in constant expectation of further war with England or Mexico. In 1846 court martial proceedings were unsuccessfully instituted against him for raising volunteers without authority to serve in the Mexican War. Dickens met him during his 1842 American tour and found him an intolerable bore, though not uninteresting in appearance.

CHOULETTE, in Anatole France's *Le Lys rouge* (1894), is the poet Paul Verlaine (1844–96), whose unhappy career included a two-year prison sentence for shooting in the wrist his friend the poet Rimbaud, who influenced him to the extent that he left his home and wife to lead a vagrant life with Rimbaud in England and Belgium.

CHRISTIAN, Charlie, in Hugh Walpole's *John Cornelius* (1937), is Harold Cheevers (1893–   ). Walpole first met him in 1924 and Cheevers became the author's friend and companion, serving as his secretary and chauffeur, for the rest of Walpole's life. A former Metropolitan Police constable, he had been the British Isles police revolver champion and was an outstandingly strong swimmer. In 1931 he swam the pool beneath Piper's Hole, St Mary's, Scilly, a feat which inspired a passage in William Plomer's *The Case is Altered* (1932). Walpole's *Rogue Herries* and *Roman Fountain* are dedicated to Cheevers.

CHRISTOPHER ROBIN, in A.A. Milne's *When We Were Very Young* (1924), *Winnie-the-Pooh* (1926), *Now We Are Six* (1927) and *The House at Pooh Corner* (1928), is the author's son, Christopher Robin Milne (1920–   ), who was also the model for Ernest H. Shepard's illustrations. Wounded at Salerno while serving with the Army in the Second World War, he subsequently became a bookseller in Dartmouth, mentally wincing when mothers in his shop urged their children to shake hands with 'the real Christopher Robin'. In his autobiography, *The Enchanted Places* (1974), he declares he grew up to wish his name were Charles Robert.

CHRONOMASTIX, in Ben Jonson's *Time Vindicated to Himselfe and to his Honors* (1623), is the poet George Wither (1588–1667). As a Parliamentarian on the run, he was captured by Royalists, but his life was spared upon the intervention of Sir John Denham, who gave as his reason that so long as Wither lived, he (Denham) could not be branded the worst poet in England.

CHRYSTAL, Charles P., in C.P. Snow's *The Light and the Dark* (1947) and *The Masters* (1951), is part-inspired by Travers Carey Wyatt (1887–1954), who in 1937 became bursar of Christ's College, Cambridge, of which he was vice-master from 1950 to 1952, as Philip Snow records in *Stranger and Brother: a Portrait of C.P. Snow* (1982).

CHYCHESTER, Uncle Sufford, in Henry Williamson's *The Pathway* (1928), is Charles Calvert Hibbert, of Chalfont Park, Buckinghamshire, and Landcross, Devon. Father of the author's first wife, he was the senior member of the Cheriton Otter Hunt, and uncle of the navigator Sir Francis Chichester.

CIBBER, Jeremy Pratt and Adèle, in Richard Aldington's *Stepping Heavenward* (1931). Pouring hot chocolate through one's estranged husband's letter-box is not a recommended way of persuading him to return. This and other desperate, attention-seeking devices served only to strengthen the resolve of T.S. Eliot (see Horty, Mr) never to see his first wife again. Portraying them as Jeremy and the melancholy Adèle, Aldington's novella foreshadows the break-up of the marriage of Eliot and his schizophrenic wife, Vivienne Haigh Wood (1888–1947), from whom Eliot separated in 1933. In 1938 she entered a private mental hospital where she spent the rest of her life. Peter Ackroyd's *T.S. Eliot* (1984) records how Vivienne had earlier alarmed Virginia Woolf and Ottoline Morrell and had prompted Edith Sitwell's maid (a former mental hospital employee) to warn her mistress, 'If she starts anything, Miss, get her by the wrists, sit on her face and don't let her bite you.'

CIRCUMFERENCE, Lady, in Evelyn Waugh's *Decline and Fall* (1928), is Jessie Graham (*d.* 1934), American mother of Alastair Graham (see Lennox, Hamish). Waugh's *Diaries* (1976) portray her as a daunting woman who once gave him a dressing-down for his rudeness. She was the daughter of Andrew Low, of Savannah, a Scot who emigrated to America, made his fortune in cotton, and in the Civil War was arrested and imprisoned as a Northern spy.

CLANDON, Mrs Lanfrey, in George Bernard Shaw's *You Never Can Tell* (1898), is an amalgam of Mrs Annie Besant (see Petkoff, Raina) and the author's mother, Lucinda Elizabeth Shaw (née Gurly, 1830–1913), who in 1852 married George Carr Shaw, an alcoholic who on being made redundant as a civil servant became equally unsuccessful as a grain merchant. Shortly after the marriage, the couple were joined in Dublin by George Vandaleur Lee (see Higgins, Henry), forming a *ménage à trois*. Lucinda Shaw left her husband in 1873, following Lee to London where until five years before her death she was singing mistress at the North London Collegiate School for women.

CLARE, Angel, in Thomas Hardy's *Tess of the D'Urbervilles* (1891), is in part the author's boyhood friend and early literary mentor Horace Moule (*d.* 1873), son of the Revd Henry Moule (1801–80), vicar of Fordington, Dorset, who acquired a national reputation through his inventive efforts to combat cholera epidemics. Eight years Hardy's senior, and temperamentally unstable, with a weakness for drink, Horace Moule was a classics master at Marlborough College (1865–8), sired an illegitimate child in his father's parish and committed suicide by cutting his throat with a razor. One of his brothers became Bishop of Durham, another was the first Anglican Bishop of Mid-China, and a third was president of Corpus Christi College, Cambridge.

CLARINDA, in the poems of Robert Burns, is Agnes ('Nancy') M'lehose (1759–1841). A Glasgow surgeon's daughter, at seventeen she married a law agent who, ordered from the house by her father, had contrived to see her alone by purchasing all the seats but one on a Glasgow-to-Edinburgh coach in which he knew she would be travelling. After bearing him four children she left him, subsequently living alone in Edinburgh. It was there that she met Burns, whose attentions she encouraged – provided they stopped short of the physical.

CLARISSA, in Ford Madox Ford's *Mister Bosphorous and the Muses* (1923), was inspired by Stella Bowen. See Wannop, Valentine.

CLARISSE, in Robert Musil's *The Man Without Qualities* (1930—43), is Alice Donath, wife of the author's childhood friend, Gustav Donath (1878—1965). Over a period of months, Musil watched her lapse into insanity.

CLARISSE, in Madeleine de Scudéry's *Clélie* (1654—60), is Anne ('Ninon') de Lenclos (1620—1705), a Paris hostess whose salon was frequented by the leading writers of her day. She was noted for her distinguished lovers, of whom the first, according to Voltaire, was Richelieu.

CLARKE, St. John, in Anthony Powell's *A Dance to the Music of Time* sequence (1951—75). Upon the publication of Powell's fourth and final volume of memoirs, *The Strangers All are Gone* (1982), the critic Hilary Spurling remarked in the *Observer*: 'The rich compost of false sentiment, trite thought, bogus aesthetics and genuine vanity so fruitfully fermenting in the Edwardian clubman St. John Clarke (bestselling author of *Fields of Amaranth, The Heart is Highland*, etc. etc.) originated, presumably, in a single, startling brush with Galsworthy recorded in *Messengers of Day*.' Few can know their Powell better than Spurling, author of the guide to Anthony Powell's *Music of Time* (1977), but what does the author himself have to say? 'I should not have thought that St. John Clarke bore the smallest resemblance to Galsworthy in any respect. St. John Clarke was just a type-figure of the men of letters of his period . . . That is why it is irritating to have people saying he (and others) are "meant to be" so-and-so.' For John Galsworthy proper, see Morland, Thomas.

CLAYHANGER, Darius, in Arnold Bennett's *Clayhanger* (1910). 'All the time my father was dying, I was at the bedside making copious notes,' the author recorded. 'You can't just slap these things down.' Enoch Bennett (1843—1902), in part the model for Darius, worked his way up from potter and pawnbroker to become a solicitor and part-proprietor of a Burslem newspaper, Burslem being one of the Staffordshire towns that feature in the author's Potteries stories. A tyrannical, sneering parent believed to have been responsible for Arnold Bennett's stammer, he became prematurely senile and was finally reduced to imbecility.

CLEEVER, Eustace, in Rudyard Kipling's 'A Conference of the Powers' (*Many Inventions*, 1893). In his *The Strange Ride of Rudyard Kipling: His Life and Work* (1977), Angus Wilson suggests that in

Cleever the author had in mind Thomas Hardy (see Driffield, Edward). Cleever is presented by Kipling as seen through practical eyes, an author who has only written, never *done* anything. His works include *As It Was in the Beginning*, a title which has a Hardy 'ring'.

CLÉRENCES, Gilbert de, in Pierre Drieu la Rochelle's *Gilles* (1939). According to *Drieu la Rochelle and the Fiction of Testimony* (1958), by Fréderic J. Grover, Clérences is the French Radical Socialist statesman Gaston Bergery (?1892–1974), head of Édouard Herriott's cabinet in 1924 and a founder of the Popular Front which swept all before it in the elections of 1936. In the Second World War, in which he supported the collaborationist government of Pierre Laval, he was Vichy France's ambassador to the Soviet Union and Turkey. Subsequently accused of collaborating with the Germans, he was acquitted in 1949.

CLERY, Emma, in James Joyce's *A Portrait of the Artist as a Young Man* (1916) and *Stephen Hero* (1944), is supposedly an amalgam of Mary Kettle (née Sheehy) and Amalia Risolo (née Popper). Mary was the daughter of David Sheehy, a Dublin MP. A sweetheart of the author's adolescence, she married Thomas Kettle (see Hand, Robert). Amalia, daughter of a Jewish businessman, was a pupil of Joyce in Trieste in 1913. Upon her marriage, she moved to Florence.

CLEVELAND, Clement, in Sir Walter Scott's *The Pirate* (1822), has as prototype John Gow (*d.* 1725), whose career was also chronicled by Defoe. Son of a Scot who had settled at Stromness in the Orkney Islands, Gow incited a crew to mutiny on a vessel of which he was second mate. Killing the chief officers, they placed Gow in command and became pirates. When he sought to extend his plundering ashore, Gow was captured, tried, and executed in London.

CLIFFORD, Martha, in James Joyce's *Ulysses* (1922), was part-inspired by Marthe Fleischmann (see MacDowell, Gerty), who preferred 'to arouse rather than to requite desire', according to Joyce's biographer, Richard Ellmann.

CLINE, Frances, in Ernest Hemingway's *The Sun Also Rises* (1926; published in England as *Fiesta*). So annoyed was Frances ('Kitty') Cannell by her portrayal as Frances Cline that she took to her bed for three days, according to Hemingway's biographer, Carlos Baker. A former professional dancer, she had an apartment next door to Harold Loeb (see Cohn, Robert) in Paris, and was outraged by Hemingway's vilification of Loeb and by the presentation of herself as Loeb's jealous mistress. Hemingway took Cannell's conversational style, says Baker, and grafted it on to the character and experience of a Jewish secretary who had worked for Loeb on the magazine *Broom*.

CLINTON, Oscar, in H. Russell Wakefield's 'He Cometh and He Passeth By' (*The Best Ghost Stories of H. Russell Wakefield*, 1978), is Aleister Crowley (see Haddo, Oliver), according to Richard Dalby's introduction to this collection. Others might find it difficult to recognise Crowley in 'one of the most dangerous and intellectual men in the world', but overstatement was Wakefield's forte . . . and Crowley would not have disputed the description, for it was precisely how he liked to see himself.

CLITORESSA of Natescourt, the Duchess, in Djuna Barnes's *The Ladies' Almanack* (1928), is Élisabeth de Gramont, Duchesse de Clermont-Tonnerre, whose adoption of a bobbed hairstyle prompted Gertrude Stein (see Percival, Mrs) to wear her hair short ever after. Daughter of the Duc de Gramont (see Guermantes, Basin, Duc de) and half-sister of Armand, Duc de Guiche (see Saint-Loup, Robert de), she was among the lovers of Natalie Barney (see Flossie). She wrote two volumes of memoirs, *Pomp and Circumstance* (1929) and *Years of Plenty* (1932).

CLIVE, in Christopher Isherwood's *Goodbye to Berlin* (1939), is John Blomshield, an American artist who when Isherwood met him in Berlin in 1929 was occupying a suite at the Adlon Hotel at the expense of his estranged wife, who was divorcing him. Breakfasting with champagne − tea, he said, did not agree with an empty stomach − he had a love-hate relationship with a Norwegian boyfriend who subsequently accompanied him to America.

CLORINDA, in George Sand's *Consuelo* (1842−3), is Marie de Flavigny, Comtesse d'Agoult (see Rochefide, Béatrix de), who left her husband to live with Franz Liszt (see Conti, Gennaro).

CLOTILDE, in Émile Zola's *Le Docteur Pascal* (1893), is Jeanne Rozerot. Joining the author's household as a seamstress in 1888, she became his mistress, bearing him two children.

CLUTTON, in W. Somerset Maugham's *Of Human Bondage* (1915), is Roderick O'Conor (see O'Brien). Here, seven years after his first appearance in a Maugham novel, O'Conor is seen alerting the author to the fictional possibilities of Gauguin (see Strickland, Charles), just as he apparently did in real life.

COATES, Adrian, in Angela Thirkell's *High Rising* (1933), according to Margot Strickland's *Angela Thirkell: Portrait of a Lady Novelist* (1977), is Hamish Hamilton (1900–   ), founder in 1931 and managing director until 1972 of the London publishing house which bears his name.

COCKSHOT, in R.L. Stevenson's 'Talk and Talkers' (1882; *Memories and Portraits*, 1887), is Fleeming Jenkin (1833–85), Professor of Engineering at Edinburgh University. Stevenson was his secretary when he attended the International Exposition in Paris in 1878 as a juror (Jenkin's wife and Stevenson's mother were friends, the acquaintanceship leading to the author's introduction to the professor). A lively polymath, Jenkin was a pioneer of submarine telegraphy and in 1882 devised a system for the automatic electric transport of goods by what he termed 'telpherage'. Although details of this system were incomplete when he died, a 'telpher' line based on his notion was built at Glynde, in Sussex.

CODLIN, Thomas, in Charles Dickens's *The Old Curiosity Shop* (1841), may owe his name to the Codman family, Punch and Judy practitioners since at least 1830 and the subject of a public outcry when Liverpool Corporation tried to banish them from their St George's Plateau pitch in the 1950s. An early Codman travelled the country with his canvas booth on his back. Alternatively, the name may have been suggested by 'Hot Codlins', a song made famous by the clown, Grimaldi, whose biography Dickens wrote. A codlin is a cooking apple.

CODRINGTON, Christopher, in Philip Gibbs's *The Street of Adventure* (1923). Nowadays, anything goes; but there was a time when a tacit 'dog doesn't eat dog' code meant that it was unusual for one journalist to sue another. His portrayal as Codrington, however, was more than Randall Charlton could stomach. He sued Gibbs, his colleague on the London *Tribune*. 'One day in Fleet Street the two met, raised their hats to each other, and then laughed', Hamilton Fyfe records in *Sixty Years of Fleet Street* (1949). 'Gibbs suggested they should have lunch together. The other hesitated. "One must eat," Gibbs urged. The other accepted the invitation. When the solicitors heard of it, they were aghast. "That ends the case," they said, and it did, for Gibbs persuaded his friend to withdraw the action.'

CODY, Dan, in F. Scott Fitzgerald's *The Great Gatsby* (1925), has a possible prototype in the New York financier Charles A. Stoneham (*d.* 1936), who progressed from broker's office-boy to become president of his own brokerage firm. With two partners, in 1919 he bought the New York Giants Baseball Club. After selling his business in 1921, he acquired a newspaper, a gambling casino and a race-track.

COEURDELION, the Duke of, in W.M. Thackeray's *The Book of Snobs* (1846–8), is supposedly Richard Plantagenet Temple Nugent Brydges Chandos Grenville (1797–1861), Second Duke of Buckingham and Chandos, and Lord Privy Seal from 1841 to 1842. He was the author of a number of books of memoirs of the courts of George III, George IV, William IV and Victoria.

COHEN, Mordecai, in George Eliot's *Daniel Deronda* (1876), is an amalgam of Emmanuel Deutsch (see Deronda, Daniel) and Judah Ben Samuel Halevi (?1085–1140), Hebrew poet and hymn-writer. The identification of Deutsch was made by the Eliot biographer Gordon S. Haight, and that of Halevi by Barbara Hardy, author of *Particularities: Readings in George Eliot* (1982).

COHN, Robert, in Ernest Hemingway's *The Sun Also Rises* (1926; published in England as *Fiesta*), is Harold Loeb (1891–1974), member of a Wall Street banking family, publisher of the arts magazine *Broom* (1921–4), economist, and author of three novels. Living in Weston, Connecticut, he died on holiday in Morocco.

COLCHICUM, Lord, in W.M. Thackeray's *The History of Pendennis* (1848–50), has as prototype William Lowther, Third Earl of Lonsdale (1787–1872). A life-long bachelor, he was a patron of opera (and opera singers) and a dedicated hunting man who twice refused to become prime minister, explaining that the office would impinge too much upon his private life. Affairs of state – he held a number of government posts – claimed his attention only when the ground was frozen and hunting with his hounds at Tring was out of the question.

COLEMAN, in Aldous Huxley's *Antic Hay* (1923). Jocelyn Brooke's *Aldous Huxley* (1954) finds Coleman 'easily recognisable' as the composer Peter Warlock (Philip Heseltine). See Halliday, Julius.

COLLIN, Jacques. See Vautrin.

COLUMBINE, in Leon Uris's *Topaz* (1962), has been taken to have a prototype in Jacques Foccart (1913–), ostensibly France's Secretary-General for French Community, African and Madagascar Affairs, but in reality principal Intelligence adviser to the then President Charles de Gaulle. His popular identification with Columbine caused a scandal which cost him his job, although he was later reinstated.

COMBERBACH, Private Silas Tomkyn, in Charles Lloyd's *Edmund Oliver* (1798), is Samuel Taylor Coleridge, according to Claude A. Prance's *Companion to Charles Lamb* (1983). See Skionar, Mr.

COMIC, Sir Farcical, in Henry Fielding's *The Author's Farce* (1730), is Colley Cibber. See Bays.

COMPOSTELLA, Miss, in Ronald Firbank's *Vainglory* (1915), is Mrs Patrick Campbell (see Hushabye, Hesione), one of whose Christian names was Stella.

COMUS, in Max Beerbohm's 'Laughter' (*And Even Now*, 1920), is Reggie Turner (1869–1938), illegitimate son of the first Lord Burnham. He wrote the 'London Day by Day' column in the *Daily Telegraph*, was drama critic of *The Academy*, and on Oscar Wilde's release from prison in 1897 joined him in Dieppe to share his exile. He was noted for his ugliness and for his wit. 'Last night I dreamed that I was at the banquet of the dead,' Wilde remarked one morning. 'I'm sure you were the life and soul of the party,' said Turner. On Herbert Horne's biography of Botticelli: 'Dear Herbert Horne! Poring over Botticelli's washing bills – and always a shirt missing.' On his own career as an unsuccessful novelist, Turner remarked that while others' first editions were rare, *his* second editions were unobtainable — 'in fact, they don't exist.'

CONINGSBY, Harry, in Benjamin Disraeli's *Coningsby* (1844), was claimed by the Revised Key to the work (1845) to be Lord Littleton (*sic*), presumably George William Lyttelton, Fourth Baron Lyttelton (1817–76), Under-Secretary of State for the Colonies in 1846. Coningsby is also part-inspired by the Hon. George Smythe (1818–57). Subsequently Seventh Viscount Strangford and Second Baron Penshurst, he was a founder member of the Young England party in which Disraeli was prominent. His collection of poems and essays, *Historic Fancies*, was published in 1844, and in 1852 he fought at Weybridge what was reputed to be the last duel in England.

CONNAGE, Rosalind, in F. Scott Fitzgerald's *This Side of Paradise* (1920). Rosalind is this novel's Zelda figure: one of the 'smart set', a desirable debutante, a feather in the cap of any young fellow fortunate enough to date her. Like Zelda Sayre (see Diver, Nicole), she has doubts about the man who loves her, the novel's Amory Blaine. Knowing she cannot be happy with a man without money, she marries another — just as Zelda doubtless would have done had Fitzgerald not achieved financial success. See also Cary, Jonquil.

CONNIE, in D.H. Lawrence's 'The Witch à la Mode' (*A Modern Lover*, 1934), is Jessie Chambers. See Leivers, Miriam.

CONRAD, in Lord Byron's *The Corsair* (1814), is the French pirate and smuggler Jean Lafitte (1780–?1825). His operations off the coast of Louisiana prompted the British government in 1814 to offer him a commission in the Royal Navy and £30,000 if he would take part in an attack on New Orleans. He responded by passing documentary evidence of this offer to the American authorities, who accepted his assistance in the Battle of New Orleans and pardoned his previous piratical activities.

CONROY, Gabriel and Gretta, in James Joyce's 'The Dead' (*Dubliners*, 1914). The author's brother, Stanislaus, said that Gabriel owed his oratorical style to their father, John Joyce (see Dedalus, Simon). Gabriel is also part-inspired by Constantine P. Curran (see Donovan). Gretta is based in part on Nora Barnacle (see Bloom, Molly).

CONSTABLE, Algy, in D.H. Lawrence's *Aaron's Rod* (1922), is Reggie Turner (see Comus). Lawrence apparently thought him lacking in application – in a letter to Dorothy Brett he remarked that Turner was 'doing a book but I doubt if he'll finish it.'

CONSTANCE, in Gertrude Stein's *Yes Is For a Very Young Man* (1946), has as prototype the dramatist Clare Boothe Luce (1903–), according to James R. Mellow's *Charmed Circle: Gertrude Stein and Company* (1974).

CONSTANTINE, Leo, in C.P. Snow's *The Search* (1934), is Professor John Desmond Bernal (1901–71), Professor of Crystallography at Birkbeck College, London University, from 1963 to 1968. A Marxist, he was an assistant to Lord Mountbatten (see Gilpin, Commander Peter) in the Second World War.

CONSUELO, in George Sand's *Consuelo* (1842–3), is Pauline Viardot. See Natalya Petrovna.

CONTI, Gennaro, in Honoré de Balzac's *Béatrix* (1844), is a composite of three composers: Frédéric Chopin (see Roswald, Prince Karol de); Franz Liszt (1811–86), lover of Marie d'Agoult (see Rochefide, Béatrix de), who bore him three children; and Gioacchino Rossini (1792–1868).

CONTINENTAL OP, the, in Dashiell Hammett's stories and collection of that name (1974), is based on James Wright, assistant manager of the Baltimore office of Pinkerton's National Detective Agency, and Hammett's mentor when the author became a Pinkerton detective in 1915, at the age of twenty-one.

COOGAN, Mike, in Viviane Ventura's *April Fool* (1983), is supposedly part-inspired by the Hollywood film actor Anthony Quinn (1915–), with whom the author appeared in *High Wind in Jamaica*.

COOKE, Betty, in C.P. Snow's *Homecomings* (1956) and *The Sleep of Reason* (1968), is Anne Seagrim, post-war secretary to the author and, for about thirty years, his mistress. She was secretary to the Duke of Windsor from 1950 to 1954, and subsequently to Field Marshal Earl Alexander of Tunis (see Gilbey, Lord).

COOLEY, Ben ('Kangaroo'), in D.H. Lawrence's *Kangaroo* (1923). The author's wife said that Cooley was Dr M.D. Eder (1865–1936), a pioneer Freudian psychoanalyst and Zionist leader who was the political chief of the Zionist Executive in Jerusalem from 1918 to 1923; Lawrence first met him in 1914. Cooley's appearance, the Lawrence biographer Harry T. Moore believes, was modelled upon that of General Sir John Monash (1865–1931), vice-chancellor of Melbourne University. Lawrence himself denied suggestions that Cooley was S.S. Koteliansky (see Perekatov, Mr).

COOPER, Margaret, in William Gilmore Simms's *Charlemont; or The Pride of the Village* (1856), is Ann Cook. See Octavia.

COPPER, Lord, in Evelyn Waugh's *Scoop* (1938), is Lord Beaverbrook (see Ottercove, Lord), who briefly employed the author on the *Daily Express* in 1927.

CORBIE, Hamish, in Dylan Thomas and John Davenport's *The Death of the King's Canary* (written 1940, published 1976), is Aleister Crowley. See Haddo, Oliver.

CORD, Jonas, in Harold Robbins's *The Carpetbaggers* (1961), is Howard Hughes. See Hackamore, Henry.

CORDWAINER, Peter, in Malcolm Lowry's *October Ferry to Gabriola* (1970), is Paul Fitte, a Cambridge undergraduate contemporary of the author. His homosexual relationship with Lowry led to his suicide, for which the author ever after blamed himself.

CORINNA, La, in George Sand's *Consuelo* (1842–3), is the Italian prima donna Giulia Grisi (1811–69), whose jealousy made life difficult for her young rival, Pauline Viardot (see Natalya Petrovna).

COROMBONA, Vittoria, in John Webster's *The White Devil* (produced as *The White Divel c.*1608 and published in 1612) is Vittoria Accoramboni (1557–85), a Rome beauty who married Paolo Giordano Orsini, Duke of Bracciano, following the murder of her husband, Francesco Peretti, in which the couple were suspected of being implicated. Also suspected of murdering his first wife, Isabella de' Medici, Bracciano moved with Vittoria to Salo, where he died in 1585. Five weeks later, his widow was killed by one of

Bracciano's relatives who had commenced litigation over the inheritance of the estate.

CORRÈZE, Raphael de, in Ouida's *Moths* (1880), has as prototype the Italian tenor Giovanni Mario di Candia, with whom the author fell in love when she was thirty-two. Married to Giulia Grisi (see Corinna, La), the singer failed to respond to Ouida's overtures.

CORTWRIGHT, Edith, in Sinclair Lewis's *Dodsworth* (1929), is the author's second wife, the foreign correspondent and New York *Herald Tribune* columnist Dorothy Thompson (1894–1961). A fugitive from the failure of his first marriage, Lewis met her in Berlin. He was in Europe seeking material for his next novel; she was there as a journalist – her *I Saw Hitler* (1932), which said that Hitler would never become his country's leader, did not prevent her from later becoming an influential political commentator. See also Homeward, Winifred.

COSSINGTON, in H.G. Wells's *The New Machiavelli* (1911), is Lord Northcliffe. See Tilbury, Lord.

COTTARD, Dr, in Marcel Proust's *À la recherche du temps perdu* (1913–27). 'I wouldn't have trusted him to cut my hair, especially if there'd been a mirror in the room.' That was Léon Daudet's view of the medical ability and conceit of Dr Samuel Jean Pozzi (1846–1918), one of the models for Cottard. He was a Bonapartist and Dreyfusard friend of the author's parents and was noted for his vanity and his affairs with fashionable patients – 'I don't deceive you, my dear,' he would reassure his wife, 'I supplement you.' Portrayed by Sargent and a friend of Henry James, he took the teenage Proust out to his first dinner and in 1914 secured his exemption from military service. He was murdered by an insane patient. Cottard owes his pince-nez and nervous wink to Albert Vandal (1853–1910), under whom Proust studied political history in Paris in 1890. Also perceived in this character have been Professor Georges Dieulafoy (1839–1911), physician to Princesse Mathilde, who also appears under his own name; Dr Eugène-Louis Doyen (1859–1916), noted for the originality of his surgical methods and his gaucherie in society; and Professor Félix Guyon (1831–1920), a urologist given to lacing his lectures with puns.

COUAËN, Madame de, in Charles-Augustin Sainte-Beuve's *Volupté* (1834), is Adèle Hugo (née Foucher, 1803–68), wife of the novelist Victor Hugo (see Hulot, Baron). Abandoning marital relations with her philandering husband after the birth of their fifth child she was from 1831 to 1837 Sainte-Beuve's mistress. Dickens found her to be 'a handsome woman with flashing black eyes, who looks as if she might poison her husband's breakfast any morning the humour seized her.'

COUCY, Lady Blanche de, in Ford Madox Ford's *Ladies Whose Bright Eyes* (1911), is part-inspired by Elsie Martindale (see Macdonald, Countess), according to Thomas C. Moser's *The Life in the Fiction of Ford Madox Ford* (1980).

COUPEAU, Anna ('Nana'), in Émile Zola's *Nana* (1879–80). In *Things I Shouldn't Tell* (1924), the American writer Julian Osgood Field remarked, 'Blanche d'Antigny was, of course, Nana — everyone knew that; and, in fact, Zola told me so himself.' The identification was supported by L. Auriant's *La Véritable Histoire de 'Nana'* (1942). Blanche d'Antigny (Marie Ernestine Antigny, 1804–74) was an actress and cocotte whose wealth became such that in 1873 she was able to buy 101, rue de Chaillet, Paris, from the courtesan Cora Pearl (Emma Elizabeth Crouch). The house had been given to Pearl by her lover, Prince Jerome, nephew of Napoleon I. Nana may also be part-inspired by the actress Henriette Hauser, known as 'Citron' and the model for Manet's painting, 'Nana'. Although this portrait predated the novel, it may have been prompted by Anna Coupeau's earlier appearance in Zola's *L'Assommoir* (1876–7).

COURTENEY, Sir Samson, in Evelyn Waugh's *Black Mischief* (1932). Sir Sidney Barton (1876–1946), Britain's Envoy Extraordinary and Minister Plenipotentiary to Abyssinia from 1929 to 1937, identified himself as Courteney, recalls William Deedes in his introduction to the Folio Society edition of this novel (1981). One of Barton's daughters, believing herself to be the novel's Prudence, dashed a glass of wine in the author's face upon encountering him in 1935 in a night club in Addis Ababa.

COURTIER, Charles, in John Galsworthy's *The Patrician* (1911), is an amalgam of R.B. Cunninghame Graham (see Hushabye, Hector) and the foreign correspondent and author H.W. Nevinson (1856–1941). Although he found the caricature flattering, Nevinson told Galsworthy his portrayal as a devotee of lost causes was erroneous: Indian nationalism, the emancipation of women and a Russian revolution were winning causes, or would be. Galsworthy replied that his acquaintance with Nevinson had been an impediment rather than a help in portraying a man of Nevinson's type: Courtier had been created in spite of, rather than because of, Nevinson.

COVERLEY, Sir Roger de, in the contributions of Joseph Addison to *The Spectator* (1711–14), has a suggested original in the writer's friend, the Worcestershire bachelor MP and poet William Walsh (1663–1708), of Abberley Lodge, Abberley, where Addison was often a guest. Another Worcestershire village, Hampton Lovett, contends that its squire, Sir John Pakington MP (1671–1727), was the model for Sir Roger, but this is less likely: twice-married, Sir John was noted as being 'of a violently controversial nature'. Another suggested original is William Boevey (*d.* 1692), of Flaxley Abbey, Gloucestershire, whose widow Katherine (*d.* 1726, aged fifty-six) is supposedly the widow impervious to Sir Roger's attentions.

COWPERWOOD, Frank Algernon, in Theodore Dreiser's *The Financier* (1912), *The Titan* (1914) and *The Stoic* (1947). 'It's the strap-hanger that pays the dividends,' observed the Chicago street-car magnate and financier Charles Tyson Yerkes (1837–1905), who was Dreiser's model for Cowperwood. Leaving the United States in 1900 following allegations that he had secured franchises through political corruption, he settled in London and was largely responsible for the development of the city's underground railway system. His early career included a term in prison . . . so when you travel by London Underground or by elevated railway in Chicago, you have a former embezzler to thank.

COX, Charlemagne and Mrs, in Richard Aldington's 'Nobody's Baby' (*Soft Answers*, 1932), are Ezra Pound (see Forbes, Duncan) and Nancy Cunard (see Storm, Iris).

COZENS, Nancy, in Wyndham Lewis's *The Roaring Queen* (1936), is Daisy Ashford (1881–1972), author of *The Young Visiters*, written when she was nine and published twenty-nine years later. As Lewis's biographer, Jeffrey Meyers, records, *Splashing into Society* (the first novel by Iris Barry, Lewis's mistress) was a parody of *The Young Visiters*.

CRABBE, Tom Waterhouse, in Sir Arthur Conan Doyle's 'Crabbe's Practice' (1884; *Tales of Adventure and Medical Life*, 1922), is Dr George Turnavine Budd. See Challenger, Professor George Edward.

CRABTREE, Joel, in Anita Loos's *But Gentlemen Marry Brunettes* (1927), is the poet and New York journalist Franklin Pierce Adams (1881—1960), contributor of the influential column 'The Conning Tower' to the New York *Herald Tribune*.

CRAMIER, Olive, in John Galsworthy's *The Dark Flower* (1913), is Ada Galsworthy. See Forsyte, Irene.

CRANLY, in James Joyce's *A Portrait of the Artist as a Young Man* (1916) and *Stephen Hero* (1944), is J.F. Byrne, a University College, Dublin, contemporary and confidant of the author. The Blooms' home in *Ulysses* is based on his house. His memoir of Joyce, *Silent Years*, was published in 1953.

CRAUFORD, Richard, in Bulwer Lytton's *The Disowned* (1828), is Henry Fauntleroy (1758—1824), a banker sentenced to death for forgery. He was executed despite the protests of numerous members of his profession and men of commerce who extolled his integrity, and despite the offer of an Italian gentleman to take his place on the scaffold ... from which, it was fallaciously rumoured, Fauntleroy escaped to live in comfort abroad, having inserted a silver tube in his throat to thwart strangulation.

CRAVEN, Julia, in George Bernard Shaw's *The Philanderer* (1905). On his twenty-ninth birthday, Shaw lost his virginity to Jenny Patterson (1839—1924), a well-to-do Irish widow fifteen years his senior, and his model for Julia Craven. One of his mother's singing pupils, she lived in London's Brompton Square and subsequently at 'Bookhams', Churt, in Surrey. She was supplanted in Shaw's affections by Florence Farr (see Tranfield, Grace), with whom she consequently engaged in fisticuffs. Despite this and other scenes, she remained a friend of the Shaw family for the rest of her life.

CRAVISTER, Mrs, in Aldous Huxley's 'The Farcical History of Richard Greenow' (*Limbo*, 1920), is Blanche Cornish, wife of Francis Warre Cornish, Vice-Provost of Eton College from 1893 to 1916. Noted for wrong-footing others in conversation, she was also proficient in the perfect put-down — thus, to one of a gathering of masters' wives meeting to read French drama, 'How wise of you, dear, not to attempt the French accent.' Her daughter, Mary, married the author and literary critic Sir Desmond MacCarthy. See Bernard.

CRAW, Bill, in John le Carré's *The Honourable Schoolboy* (1977). Identified as Craw upon this novel's publication, Richard Hughes (see Henderson, Dikko) told the *Sunday Times*, 'Craw works ten times as hard and far more effectively than I do. I must also insist that he drinks ten times as much as I, and takes far more interest in ladies than my stern Chinese wife allows me to. His grossly improper association with MI6 — or is it SIS? — is something of course completely beyond my ken.'

CRAW, Thomas Carlyle, in John Buchan's *Castle Gay* (1930), is an amalgam of Lord Rothermere (see Youngbrother, Lord) and Sir William Robertson Nicoll (1851–1923), a Scottish Nonconformist minister and man of letters, and founder-editor of *The British Weekly* (1886) and *The Bookman* (1891). Nicoll credited the Scots novelist S.R. Crockett with more strength in his little finger than was to be found in Buchan's entire body.

CRAWFORD, Homer T. ('Chuck'), in John Dos Passos's *Number One* (1943), is Huey Long. See Stark, Willie.

CRAWFORD, Myles, in James Joyce's *Ulysses* (1922), is probably Patrick J. Mead, editor of the Dublin *Evening Telegraph*, though Crawford's expression 'kiss my royal Irish arse' was that of another *Telegraph* journalist, John Wyse Power, according to Joyce's biographer, Richard Ellmann.

CRAWFORD, Redvers Thomas Arbuthnot, in C.P. Snow's *The Masters* (1951) and *The Affair* (1960). The critic Julian Symons has remarked that many identifications of Snow originals have little importance except for those who knew them. So here's hoping you were acquainted with the two models for Crawford: Sir Robert Alexander Watson-Watt (1892–1973), a pioneer of radar and

Scientific Adviser to the Air Ministry in the Second World War; and the mathematical physicist Sir Charles Galton Darwin (1887–1962), grandson of Charles Darwin (see Hamley, Roger), Master of Christ's College, Cambridge, from 1936 to 1938 and Director of the National Physical Laboratory from 1938 to 1949.

CRAWLEY, Con, in Lady Morgan's *Florence Macarthy* (1818), is John Wilson Croker (see Rigby, Mr). This was the author's revenge for a rancorous review of her *France* (1817) in the *Quarterly Review*.

CRAWLEY, Miss Matilda, in W.M. Thackeray's *Vanity Fair* (1847–8), is the author's maternal grandmother, Harriet Butler (née Cowper, ?1770–1847), who in 1786 married John Harman Becher (d. 1800), a collector of the East India Company, who became bankrupt and by whom she had four children. After her husband's death she lived in Bengal as the wife of Captain Charles Christie (d. 1804), and in 1806 she married Captain (later Lieutenant-Colonel) Edward William Butler (d. 1819), of the Bengal Artillery, father of four illegitimate children by Indian mistresses. Cantankerous and restless – in her old age she seldom settled long in one place – she was a generous benefactor to Thackeray and apparently approved of her portrayal as Miss Crawley, for she adopted the first name Matilda.

CRAWLEY, Sir Pitt, *idem*, is supposedly Lord (John) Rolle of Stevenstone (1750–1842), who as a politician was a supporter of William Pitt (1759–1806). The Whig satire, *The Rolliad* (1784), derived its name from Rolle.

CRAYE, Lady Florence, in P.G. Wodehouse's *Carry On, Jeeves* (1925), *Joy in the Morning* (1947), *Jeeves and the Feudal Spirit* (1954) and *Much Obliged, Jeeves* (1971). Girton College, Cambridge, figures in the background of several of the formidable young women who cause Bertram Wooster to quail, as the Wodehouse commentator N.T.P. Murphy has noted. They include Heloise Pringle and Honoria Glossop, but it is in Wooster's cousin, Lady Florence Craye, that a pointer to a model can be discerned. Wodehouse's cousin, Dr Helen Marion Wodehouse (1880–1964), Mistress of Girton from 1931 to 1942, was the author of *The Logic of Will* (1908), which is echoed by *Types of Ethical Theory* in *Carry On, Jeeves*. Dr Wodehouse was a niece of Graham Wallas (see Willersley). Her career suggests that, like Florence, she was 'one of those intellectual girls, her bean crammed to bursting point with little grey cells.'

CRAYE, Miss, in Virginia Woolf's 'Slater's Pins Have No Points' (*A Haunted House*, 1943), is Clara Pater, sister of Walter Pater (see Rose, Mr) and Greek tutor to the author, suggests Woolf's biographer, Quentin Bell.

CREAKLE, Mr, in Charles Dickens's *David Copperfield* (1849–50). Speaking in 1857 at a Warehousemen and Clerks' Schools' charity banquet, Dickens described Creakle's original as 'by far the most ignorant man I have ever had the pleasure to know, who was one of the worst-tempered men perhaps that ever lived, whose business it was to make as much out of us and put as little into us as possible.' He was William Jones, the Welsh proprietor of Wellington House Academy, Mornington Place, Hampstead Road, London, which the author attended as a pupil in 1824. Jones had the reputation of knowing little himself but employing an assistant who knew almost everything; and of being rather more kindly than Creakle. His establishment was also the model for 'Our School', a sketch written by Dickens for *Household Words* in 1851.

CRÉCY, Odette de, in Marcel Proust's *A la recherche du temps perdu* (1913–27), is supposedly an amalgam of the Comtesse de la Beraudière, last mistress of Comte Henri Greffulhe (see Guermantes, Basin, Duc de), who unsuccessfully tried to prevent her from seeing others and who left her a considerable legacy; the Parisian courtesan Léonie Closmesnil, known as 'the butcheress' because her first lover was a butcher; Laure Hayman (1851–1932), celebrated courtesan, collector of Saxe figurines (she called Proust 'my little porcelain psychologist') and mistress of Louis Weil, Proust's mother's uncle; Méry Laurent (née Louviot, *b.* 1849), Parisian cocotte, actress, artist's model, and mistress of Édouard Manet (see Lantier, Claude), Stéphane Mallarmé and Dr Thomas Evans, American dentist to Napoleon III; Baronne Aimery Harty de Pierrebourg (née Marguerite Thomas-Galline, 1856–1943), who lived apart from her husband, deserted the salon of Lydie Aubernon (see Verdurin, Mme) to start one of her own, wrote novels under the name Claude Ferval, and was mistress of Paul Hervieu (see Swann, Charles); and Mme Émile Straus (see Guermantes, Oriane, Duchesse de).

CRICH, Gerald, in D.H. Lawrence's *Women in Love* (1920), is a composite of Major (later Sir) Thomas Philip Barber, John Middleton Murry, and George Neville (see Tempest, Leslie). Barber (1876–1961), Lawrence's main source for Crich's physical appearance, was a Nottinghamshire colliery owner who increased mechanisation in his Eastwood pits at the expense of humanity. In 1890 he accidentally shot and killed his younger, thirteen-year-old brother; and in 1892 his seven-year-old sister drowned in Moorgreen reservoir after falling from her father's houseboat, dragging to his death a doctor's son who dived in to rescue her. Murry (1889–1957), critic, novelist and poet, was the husband of Katherine Mansfield (see Brangwen, Gudrun), edited the *Athenaeum* and in 1923 founded the literary magazine *Adelphi*. Although physically attracted to Murry, Lawrence decided early in their acquaintanceship that he was untrustworthy. When Lawrence was dying, he heard that Murry had decided there was no God. 'Now I know there is,' said Lawrence.

CRIMBLE, Hugh, in Henry James's *The Outcry* (1911), is part-inspired by Hugh Walpole (see Kear, Alroy). 'Certainly the physical description is something like,' commented Walpole. 'The rest, not at all.'

CRISCROSS, Professor James, in Osbert Sitwell's *Triple Fugue* (1924), is the poet and critic Sir Edmund Gosse (1849–1928), according to his fellow critic Cyril Connolly.

CROCODILE, Lady Kitty, in Samuel Foote's *A Trip to Calais* (1776), is Elizabeth Chudleigh, Duchess of Kingston (1720–88). After secretly marrying Augustus John Hervey (later to become Third Earl of Bristol), she attempted to repudiate this union and persuaded a court to declare her a spinster, whereupon she married Evelyn Pierrepont, Second Duke of Kingston, whose mistress she had been. After his death she was convicted of bigamy following a case brought against her by the late Duke's nephew who had a reversionary interest in the estate.

CROMLECH, David, in Siegfried Sassoon's *Memoirs of an Infantry Officer* (1930), is the poet Robert Graves (1895–   ), who as an officer in the Royal Welch Fusiliers shared an army hut in Litherland, Liverpool, with Sassoon. See also Casselis, David, and Patient B.

CROSBIE, Leslie, in W. Somerset Maugham's 'The Letter' (*The Casuarina Tree*, 1926). In 1911, on the verandah of her home in Malaya, Ethel Mabel Proudlock shot dead the manager of a local tin-mine, allegedly her lover. Was she defending her honour or reacting to the discovery that he had a Chinese mistress? The trial of Mrs Proudlock — Maugham's Leslie Crosbie — became a Malayan *cause célèbre*. Convicted of murder and sentenced to death, she was pardoned by the Sultan of Selangor after local residents had petitioned for a reprieve and a plea for clemency had been cabled to the Secretary of State for the Colonies by her husband, the acting headmaster of the Victoria Institute school, Kuala Lumpur. Upon her release she returned alone to England, where she died in an asylum, deranged by her time spent awaiting execution. Made into a play and a film (starring, respectively, Gladys Cooper and Bette Davis), 'The Letter' is among Maugham's most successful stories. To the Singapore lawyer's wife who brought the affair to his attention he sent an inscribed copy of the play. Thanks to her, and to Maugham's dramatic skill, the six shots fired by Mrs Proudlock echoed round the world.

CROY, Kate, in Henry James's *The Wings of the Dove* (1902), is the author's aunt, Mrs Catherine Walsh. She lived with her sister in the household of Henry James senior, whom she revered, despite her own otherwise independent character.

CROYSADO, the Great, in Samuel Butler's *Hudibras* (1663–78), is Thomas Fairfax, Third Baron Fairfax (1612–71), commander of the Parliamentary army which defeated Charles I at Naseby in 1645. Five years later, unable to agree to the invasion of Scotland, he resigned his command.

CRUMMLES, Vincent, in Charles Dickens's *Nicholas Nickleby* (1838–9). It was as an aspiring amateur actor in Portsmouth that Dickens met the man upon whom Crummles is believed to have been based: T.D. Davenport, lawyer turned actor-manager of London's Westminster Subscription Theatre. The contemporary journal *Figaro in London* described him as a 'man of about 20 stone with lungs *en suite* and a face of alarming fatness which he screwed into the most distorted shape, presenting a series of grimaces equally unmeaning and horrible.' He advised Dickens to stick to writing: acting was not his forte.

CRUMP, Lottie, in Evelyn Waugh's *Vile Bodies* (1930), is Rosa Lewis (née Ovenden, 1867—1952), proprietor of the Cavendish Hotel, Jermyn Street, which she bought, with money earned as a first-class cook, in 1901. She was a former kitchen maid whose marriage in 1893 to a butler, Excelsior Lewis, was one of convenience. Although she ran her establishment on liberal lines, she declared that she herself slept with only three men: King Edward VII (for whom she also acted as madame when he was Prince of Wales); the Kaiser (whose portrait she consigned to the men's lavatory upon the outbreak of war); and Lord Ribblesdale, Queen Victoria's Master of Buckhounds (who in his old age became a semi-permanent and very dependent guest). Her practice of greeting aged peers with 'Hello, mutton chops, still fancy a nice clean whore?' or 'Hello, droopy drawers, when are you coming round the Cavendish to bounce a cheque?' caused her banishment from London's Ritz Hotel. 'Get out!' she ordered Waugh on his first visit after the publication of *Vile Bodies*. 'There's two little swine I'm not going to have in here,' she later declared. 'One's Donegal [the Marquis of Donegal, who worked as a newspaper gossip columnist] and the other's that little Evelyn Waugh.'

CRUPP, in H.G. Wells's *The New Machiavelli* (1911), is the Tory statesman Leo Amery (1873—1955), who in 1924 became Secretary for the Colonies. An All Souls' don who as a reporter covered the Boer War for *The Times*, he was said to have had the makings of a great man ... if only he had been half a head taller and his speeches half an hour shorter.

CRUSOE, Robinson, in Daniel Defoe's *The Adventures of Robinson Crusoe* (1719), has as prototype Alexander Selkirk (1676—1721). Born in Largo, Fife, he ran away to sea and while serving as sailing master of the privateer *Cinque Ports* quarrelled with his captain, claiming the vessel was unseaworthy and that he would sail no more in her. He was promptly put ashore and abandoned on Mas-a-Tierra, one of the Juan Fernández group of islands 350 miles west of Valparaiso. *Cinque Ports* later foundered, and Selkirk spent four years and four months on his island before he was discovered by a Bristol privateer on 2 February 1709. Back in Britain, the novelty of his initial lionisation soon wore off. Near Largo he built a replica of his island cave, where he would sit for hours bewailing the loss of his earthly paradise, his island home. He subsequently went to London, married a barmaid, joined the navy, died of fever, and was buried at sea off West Africa. Defoe had interviewed him in Bristol, and the celebrated castaway later said he had given the author his papers. In 1968 the Chilean government named one of the Juan Fernández islands 'Isla Alexander Selkirk', and another 'Isla Robinson Crusoe' – a name spotted on a tombstone by Defoe while hiding in a churchyard as a fugitive from the aftermath of Monmouth's rebellion, which he had supported.

CRUTTWELL, Sebastian and Lydia, in Terence Rattigan's 'After Lydia' (*In Praise of Love*, 1973). This play was part-inspired by the situation of the actor Rex Harrison (1908–) and his third wife, the actress Kay Kendall (d. 1959, aged thirty-two). Like Lydia, Kay Kendall died from leukaemia; like Sebastian, Rex Harrison strove to keep the nature of her illness from his wife. He appeared as Sebastian in the 1974 New York production of the play. 'After Lydia' also stemmed from Rattigan's own experience. In 1964 he was told he had leukaemia, with only a year or two to live. Deciding to have a good time, he went on a world cruise, only to be told on his return that there had been a mistake: he had not got leukaemia. He died thirteen years later, from bone cancer.

CUFF, Sergeant Richard, in Wilkie Collins's *The Moonstone* (1868), is modelled upon Inspector Jonathan Whicher (d. 1871), of Scotland Yard. He joined the police force in 1840 and two years later, upon the creation of the nation's first detective force, became one of Britain's first six detective sergeants. His cases included the celebrated Road (Wiltshire) affair of 1860, in which the infant son of a civil servant was taken from his cot and carried to an outside privy, where his throat was cut. On Whicher's insistence, the murdered child's half-sister, Constance Kent (see also North, Valentine; Thompson, Helen), appeared before the local magistrate, who found there was insufficient evidence to commit her for trial. Whicher's case was that there was no sign that entry had been gained from outside; that the killer must have bloodstained clothes; and that one of Constance Kent's nightdresses was missing. Five years later, having become a nun, she confessed and was committed to prison. She was released in 1885, at the age of forty-one, and is believed to have emigrated to the United States, marrying a San Francisco lawyer. The public outcry and press criticism attracted by Whicher's arrest of the girl, together with a subsequent case in which he was unjustly criticised, caused him to sink into a deep depression from which he never recovered.

He spent his declining years in desk-work, his active detective career over.

CULLINGWORTH, in Sir Arthur Conan Doyle's *The Stark Munro Letters* (1895), is Dr George Turnavine Budd. See Challenger, Professor George Edward.

CUNNINGHAM, in Sir Charles Sedley's *Bellamira* (1687), is John Churchill, First Duke of Marlborough (1650–1722), who in 1677, at the instigation of his parents, was a contender for the hand of the author's daughter. Sarah Jennings (see Atossa) persuaded Churchill to have second thoughts and to marry for love rather than for Katherine Sedley's money.

CUNNINGHAM, Julia and Robert, in D.H. Lawrence's *Aaron's Rod* (1922), are Hilda Doolittle (see Masters, Miranda) and Richard Aldington (see Ashton, Rafe).

CURATOR, the, in Rudyard Kipling's *Kim* (1901), is the author's father, John Lockwood Kipling (1837–1911), whose plaster-reliefs illustrated this book. From a Yorkshire Methodist background, he became a pottery designer and, as a stonemason, worked on the building of London's Victoria and Albert Museum. He later became Professor of Architectural Sculpture at the Bombay School of Art, Curator of Lahore Museum and Head of Lahore Art School.

CURÉ, the, of Combray, in Marcel Proust's *A la recherche du temps perdu* (1913–27), is Canon Joseph Marquis, who as parish priest of Illiers taught the author Latin, also passing on something of his own love for etymology. In 1907 he published a substantial monograph on Illiers and its history.

CURRY, William, in John Ehrlichman's *The Company* (1976), is John F. Kennedy (see Baltimore, Scott). As John Sutherland notes in *Best Sellers* (1981), '*The Company* is based distantly, but unmistakably, on the alleged CIA murder of Diem, which (again allegedly) Kennedy connived in. The other Kennedy Presidential misdemeanour, the Bay of Pigs invasion, is fictionally combined with this earlier assassination.' Curry dies prematurely in a plane crash.

CURTIS-DUNNE, in Evelyn Waugh's 'Charles Ryder's Schooldays' (written 1945, published 1982), is Hugh Molson, Baron

Molson (1903–), a contemporary of the author at Lancing College. A Unionist MP, he was Minister of Works from 1957 to 1959. For this and other 'Charles Ryder's Schooldays' identifications, I am indebted to B.W. Handford, keeper of the Lancing archives, who explored the story's background in a letter to the *Times Literary Supplement* on 9 April 1982.

CUSINS, Professor Adolphus, in George Bernard Shaw's *Major Barbara* (1905). At Shaw's request, in the first production of this play the actor cast as Cusins made-up to resemble the author's model: Gilbert Murray (1866–1957), Regius Professor of Greek at Oxford from 1908 to 1936, husband of Lady Mary Murray (see Undershaft, Barbara) and father of Basil Murray (see Seal, Basil). A popular translator of Euripides, Aeschylus and Sophocles, Murray also produced a number of works on pacifism and was chairman of the League of Nations Union from 1923 to 1938.

CUTE, Alderman, in Charles Dickens's *The Chimes* (1845), is Sir Peter Laurie (1779–1861), a magistrate and alderman who was knighted in 1824 and in 1831 became Lord Mayor of London. His campaign to 'put down' suicide had irritated the author. Laurie sought revenge for the portrait by describing the Folly Ditch and Jacob's Island of *Oliver Twist* as gross exaggeration.

CUTHBERTSON, Cecil, in Harold Acton's 'A Morning at Upshott's' (*The Soul's Gymnasium*, 1982), is Cyril Connolly. See Quiggin, J.G.

CUTHBERTSON, Joseph, in George Bernard Shaw's *The Philanderer* (1898), is the *Daily Telegraph* drama critic Clement Scott (1841–1904), according to St John Ervine's *Bernard Shaw: His Life, Work and Friends* (1956).

CUTPURSE, Moll, in Thomas Middleton and Thomas Dekker's *The Roaring Girle* (1611), is Mary Frith (?1589–?1689), a notorious London pickpocket and prostitute who dressed as a man and is reputed to have been the first woman smoker. 'Moll Cutpurse' was her nickname. She also appears in Nathaniel Field's *Amends for Ladies* (1618).

CYCLOPS, in James Joyce's *Ulysses* (1922), is Michael Cusack (*b.* 1847), who in 1884 founded the Gaelic Athletic Association. His mind appears to have been as narrow as his shoulders were broad, and he was introduced to Joyce by George Clancy (see Davin). It was his custom to announce his entry to a public house by shouting at the nearest waiter: 'I'm Citizen Cusack from the Parish of Carron in the Barony of Burren in the County of Clare, you Protestant dog!'

CYNIC SAL, in Djuna Barnes's *The Ladies' Almanack* (1928), is Romaine Brooks. See Leigh, Olimpia.

CYNTHIUS, in Sir Edmund Gosse's 'The Island of the Blest' (1879; *Firdausi in Exile and Other Poems*, 1885), is Robert Louis Stevenson (see Woodseer, Gower), portrayed at the age of twenty-nine. Gosse did not reveal the identity of Cynthius ('most indiscreet he was, though kind and true') until 1913. The two were close friends, and it was to Gosse that Stevenson wrote his last letter, two days before he died.

CYPRESS, Mr, in Thomas Love Peacock's *Nightmare Abbey* (1818), is Lord Byron (see Cadurcis, Lord). The portrait prompted Byron to send the author a rosebud, which Peacock had mounted in an inscribed gold locket.

D

DACH, Simon, in Günter Grass's *The Meeting at Telgte* (1981), has as prototype the book's dedicatee, the German novelist and editor Hans Werner Richter (1908–), who in 1947 convened the first meeting of what became known as Group 47, a discussion forum for West German writers which Grass first attended in 1955, winning its Preis der Gruppe 47 with *The Tin Drum* in 1958.

DAHDAH, Habbas, in Hans Christian Andersen's *The Improvisatore* (1835), is an amalgam of C. Molbech, a critic who savaged Andersen's poetry in the journal *Maanedsskrift for Litteratur*, and Dr Simon Meisling, headmaster of Slagelse and Elsinore grammar schools, both of which Andersen attended. Meisling was such an ogre in Andersen's eyes that he haunted his dreams throughout his life – even though a decade after Andersen left school he received a fulsome apology from his old headmaster, who acknowledged that he had misjudged him.

DAHLIA, Aunt. See Travers, Dahlia Portarlington.

DALE, Edith, in Carl Van Vechten's *Peter Whiffle: His Life and Work* (1922), is the American patron of the arts, Mabel Dodge Luhan (1879–1962), who is also caricatured in D.H. Lawrence's 'The Woman Who Rode Away' (1925; *The Woman Who Rode Away*, 1928).

DALGETTY, Dugald, in Sir Walter Scott's *A Legend of Montrose* (1819), had as prototype Sir James Turner (1615–?1686), a soldier of fortune whose memoirs Scott consulted in researching his novel.

DALLOWAY, Richard and Clarissa, in Virginia Woolf's *The Voyage Out* (1915) and *Mrs Dalloway* (1925). Richard is part-inspired by Philip Morrell (see Wimbush, Henry). Clarissa, according to Woolf's biographer, Quentin Bell, is primarily Kitty Maxse (1867–1922), wife of Leo Maxse, owner-editor of the *National Review*, and daughter-in-law of Rear-Admiral Frederick Augustus Maxse (see Beauchamp, Nevil). She was an old friend of the author's family. Julia Stephen (see Ramsay, Mrs) had been her matchmaker, and she was particularly close to Virginia Woolf's sister, Vanessa (see Ambrose, Helen), helping her to enter London society. Virginia Woolf regarded Kitty Maxse's death – she fell down a flight of stairs – as suicide. Traces of Lady Ottoline Morrell (see Roddice, Hermione) may also be discerned in Clarissa. 'I want to bring in the despicableness of people like Ott', the author noted in her diary.

DAN, in Ernest Hemingway's *The Green Hills of Africa* (1935), is Ben Fourie, assistant to Philip Percival (see Wilson, Robert).

DAN, in Rudyard Kipling's *Puck of Pook's Hill* (1906), is the author's son, John Kipling (1897–1915). On leaving Wellington School he was rejected for military service because of his poor eyesight, but through his father's influence obtained a commission in the Irish Guards. He was killed, aged eighteen, in the Battle of Loos – a blow from which his father never fully recovered. *Puck of Pook's Hill* stemmed from John and his sister Elsie's production with their father, in 1904, of a scene from *A Midsummer Night's Dream*, in a former quarry overlooked by a slope which they called Pook's Hill.

D'ANGELI, David, in Jack Kerouac's *Desolation Angels* (1965), is Philip Lamantia. See Pavia, Francis Da.

DANIEL, in Malcolm Lowry's *Dark as the Grave Wherein my Friend is Laid* (1967), is Conrad Aiken. See Taskerson, Abraham.

DANIEL, in Thomas Mann's 'At the Prophet's' (*Stories of Three Decades*, 1936), is the German poet Ludwig Derleth (1870–1948), who is described in Katia Mann's memoirs as habitually attempting to transform everything into something extraordinary and intense. In 'At the Prophet's' he relentlessly ploughs on with a reading of his work until the story's narrator can think only of the supper he is missing.

DANNISBURGH, Lord, in George Meredith's *Diana of the Crossways* (1885), is the British statesman William Lamb, Second Viscount Melbourne (1779–1848). See also Merion, Diana.

DANVERS, James, in Angela Thirkell's *O, These Men, These Men!* (1935), according to Thirkell's biographer, Margot Strickland, is the author's first husband, the singer James Campbell McInnes (*b.* 1874), son of a Ramsbottom textile design-engineer. Studying under Jacques Bouhy in Paris, he made his London début in 1899, subsequently becoming one of the best known soloists of his day. Angela Thirkell met and married him in 1911, divorcing him in 1917 for cruelty and adultery – the judge described the behaviour of McInnes (a bisexual alcoholic) as that of a drunken beast. Their children included the novelist Colin MacInnes. See also Murray, Alexander.

DARBY, Lou, in Frank Hardy's *Power without Glory* (1950). As the author has acknowledged, the prototype for Darby is James Leslie (Les) Darcy (1895–1917), a blacksmith's apprentice who became Australian light-, middle- and heavyweight boxing champion. He travelled to the United States as a stowaway with the intention of establishing himself as a world-ranking boxer, but died, from blood poisoning, shortly after his arrival.

D'ARCY, Bartell, in James Joyce's 'The Dead' (*Dubliners*, 1914), has a suggested model in Barton M'Guckin, leading tenor in the Carl Rosa Opera Company, although this identification is suspect – Flann O'Brien claimed to have invented it. Another contender is P.J. Darcy, a post-office worker who sang with Joyce's father under the name Bartholomew D'Arcy.

DARCY, Father Thayer, in F. Scott Fitzgerald's *This Side of Paradise* (1920), is Father Cyril Sigourney Webster Fay (*d.* 1919), an Episcopalian convert to Roman Catholicism who took an interest in the author when Fitzgerald was a student. A wealthy socialite and something of a dandy, Fay died in an influenza epidemic.

DARDENTOR, Clovis, in Jules Verne's *Clovis Dardentor* (1896), is Louis Salvator. See Antekirtt, Dr.

DARK LADY, the, of William Shakespeare's sonnets, has several putative originals. They include the wife of an Oxford innkeeper named Davenant; Penelope Devereux (see Stella); Mary Fitton (1578–1647), daughter of Sir Edward Fitton of Gawsworth, Cheshire, maid of honour to Queen Elizabeth I, mistress of William

Herbert, Third Earl of Pembroke (see W.H.), by whom she had a child, and subsequently wife first of Captain William Polwhele, and secondly of Captain John Lougher; Emilia Lanier (née Bassano), daughter of an Italian musician in the court of Queen Elizabeth, mistress of Lord Hunsdon (founder of the players' company to which Shakespeare belonged), and wife of a musician, William Lanier; and Lucy Parker (née Morgan), alias Black Luce and Lucy Negro, prostitute and Clerkenwell brothel-keeper. 'Anyone who wastes his time trying to identify the dark lady', W.H. Auden remarked in 1964, 'seems to me to be a fool.'

DARLING, Mr and Mrs and family, in J.M. Barrie's *Peter Pan* (1904) and *Peter and Wendy* (1911). At a dinner party in 1897, Barrie sat next to 'the most beautiful creature' he had ever seen. She was Sylvia Llewelyn Davies (1866–1910), daughter of the novelist and *Punch* cartoonist George Du Maurier, and Barrie discovered that he had already made the acquaintance of two of her children during his strolls in Kensington Gardens. He quickly became infatuated with her and her family, whom he used as his models in *Peter Pan*. Mr Darling is an amalgam of Arthur Llewelyn Davies (1863–1907), a London barrister, and his son George (see David); Mrs Darling is a composite of Arthur's wife, Sylvia, and Barrie's mother. Upon the couple's death from cancer, Barrie became the children's guardian. Jack Llewelyn Davies (1894–1959) is John Darling; Michael Llewelyn Davies (see Peter Pan) is Michael Darling. The name Wendy, which Barrie coined, was derived from the habit of Margaret, daughter of W.E. Henley (see Silver, Long John), of calling Barrie 'my friendy' (pronounced 'wendy' because of her inability to sound her r's). She died in infancy.

DARRELL, Larry, in W. Somerset Maugham's *The Razor's Edge* (1944), is part-inspired by Sir Henry 'Chips' Channon (see Templeton, Elliott), with traces of Gerald Haxton (see Flint, Rowley), Gerald Heard (see Par, Augustus) and Christopher Isherwood (see Pimpernell).

D'ARTAGNAN. See Artagnan, D'.

DARTLE, Rosa, in Charles Dickens's *David Copperfield* (1849–50), owes her penchant for innuendo and her argumentativeness to Mrs William Brown (née Hannah Meredith, *d.* 1878), governess and companion to Angela Burdett Coutts (see Wickfield, Agnes). Also discerned in Rosa Dartle is Marianne Leigh, daughter of John Porter Leigh (see Budden, Octavius) and Mrs Leigh (see Porter, Mrs Joseph). A gossip with a relish for scandal, she incensed Dickens by passing on his confidences to Maria Beadnell (see Spenlow, Dora).

DAUBENY, Mr, in Anthony Trollope's *Phineas Finn* (1869), *Phineas Redux* (1874) and *The Prime Minister* (1876). Trollope himself gave Daubeny's model as the English statesman and novelist Benjamin Disraeli, Earl of Beaconsfield (1804—81), who was prime minister in 1868 and in 1874—80. He was a favourite of Queen Victoria, not only because he was an accomplished flatterer: he was also a more 'human' prime minister than the frosty Gladstone (see Gresham, Mr). Calling on Lady Bradford, he was informed by a servant that, as was her custom on a Monday, her ladyship had gone to town. 'I thought you would know that, sir,' the servant added. 'I did not,' the prime minister replied, 'nor did I know it was Monday.'

DAUBER, in Alexander Zinoviev's *The Yawning Heights* (1979), is the anti-establishment Russian sculptor Ernst Neizvestny (1926—).

DAVENANT, Claude, in *Mirage* (1877), by George Fleming (Julia Constance Fletcher), is supposedly Oscar Wilde (see Amarinth, Esme), who dedicated his poem 'Ravenna' (1878; winner of the Newdigate Prize) to the author and had *Mirage* in his library, according to Sir Rupert Hart-Davis, editor of Wilde's letters.

DAVENANT, Lady, in Henry James's 'A London Life' (1887; *A London Life*, 1889), is the author's London society friend, Mrs Duncan Stewart, whose daughter, Christina Rogerson, was named in a celebrated 1885 divorce action (see Grace).

DAVID, in J.M. Barrie's *The Little White Bird* (1902), is George Llewelyn Davies (1893—1915), eldest son of Arthur Llewelyn Davies (see Darling, Mr). He took a copy of *The Little White Bird* with him to France, where he was killed in the trenches.

DAVID, in Charles Dickens's *Nicholas Nickleby* (1838—9), is supposedly Alfred Boot, butler to the Grant brothers (see Cheeryble) in Manchester.

DAVIDSON, Austin, in C.P. Snow's *Homecomings* (1956), *The Sleep of Reason* (1968) and *Last Things* (1970). 'His was the most beautiful mind that I have ever been in close contact with, and I learned more from him intellectually than from any single person', said Snow of the mathematician Godfrey Harold Hardy (1877–1947) who, like Austin Davidson, collected barbiturates for a suicide attempt, and was acknowledged by Snow to be Davidson's model. Hardy was a Fellow of Trinity College, Cambridge; Savilian Professor of Geometry, Oxford, from 1919 to 1931; and Sadleirian Professor of Pure Mathematics, Cambridge, from 1931 to 1942. He classed himself in his prime as probably the world's fifth or sixth best analyst. Like Snow, he was a cricket enthusiast. 'I had the luck to know him well during the last 16 years of his life,' said Snow. 'That was the one good result that has ever come to me through an excessive addiction to the game of cricket.'

DAVIDSON, Margaret, in C.P. Snow's *Homecomings* (1956), is in part the author's wife, Lady Snow (1912–81), better known as the novelist Pamela Hansford Johnson. Her first contact with Snow was in 1940, when she reviewed his *Strangers and Brothers* in the *Liverpool Daily Post*. He wrote her a letter of thanks, further correspondence ensued, and in 1950 he became her husband. The marriage was successful although (or perhaps because) Snow also had a mistress (see Cooke, Betty). Earlier, when she was nineteen, Pamela Hansford Johnson had another literary correspondence which led to a proposal. Having won a *Sunday Referee* poetry prize, she thought the winning poem in the following week's edition so much better than hers that she wrote to congratulate the poet. They met and he proposed, but it came to nothing. He was Dylan Thomas.

DAVIES, Peter, in Gilbert Cannan's *Peter Homunculus* (1909). Diana Farr, Cannan's biographer, identifies a model for Davies as the essayist, novelist, poet and biographer E.V. Lucas (1868–1938), assistant editor of *Punch*.

DAVIN, in James Joyce's *A Portrait of the Artist as a Young Man* (1916), is George Clancy, a fellow-student of the author at University College, Dublin, who became Mayor of Limerick. He was shot by the Black and Tans.

DAWES, Clara, in D.H. Lawrence's *Sons and Lovers* (1913). How did Lawrence overcome writer's block? His experience with his model for Clara Dawes suggests an answer. She was Alice Mary Dax (1878–1959), a Liverpool-born suffragette and socialist, and the wife of a chemist from Eastwood, Nottinghamshire, Henry Dax (1873–1962), whom she married in 1905. After Lawrence's elopement with Frieda Weekley (see Somers, Harriet), she wrote to the couple wishing them happiness and confessing that she had herself nurtured for Lawrence a passion so unendurable that it had reduced her to yielding to her husband and bearing him a child. It was her earlier affair with Lawrence that seems to have lubricated his mental processes: after she had given him sex, she wrote to a friend, he had been able to complete a poem over which he had been struggling. Alice Dax and her husband emigrated to Australia in the early 1950s.

DAWSON, Nigel, in Compton Mackenzie's *Vestal Fire* (1927), is Vernon Andrews, an American expatriate from Honolulu who settled in Capri. In 1909, as a young man, he accompanied Norman Douglas (see Argyle, James) to Calabria, to deliver money collected for the relief of earthquake victims. Douglas's biographer, Mark Holloway, records how the muleteer on the trip was scandalised by Andrews's use of make-up.

DAWSON, Ophelia (Mrs Charlemagne Cox), in Richard Aldington's 'Nobody's Baby' (*Soft Answers*, 1932), is Nancy Cunard. See Storm, Iris.

DAWSON-HILL, in C.P. Snow's *The Affair* (1960), is the literary critic Alan Pryce-Jones (1908–   ), editor of *The Times Literary Supplement* from 1948 to 1959.

DAY, Clara, in Gilbert Cannan's *Mummery* (1918), is Gwen Wilson (later Lady Melchett), a South African from Johannesburg with whom the author, according to Diana Farr, his biographer, fell in love at first sight on meeting her in a London bookshop in 1916. In 1920 she married Henry Mond, subsequently Second Baron Melchett, with whom the two had been living. This helped to push Cannan over the brink into insanity, and his last thirty years were spent in private mental institutions; Lord Melchett – chairman of Barclays Bank and deputy chairman of ICI – paid the bills.

DEADWOOD DICK, in the 'Deadwood Dick' dime novels of Edward L. Wheeler, which made their début in 1877, is Richard W. Clarke (1845−1930), South Dakota frontiersman, Indian fighter and gold shipments' guard. 'Deadwood Dick' was his real-life nickname.

DEAN, Mattie, in Osbert Sitwell's *Triple Fugue* (1924), is Sir Edward ('Eddie') Marsh (1872−1953), editor of *Georgian Poetry* and a discerning patron of the arts who used what he called his 'murder money' to build up an impressive collection. This modest sum was disbursed to him periodically as an heir to the estate of his maternal great grandfather, Spencer Percival, the prime minister who was assassinated in 1812. Marsh's inheritance came from a fund established by the British government as compensation for the murdered premier's family. Private secretary to Winston Churchill (see Catskill, Rupert) for more than twenty years, he was knighted on his retirement in 1937. Marsh was never a rich man − he often bought by hire-purchase − but he is remembered for his perceptive talent-spotting and for his many kindnesses to impecunious artists; those he befriended included John Currie (see Logan), who shot his mistress and killed himself shortly after staying with Marsh.

DEANE, Lucy (as a child), in George Eliot's *The Mill on the Floss* (1860), is the author's eldest sister, Christiana Evans (1814−59), who in 1837 married Edward Clarke (see Lydgate, Tertius).

DEANS, Jeanie, in Sir Walter Scott's *The Heart of Midlothian* (1818), has as prototype Helen Walker (1712−91), the daughter of a labourer from Cluden, Kirkcudbrightshire. In 1738 her younger, unmarried, sister was convicted of infanticide and sentenced to death − under Scottish law, execution was the penalty when a child's death occurred through a birth being unattended, no assistance having been sought. Helen Walker could have sworn she attended the birth, thus saving her sister from the gallows, but her conscience would not permit her to lie. Instead, she walked to London where she successfully petitioned for a reprieve.

DEARBORN, Hugh, in Osbert Sitwell's 'The Machine Breaks Down' (*Triple Fugue*, 1924). John Pearson's *Façades: Edith, Osbert and Sacheverell Sitwell* (1978) identifies Dearborn's model as Harry Melvill (1861−1936), whose nickname was 'Mr Chatterbox'.

DEASY, in James Joyce's *Ulysses* (1922), is an amalgam of Francis Irwin and Henry N. Blackwood Price. Irwin was an Ulster Scot, a graduate of Trinity College, Dublin, and founder-headmaster of Clifton School, Dalkey, where Joyce was a temporary teacher shortly before Irwin's addiction to drink caused the academy's closure. Price was assistant manager of the Eastern Telegraph Company in Trieste and was keenly interested in foot and mouth disease, seeking to share his interest with the author.

DEBINGHAM, Henry, in Edith Sitwell's *I Live Under a Black Sun* (1937). Look — no hands! Why are they missing from Wyndham Lewis's Tate Gallery painting of Edith Sitwell? Because she walked out on him after a sitting spanning ten months in the mice-infested studio in which, by one mouse-hole, he positioned a gong which he beat periodically to rout the rodents. During that sitting he apparently made a pass at her — 'the only man on record as doing so,' as Anthony Powell once noted. Starting out as an ally of the Sitwells, Lewis (see Lypiatt, Casimir) became one of their most vociferous critics ... and Edith's model for Henry Debingham. Life was one long, polemical battle between the two camps, Edith complaining that Lewis provoked her beyond endurance, Lewis retorting, in *The Apes of God*, that she was 'still making mud pies at forty.'

DEBORAH, in Philippe Sollers's *Femmes* (1983), is the author's wife, Julia Kristeva, semiologist and psychoanalyst.

DEDALUS, Simon, in James Joyce's *Ulysses* (1922), is the author's tippling, improvident father, John Stanislaus Joyce (1849–1931), who as a result of being made redundant became a fugitive from bailiffs.

DEERING, Vincent, in Edith Wharton's 'The Letters' (*Tales of Men and Ghosts*, 1910). A bisexual American journalist, Morton Fullerton (1865–1952) had a liaison with Edith Wharton and thus became her Vincent Deering. Divorced from an actress, he was chief Paris correspondent of *The Times* from 1902 to 1907. Oscar Wilde was among his friends, and his lovers included Lord Ronald Gower (see Wootton, Lord Henry). When he was blackmailed by a French mistress, friends including Henry James rallied to help him meet her demands.

DE LA MOLE, Mathilde, in Stendhal's *Le Rouge et le Noir* (1830), is part-inspired by Matilde Dembowski (née Viscontini, d. 1825), the estranged wife of a Polish officer, Jan Dembowski, a naturalised Italian by whom she had two sons. Stendhal began his three years' infatuation with her in 1818, in Milan, shortly after her return from Switzerland, where she had been taking refuge from her husband. She was involved in revolutionary politics, and her intimates included the poet Foscolo.

DELIA, in the poems of William Cowper (1731–1800), is the poet's cousin, Theodora Cowper, daughter of Ashley Cowper, of Southampton Row, London. Their relationship was terminated by her father. Both remained single, although Cowper was contemplating matrimony when in 1773 he became deranged following the death of his brother.

DELMARE, Colonel, in George Sand's *Indiana* (1832), is the author's husband, Casimir Dudevant (1795–1871). The illegitimate son of an army colonel who was created a baron by Napoleon I, he was the outcome of his father's liaison with a housemaid. His marriage to Sand in 1822 was followed by separation in 1831. Although himself a far from model spouse, shortly before his death he wrote to the Emperor suggesting that his sufferings as George Sand's husband qualified him for the Grand Cross of the Legion of Honour.

DENISOV, Vasily, in Leo Tolstoy's *War and Peace* (1865–72), is Denis Davidov, poet and exponent of guerrilla tactics against the French in the Russian campaign of 1812.

DENNIS, Ned, in Charles Dickens's *Barnaby Rudge* (1841), has a suggested original in William Calcraft (1800–79), a shoemaker who was paid ten shillings a week for flogging boys at Newgate prison, and who was the City of London hangman from 1829 to 1874. Maria Manning (see Hortense, Mlle) was among those he executed. In private life, he was reputed to be much attached to his children, grandchildren and pets. But Dickens — who witnessed a Calcraft execution in 1840 as well as the Manning hanging — wrote a letter to *The Times* saying that 'Mr Calcraft should be restrained in his unseemly briskness, in his jokes, his oaths and his brandy.'

DENNISON, Will and Mary, in Jack Kerouac's *The Town and the City* (1950), are the American novelist William S. Burroughs

(1914–) and his wife, Joan Vollmer Adams Burroughs (*d.* 1952), whom he accidentally killed at a party when she commanded him to shoot a champagne glass off her head and his bullet missed the glass, passing instead through her brain. Kerouac lived with Burroughs in Mexico City in the early 1950s.

DENSHER, Merton, in Henry James's *The Wings of the Dove* (1902), was claimed by Ford Madox Ford (see Braddocks, Henry) to be a portrait of himself, but the identification is doubtful.

DENVER, the Dowager Duchess of, in Dorothy L. Sayers's Lord Peter Wimsey detective novels (1926–37), is part-inspired by the author's mother, Helen Mary Sayers (née Leigh, *d.* 1929), daughter of a Southampton solicitor and niece of Percival Leigh, deputy editor of *Punch*.

DERONDA, Daniel, in George Eliot's *Daniel Deronda* (1876). Gordon S. Haight's *George Eliot* (1968), Marghanita Laski's *George Eliot and Her World* (1973) and Trevor H. Hall's *The Strange Case of Edmund Gurney* (1964) give three putative models for Deronda: Sir Edward Augustus Bond (1815–98), British Museum librarian and joint-founder of the Palaeographical Society; Emmanuel Deutsch (1829–73), a German orientalist and Talmudic scholar who in 1867 resigned his British Museum appointment to lead a 'Back to Palestine' movement; and Edmund Gurney (1847–88), Fellow of Trinity College, Cambridge, and all-too-credulous honorary secretary of the Society for Psychical Research. Gurney was discovered dead in a Brighton hotel, a sponge-bag over his nose and a bottle of colourless fluid at his side. Although he was at the time officially stated to have died from an overdose of a narcotic taken to induce sleep, suicide was suspected. His private secretary, on whose experiments much of his research relied, had just been exposed as a fraud; and Gurney was also believed to have feared a homosexual scandal arising from his own thought-transference experiments with working-class boys.

DERRINGHAM, John, in Elinor Glyn's *Halcyone* (1912). 'Would you like to sin / With Elinor Glyn / On a tiger-skin? Or would you prefer / to err / with her / on some other fur?' Those (anonymous) lines were inspired by the scenes involving a tiger-skin rug in the author's *Three Weeks* (1907), which also prompted both Lord Milner and Lord Curzon to present her with tiger-skin rugs. George Nathaniel Curzon, First Marquess of Kedleston and Fifth Baron

Scarsdale (1859–1925), duly became her model for Derringham. As imperious as he was ambitious, he took such great pride in his exalted ancestry and rank that upon seeing soldiers bathing he was said to have expressed surprise that the skins of the lower orders were so white. He was Viceroy of India from 1898 to 1905, a member of the British War Cabinet, Secretary of State for Foreign Affairs from 1919 to 1924, and Leader of the House of Lords from 1916 to 1925. Although the author fell in love with him, as her grandson Anthony Glyn recorded in *Elinor Glyn* (1955), she was not blind to the imperfections of the man she called her 'idol'. 'We cannot think', her biographer notes, 'that Curzon, when he read *Halcyone*, failed to recognise himself; and, equally, we cannot think that he can have been very pleased with the character displayed there, a selfish egotistical man who was prepared to put his own aims and ambitions before anything else; who believed, at any rate initially, that only the male sex could have souls; and who was told forcibly . . . at the end that he was not worthy of Halcyone.' In acknowledging receipt of the copy of *Halcyone* sent him by Elinor Glyn, he pointed out two spelling mistakes in her covering letter.

DES ESSEINTES, Duc Jean Floressas, in J-K Huysmans's *A rebours* (1884), is primarily Comte Robert de Montesquiou-Fezensac (see Charlus, Baron Palamède de). Also contributing, it has been suggested, are Jules-Amédée Barbey d'Aurevilly (1808–89), novelist, critic, dandy and biographer of Beau Brummell; Charles Baudelaire (see Spandrell, Maurice), who was noted for his exotic taste in interior décor; Edmond de Goncourt (1822–96), highly-strung novelist and collector of *objets d'art*; Ludwig II of Bavaria (1845–86), who liked to take his ease in an indoor artificial forest with mechanical lizards; and Francis Poictevin (*d.* 1904), an eccentric, wealthy, dilettante writer.

DESMOND, Professor, in C.P. Snow's *The Search* (1934), is supposedly an amalgam of Professor Frank Philip Bowden (see Getliffe, Francis) and Professor Sir Eric Rideal (see Getliffe, Herbert).

DESPARD-SMITH, Albert Theophilus, in C.P. Snow's *The Masters* (1951). As the novelist and critic Francis King has remarked, the reaction of most readers to the revelation that some half-forgotten Snow character is a totally-forgotten character in real life is likely to be a weary 'So what?' Those with a high boredom threshold, however, might like to know that Despard-Smith is in part Sir Franklin Sibly (1883–1948), Vice-Chancellor of Reading University from 1929 to 1946.

DEXTER, Benjamin, in Graham Greene's *The Third Man* (1950). Dexter 'has been ranked as a stylist with Henry James, but he has a wider feminine streak than his master — indeed his enemies have sometimes described his subtle, complex, wavering style as old-maidish. For a man still on the right side of fifty his passionate interest in embroidery and his habit of calming a not very tumultuous mind with tatting — a trait beloved by his disciples — certainly to others seems a little affected.' Who would you suppose that is? Greene himself has supplied the answer, acknowledging that Dexter's 'literary character bore certain echoes of the gentle genius' of E.M. Forster (1879–1970).

DICK THE SCHOLAR, in W.M. Thackeray's *The History of Henry Esmond* (1852), is the essayist Sir Richard Steele (1672–1729), founder of the *Tatler*.

DIDDLER, Dionysius, in W.M. Thackeray's *The History of Dionysius Diddler* (1864), is Dionysius Lardner (1793–1859). Appointed Professor of Natural Philosophy and Astronomy, University of London, in 1827, in 1829 he began work on his Cabinet Cyclopaedia, completed twenty years later, in 133 volumes. In addition to this and his role as a popular scientific writer and lecturer, he found time to elope to North America, with, and have a child by, another man's wife. The Irish dramatist Boucicault (1820–90) was named after him.

DIGBY-VANE-TRUMPINGTON, Sonia, in Evelyn Waugh's *Put Out More Flags* (1942). *The Diaries of Evelyn Waugh*, edited by Michael Davie (1976), give Sonia's original as Wanda Baillie-Hamilton (née Holden), wife of the Hon. Charles William Baillie-Hamilton, MP for Bath from 1929 to 1931 and brother of the Earl of Haddington. They married in 1929, and divorced in 1932. One of the 'bright young things' of the 1920s, she is remembered for having a cocktail thrown in her face by Randolph Churchill (son of Winston Churchill — see Catskill, Rupert), who claimed that her husband abandoned his political career after she threw a bun at a mayor in his constituency.

DINMONT, Dandie, in Sir Walter Scott's *Guy Mannering* (1815). Supposed models proliferate in ratio to a character's popularity, and Dinmont's early establishment as a Scott favourite was followed, with the inexorability of the rising of the sun, by 'originals' popping up all over the place. They include Willie Elliot (1755–1827), of Millburnholm, a Borders sheep-farmer visited by the author; William Laidlaw (1750–1845), who first met Scott in 1802 and in 1817 became his steward and amanuensis at Abbotsford; Archie Park (*d.* 1831), of Lewisthorpe, an exciseman from Tobermory, Strathclyde, and brother of Mungo Park (see Gray, Gideon); and John Thornburn, of Juniper Bank, Walkerburn, Borders. One of them could have been the inspiration for Dinmont; or Scott could be chuckling in his grave . . .

D'INVILLIERS, Tom Parke, in F. Scott Fitzgerald's *This Side of Paradise* (1920), is generally thought to be the American poet, essayist, novelist and short-story writer, John Peale Bishop (1892–1944).

DIOGÈNE, in Paul de Musset's *Lui et elle* (1859), is the *Revue des deux mondes* critic Gustave Planche (1808–57). He was alleged by George Sand's husband (see Delmare, Colonel) to have slept not only with her but also, at the same time, and in the same bed, with her four-year-old daughter. In 1833 Planche fought a duel with another journalist who had described Sand's *Lélia* as obscene.

DIRKES, Prism, in Wyndham Lewis's *Tarr* (1918). Living with Lewis for about two years, the critic and novelist Iris Barry (née Crump, 1895–1969) became his Prism Dirkes and bore him two children who were promptly put into care. After periods of acute poverty she became film critic of the *Spectator*, film editor of the *Daily Mail* and founder-curator of the film library of the Museum of Modern Art, New York. Her husbands included the poet Alan Porter, whom she married in 1923, and the Wall Street financier John Abbott, from 1934. She was the model for Lewis's painting 'Praxitella' (1921). Jeffrey Meyers, Lewis's biographer, records her most painful memory of life with the artist: returning from hospital with her new-born baby girl and having to wait on the steps outside his studio while he finished having sex with Nancy Cunard (see Storm, Iris).

DIVER, Dick and Nicole, in F. Scott Fitzgerald's *Tender is the Night* (1934), are part-inspired by Gerald Murphy (1888–1964), whose entrepreneurial father introduced the Thermos flask to the United States, and his wife, Sara (née Wiborg), daughter of a Cincinnati ink-manufacturer. A graduate of Yale who also studied landscape architecture at Harvard, Murphy was a talented artist who went with his wife to France to paint. They became noted hosts, at their Riviera villa and in Paris, of the American artistic fraternity in France, and they have been credited with initiating the fashion for sunbathing. Much affected by the loss of children through tuberculosis and spinal meningitis, they returned to the United States in 1933, Gerald Murphy rejoining the family leather-goods business, Mark Cross of Fifth Avenue. Nicole Diver is also part-inspired by the author's wife, Zelda (née Sayre, *d.* 1947), daughter of an Alabama judge. With her husband, she epitomised the Jazz Age's youthful disregard for convention, but their gaiety had more than a hint of desperation. By 1927 Zelda had begun to show signs of insanity, and in 1930 she had her first mental breakdown. She spent the greater part of the rest of her life in mental institutions, dying in an asylum fire. Her *Save Me the Waltz* (1932), written in six weeks, between breakdowns, is poignant testimony of talent gone to waste.

DIXON, Jim, in Kingsley Amis's *Lucky Jim* (1954), at least with regard to his attitude to Mozart, is the poet and jazz authority Philip Larkin (1922–   ), an Oxford contemporary of the author. 'It is the voice of Larkin which rings, rancorous and clear, in the diatribes against "filthy Mozart" in *Lucky Jim*', noted Philip Oakes in a profile of the poet (*Sunday Times*, 27 March 1966). '"Actually," says Larkin, "Kingsley adored Mozart ... I detested him but I suppose he's not quite so bad as I used to think."' Jim Dixon's surname derives from Dixon Drive, Leicester, where Amis stayed with Larkin in the late 1940s, when the latter was living there in digs.

DOBSON, Zuleika, in Max Beerbohm's *Zuleika Dobson* (1911). John Felstiner's *The Lies of Art: Max Beerbohm's Parody and Caricature* (1973) gives a suggested model for Zuleika in Adah Isaacs Menken (1835–68), circus equestrienne, actress, putative mistress of Algernon Swinburne (see Runningbrook, Tracy) and author of verse recording her unsuccessful quest for the perfect lover.

DOC, in John Steinbeck's *Cannery Row* (1945) and *Sweet Thursday* (1954), is Edward F. Ricketts (*d.* 1948), a marine biologist with whom Steinbeck fled on a sea expedition in 1939 to escape the publicity that followed publication of *The Grapes of Wrath*. With Steinbeck, Ricketts was co-author of *Sea of Cortez* (1941). His Pacific Biological Laboratory supplied West Coast biological specimens to clients throughout the United States. He died after a car he was driving across the Southern Pacific tracks was struck by an evening train from San Francisco.

DOCRE, Canon, in J-K Huysmans's *Là-bas* (1891). On the evidence of two acquaintances — both later committed to lunatic asylums — the author decided that Abbé Louis Van Haecke (d. 1912, aged eighty-three) was a Satanist, and accordingly portrayed him as Canon Docre. In reality, says Robert Baldick, Huysmans's biographer, this Bruges priest was loved and respected by his parishioners, who would have 'laughed to scorn any accusations of devil-worship' levelled against him.

DOCTOR, the, in Thomas Hughes's *Tom Brown's Schooldays* (1857), is Dr Thomas Arnold (1795—1842), celebrated headmaster of Rugby from 1828 to 1842, father of Matthew Arnold (see Luke, Mr) and the Revd Thomas Arnold (see Hewson, Philip), grandfather of Mrs Humphry Ward (see Foxe, Mrs), and great-grandfather of Aldous Huxley (see Erasmus, William).

DOCTOR, the, in Tobias Smollett's *The Adventures of Peregrine Pickle* (1751), is the poet, physician and pedant Mark Akenside (1721—70), a Newcastle butcher's son who qualified as a doctor after first studying theology, practised in Northampton and London and became physician to the Queen. He wrote *Pleasures of the Imagination* (1744).

DOCTOR, the, in W.M. Thackeray's *The History of Pendennis* (1848—50), is Dr John Russell. See Birch, Dr.

DODD, Lewis, in Margaret Kennedy's *The Constant Nymph* (1924), is the artist Henry Lamb (1883—1960), a trustee of the National Portrait Gallery, husband of Lady Pansy Pakenham and brother-in-law of the novelist Anthony Powell.

DODO, in E.F. Benson's *Dodo* (1893). 'But of course your heroine could not be me, dear Mr Benson,' replied Margot Tennant (1864—1945) to the author's denial that she had been his model. 'I am not beautiful and I certainly don't hunt in June.' The keener acid of her wit was reserved for more substantial targets, like Lloyd George (see Burge, Joyce): 'He could not see a belt without hitting below it.' The great-granddaughter of Charles Tennant (see Wabster Charlie), she became Lady Oxford, second wife of Herbert Asquith (see Lubin) and mother of the film director Anthony Asquith. She was the dedicatee of Oscar Wilde's 'The Star-Child', her wardrobe included a nightdress in an admirer's racing colours, and in her autobiography she recalled that when she was Asquith's fiancée he was warned against her by Lord Rosebery (see Carteret, Charles), who advised him to read *Dodo* as there was a great deal of truth in it. In portraying this daughter of a baronet as Dodo, Benson — the son of an archbishop of Canterbury — was felt to have betrayed his class.

DODS, Meg, in Sir Walter Scott's *St Ronan's Well* (1823), is Marion Ritchie (*d.* 1822), spinster hostess of the Cross Keys Inn in North-gate, Peebles. The daughter of Walter Ritchie, a provost of Peebles, she was noted for her no-nonsense, domineering attitude towards guests. When she heard a party of French officers exclaiming 'bon, bon' upon tasting her barley broth, she ordered them out of the house, thinking they were alleging her kail contained bones. The name of this character, however, Scott borrowed from another hotelier, Mrs Margaret Dods, who kept a small inn at Howgate, Lothian.

DODSON, the Misses, in George Eliot's *The Mill on the Floss* (1860), are the three well-married Warwickshire sisters of the author's mother. 'Aunt Deane' is Mrs George Garner (née Ann Pearson), of Sole End, Astley. 'Aunt Glegg' is Mrs John Evarard (née Mary Pearson, ?1771—1844), of Attleborough, Nuneaton. Her husband's second wife, she saved her best clothes, unworn, so that they could be admired after her death. 'Aunt Pullet' is Mrs Richard Johnson (née Elizabeth Pearson), of Marston Jabbett.

DODSWORTH, Fran. See Voelker, Frau.

DOGSBOROUGH, in Bertolt Brecht's *The Resistible Rise of Arturo Ui* (written 1941, first performed 1958). As President of the German Republic, Paul von Hindenburg (1847—1934) was believed by Brecht to have accepted Adolf Hitler (see Ui, Arturo) as Chancellor in the face of blackmail threats. According to Ronald Hayman's

Brecht (1983) and Ronald Gray's *Brecht the Dramatist* (1976), Brecht represents him as Dogsborough, Mayor of Chicago, who is sold a shipyard at a knock-down price by the Cauliflower Trust, just as Hindenburg was presented with an estate by noblemen seeking government assistance. Hindenburg was also involved in the evasion of tax on a presidential estate and in a scandal concerning the misuse of landowners' subsidies. Fearing exposure, Dogsborough gives Ui his support: Brecht's interpretation of Hindenburg's acceptance of Hitler, whom he had previously opposed.

DOLAN, Father, in James Joyce's *A Portrait of the Artist as a Young Man* (1916) and *Ulysses* (1922), is Father James Daly, prefect of studies during the author's time as a pupil at Clongowes Wood College. When another boy smashed Joyce's spectacles, Daly beat the author for breaking them to avoid studying, and Joyce complained to the College's rector.

DOLOKHOV, Fyodor Ivanovich, in Leo Tolstoy's *War and Peace* (1865–72), is the author's uncle, Fyodor Ivanovich Tolstoy (1782–1846), a notorious libertine, cardsharp and duellist credited with killing eleven men. He had tattoos all over his body, and was nicknamed 'The American' after he was abandoned on one of the Russo-American Aleutian Islands following his spear-heading of a mutiny on a Russian ship making a round-the-world expedition. As a castaway, he was reputed to have made love to a female ape, which he subsequently killed and ate. The character's name is supposedly inspired by that of the Russian partisan Dorokhov.

DOLORES, in Algernon Swinburne's 'Dolores' (*Poems and Ballads*, 1866). Sharing Swinburne's interest in flagellation, his first cousin, Mary Gordon, left his life 'a barren stock' when she married Colonel Disney Leith. On the evidence of their letters, she has been taken by the Swinburne biographer, Jean Overton Fuller, to be Dolores. A novelist whose accomplishments included teaching herself Icelandic, she wrote *The Boyhood of Algernon Charles Swinburne* after her cousin's death. Their mutual sado-masochistic tendencies are not mentioned, but have emerged from their correspondence, conducted in a childish code and disclosed in Fuller's *Swinburne* (1968). When Swinburne died his cousin described him as a staunch supporter of the Church of England (he detested Christianity, refusing to kneel at his mother's funeral), claimed he had never been intoxicated (he was a celebrated drunkard) and said he was 'far too well-bred a gentleman ever to *speak* to a woman of that class' — this referring to his relationship with Adah Menken (see Dobson, Zuleika), who claimed to be the original 'Dolores'. Swinburne wrote the poem before he met Menken, but she is believed to have part-inspired a later, revised version.

DOLPHIN, Mr, in W.M. Thackeray's *The History of Pendennis* (1848—50), is Alfred Bunn (1796—1860), manager of London's Drury Lane and Covent Garden theatres. Although he became bankrupt in 1840, his career was artistically a success, most of the principal players of the day appearing under his management. He also encouraged acceptance of opera by English composers, himself producing the works of Michael Balfe, whose libretti he translated.

DOMBEY, Florence and Paul, in Charles Dickens's *Dombey and Son* (1847—8). The author's sister and childhood confidante, Mrs Henry Burnett (see Nickleby, Kate) is believed to be in part the model for Florence. Paul is reputedly Dickens's nephew, Henry Augustus (Harry) Burnett (1839—49), a cripple with a spinal deformity. He was said by his father, Henry Burnett (see Nickleby, Nicholas), to be remarkably observant, with something of his uncle Charles's eye for detail.

DON, Remote and ineffectual, in Hilaire Belloc's 'Lines to a Don' (*Sonnets and Verse*, 1923), is the historian G.G. Coulton (1858—1947), Fellow of St John's College, Cambridge, and Rhind lecturer at Edinburgh. He engaged in a long feud with Belloc, accusing him — and not without reason — of falsifying history. In taking this view, Coulton was not alone: G.M. Trevelyan considered Belloc to be a liar, as did A.L. Rowse — although the latter conceded that Belloc had genius. 'The professors did not relish Mr Belloc's dramatic reading and rendering of history', remarked Frank Swinnerton. 'Being incapable of imagining a scene that brought the past leaping to mind and eye, they did not understand, did not envy, his gift. They brought out their Pipe Rolls, their documents, their dates.'

DON JUAN, in Robert Browning's *Fifine at the Fair* (1872), was taken by an outraged Dante Gabriel Rossetti (1828—82), Pre-Raphaelite painter and poet, to be a portrait of himself, according to William Irvine and Park Honan's *The Book, The Ring and The Poet: a biography of Robert Browning* (1975).

DONALD, Geoffrey, in Jack Kerouac's *Desolation Angels* (1965), is the San Francisco poet, Robert Duncan (1919–   ).

DONEGAL, Marietta, in Gore Vidal's *Two Sisters* (1970). When he was twenty Vidal was taken up by and lived with the writer Anaïs Nin (1914–77), who featured him in her *Journals*. But Vidal claims that the elderly writer Marietta Donegal is not Nin, rather unconvincingly in view of the obvious autobiographical aspects of *Two Sisters* . . . in which he notes, 'Only writers know how they use the "real" in their fictions, and no writer has yet been willing or able to explain how he does it.'

DONNE, Mr, in Charlotte Brontë's *Shirley* (1849), is the Revd Joseph Brett Grant, headmaster of Haworth Grammar School and curate to the author's father, Haworth's vicar. After initial indignation at his portrayal, Grant swallowed the insult . . . with a spoonful of sugar in the form of the fame the caricature brought him. 'It is a curious fact', remarked the author, 'that since he read *Shirley*, he has come to the house oftener than ever, and been remarkably meek, and assiduous to please. Some people's natures are veritable enigmas: I quite expected to have had one good scene at least with him . . . '

DONNITHORPE, Squire, in George Eliot's *Adam Bede* (1859), has a suggested original in Francis Parker Newdigate I (*d.* 1835) of Wootton Hall, Staffordshire, father of Francis Parker Newdigate II (see Wybrow, Captain Anthony). He succeeded to the Arbury Hall estates in Warwickshire in 1806, on the death of his cousin, Sir Roger Newdigate (see Cheverel, Sir Christopher).

DONOVAN, in James Joyce's *A Portrait of the Artist as a Young Man* (1916), is Constantine P. Curran, a contemporary of the author at University College, Dublin. He subsequently became Registrar of the Supreme Court.

DONSANTE, Rosalba, in Compton Mackenzie's *Extraordinary Women* (1928), is Mimi Franchetti, would-be poet, daughter of a baron who composed operas, and, according to Meryle Secrest's *Between Me and Life: a biography of Romaine Brooks* (1976), a member of a Capri group of lesbians in the 1920s.

DOONE FAMILY, the, in R.D. Blackmore's *Lorna Doone* (1869), is supposedly based on a family of fugitives from Scotland. In 1618 Ensor James Stuart, cousin of James Stewart, Second Earl of Moray and eldest son of Lord Doune, assumed the surname Doune. This so enraged the Third Earl that Ensor was forced to quit Scotland. Accompanied by his wife and a retainer, he settled on Exmoor, in the village of East Lyn, raising four sons who all led the life of outlaws. Ensor died in 1684, aged eighty-seven. His sons returned to Scotland in 1699, having received an offer of compensation from Alexander, Fifth Earl of Moray. The full story is recounted in 'The Original Doones of Exmoor', by Ida M. Browne, *West Somerset Free Press*, 12 October 1901.

DOONE, Sylvia, in John Galsworthy's *The Dark Flower* (1913), is the author's wife (see Forsyte, Irene), with regard to the fading period of their marriage.

DORMER, Nick, in Henry James's *The Tragic Muse* (1890), is Cyril Flower, Lord Battersea (1843–1907). Although artistically inclined, he was persuaded by his wife to pursue a political career. He was an MP from 1880 to 1892, and Lord of the Treasury in Gladstone's last administration.

DORON, in Robert Greene's *Menaphon* (1589), has a suggested original in William Shakespeare (1564–1616), who was also attacked by Greene in his *Groatsworth of Wit bought with a Million of Repentance* (1592). Describing him as 'in his owne conceyt the onely shake-scene in a countrey', Greene apparently considered Shakespeare a plagiarist and saw in the actor a threat to dramatists' monopoly of playwriting.

DORRIT, Amy and William, in Charles Dickens's *Little Dorrit* (1855–7), are respectively Mary Scott Hogarth (see Maylie, Rose) and John Dickens (see Micawber, Wilkins).

DOUGLAS, Ellen, in Sir Walter Scott's *The Lady of the Lake* (1810). See Fifine.

DOWD, James, in Charlotte Haldane's *I Bring Not Peace* (1932), is in part the novelist Malcolm Lowry (1909–57), according to Douglas Day's biography of Lowry (1974). As a Cambridge undergraduate he was in 1929 introduced to the author's salon. (For Charlotte Haldane's husband, see Shearwater, James.)

DOWELL, Florence, in Ford Madox Ford's *The Good Soldier* (1915), is an amalgam of Violet Hunt (see Nesbit, Norah) and Elsie Martindale (see Macdonald, Countess).

DOWLER, Mr, in Charles Dickens's *The Posthumous Papers of the Pickwick Club* (1836–7), has a putative prototype in John Forster (see Podsnap, Mr). Dickens took the character's name from Vincent Dowling, a fellow reporter.

DOYE, Basil, in Rose Macaulay's *Non-Combatants and Others* (1916). According to Constance Babington Smith's *Rose Macaulay* (1972), Doye had an original in Rupert Brooke (see Brookes, Winsome), whom the author first met when he was an undergraduate and who subsequently introduced her to literary London. It is probable that she loved him.

DRACULA, Count, in Bram Stoker's *Dracula* (1897), is part-inspired by 'Vlad the Impaler' — the Walachian tyrant Vlad Tepes, scourge of the Turks, who ruled from 1456 to 1462 and again in 1476. He was otherwise known as Dracula, meaning 'son of the dragon', or 'son of the devil'. His father, Dracul, also a notorious war-lord, was a member of the Order of the Dragon, established in 1418 to defend the Church of Rome. It was from a Hungarian acquaintance, Professor Arminius Vambery of Budapest, that Stoker learned of Dracula. The name appealed to him and he consequently consulted works on the history of Walachia. Stoker was manager of Sir Henry Irving's theatrical company, and the visage of his Dracula is believed to have been inspired by Irving's portrayal of the principal character in *The Flying Dutchman*. In his own way, Irving (1838–1905) was as uncompromising as Dracula. After his outstanding first-night success in *The Bells*, he was returning home in a carriage with his wife when she asked, 'Are you going to go on making a fool of yourself like this all your life?' Ordering the driver to stop, Irving left the brougham without a word. He neither spoke to his wife nor saw his home again.

DRAX, Sir Hugo, in Ian Fleming's *Moonraker* (1955), is believed to be based on Otto Skorzeny (*d.* 1975), a German SS colonel who in 1943 led a glider attack on a hotel in the Abruzzi Mountains where

Mussolini (see Arango, General Tereso) was the prisoner of anti-Fascist Italian troops. Skorzeny escaped with Mussolini in a light plane, and later led German commandos in GI uniforms in an abortive bid to capture Eisenhower (see Starbuck, General Lucas P.). At the age of sixty-seven, Skorzeny died in Madrid, from cancer. In *The Life of Ian Fleming* (1966), John Pearson tells how, as a naval Intelligence officer, the author took a special interest in Skorzeny's leadership of what were in effect the first Intelligence commandos. In 1941 Skorzeny's men raided two British head-quarters on Crete, snatching secret material. This exploit gave Fleming the idea for his own Assault Unit, in which the naval element was commanded by Dunstan Curtis (see Bond, James).

DREUTHER, Herbert, in Graham Greene's *Loser Takes All* (1956). 'My dear boy, it is not easy to lose a good woman. If one must marry, it is better to marry a bad woman.' When Dreuther gives that advice, it is the film producer Sir Alexander Korda (1893–1956) speaking. The tip on marriage was originally addressed to Greene by Korda, 'in that hesitant Hungarian accent which lent a sense of considered wisdom to his lightest words.' Although the author often adversely criticised his films, Korda became a close friend – 'There was never a man who bore less malice, and I think of him with affection – even love – as the only film producer I have ever known with whom I could spend days and nights of conversation without so much as mentioning the cinema.' Dreuther is, he noted in *Ways of Escape* (1980), the only principal character in one of his novels to have been drawn from life.

DRIFFIELD, Edward, in W. Somerset Maugham's *Cakes and Ale* (1930). The author protested that in the creation of Driffield the novelist Thomas Hardy (1840–1928) had been no more in his mind than George Meredith or Anatole France. But he lied about the novel's portrayal of Walpole (see Kear, Alroy), and the similarities between Driffield and Hardy are surely beyond coincidence, including as they do Driffield's dislike of water, even in a bath – Hardy's housemaid from 1921 until his death never knew him to take a bath. Certainly Hardy's second wife, Florence Dugdale (1879–1937), identified herself as the second Mrs Driffield, Maugham's portrait so upsetting her that she declined to unveil a stained-glass window memorial to her husband in his family's local church. They married in 1914 when she – the daughter of a London headmaster, and Hardy's secretary/mistress — was thirty-five, and Hardy seventy-three.

DRIFFIELD, Rosie, *idem*. Maugham's well-known homosexuality has tended to obscure the fact that there was a time when he was interested primarily in women. His model for Rosie was the actress Ethelwyn Sylvia ('Sue') Jones (1883–1948). Maugham first met her in 1906 and they had an affair which lasted several years, during which, as he later recorded, he proposed to her, travelling to Chicago where she was on tour. She would sleep with him, she said, but she would not marry him. The second daughter of the playwright Henry Arthur Jones, she was divorced from a producer, Montague Vivian Leveaux, whom she had married in 1902. She subsequently became the wife of Angus McDonnell, second son of the Sixth Earl of Antrim, whom she married in 1913, retiring from the stage in the following year. It is to her that Rosie owes her warmth and sexual honesty.

DRITTER, Richard, in Wyndham Lewis's *The Roaring Queen* (1936), is the painter Walter Richard Sickert (1860–1942), whose portraits Virginia Woolf found more revealing than any biography.

DRIVER, Fabian, in Barbara Pym's *Jane and Prudence* (1953), is the writer and broadcaster C. Gordon Glover (1908–75), with whom the author had a brief, traumatic affair. He was at that time in the process of becoming divorced from the writer Honor Wyatt, in whose home in Bristol Pym lived before she volunteered for the WRNS. Glover turned the end of their romance to advantage in his radio play *Farewell, Hilda*.

DROMORE, Nell, in John Galsworthy's *The Dark Flower* (1913), is the dancer Margaret Morris, head of the Margaret Morris School of Dancing, London, and founder-director of the Celtic Ballet of Scotland. She first met Galsworthy in 1910, when she was nineteen and the novelist forty-three. She became his secretary, and Galsworthy — who first saw her on the stage of the Savoy Theatre — took an interest in her dancing career, helping her financially when she established her school. In 1913 she met the artist J.D. Ferguson (*d.* 1961), whom she later married.

DROOD, Julian, in V.S. Pritchett's 'The Lady from Guatemala' (*Collected Stories*, 1982). Becoming a reviewer for the *New Statesman* in the 1930s (at £5 a column), the author was able to observe Kingsley Martin (see Wilberforce) at work. This he turned to advantage in his portrait of Drood, the vain editor who 'knew how to appear to listen, to charm, ask a jolly question and then lead his visitors to the door before they knew the interview was over.' Reviewing *Collected Stories* in the *Listener*, Clancy Sigal described Drood as 'a wicked caricature' of Kingsley Martin. Pritchett did not deny it.

DRUID ('A little druid wight,/Of withered aspect'), in the second canto of James Thomson's *The Castle of Indolence* (1748), is the poet Alexander Pope (1688–1744), who in childhood suffered an illness which deformed his spine, stunting his growth.

DRUMMOND, Captain Hugh, in Sapper's *Bull-Dog Drummond* (1920) and nine subsequent novels, is in part the author's friend Gerard Fairlie (1899–1983), who after the death of Sapper (Lt-Col. H.C. MacNeile) wrote seven further novels extending Drummond's career. Fairlie was a six-foot-two army heavy-weight boxing champion (1919) who also captained the army at rugby football and golf. After serving in the Scots Guards (1917–24) he became a novelist and film script-writer. In the Second World War he took charge of a commando training school and parachuted into occupied France to make contact with the Maquis. He spent his retirement in Malta.

DRUMMOND, Lord, in Anthony Trollope's *The Prime Minister* (1876) and *The Duke's Children* (1880), has a suggested prototype in the Fourteenth Earl of Derby. See Terrier, Lord de.

DUB, Lieutenant, in Jaroslav Hašek's *The Good Soldier Švjek* (1921–3), is a subaltern named Mechálek, with whom the author served in the Czech 91st Infantry Regiment in 1915. Making the identification, Hašek's biographer, Sir Cecil Parrott, remarked that – like Dub – Mechálek was always saying 'You don't know me yet, but when you get to know me you'll howl.' Armies, it would seem, are much the same the world over …

DUBEDAT, Jennifer, in George Bernard Shaw's *The Doctor's Dilemma* (1906), is part-inspired by the actress Lillah McCarthy (1875–1960), first wife of the actor-dramatist Harley Granville-

Barker. Shaw wrote the role for her, and she appeared in the play's first production.

DUBEDAT, Louis, *idem*, is an amalgam of Edward Bibbins Aveling (1851–98), translator of *Das Kapital* and common-law husband of Marx's daughter, Eleanor, who committed suicide on learning he had married a woman twenty-one years her junior – his record as a borrower of money, swindler and seducer of women Shaw considered to be unimpeachable; the tubercular *fin de siècle* artist Aubrey Beardsley (1872–98); Charles Charrington (see Morrell, Revd James Mavor), for his familiarity with pawnbroking; and the sculptor Sir Alfred Gilbert (1854–1934), creator of the Eros fountain in London's Piccadilly Circus, who resigned from the Royal Academy following a scandal concerning his acceptance of payments in advance for a commission which he failed to execute. When Shaw's support for Gilbert was solicited, he replied that the sculptor should be drowned in the fountain with which he had defaced Piccadilly Circus.

DUBREUILH, Robert, in Simone de Beauvoir's *The Mandarins* (1954). Although the author insisted that this was no *roman à clef*, her circle had no difficulty in identifying the models for the novel's characters. Dubreuilh is primarily the philosopher and writer Jean-Paul Sartre (1905–80), Beauvoir's lover for half a century. See also Perron, Henri.

DUCAYNE, Gerald, in Dorothy M. Richardson's *Pilgrimage* novel cycle (1915–67), is Robert Thomas Hale. See Henderson, Harriett.

DUCHEMIN, Edith Ethel, in Ford Madox Ford's *Parade's End* tetralogy (1924–8), is Elsie Martindale. See Macdonald, Countess.

DUCK, Peter, in Arthur Ransome's *Peter Duck* (1932), is Captain Sehmel, of Riga, a veteran sailor who, with the author's second wife (previously Trotsky's secretary at the time of the Russian Revolution of 1917), crewed Ransome's yacht, *Racundra*, on its first voyage in 1922. He appears as the Ancient Mariner in Ransome's *Racundra's First Cruise* (1923) ... and, photographed looking precisely as one would expect Peter Duck to look, in Hugh Brogan's *The Life of Arthur Ransome* (1984), which makes the identification.

DUCK, Ronald, in David Lodge's *Changing Places* (1975). No prizes are offered for naming the prototype for Ronald Duck, former movie actor and right-wing State Governor of Euphoria. But for the benefit of any Rip Van Winkle, he is Ronald Reagan (1911–), film actor turned statesman, Governor of California when this novel was written, and subsequently President of the United States.

DUCK, the, in Lewis Carroll's *Alice's Adventures in Wonderland* (1865), is the Revd Robinson Duckworth, who introduced the author to Alice Liddell (see Alice). A Fellow of Trinity College, Oxford, Duckworth was a friend of Alice's father. He later became a canon of Westminster.

DUCROS, Stanislas Richard, in Maurice Baring's *Friday's Business* (1932), is James David Bourchier (d. 1920), an Eton master who, unable to keep his pupils in order, gave up teaching and in 1888 became Balkans correspondent of *The Times*. A boulevard in Sofia is named after him.

DUDLEY, Lady Arabella, in Honoré de Balzac's *Le Lys dans la vallé* (1835), is Jane Elizabeth Digby (1807–81), daughter of an admiral and a celebrated beauty whose admirers included the Prince of Wales. She scandalised Victorian society by her proclivity for falling into and out of love – and bed: she had six children by four fathers. Originally married to Edward Law, Lord Ellenborough, she subsequently had lovers including Balzac; Prince Felix Schwarzenberg, an Austrian diplomat who was the cause of her first divorce in 1829; Ludwig II (see Des Esseintes, Duc Jean Floressas); General Xristodolous Hadji-Petros, a Greek brigand; and finally, Medjuel of the Mesrab tribe, a Bedouin sheikh whom she married.

DUDLEY, Esther, in Henry Brooks Adams's *Esther* (1884) – written under the pseudonym Frances Snow Compton – is the author's wife, Marian Hooper, whom he married in 1872. She committed suicide in 1885.

DUFFERIN-CHAUTEL, Maxime, in Colette's *La Vagabonde* (1910), is supposedly Auguste Hériot, orphan heir to the Galeries Lafayette fortune. The lover of the Algerian singer-actress Polaire (Émilie-Marie Bouchard, d. 1939), he transferred his affections to Colette with but limited success, although they holidayed together in Naples and he was for a time constantly in her company.

DUGDALE, Mary, in Gilbert Cannan's *Peter Homunculus* (1909), is Mary Ansell. See Rodney, Jane.

DULLFEET, Ignatius, in Bertolt Brecht's *The Resistible Rise of Arturo Ui* (written 1941, first performed 1958). Ronald Gray's *Brecht the Dramatist* (1976) identifies Dullfeet as Engelbert Dollfuss who was Chancellor of Austria until 1934, when he was murdered by Austrian Nazis.

DUMONTET, Horace, in George Sand's *Horace* (1841), is part-inspired by Jules Sandeau. See Sténio.

DUNKERLEY, Daniel, in Howard Spring's *Hard Facts* (1944), has probable prototypes in two Manchester publishers who both achieved national success and moved to London: the newspaper proprietor Sir Edward Hulton (1869–1925) and the periodical proprietor Sir George Newnes (1851–1910). Spring spent seventeen years in Manchester with the *Manchester Guardian*, and would have been familiar with the careers of Newnes and Hulton.

DUNMARTIN, Ivor, Sir Robert and Lady, in Caroline Blackwood's *Great Granny Webster* (1977), are based on the author's father, the Fourth Marquess of Dufferin and Ava (see Seal, Basil); and her paternal grandparents, Sir Frederick Hamilton-Temple-Blackwood, Third Marquess of Dufferin and Ava (1875–1930), and Lady Hamilton-Temple-Blackwood (née Brenda Woodhouse, *d.* 1946). From 1921 until his death in an aeroplane accident, Sir Frederick was Speaker of the Senate of Northern Ireland.

DUNN, Miss Joan Hunter, in John Betjeman's 'A Subaltern's Love Song' (*New Bats In Old Belfries*, 1945). 'Look at that marvellous girl!' said Betjeman to a colleague in the Ministry of Information canteen in London during the 1940 blitz. Her name, he learned, was Joanna Hunter Dunn. 'I bet she's a doctor's daughter from Aldershot,' he said. And so she was – at least, the practice of her father, Dr George Hunter Dunn, was at Farnborough, which is near enough. Educated at a convent school in St Leonard's-on-Sea, at Queen Anne's, Caversham, and at Queen Elizabeth College, London University, she had become deputy catering manageress at London University's Senate House, which had been occupied by the Ministry of Information. 'I used to wish, desperately, for a small wound from a bomb so that she would minister to me,' Betjeman later recalled. Taking her out to lunch, he showed her the poem he had written about her, with 'Joanna' shortened to 'Joan' to fit the metre. She married a civil servant, H. Wycliffe Jackson, in 1945, had three children and was widowed in 1963. In 1983, an *Observer* columnist spotted an announcement in an Old Girls' Association magazine saying that she 'would welcome any OGs to her house in Hampshire'. 'Unfortunately,' he reported, 'Miss Hunter Dunn is even more fed up with nostalgia than I am. It's probably because I never went to Queen Anne's school, but as soon as I started to ask her about the remembrance of things past, she said, "No, thank you," and put the 'phone down. But her voice, that bygone blend of firmness, authority and politeness — that was real nostalgia.' In 1984 she was among those who attended Betjeman's memorial service in London, but she declined to be interviewed or photographed for *John Betjeman: a Life in Pictures* (1984) . . . though out of regard for Betjeman she supplied a photograph of herself in her youth, on the understanding that the publishers would lend it to no one.

DUPIN, C. Auguste, in Edgar Allan Poe's *The Murders in the Rue Morgue* (1841), *The Mystery of Marie Roget* (1842–3) and *The Purloined Letter* (1845), has two suggested prototypes: Jesquet, a Paris police chief in the reign of Louis Philippe, and François-Eugène Vidocq (see Vautrin, Jacques Collin). Both Jesquet and Vidocq wrote memoirs, and Poe is known to have read those of the latter.

DUQUETTE, Raoul, in Katherine Mansfield's 'Je ne parle français' (*Bliss*, 1920), is the French poet and novelist Francis Carco (François Carcopino-Tussoli, 1886–1958). In 1915 Mansfield left her lover, Murry (see Crich, Gerald), to join Carco in Paris. Six days later she returned, disillusioned. The episode is recorded in Antony Alpers's *The Life of Katherine Mansfield* (1980).

DURBEYFIELD, Tess, in Thomas Hardy's *Tess of the D'Urbervilles* (1891), is in appearance modelled upon Lady Thornycroft (née Agatha Cox), wife of the author's sculptor acquaintance Sir (William) Hamo Thornycroft (1850–1925).

DUSA, Corrado, in Allan Massie's *The Death of Men* (1981), has as prototype the lawyer and statesman Aldo Moro (1916–78), who was five times prime minister of Italy between 1963 and 1976. He was kidnapped and assassinated by the Red Brigades.

E

E, Professor, in Marcel Proust's *A la recherche du temps perdu* (1913–27), is Dr Édouard Brissaud. See Boulbon, Dr du.

EAGLET, the, in Lewis Carroll's *Alice's Adventures in Wonderland* (1865), is Edith Mary Liddell (1854–76), sister of Alice Liddell (see Alice). Within two weeks of becoming engaged, she died from peritonitis, following measles. Her father attributed her death to a fruit stone or pip lodging in her intestine.

EAMES, Ernest, in Norman Douglas's *South Wind* (1917), is John Ellingham Brooks. See Hayward.

EARWICKER, Humphrey Chimpden, in James Joyce's *Finnegans Wake* (1939), is the author's father. See Dedalus, Simon.

EAST, Harry ('Scud'), in Thomas Hughes's *Tom Brown's Schooldays* (1857). Trains were a novelty when Hughes attended Rugby School. He later recalled that the 'most reckless of all' the boys making the railway journey to Rugby, climbing down between the carriages while the train was in motion, was his model for East: William Patrick Adam (1823–81). Graduating from Trinity College, Cambridge, Adam became a barrister, was the Liberal chief whip in the House of Commons and ended his career as Governor of Madras.

E.B., in George Gissing's *The Private Papers of Henry Ryecroft* (1903), is Eduard Bertz. See Eggers.

EBBSMITH, Agnes, in Sir Arthur Wing Pinero's *The Notorious Mrs Ebbsmith* (1895). Ill-informed gossip about Mrs Annie Besant (see Petkoff, Raina) was the inspiration for this play, in which she is the model for Mrs Ebbsmith. The speculation concerned her relationship with her husband, the Revd Frank Besant (*d.* 1917), younger brother of the novelist Sir Walter Besant. As 'she could not be the bride of Heaven', W.T. Stead commented, she 'therefore became the bride of Mr Frank Besant, who was hardly an adequate substitute.' They separated, Mrs Besant rebelling against her husband's unquestioning, doctrinaire observance of his faith. She was subsequently associated with Charles Bradlaugh (see Stockmann, Dr) in a campaign for birth control. In this connection they were together convicted — against the Lord Chief Justice's advice to the jury — of publishing a work calculated to deprave public morals.

EDDIE, in Elizabeth Bowen's *The Death of the Heart* (1938). In the 1930s the author had an affair with Goronwy Rees (1909–79), who thus became in part the model for Eddie, according to Peter Quennell's *Customs and Characters* (1982). At the time of his romance with Bowen he was assistant editor of the *Spectator*. In 1951 he became Estates Bursar of All Souls College, Oxford, of which he was a Fellow, and in 1953 he was appointed Principal of the University College of Wales, Aberystwyth, resigning in 1957 following controversy over his revelation that he had been a friend of Guy Burgess, who had unsuccessfully tried to recruit him to work for Russia. In the year of his death he was involved in the exposure as a spy of Anthony Blunt.

EDWARD, in Christopher Isherwood's *The Memorial* (1932), is John Layard. See Barnard.

EDWARDS, Foxhall Morton, in Thomas Wolfe's *You Can't Go Home Again* (1940), is the author's publisher, Maxwell Perkins (1884–1947), of Scribner's, who displayed an almost saintly patience with the wayward novelist. Their association ended with blows after critics suggested that a large part of the success of Wolfe's *Look Homeward, Angel* (1929) had belonged to Perkins, who, his monumental patience finally exhausted, had taken the novel away from Wolfe and sent it to the printers before the author felt he had satisfactorily completed it. Carlos Baker records that Hemingway, unimpressed by Wolfe's portrait of Perkins as Edwards, bragged that he could get Perkins straighter in 1,000 words than Wolfe had done in 10,000.

EEYORE, in A.A. Milne's *Winnie-the-Pooh* (1926) and *The House at Pooh Corner* (1928). 'A strange, unlucky man' was Milne's description of Sir Owen Seaman (1861–1936), editor of *Punch* from 1906 to 1932. Milne was for eight years his assistant. This connection and Seaman's dour disposition prompt the suspicion that here is the model for the lugubrious Eeyore. In his autobiography, Milne says Seaman had 'not only the will to win but the determination to explain why he hadn't won. There is a story of him as a golfer, making an excuse for every bad shot until he got to the last green, when he threw down his putter and said: "That settles it, I'll never play in knickerbockers again."'

EGAN, Kevin, in James Joyce's *Ulysses* (1922), is Joseph Casey, a *New York Herald* compositor in Paris. Prior to settling in France, he was imprisoned in England on suspicion of assisting the escape of captive Fenians in Manchester in 1867, but was acquitted.

EGBERT, in D.H. Lawrence's 'England, My England' (1915; *England, My England*, 1922), is Perceval Lucas (1879–1916), brother of E.V. Lucas (see Davies, Peter). When Lawrence wrote this story he was unaware that Lucas had volunteered for military service, although he was middle-aged, with several children. He was killed in France.

EGERIA, in Maria Jane Jewsbury's *The Three Histories* (1830), is the poet Mrs Felicia Dorothea Hemans (1793–1835), best remembered for 'The boy stood on the burning deck . . . ' ('Casabianca').

EGERTON, Lady Dionissia de, in Ford Madox Ford's *Ladies Whose Bright Eyes* (1911), is part-inspired by Violet Hunt. See Nesbit, Norah.

EGG, Joe, in Peter Nichols's *A Day in the Death of Joe Egg* (1967), stems from the author's experience with his birth-damaged daughter, Abigail Nichols (*d.* 1971, aged eleven), who spent most of her life in a mental hospital, barely attaining consciousness. 'We had to make jokes about her to keep sane and to give a character to someone who could never have a character,' Nichols recalled. 'We got to hate the hypocrisy of people who felt that such children have to be kept alive at all costs.' When Abigail died, 'I shed no tears over what we all knew was a happy event.'

EGGAR, Houston, in C.P. Snow's *The Light and the Dark* (1947), is part-inspired by Baron Zuckerman (Professor Solly Zuckerman, 1904–   ), Chief Scientific Adviser to the British Government from 1964 to 1971 and President of the Zoological Society of London since 1977.

EGGERS, in George Gissing's *The Unclassed* (1884), is Eduard Bertz (*d.* 1931), a German exile teaching in London who met the author in 1879, when Gissing answered his newspaper advertisement seeking intellectual companionship. Bertz became Gissing's lifelong correspondent, valued critic and confidant.

EGINHARD, in Carsten Hauch's *The Castle on the Rhine* (1845). 'Here all my weaknesses are gathered together!' confessed the Danish writer, Hans Christian Andersen (1805–75), acknowledging the accuracy of this caricature of himself as an extravagantly egotistical poet. 'I hope and believe that I have lived through that period, but everything that this poet says and does I could have said and done.'

EGLETT, Lady Charlotte, in George Meredith's *Lord Ormont and his Aminta* (1894), is Lady Caroline Maxse (née FitzHardinge, *d.* 1886), daughter of the Fifth Earl of Berkeley and mother of Rear-Admiral Frederick Augustus Maxse (see Beauchamp, Nevil). It was from her that Meredith heard the story of Caroline Norton (see Merion, Diana).

EGO, Pomponius, in R.S. Surtees's *Handley Cross* (1843). Snob and egotist though he was, the sporting journalist 'Nimrod' – Charles James Apperley (1777–1843) – had a devoted following and pioneered 'country house' journalism. Though Surtees guyed him without mercy, he wrote a not ungenerous memoir of 'Nimrod' after his death.

EJNAR, in Henrik Ibsen's *Brand* (1866), is believed by the Ibsen biographer, Michael Meyer, to be Walter Runeberg, Finnish sculptor and son of the Swedish poet Johan Ludvig Runeberg. In the summer of 1864 he fell in love with Thea Bruun (see Agnes), in Italy.

EKDAL, Hjalmar, in Henrik Ibsen's *The Wild Duck* (1884), has suggested originals including Kristofer Janson, a young novelist acquaintance of Ibsen in Rome in the 1860s; and C.D. Magelssen, a sculptor in Rome at that time, obsessed with a technique he was perfecting to revolutionise both bronze-casting and torpedo manufacture. The hypersensitive Swedish dramatist, August Strindberg (1849–1912), erroneously took this character to be a portrait of himself.

EKDAL, Old, *idem*, is the author's father, Knud Plesner Ibsen (1797–1877), son of the owner-captain of a ship lost with all hands in the year of his birth. He was the proprietor of a general store at Skien, Norway, and a distiller of schnapps.

ELEONORA, in Edgar Allan Poe's 'Eleonora' (1842), is Virginia Clemm. See Lee, Annabel.

ELIA, Bridget, in Charles Lamb's 'Mackery End' (1821), 'Mrs Battle's Opinions on Whist' (1821), 'My Relations' (1821) and 'Old China' (1823), collected in *Essays of Elia* (1823), is the author's sister, Mary Lamb (1764–1847). In a passing fit of insanity, she in 1796 murdered her mother and was subsequently cared for by Charles, under whose guardianship she was placed, although her brother John wished her to be put in an asylum. With Charles, she was co-author of *Tales from Shakespeare* (1807).

ELIA, James, in Charles Lamb's 'My Relations' (1821) and 'Dream Children' (1822), collected in *Essays of Elia* (1823), is the author's brother, John Lamb (1763–1821). Accountant of the South Sea Company in London, he was an art lover who once knocked down the critic and essayist William Hazlitt during an argument about the colours of Holbein and Van Dyck. He did not mind the blow, Hazlitt later remarked, 'nothing but an *idea* hurts me.' In the year after his death, John Lamb's collection of pictures fetched £336 at Christie's.

ELIOT, Charles, in C.P. Snow's *The Sleep of Reason* (1968) and *Last Things* (1970), is the author's son, Philip Charles Hansford Snow (1952–   ), a Chinese scholar. The author's brother, Philip Snow, makes the identification in *Stranger and Brother: a Portrait of C.P. Snow* (1982).

ELIOT, Hubert Edward (Bertie), in C.P. Snow's *Time of Hope* (1949) and *Last Things* (1970), is the author's father, William Edward Snow (?1869–1954), a Fellow of the Royal College of Organists who, unable to make a living from music, became a clerk in a Leicester boot and shoe factory.

ELIOT, Lena, in C.P. Snow's *Time of Hope* (1949), is the author's mother, Ada Sophia Snow (née Robinson, *d*. 1944), a Leicester seamstress at the time of her marriage in 1897.

ELIOT, Martin F., in C.P. Snow's *Time of Hope* (1949), *The New Men* (1954), *The Affair* (1960), *Corridors of Power* (1964), *The Sleep of Reason* (1968) and *Last Things* (1970), is part-inspired by the author's brother, Philip Albert Snow (1915–), an administrator in Fiji and the Western Pacific for fourteen years, bursar of Rugby School for twenty-five, and author of works including *Stranger and Brother: a Portrait of C.P. Snow* (1982).

ELIZA, in Laurence Sterne's *Bramine's Journal* (1767) and *Letters from Yorick to Eliza* (written 1766–7; published 1775), is Mrs Eliza Draper (1744–78), with whom the author had an affair. She was the wife of an East India Company official, and following Sterne's death in insolvency she was instrumental in raising a subscription to assist his widow and daughter.

ELIZABETH, in Stephen Spender's *World within World* (1951), is Dr Muriel Gardiner (see Julia), with whom the author had a brief affair in Vienna in the 1930s.

ELLÉNORE, in Benjamin Constant's *Adolphe* (written 1807, published 1816), is believed to be modelled upon two of the author's lovers, having the physical characteristics of Mme Agnès Isabelle Émilie de Charrière (1740–1805), a Dutch novelist and essayist twenty-seven years the author's senior, and deriving in other respects from the writer Mme de Staël (née Anne-Louise-Germaine Necker, 1766–1817). Mme de Charrière, who had rejected James Boswell (Samuel Johnson's biographer) as her suitor and married her brother's Swiss tutor, a distant relative of Constant, was the author's mistress from 1787 to 1796. She was supplanted by Mme de Staël, celebrated for her Paris salon, and the wife of a Swedish diplomat from whom she separated in 1798, her affair with Constant lasting until her death.

ELLIOT, Captain, in Joseph Conrad's *Lord Jim* (1900) and 'The End of the Tether' (*Youth*, 1902), is Captain Henry Ellis (1835–

1908), who in 1873 was appointed Harbour Master of Singapore. An autocratic Irishman from Bundoran, County Donegal, he retired in 1888 and died after refusing to have a broken leg put in splints.

ELLIOT, Hubert, in Ernest Hemingway's 'Mr and Mrs Elliot' (*In Our Time*, 1925), is the American novelist Chard Powers Smith (1894–1977), a contemporary of the author in Paris in the 1920s. The portrait provoked a letter from Smith calling the author a contemptible worm. Hemingway responded by offering to knock him down a few times, or maybe once, depending on his capacity to get up again.

ELLIOTT, Christina (Kirstie), in Robert Louis Stevenson's *Weir of Hermiston* (1896). 'The story is all the more thrilling as he says he has taken me for young Kirstie,' noted Isobel Strong (née Osbourne, d. 1957) in her diary. She was the daughter of Stevenson's wife by her first marriage, and at Vailima, Samoa, she acted as his secretary. It was to her that he dictated the *Weir*. Earlier, in 1879, she had eloped with a spendthrift alcoholic San Francisco artist, Joe Strong, by whom she had a son. They were divorced in 1892 and she subsequently married Salisbury Field, a former beau of her mother. Her memoirs, *This Life I've Loved*, were published in 1937.

ELLIS, Captain, in Joseph Conrad's *The Shadow-Line* (1917), is Captain Henry Ellis. See Elliot, Captain.

ELLISON, Mr, in Flora Thompson's trilogy *Lark Rise to Candleford* (1939–43), is the Revd Charles Sawkins Harrison, rector of Cottisford from 1853 to 1896, according to Thomas Hinde's *A field guide to the English Country Parson* (1983).

ELMS, Alfred, in Frederick Rolfe's *Hadrian the Seventh* (1904), is Trevor Haddon (1864–1941), a Cambridge portrait painter. When he first met Rolfe, Haddon was living in London, at Elms Road, Clapham Common, and had a studio in Westminster, says Donald Weeks, in *Corvo* (1971). As with most of Rolfe's friendships, the acquaintance ended in a quarrel.

ÉLOMIRE, in *Zélinde* (1663), by Jean Donneau de Visé, is the rival French dramatist Molière (Jean-Baptiste Poquelin, 1622–73). The anagram is also applied to Molière in the play *Élomire hypochondre, ou Les Medicins vengés* (1670), by Le Boulanger de Chalussay.

ELSA, in Louis Aragon's *Les Yeux d'Elsa* (1942), *Elsa* (1959), *Le Fou d'Elsa* (1963) and *Il ne m'est Paris que d'Elsa* (1964), is the poet's companion Elsa Triolet (1896–1970), a Russian-born novelist and journalist whom he first met in 1928.

ELSA, in Kay Boyle's 'The Rest Cure' (*Thirty Stories*, 1948), is Frieda Lawrence (see Somers, Harriet). D.H. Lawrence (see Rampion, Mark) is the story's un-named principal character.

ELSHENDER, in Sir Walter Scott's *The Black Dwarf* (1816), is the recluse David Ritchie (?1740–1811). Born at Easter Happrew, Peeblleshire, he was the son of a quarryman. His deformity (he was little more than three-foot-three) caused him to withdraw to a cottage at Manor, where Scott visited him in 1797.

ELSIE, in Lewis Carroll's *Alice's Adventures in Wonderland* (1865), is Lorina Charlotte Liddell (see Lory, the), Elsie being a play on her initials, L.C.

ELSTIR, in Marcel Proust's *A la recherche du temps perdu* (1913–27), is supposedly a composite of the artists Jacques Émile Blanche (1861–1942); Alexander Harrison (1853–1930), an American marine painter encountered by Proust at Beg-Meil in 1895; Paul-César Helleu (1859–1927); Claude-Oscar Monet (1840–1926); Gustave Moreau (1826–98); J.M.W. Turner (1775–1851); James Abbott McNeill Whistler (see Sibley, Joe); and Édouard Vuillard (1868–1940).

ELVIRE, in Alphonse Lamartine's *Méditations poétiques et religieuses* (1820), is Julie Charles, the invalid spouse of a Paris doctor. Lamartine met her at Aix-les-Bains in 1816, and she died in the following year. He married in 1823, and named his daughter after her.

EMMANUEL, Paul, in Charlotte Brontë's *Villette* (1853). Although it has yet to be recognised by the payment of danger money, an occupational hazard of male teachers is the tendency of women students to fall in love with them. To this, were he still around, Constantin Georges Romain Heger would doubtless testify. The model for Paul Emmanuel, he was principal of the Pensionnat Heger in the Rue Isabelle, Brussels. It was to this establishment that Charlotte Brontë (then aged twenty-six) and her sister, Emily, went to improve their French and acquire some German with a view to starting their own school. Charlotte became infatuated with Heger, staying on beyond her arranged date of departure from Brussels and subsequently writing desperate letters to him from England — letters which he did not answer but must have kept, for his descendants gave them to the British Museum.

EMMOTT, David, in Agatha Christie's *Murder in Mesopotamia* (1936). The author's second husband, the archaeologist Sir Max Mallowan (1904–78), recognised himself as this 'minor but decent character', as he noted in his memoirs. He met his bride in 1930, when the imperious Katherine Woolley (see Leidner, Louise) commanded him to take a woman visitor — Agatha Christie — on a tour of Baghdad and the desert. Their car became bogged down in the sand, Agatha accepted this cheerfully as all in a day's work, and Mallowan decided that here was a remarkable woman. They married a few months later.

EMSWORTH, Colonel, in Sir Arthur Conan Doyle's 'The Adventure of the Blanched Soldier' (1926; *The Case-book of Sherlock Holmes*, 1927). During the Boer War the author was in charge of a military hospital at Bloemfontein. When this was overwhelmed by a typhoid epidemic, Doyle underwent a gruelling cross-examination by Field Marshal Lord Roberts (1832–1914). This encounter has prompted Charles Higham to suggest Roberts as a model for Emsworth (*The Adventures of Conan Doyle*, 1976).

EMSWORTH, the Earl of (Clarence Threepwood), in P.G. Wodehouse's 'Blandings' stories (1915–77). It is no more than a guess, but so pronounced are the similarities between the pig-doting Clarence and Spencer Compton Cavendish, Eighth Duke of Devonshire (see Chiltern, Lord), that if the Duke were not Emsworth's prototype, then he was virtually his double. His legendary absent-mindedness included forgetting he had invited Edward VII to dinner (when the King arrived, the Duke had gone to the Turf Club). He was also noted for falling asleep on public occasions. In the House of Lords, when a member was speaking on the greatest moments in life, the Duke is reputed to have woken to remark to a neighbour, 'My greatest moment was when my pig won first prize at Skipton Fair.'

E.N., in Alexander Zinoviev's *Ante-room to Paradise* (1980), is Ernst Neizvestny, according to Geoffrey Hosking's review of the book in *The Times Literary Supplement* (23 May 1980). See Dauber.

ENDE, Ute, in Heinrich Mann's *The Hunt for Love* (1903), is the author's actress sister, Carla Mann (1881–1910), who terminated an unsuccessful stage career with suicide, following a row with her fiancé.

ENFELON, T.L., in Osbert Sitwell's *Miracle on Sinai* (1933). With a 'mild but petulant beard' and 'loose, shaggy clothes clinging to a giraffe-like body', Enfelon is D.H. Lawrence (see Rampion, Mark) – 'portrayed with surprising charity', remarks the Sitwells' biographer, John Lehmann, 'if one remembers the bitterness with which Edith was to speak of Lawrence in *Taken Care Of* and her conviction that *Lady Chatterley's Lover* was an attack on her own family.'

ENID, in R.H. Benson's *Initiation* (1914), is Frederick Rolfe (1860–1913), writer, artist, paranoiac, homosexual, failed schoolmaster and reject of the Catholic priesthood. He adopted the title 'Baron Corvo'. The two quarrelled when Benson (see Bonsen, the Revd Bobugo) suggested that Rolfe's name should not appear on a book on which they were collaborating.

EPPIS, Howard, in Roger L. Simon's *The Big Fix* (1973), has a probable prototype in the American radical Abbie Hoffman (1936–), suggests David Geherin in *Sons of Sam Spade* (1980). The author of *Steal This Book*, Hoffman was prominent in the 1960s.

ERASMUS, William, in Osbert Sitwell's 'The Machine Breaks Down' (*Triple Fugue*, 1924), is the novelist Aldous Huxley (1894–1963). The story stems from Sitwell, in the company of Huxley, overhearing Harry Melvill (see Dearborn, Hugh) talking to himself. It was Sitwell's revenge for Huxley's 'The Tillotson Banquet' (see Badgery, Lord). 'I've always thought it faintly odd that Osbert should have written that story,' remarked Huxley in 1932, 'because in some ways he himself was not totally unlike Harry Melvill.'

ERIKSON, in Malcolm Lowry's *Dark as the Grave Wherein My Friend is Laid* (1967). So impressed was Lowry by the novel *The Ship Sails On* (1924) that he joined a Norwegian tramp ship sailing from

Preston, signing on as a fireman, and made his way to Oslo to meet the author, Nordahl Grieg (1902—43), who became Lowry's Erikson. A former seaman, Grieg worked in broadcasting and journalism in Britain and Iceland following the German invasion of Norway in 1940. He was killed over Berlin on a bombing mission.

ERRIDGE, Viscount, Earl of Warminster (Alfred Tolland), in Anthony Powell's *A Dance to the Music of Time* sequence (1951—75), owes something of his appearance to the author's friend George Orwell (see Tait, Basil). 'It argues a great restraint on Powell's part', remarks Orwell's biographer, Bernard Crick, 'that there is only the merest whiff of Orwell, small but distinct, in the twelve volumes of his *A Dance to the Music of Time* — in the physical description of Alf, Viscount Erridge, Earl of Warminster, the eccentric, and erratic, high-minded revolutionary, living in squalor and an old corduroy jacket and surrounded by spongers and Left-wing hangers-on.' Powell has himself conceded that Erridge has 'vaguely Orwellian lineaments'.

ERROL, Cedric, See Fauntleroy, Lord.

ERSKINE, Chichester, in George Bernard Shaw's *An Unsocial Socialist* (1887), is the minor Irish poet Pakenham Beatty (1855—1930), a drink-addicted boxing champion of Shaw's twenties. They first met in London in 1876 when Beatty — an old Harrovian who had completed his education in Bonn — was busy squandering his inheritance.

ESHETFORD, Lady, in Ford Madox Ford's *The Portrait* (1910), is Violet Hunt. See Nesbit, Norah.

ESKDALE, Lord, in Benjamin Disraeli's *Tancred* (1847), is William Lowther, Third Earl of Lonsdale. See Colchicum, Lord.

ESOR, Stanley, in Osbert Sitwell's *Those Were The Days* (1938). The Sitwells couldn't stand the sight of him, but Wyndham Lewis (see Lypiatt, Casimir) is indispensable to this novel as Esor, its strongest character. He is presented irresistibly attracting women to his squalid studio — as he did in real life — and is accorded 'the pose of a herdsman, a lonely figure far above the flock'. This is an allusion, says Lewis's biographer, Jeffrey Meyers, to his manifesto, 'The Code of a Herdsman'.

ESSIE. See Harding, Hester.

ESSLING-STERLINGHOVEN, Lolotte, Gräfin, in Anthony West's *Heritage* (1955). 'An older woman', Odette Keun (see Campbell, Clementina) informed West's father, 'can play a very important role in the life of a boy of a certain age. She can do for him something that no little miss, all gaucherie, and inexperience, and self-regard, can ever do. If you wish to be happy in your love life, you should start off with an older woman who knows what she is about in a hard, hard bed. She will put you on the right path, and bring an end to all your confusions and hesitations.' West was then fourteen and 'very uncertain of my sexual identity', as he records in his biography of his father, *H.G. Wells* (1984). From this, Keun (his Lolotte in *Heritage*) emerges as a person of integrity whom Wells failed utterly to understand.

ESTE, Princesse d', in Joséphin Péladan's *Le Vice suprême* (1884), is the author's mistress, Henriette Maillat. See Chantelouve, Mme.

ESTHER, in Eliza Lynn Linton's *The Autobiography of Christopher Kirkland* (1885), is the author's husband, William James Linton (1812–97), a talented wood-engraver who might have achieved greater fulfilment in his art had he not, in the words of his wife, bitten the Dead Sea apple of impracticable politics. Both were republicans, but his obsession with that cause to the exclusion of all else resulted in their early separation. He was among the first artists engaged in the production of the *Illustrated London News*. In her autobiographical novel, the author transposes the sexes of herself and her husband.

EUGENIUS, in Laurence Sterne's *The Life and Opinions of Tristram Shandy* (1759–67), is John Hall-Stevenson (1718–85), extrovert, wit and a Cambridge contemporary of the author. Calling his home (Skelton Hall, Yorkshire) 'Crazy Castle', he made it the base for a high-spirited circle of squires and clerics known as 'The Demoniacks'. He was the author of a number of sketches and wrote a continuation of Sterne's *Sentimental Journey*.

EUPHORION, in Johann Wolfgang von Goethe's *Faust*, part 2 (1832), is Lord Byron. See Cadurcis, Lord.

EVA, Lady, in D.H. Lawrence's *The First Lady Chatterley* (written 1926–7, published 1944), is Lady Ida Sitwell (*d.* 1937), daughter of the First Earl of Londesborough and mother of Edith, Osbert and Sacheverell Sitwell (see Whittlebot, Hernia, Gob and Sago). In 1915 her husband (see Rotherham, Sir Henry) refused to settle her gambling debts and she was sent to Holloway Prison for three months. Lawrence met her briefly when he visited the Sitwells in Italy in 1926.

EVANGELIST, in John Bunyan's *The Pilgrim's Progress* (1678), is believed to have been inspired by John Gifford (*d.* 1655), a former Royalist army officer, gambler and libertine, who after losing heavily at cards cursed God ... and then found himself drawn to religion. Obtaining the living of the Nonconformist church of St John, Bedford, in 1653, he became a profound influence on Bunyan, a member of his congregation.

EVANS, Amy, in Henry James's 'The Velvet Glove' (1909; *The Finer Grain*, 1910), is the author's novelist friend, Edith Wharton (1862–1937).

EVANS, Sirrie, in H.G. Wells's *The World of William Clissold* (1926), is part-inspired by the author's wife, Jane Wells. See Stanley, Ann Veronica.

EVELYN, in Jack Kerouac's *Visions of Cody* (1960), is Carolyn Cassady. See Camille.

EVERARD, in George Sand's *Les Lettres d'un voyageur* (1834–6), is Michel de Bourges, a lawyer who in 1836 negotiated the author's separation from her husband and with whom she lived briefly, fleeing eventually from his perpetual preaching and his practice of locking her in her bedroom to ponder his sermons.

EVERARD, George, in Ford Madox Ford's *The Simple Life Limited* (published under the pseudonym Daniel Chaucer, 1911). Thomas C. Moser's *The Life in the Fiction of Ford Madox Ford* (1980) suggests that Everard owes his physical characteristics to Frank Harris (see Parker, Ralph), of whom Shaw said, 'He is neither first rate, nor second rate, nor tenth rate. He is just his horrible unique self.' Perhaps, for Ford, this was Harris's attraction.

EVESHAM, Sir Arthur, in H.G. Wells's *The New Machiavelli* (1911), is the British statesman Arthur James Balfour, First Earl Balfour (1848–1930), best remembered for the Balfour Declaration, favouring Palestine as a national home for the Jews, which he signed as Foreign Secretary in 1917. He was Prime Minister from 1902 to 1905.

EWART, Bob, in H.G. Wells's *Tono-Bungay* (1909). According to Lovat Dickson's *H.G. Wells: His Turbulent Life and Times* (1969), Ewart is the author's friend Walter Low, editor of the *Educational Times*.

F

FAGAN, Dr Augustus, in Evelyn Waugh's *Decline and Fall* (1928). It is tempting to equate Fagan with one Banks, head of Arnold House School, Llanddulas, where Waugh taught in 1925 upon leaving Oxford. On the evidence of those who knew him, however, Banks bore no resemblance to Fagan. A more likely model is John Ferguson Roxburgh (1888–1954), a Lancing housemaster when Waugh was a pupil at that school. The author disliked him. Roxburgh was subsequently founder-headmaster of Stowe School (1923–49), where he is remembered for his exemplary courtesy to a call-girl brought to a speech day by a youthful Old Boy, the actor David Niven. An unequivocal statement that Roxburgh was Fagan, in the *Observer* on 29 October 1978, went unchallenged.

FAGIN, in Charles Dickens's *Oliver Twist* (1837–8), has a putative prototype in Iky Solomons, a receiver of stolen goods imprisoned at Newgate Gaol in 1831. He was sufficiently notorious for Barney Fence, in *Van Diemen's Land* (1830), to be renamed after him when the play was revived.

FAILING, Mrs, in E.M. Forster's *The Longest Journey* (1907). Can you imagine Mrs Failing stripping under the trees and making love with H.G. Wells on a copy of *The Times*, spread out at a page containing a narrow-minded letter from the novelist Mrs Humphry Ward? Or at her Swiss home, welcoming Wells as he enters her room via a secret door concealed by a wardrobe? These, according to Wells, were among his exploits with Elizabeth von Arnim (1866–1941), who is suggested by Forster's biographer, P.N. Furbank, to be in part the model for Mrs Failing. As her children's tutor, Forster distrusted her and was repelled by her false teeth; she, in turn, was repelled by his taste in ties. Born Mary Annette Beauchamp, in Australia, she was a cousin of Katherine Mansfield (see Brangwen,

Gudrun). She married a German count and on his Pomeranian estate cultivated the grounds that were the inspiration for her best-selling *Elizabeth and Her German Garden* (1898). After the death of the count she had an affair with Wells and became the third wife of the Second Earl Russell, brother of Bertrand Russell (see Mattheson, Sir Joshua). Forster, however, said that Mrs Failing was based on his domineering Uncle Willie — William Howley Forster (1855—1910), a Northumberland squire who devoted himself to shooting, hunting and fishing, his father having denied him the military career that was his preference.

FAIRCHILD, Dawson, in William Faulkner's *Mosquitoes* (1927), according to Joseph Blotner's *Faulkner* (1974), is the American novelist and short-story writer Sherwood Anderson (1876—1941), whom Faulkner met while working on a New Orleans newspaper. Anderson helped him to achieve his first novel's publication.

FAIRFORD, Saunders, in Sir Walter Scott's *Redgauntlet* (1824), is the author's father, Walter Scott (1729—99), an Edinburgh attorney who married the eldest daughter of Edinburgh University's Professor of Medicine in 1758 and had twelve children, six of whom died in infancy.

FALCONEY, Édouard de, in Paul de Musset's *Lui et elle* (1859), is the author's brother, Alfred. See Laurent; Olympe.

FALS, in Philippe Sollers's *Femmes* (1983), is the psychoanalyst Jacques Lacan (1901—81). Both died pitiable deaths.

FALSTAFF, Sir John, in William Shakespeare's *Henry IV* (1597—8) and *The Merry Wives of Windsor* (1600—1), has a suggested model in Adrian Gilbert, younger brother of the soldier and navigator Sir Humphrey Gilbert (?1539—83). Corpulent and addicted to deer-poaching and to dabbling in medicine, Adrian Gilbert was described by the antiquary John Aubrey as 'the greatest Buffoon of the Nation'. Falstaff was originally named Oldcastle, Shakespeare having apparently unwittingly used the name of a Lollard martyr, Sir John Oldcastle, who was executed in 1417. The name was changed to Falstaff upon representations by Lord Cobham, a descendant of Oldcastle. Despite Shakespeare's denial of any intention to portray Oldcastle, Roman Catholics persisted in claiming Falstaff to be a portrait of the heretic. In choosing the name Falstaff, it is possible that Shakespeare had in mind the name of Sir John Fastolf (1378—1459), warrior and benefactor of the universities of Oxford and Cambridge.

FANE, Walter, in W. Somerset Maugham's *The Painted Veil* (1925), was admitted by the author to be his lawyer brother, Frederic Herbert Maugham, First Viscount Maugham of Hatfield (1866—1958), Britain's Lord Chancellor from 1938 to 1939.

FANG, Mr, in Charles Dickens's *Oliver Twist*, (1837—8), is Allan Stewart Laing (1788—1862), a notoriously brutal magistrate in London's Hatton Garden Police Court who was removed from his post by the Home Office following his involvement in a street fracas with a doctor.

FANNING, Long John, in James Joyce's *Ulysses* (1922), is Long John Clancy, sub-sheriff of Dublin and a neighbour of the Joyce family during the author's youth. Too squeamish for executions, he would find a pretext for going to London whenever a man was to be hanged, leaving the preparations to his assistant. He appears under his own name in *Finnegans Wake* (1939).

FANNY, in Richard Aldington's *Death of a Hero* (1929). 'One felt that her morning bath had something Lethean about it, and washed away the memory of last night's lover along with his touch', remarks Aldington of Fanny, who in real life was Dorothy Yorke (see Carter, Bella), for whom he left his wife (see Winterbourne, Elizabeth).

FANNY, Lord, in Alexander Pope's 'Bathos, the art of sinking in Poetry' (*Miscellanies*, 1727—8) and *The Dunciad* (1728), is Lord Hervey (see Sporus). Lord Fanny was Hervey's nickname, inspired by his effeminate bearing.

FARINTOSH, the Marquis of, in W.M. Thackeray's *The New-comes* (1853—5). In his *Memories* (1874), Maunsell B. Field says that Thackeray told him that his model for Farintosh was John Alexander Thynne, Fourth Marquis of Bath (1831—96). Whatever figure Thynne cut in his youth to inspire this portrait of a worthless puppy, he went on to chair Wiltshire County Council and to produce *Observations on Bulgarian Affairs* (1880).

FARNON, Siegfried and Tristan, in the 'Vet' books of James Herriot (James Alfred Wight), commencing with *If Only They Could Talk* (1970). 'What Herriot has written is pretty accurate. The relationship we had with each other is well-portrayed — it comes across as a very happy time, and that is what it was', says Brian Sinclair (1912–), of Harrogate, who as the original of Tristan has become something of a celebrity, frequently invited to be guest speaker at farmers' functions in the north of England. As a trainee vet, he worked for his elder brother, Donald Sinclair (Siegfried), in the Thirsk practice which Herriot joined upon qualifying as a veterinary surgeon in 1939. Brian Sinclair qualified in 1943, was first employed in Ulverston, Cumbria, and after war service with the Royal Army Veterinary Corps in India worked in Scotland and Yorkshire for the Ministry of Agriculture, retiring in 1977. Herriot's *It Shouldn't Happen to a Vet* (1972) is dedicated to the two brothers.

FAROU, in Sidonie-Gabrielle Colette's *La Seconde* (1929), is supposedly Henri de Jouvenel. See Jean.

FARQUHAR, Mr, in George Eliot's 'Amos Barton' (*Scenes of Clerical Life*, 1858), is supposedly Henry Harpur, squire of Chilvers Coton, Warwickshire, during the author's youth, when he lent her books to counterbalance her pronounced evangelicalism.

FARQUHAR, Philip and Katherine, in D.H. Lawrence's 'The Border Line' (*The Woman Who Rode Away*, 1928), are John Middleton Murry (see Crich, Gerald) and Frieda Lawrence (see Somers, Harriet).

FARRANT, Anthony, in Graham Greene's *England Made Me* (1935), is an idealised portrait of the author's eldest brother, Herbert Greene, 'to whom unemployment was like recurring flu'. He was a family failure, his *Secret Agent in Spain* dismissed by Graham Greene as being of doubtful authenticity.

FAT BOY, the, in Charles Dickens's *The Posthumous Papers of the Pickwick Club* (1836–7), it has been claimed, was a servant at the Turk's Head Inn, Exeter (*Western Morning News*, June, 1910), and, 'on his own statement' (*Manchester Guardian*, April, 1905), the murderer Charles Pearce. But the Dickens biographer Frederic G. Kitton, as well as Alex J. Philip and Lt-Col. Laurence W. Gadd in their *Dickens Dictionary* (1928) are unanimous in naming the Fat Boy as James Budden, son of the landlord of the Red Lion Inn, Chatham, Kent. As Major James Budden, he lived in the 1880s in Higham, Rochester, where he was recalled by the artist Fred Roe as 'a short, thick-set, elderly man with a small dark moustache: not corpulent, if inclining to stoutness; who was inclined to hold his head on one side and who held his arms straight by his body when walking.'

FATHER, in Graham Greene's *Carving a Statue* (1964). Indifferent artist though he was, Benjamin Robert Haydon (see Skimpole, Harold) served as an inspiration for both Dickens and Greene. Here he is Greene's sculptor — 'you cannot read the diaries of Haydon', the author has noted, 'without realizing that he had a true daemon and yet he had no talent at all — surely a farcical character, though he came to a tragic end.'

FAUNTLEROY, Lord, in Frances Hodgson Burnett's *Little Lord Fauntleroy* (1885). In the days when triple-decker headlines made the subsequent reports almost superfluous, a newspaper announced: 'ORIGINAL "FAUNTLEROY" DIES IN BOAT AFTER HELPING RESCUE FOUR IN SOUND. Vivian Burnett, Author's Son who Devoted Life to Escaping Cissified Role is Stricken at Helm — Manoeuvres Yawl to get two Men and two Women from Overturned Craft, then Collapses.' This recorded the passing of Vivian Burnett (1876–1937), the author's younger son and her model for Cedric Errol, Lord Fauntleroy. Like Fauntleroy, as a child he addressed his mother as 'Dearest'; and like Fauntleroy he wore a velvet knickerbocker suit. His clothes, suggests the author's biographer, Ann Thwaite, may have been prompted by Oscar Wilde's visit to Burnett in Washington in 1882, wearing 'a black silk claw-hammer coat, fancily flowered dark waistcoat, knee breeches, silk stockings and patent leather pumps with broad buckles'. But, as Roger Lancelyn Green points out in *Tellers of Tales* (1946), 'Mrs Burnett did not invent the costume: it had become a recognized dress for small boys as a variant from the ordinary "sailor suit" of every day, and may be seen in illustrations to *Aunt Judy's Magazine* and *Little Folk* from the beginning of the 1880s.' Nevertheless, when *Little Lord Fauntleroy* was staged the costume became known as the Fauntleroy suit. Those thrust into it included Compton Mackenzie and A.A. Milne (whose wife was to inflict girlish clothes upon Christopher Robin). In Davenport, Iowa, Thwaite records, 'an eight-year-old burned down his father's barn in protest at being dressed as Little Lord Fauntleroy'. The play, rather than the book, was responsible for the cissy image which was to blight Vivian Burnett's life — his mother having admitted him to be Fauntleroy's model, and a photograph taken in 1884 the basis for Reginald Birch's illustrations. Not that this stopped him from becoming a reporter on the *Denver Republican,* later entering magazine publishing, marrying at thirty-eight, having two daughters . . . and dying an honourable death.

FAUSTINE, in Algernon Swinburne's 'Faustine' (*Poems and Ballads,* 1866), is supposedly Mary Leith. See Dolores.

FAUSTUS, Dr, in Christopher Marlowe's *Dr Faustus* (1604), is seen by Frances A. Yates, in *The Occult Philosophy in the Elizabethan Age* (1979), as an attack on Dr John Dee (see Prospero). Dee lived well for a time on his reputation for turning base metal into gold, an activity in which Marlowe was less successful: when he produced and tried to pass a forged pewter coin as gold, he was arrested.

FAX, Mr, in Thomas Love Peacock's *Melincourt* (1817), is supposedly Thomas Robert Malthus (1766—1834), remembered as a writer on economics and population control.

FEATHERNEST, Mr, in Thomas Love Peacock's *Melincourt* (1817), is the poet and biographer Robert Southey (1774—1843), whose rebellious youth was succeeded by conformist middle age: from being a supporter of revolution, he gradually changed into a Tory establishment figure, was granted a government pension, and in 1813 became poet laureate.

FELL, Carlotta, in D.H. Lawrence's 'Glad Ghosts' (1926; *The Woman Who Rode Away*, 1928), is Lady Cynthia Asquith (see Pervin, Isabel), according to the Lawrence biographer Harry T. Moore, who notes, however, that the character started out as Dorothy Brett (see Mullion, Jenny).

FELL, Dr Gideon, in the detective novels of John Dickson Carr, commencing with *Hag's Nook* (1933), is a caricature of the novelist, essayist and poet Gilbert Keith Chesterton (1874—1936), upon whose 'Father Brown' stories Carr modelled his earliest, unpublished work. Carr was honorary secretary of the Detection Club, founded in London in 1932 with Chesterton as its first president.

FENTIMAN, George, in Dorothy L. Sayers's *The Unpleasantness at the Bellona Club* (1928), is based — says the author's biographer, Janet Hitchman — on Sayers's husband, Oswald Arthur Fleming (1881–1950), whom she married in 1926, after his first wife had divorced him for adultery, and supported for the rest of his life. Dissatisfied with his prosaic Christian names, he changed them to Oswold Atherton when he was seventeen. In South Africa he worked briefly as a special war correspondent for the magazine *Black and White*, and in the First World War he served as an Army Service Corps captain, subsequently posing as a former Royal Dragoon Guards' major with a colourful war record. A good cook, he was the author of *The Gourmet's Book of Food and Drink* (1933), in which he incorporated material from a Colman's Mustard recipe booklet. He also wrote on motoring for the *News of the World* and was the author of *How to See the Battlefields* (1919) and *The Craft of the Short Story* (under the pseudonym Donald Maconochie).

FENWICK, Arthur, in W. Somerset Maugham's *Our Betters* (1917), is Gordon Selfridge (1856–1947), the American-born proprietor of a celebrated London department store, which he opened in 1909. He was the lover of Syrie Wellcome (see Middleton, Constance) before her marriage to Maugham.

FEODOROVA, Olga, in Dorothy Richardson's *Pilgrimage* novel cycle (1915–67), is Olga Sokolov (*d. c.*1911). A friend of Kropotkin (see Leonidov, Anastasia Alexandrovna), she was herself inspired by revolutionary ideals despite her wealthy Russian background. Abruptly leaving London (where she was a student), she went to Paris with a lover and shortly afterwards committed suicide, despairing of the affair.

FERGAN, Captain, in Claude Farrère's *La Bataille* (1909), is Admiral Sir William Pakenham (1861–1933). British Naval Attaché, Tokyo, from 1904 to 1905, he was on deck observing the Battle of Tsushima through binoculars, but retired below when a shell burst nearby, spattering his uniform with the blood of casualties. Moments later, he reappeared in immaculate white trousers. He was subsequently ADC to King George V and in the First World War commanded a cruiser squadron and a battle cruiser fleet. President of the Royal Naval College, Greenwich, from 1919 to 1920, he retired in 1923 as Commander-in-Chief, North America and West Indies Station.

FERRARS, Myra, in Benjamin Disraeli's *Endymion* (1880), is the author's sister, Sarah (*b.* 1802). The two were particularly close, brother encouraging sister to be co-author of *A Year at Hartlebury, or The Election* (1834), published under the pseudonyms Cherry and Fair Star, as a therapy following her fiancé's death from smallpox.

FEUERMAUL, in Robert Musil's *The Man without Qualities* (1930—43), is the Austrian poet, novelist and playwright Franz Werfel (1890—1945), according to Musil's biographer, David S. Luft.

FIAMMA, in George Sand's *Simon* (1836), is Marie de Flavigny, Comtesse d'Agoult. See Rochefide, Béatrix de.

FIAMMETTA, in Giovanni Boccaccio's *L'amorosa Fiammetta* and *Elegia di madonna Fiammetta*, is supposedly Maria d'Aquino, wife of Count d'Aquino and illegitimate daughter of Robert of Anjou, King of Naples. Boccaccio first saw her in the church of San Lorenzo on Easter eve, 1341. She is believed to have predeceased him by many years, although he was still writing of her shortly before his death.

FIDDES, Dr, in James Kennaway's *Some Gorgeous Accident* (1967). When Kennaway introduced his wife, Susan, to his close friend, the novelist John le Carré, did he consciously set up the triangular relationship which transpired, simply to provide the raw material for his novel? The suspicion is invited by *The Kennaway Papers* (1981), the Kennaways' joint account of the affair, James Kennaway's contribution taking the form of posthumous extracts from the diary he kept at the time — 'How wonderfully close fiction and life have suddenly become', he noted. Le Carré — the story's Fiddes — also got a novel out of it: *The Naïve and Sentimental Lover* (see Shamus). Susan fell in love with him, but not out of love with her husband. Kennaway, having previously suggested that his wife should have affairs, responded by going berserk and taking off for the Continent, writing home that he was contemplating killing her. She found herself making love with le Carré in hotel bedrooms, while ostensibly studying German; holding hands simultaneously with both men in the cinema; nearly being torn apart by the two of them in a scene at a railway station. Pacing events all the while in *Some Gorgeous Accident*, which he wrote as the affair progressed, Kennaway appears to have been genuinely upset by it all, but to have felt it to be an emotional hoop through which he had to put himself to further his development as a writer. Madness threatened as he strove to swallow the medicine he had so often dispensed to his wife with his insatiable appetite for other women. But he was, as she later noted, a great manipulator: 'He enjoyed playing with people's lives, and it was inevitable that sooner or later he would begin to play with my life and with David's [le Carré's] life, and it was inevitable, too, the turn that that would take.' The affair ended when le Carré was unable to leave his wife and children.

FIFINE, in Robert Browning's *Fifine at the Fair* (1872), is part-inspired by the tempestuous beauty Louisa, Lady Ashburton (*d.* 1903), second wife of the Second Baron Ashburton and daughter of the Rt Hon. James Stewart Mackenzie, nephew of the Earl of Galloway. Her mother was the putative model for Ellen Douglas in Sir Walter Scott's *The Lady of the Lake*. Browning never forgave her for summarily rejecting his proposal of marriage, which he infelicitously coupled with the information that, of course, his heart was buried with his late, beloved wife in Florence, but that Lady Ashburton's marrying him would be greatly to his son's advantage.

FILSON, Nathaniel, in Norman Douglas's *Looking Back* (1933), is Nelson Foley, brother-in-law of Sir Arthur Conan Doyle and a neighbour of the author on Capri.

FINCHING, Flora, in Charles Dickens's *Little Dorrit* (1855-7). For twenty years, the author saw little of Maria Sarah Beadnell (see Spenlow, Dora), the flame of his youth. Then the acquaintance was renewed, and this is a portrait of Maria 'twenty years after'. Though it is not unaffectionate, one senses that Dickens must have felt he'd had a lucky escape.

FINESPUN, Mr, in Anthony Trollope's *Can You Forgive Her?* (1864), is supposedly William Ewart Gladstone (see Gresham, Mr), who was Chancellor of the Exchequer when this novel appeared.

FINN, Huckleberry, in Mark Twain's *The Adventures of Tom Sawyer* (1876) and *The Adventures of Huckleberry Finn* (1885), is Tom Blankenship, son of the local drunk in Hannibal, the Missouri home-town of the author's youth. In 1906 Twain noted in his autobiography, 'I have drawn Tom Blankenship exactly as he was. He was ignorant, unwashed, insufficiently fed; but he had as good a heart as ever any boy had. His liberties were totally unrestricted. He was the only really independent person — boy or man — in the community, and by consequence he was tranquilly and continuously happy and was envied by all the rest of us. We liked him; we enjoyed his society. And as his society was forbidden us by our parents the prohibition trebled and quadrupled its value . . . I heard, four years ago, that he was justice of the peace in a remote village in Montana and was a good citizen and greatly respected.'

FINN, Phineas, in Anthony Trollope's *Phineas Finn* (1869), *Phineas Redux* (1874), *The Prime Minister* (1876) and *The Duke's Children* (1880), has suggested originals including Sir William Gregory (1817–92), a friend of the author, and a Tory MP who opposed his party's Irish policy and became Governor of Ceylon; Chichester Samuel Fortescue (1823–98), an Irish MP who in 1874 became Lord Carlingford and who was the fourth husband of Frances, Dowager Countess Waldegrave, whom he married in 1863; and Sir John Pope Hennessy (1834–91), a Cork politician who was the first Roman Catholic Conservative to sit in parliament, and who became Governor of Labuan, the Gold Coast, the Windward Islands, Hong Kong and Mauritius. Finn's physical appearance, Michael Sadleir suggests, was taken from an English journalist, Joe Parkinson, who after marrying a millionaire's daughter became a company director.

FIRMIANI, Mme, in Honoré de Balzac's *Madame Firmiani* (1832), is part-inspired by Mme de Berny. See Mortsauf, Mme de.

FISBO, in Robert Nichols's *Fisbo, or The looking-glass loaned* (1934), is Osbert Sitwell. See Whittlebot, Gob.

FISH, Rose, in Terence Rattigan's *Variation on a Theme* (1958), has as prototype the actress Margaret Leighton (1922–76), for whom the part was written and who starred in the play's London première. Rattigan's inspiration was Margaret Leighton's short-lived second marriage, with Laurence Harvey (see Vale, Ron). As a young, unknown but precocious actor at Stratford, Harvey laid siege to Leighton, already an established star, although their marriage meant him risking his career by losing the interest of a protective film producer. After the marriage was dissolved, Margaret Leighton married the actor Michael Wilding.

FISHER, Horne, in G.K. Chesterton's *The Man Who Knew Too Much* (1922), is suggested by Penelope Fitzgerald (*The Knox*

Brothers, 1977) to be Maurice Baring (1874–1945), novelist, poet, essayist and dramatist. Fourth son of the First Lord Revelstoke, he was a diplomat turned newspaper foreign correspondent in Russia and the Balkans. His novels were concerned with Edwardian society, and he was noted for his worldly-wise urbanity; his accomplishments also included balancing a wineglass on his head and diving from Brighton pier in evening dress.

FISHER, Max, in William Gerhardi's *Pending Heaven* (1930), has been identified by Philip Toynbee ('A Forgotten Talent Reclaimed', *Observer*, 21 January 1962), as the author's friend, Hugh Kingsmill (Hugh Kingsmill Lunn, 1889–1949), novelist, biographer and son of the pioneer London travel agent, Sir Henry Lunn.

FITZFASSENDEN, Alastair and Epifania, in George Bernard Shaw's *The Millionairess* (1935). John Roe suggests that Alastair's fighting style, and perhaps also the 'Fitz' element of his surname, is owed to Robert Fitzsimmons, a Cornishman who in 1897 relieved 'Gentleman Jim' Corbett of his world heavyweight title. Writing to the *Times Literary Supplement* (2 June 1978) from the British School in Rome, Roe cited Epifania's commendation of the power of her fiancé's solar-plexus punch. 'It was with this punch', wrote Roe, 'that Fitzsimmons knocked out Corbett, following the advice of his wife who called out from the ringside: "Hit him in the slats, Bob." That must have appealed to Shaw.' Epifania, say the Shaw biographers Margot Peters and Stanley Weintraub, is based on Beatrice Webb (see Bailey, Altiora). Like Epifania, she left a privileged, wealthy background to investigate and experience slum conditions in London's East End, and found a husband with, in Shaw's words, 'the sort of genius that she wanted'.

FITZGERALD, Burgo, in Anthony Trollope's *Can You Forgive Her?* (1864), has a suggested model in the poet, traveller, and diarist Wilfrid Scawen Blunt (1840–1922), a Byronic figure, notorious as a womaniser with a penchant for his cousins.

FITZPATRICK, Walt, in Jack Kerouac's *The Subterraneans* (1958), is Whit Burnett, founder-editor (with his wife, Martha Foley) of the American *Story* magazine (1931–53).

FLAM, Mr, in W.M. Thackeray's 'Mrs Perkins's Ball' (1847; *Christmas Books*, 1857), is supposedly Abraham Hayward

(1801–84), an influential English man of letters. Editor of *Law Magazine* from 1829 to 1844, he was also a noted London host and as a critic contributed to the *Edinburgh Review* a favourable notice of Thackeray's *Vanity Fair*, thus assisting its launching. He was persuaded to write the review only after much prodding by a Thackeray admirer who, to save the reluctant critic time, thoughtfully supplied short, selected passages for his attention. This did not, however, stop Hayward from later taking credit for 'discovering' Thackeray.

FLAMSON, Mr, in George Borrow's *The Romany Rye* (1857). This character owes his creation to a row – between Borrow and the politician, railway contractor and civil engineer Sir Samuel Morton Peto (1809–89), who is Flamson. In the 1840s, as the Borrow biographer Michael Collie records, Peto outraged the author by building a railway from Lowestoft to Reedham in Norfolk, bisecting Borrow's Oulton Hall estate. A Liberal MP, Peto was in 1854 awarded his baronetcy for building, without payment, the first military railway from Balaclava to Sebastopol. In addition to building railways in Canada and Australia, he was responsible for one of England's largest railway cuttings (on the Oxford–Birmingham line), and as a builder was involved in the erection of the new Houses of Parliament in London.

FLAVELL, in Malcolm Muggeridge's *In a Valley of this Restless Mind* (1938), is the poet, novelist and critic Gerald Bullett (1893–1958), as Muggeridge disclosed when the book was republished in 1978.

FLEISHER, Von Humboldt. See Humboldt.

FLEMING, Berenice, in Theodore Dreiser's *The Titan* (1914), is Emilie Busbey Grigsby, the mistress of Charles T. Yerkes (see Cowperwood, Frank Algernon), who installed her in a New York Park Avenue mansion and paid the rent for her London residence in Mayfair. She claimed to be the original of Milly Theale in Henry James's *The Wings of the Dove*, but was not: James did not meet her until after the novel's publication – 'before', he declared, 'I had ever heard of her apparently extremely silly existence.'

FLIGHTY, Mrs, in *1844, or The Power of the 'S.F.'*, written under a pseudonym by Thomas Dunn English (1819–1902). The Poe biographer Julian Symons identifies Mrs Flighty as the Massachusetts poet Frances Sargent Osgood (1811–50), who was the subject of extravagant praise by Edgar Allan Poe in 'The Literati', which ridiculed English.

FLIMNAP, in Jonathan Swift's *Gulliver's Travels* (1726), is supposedly Sir Robert Walpole (see Wild, Jonathan), although it is possible that Swift's target was not Walpole in particular but prime ministers in general.

FLINT, Rowley, in W. Somerset Maugham's *Up at the Villa* (1941). 'Of course he's a bad lot,' said the Princess San Ferdinando, 'but if I were thirty years younger and he asked me to run away with him I wouldn't hesitate for a moment even though he'd chuck me in a week and I'd be wretched for the rest of my life.' She was referring to Maugham's lover, Gerald Haxton (1892–1944), who is the model for Flint. He is also discerned by Maugham's biographer, Ted Morgan, in the character of the drunken, gambling husband of Mary Panton in this novel. Maugham and Haxton met while serving with the same ambulance unit in Flanders in the First World War. Haxton's deportation from England in 1919 as an undesirable alien prompted Maugham to live with him in exile, and they settled on the French Riviera. His practical value to the author was that of a good mixer and wideawake bar-fly who picked up real-life stories which Maugham used as a basis for his fiction. Haxton died in the alcoholics ward of a New York hospital.

FLINT, Solomon, in Samuel Foote's *The Maid of Bath* (1771), is Walter Long, of Whaddon, Wiltshire, a wealthy squire who in late middle-age was marked down by the father of Elizabeth Ann Linley (see Linnet, Kitty) as an advantageous match for his sixteen-year-old daughter. Long agreed to pay the girl's father £1,000 for the loss of his daughter's services, but she, in love with another, begged her fiancé to release her and for appearances' sake to take the blame. He agreed, and was promptly dunned by her father for another £2,000, his extrication from the situation already having cost him a further £1,000 in jewellery which he had given his betrothed. Foote's portrait was prompted by the public figure cut by the unhappy Long. There are several versions of this episode, those emanating from the Linley camp portraying Long as a lecherous villain. My account relies upon the one to be found in Kenelm Foss's *Here Lies Richard Brinsley Sheridan* (1939) which, for me, has the ring of truth.

FLORENCE, in Lord Byron's *Childe Harold's Pilgrimage* (1812–18), is Mrs Constance Spencer Smith, with whom the poet had an affair in Malta in 1809 – the year in which he began writing *Childe Harold*. Her father was Austrian ambassador in Constantinople, her husband British minister in Stuttgart. Three years Byron's senior, she claimed she had made an enemy of Napoleon, who suspected her of being involved in a conspiracy against him and twice caused her to flee from French-occupied territory. When the French occupied Venice, her escape was effected by a Sicilian nobleman, or so she told Byron, who thrilled to the romance of such high drama.

FLORESTAN, Prince, in Benjamin Disraeli's *Endymion* (1880), is Napoleon III – Charles Louis Napoleon Bonaparte (1808–73), Emperor of France when his country was Britain's ally in the Crimean War. He was taken prisoner in the Franco-Prussian War, spent a period in captivity in Germany, and was then exiled to England, where he died.

FLOSKY, Mr, in Thomas Love Peacock's *Nightmare Abbey* (1818), is part-inspired by Samuel Taylor Coleridge. See Skionar, Mr.

FLOSSIE, in Sidonie-Gabrielle Colette's *Claudine* novels (1900–3) and Liane de Pougy's *Idylle saphique* (1901). 'From a stranger who would like to cease being one to you', said the note accompanying the flowers sent to Liane de Pougy, the celebrated Paris courtesan. The sender followed her note with a visit, and before long Liane was exerting herself to earn 8,000 francs to enable the two of them to set up home together. Sighting Liane in her carriage, Natalie Clifford Barney (1877–1972), had decided to seduce her, to save her from her life of degradation, as she put it, at the hands of men. But as Natalie was still dependent on her father – a financier from Dayton, Ohio – the women's plan required Liane to work harder. Flossie was Liane's nickname for Natalie, and it is as Flossie (otherwise Emily Florence Temple Bradfford) that she appears in *Idylle saphique*, while in Colette's *Claudine* stories she is Miss Flossie, as her biographer George Wickes records. She had arrived in Paris in the 1890s, and her romance with Liane was neither her first nor her last, although their relationship continued for forty years, ending when Liane turned to religion. Meanwhile, Natalie had become a noted Paris hostess whose circle included Colette, Ezra Pound and Ford Madox Ford. She claimed to have had more than forty lovers. Among them were

Romaine Brooks (see Leigh, Olimpia) and the Duchesse de
Clermont-Tonnerre (see Clitoressa).

FLYTE, Lord Sebastian, in Evelyn Waugh's *Brideshead Revisited*
(1945). In the early 1920s Waugh was taken by an Oxford friend to
his family seat. That and subsequent visits can now be seen to have
sown the seed for *Brideshead*. A fellow undergraduate, Waugh's
friend was the Hon. Hugh Lygon (1904–36), second son of the
Seventh Earl Beauchamp. His home, which made a great impression
on Waugh, was Madresfield Court, Great Malvern, Worcestershire.
In creating Brideshead more than twenty years later, Waugh clearly
had the Lygons' seat in mind, though he may well have blended it
with subsequent memories of other stately homes. Certainly,
Brideshead's chapel is the chapel of Madresfield Court. And the
Lygon family? The earl's exile is reflected in *Brideshead* (see
Marchmain), and Sebastian Flyte, as Waugh admitted, was part-
inspired by Hugh – although the author's biographer Christopher
Sykes notes that he was the model only to a very limited extent. By
the time *Brideshead* appeared he had been dead for nearly a decade: on
a motoring holiday in Germany, he had fallen and fractured his skull
while getting out of his car. Flyte owed his circumstances and
something of his appearance to Lygon, says Sykes, but memories of
Alastair Graham (see Lennox, Hamish) were a stronger factor, on
Waugh's own testimony. In fact, as Sykes reveals, in the manuscript
of *Brideshead* the name Alastair occasionally occurs instead of
Sebastian.

FOEDORA, in Honoré de Balzac's *La Peau de chagrin* (1830–1).
'The total of the women who have had the impertinence to recognise
themselves as Foedora now stands at seventy-two', remarked Balzac
in a letter. He drew her, he said, 'from two women I have known.'
Beth Archer Brombert's *Cristina* (1978) suggests Princess Cristina
Belgiojoso (née Trivulzio, 1808–71) as one of the models. A champion of women's rights, she opposed the Austrian domination of
Italy and on being invited to Rome by Giuseppe Mazzini to run the
city's hospitals she recruited prostitutes, training them into excellent
nurses. Balzac doted upon her, as did Liszt and the German poet
Heinrich Heine.

FOGG, Phileas, in Jules Verne's *Around the World in Eighty Days*
(1873). In 1870 George Francis Train (1829–1904) of Boston became
the prototype for Phileas Fogg by travelling round the world in

eighty days . . . excluding a hiatus in a Lyons gaol when he became involved in the Communes: draped in the Tricolour, he challenged provisional government troops to fire on their nation's flag and was arrested. *En route*, he also raised Japanese eyebrows by bathing naked in a public bath. In 1860 he had pioneered the introduction of tramways in Britain; and in 1862–9 he built the first Pacific railway. He claimed to have been imprisoned in fifteen gaols without committing a crime, to have been declared a lunatic by six courts, and to have doubled his life-span through psychic-telepathy, describing himself as 'seventy-five years young'. The name of Verne's hero apparently derives from William Perry Fogg, of Cleveland, Ohio, author of *Around the World* (1872), an account of his comparatively leisurely 1869–71 journey from San Francisco to Japan and thence (via China, India and Egypt) to Europe for a year's sojourn, before returning home across the Atlantic.

FOIX, Prince de, in Marcel Proust's *A la recherche du temps perdu* (1913–27), is Prince Constantin Radziwill. See Guermantes, Gilbert, Prince de.

FOKER, Harry, in W.M. Thackeray's *The History of Pendennis* (1848–50), is Andrew Arcedeckne, a Norfolk landowner and member of the Fielding Club in London, to which Thackeray also belonged. Nicknamed 'Phoca', Arcedeckne was a cock- and prize-fighting enthusiast, small in stature and eccentric in dress. His all too obvious portrait (even the book's woodcut illustration was a good likeness) supposedly prompted the Travellers' Club to reject Thackeray's application to join in 1856, members intimating that they did not wish to appear in a subsequent novel.

FOLYAT, Serge, in Gilbert Cannan's *Round the Corner* (1913), is the author's uncle, Henry Charles Seppings Wright, son of the Revd Francis Hill Arbuthnot Wright, vicar of St Paul's, Paddington, Salford. Sent to sea at the age of thirteen, Wright was later a diamond prospector and a war artist, covering the Russo-Japanese war for the *Illustrated London News*.

FONTANE, Johnny, in Mario Puzo's *The Godfather* (1969). The subject of an FBI report on his alleged links with the Mafia, the American singer Frank Sinatra (1915–   ) successfully sued a British newspaper which suggested he might have mob connections similar to those of Johnny Fontane. 'The ubiquitously reported scene of

Sinatra bawling Puzo out in a Hollywood restaurant fuelled the sales-promoting conviction that here was a novel/film which spilled some interesting beans,' notes John Sutherland's *Best Sellers* (1981).

FORBES, Duncan, in D.H. Lawrence's *Lady Chatterley's Lover* (1928), is the Post-Impressionist artist Duncan Grant (1885–1978), according to the novelist David Garnett. A cousin of Lytton Strachey (see Plunkett, Matthew), Grant was the bisexual lover of Vanessa Bell (see Ambrose, Helen). Following the birth of their daughter, Angelica, he left Vanessa's bed for David Garnett, who subsequently married Angelica. Also discerned in Duncan Forbes are traits of Wyndham Lewis (see Lypiatt, Casimir) and the American poet Ezra Pound (1885–1972), promoter of the verse of T.S. Eliot, Robert Frost and Marianne Moore, and of the Vorticist movement in which Lewis was pre-eminent as a painter.

FORD, Josephine, in D.H. Lawrence's *Aaron's Rod* (1922), is Dorothy Yorke (see Carter, Bella), whom Lawrence came to know when he lodged in the home of Hilda Doolittle (see Masters, Miranda), since Yorke was living in Doolittle's attic. She subsequently departed with Doolittle's husband, thus – in more ways than one – leaving her flat.

FORELAND, Lord, in H. Russell Wakefield's 'A Black Solitude' (*The Best Ghost Stories of H. Russell Wakefield*, 1978), is Lord Northcliffe (see Tilbury, Lord). Wakefield was Northcliffe's personal private secretary from 1911 to 1914.

FORESTER, Sylvan, in Thomas Love Peacock's *Melincourt* (1817), is supposedly Percy Bysshe Shelley. See Glowry, Scythrop; see also Adrian.

FORNO, in Christopher Isherwood's *Lions and Shadows* (1938), is the conductor Sir John Barbirolli (1899–1970), who as a cellist in the early 1920s was a member of André Mangeot's International String Quartet (see Cheuret, Édouard).

FORSYTE, Old Jolyon, Irene and June, in John Galsworthy's *The Forsyte Saga* (1906–21). 'So many people have written and claimed that their families were the originals of the Forsytes', remarked Galsworthy in 1922, 'that one has been almost encouraged to believe in the typicality of that species.' Most of the models were rounded up in Dudley Barker's biography of Galsworthy (1963). Old Jolyon is the author's father, John Galsworthy (*d.* 1904), a London solicitor and company director with mining interests, whose assets upon his death were valued at £110,000. His wife left him when he was eighty-six, taking umbrage at the interest he was displaying in the governess of one of their grandchildren. Irene is primarily the author's wife, Ada Nemesis Cooper (1864–1956), the illegitimate child of an unknown father. Adopted by Dr Emanuel Cooper, who delivered her, she in 1891 married Galsworthy's cousin, Major Arthur Galsworthy of the Essex Yeomanry. She first met the author in 1895, in Paris. They became lovers, and to prompt John Galsworthy to take her away from her husband she related highly coloured stories of physical cruelty which she claimed the Major was inflicting upon her. These were the inspiration of Soames Forsyte's rape of Irene in *The Man of Property*, published in 1906, the year after John and Ada Galsworthy married, following the Major's institution of divorce proceedings in 1904. June is the author's musical sister, Mabel, whose protégées included the pianists Myra Hess and Harriet Cohen. In her youth she fell in love with the painter Georg Sauter (see Harz, Alois), but he married her sister, Lilian. In 1897 Mabel Galsworthy married an engineer, Thomas Blair Reynolds, living in the former Kensington home of the artist Holman Hunt. She published her *Memories of John Galsworthy* in 1936.

FORTH, Professor James, in Rhoda Broughton's *Belinda* (1883). Recognising himself as this mean and withered pedant, Mark Pattison (see Casaubon, Revd Edward) called on the author and had himself announced as 'Professor Forth'. Rhoda Broughton must have feared the worst for she had caricatured him as a cheeseparing, 'slovenly middle-aged figure' who upon marrying informs his young bride, 'The press of my occupations and the condition of my health forbid my indulging in many amusements and enjoyments enjoyed by other persons, but from which I shall be compelled to require you, as well as myself, to abstain,' After an inevitable coolness, however, their friendship survived the portrait. For an account of its background I recommend *Oxford Common Room* (1957) by V.H.H. Green . . . who was himself to become an original (see Smiley, George).

FORTINBRAS, General Flanco de, in George Bernard Shaw's *Geneva* (1938), is the Spanish ruler, General Franco – General Francisco Franco-Bahamonde (1892–1975).

FOSSILE, Dr, in John Gay's *Three Hours After Marriage* (1717), is Dr John Woodward (1665–1728), physician, geologist and Professor of Physics at Gresham College, London. In addition to amassing a notable collection of fossils, he devoted much time to being wrong at the top of his voice. Thus, he 'established' that Stonehenge was built by the Danes, supported the biblical account of the deluge, and claimed that smallpox could be cured by vomiting. His story is told in Joseph M. Levine's *Dr Woodward's Shield* (1977).

FOSTER, Miss, in Marcel Proust's *A la recherche du temps perdu* (1913–27). Though she became Duchess of Marlborough, it is as Proust's model for Miss Foster that Gladys Marie Deacon (1881–1977) will be remembered. She was the daughter of a Boston banker, Edward Parker Deacon, and she became a principal figure of the *belle époque* and the heiress to 500,000 francs left by her mother's lover. This benefactor, Émile Abeille, had been shot dead by her father in 1893 while attempting to jump from her mother's window. Proust – who first sighted her in 1906 ('I never saw a girl with such beauty, such magnificent intelligence, such goodness and charm') –. was involved in a scheme to marry her to Count Loche Radziwill. D'Annunzio, the Italian poet, was said to have been so bowled over by her beauty that he fainted, but she later became grotesque, the result of her indulgence in unnecessary and injudicious plastic surgery. In 1921, Gladys Deacon became the second wife of the Ninth Duke of Marlborough, with whom she had had a twenty-year affair.

FOTHERINGAY, Miss, in W.M. Thackeray's *The History of Pendennis* (1848–50), is the Irish tragic actress Eliza O'Neill (1791–1872), who was regarded in her day as the successor to Mrs Siddons (Sarah Siddons, 1755–1831). The daughter of the manager of an itinerant theatre company, she made her Covent Garden début in 1814. Five years later she married Mr (later Sir) William Becher.

FOTHERINGHAM, in Anthony Powell's *Afternoon Men* (1931), is revealed in the author's memoirs to have been part-inspired by Cecil A. ('Bobby') Roberts, an eccentric Old Wellingtonian whose success at talking himself into jobs was equalled by his aptitude for drinking himself out of them – his personal disciplines included an insistence upon hearing 'time' called every night in a public house, wherever he happened to be. A friend of Evelyn Waugh (see Blow, Christopher) and John Heygate (see Beaver, John), he worked briefly for the *London Mercury* and, in its infancy, for the BBC, subsequently becoming assistant manager at London's Sadler's Wells Theatre. After service in the Second World War as a squadron leader in public relations with the RAF Volunteer Reserve in India and Ceylon, he returned to theatre management in England, in the provinces.

FOTHERINGHAM, Mary, in *Cuthbert Learmont* (1910), by J.A. Revermort (J.A. Cramb), is the ubiquitous Lady Ottoline Morrell (see Roddice, Hermione). If originals were entitled to modelling fees, she would have made a fortune.

FOXE, Brian, in Aldous Huxley's *Eyeless in Gaza* (1936), is the author's brother, Trevenen Huxley, who in 1914 committed suicide at the age of twenty-four by hanging himself from a tree near the psychiatric nursing home where he had been receiving treatment following a nervous breakdown. An outstanding mathematician, he had not sustained his early promise, achieving only a Second in Greats at Oxford.

FOXE, Mrs, *idem*, according to Enid Huws Jones's *Mrs Humphry Ward* (1973), is the author's aunt, the novelist Mrs Humphry Ward (1851–1920), who cared for him when he was a child, following the death of his mother. Huxley's choice of name probably derives from his aunt's home in Cumbria, Fox Howe, Ambleside, which her grandfather, Dr Thomas Arnold (see Doctor, the), built in 1833.

FR——, in Charles Lamb's 'Christ's Hospital Five and Thirty Years Ago' (1820; *Essays of Elia*, 1823), is the Revd Frederick William Franklin (*d.* 1836), a Christ's Hospital contemporary of the author who went on to Pembroke College, Cambridge, and then became a teacher at the Blue Coat School, Hertford. Subsequently vicar of Albrighton, in Shropshire, he was chaplain to the county prison and attended John Thurtell (see Turtle, Tom) at his execution. In appreciation, Thurtell gave him his gold watch.

FR——, Mr John, in Henry Fielding's *Tom Jones* (1749), is John Freke (1688–1756), a surgeon and Fellow of the Royal Society whose public display of experiments with electricity excited much interest. He became involved in controversy with the physician and naturalist Sir William Watson, FRS (1715–87), over the nature of electricity.

FRANCIS, Ad, in Ernest Hemingway's 'The Battler' (*In Our Time*, 1925). Two of the author's prize-fighting acquaintances, 'Bat' Nelson and Ad Wolgast, are combined in Francis. 'Battling' Nelson (*b.* 1882) was of Danish extraction. Wolgast, born in Cadillac, Michigan, held the world lightweight title from 1910 to 1912, acquiring it by defeating Nelson with a technical knock-out after forty rounds. Committed to a mental hospital in 1927, Wolgast died in 1955, aged sixty-seven.

FRANÇOISE, in Marcel Proust's *A la recherche du temps perdu* (1913–27), is an amalgam of domestic servants including Céleste Albaret (*d.* 1984, aged ninety-two), a taxi-driver turned innkeeper's wife who was Proust's cook and housekeeper-secretary for eight years, attending him on his deathbed and publishing her reminiscences in 1976; Félicie Fitau, a Proust family retainer; and Ernestine Gallou, of Illiers, the cook in the author's childhood home.

FRANK, in Evelyn Waugh's 'Charles Ryder's Schooldays' (written 1945, published 1982), is W.B. Harris, housemaster of Gibbs House, Lancing College, during the author's school-days.

FRANKENSTEIN, Victor, in Mary Shelley's *Frankenstein* (1818). 'I passed the summer of 1816 in the environs of Geneva', the author recorded. 'The season was cold and rainy, and in the evenings we crowded around a blazing wood fire, and occasionally amused ourselves with some German stories of ghosts. These tales excited in us a playful desire for imitation. Two other friends and myself agreed to write each a story founded on some supernatural occurrence ... ' The 'two other friends', Byron and Shelley, failed to complete their stories. Mary Shelley persevered, and created in Victor Frankenstein a character having much in common, both in philosophy and in personality, with her husband, Percy Bysshe Shelley (see Glowry, Scythrop), who urged her to develop her tale into a longer story. Shelley's affinity with Frankenstein is explored by Christopher Small in *Ariel Like a Harpy* (1972). Another possible influence was Konrad Dippel (1673–1734), who spent his youth at Castle Frankenstein, near Darmstadt (where it stands to this day). According to Radu Florescu's *In Search of Frankenstein* (1975), Dippel enrolled at Giessen University as 'Franckensteina' and later became a noted alchemist, believing that the body was 'an inert substance animated by an errant spirit that could leave it at any time to infuse life into another.' Peter Haining's *The Man Who Was Frankenstein*

(1979) suggests a further source of inspiration: Andrew Crosse (1784–1855), a Brasenose-educated amateur scientist. At Fyne Court, Broomfield, his Somerset home, Crosse strung copper wire round the trees, using lightning to perform electrical experiments. Electro-crystallisation and metallurgy were his passions, and he became notorious when he announced the appearance of strange insects after he had passed electricity through a piece of volcanic rock. 'It is an attractive idea', wrote William St Clair, reviewing Haining's book in the *Sunday Telegraph*. 'Shelley and Mary were keenly interested in the latest electrical discoveries and read the works of Sir Humphry Davy. But the lecture they attended on December 28, 1814 (which is the critical link in Mr Haining's theory) was not delivered by Crosse, as he asserts, but by the French scientist Garnerin, so the theory collapses.'

FRANKL, Sam, in George S. Kaufman and Moss Hart's *Merrily We Roll Along* (1934), was taken to be a caricature of the American composer George Gershwin (1898–1937). Kaufman's biographer, Scott Meredith, records that a Broadway columnist wrote, 'Gershwin saw the play from the second row center ... and seemed, according to an eager observer, to be slightly embarrassed now and then.' Kaufman 'contented himself with a broad grin when asked if Sam Frankl was intended as a playful portrait of George Gershwin.' Not that Kaufman had anything to worry about: Frankl was presented as a highly talented popular composer and a genius at the keyboard.

FRANKS, Sir William, in D.H. Lawrence's *Aaron's Rod* (1922), is the English ship-owner Sir Walter Becker (1855–1927). In 1919 Lawrence was a guest at his villa near Turin, where Becker founded a maternity home and established a hospital for the British Expeditionary Force in Italy.

FREDERICK, Elsa, in Hilda Doolittle's *Bid Me to Live* (1960). Admitted by the author to be a *roman à clef*, this novel recalls the time D.H. Lawrence and his wife spent under Doolittle's roof in London in 1917. Doolittle's account has Elsa (Frieda Lawrence) encouraging Julia (Doolittle) to make love with Rico (Lawrence), thus leaving Elsa free for Vanio (Cecil Gray; see Sharpe, James). In real life, however, Gray became Doolittle's lover.

FREDERICK, Lady, in W. Somerset Maugham's *Lady Frederick* (1907). Had she been beautiful and sane she would have been one of the world's great wicked women, said Henry James of the model suggested by Maugham's biographer, Ted Morgan, for Lady Frederick. Mrs G.W. Steevens (née Christina Stewart) was the widow of a *Daily Mail* foreign correspondent killed at the siege of Ladysmith and a mistress of the Liberal statesman Sir Charles Dilke (see Grace). An energetic organiser of charitable ventures, she held court for writers and artists at her London home, Merton Abbey, near Clapham Common, and was suspected of setting fire to the house for insurance. To Henry James she intimated she had poisoned her first husband. It was at her home that Maugham first encountered Sue Jones (see Driffield, Rosie).

FREELAND, Frances, in John Galsworthy's *The Freelands* (1915), is Blanche Galsworthy. See Small, Mrs Septimus.

FREEMANTLE, Catherine. See Bendick, Catherine.

FRÉLON, in Voltaire's *L'Écossaise* (1760), is the critic Élie Catherine Fréron (1718–76), who attacked Voltaire on a number of occasions.

FRIEDA, in Franz Kafka's *The Castle* (written 1921–2, published 1926). Most of Kafka's writings contain a 'Felice' figure, symbolising Felice Bauer (see Bürstner, Fräulein). 'I cannot live with her and I cannot live without her', the author confessed. Here she is represented by Frieda – childish, vain and sad. If these were aspects of Felice, what was the attraction? The critic Rosemary Dinnage suggests that Felice was, in a sense, Kafka's own invention. Examining his love-letters (in *The World of Franz Kafka*, 1981) she concludes that Felice suffered greatly from Kafka's refusal to recognise her real self. He preferred the 'written-to, invented' Felice to whom he often penned two letters a day, becoming caught – says Dinnage – 'in the addict's vicious, masturbatory vortex'. Regarded in this way, all those letters were not really to Felice: they were written to and for Kafka himself.

FRIEND, the, in William Shakespeare's Sonnets nos. 33, 95, 135 and 136, has a suggested original in William Hatcliffe (1568–?1631). The son of a Lincolnshire landowner, he graduated from Jesus College, Cambridge, and as a young lawyer was in 1587 elected

Prince of Purpoole for the Christmas festivities of London's Inns of Court. This, Leslie Hotson argues in *Mr W.H.* (1964), explains Shakespeare's reference to the Friend as a sovereign. Hatcliffe (also spelt Hatliffe) subsequently squandered his family fortune and lapsed into obscurity.

FRIETCHIE, Barbara, in John Greenleaf Whittier's 'Barbara Frietchie' (*In War Time and Other Poems*, 1864). A friend told Whittier the story which inspired this poem, in which Barbara Frietchie is portrayed bravely brandishing a Union flag in the face of Confederate troops. It was not long before residents of Frederick, Maryland — the poem's setting — let it be known that the poet had named the wrong woman, the flag-waver, they claimed, being Barbara Frietchie's neighbour, Mrs May Quantrell. Union troops had promptly broken the staff of her flag, and when she acquired a replacement the soldiers' leader, General Ambrose Powell Hill, had ordered them to allow her to keep it. Whittier prefaced later print-ings of the poem with an acknowledgement that conflicting versions of the Frederick incident had been brought to his attention. Loth to accept that he had named the wrong woman, he implied that there might have been two flag-wavers — 'it is possible', he wrote, 'that there has been a blending of the two incidents.'

FROST, Jerry, in F. Scott Fitzgerald's *The Vegetable* (1923), has as prototype Warren Harding (1865–1923), a small-town news-paperman who became a senator and was President of the United States from 1921 to 1923. Frost 'puts his cronies in key posts, as Harding did', notes the Fitzgerald biographer, André Le Vot. Becoming known as 'the Ohio gang', Harding's corrupt friends discredited his administration.

FRUIT-NORTON, Elliot, in Howard Brenton and David Hare's *Pravda: A Fleet Street comedy* (1985). 'As at a university revue, the audience is distracted by allusion-spotting', remarked Michael Davie, reviewing this play for the *Times Literary Supplement*. 'The *Tide* must be the *Sun*; *Victory* must be *The Times*. The pompous deposed "Fruit-Norton" must be Sir William Rees-Mogg and the northern editor come south must be Mr Harold Evans and "Cliveden Whicker-Basket" must be Mr Charles Douglas-Home, the present editor of *The Times*. (Apart from the way his trousers hang round his ankles, Le Roux alone bears no resemblance to any living Fleet Street figure, such as Mr Rupert Murdoch.)' Certainly, there are career similarities between the bookish Rees-Mogg (see Lloyd-James, Somerset) and Fruit-Norton, a connoisseur of Addison and Steele who after editing *Victory* becomes chairman of the National Greyhound Racetrack Inspection Board, just as Rees-Mogg took public office (as chairman of the Arts Council of Great Britain) on leaving the editorship of *The Times*. But then, this is a play in which coincidences abound. Lambert Le Roux is a South African who owns a down-market British tabloid and takes over the nation's most prestigious but ailing national daily, just as Murdoch, an Australian, added *The Times* to his stable after acquiring *The Sun*.

FULLER, Franny, in Doris Grumbach's *The Missing Person* (1981), has as prototype Marilyn Monroe. See Maggie.

FURBER, Cedric, in Wyndham Lewis's *The Vulgar Streak* (1941), is part-inspired by Douglas Duncan (1902–68), a Michigan-born graduate of Toronto University who after residing in Paris in the 1920s established the Picture Loan Society, whose clients rented paintings by the month, purchasing if they wished. The homosexual son of the president of Provincial Paper Ltd, he was formerly a craftsman bookbinder.

FURBER, Cedric, in Wyndham Lewis's *Self-Condemned* (1954), is Lytton Strachey. See Plunkett, Matthew.

FURIOUS, Doll, in Djuna Barnes's *The Ladies' Almanack* (1928), is Dorothy ('Dolly') Wilde, the drug-addicted, lesbian niece of Oscar Wilde (see Amarinth, Esme) and a Paris contemporary of the author. Her affair with Natalie Barney (see Flossie) twice drove her to attempt suicide.

G

G, in Edmund Wilson's *Europe without Baedeker* (1947). Had she said 'Yes', Wilson would have married Mamaine Paget, the G of this travel book. But she rejected him, in favour of Arthur Koestler (see Scriassine, Victor). Living with Koestler for six years before they married in 1950, she put up with his infidelity, violence and drinking, and shared his crusades and enthusiasms. They separated in 1951, but remained friends, seeing each other frequently until her death in 1954 at the age of thirty-seven — she had long been plagued by bronchial asthma. Eighteen months earlier, she declared in a letter (collected in *Living with Koestler*, 1985), 'I shall consider my life has been well spent since I have spent years of it with K . . . I would do anything, even leave him if it were necessary, to help him fulfil what I consider to be his destiny. I should count myself and my life of little importance in such a case.'

GABLER, Hedda, in Henrik Ibsen's *Hedda Gabler* (1890). It was in 1889 that Ibsen met Emilie Bardach (1873–1955), the model for Hedda Gabler. He was in Gossensass, at a reception in his honour to mark the naming of the Tyrolean town's Ibsenplatz; also present was Emilie — Viennese, eighteen, elegant, and bored. Ibsen later alleged that she shocked him with her declared readiness to purloin other women's husbands. Although he was sixty-one, he became infatuated with her, calling her 'the May-day of my September life'. Her diary — published in 1923 — shows that she was not unaffected by him: 'The obstacles! How they grow more numerous, the more I think of them! The difference of age! His wife! His son! All that there is to keep us apart! Did this have to happen?' After several months' correspondence, however, Ibsen asked her not to write again — 'When conditions have changed, I will let you know.' On his seventieth birthday, she sent him a congratulatory telegram, to which he replied, 'The summer in Gossensass was the happiest, the

most beautiful in my whole life.' She died, unmarried, in Switzerland, the authorities allowing her to remain there, on account of her
age and poor health, when the Nazi regime summoned her to Vienna
to investigate her Jewish birth.

GALANT, Cyrille, in Pierre Drieu la Rochelle's *Gilles* (1939), is
part-inspired by the French Communist poet and novelist Louis
Aragon (1897–1982), whose friendship with André Breton (see
Caël) ended in 1930 with a political row. Aragon was a lover of
Nancy Cunard (see Storm, Iris). When she left him for a black jazz
pianist, he attempted suicide. Seven weeks later he met Elsa Triolet
(see Elsa).

GALAS, Maria Magdalena, in Charles Ludlam's *Galas* (1983).
'The characters in the play are real. Only their names have been
changed to protect the playwright', announced a programme note
for this camp life of Maria Callas (1923–77), who confides to the
audience, 'What I really wanted to be was a dentist.'

GALE, Martin, in Peter Jenkins's *Illuminations* (1980). Although he
was much respected as a Labour minister, the English statesman
Anthony Crosland (1918–77) was almost pathologically sensitive to
Press criticism, as the Lobby correspondent turned theatre critic,
James Fenton, recalled on reviewing this play in the *Sunday Times* (16
November 1980). Crosland, he said, was 'obviously the original for
Martin Gale'. This was not disputed.

GALL, Alice, in D.H. Lawrence's *The White Peacock* (1911).
Outraged by the portrayal of his wife as Alice Gall, the model's
husband threatened to sue. Alice Beatrice Holdich (née Hall) was the
original. She had been a pupil-teacher with the author in Eastwood,
Nottinghamshire, in the early 1900s. If the couple felt their chapel-
going image had been impugned, Lawrence told them, he would
contrive in the novel's next impression to have the character's name
changed to Margaret Undine Widmerpuddle or any other fantasy of
their choice. It did not come to that . . . but if it had, Anthony Powell
might have felt it necessary to choose a different name for the
character Widmerpool in his *Music of Time* sequence. Powell took
Widmerpool, he tells me, from Hutchinson's Memoirs of the Civil
War — 'it was a Nottinghamshire family, and a village exists of the
same name, which was of course why Lawrence knew it.'

GALLEON, Henry, in Hugh Walpole's *Fortitude* (1913), is Henry James (see Boon, George), who befriended Walpole when he began his literary career.

GAMIAMI, Comtesse, in *Gamiami ou Deux nuits d'excès* (1833—5), by 'Alcide de M——' (supposedly Alfred de Musset), is believed by Francis Steegmuller — editor of Flaubert's letters — to be George Sand (see Maupin, Camille) as portrayed by her ex-lover.

GAMMA, the Slave of History, in Czesław Miłosz's *The Captive Mind* (1953), is Jerzy Putrament, Polish statesman, ambassador, and editor of *Literaturea*; he was a contemporary of the author at Vilnyus University. Reporting from Warsaw on the author's return to Poland in 1981, after thirty years' exile, W.L. Webb noted in the *Guardian* that this 'subtle but ferocious portrait of the still powerful Communist Party figure' spans his time from '"an ungainly, red-faced boy, coarse and boisterous" and violently anti-semitic, to Putrament's latter days as a brilliant ambassador and literary law giver of post-war Poland.'

GANDISH, Professor, in W.M. Thackeray's *The Newcomes* (1853—5), has a possible prototype in the English portrait painter Henry Sass (1788—1844), whose Bloomsbury drawing academy was the first of its kind in England. His pupils included Millais and Frith.

GANT, Ben; Eliza; Helen; Oliver and Steve, in Thomas Wolfe's *Look Homeward, Angel* (1929), are respectively the author's elder brother, Ben (*d.* 1918), a member of the circulation staff of a North Carolina newspaper; his mother, Julia (née Westall, *b.* 1860), a school teacher in Asheville, North Carolina; his sister, Mabel (Mrs Ralph Wheaton), ten years his senior; his father, William Oliver (1851—1922), an Asheville monumental mason; and his eldest, ne'er do well, brother, Frank. Wolfe's biographer, Andrew Turnbull, makes the identifications.

GARDEN, Irwin, in Jack Kerouac's *Visions of Cody* (1960), *Book of Dreams* (1961), *Big Sur* (1962), *Desolation Angels* (1966) and *Vanity of Dulouz* (1968), is the American poet and pioneer of overt homosexuality, Allen Ginsberg (1926—   ). In 1945 he was suspended by Columbia University for sharing his room overnight with Kerouac, whom he described as 'the new Buddha of American prose'. Oddly, while Kerouac seems to have put into his books just about everyone he knew, there was no rush to put *him* in a novel. Perhaps this was because his circle was not strong in novelists, William Burroughs excepted. Or because his Beat Generation image was somewhat larger than life . . . shortly before his death, at forty-seven, he saw a girl on a beach reading his *On the Road*. He went up to her, saying he was Jack Kerouac. She called the police and had him arrested.

GARTH, Caleb, in George Eliot's *Middlemarch* (1872). For Caleb, work is a kind of religion . . . just as it was for Eliot's father, Robert Evans (see Bede, Adam), who is Caleb's original.

GASHFORD, Mr, in Charles Dickens's *Barnaby Rudge* (1841). Just as the Lord George Gordon of this novel is clearly intended to resemble the Lord George Gordon of the anti-popery riots in London in 1780, so is Gashford, the peer's secretary, believed to be based on Robert Watson (1746–1838), secretary to the real-life Lord George Gordon during the riots. Like Gashford, he committed suicide at an inn.

GATSBY, Jay, in F. Scott Fitzgerald's *The Great Gatsby* (1925). The author said that Gatsby began as a man he knew and then became himself. The initial inspiration is believed to have been Max Gerlach, a bootlegger and a Long Island neighbour of Fitzgerald. Seeking further background, Fitzgerald enlisted the help of George Jean Nathan (see Noble, Maury), and he is known also to have studied the career of Edward M. Fuller, of Great Neck, Long Island. From obscure beginnings, Fuller appeared on Wall Street in 1916 as a member of the Consolidated Stock Exchange, heading his own New York brokerage company. From his Great Neck estate he commuted weekly by air to Atlantic City during the horse-racing season. A bachelor socialite, he served a twelve-month sentence in Sing Sing prison after his firm became bankrupt in 1922 in circumstances suggesting corruption in high places – the president of the CSE was implicated in one of Fuller's trials for fraud.

GAUTIER, Marguerite, in *La Dame aux camélias* (1848), by Alexandre Dumas *fils*, is Marie Duplessis (née Rose-Alphonsine Plessis, 1824–47), daughter of an alcoholic Normandy tinker. Losing her innocence as a child to a farm labourer, and subsequently taken up by an elderly man who abandoned her in Paris, she worked as a corset maker before walking the streets and becoming a celebrated courtesan. Seven young admirers proposed forming themselves into a syndicate to share her, one for each day of the week; Liszt (see Conti, Gennaro) was among her lovers; and an elderly count, struck by her resemblance to his deceased daughter, paid her to forsake prostitution, but she soon returned to her old life. Dumas adored her, persuading her to live with him in the country to improve her health (she was consumptive). Their parting was bitter; he was neither rich enough to keep nor poor enough to be kept, he declared. Returning to Paris, she suffered a further deterioration in her health and died at the age of twenty-three.

GAY, Lucian, in Benjamin Disraeli's *Coningsby* (1844). This character's name sign-posts the original: the joker Theodore Hook. See Wagg, Mr.

GAY, M.H.L., in C.P. Snow's *The Light and the Dark* (1947), *The Masters* (1951), and *The Affair* (1960), is Professor John Holland Rose (1855—1942), Professor of Naval History at Cambridge from 1919 to 1933, and Fellow of Christ's College, Cambridge.

GAZAY, Cléo, in Compton Mackenzie's *Extraordinary Women* (1928), is the pianist Renata Borgatti, daughter of the Wagnerian tenor Giuseppe Borgatti and, according to Meryle Secrest's biography of Romaine Brooks (1976), a member of a lesbian clique on the island of Capri in the 1920s.

GEE, Cameron, in D.H. Lawrence's 'Two Blue Birds' (1927; *The Woman Who Rode Away*, 1928). Did Lawrence's model for this self-satisfied, narcissistic writer really fail to recognise himself? His wife identified him instantly, and Lawrence's biographers are agreed that Cameron Gee is Compton Mackenzie (see Cathcart, Mr). But Mackenzie, self-protectively perhaps, would have none of it. In vain did Faith, his wife, write of how she had talked with Lawrence, 'warmed by Capri wine, and his sensitive understanding and the glow of kindness in his deep eyes. To me that night he seemed an angel, and I gave him some of the secrets of my heart which hitherto had never been let loose.' The outcome, she recorded, was this story which 'he could not have written if I had not dined with him that night in Capri. A malicious caricature of Monty, and a monstrous perversion of facts, yet the source of it is clearly recognisable.' Mackenzie blandly refused to believe it. 'When Faith was upset by this story', he noted in his memoirs, 'I thought she was imagining a grievance, for I could not see in it the faintest resemblance to her or to me and as there was no resemblance to our background, which, as I told Faith, there certainly would have been if Lawrence had been writing about her and me, I urged her to give up worrying.' Cameron Gee's reaction would surely have been much the same.

GEHAZI, in Rudyard Kipling's 'Gehazi' (*The Years Between*, 1919). 'Sticky fingers!' cried his opponents in the House of Commons. But this did not hinder the career of Rufus Isaacs, First Marquess of Reading (1860—1935). If anything, those allegations of corruption assisted him, for when the position of Lord Chief Justice became vacant, Isaacs, as one of the most able lawyers of his day, was not only a natural choice: the appointment of anyone else would have been seen as an admission of guilt on the part of an already embarrassed government. Questionable dealings in Marconi shares were the source of that embarrassment. As Attorney General, Isaacs had investigated the Marconi scandal which involved government contracts and with which, it transpired, he was himself associated as a speculator. So when Isaacs's appointment as Lord Chief Justice was announced, Kipling attacked him as Gehazi. Describing him as a leper, the poem was circulated privately until Kipling felt it safe to publish, four years later. Isaacs went on to become Viceroy of India, a country he had last visited as a ship's boy in an earlier, less publicised career. The son of a fruit merchant, he left school at fourteen, became a deckhand, jumped ship in Rio, and on being caught was set to work with a team of Negro stokers. He subsequently entered the Stock Exchange, lying about his age in the process and becoming noted for his ability to applaud music-hall turns by standing on his head and clapping with his feet. Hammered from the Exchange at twenty-five, he at last turned to the law, becoming arguably the only Lord Chief Justice to have had his nose broken by a prize-fighter, a legacy of his seafaring days. He presided at the trial of Sir Roger Casement (see Roxton, Lord John), and his second wife founded the WVS.

GELLATLEY, Davie, in Sir Walter Scott's *Waverley* (1814), is supposedly 'Daft' Jock Gray (?1776—1837), the son of an Ettrick (Borders) weaver turned itinerant pedlar. He accompanied his father on his travels and outlived him by only a few months, dying at Selkirk. Both were addicted to lay preaching.

GELLYBORE-FRINTON, Victoria. See Chilleywater, Mrs Harold.

GEORGE, in Jerome K. Jerome's *Three Men in a Boat* (1889) and *Three Men on the Bummel* (1900), is George Wingrave (*d*. 1941, aged seventy-nine), a bank clerk who subsequently became manager of Barclay's Bank, 366 The Strand, London. He died in Hertfordshire, at Cheshunt Cottage Hospital. Sharing lodgings with Jerome, he and the author first met Carl Hentschel (see Harris) at a theatre. The three subsequently spent weekends together on the River Thames.

GEORGIANA and MR GEORGIANA, in Roy Campbell's *The Georgiad* (1933). 'Fancy being cuckolded by a woman!' chortled the writer C.S. Lewis on hearing from Campbell that his wife had been seduced by Victoria Sackville-West. As Campbell's biographer Peter Alexander records, *The Georgiad* was the poet's revenge, portraying Sackville-West and her husband, Harold Nicolson (see Chilleywater, the Hon. Harold and Mrs), as Georgiana and Mr Georgiana.

GERARD, in Marcus Clarke's 'Holiday Peak or Mount Might-ha-been' (1873), is Gerard Manley Hopkins (see Manley, Gerontius). Clarke and Hopkins first met as children, in 1855, and the two became school-fellows at Highgate School, London. After emigrating to Australia, Clarke was unaware that Hopkins had become a poet, imagining him instead to be an artist.

GERARD, Brigadier Étienne, in Sir Arthur Conan Doyle's *The Exploits of Brigadier Gerard* (1896). In 1892, Doyle read the memoirs of an absurdly egotistical French general whose book revealed him to be as blunderingly naive as he was courageous. Their author — records Doyle's biographer, Charles Higham — was Lieutenant-General Jean Baptiste Antoine Marcelin, Baron de Marbot (1782—1854). A ready-made Gerard, he was a veteran of France's war with Prussia and Russia (1806—7), in which he was aide-de-camp to Marshal Augerau; the Peninsular War (1808—14), in which he served under Marshals Lannes and Masséna; the Russian and German campaigns of 1812 and 1813 respectively; the battle of Waterloo (1815), in which he was wounded; and the siege of Antwerp (1832). 'I am an excellent soldier', he declared. 'I do not say so because I am prejudiced in my own favour, but because I really am so.'

GERETH, Mrs, in Henry James's *The Spoils of Poynton* (1897), is Mrs Frederic Morrell, mother-in-law of Lady Ottoline Morrell (see Roddice, Hermione), suggests Ottoline's biographer, Sandra Jobson Darroch.

GERRETT, in Sinclair Lewis and Dore Schary's *Storm in the West* (written 1943, published 1963), is Hermann Goering (1893–1946), creator and commander of Nazi Germany's Luftwaffe. Sentenced to death at the Nuremberg war-crimes' trials, he committed suicide.

GERTRUDE, Sister, in Muriel Spark's *The Abbess of Crewe* (1974). The guttural Gertrude, who restores the discredited reputation of her Order through her global missionary efforts, is the Kissinger figure in this satire on the Watergate scandal. Henry Kissinger (1923–   ) was the United States Secretary of State from 1973 to 1977.

GETLIFFE, Francis, in C.P. Snow's *The Light and the Dark* (1947), *The Masters* (1951), *The New Men* (1954), *The Conscience of the Rich* (1958), *The Affair* (1960), *Corridors of Power* (1964), *The Sleep of Reason* (1968) and *Last Things* (1970), owes his personality to Professor Frank Philip Bowden (1903–68), Professor of Surface Physics at Cambridge from 1966 to 1968, and a Fellow of Caius College, Cambridge. From 1958 to 1968 he was a director of the English Electric Company. Externally, Francis Getliffe is inspired by Baron Blackett (Patrick Blackett, 1897–1974), who won the Nobel prize for physics in 1948 and was Professor of Physics at the Imperial College of Science and Technology from 1953 to 1965, and president of the Royal Society from 1965 to 1970.

GETLIFFE, Herbert, in C.P. Snow's *George Passant* (originally published as *Strangers and Brothers*, 1940), is Sir Eric Rideal (1890–1974), Professor of Colloid Science at Cambridge from 1930 to 1946, and Professor of Physical Chemistry at King's College, London, from 1950 to 1955.

GÉVRESIN, Abbé, in J-K Huysmans's *En route* (1895), is supposedly an amalgam of Joseph-Antoine Boullan (see Johannès, Dr) and Abbé Arthur Mugnier (1853–1944), a Benedictine priest in Paris who influenced many writers of his day and in 1891 became Huysmans's spiritual adviser.

GIBBONS, Jasper, in W. Somerset Maugham's *Cakes and Ale* (1930), is identified by Robert Lorin Calder in *W. Somerset Maugham and the Quest for Freedom* (1972) as Stephen Phillips (1868–1915), a poet who was taken up by Lady Colvin (see Trafford, Mrs Barton) but lost his swiftly gained reputation as rapidly as he had acquired it.

GIBSON, Mr, in Elizabeth Gaskell's *Wives and Daughters* (1864–6), is inspired partly by the author's husband, the Revd William Gaskell (1805–84), a Unitarian who was minister at Cross Street Chapel, Manchester, for fifty-six years; and partly by the author's father, William Stevenson (1772–1829), a native of Berwick-on-Tweed who became a Unitarian preacher in Failsworth, Manchester. He was subsequently classics master at Manchester Academy; an Edinburgh-based freelance journalist; editor of the *Scots Magazine*; a prolific author; and, from 1806 until his death, Keeper of Records at the Treasury in London. Gaskell's uncle, Dr Peter Holland (1766–1855), a Knutsford surgeon, is also a suggested model for Gibson.

GIBSON, Mrs, *idem*, owes some of her disagreeable characteristics to the author's stepmother, Catherine Stevenson (née Thomson), sister of the Chelsea physician responsible for Elizabeth Gaskell's delivery. She became the second wife of the author's father in 1814.

GIGI, in Sidonie-Gabrielle Colette's *Gigi* (1944), according to the Colette biographer Yvonne Mitchell, has as prototype Yola Henriques, who as a girl fell in love with the fifty-year-old editor of *Le Journal*. Colette first met her in 1926.

GILBEY, Lord, in C.P. Snow's *Corridors of Power* (1964). 'He has some faint resemblances to Lord Alexander, one of our greatest military commanders', said Gilbey's creator, referring to Field Marshal Earl Alexander of Tunis (1891–1969). 'He was hopeless in this place' (the Ministry of Defence), Snow told his oral biographer, John Halperin. 'He was a good general and a very nice man, but in fact he was a friend of Winston's who persuaded him much against his will to appoint him Minister of Defence. He wasn't very effective.' On my own meeting with Alexander, in 1958, I received the impression of a cautious man slightly out of touch with the mundane realities of life: on a liner about to depart for Canada he was wearing both belt and braces, and as our interview drew to a close he asked me to post a letter for him, giving me twopence-halfpenny for the stamp ... which for several months had cost threepence.

GILDA, in Noël Coward's *Design for Living* (1933). Gilda's professional aspect, if nothing else, must surely have been suggested by Syrie Maugham (see Middleton, Constance), like Gilda an attractive, intelligent, successful and expensive interior decorator. Syrie was Coward's friend and furnished his home, Goldenhurst Farm, Aldington, Kent. One could test the intelligence of one's friends, he remarked, by seeing if they had noted that Syrie was much brighter than her husband, Willie. And long after the white décor she pioneered had ceased to be fashionable and others had turned to less clinical colours, Coward continued to endure a white-walled monotony out of loyalty to Syrie.

GILPIN, John, in William Cowper's *The Diverting History of John Gilpin* (1782), is supposedly William Beyer (1693−1791), a London linen-draper in business at the junction of Cheapside and Paternoster Row. His story was told to Cowper by the poet's neighbour at Olney, Buckinghamshire, Lady Austen.

GILPIN, Commander Peter and Lady Maureen, in Noël Coward's 'Hands Across the Sea' (*Tonight at 8.30*, 1935). Two of Coward's closest friends are portrayed here: Earl Mountbatten of Burma (1900−79) and Lady Mountbatten (see Prynne, Amanda). It was a conversation with Mountbatten, who had just lost his ship in enemy action, that gave Coward the idea for his wartime film *In Which We Serve*. Becoming Supreme Allied Commander, South East Asia, Mountbatten survived the war ... only to be killed by a bomb planted by Irish terrorists on his boat at his holiday residence in County Sligo.

GIRI, in Bertolt Brecht's *The Resistible Rise of Arturo Ui* (written 1941, first performed 1958), is Hermann Goering (see Gerrett), presented as a cross between a dandyish clown and a mafia-style hit man, as Ronald Hayman remarks in *Brecht: a biography* (1984), which explores the background of the play.

GIROUETTE, Miss Emily, in Thomas Love Peacock's *Nightmare Abbey* (1818), is supposedly Harriet Grove, cousin of the poet Percy Bysshe Shelley (see Glowry, Scythrop), who was much attached to her. She rejected him because of his heterodoxies ... or because she preferred another, for she was not slow to switch her affections: hence, perhaps, Peacock's choice of the name 'Girouette' – weathercock.

GIVOLA, in Bertolt Brecht's *The Resistible Rise of Arturo Ui* (written 1941, first performed 1958), is Joseph Goebbels (see Gribbles). Just as Goebbels edited Hindenburg's last thoughts on Hitler, so does Givola revise the will of Dogsborough (Hindenburg) and its indictment of Ui (Hitler).

GLAYDE, in Hugh Kingsmill's 'The End of the World' (*The Dawn's Delay*, 1924), is identified by the author's biographer, Michael Holroyd, as the novelist Alec Waugh (1898–1981), brother of Evelyn Waugh (see Blow, Christopher).

GLEGG, Aunt. See Dodson, the Misses.

GLENARVON, Lord, in Lady Caroline Lamb's *Glenarvon* (1816; republished as *The Fatal Passion*, 1865), is Lord Byron (see Cadurcis, Lord). The author was Byron's lover until 1813, when he left her. Eleven years later she accidentally encountered his funeral procession, and the experience permanently deranged her mind. She survived him by four years.

GLENDINNING, Mrs, in Herman Melville's *Pierre* (1852), is the author's mother, Maria Melville (née Gansevoort, *d.* 1871).

GLENN, Julia, in George S. Kaufman and Moss Hart's *Merrily We Roll Along* (1934), is largely modelled upon the American writer and waspish wit, Dorothy Parker (1893–1967), whose preference for men somewhat younger than herself is mirrored in Julia. Asked why she had not troubled to see the play, she replied: 'I've been too fucking busy and vice versa.'

GLIGORIC, Yuri, in Jack Kerouac's *The Dharma Bums* (1958), is the American 'Beat Generation' poet, Gregory Corso (1930–   ).

GLORIANI, in Henry James's *Roderick Hudson* (1876). The author's biographer, Leon Edel, suggests that Gloriani is based on William Wetmore Story (1819–95), an American lawyer who became a fashionable sculptor and poet and was living in Rome in considerable splendour when James first met him in the early 1870s, later writing Story's biography. Nathaniel Hawthorne was much impressed by his statue 'Cleopatra' and refers to it in *The Marble Faun*, in which Story's workplace becomes Kenyon's studio.

GLOWRY, Scythrop, in Thomas Love Peacock's *Nightmare Abbey* (1818), has been taken to be the poet Percy Bysshe Shelley (1792–1822), who as a young man was a noted disciple of free love. Peacock later recorded that Shelley 'took to himself the character of Scythrop', but if this was in fact intended as a portrait of the poet and his two loves (one of whom was drowned in 1816), then it was in dubious taste ... and Peacock was fastidious in such matters.

G—— M——, Mme, in Archibald MacLeish's 'Sketch for a Portrait of Mme G—— M——' (*Streets in the Moon*, 1926), is Mrs Gerald Murphy. See Diver, Dick and Nicole.

GOLD, Jeremy, in Desmond Briggs's *The Partners* (1982). 'The character of Jeremy Gold is obviously me', said the publisher and novelist Anthony Blond, complaining that he had been presented as 'some sort of over-sexed monster – I would never have done some of those things.' But then, as Godfrey Smith remarked in the *Sunday Times*, 'Anthony is one of those rare souls who is so much larger than life that he verges on the fictional.' The novel stems from Blond's publishing partnership with the author – 'Anthony is part of the Gold character,' Briggs admitted, 'but not all of it.'

GOLDBOOK, Alvah, in Jack Kerouac's *The Dharma Bums* (1958). If all the Kerouac characters based on Allen Ginsberg were laid end to end, they'd doubtless enjoy it. This is one of them. See Garden, Irwin.

GOLDFINGER, Auric, in Ian Fleming's *Goldfinger* (1959). A large man said to display all the concentrated power and dignity of a Roman emperor, Charles W. Engelhard (1917–71) was in 1965 suggested by *Forbes*, the American financial magazine, to be the inspiration for Goldfinger. This American financier was reputed to have come as near to controlling the world's gold industry as any one man could. He was chairman of Engelhard Minerals and Chemicals Corporation, was described as 'a walking conglomerate', and had a string of more than fifty racehorses under five different trainers in England and Ireland, including Nijinsky, the 1970 winner of the

Derby, the St Leger, the 2000 Guineas and the Irish Derby. Engel-hard represented President Lyndon Johnson at Pope Paul's coronation ... and, yes, he admitted to having met Fleming. Making a joke of his identification with Goldfinger, he claimed to have a stewardess on his private plane called Pussy Galore.

GOLDSTEIN, Emmanuel, in George Orwell's *Nineteen Eighty-Four* (1949), is said by the author's biographer, Bernard Crick, to be part-inspired by Andres Nin, leader of Spain's POUM (United Marxist Workers' Party), which rivalled the Communist Party. He was expelled from the Spanish government in 1936, and subsequently became a martyr to his cause, when he was kidnapped and murdered by Russian agents.

GOLZ, General, in Ernest Hemingway's *For Whom the Bell Tolls* (1940), is Karol Swierczewski, a Pole who commanded the Four-teenth International Brigade in the Spanish Civil War. A native of Warsaw, he had served in the Red Army and had been on the staff of Frunze Military Academy at the start of the Spanish conflict. He was assassinated in 1947.

GOMBAULD, in Aldous Huxley's *Crome Yellow* (1921), is believed to be based on Mark Gertler (see Loerke), one of Huxley's fellow guests at Garsington Manor, the setting for this novel (see also Roddice, Hermione).

GOOD, Captain John, in H. Rider Haggard's *King Solomon's Mines* (1885), is supposedly an amalgam of the author's lifelong friend, Sir Frederick Jackson (1860–1929), brother of Mary Eliza-beth Archer (see Ayesha); and the author's brother, John G. Haggard (*d.* 1908). The author was indebted to both for background infor-mation, anecdotes and technical detail from their experiences in Africa. Jackson led a British expedition to Uganda in 1889, was Lieutenant-Governor of the East Africa Protectorate from 1907 to 1911, and was Governor and Commander-in-Chief, Uganda, from 1911 to 1917. John Haggard was vice-consul at Lamu, East Africa.

GOODENOUGH, Dr, in W.M. Thackeray's *The History of Pen-dennis* (1848–50), is the book's dedicatee, Dr John Elliotson (1791–1868). Attending Thackeray while *Pendennis* was being written, he refused to take a fee. The actor William Charles Macready was also among his patients. An interest in mesmerism –

he held seances, established a mesmeric hospital and founded a magazine, *The Zoist* — caused him to resign a London University professorship and his appointment as physician to University College hospital. He was president of the Phrenological Society, a Fellow of the Royal Society and of the Royal College of Physicians, a pioneer advocate of the use of the stethoscope, and the author of *Surgical Operations in the Mesmeric State without Pain* (1843).

GOODLEY, Lady Septuagesima, in Osbert Sitwell's *Triple Fugue* (1924). So tall that she seemed like 'an animated public monument', Lady Septuagesima had 'an almost masculine face', an absurd voice blending 'the peaceful lowing of cattle and the barbed drone of wasp and hornet' and a dress-sense which prompted onlookers to suppose 'she was staggering by under the weight of odd-lots that, now past their use, had been bestowed upon her by a charitable theatrical costumier.' Yes, this is Garsington's answer to the 1920s' novelist's prayer: Lady Ottoline Morrell. See Roddice, Hermione.

GORDON, Richard, in Ernest Hemingway's *To Have and Have Not* (1937). Worried by the possibility of libel, the author showed his manuscript to Arnold Gingrich (see MacWalsey, Professor John). Gingrich, says Hemingway's biographer, Carlos Baker, suggested the deletion or reworking of passages which might give offence, for he had quickly identified Gordon as the novelist John Dos Passos (1896–1970). Loth to take this advice, Hemingway decided to risk the book as it was. If he told Dos Passos that Gingrich objected to certain sections, he reasoned, then Dos Passos (who disliked Gingrich) would be sure to give his approval.

GORDON, Squire and Mrs, in Anna Sewell's *Black Beauty* (1877), are supposed by Sewell's biographer, Susan Chitty, to be the author's uncle and aunt, John Wright and his wife, Anne (née Harford), of Dudwick House, Buxton, Norfolk. John Wright was the heir to the fortune of a London Quaker banker; his wife was the author of a children's book on geology, a commentary on Leviticus and two natural-history books for children — *The Observing Eye* (1850), which was personally approved by Queen Victoria, and *What is a Bird?* (1858).

GORSE, Mr, in Christopher Isherwood's *Lions and Shadows* (1938). 'I'll say this for you,' said Kenneth Pickthorn, Isherwood's tutor at

Corpus Christi, Cambridge, delivering judgement on the author's first, inadequate essay: 'it's not the work of an entirely uneducated fool.' With the passage of time, as the Isherwood biographer Jonathan Fryer records, Pickthorn (1892—1975) became not only Mr Gorse but also Sir Kenneth Pickthorn, Parliamentary Secretary at the Ministry of Education.

GORTON, Bill, in Ernest Hemingway's *The Sun Also Rises* (1926; published in England as *Fiesta*), is the American humorist Donald Ogden Stewart (1894—1980), a companion of the author in Paris in the 1920s.

GOTOBED, Maddie, in Tom Stoppard's *Dirty Linen* (1976). 'I was never a lawnmower in knickers', Mandy Rice-Davies assured *The Times* when her appearance as Maddie in a 1981 revival of this play prompted the suspicion that she was Maddie's prototype. 'Really, there is nothing of Maddie in me, or at least I like to think so.' As the flat-mate of Christine Keeler, she was in 1963 involved in the British political scandal which caused the resignation of John Profumo (see Price, John), Secretary for War. Rice-Davies (1944—   ) is best remembered for a rejoinder during the vice trial which arose from the Profumo affair. Told by counsel that Viscount Astor denied having slept with her, she replied, 'Well, he would, wouldn't he?' When she said she was not Maddie, some 'Well, she would, wouldn't she?' scepticism was inevitable ... but when the play was first produced, Stoppard declared Maddie to be 'off the shelf — she's not a real character. What interests me is getting a cliché and then betraying it. Miss Gotobed is a busty lady who triumphs in the play and she's sharper and brighter about a lot of things and that's fine, but it doesn't mean she's a real character at all. In fact, it probably means that she's less real than anybody else.'

GOULD, Charles, in Joseph Conrad's *Nostromo* (1904). One of Conrad's staunchest friends, R.B. Cunninghame Graham (see Hushabye, Hector) helped the author with the background of *Nostromo*. Like Gould, he prospected for gold in ancient Spanish mines; his wife, sketch-book in hand, accompanied him on his Latin American travels; and he had family links in South America. Small wonder, therefore, that the Conrad biographer Norman Sherry suggests him as Gould's model.

GOVERNOR OF NEW YORK, the, in James Reichley's *Hail to the Chief* (1960). It came as quite a surprise to the *Chicago Tribune* when Thomas E. Dewey (1902—71) was not elected President of the United States — before the 1948 count was complete, the newspaper carried the headline, 'DEWEY DEFEATS TRUMAN'. Instead, Dewey was accorded a different chance of immortality as Reichley's Governor of New York, an office held by this lawyer-politician from 1942 to 1954.

GRACE, in W.H. Mallock's *The New Republic* (1877), according to Thomas Wright's *The Life of Walter Pater* (1907), is Mrs Mark Pattison (née Emilia Frances Strong, *d.* 1904), art critic wife of the Rector of Lincoln College, Oxford (see Casaubon, Revd Edward). Her perfume, fashionable dress, addiction to cigarettes and advocacy of fencing for women both scandalised and allured the Oxford of her day. Following the death of Pattison she married Sir Charles Dilke (1843—1911), Under-Secretary for Foreign Affairs from 1880 to 1882, whose political career was in 1885 ruined by his involvement as co-respondent in a sensational divorce action.

GRAHAM, Mary, in Charles Dickens's *Martin Chuzzlewit* (1843—4). Naming Mary Hogarth (see Maylie, Rose) as Mary Graham, Michael Slater's *Dickens and Women* (1983) contends that, like Rose Maylie, Mary Graham 'is an embodiment of that youthful sweetness and purity that Dickens identified with Mary Hogarth, but she is an altogether calmer recollection of the original', and is spared her model's sudden illness.

GRAMMONT, V.V., in H.G. Wells's *The Secret Places of the Heart* (1922), is the author's friend Margaret Sanger (1883—1966), American feminist and birth-control campaigner, suggests J.R. Hammond in *An H.G. Wells Companion* (1979).

GRAMPOUND, Lord. See Bevill, Thomas.

GRAND, Jamie, in Antonia Fraser's *A Splash of Red* (1981) and *Cool Repentance* (1982). Some originals are slow to emerge, their recognition being heralded by a fanfare of hints until at last somebody names them. *Cool Repentance* was teasingly reviewed in the *Times Literary Supplement* by T.J. Binyon: 'On whom could Jamie Grand, a suave and debonair background figure, described as the powerful editor of *Literature*, possibly be modelled?' A year later, when *A Splash of Red* was dramatised for television, Anne Chisholm noted in the *Observer*: 'Antonia Fraser admits that there are private jokes and references to friends of her own in the books. Jamie Grand, a sociable, amusing literary man, has the same initials as a former editor of the *Times Literary Supplement* who is an old friend.' This as good as confirmed the identity of Grand's model for anyone putting two and two together . . . although in this game *faux pas de deux* have been known. In 1984, Mark Amory, in the *Tatler*, named John Gross (1935—), editor of the *Times Literary Supplement* from 1974 to 1981.

GRANDET, Eugénie, in Honoré de Balzac's *Eugénie Grandet* (1833), is an amalgam of Maria du Fresnay and Evelina Hanska (*b.* 1800). The novel's dedicatee, du Fresnay was a married woman who had a child by Balzac in 1834 — a daughter, who died in 1930. Hanska was a Pole, the daughter of Count Adam Rzewuski. Balzac courted her intermittently for nearly twenty years, on the understanding that they would marry when her husband died. After much prevarication, she finally became Balzac's wife a few months before his death.

GRANDISON, Cardinal, in Benjamin Disraeli's *Lothair* (1870), is Cardinal Manning (Henry Edward Manning, 1808—92), who transferred his support from Disraeli to Gladstone (see Gresham, Mr) in the belief that Roman Catholics might expect more favourable treatment from the Liberals.

GRANDMA, in Fyodor Dostoevsky's *The Gambler* (1866). Both Grandma and the author's aunt, Aleksandra Kumanina, returned from the grave. Thought to be dead, Grandma made her come-back at a casino where she flamboyantly lost much of her fortune while her principal heir looked on. Aleksandra, presumed dead, turned out to be inconveniently still alive when Dostoevsky challenged the will in which she left 40,000 roubles to a monastery. To that extent, if no more, Grandma mirrors Aleksandra . . . who died in 1871, the division of her estate involving her heirs in litigation for several years.

GRAVES, in Evelyn Waugh's 'Charles Ryder's Schooldays' (written 1945, published 1982), is E.B. Gordon, the author's house tutor in Head's House, Lancing College.

GRAY, Dorian, in Oscar Wilde's *The Picture of Dorian Gray* (1891). Using blue and black bed-linen, keeping a tortoise and growing purple hyacinths for the altar, Canon John Gray (see Brown, Father) pursued a life-style reminiscent of Montesquiou (see Charlus). His acquaintances included a male prostitute who gave evidence against Wilde, and since he signed his letters 'Dorian' he was taken to be Dorian Gray's model. Although it has been claimed that Wilde did not meet him until after the novel's publication, the two are known to have been fellow guests at a dinner party more than a year before the book appeared, and so striking was Gray's boyish beauty that Wilde would surely have hastened to make his acquaintance at first sighting. According to one account, the two were introduced at a meeting of the Rhymers' Club in 1889.

GRAY, Gideon, in Sir Walter Scott's 'The Surgeon's Daughter' (*Chronicles of the Canongate*, 1827), is an amalgam of Mungo Park (1771−?1806), Scottish explorer of Africa, who for a time was a Peebles medical practitioner; and Ebenezer Clarkson (1763−1847) of Selkirk, the author's family doctor, whose physician son attended Scott on his death-bed.

GRAY, Jane, in Margaret Drabble's *The Waterfall* (1969). 'Jane is partially based on the poet Sylvia Plath', said the author in a *Radio Times* interview when this novel was dramatised in 1980. 'A lot of intelligent, self-aware women experience a tremendous alienation and loss of confidence while they are bringing up young children. There is a lot going on in Jane's mind, but she can't express it creatively because that would involve plunging herself into an extreme state of mind, and you can't do that when you've got young kids. They bring you back to normality and the routine of daily life. Unfortunately, the creative state is opposed to routine.' The career of Plath (1932−63) was for a time overshadowed by the reputation of her poet husband, Ted Hughes, and by the demands made upon her by looking after their two young children. Husband and wife parted in 1962, she persevering with her writing by rising early and working before her two-year-old daughter and baby son awoke. In the following year she committed suicide.

GREEK, the, in George Du Maurier's *Trilby* (1894), is identified by the author's biographer, Leonée Ormond, as Alexander A. Ionides, a student acquaintance during Du Maurier's youth in Paris and subsequently a lifelong friend. He was the son of a London-based

Greek merchant prince, and his family — who lived at Tulse Hill — were noted patrons of the arts in general and of young, indigent artists in particular.

GREENE, Sir Nicholas, in Virginia Woolf's *Orlando* (1928). 'I know a mean skunk when I see one, or rather smell one', said Woolf in a letter to Lytton Strachey, referring to her model for Greene: Sir Edmund Gosse (see Criscross, Professor James). Describing him as 'that little grocer', she thought him a low-brow, dowagers' toady, as Gosse's biographer, Ann Thwaite, records. Thwaite also notes that Woolf was aware that Gosse thought she showed insufficient respect for the memory of his friend, her father; and that she had heard that he had referred to her as a nonentity. On his death she described him in a letter as 'a crafty, worldly, prim, astute little beast'. Then, on seeing Press reports that he had chosen to risk a hazardous operation rather than become an invalid, she noted in her diary that she was 'half-reconciled' to him.

GREENGLASS, Meyer, in Roger L. Simon's *Wild Turkey* (1975). 'We are bigger than US Steel', boasted Greenglass's prototype, the Russian-born American racketeer Meyer Lansky (?1902—83), allegedly one-time director of 'Murder Incorporated'. Although recognised as the 'Mr Big' of organised crime in the United States for several decades, he served only one prison sentence — two months, for a 1953 gambling conviction.

GREEN-MANTLE. See Redgauntlet, Lilias.

GREGORY, in Henry Fielding's *The Mock Doctor* (1732), is said by the Fielding biographer, Austin Dobson, to be the work's dedicatee, John Misaubin (*d.* 1734), medical practitioner, manufacturer of a celebrated pill and one of the personages delineated in William Hogarth's 'The Harlot's Progress'.

GRESHAM, Mr, in Anthony Trollope's *Phineas Finn* (1869), *The Eustace Diamonds* (1873), *Phineas Redux* (1874) and *The Prime Minister* (1876), is William Ewart Gladstone (1809—98), who was four times prime minister of Britain. Impervious to constant criticism from Queen Victoria, he was a master of the barbed put-down. He was in Lancashire when she wired him to express her dismay at the news from Khartoum — 'and to think that all this might have been prevented and many lives saved by earlier action is too fearful.' The premier replied: 'Mr Gladstone has had the honour this day to receive your Majesty's telegram. Mr Gladstone does not presume to estimate the means of judgement possessed by your Majesty but as far as his information goes he is not altogether able to follow the conclusion which your Majesty has been pleased thus to announce to him.'

GRETCHEN, in Johann Wolfgang von Goethe's *Faust* (1808–32). As Richard Friedenthal notes in his *Goethe* (1965), Gretchen is part-inspired by Friederike Brion (1752–1813), the daughter of a Lutheran pastor in Sesenheim, Strasbourg. In addition to Goethe – who met her in 1771 – her admirers included the dramatist and poet Jakob Lenz, but she died a spinster. She is also the Friederike of Goethe's 'Friederike in Sesenheim' (*Aus meinem Leben: Dichtung und Wahrheit*, 1811–33).

GREY, Edward, in Mrs Humphry Ward's *Robert Elsmere* (1888), is Thomas Hill Green (1836–82), who in 1878 was appointed Whyte's Professor of Moral Philosophy at Oxford.

GREY, Farmer, in Anna Sewell's *Black Beauty* (1877), is supposedly the author's grandfather, John Wright, a Quaker farmer of Felthorpe, Norfolk, where he pioneered the use of the threshing machine and the introduction of merino sheep.

GREYSLAER, Max, in C.F. Hoffman's *Greyslaer* (1840), is part-inspired by Jeroboam O. Beauchamp. See Octavia.

GRIBBLES, in Sinclair Lewis and Dore Schary's *Storm in the West* (written 1943, published 1963), is Joseph Goebbels (1897–1945), Nazi Germany's Minister for Propaganda.

GRIEVE, Sandy, in Mrs Humphry Ward's *The History of David Grieve* (1892), is a childhood portrait of the author's nephew, Sir Julian Huxley (1887–1975), biologist grandson of T.H. Huxley (see Storks, Mr) and brother of Aldous Huxley (see Erasmus, William), according to the author's biographer, Enid Huws Jones.

GRIFFENBOTTOM, in Anthony Trollope's *Ralph the Heir* (1871), is Sir Henry Edwards, chairman of the Yorkshire railway-truck manufacturers, the Beverley Waggon Company, and one of Beverley's two Tory MPs. He resoundingly defeated Trollope and a fellow Liberal when the two contested Beverley in the parliamentary election of 1868. Trollope's Beverley campaign is detailed in John Halperin's *Trollope and Politics* (1977).

GRIFFITHS, Clyde, in Theodore Dreiser's *An American Tragedy* (1925), is Chester Gillette (1883–1908). Working in a shirt factory owned by his uncle at Cortland, New York, he found his high-society aspirations were threatened when he made a factory secretary pregnant. Taking her on holiday, he hired a boat for a picnic outing on Big Moose Lake (Herkimer County) . . . and her body was found the next day. Saying first that she had committed suicide and then that the boat had capsized and she had drowned by accident, he was sentenced to death and executed.

GRIMES, Captain, in Evelyn Waugh's *Decline and Fall* (1928). Although Waugh's diaries provided clues, the identity of the model for Grimes did not emerge until 1976, when it was revealed in the *Sunday Telegraph*. He turned out to be William (Dick) Young (1895–1972), a colleague of Waugh in 1925 at Arnold House school, Llanddulas, Denbighshire. Educated at Wellington and Keble College, Oxford, he served in the Welch Regiment in the First World War and was mentioned in despatches. After an unsuccessful teaching career (Waugh's diaries mention his precipitate departure from four schools), he became a solicitor. He also wrote a thriller, under the name Richard Macnaughton: *The Preparatory School Murder* (1934), with Arnold House as the setting and Waugh among the characters. In 1961 he was admitted to St Cross Hospital, Winchester, a Church of England home for the destitute. Eleven years later, he surprised his benefactors by leaving £58,557 – but only £100 to them. His effects included a collection of porcelain valued at £20,000, his Worcester being bequeathed to Hastings Museum, his Meissen and Chelsea to Oxford's Ashmolean. Waugh's diaries record: 'Young and I went out and made ourselves drunk and he confessed all his previous career. He was expelled from Wellington, sent down from Oxford and forced to resign his commission in the army.' Perhaps Young was spinning the kind of yarn he sensed Waugh wanted to hear. He may well have been expelled – he left Wellington at fifteen – but he took a degree at Oxford.

GROAN, Lady, in Mervyn Peake's *Titus Groan* (1946), is said by Peake's biographer, John Watney, to be Margaret Gilmour Dunlop (*d.* 1947), first wife of the sculptor Sir Jacob Epstein. The author met her in 1938, after *Picture Post* published a poem he had written in defence of Epstein's much-criticised statue, 'Adam'.

GROVELL, Dick, in Osbert Sitwell's *Those Were The Days* (1938). Until the Sitwells fell out with Wyndham Lewis (see Lypiatt, Casimir), their friends included the South African poet Roy Campbell (1902–57). After that rift, Campbell's continued association with the Sitwells' enemy prompted this Dick Grovell caricature, says Lewis's biographer, Jeffrey Meyers.

GRUBSTREET, in W.M. Thackeray's *The Virginians* (1857–9). Annoyed by a sketch in *Town Talk*, Thackeray avenged himself by creating Grubstreet, a caricature of the offending article's author, Edmund Hodgson Yates (1831–94), a journalist and novelist who was editor of *Town Talk* at that time. Further reprisals included having Yates struck off the members' list of the Garrick Club – where Thackeray must have mixed his colours for the Grubstreet portrait. It was a somewhat hypocritical revenge – see Foker, Harry.

GUERMANTES, Basin, Duc de, in Marcel Proust's *A la recherche du temps perdu* (1913–27). Like many another chronically unfaithful husband, Comte Henri Greffulhe (*d.* 1932) was zealous in ensuring that his wife enjoyed none of his own freedom, requiring her always to return home by 11.30 p.m. A naturalised French member of a Belgian family of bankers, he died at eighty-four, leaving his last mistress an indiscreetly generous legacy . . . and assured of a place in literary history as one of the models for Guermantes. Also discerned in the character are Agénor, Duc de Gramont (*d.* 1925), father of the Duchesse de Clermont-Tonnerre (see Clitoressa of Natescourt, the Duchess) and builder of the *château* of Vallières (thanks to the fortune of his second wife, Marguerite de Rothschild); and Comte Gabriel Othenin d'Haussonville (1843–1924), a grandson of Mme de Staël (see Ellénore) and a member of the Jockey Club and the Académie Française (for his wife, see Cambremer, Marquise de).

GUERMANTES, Gilbert, Prince de, *idem*. 'A few nights of passion, and then a whole lifetime at the wrong end of the table,' commented Comte Aimery de La Rochefoucauld (1843–1928) on hearing of a girl who had married beneath her for love. The principal model for the status-conscious Gilbert, he was inordinately proud of his rank, his obsessive concern with precedence earning him the sobriquet 'Place at Table'. If he was not seated to his satisfaction, he would call for his carriage. Also present in Gilbert is Prince Constantin Radziwill, whose homosexual proclivities cost him an average of 70,000 francs a year in blackmail ... or so he told Montesquiou.

GUERMANTES, Marie, Princesse de, *idem*, is an amalgam of Comtesse Henri Greffulhe (see Guermantes, Oriane, Duchesse de) and Comtesse Jean (Dolly) de Castellane (née Dorothée de Talleyrand-Périgord). The widow of Karl Egon, Prince von Fürstenburg, she in 1898 married Comte Jean de Castellane and became a leader of Paris society.

GUERMANTES, Oriane, Duchesse de, *idem*. 'She won't read me. She says she stabs her foot in my sentences,' Proust complained to Jean Cocteau, asking him to intercede with his reluctant reader and model for Oriane: Comtesse Adhéaume de Chevigné (née Laure de Sade, 1860–1936). He might as well ask an ant to read Fabre, Cocteau replied; one didn't invite an insect to read entomology. A witty, aquiline-featured descendant of the Marquis de Sade, the Comtesse presided over a salon at her home in Paris in the rue de Miromesnil. Oriane also displays elements of Comtesse Henri Greffulhe (née Princesse Élisabeth de Caraman-Chimay, 1860–1952), the eldest daughter of the Franco-Belgian Prince Joseph de Caraman-Chimay. She married Comte Henri Greffulhe (see Guermantes, Basin, Duc de) in 1878. A narcissistic, celebrated beauty, she was thirty-four when Proust was introduced to her by her cousin, Comte Robert de Montesquiou-Fezensac (see Charlus, Baron Palamède de). Among those dancing attendance on her was Charles Haas (see Swann, Charles). A further ingredient of Oriane is Mme Émile Straus (née Génevière Halévy, ?1846–1926), daughter of one composer, Jacques Halévy, and widow of another, Georges Bizet. A noted hostess and wit, she married Émile Straus (see Swann, Charles) in 1886. For these Guermantes identifications and many other Proust entries I am primarily indebted to George D. Painter's definitive Proust biography.

GUEST, Stephen, in George Eliot's *The Mill on the Floss* (1860). Nicknamed 'Byron' for his good looks and also, perhaps, for his womanising, the London publisher John Chapman (1821–94) is a suggested model for Guest. As his assistant, Eliot lived in his home ... and became involved in his philandering. Also in the household were his wife and his mistress (ostensibly his children's governess), and Chapman found his affections torn between the three. When he bought a piano for Eliot's room, to enjoy her playing, his wife promptly purchased another for the dining-room so that Eliot's musical gifts could be aired more publicly; and when Eliot started teaching Chapman German, his mistress also decided to learn the language – from him. The novel's Maggie Tulliver was popularly believed to be Eliot herself. The Eliot biographer Marghanita Laski notes the *Saturday Review*'s observation that Stephen kissing Maggie's arm was not 'a theme that a female novelist can touch on without leaving a feeling of hesitation, if not repulsion, in the reader ... There are emotions over which we ought to throw a veil' (an allusion, I suspect, to Eliot's then recently published story 'The Lifted Veil'). Swinburne later said that no man could encounter Stephen Guest without 'a twitching in his fingers and a tingling in his toes' as he longed to horsewhip 'the cur' – but then, Swinburne had his own private interest in whipping (see Dolores). The journalist T.P. O'Connor recalled walking down the Strand with Chapman, then in his old age. Their conversation turned to Eliot and, giving his arm an eloquent squeeze, Chapman said she had been more than a little fond of him.

GUINEA, Philomena, in Sylvia Plath's *The Bell Jar* (1963), is the author's benefactor, the American novelist Olive Higgins Prouty (1882–1974). She endowed Plath's Smith College scholarship, and in 1953 paid for her treatment at a private institution following her first suicide attempt. Prouty's interest in Plath is recorded in *Sylvia Plath: The Woman and the Work*, edited by Edward Butscher (1979).

GUISHAR, Larissa Fyodorovna '(Lara')', in Boris Pasternak's *Dr Zhivago* (1957). 'Lara exists. I want you to meet her. Here is her telephone number,' said Pasternak to a visitor. The number he gave was that of Olga Vsevolodovna Ivinskaya (1912–   ), his mistress for the last fourteen years of his life. They met in 1946, when she was thirty-four, twice-widowed, the mother of two children and working for the Moscow literary magazine *Novy Mir*. He was fifty-six and could not bring himself to leave his wife, but his relationship with Ivinskaya thrived until the Soviet authorities in 1949 took revenge on his unwelcome literary activities by arresting his mistress (who had become his secretary/agent), sending her for four years to a labour camp in Siberia. The affair resumed upon her return in 1953. In 1960, a few weeks before Pasternak's death,

Ivinskaya was arrested and sentenced to eight years' imprisonment for illegally receiving 800,000 roubles in royalties from her lover's Italian publisher. There were protests from leading Western intellectuals including Bertrand Russell, and in 1964 she was released. In 1978 she told her story in *A Captive of Time: My Years with Pasternak*. 'That Lara was none other than Ivinskaya was accepted within Pasternak's own family,' says his biographer, Guy de Mallac. 'The truth is, however, more complex ... ' Also contributing to Lara, said Pasternak, were Zinaida Nikolaevna Eremeev (1898–1966), who became his wife in 1934, having earlier left her first husband – by whom she had two sons – to live with the author; and Nina Aleksandrovna Tabidze, wife of the poet Titian Tabidze.

GUNDERMANN, in Émile Zola's *L'Argent* (1891), is Baron James (Jacob) Rothschild (1792–1868), youngest son of the founder of the Rothschild family banking dynasty. Sent to Paris to open a branch of the business, he financed the French railway system, negotiated loans for the Bourbons and became celebrated for his opulent life-style. His story is told, and the Zola identification made, in Anka Muhlstein's *Baron James* (1983).

GUNGA DIN, in Rudyard Kipling's 'Gunga Din' (*Barrack Room Ballads*, 1892). The example of Juma, a low-caste Indian employed by the Corps of Guides in India as a regimental water-carrier, is believed to have been the inspiration for this poem. His disregard for his own safety during the siege of Delhi in 1857 led to his being decorated for bravery, and his courage won him further awards in the Afghan War of 1878, in which he served as a Guides' officer.

GUNN, Gilbert, in George Bernard Shaw's *Fanny's First Play* (1911), is Gilbert Cannan (1884–1955), novelist, playwright and drama critic of the *Star*. As his biographer, Diana Farr, relates, he eloped with and subsequently married the wife of J.M. Barrie (see Wilson, Murray; Rodney, Jane); fathered a child by her maid; was diagnosed schizophrenic in 1924; and spent the remainder of his life in an asylum where his fees were paid by Lord Melchett, whose wife had been Cannan's last love.

GUNNER, Ambrose, in Olivia Manning's *The Rain Forest* (1974). 'Do you recognise Ambrose?' asked the author, when this novel was published. He was based, she said, on a late literary journalist who was the brightest man of his year at university but subsequently failed to live up to his promise. Given that clue, one hardly needed to open the book to find in Ambrose an unmistakable resemblance to Cyril Connolly. See Quiggin, J.G.

GUSTAVUS, George. See Steyne, Marquis of.

GWEN, in F. Scott Fitzgerald's 'Too Cute for Words' and 'Inside the House' (1936; *The Price Was High*, 1979), is Frances Scott ('Scottie') Fitzgerald. See Brady, Cecilia.

GWYNNE, Winifred, in John Cournos's *Miranda Masters* (1926), is the author's mistress, Dorothy Yorke (see Carter, Bella), who came from Reading, Pennsylvania.

GYNT, Jon, in Henrik Ibsen's *Peer Gynt* (1867), is based on the author's father, Knud Ibsen (see Ekdal, Old). Near-bankruptcy stemming from tax problems turned him from a genial raconteur into a litigious, embittered man.

H

H, in Jean Cocteau's *Le Livre blanc* (1928). 'There's a child with a walking stick wishing to see you', said Cocteau's valet, showing in a short, pale boy with a sulky mouth and unkempt hair. He had been sent by Cocteau's friend, the poet Max Jacob. Cocteau read the young visitor's poems and decided he had genius. He also fell in love with the boy, and their stormy relationship is recorded in this autobiographical novel in which H is the youth with the walking stick: the novelist and poet Raymond Radiguet (1903–23). Rebelling against Cocteau's jealous possessiveness, the maturing Radiguet turned to women. Then, following a meal of suspect oysters, he succumbed to typhoid fever and died at twenty. Too distressed to join Picasso, Brancusi, Chanel and Radiguet's other friends and admirers at the funeral, Cocteau was haunted by the memory of his young lover for the rest of his life. For the teacher had become the taught, Cocteau being influenced by a Radiguet who was revered by his elders and who recoiled from the inevitable 'infant prodigy' label. But what else could they call a youth whose writing displayed such extraordinary maturity and sophistication? Radiguet had an answer: 'All great poets have written at seventeen. The greatest are those who succeed in making one forget it.'

HAAKONSSON, Haakon, in Henrik Ibsen's *The Pretenders* (1863), is identified by the Ibsen biographer Michael Meyer as the Norwegian poet, novelist and dramatist Bjørnstjerne Bjørnson (1832–1910), whose early self-confidence contrasted with Ibsen's sense of personal failure.

HACKAMORE, Henry, in Sam Shepard's *Seduced* (1979). 'If Howard Hughes had not existed no dramatist would have dared invent him', wrote Michael Billington in the *Guardian* when this play was presented in London in 1980. 'The one exception perhaps is

Sam Shepard, that specialist in American Gothic, who in *Seduced* focuses on the last hours of a white-maned, long-taloned Hughesian recluse called Henry Hackamore.' Also taken by *Current Biography Yearbook* to be Hackamore, the American millionaire Howard Hughes (1905–76) inherited a fortune which he deployed largely in aviation. He became a noted pilot, aircraft designer (Lockheed Constellation), airline owner (TWA) and film-maker (*Hell's Angels; The Outlaw*). In his last twenty years he became prey to an obsessive fear of germs, retiring to a specially decontaminated Las Vegas penthouse where, it was said, he lived naked, his privacy ensured by electronic alarms and bodyguards.

HACKETT, in Flann O'Brien's *The Dalkey Archive* (1964), is Oliver St John Gogarty (see Mulligan, Buck), according to Anne Clissmann's *Flann O'Brien: A Critical Introduction to his Writing* (1975).

HADDO, Oliver, in W. Somerset Maugham's *The Magician* (1908). The model for Haddo was proud of a fancied resemblance to Winston Churchill, although one acquaintance likened his face to a penis. He was Aleister Crowley (1875–1947), and Maugham first met him in Paris in 1897, at the studio of their mutual friend Gerald Kelly (subsequently president of the Royal Academy), whose sister Crowley married. Reviewing the novel in *Vanity Fair*, Crowley signed his notice 'Oliver Haddo'. He was not without talent but was considered something of a mountebank. When he was not striding about London in green plus-fours, the novelist Anthony Powell has recalled, Crowley would be garbed in swallow-tail coat and sponge-bag trousers, like some ducal refugee from a musical comedy. In furtherance of his occultism and his creed 'Do what thou wilt shall be the whole of the Law', he recruited disciples and in 1920 founded an 'abbey' in Sicily, from which he was expelled in 1923 following allegations of sacrifices and sexual aberration. In his later years he became a somewhat pathetic figure, hardly to be taken seriously. But in the 1930s there were those who regarded him as the ultimate in depravity. When he brought an unsuccessful action for defamation in 1934, the judge summed up: 'I have been over forty years engaged in the administration of justice in one capacity or another. I thought that I knew of every single form of wickedness. I thought that everything which was vicious had been produced at some time or another before me. I have learned in this case that we can always learn something more if we live long enough . . . I have never heard such dreadful, horrible, blasphemous and abominable stuff as that which has been produced by the man who describes himself to you as the greatest living poet.' In his autobiography, Crowley noted: 'I have never lost the childlike humility which characterizes all truly great men.'

HAIK, General Dewey, in Sinclair Lewis's *It Can't Happen Here* (1935). This novel was written to warn America against the fascism Lewis had witnessed in Germany, and the characters are modelled on American figures seen by Lewis as counterparts of the Nazi leaders. In *The Age of Roosevelt: The Politics of Upheaval* (1960), Arthur M. Schlesinger jun. believes that Dewey Haik, the collaborating general, may have been suggested by General Douglas MacArthur (1880–1964), who was Chief of Staff in Washington from 1930 to 1935. A Second World War hero considered largely responsible for Japan's surrender, he went on to become quite the reverse of the collaborative Haik. In the Korean War he appealed to the public against President Harry Truman's prohibition on attacking Chinese territory, and was dismissed.

HAINES, Celtophile, in James Joyce's *Ulysses* (1922). When he found his sleeping quarters had become a shooting range, Joyce made an abrupt departure. He was staying at the Martello tower rented by Oliver St John Gogarty (see Mulligan, Buck), and his fellow guest was the model for Celtophile Haines: Samuel Chenevix Trench, a member of an old Anglo-Irish family and an Oxford acquaintance of Gogarty. Trench had nightmares in which he was about to be attacked by a black panther. Screaming, he awoke, grabbed his revolver and shot at the phantom, his bullet hitting the fireplace by Joyce's bed. As the dreamer resumed his sleep, Gogarty took the gun. Trench began screaming again and once more reached for his revolver. 'Leave him to me!' cried Gogarty, shooting down some pans hanging above Joyce ... who felt that, despite the earliness of the hour, it was time for him to leave. Dressing quickly, he set out on foot for Dublin. Five years later, Trench blew his brains out – 'perhaps', says the Joyce biographer Richard Ellmann, 'with the very weapon with which he and Gogarty had so nearly blown out Joyce's.'

HALCYON, Helen, in F. Scott Fitzgerald's 'The Debutante' (1917; *The Apprentice Fiction of F. Scott Fitzgerald*, 1965). Prompted by her break with the author, this story presents Ginevra King (see Borgé, Isabelle) as a self-centred society belle.

HALE, Frederick; Mr and Margaret, in Elizabeth Gaskell's *North and South* (1855). The Gaskell biographer Winifred Gérin supposes Frederick to be the author's brother, John Stevenson (1798–?1828). A merchant seaman sailing regularly between England and India, he was presumed lost at sea. Mr Hale and his wife, Margaret, are believed by the Gaskell authority J.G. Sharps to be based on the historian J.A. Froude (1818–94) and his first wife, Charlotte. Froude edited *Fraser's Magazine* from 1860 to 1874 and – like Hale – was tutor to the children of a manufacturer (Samuel Dunkinfield Darbishire, of Manchester). Gaskell was intrigued by his marriage to Charlotte, who was reputed to have decided to accept him when about to enter a convent as a nun. Her sister married the writer Charles Kingsley.

HALL, Revd Cyril, in Charlotte Brontë's *Shirley* (1849). The author was 'perfectly welcome to what she can make of so unprom-ising a subject', wrote her model for Hall in a letter to Charlotte Brontë's friend, Ellen Nussey (see Helstone, Caroline). He was the Revd William Margetson Heald, vicar of Birstall, Leeds, and his letter went on to say that he recognised himself as 'black, bilious, and of dismal aspect, stooping a trifle, and indulging a little now and then in the indigenous dialect. This seems to sit very well on your humble servant ... '

HALLIDAY, Julius, in D.H. Lawrence's *Women in Love* (1920). Threatening to sue for libel, the model for Halliday was bought off by Lawrence's publishers with a payment of £50. He was the composer Philip Heseltine (1894–1930), who changed his name to Peter Warlock. When the manuscript of some philosophical essays by Lawrence came into his hands, he took the opportunity to avenge himself for the Halliday portrait. In the words of Lawrence's Dublin publishing associate, Joseph Hone, Heseltine 'put the pages to the base uses of the water-closet.' No other copy of those essays survives. Heseltine was a pioneer campaigner for real ale – one of his pseudonyms was Rab Noolas (saloon bar, backwards) – but so pickled in alcohol was his system that he could be incapacitated by as little as half a pint of beer. His friends included Michael Arlen (see Michaelis), the composer Frederick Delius and Lady Ottoline

Morrell (see Roddice, Hermione). Excitable and pathologically susceptible to women (of whom he spoke as if they were cats, for which he had a great affection; see also Pussum), he apparently died by his own hand, putting the cat out before gassing himself.

HALLIDAY, Manley, in Budd Schulberg's *The Disenchanted* (1950). The author has insisted that Halliday is a composite of several writers, but the character is clearly based primarily on the American novelist F. Scott Fitzgerald (1896–1940), with whom Schulberg worked as a screen-writer. *The Disenchanted* is largely auto-biographical: Schulberg is Shep, his meeting with Halliday mirroring what happened when the two met in real life; and, like Fitzgerald, Halliday has an unbalanced wife. Looking back on Fitzgerald and Halliday, Schulberg said in 1982, 'Scott was different. Most writers came there because they knew there was lots of money. But he was the only one who thought films could be an art form.'

HALLWARD, Basil, in Oscar Wilde's *The Picture of Dorian Gray* (1890), takes his name from the author's artist friend Basil Ward, in whose studio in 1884 Wilde found the story's inspiration. Watching Ward at work on a portrait of an outstandingly handsome young man, Wilde remarked – after the sitter had left – that it was a pity such a glorious creature should ever grow old. Yes, agreed Ward, how delightful it would be if the youth could remain as he was, the portrait ageing in his stead. Ward subsequently contributed an introduction to an edition of the novel.

HALM-EBERSTEIN, Princess Leonora, in George Eliot's *Daniel Deronda* (1876), is suggested by the Eliot biographer Blanche Colton Williams to have a prototype in Mrs Isaac D'Israeli (née Maria Basevi), mother of the Earl of Beaconsfield (see Daubeny, Mr). She was noted for her resentment of the social disadvantages of being Jewish.

HAMBO, in Conrad Aiken's *A Heart for the Gods of Mexico* (1939) and *Ushant* (1952). 'The sheer malice which has been spat upon it has taken me aback – odd the way my books time after time have the faculty of making so many people *angry*', wrote Aiken in a letter, noting the bad but extensive reviews of *A Heart*. Not that it upset his model for Hambo, his protégé Malcolm Lowry (see Dowd, James). A few months later 'Hambo', fallen on hard times, was asking Aiken to 'save my life'. In a BBC Third Programme broadcast in 1967,

Aiken recalled his first meeting with Lowry, then nineteen: 'He arrived with a little broken suitcase in one hand and a ukulele in the other. The suitcase had practically nothing in it except for the exercise book in which he was writing *Ultramarine*. We spoke exactly the same language, so we celebrated right off — we in fact celebrated too well and after a few drops taken we staged a series of wrestling matches. He was a very powerful fellow — extraordinary — and I somehow fell over backwards into the fireplace and fractured my skull. That was the beginning of a beautiful friendship.'

HAMILTON, Derrick, in Helen Corke's *Neutral Ground* (1933), is D.H. Lawrence (see Rampion, Mark), who as a schoolteacher was a colleague of the author in Croydon. *Neutral Ground* was Corke's account of her tragic love affair, which Lawrence used as the basis of *The Trespasser* (see Verden, Helena). Interviewed in 1968 by Malcolm Muggeridge — who as a child had been one of her pupils — Helen Corke recalled how Lawrence's sympathetic interest had brought her back from a cul-de-sac of mourning into a main road of life: 'At the time there was a good part of my life which I couldn't share with anyone. But I found that instinctively Lawrence would bring an understanding to it which no one else could.'

HAMILTON, Olive and Samuel, in John Steinbeck's *East of Eden* (1952), are identified by the Steinbeck biographer Peter Lisca as the author's mother, Olive Steinbeck (*d.* 1934), and her father, Samuel Hamilton, who emigrated from northern Ireland to California in 1851. A schoolteacher in the Salinas Valley, Olive married the author's father in 1890.

HAMLEY, Roger, in Elizabeth Gaskell's *Wives and Daughters* (1864—6). According to Coral Lansbury's study of Gaskell (1975), the author 'was not unconscious of Darwin's eccentricities of behaviour, and a clumsiness that was the bane of ladies conducting tea parties among the bric-à-brac and *objets d'art* of the Victorian drawing-room, but she never forgot his genius even in the middle of broken china.' She presented a young version of the naturalist Charles Darwin (1809—82) in Roger Hamley, in whom another of her friends is also depicted: the Irish botanist and zoologist, Dr George James Allman (1812—98), Professor of Natural History at Edinburgh University.

HAMMER, Patrick, in William Saroyan's *Get Away Old Man* (1943), is the film producer Louis B. Mayer (see Brinkmeyer), who had the satisfaction of seeing the play close after only thirteen performances.

HAMMERGLOW, Lady, in H.G. Wells's *The Wonderful Visit* (1895). The original of Lady Hammerglow was not to the manor born: she came by it in a way most novelists would have hesitated to invent. She was Miss Frances Bullock Fetherstonhaugh (*d.* 1895), who assumed her surname when she inherited Uppark, Petersfield, on the death of her sister, an estate worker who had taken the fancy of Sir Harry Fetherstonhaugh when he was seventy and she was twenty. Sir Harry in love was in every sense a great leveller, to whom differences in station were of no consequence: it was one level-crossing after another. Infatuated by a miller's daughter, he had to be sent abroad; then it was a servant girl of fifteen, despatched pregnant from Uppark and later to become Nelson's Lady Hamilton; an affair with a footman was resolved when the flunkey was paid off to settle in Ireland. Then, after a lifetime's domestic dalliance, wedding bells ... for Sir Harry and Mary Ann Bullock, Uppark's head dairymaid. When he chanced upon her singing at her work, Sir Harry's heart churned. Tradition has it that, taken aback by his proposal, she was told to think it over and then to send her reply. As she could not write and had no access above-stairs, it was arranged that if her answer were 'Yes' she would cut a slice from a leg of mutton before it left the kitchen for Sir Harry's table. Mary Ann attended to the mutton — it was a prime cut she could not afford to miss. In 1850, Wells's mother went to Uppark as Frances's maid, leaving in 1853 and returning as housekeeper in 1880. Twelve years later she was dismissed for incompetence. By then, Wells had mentally filed not only Miss Frances for Lady Hammerglow but also Uppark as a setting for *Tono-Bungay*. And Sir Harry? He soldiered on to ninety-two, just in case you were wondering.

HAMMOND, Geoff, in W. Somerset Maugham's 'The Letter' (*The Casuarina Tree*, 1926), is William Crozier Steward, manager of a Malayan tin-mine, who in 1911 was shot dead by a woman believed to be his mistress, on the verandah of her home. See also Crosbie, Leslie.

HAND, Robert, in James Joyce's *Exiles* (1918). Two men who fancied Joyce's wife are discerned in Hand, the would-be cuckolder.

They are Vincent Cosgrave (see Lynch) and Roberto Prezioso, editor of the Trieste newspaper *Il piccolo della sera*. Hand's joviality is drawn from Oliver St John Gogarty (see Mulligan, Buck); and his journalism echoes that of Thomas Kettle (*d.* 1916), a friend of Joyce's youth who became an MP, was a contributor to *Freeman's Journal* and was killed while serving in the British army.

HANNAY, Richard, in John Buchan's *The Thirty-Nine Steps* (1915), *Greenmantle* (1916), *Mr Standfast* (1919), *The Three Hostages* (1924) and *The Island of Sheep* (1936). It was while Buchan was working for Lord Milner, High Commissioner for South Africa, that he in 1901 met his model for Hannay: a six-foot-four lieutenant engaged in Intelligence. William Edmund Ironside – Field Marshal Lord Ironside of Archangel (1880–1959), as he became – was fluent in fourteen languages. including Afrikaans. His decorations included a German military medal, won when he disguised himself as a Boer transport driver and worked as a spy behind German lines in south-west Africa. Intelligence work in Russia followed, and in 1938 he became Chief of the Imperial General Staff. After Dunkirk he was briefly Commander-in-Chief, Home Forces, a role in which he was noted for taking the War Office steps three at a time and for his penchant for pontificating – though he spoke many languages, Jakie Astor remarked, he made sense in none of them. His barony, conferred in 1941, was presumably Churchill's way of pensioning him off.

HANSEN, Hans, in Thomas Mann's 'Tonio Kroger' (*Stories of Three Decades*, 1936), is Armin Martens, the son of a Lübeck sawmill owner and the author's first love. According to Mann's autobiography, Martens became an alcoholic and 'made a melancholy end in Africa.'

HAPPER, Sally Carrol, in F. Scott Fitzgerald's 'The Ice Palace' (*Flappers and Philosophers*, 1920), is Zelda Fitzgerald (see Diver, Nicole). Recalling his start as a writer, the author noted, 'I was a professional and my enchantment with certain things that she felt and said was already paced by an anxiety to set them down in a story – it was called "The Ice Palace".'

HARDING, Hester, in Wyndham Lewis's *Self Condemned* (1954), is Gladys Anne Hoskyns (see Stamp, Margot), whom Lewis described as his 'wife in a thousand'.

HARDLINES, Sir Gregory, in Anthony Trollope's *The Three Clerks* (1858). Had you aspired in 1853 to a career in the Post Office, you might have had second thoughts on discovering the proposed requirements. It was in that year that a report on the Civil Service advocated competitive examinations requiring seventeen-year-old Post Office clerks to be proficient in history, jurisprudence, political economy, modern languages, political and physical geography, mathematics and the classics. Sir Charles Trevelyan (1807–86), joint author of that 1853 report, is suggested by R.H. Super's *Trollope in the Post Office* (1981) to be the model for Sir Gregory Hardlines. Subsequently governor of Madras and Indian finance minister, Trevelyan was grandfather of the historian G.M. Trevelyan. John Halperin's *Trollope and Politics* (1977), however, names as Hardlines's original another supporter of competitive examinations: Sir Rowland Hill (1795–1879), pioneer of Britain's penny post and from 1854 to 1864 secretary to the Post Office, for which Trollope (as an inspector) is reputed to have invented the pillar-box. As Super has made the closer study of Trollope's Post Office background, his candidate perhaps carries the greater weight.

HARDY, Thomas ('Bill'), in P.G. Wodehouse's *Company for Henry* (1967), is William Townend (see Lickford). Like Townend, Hardy is known as Bill, has a broken nose, is a writer who has been to sea and has been a lemon-picker in California.

HARE, Jonathan, in Edith Sitwell's *I Live under a Black Sun* (1937), is an amalgam of the homosexual Russian émigré and neo-Romantic artist Pavel Tchelitchew (*d.* 1957), for whom the author had an unrequited love, and the English satirist Jonathan Swift (1667–1745).

HARLETH, Gwendolen, in George Eliot's *Daniel Deronda* (1876), owes her creation to the author's observation of 'Byron's grandniece, Miss Leigh', at the roulette table in Homburg in 1872. 'The saddest thing to be witnessed is the play of Miss Leigh, Byron's grandniece, who is only twenty-six years old, and is completely in the grasp of this mean, money-making demon', George Eliot wrote in a letter. 'It made me cry to see her young fresh face among the hags and brutally stupid men around her.' Miss Leigh, who lost £500, was possibly Geraldine Leigh, daughter of George Henry John Leigh (*b.* 1812), eldest son of Augusta Leigh (see Astarte).

HARMON, Dick, in Katherine Mansfield's 'Je ne parle français' (*Bliss*, 1920), is John Middleton Murry (see Crich, Gerald). The story chronicles Mansfield's brief fling with Francis Carco (see Duquette, Raoul).

HARRALD, Dame, in *A Year at Hartlebury, or The Election* (1834), by Benjamin Disraeli and his sister, Sarah (under the pseudonyms Cherry and Fair Star). 'Something between Jeremy Bentham and Meg Merrilies, very clever but awfully revolutionary', was how Disraeli described the woman who is believed to be the model for Dame Harrald. The description occurs in a letter to his sister, written after he had dined with Edward Bulwer Lytton (see Bulwig) and had been overwhelmed by his host's mother-in-law, Mrs Francis Wheeler (née Doyle). From Ballywire, near Limerick, she was a niece of the Lt-Governor of Guernsey and was a noted feminist. Disraeli's letter records her forceful advocacy of the rights of women, pouring forth 'all her systems upon my novitiate ear.'

HARRAS, General, in Carl Zuckmayer's *The Devil's General* (1946), has as prototype Lt-General Ernst Udet (1896–1941), a First World War German fighter pilot who subsequently commanded the Technical Bureau of the Luftwaffe. He committed suicide following the Luftwaffe's defeat in the Battle of Britain, for which Hitler (see Ui, Arturo) held him partly to blame.

HARRIET, Archduchess, in Virginia Woolf's *Orlando* (1928). According to Harold Nicolson's biographer, James Lees-Milne, an unsuccessful suitor for the hand of Vita Sackville-West (see Orlando) was the model for Archduchess Harriet. Rejected by Vita, Henry George Charles Lascelles, Sixth Earl of Harewood (1882–1947), married Princess Mary, the Princess Royal . . . and had the distinction of *Who Was Who* recording his demise when he still had thirty-six years to live.

HARRINGTON, Evan and Melchizedek, in George Meredith's *Evan Harrington* (1861). Aspects of the author's father, Augustus Urmston Meredith (1797–1871), are to be found in Evan Harrington. A reluctant tailor, Augustus inherited his father's naval outfitters business in Portsmouth. In 1849 he emigrated, setting up in business in Cape Town where he announced himself 'not so bigoted to his own style but that he willingly yields to gentlemen's own peculiarities'. Melchizedek Harrington is Augustus's father, Melchizedek Meredith (*d.* 1814). In 1796 he became a freeman of Portsmouth, where he was known as 'the Count', cutting such a fine figure that he was reputed to have been mistaken in Bath for a marquess.

HARRIS, in Jerome K. Jerome's *Three Men in a Boat* (1889) and *Three Men on the Bummel* (1900). Remarking on how many ancient inns claimed to have been visited by Queen Elizabeth, the author speculates in *Three Men in a Boat* on what would happen if Harris 'turned over a new leaf, and became a great and good man, and got to be Prime Minister'. Would signs be displayed in the public houses he patronised? 'No, there would be too many of them! It would be houses that he never entered that would become famous. "Only house in South London that Harris never had a drink in!"' This was a private joke, aimed at the model for Harris: Carl Hentschel, the trio's teetotaller, who with George Wingrave (see George) was Jerome's companion on excursions on the Thames. His father, Carl Hentschel, revolutionised newspaper production in England with his introduction of photo-etching and was the inventor of the Hentschel-Colourtype Process. The family reputedly suffered financially during the First World War as victims of business rivals' suggestions that they were German. They were in fact Polish.

HARRIS, in Mark Twain's *A Tramp Abroad* (1880). On being charged eight dollars for a boat trip on the Sea of Galilee, Mark Twain asked, 'Do you wonder that Christ walked?' Happily, he was not then inhibited by the presence of his companion on his 1878 European tour, the Revd Joseph Hopkins Twichell (1838–1918), his model for Harris. The Yale-educated son of a Connecticut farmer, Twichell was chaplain to the New York Zouaves in the Civil War and spent the rest of his life as pastor of Asylum Hill Congregational Church, Hartford, Connecticut, with a flock so well-heeled that Twain called the chapel 'The Church of the Holy Speculators'. .

HARRIS, Andrew Crocker, in Terence Rattigan's *The Browning Version* (1948). 'In his first two years at Harrow one master had a particular fascination for Rattigan – his ageing, dry-as-dust Greek teacher, Mr Coke Norris', Michael Darlow and Gillian Hodson's *Terence Rattigan* (1979) records. A humourless disciplinarian, Coke Norris retired during Rattigan's second year. Upon being given a leaving present by one of the boys, he received it 'with hard words rather than any apparent pleasure. Rattigan could not understand how anyone could return kindness with unkindness.' This present-giving became the climax of *The Browning Version*, although in Crocker Harris it provoked a different reaction.

HARRIS, George, in Harriet Beecher Stowe's *Uncle Tom's Cabin* (1852), is part-inspired by Lewis Clark, a former slave employed in the household of the author's sister-in-law.

HARROWDEAN, Mrs, in H.G. Wells's *Mr Britling Sees It Through* (1916). Under the pine-trees, she gave herself to the author with abandon (see Failing, Mrs) . . . so what went wrong? The answer is to be found in Wells's portrait of Elizabeth von Arnim as Mrs Harrowdean, who 'was determined that the path of true love should not, if she could help it, run smooth'; who found it intolerable that she could be taken 'easily and happily' and was determined that her lover should pay heavily for her, 'in time, in emotion, in self-respect'. Elizabeth von Arnim humiliated Wells in company and later treated him with disdain: the coolness of a discarded woman.

HARVEY, Gladys, in Paul Bourget's 'Gladys Harvey' (*Pastels*, 1885), is Laure Hayman (see Crécy, Odette de), a cocotte adept in both the language of love and the love of language. When a client wrote that the heat in Biarritz was torrential, she replied, 'The rain here has been positively torrid.'

HARVILLE, Captain, in Jane Austen's *Persuasion* (1818). Like Captain Harville, for whom he was the model, Jane Austen's elder brother, Frank, was a precise man with an eye for detail. On board his ship at anchor, he was watching a fellow officer bathing in the sea when he saw that the swimmer was being pursued. 'Mr Pakenham!' he cried. 'You are in danger of a shark — a shark of the blue species!' Just as Harville busied himself ashore, making children's toys and fishing nets, so were the spare moments of Admiral Sir Francis William Austen (1774–1865) similarly occupied, his grandchildren recalled. His career included taking part in the blockade of Boulogne in 1804 and serving as flag captain to Admiral Lord Nelson's second-in-command. He was appointed Commander of the Fleet in 1863 and said that Harville's 'domestic habits, tastes and occupations have a considerable resemblance to mine.'

HARZ, Alois, in John Galsworthy's *Villa Rubein* (1900), is said by the author's biographer, Dudley Barker, to be part-inspired by

Galsworthy's brother-in-law, the Bavarian portrait painter Georg Sauter (1866–1937), who married Lilian Galsworthy (*d.* 1924) in 1894. The marriage broke up after Sauter's internment as an enemy alien early in the First World War. Repatriated, he settled in Berlin with an antipathy for all things English . . . although in 1926 he chose for his second wife another Englishwoman. His portrait of the author's wife (1898) was Galsworthy's inspiration for his physical description of Irene Forsyte, just as one of his portraits of the author's father inspired Galsworthy's image of Old Jolyon Forsyte.

HASTINGS, Lord Reggie, in Robert Hichens's *The Green Carnation* (1894). When this novella first appeared, anonymously, Lord Alfred Douglas (1870–1945) and Oscar Wilde not only recognised themselves as Lord Reggie Hastings and Esme Amarinth; they also guessed the author to be Hichens and sent him leg-pulling telegrams, as he recalled when *The Green Carnation* was republished in 1949. Hichens first met Douglas in Cairo and through him came to know Wilde. In 1895 the book was withdrawn when Wilde found himself at the centre of a scandal that led to his imprisonment and ruin. Objecting to Wilde's association with his son, Lord Alfred, the Marquess of Queensberry made accusations which provoked the dramatist to sue for criminal libel. Queensberry was acquitted. Wilde was arrested, charged with homosexual offences, convicted and gaoled. *The Green Carnation* stemmed from Hichens's wish to produce a book to rival *Dodo*, E.F. Benson's best-selling *roman-à-clef*. His experience in writing about Douglas contrasts with that of the author Arthur Machen, who lost his job on the London *Evening News* when in an obituary notice of Lord Alfred he called him degenerate and involved the paper in a libel action which cost it £1000. True, you cannot libel the dead. Lord Alfred Douglas was still alive. See also Amarinth, Esme.

HATTIGÉ, in G. de Bremond's *Hattigé ou La Belle Turque* (1676). With a reputation for outrageous lewdness, the model for Hattigé was Barbara Villiers (1641–1709), who was successively Lady Castlemaine and Duchess of Cleveland. Lord Coleraine is credited (or discredited) with noting, on 10 December 1675, a visit paid by the Duchess to the mummified body of Bishop Braybrook in St Paul's Chantry. Crossing herself, the note recorded, she served the body 'like a Turkish Eunuch & dismembered as much of the Privity as the Lady could get into her mouth to bite (for want of a circumcising Penknife to cut).' She was a notorious mistress of

Charles II, by whom she had a number of children, and her lovers also included the Second Earl of Chesterfield, the Duke of Buckingham and the dramatist William Wycherley.

HAUKSBEE, Lucy, in Rudyard Kipling's *Plain Tales from the Hills* (1888), 'The Education of Otis Yeere' (*Under the Deodars*, 1888), 'Mrs Hauksbee Sits Out' (1890; *Under the Deodars* – Outward Bound edn, 1897) and 'A Supplementary Chapter' (1888; *Abaft the Funnel*, 1909), is Mrs F.C. Burton, wife of a colonel in the Indian army and friend of the author, with whom she appeared in amateur dramatics. They first met in 1886.

HAVISHAM, Miss, in Charles Dickens's *Great Expectations* (1860–1). After spending eighteen years as a recluse, dressed in white and never venturing out, Martha Joachim died aged sixty-two in 1849 at her London home, York Buildings, Marylebone. She is believed to have been the inspiration for Miss Havisham, for her death was recorded in Dickens's magazine, *Household Narrative*, in January 1850. This noted that in 1825 'a suitor of the deceased, whom her mother rejected, shot himself while sitting on the sofa with her, and she was covered with his brains. From that instant she lost her reason.' The report also recorded that Miss Joachim's father, a Life Guards' officer, had been robbed and murdered in Regent's Park in 1808. Instead of suffering Miss Havisham's fiery fate, however, Miss Joachim died from bronchitis. There is also a Cheshire tradition that the inspiration for Miss Havisham may have come from that county. Dickens spent a night at Stanthorne Lodge, Middlewich, while visiting the novelist Harrison Ainsworth's three daughters at a nearby school. He is reputed to have found that the daughter of the house had recently been jilted, her wedding cancelled at the last moment, her wedding breakfast being left untouched for many months in the drawing-room.

HAWKE, Bascom, in Thomas Wolfe's 'A Portrait of Bascom Hawke' (1932; *Of Time and the River*, 1935), was part-inspired by Henry Westall, a Unitarian minister who became a Boston real-estate conveyancer. When he complained of his portrait, Wolfe replied that the character was a composite in whom several acquaintances were present. A writer, he explained, did not simply change the names of Brown and Smith to Black and White. Were it that easy, everyone might as well set out for the nearest town with a trunk full of notebooks and pencils, to record the inhabitants' words and movements from a convenient corner.

HAWKE, Youngblood, in Herman Wouk's *Youngblood Hawke* (1962), has been taken to be the American novelist Thomas Wolfe (1900–38). This identification was denied by Wouk, who said his model was the French novelist Honoré de Balzac (1799–1850), with whom Wolfe had much in common. Wouk's choice of his character's surname, coinciding with Wolfe's Hawke (see above), suggests that there may have been at least a subconscious Wolfe influence.

HAWKEYE. See Bumppo, Natty.

HAYDEN, Anita, in Christopher Isherwood's *Prater Violet* (1945), is the English actress Lydia Sherwood (1906–   ), who starred in the film *Little Friend* (1933), for which Isherwood wrote the screenplay.

HAYDON, Bill, in John le Carré's *Tinker, Tailor, Soldier, Spy* (1974). There is much about Haydon that suggests a prototype in the double-agent Kim Philby (1912–   ), and on the novel's publication Haydon was described by the critic Maurice Richardson as a Philby-style figure. But *is* Haydon Philby? The question was posed by Miriam Gross, interviewing le Carré for the *Observer* in 1980. 'I don't think that I was consciously pursuing any particular original when I wrote about Bill Haydon', said the author. 'I had all the traitors in mind ... Philby had an innate disposition to deceive, which preceded his Marxism ... His deceitful nature derived, I suspect, from that rather horrendous father of his, St John Philby, and also from an overwhelming vanity about his own worth. He grew up with the idea that he was born, as Connie Sachs says of Bill Haydon, as an Empire baby, to rule; and he entered a world where all his toys were being taken away by history. It seems to me that for that kind of Establishment person this is a much more cogent motive for betrayal than any half-cock pro-Stalinist Marxism which could not be seriously sustained after University ... Philby was a bent voluptuary. Come to think of it – yes, I gave that quality to Haydon, and perhaps I did pinch it from Philby.' Recruited by Russia in 1933, Philby in 1944 established Britain's Soviet counter-intelligence system, thereby filling a role in which he was supposed to catch himself. After the betrayal to Russia of an Albanian mission he came under increasing suspicion with the defection of the spies

Burgess and Maclean in 1951. He finally fled to Russia in 1963. Of impeccable background — the son of a distinguished explorer, educated at Westminster and Cambridge, a foreign correspondent of the *Observer* — Philby demonstrated that upbringing and class could no longer be relied upon as guarantees of ideological trustworthiness.

HAYWARD, in W. Somerset Maugham's *Of Human Bondage* (1915). The author's first homosexual lover is the model for Hayward: John Ellingham Brooks (*d.* 1929), who first met Maugham in Heidelberg in 1890 when they were lodgers in the same pension. Brooks was aged twenty-six at that time, and Maugham was sixteen. In *Looking Back*, Maugham claims he was too innocent to realise that Brooks desired him physically, wanting more than just his company. 'In fact,' says Maugham's biographer, Ted Morgan, 'he is covering up his first homosexual experience, for it was Brooks who took his virginity. He kept this first love affair a secret all his life, but admitted it to his close friend Glenway Wescott.' Having abandoned law studies for a literary career, Brooks wrote and translated much but was content to remain unpublished, his scholarship its own end, though it proved of use to Norman Douglas (see Argyle, James) in his *Birds and Beasts of the Greek Anthology* (1927), of which Brooks is the dedicatee. In his later years he lived in Capri on an allowance from his estranged wife (see Leigh, Olimpia). He also appears in Maugham's 'The Lotus-Eater' (*The Mixture as Before*, 1940) and *The Summing Up* (1938, as Brown).

HAZEL in Richard Adams's *Watership Down* (1972). Adams's respect for his wartime commanding officer is reflected in Hazel, who is modelled upon John Gifford, an architect with whom the author served in an airborne unit of the Royal Army Service Corps. Gifford's every quiet word, Adams has recalled, was instantly heeded. After the war he lived in Bucklebury, Berkshire.

HAZELROD, Lord Chief Justice, in Mercy Otis Warren's *The Group* (1775), is Peter Oliver (1713–91), who was appointed chief justice of Massachusetts in 1771, and impeached in 1774; he was a Tory in the Revolution.

HEARTFREE, Thomas, in Henry Fielding's *The Life of Mr Jonathan Wild the Great* (1743). Believed to have been a London jeweller, the dramatist George Lillo (1693–1739) is suggested as the model for Heartfree in Brian McCrea's *Henry Fielding and the Politics of Mid-18th Century England* (1981). Lillo pioneered domestic tragedy with *The London Merchant, or The History of George Barnwell* (1731).

HEATHCLIFF, in Emily Brontë's *Wuthering Heights* (1847). Some trails never go quite cold. As recently as 1984 another 'Heathcliff' was discovered, but I think there can be little doubt that the Brontë biographer Winifred Gérin got it right in 1971 when she suggested Jack Sharp as Heathcliff's prototype. In 1837, Emily Brontë took up a teaching post near Halifax at a girls' school, Law Hill, South-owram. She soon discovered that Law Hill, formerly a private house, had been built by Jack Sharp, the fatherless nephew of a wool manufacturer who had adopted him as a child. The charitable uncle, John Walker, gradually found himself displaced in his own house and business by the increasingly arrogant Sharp, who became so domineering that Walker retired early from the mill and left home. Sharp later brutalised Samuel Stead, a young cousin of Walker, in much the same way that Heathcliff corrupted Hareton Earnshaw. By the time Emily arrived, Sharp had long since become bankrupt, left the district and died. But still living nearby at Walterclough Hall was one of Walker's granddaughters, with plenty to say about Sharp and little of it to his credit. Another source for Heathcliff is suggested by William Wright's *The Brontës in Ireland* (1893), which relates a fanciful story presented by the author as a Brontë family tradition. This concerns 'Welsh' Brunty (an earlier spelling of Brontë). As a child of unknown origin, he was reputed to have been adopted by Emily Brontë's great-great-grandfather, Hugh Brunty, during a cattle-dealing visit to Liverpool. On Hugh Brunty's death, 'Welsh' Brunty assumed control of the family farm in Ireland, marrying one of his adoptive father's daughters against her wishes and adopting Emily's grandfather, Hugh Brunty, on the understanding that the child's father must never make contact with his son again. The boy's complete separation from his parent was ensured by the round-about route of his journey to his new home, planned so that young Hugh Brunty would be unable to find his way back. 'Welsh' Brunty subsequently exploited him as slave labour on the farm . . . or so the story goes. Certainly Grandfather Brunty is known to have been a colourful raconteur, and perhaps he was matched by Wright, whose account, if not entirely discredited, has come to be regarded with great reservation. The Heathcliff 1984 model emerged when Kim Lyon began researching the history of her home, Whernside Manor, Dent, in that part of Cumbria which was formerly in the West

Riding of Yorkshire. As the *Observer* reported on 30 September 1984, she found that a former owner, Richard Sutton (1782–1851), had been adopted as an orphan by a local, slave-owning family whose interests included plantations in the West Indies. Although apparently treated like a slave in his youth, Sutton inherited part of the family's property and prospered, with a wife and eleven children, and a mistress by whom he had two illegitimate sons. Further research led Mrs Lyon to identify Dent's Mason family with the Lintons of *Wuthering Heights* and the Sill family, who adopted Sutton, with the novel's Earnshaws. Sutton's story was told in William Howitt's *Rural Life in England* (1837), and the theory is that Emily Brontë read it. Well, maybe . . . but there is no record, as far as I am aware, of Emily interesting herself in Dent. Adopted foundlings were not uncommon in the late eighteenth century, and I suspect that many a rural district had a Heathcliff.

HECHT, Jock, in Roger L. Simon's *Wild Turkey* (1975), is suggested in David Geherin's *Sons of Sam Spade* (1980) to have Norman Mailer (see Marker, Harvey) as prototype.

HEIDLER, Hugh (H.J.), in Jean Rhys's *Postures* (1928; later retitled *Quartet*), is Ford Madox Ford (see Braddocks, Henry), with whom Rhys had a brief affair in Paris in the mid 1920s, when he was living with Stella Bowen (see Lois; Wannop, Valentine).

HEIMANN, George, in Ford Madox Ford's *The Marsden Case* (1923). 'It's the story of Ralston, the first translator of Turgenev', Ford wrote to his friend, the author Edgar Jepson, describing Ralston's career as 'one that has haunted me certainly ever since I was 18, on and off.' William Ralston Shedden Ralston (1828–89), the model for Heimann, was a pioneer among English translators of Russian. His father, W.P. Ralston Shedden, a Calcutta merchant, lost his fortune through his prolonged prosecution of an unsuccessful claim to the Ralston estate in Ayrshire. This became a family obsession, the litigant's daughter taking up the cause and conducting pleadings before a committee of the House of Lords for more than a month. The family's financial plight obliged her brother to abandon his chosen legal career and seek another. He changed his name by adding a second Ralston to disassociate himself from the notorious Shedden lawsuit, and obtained a post at the British Museum, where he applied himself to mastering Russian. Heimann is also, however, in part a self-portrait of the author . . . with the apparel of Wyndham Lewis (see Lypiatt, Casimir).

HEJRE, Daniel, in Henrik Ibsen's *The League of Youth* (1869), is the author's father, Knud Plesner Ibsen. See Ekdal, Old.

HELEN, in the poems of D.H. Lawrence, is Helen Corke. See Verden, Helena.

HELEN, in John le Carré's *The Naive and Sentimental Lover* (1971), is Susan Kennaway, wife of James Kennaway (see Shamus). In *The Kennaway Papers* (1981), she published her account of her affair with le Carré (see Fiddes, Dr.)

HELEN, in Edgar Allan Poe's 'To Helen' (1831), is supposedly Mrs Sarah Helen Whitman, a spiritualist from Providence, Rhode Island, who erroneously claimed to be Poe's last love.

HELEN, in H.G. Wells's *The World of William Clissold* (1926), is part-inspired by the novelist and critic Rebecca West (1892–1983), who was for more than ten years Wells's lover. Their son, the writer Anthony West, also used Rebecca West as a model. See Savage, Naomi.

HELENA, in Evelyn Waugh's *Helena* (1950), is Penelope, Lady Betjeman (1910–), widow of Sir John Betjeman (see Wignall, Dawson). An expert horsewoman, she assisted Waugh with the novel's equestrian details.

HELGIN, Ben, in Maxwell Bodenheim's *Ninth Avenue* (1926), is Ben Hecht (see Herring, Duke Arturo), according to Jack B. Moore, Bodenheim's biographer.

HELMER, Nora, in Henrik Ibsen's *A Doll's House* (1879). Although he was unable to help her in a predicament, Ibsen found Laura Kieler useful as a model, as his biographer Michael Meyer records. The inspiration for Nora Helmer, she in 1870 published *Brand's Daughters*, a women's rights tract in the form of a sequel to Ibsen's *Brand*. Subsequently, when her husband — a Danish schoolmaster — succumbed to tuberculosis, she was told he would die if he were not taken to a warmer climate. She borrowed sufficient money to enable her to take him to Italy, where he recovered. But she still had the problem of repaying the loan, of which he knew nothing and for which her creditor was now pressing. In desperation, she wrote a quick pot-boiler and sent the manuscript to Ibsen in the hope that he might use his influence to have it published, thereby raising enough money to repay her debt. Ibsen was unable to oblige, so she forged a cheque, the fraud was discovered, and when she confessed her predicament to her husband he upbraided her with being unfit to look after their children. This caused her to have a nervous breakdown, whereupon he placed her in a lunatic asylum. Released a month later, she persuaded her husband to take her back, for the sake of the children. He agreed, but with reluctance.

HELSTONE, Caroline, in Charlotte Brontë's *Shirley* (1849), has a putative prototype in the author's school-friend and lifelong correspondent, Ellen Nussey (*d.* 1897), the daughter of a cloth manufacturer from Birstall, Yorkshire. Certainly, Caroline Helstone has Nussey's physical appearance; but the character has also been seen as a tribute to the author's sister, the novelist Anne Brontë (1820–49).

HEMPLE, Luella, in F. Scott Fitzgerald's 'The Adjuster' (1925; *All the Sad Young Men*, 1926), portrays Zelda Fitzgerald (see Diver, Nicole), and in particular her naive belief in her entitlement to the good things of life, at somebody else's expense.

HENDERSON, Dikko, in Ian Fleming's *You Only Live Twice* (1964). When his model for Dikko threatened to sue, Fleming replied, 'Go ahead, Dikko – but I warn you that I will then write the real truth about you.' He was Richard Hughes (1906–84), an Australian newspaperman based in Hong Kong who accompanied Fleming on his fact-finding tour of Japan for *You Only Live Twice* – the novel is dedicated to him. Representing Britain's *Sunday Times* and *The Times* in the Far East, he had previously worked for the Sydney *Daily Telegraph*, acquiring the nickname 'the Monk' because of his ecclesiastical manner and fondness for biblical quotations. Colleagues addressed him as 'Your Grace'.

HENDERSON, Mr and Mrs; Eve; Harriett and Sarah, in Dorothy Richardson's *Pilgrimage* novel cycle (1915–67), have been identified by Richardson's biographer, John Rosenberg. Mr Henderson is the author's father, Charles Richardson, a grocer from Abingdon, Berkshire, who upon inheriting his father's estate in 1874 left 'trade' to become a gentleman of independent means and was subsequently made bankrupt. Mary Richardson (*d.* 1895), the author's mother and the model for Mrs Henderson, was the daughter of a canvas manufacturer from East Coker, Somerset; she killed herself by cutting her throat with a kitchen knife while convalescing in Hastings. Eve is the author's elder sister, Alice Mary Richardson (1868–1910), who became governess to the Harris family of bacon-curers and pork-sausage manufacturers in Calne, Wiltshire, while Harriett and Sarah are, respectively, the author's younger sister, Jessie Abbott Richardson (1874–1962), who in 1895 married Robert Thomas Hale (see Ducayne, Gerald) and ran a Hastings boarding house with him before emigrating to Texas in 1903, and her eldest sister, Frances Kate Richardson (1867–1941), who in 1895 married John Arthur Batchelor (*d.* 1938), agent for a bookbinding materials manufacturer and organist of the Church of St Anne and St Agnes, Gresham Street, in the City of London. He appears in *Pilgrimage* as Bennett Brodie.

HENNEKER, Mrs, in C.P. Snow's *Corridors of Power* (1964). Just as Mrs Henneker pesters Lewis Eliot to read passages from her eulogistic biography of her dead husband, so did Jessica Brett Young, widow of Francis Brett Young (see Knight, Laurence), trouble Snow to read excerpts from her study of Young (1962) – 'at critical moments, and it was maddening', he told his oral biographer, John Halperin. He suppressed his irritation, however, and contributed a preface.

HENRY, Lieutenant Frederic, in Ernest Hemingway's *A Farewell to Arms* (1929), is part-inspired by Lieutenant Edward McKey, an artist who before the First World War had lived in France and Italy. According to Michael S. Reynolds's *Hemingway's First War* (1976), McKey became an ambulance driver for the Italian army and was in 1918 the first Red Cross member to die in Italy, killed near Piave by an Austrian shell.

HERBERT, in Sidonie-Gabrielle Colette's *Julie de Carneilhan* (1941), is supposedly Baron Henri de Jouvenel. See Jean.

HERBERT, Marmion, in Benjamin Disraeli's *Venetia, or The Poet's Daughter* (1841), according to Bevis Hillier's article 'Byronic Attitudes' which appeared in the *Illustrated London News* of June 1974, is Percy Bysshe Shelley. See Glowry, Scythrop.

HERBERT, Mr, in William Hurrell Mallock's *The New Republic* (1877), is the English art critic and social reformer, John Ruskin (1819–1900).

HERMINIUS, in Madeleine de Scudéry's *Clélie, histoire romaine* (1656), is the French littérateur Paul Pellisson (1624–93). As secretary to the financier Nicolas Fouquet, he was imprisoned for five years in the Bastille following his employer's arrest and incarceration for life for embezzlement. He was released by the king, who appointed him historiographer. His history of the Académie Française won him membership of that body.

HERMISTON, Lord, in Robert Louis Stevenson's *Weir of Hermiston* (1896), is supposedly inspired by the account of Robert Macqueen, Lord Braxfield (1721–99), in Lord Cockburn's *Memorials* (1856). Known as 'the Hanging Judge', Braxfield presided over the trial of William Brodie (see Jekyll, Dr).

HERRING, Duke Arturo, in Maxwell Bodenheim's *Duke Herring* (1931), is the author's friend and occasional collaborator, the American dramatist and novelist Ben Hecht (1894–1964), who more than thirty years later declared Bodenheim to have been 'more disliked, derided, denounced, beaten up, and kicked down more flights of stairs than any other poet of whom I have ever heard or read.' *Duke Herring* was Bodenheim's reply to the portrayal of himself in Hecht's *Count Bruga* (1926). Hecht admired Bodenheim's work 'more than the poetry of most of his famed contemporaries', he said in *Letters from Bohemia* (1965), going on to recall how 'it pleased Bodenheim immensely to turn down social invitations. "Thank you for inviting me to dine at your house," he wrote a well-to-do lady who fancied she was running a salon, "but I prefer to dine in the Greek restaurant at Wabash Avenue and 12th Street where I will be limited to finding dead flies in my soup."'

HERRITON, Philip, in E.M. Forster's *Where Angels Fear to Tread* (1905). 'Philip Herriton I modelled on Professor Dent. He knew this, and took an interest in his own progress', said Forster in a *Paris Review* interview (collected in *Writers at Work*, 1958). He was referring to his friend, Edward J. Dent (1876–1957), Professor of Music at Cambridge from 1926 to 1941. '*Where Angels Fear to Tread* should have been called "Monteriano"', said Forster, 'but the publisher thought this wouldn't sell. It was Dent who gave me the present title.'

HERSLAND, David and Fanny, in Gertrude Stein's *The Making of Americans* (1925), are identified by Stein's biographer, James R. Mellow, as the author's parents, Daniel Stein (1832–91) and his wife, Amelia (née Keyser, 1842–85). A German Jew, Daniel arrived in America with his parents in 1841. In 1862 he opened a clothing store in Pittsburgh, and in 1874 he went to Austria to pursue a new business career, returning a few years later to settle in San Francisco where he became vice-president of a street railroad company. Amelia was a member of a Baltimore German-Jewish family.

HERTFORDSHIRE, the Duchess of, in Max Beerbohm's 'Maltby and Braxton' (*Seven Men*, 1919). At Taplow Court, her Buckinghamshire home, Lady Desborough (1867–1952) was the principal hostess of her Edwardian day. Beerbohm was often a guest, taking a quiet pride – as his biographer, David Cecil, records – in the distinguished company he kept. 'Ettie' Desborough, his Duchess of Hertfordshire, was celebrated for both her beauty and her charm. Her husband, William Grenfell, First Baron Desborough, rowed the English Channel in an open boat and twice swam Niagara below the falls. Appropriately, for one so at home with water, he was chairman of the Thames Conservancy Board.

HESSEL, Lona, in Henrik Ibsen's *The Pillars of Society* (1877), is Asta Hansteen, a prominent Norwegian women's rights campaigner who met with such antagonism that in 1880 she left to settle in the United States.

HEWSON, Philip, in Arthur Hugh Clough's *The Bothie of Tober-na-Vuolich* (1848; originally *The Bothie of Toper-na-Fuosich*), is the Revd Thomas Arnold (1823–1900), second son of Thomas Arnold (see Doctor, the), brother of Matthew Arnold (see Luke, Mr), father of Mrs Humphry Ward (see Foxe, Mrs) and grandfather of Aldous Huxley (see Erasmus, William). As a young man he emigrated to New Zealand to farm land bought by his father. He failed in this, married a girl of Huguenot descent, became Inspector of Schools in Tasmania and entered the Catholic Church – a conversion which cost him his job. Returning to England, he settled in Oxford where he edited Wycliffe and Beowulf and produced *A Manual of English Literature*.

HIAWATHA, in Henry Longfellow's *The Song of Hiawatha* (1855), owes his name, but little else, to Hiawatha (*fl. c.* 1570), a Mohawk Iroquois Indian chief who was an organiser of the Iroquois confederacy. The character is partly drawn from legends of Manabozho, a hero of Algonquin Indian tradition. Longfellow's inspiration came from sources including Henry Rowe Schoolcraft's published researches (1839–57) in North American Indian history. Cecil B. Williams's *Longfellow* (1964) notes that the author sent a copy of the poem to Schoolcraft, whose wife was part Chippewa and who had lived for years among Indians. Schoolcraft replied, praising the work's fidelity to the Indian, 'a warrior in war, a savage in revenge, a stoic in endurance, a wolverine in suppleness and cunning. But he is also a father at the head of his lodge, a patriot in the love of his country . . . There has been no attempt, my dear sir, before *Hiawatha* to show this.'

HIGGINS, Henry, in George Bernard Shaw's *Pygmalion* (1913). Shaw was introduced to Henry Sweet (1845–1912), a philologist known today mainly for his Anglo-Saxon Primer and Reader, by James Lecky, who first interested the dramatist in phonetics in 1879. At Oxford, where he was Anglicist Reader in Phonetics, Sweet showed such contempt for colleagues in other disciplines that he became an unpopular figure. In his dotage, his ambition was to do some 'real flying – not with bags and stoves'. Shaw admitted that Henry Higgins displayed 'touches' of Sweet, but this did not stop another phonetician from claiming to be the model. Daniel Jones (1881–1967) – a cousin of Rupert D'Oyly Carte (see Psmith) – founded the Phonetics Department of University College, London, in 1907 and was Professor of Phonetics at London from 1921 to 1949. Jean Overton Fuller, in a letter to the *Observer* (8 January 1978), recalled Jones saying that 'so long as Shaw lived, a box was permanently reserved to his use, free of charge, for any performance of any production of *Pygmalion*. This, Jones understood, was a reward for his having accepted in good part the fiction Shaw had woven around him after a visit to his department, of which he knew nothing until it was sprung on him at the first night. Shaw afterwards told him that it was whilst riding on the deck of a bus through south London, wondering what name he should give him, that he saw over a shop Jones & Higgins. As, because of the fiction, "he could not call me Jones, he called me Higgins".' Other suggestions for Higgins originals are made by Michael Holroyd, the authorised biographer of Shaw, who points to George John Vandaleur Lee (*d.*

1886), mesmeric music-teacher and possibly Shaw's natural father (see Clandon, Mrs Lanfrey), who applied his idiosyncratic teaching method to a pupil called Eliza; and Anthony Masters, who in his biography *Rosa Lewis* (1977) declares that Thomas Lister, Fourth Baron Ribblesdale (1854–1925), 'was taken by Shaw as the prototype for Professor Higgins in *Pygmalion*. Higgins was arrogant but his arrogance was based on a major lack of self-confidence – and Ribblesdale's own personality was not far away from that'. Masters gives no source to substantiate this. Ribblesdale was a lover of Rosa Lewis (see Crump, Lottie). Did he try to eradicate her cockney? Shaw's inspiration may also owe something to 'The Child of the Children', a story by Ethel Turner which appeared in the *Windsor Magazine* in 1897 and was republished in book form in 1959. This described attempts to transform a slum girl into a 'little lady'. The heroine was called Eliza Huggins. True, sixteen years were to pass before the first production of *Pygmalion*. But in 1897 Shaw wrote to Ellen Terry, 'Caesar and Cleopatra has been driven clean out of my head by a play I want to write for them (Forbes-Robertson and Mrs Patrick Campbell) in which he shall be a west end gentleman and she an east end dona in an apron and three orange and red ostrich feathers . . .'

HIGGS, in P.G. Wodehouse's *The Head of Kay's* (1905), is the actor-manager Sir Seymour Hicks (1871–1949), whose Hicks Theatre in London subsequently became the Aldwych. See also Briggs, Stanley.

HIGHMORE, Mrs, in Henry James's 'The Next Time' (1895; *Embarrassments*, 1896). James's friend Mrs Humphry Ward (see Foxe, Mrs) is suggested by her biographer, Enid Huws Jones, as the probable prototype. Like Mrs Highmore, she was a successful novelist, her best-selling *Bessie Costrell* being published in 1895, shortly before 'The Next Time'.

HILARY, Mrs, in Rose Macaulay's *Dangerous Ages* (1921). This novel is dedicated 'To my mother, driving gaily through the adventurous middle years'. But that drive, for Grace Macaulay (née Conybeare, 1855–1925), was hardly gay. According to Rose Macaulay's biographer, Constance Babington Smith, the widowed Grace exasperated her children. Rose lived with her mother out of a misguided sense of duty, blinding herself – in the view of her sister, Jean – to the fact that her mother was miserably aware of being despised. Rose's irritation found expression in *Dangerous Ages*, in which her mother, as Mrs Hilary, is scorned by her children as a 'muddled bigot'. Reading the novel in manuscript, Grace was not so muddled as to fail to recognise herself. Distressed, she asked — apparently without success — for the portrait to be softened. So what are we to make of that dedication? The author's biographer suggests that Rose may have been trying to make amends. Another explanation could be that this was an attempt to allay suspicion, in the minds both of readers and of her mother: a way of saying 'It isn't *really* you'.

HILBERY, Mrs Katherine, in Virginia Woolf's *Night and Day* (1919). 'Preposterous!' cried the artist John Millais on hearing that the novelist Anne Thackeray (1837–1919) had married her godson, who was also her cousin and seventeen years her junior. But Lady Ritchie (as she became) outlived her husband by six years. The eldest daughter of the novelist William Makepeace Thackeray, she was the sister-in-law, by his first marriage, of Virginia Woolf's father and is named by Woolf's biographer, Quentin Bell, as the model for Katherine Hilbery. Lyndall Gordon's *Virginia Woolf* (1984), however, suggests that Mrs Hilbery owes her dependence on reason and her silent stoicism to Vanessa Bell (see Ambrose, Helen), whose painting Gordon equates with Mrs Hilbery's commitment to mathematics.

HILLIARD, Mary, in George Oppenheimer's *Here Today* (1932), is Dorothy Parker (see Glenn, Julia), according to her biographer, John Keats. In the play's first production she was portrayed by the actress Ruth Gordon, who later wrote and starred in *Over Twenty-One*, another play built around a character modelled on Parker. Much though she would like to write her autobiography, Parker is said to have remarked, she hesitated to do so lest George Oppenheimer and Ruth Gordon sue her for plagiarism.

HILLMORTON, Lord, in C.P. Snow's *In Their Wisdom* (1974). 'He hadn't the enormous substance — the hard, rather uniform substance — of Churchill, but he was far more various and interesting', said the author of his publisher, Harold Macmillan (see C), the model for Hillmorton. Snow never knew if Macmillan recognised himself in the portrait but 'he stood me a very good dinner soon after it appeared.'

HINSLEY, Sir Francis, in Evelyn Waugh's *The Loved One: An Anglo-American Tragedy* (1948). Sir C. Aubrey Smith (see Abercrombie, Sir Ambrose) 'was said to look with special suspicion on Evelyn', notes Waugh's biographer, Christopher Sykes. He had good reason. Not only was he portrayed in *The Loved One* as Abercrombie; he was also, suggests Sheridan Morley's *Tales from the Hollywood Raj* (1983), the model for Hinsley, an actor from much the same mould as Abercrombie, but one whose failure and consequent suicide contrast with the success of his counterpart.

HLAVA, Colonel, in Anthony Powell's *The Military Philosophers* (1968), is identified by the author (*Faces in My Time*, 1980) as Colonel (subsequently Brigadier-General) Josef Kalla, Czech military attaché in London in the Second World War. A First World War aviator (having transferred to flying from the infantry of the Imperial and Royal Austro-Hungarian army), he died while under house arrest after his return to Soviet-occupied Czechoslovakia following the Second World War. Although touchy about others' identifications of his models, Powell is by no means unforthcoming in naming his originals himself.

HOBBLEDAY, Jack, in John Poole's *Little Pedlington and the Pedlingtonians* (1839), is Tom Hill. See Pry, Paul.

HOBBS, Roy, in Bernard Malamud's *The Natural* (1952), is based in part on the American baseball player Babe Ruth (?1895–1948), whose stomach trouble of 1925 is matched by Hobbs's abdominal ailment. The identification is made by Earl Wasserman (the *Centennial Review*, Fall, 1965) and is discussed by Tony Tanner in *City of Words: American Fiction 1950–70* (1971).

HOBSON, Alan, in Wyndham Lewis's *Tarr* (1918), is Clive Bell (see Bell, Jonathan). Lewis's biographer, Jeffrey Meyers, notes that Bell had criticised the author for lending his talent to 'a little backwater called English vorticism, which already gives signs of becoming as insipid as any other puddle of provincialism.'

HOCCLEVE, the Venerable Henry (the Archdeacon), in Barbara Pym's *Some Tame Gazelle* (1950). According to Hazel Holt and Hilary Pym, the editors of the author's diaries (1984), Hoccleve's original is Henry Harvey, a contemporary at Oxford with whom the author had an affair and who remained a lifelong friend.

Taking a job with the British Council, he went to Helsinki and married a Finn.

HODGE, William in A.G. Macdonnell's *England, Their England* (1933), is Sir John (J.C.) Squire (1884–1958), poet, literary critic and editor of the *London Mercury* from 1919 to 1934. In the 1920s he captained a literary cricket eleven, the Invalids. Macdonnell's portrayal of him on the field as the cricketing editor of the *London Weekly* 'was no caricature at all. It really was like that', remarked Alec Waugh in *My Brother Evelyn and Other Profiles* (1967). The first time he played against the Invalids, Waugh recalled, the match began nearly two-and-a-half hours late, 'with the last two places filled by an 11-year-old schoolboy and the taxi driver who had driven half the side from the remote station to which they had been misdirected.'

HOFF, Marcus, in Clifford Odets's *The Big Knife* (1948). Here we have the author as both creator and undertaker. Marcus Hoff, megalomaniac film producer, is believed to have been based on Harry Cohn (see Brock, Harry), says Cohn's biographer, Bob Thomas. And it was Odets who wrote the eulogy delivered by Danny Kaye at Cohn's funeral.

HÖFGEN, Hendrik and Barbara, in Klaus Mann's *Mephisto* (1936), are the author's brother-in-law and sister: the German actor Gustaf Gründgens (*d.* 1963) and his wife, Erika Mann (1905–69). Gründgens was celebrated for his interpretation of Goethe's Mephistopheles. Through his friendship with the actress wife of Hermann Goering, he gained control of the Prussian State Theatre in Berlin. He died at the age of sixty-four from an overdose of sleeping pills. An actress turned journalist, Erika was the eldest daughter of Thomas Mann (see Arnold). Her marriage to Gründgens ended in 1928. Leaving Germany in 1933, as an outspoken critic of the Nazi regime she was threatened with the loss of her German citizenship. In 1935 she asked Christopher Isherwood (see Pimpernell) to marry her so that she could become a British subject. Isherwood demurred, but suggested his friend W.H. Auden (see Weston, Hugh) instead, and Auden promptly obliged. She then settled with her father in the United States, remaining his secretary and companion for the rest of his life.

HOG, in Alexander Zinoviev's *The Yawning Heights* (1979), is Nikita Khrushchev (1894–1971), Soviet premier from 1958 to 1964.

Like Khrushchev, Hog becomes his nation's leader, makes a speech denouncing the Boss (Stalin) and is later removed from power, not to 'disappear into oblivion and disgrace as his predecessors had done', but to find his name associated with the two greatest developments in his country's history: the unmasking of the Boss and the rehabilitation of millions of the Boss's victims.

HOGARTH, Tom, in Arnold Bennett's *Lord Raingo* (1926). This novel's 'short, bald, blonde and challenging Minister of Munitions' who recalls his 1899 escape as a prisoner-of-war is Winston Churchill (see Catskill, Rupert). He is described as 'one of the finest polemical and descriptive writers in the country', with 'every gift except common sense', and the ability to 'rise victorious even from the disasters imposed upon him by an incurable foolishness.' When it was published, *Lord Raingo* was attacked in the *Daily Mail* by Lord Birkenhead. The author replied with an article and the affair became a public row. Churchill, recognising himself as Hogarth, encountered Bennett at a dinner just after the brush with Birkenhead had subsided, with Bennett the victor. 'Receive the congratulations of Tom Hogarth', said Churchill.

HOLDHURST, Lord, in Sir Arthur Conan Doyle's 'The Naval Treaty' (*The Memoirs of Sherlock Holmes*, 1893). According to Charles Higham's *The Adventures of Conan Doyle* (1976), Holdhurst is based on A.J. Balfour (see Evesham, Sir Arthur), who became a friend of Doyle. 'Knowingly,' says Higham, 'Conan Doyle places Lord Holdhurst's chambers in Downing Street, and his nephew's country place at Woking, in Surrey, the home of Balfour's brother and nephews.'

HOLMAN, Farmer, in Elizabeth Gaskell's *Cousin Phillis* (1863—4), is identified by the Gaskell biographer Winifred Gérin as the author's grandfather, Samuel Holland, farmer and preacher of Sandlebridge, Knutsford, Cheshire. He was a friend of the celebrated potter Josiah Wedgwood — the Holland and Wedgwood families were linked by marriage.

HOLMES, Colonel, in George S. Kaufman and Morrie Ryskind's *Strike Up the Band* (1930), according to Kaufman's biographer, Scott Meredith, is Colonel Edward Mandell House (1858—1938), an American diplomat who was on the staff of Governor Culberson of

Texas and who was a confidant and adviser of President Woodrow Wilson.

HOLMES, Sherlock, in Sir Arthur Conan Doyle's 'Sherlock Holmes' stories (1887–1927). Though Doyle named his model for Holmes, you would hardly expect the deductive passion of his readers to be satisfied with that. The case for at least five other prototypes has been canvassed. The author acknowledged that his inspiration for Holmes came from Dr Joseph Bell (1837–1911), a surgeon, and professor at Edinburgh University, who would deduce from a patient's appearance not only his malady but also his occupation and place of residence. As a medical student and Bell's out-patient clerk, Doyle observed the surgeon's detective ability at first hand, on one occasion witnessing his deduction that a patient had recently been a non-commissioned officer in a Highland regiment stationed in Barbados. 'The man was respectful,' Bell explained, 'but did not remove his hat. They do not in the army, but he would have learned civilian ways had he been long discharged. He has an air of authority and is obviously Scottish. As to Barbados, his complaint is elephantiasis, which is West Indian and not British.' As an independent investigator, Holmes has a possible prototype in Wendel Scherer, private consulting detective of Westbourne Grove, Bayswater, who claimed professional status in a London murder case reported in the Press four years before Holmes's creation, while Owen Dudley Edwards (*The Quest for Sherlock Holmes*, 1982) suggests that Holmes's dedication to experimental research may owe something to Professor Sir Robert Christison (1797–1882). This Edinburgh toxicologist, as medical expert witness in the trial of the Edinburgh body-snatchers Burke and Hare, beat corpses in an effort to ascertain whether a body would bruise after death. Another supposed influence is Oliver Wendell Holmes (1809–94), an American author and professor of anatomy to whose works Doyle was devoted. Holmes probably owes his manic qualities to Dr George Turnavine Budd (see Challenger, Professor George Edward), and David Garnett (*The Familiar Faces*, 1962) suggests a further model in Humphrey Lloyd, a missionary to the Maoris in New Zealand and the younger brother of Doyle's friend Mrs M.A. Marshall, who was Garnett's mother-in-law. The detective's physical appearance is part-inspired by what Doyle described in his memoirs as the 'eagle face' of Bell; and by Walter Paget, an *Illustrated London News* artist who acted as model for his brother, Sidney Paget, the Holmes stories' most popular illustrator. It is to Sidney Paget that Holmes owes his deerstalker (not mentioned in the stories); his curved pipe was added by an American illustrator, Frederick Dorr Steele, after Paget's death. Holmes's portrayal was further influenced by the stage interpretation of the detective by the American actor William Gillette. Doyle's choice of a name supposedly derives from two county cricketers – originally, it was to have been Sherrinford Holmes, until the author recalled the Yorkshire wicket-keeper Mordecai Sherlock. But there was also a well-known violinist of Holmes's day, Alfred Sherlock ...

HOLOFERNES, in William Shakespeare's *Love's Labour's Lost* (1598), has two suggested models: Alexander Aspinall (*d.* 1624), a graduate of Brasenose, Oxford, who was master of Stratford-upon-Avon grammar school from 1582 to 1624 and who married a well-to-do widow, becoming a successful Stratford businessman and alderman while continuing to teach; and John Florio (1553–1625), lexicographer and first translator of Montaigne's essays into English – 'Holofernes' supposedly being an imperfect anagram of his name.

HOLT, Felix, in George Eliot's *Felix Holt the Radical* (1866). The Dictionary of National Biography and a number of Eliot studies published in the first forty years of this century name Gerald Massey (1828–1907), a self-educated Socialist poet, as Holt's prototype. But none of the more recent works on Eliot which I have consulted – including Haight, Laski and Allen –gives Massey a mention. Could it be that nobody now wishes to be seen giving credence to the Massey identification ... but nobody is sure enough of their ground to dispute it? Now is the time for Tring (Hertfordshire) Socialists to rally to the flag. That's where Massey came from.

HOMARTYN, Lady, in H.G. Wells's *Mr Britling Sees It Through* (1916). In 1911 the author became a tenant and neighbour of Frances ('Daisy') Evelyn Greville, Countess of Warwick (1861–1938), leasing from her the Old Rectory at Little Easton, Essex. The Countess lived at Easton Lodge, playing hostess to politicians for whom her home was a popular weekend retreat. Her estate is largely the setting of this novel, just as she is the model for Lady Homartyn. A mistress of the Prince of Wales (whom she tried unsuccessfully to blackmail), in 1895 she became an instant convert to Socialism when she called on Robert Blatchford, editor of the *Clarion*, to demand an explanation for a highly critical account of a ball at Warwick Castle for which lilies were imported from the South of France, Louis XV and XVI costumes were the order of the evening, and she had appeared as Marie Antoinette (gown by Worth). Blatchford's Socialist eloquence on her extravagance won her to his cause. Step-sister of the Duchess of Sutherland (see Chell, the Countess of), she subsequently concerned herself with her tenants' education and favoured 'progressive' clergy for her livings. She established a technical school and a school of needlework (with a showroom in Bond Street), but when she forgot to pay her needlework girls for several weeks they went on strike.

HOME, Paulina, in Charlotte Brontë's *Villette* (1853), has a suggested model in Julia Bradford Gaskell (1846–1908), daughter of the author's friend, the novelist Elizabeth Gaskell. From evidence adduced by the biographer Winifred Gérin, this identification seems more likely than the claim by Ellen Nussey (see Helstone, Caroline) that Paulina is Fanny Whipp, adopted daughter of Charlotte's friends John and Sophia Hudson, of Easton House, Bridlington, Yorkshire.

HOMEWARD, Winifred, in Sinclair Lewis's *Gideon Planish* (1943), according to Sheldon N. Grebstein's *Sinclair Lewis* (1962), is a caricature of the author's second wife, Dorothy Thompson (see Cortwright, Edith), from whom he had recently been divorced.

HONEYCHURCH, Mrs, in E.M. Forster's *A Room with a View* (1908). Forster's biographer, P.N. Furbank, identifies Mrs Honeychurch's original as the author's resilient maternal grandmother, Louisa Whichelo (née Graham, 1827–1911), who in 1867, upon the death of her artist husband (Henry Mayle, junior), supported her ten children by taking in boarders.

HOOPER, Lady Artemis, in D.H. Lawrence's *Aaron's Rod* (1922), is identified by the Lawrence biographer Emile Delavenay as Lady Diana Cooper (see Stitch, Mrs Algernon). Artemis Hooper's fall through the window of a taxi is supposedly inspired by Diana Cooper's fall through a sky-light, which was widely reported in the Press. The portrait cannot have rankled: Artemis Cooper is the name of Lady Diana's granddaughter, prompted, I presume, by Lawrence's Artemis ... unless it was bestowed as a compliment to the grandmother, Artemis being the Greek counterpart of the Roman goddess, Diana – hence Lawrence's choice of name for the character.

HOPE, the Rt Hon. Trelawney, in Sir Arthur Conan Doyle's 'The Adventure of the Second Stain' (*The Return of Sherlock Holmes*, 1905), is suggested by the Doyle biographer Charles Higham to be the author's friend, the statesman Joseph Chamberlain (1836–1914).

HORACE, in Thomas Dekker's *Satiromastix, or The Untrussing of the Humorous Poet* (1602), is the dramatist Ben Jonson (1572–1637), who in *The Poetaster* (1601) had portrayed himself as Horace and attacked Dekker as 'Demetrius'.

HORTENSE, Mlle, in Charles Dickens's *Bleak House* (1852–3). Attending both the trial and the hanging of his model for Mlle Hortense, Dickens was moved to write to *The Times*, inveighing against public executions. Mlle Hortense was based on Maria Manning (née Marie de Roux, 1821–49), a former lady's maid to the Duchess of Sunderland. Swiss-born, she was hanged with her husband after the couple were convicted of murdering a money-lender whose body was found buried in quicklime beneath the floor of their Bermondsey home in London. She was arrested by Inspector Charles Field (see Bucket, Inspector) and her execution took place at London's Horsemonger Lane gaol, where she was reported to have attempted suicide by grasping her throat so tightly that the finger-nails she had specially sharpened were forced into the windpipe. Tradition has it that Mrs Manning's choice of black satin for her hanging was responsible for that material going out of fashion, but recent research suggests that the market for black satin was unaffected.

HORTY, Mr, in Wyndham Lewis's *The Apes of God* (1930), is the American-born poet, Thomas Stearns Eliot (1888–1965). The name chosen by Lewis reflects Eliot's reserved, often withdrawn temperament, which some saw as aloofness. Inclined to be pontifical, and with a remarkable capacity for boredom (even with Paris), he had a tight-buttoned personality which was echoed by his clothes – 'Come to dinner', Virginia Woolf wrote to Clive Bell, 'Eliot will be there in a four-piece suit.' Whatever he may have thought of Horty, Eliot approved of Wyndham Lewis's 1938 painting of himself – 'one by which I am quite willing that posterity should know me, if it takes any interest in me at all.'

HOSKINS, in W.M. Thackeray's *The Newcomes* (1853—5), according to the author's biographer, Lewis Melville, is John Rhodes,
landlord of the Coal Hole, a tavern in a court off the Strand, on a site
later occupied by Terry's Theatre.

HOWARD, Mr and Mrs Will, in Angela Thirkell's *Ankle Deep*
(1933), are the author's parents, Professor John William Mackail (*d.*
1945), Professor of Poetry at Oxford from 1906 to 1911, and his
wife, Margaret (1866—1953), daughter of Sir Edward Burne-Jones
and cousin of Rudyard Kipling and Stanley Baldwin. Denis Mackail,
their son, was a popular novelist who is best remembered for
Greenery Street.

HOYT, Rosemary, in F. Scott Fitzgerald's *Tender is the Night*
(1934), is the American film actress Lois Moran (1908—   ). They
met when she was twenty, he thirty. On Fitzgerald's arrival in
Hollywood, she wanted him to play opposite her as her leading man
and arranged a screen test for him. It was unsuccessful.

HUBBARD, Bull, in Jack Kerouac's *Desolation Angels* (1966), is
William S. Burroughs. See Dennison, Will.

HUBBARD, Wilson Holmes, in Jack Kerouac's *Vanity of Duluoz*
(1968), is William S. Burroughs. See Dennison, Will.

HUDIBRAS, Sir, in Samuel Butler's *Hudibras* (1662—78), has a
number of suggested models. They include the author's patron, Sir
Samuel Luke (*d.* 1670), a colonel in the Parliamentary army, governor of Newport Pagnell, Buckinghamshire, scoutmaster-general in
the army of the Earl of Essex, and MP for Bedford; Sir Henry
Rosewell, of Forde Abbey, Devon; and Colonel Rolle, a Devonshire
man who lodged with Butler. The name Hudibras was derived by
Butler from Hugh de Bras, tutelar saint of Devon.

HULL, in Theodore Hook's *Gilbert Gurney* (1836), is Tom Hill. See
Pry, Paul.

HULOT, Baron, in Honoré de Balzac's *La Cousine Bette* (1846). He
loved like a lord, and because he *was* a lord the French novelist, poet
and dramatist Victor Hugo (1802—85) got away with it. In
nineteenth-century France, if you thought your spouse was up to no
good you did not hire a private detective. You simply informed the

police, for adultery was a criminal offence. The artist Auguste Biard suspected his wife, Léonie, of infidelity with Hugo. At Biard's request, police raided a back-street apartment where Hugo and Léonie were found together in bed ... just as Balzac's Hulot is discovered by the police in bed with his mistress. Léonie was arrested and imprisoned. Hugo, claiming immunity as a peer, went free ... and hurried home to tell his wife before someone else did. Not only did Adèle Hugo forgive him; she also visited Léonie in prison ... but then, she was accustomed to her husband's philandering and had taken a lover herself (see Couaën, Madame de). Hugo was fortunate that the incident occurred in 1845; three years later, life peerages were abolished with the Revolution. As this episode and the character's name suggest, Hulot is Hugo — but only in part, for this is also a Balzac self-portrait.

HUMBOLDT (Von Humboldt Fleisher), in Saul Bellow's *Humboldt's Gift* (1975), is the American poet Delmore Schwartz (1913–66), whose mental instability led to his entering an asylum, where Bellow sought to help him by arranging a collection to pay for psychiatric treatment — a gesture which Schwartz resented.

HUMPHREY, Master, in Charles Dickens's *Master Humphrey's Clock* (1840–1) and *The Old Curiosity Shop* (1841), is Thomas Humphreys (1788–1868), a clockmaker of Barnard Castle, Durham. In 1838 Dickens stayed at Barnard Castle while researching material for *Nicholas Nickleby*, and Humphreys assisted him with information on Yorkshire boarding schools.

HUNSDEN, Yorke, in Charlotte Brontë's *The Professor* (1857), is Joshua Taylor. See Yorke, Hiram.

HUNTER, Mrs Leo, in Charles Dickens's *The Posthumous Papers of the Pickwick Club* (1836–7). So compulsive in her later years was the kleptomania of Lady Cork (1746–1840) that she became notorious for her attachment to the property of others and was even reported by the actress Fanny Kemble to have misappropriated a hedgehog, carrying it off 'from a place where the creature was a pet of the porters, and was running tame about the hall as Lady Cork crossed it to get into her carriage. She made her poor "Memory" [her companion] seize up the prickly beast, but after driving a few miles with this unpleasant spiked foot-warmer, she found means to dispose of it at a small town, where she stopped to change horses, to a baker, to whom she gave it in payment for a sponge cake, assuring him a hedgehog would be invaluable in his establishment for the destruction of black beetles, with which she knew, from good authority, that the premises of bakers were always infested.' Kemble also noted that 'fashionable London tradesmen, to whom her infirmity in this respect was well known, never allowed their goods to be taken to her carriage for inspection, but always exacted that she should come into their shops, where an individual was immediately appointed to follow her about and watch her during the whole time she was making her purchases. Whenever she visited her friends in the country, her maid on her return home used to gather together whatever she did not recognise as belonging to her mistress, and her butler transmitted it back to the house where they had been staying.' On hearing that Lady Cork had said she thought heaven would be very dull, Lady Harriet d'Orsay remarked, 'I suppose it would be rather tiresome for her, poor thing, for you know she hates music, and there would be nothing to steal but one another's wings.' Lady Cork was born Mary Monckton, daughter of the First Viscount Galway, and James Boswell noted how in her youth she enchanted Samuel Johnson with the vivacity of her conversation. Marrying the Seventh Earl of Cork and Orrery, she became a celebrated literary lion-hunter, which led to her prompt popular identification with Mrs Leo Hunter. The poetic aspect of Mrs Hunter, as author of 'Ode to an Expiring Frog', is believed to have been inspired by the verse of Elizabeth Cobbold (1767–1824), the wife of a Suffolk brewer.

HUNTINGDON, Arthur, in Anne Brontë's *The Tenant of Wildfell Hall* (1848). For the drunken, dissolute Huntingdon, the author needed to look no further than her brother, who is suggested by the Brontë biographer Margot Peters as the model. Branwell Brontë (1817–48) was a talented wastrel, whose addiction to drink and opium led to his early death.

HURLE, Leverson, in *Gin and Bitters* (1931), by A. Riposte (Evelyn May Wiehe, whose principal pseudonym was Elinor Mordaunt). 'Where will all this end?' asked Hugh Walpole, appalled by this malicious attack on W. Somerset Maugham (see Bertrand, Archie), presented as Leverson Hurle, a writer who repays the hospitality of his hosts in the Far East by putting them and the gossip about them into his stories. *Gin and Bitters* was written in retaliation for Maugham's acid portrayal of Thomas Hardy and Walpole in *Cakes and Ale* (see Driffield, Edward; Kear, Alroy), Wiehe being a friend of Hardy's second wife. Suspected of having written *Gin and Bitters* himself, Walpole was happy to help Maugham's publishers when they asked him to add his weight to their attempts to persuade Leverson Hurle's model to block the book's publication in Britain, following its appearance in the United States. *Gin and Bitters* duly arrived, retitled *Full Circle* for its English edition. Maugham sued for libel and a few weeks later the book was withdrawn.

HUSHABYE, Hector, in George Bernard Shaw's *Heartbreak House* (1917). 'A seducer on the best 18th century lines', was how H.G. Wells described Hubert Bland (1856–1914), one of Shaw's models for Hector. Wells spoke as an expert (see Wilson, Hypo), though his own attempt to seduce Bland's daughter, Rosamund, was unsuccessful. Bland was a leading Fabian whose public pronouncements on matters of morality contrasted oddly with his private life, and he is identified as an ingredient of Hector by the Shaw biographer, Stanley Weintraub. A brush-manufacturer, Bland became a left-wing journalist, the Fabians' treasurer and the husband of the children's writer, Edith Nesbit, author of *The Railway Children*. As a boxer he was Shaw's sparring partner, but it was as a womaniser that he was most remarkable. In addition to his wife's progeny, he had two children by another woman. They took the Bland name, his wife bringing them up as her own. Wilfrid Scawen Blunt (see Fitzgerald, Burgo) is another model for Hector, suggests Dan H. Laurence, editor of Shaw's *Letters*, and Weintraub also names R.B. Cunninghame Graham (1852–1936). The son of a Scottish laird who died insane, Cunninghame Graham inherited the encumbrance of Gartmore, the crumbling family mansion, and 10,000 boggy Perthshire acres. He became an anarchist (imprisoned following a riot in Trafalgar Square), a dock-strike leader, the first president of the Scottish National Party, a Socialist MP, the author of nearly thirty books and a traveller in remote places. His greatest achievement, said G.K. Chesterton, was 'the adventure of being Cunninghame Graham'.

HUSHABYE, Hesione, *idem*. We have the word of her distinguished contemporaries that Mrs Patrick Campbell (1865–1940) was a great actress, when she felt like it. But for that it would be difficult to believe, though no one would dispute that she was a great character. Shaw, who acknowledged her to be his inspiration for Hesione, became infatuated with her when she appeared in the first production of his *Pygmalion*. The part of Eliza Doolittle was written with her in mind, Shaw relishing the thought of this actress, noted for her superb diction and elegance of dress, appearing as a cockney. He also wrote her more than ninety letters, which in later years she carried with her in a hat-box, not so much out of sentiment as with regard to their market value — £200 a letter was the price she put on them. Her success as an actress was achieved despite her disruptive, capricious behaviour. She would change her lines, to throw other members of the cast; start a performance as Ophelia with her own dark hair and finish it wearing a flaxen wig; flick chocolates at the backdrop during a death scene in which she was the corpse; leave the stage without warning for a glass of water; turn her back on the audience, about whom she would make audible comments — 'Oh, the Marquis and Marchioness of Empty are in front again!' Though she appeared under her married name, it was almost a surprise that such a larger-than-life woman could have a partner. 'Your *husband*?' said Oscar Wilde, on being introduced to the overshadowed Mr Patrick Campbell. 'How *suburban*!' Widowed at the turn of the century, she remarried, expressing her appreciation of 'the deep, deep peace of the double bed after the hurly-burly of the chaise longue'. But her second husband spent all her money and left her for a mistress, and the son she idolised collected his Military Cross at Buckingham Palace and returned to his regiment, to be killed at Gallipoli. Shaw wrote, but could offer no condolence. It was just one more log for the fire of his fury against war, to be expressed in *Heartbreak House*. Mrs Patrick Campbell consoled herself. War had taught her that 'I had brought a *man* into the world — that is enough'. Becoming stout, she likened her appearance to 'an elderly wasp in an interesting condition'. Her self-destructive streak became more pronounced. Though needing help, she could do nothing but insult and repel her allies. 'She was like a sinking ship', said Alexander Woollcott, 'firing on the rescuers.'

HUTTON, Henry, in Aldous Huxley's 'The Gioconda Smile' (*Mortal Coils*, 1922). According to Tage la Cour and Harald Mogensen's *The Murder Book* (1971), Hutton's prototype was Harold Greenwood, a solicitor from Llanelly, Powys. In 1920, when he was forty-five, he was accused of murdering his wife by administering arsenic in a bottle of Burgundy. Acquitted after his daughter testified that she had drunk from the same bottle, he died nine years later, a broken man.

HYDE, Mr. See Jekyll, Dr.

HYGATT, in Sinclair Lewis and Dore Schary's *Storm in the West* (written 1943, published 1963), is Adolf Hitler (see Ui, Arturo). Lewis begrudged the time his wife, the journalist Dorothy Thompson, spent in Europe as a result of her commitment to international politics, and is reputed to have said that if he were to divorce her he would cite Hitler as co-respondent. But when divorce arrived, years later, he did not carry out the threat. Dorothy Thompson (see Cortwright, Edith) interviewed the Nazi leader and in *I Saw Hitler* (1932) portrayed him as having a countenance that was 'a caricature of a drummer-boy risen too high'. This caused her immediate expulsion from Germany when she went again to Berlin in 1934.

HYMAN, Rhoda, in Wyndham Lewis's *The Roaring Queen* (1936), is a portrait of a celebrated writer as a plagiarist. Virginia Woolf (see Aspasia) is the model. Lewis, says his biographer, Jeffrey Meyers, accused Woolf of criticising the realism of James Joyce, while relying on the description of the Viceroy's progress through Dublin in *Ulysses* for hers of the Queen's through London in *Mrs Dalloway*.

I

IBERIN, Angelo, in Bertolt Brecht's *The Roundheads and the Peakheads* (written 1932–4, first performed 1936). The demagoguery and racism of Iberin represent Adolf Hitler (see Ui, Arturo), but in the character's sexual greed the Brecht biographer Ronald Hayman sees a resemblance to Hermann Goering (see Gerrett; see also Giri).

IDA, Princess, in Alfred, Lord Tennyson's 'The Princess' (1847). Her first encounter with the poet was a meeting never forgotten by Lady Duff Gordon (née Lucie Austin, 1821–69). Stretching himself out on the carpet, Tennyson rolled across the floor to her and said 'Will you please to put your foot on me for a stool?' Suggested in John Killham's *Tennyson and 'The Princess'* (1958) to be a model for Ida, she was a writer, translator and hostess, and the mother of Janet Ross (see Jocelyn, Rose). 'I never loved a dear gazelle, but some damned brute, that's you, Gordon, had married her first', Tennyson told her husband.

IDLE, Thomas, in Charles Dickens's *The Lazy Tour of Two Idle Apprentices* (1857), is the novelist Wilkie Collins (1824–89), who accompanied Dickens on a walking-tour of Cumberland – the inspiration for this book, of which Collins was part-author. Descending in mist from Carrick Fell, Collins sprained his ankle badly and had to be carried by Dickens, who was flattered by his reception during this Lakeland excursion. Writing home to Georgina Hogarth, he said she would hardly believe the attention paid her novelist brother-in-law in the North: 'Station-masters assist him to alight from carriages, deputations await him in hotel entries, innkeepers bow down before him and put him into regal rooms, the town goes down to the platform to see him off, and Collins's ankle goes into the newspapers!!!'

INCE, Lester, in C.P. Snow's *The Affair* (1960). What was the reaction of the novelist Kingsley Amis (1922–) when it became known that he was Ince's model? Was he outraged by the portrait? Well, no . . . because, he tells me, he has not read *The Affair*. There's insouciance for you – but then, as almost every Snow character seems to have been based on one acquaintance or another, many of them less than magnetic, Amis's indifference is perhaps understandable. When Snow revealed him to be Ince, in John Halperin's oral biography, the critic Julian Symons noted, 'Ince-Amis is distinctly recognisable when we learn that he was the only person who ever called Lewis Eliot "Lew".' Contrast this, however, with Amis's comment on Ted Hughes's appointment as Poet Laureate: 'Dog doesn't bite dog, but it's a bit thick. One was gradually getting used to the idea of having a bishop called Jim Stepney – and now we find ourselves with a Poet Laureate called Ted Hughes!'

IÑEZ, Donna, in Lord Byron's *Don Juan* (1819–24), is part-inspired by Anna Isabella Milbanke (1792–1860) who after rejecting his first proposal, married Byron in 1815. Before their marriage, her interest in mathematics prompted him to call her his Princess of Parallelograms – 'we are two parallel lines prolonged to infinity side by side, but never to meet.' It would have been better had they never converged. She left him a year after their marriage, claiming he was mad and accusing him of cruelty and of incest with his half-sister (see Astarte). In 1856, she succeeded to the title of Baroness Wentworth (her mother was a daughter of Lord Wentworth, her father was Sir Ralph Milbanke). Byron's mathematical joke is echoed in Donna Iñez, 'perfect beyond all parallel'.

INFANT PHENOMENON, the, in Charles Dickens's *Nicholas Nickleby* (1838–9), is Jean Davenport, daughter of T.D. Davenport (see Crummles, Vincent).

INTRIGUER, Lord, in Ronald Firbank's *The Flower Beneath the Foot* (1923), is Courtenay Charles Evan Morgan, First Viscount Tredegar (1867–1934). The father of Evan Morgan (see Monteith, the Hon. 'Eddy', and Lombard, Ivor), he was suspected by Firbank of involvement in his son's refusal to accept the dedication of *The Princess Zoubaroff* (1920).

INVESTIGATOR, the, in Reuben Ship's *The Investigator* (1954), is Joseph McCarthy (1908–57), a Wisconsin senator notorious for his stage-management in the early 1950s of an anti-Communist purge in the United States — an investigation which became known as 'the McCarthy witch-hunt'. Finally discredited as a self-seeking opportunist, McCarthy returned to the obscurity from which he had come.

IORIS, Prince, in *Friendship* (1878), by Ouida (Louise Ramé), is the Marchese Lotteria Lotharingo della Stufa, a Florentine land-owner wooed unsuccessfully by the author — he was already provided with a domineering mistress (see Challoner, Lady Joan).

IPHIGENIE, in Johann Wolfgang von Goethe's *Iphigenie auf Tauris* (1787), is part-inspired by Charlotte von Stein, the wife of a Weimar courtier and Goethe's senior by seven years. The poet had a twelve-year affair with her, which ended in 1786.

IRÈNE, in Édouard Bourdet's *La Prisonnière* (1926). With a *ménage à trois* theme, this play concludes with the wife's lover being revealed as another woman — a situation altogether too close to home for Violet Trefusis (see Romanovitch, Princess 'Sasha'), who was taken to be Irène, and her lover, Princesse Edmond de Polignac (see Vinaigrette). To outface any scandal arising from *La Prisonnière*, the princess in 1927 took Violet and her husband, Denys Trefusis, on a much publicised visit to the United States.

IRTENYEV, in Leo Tolstoy's *Childhood* (1852), is the author's wife's grandfather, Alexander Mikhailovich Islenyev, a profligate gambler. The Tolstoy biographer Henri Troyat records that Islenyev first married the estranged wife of a count, who had the marriage annulled ... after it had produced six children. His second wife, an heiress, bore him three more children, her estate at Ivitsi becoming a refuge from creditors pressing for payment of his ever-increasing gambling debts.

ISAACS, Mr, in Francis Marion Crawford's *Mr Isaacs* (1892), is A.M. Jacob. See Lurgan Sahib.

ISABELLA, in John Keats's 'Isabella' (*Lamia, Isabella, The Eve of St. Agnes and other Poems*, 1820). Not only was 'The Eve of St. Agnes' written at the suggestion of Mrs Isabella Jones, says Robert Gittings in *John Keats: The Living Year* (1954), but Mrs Jones was also the poet's Isabella. She was handsome, sophisticated and wealthy, and Keats first met her at Hastings in 1817. There was later an attachment between them, in London, where she became a member of his circle.

ISIS, the Priestess of, in D.H. Lawrence's *The Escaped Cock* (Paris, 1929; published in Britain as *The Man Who Died*, 1931). After the author's death, Stephen Guest (later Lord Haden-Guest), the son of Lawrence's friend Mrs David Eder, gave a copy of *The Man Who Died* to Hilda Doolittle (see Masters, Miranda), telling her it had been written for her and that she was the Priestess of Isis. Doolittle's biographer, Janice S. Robinson, also notes that in his introduction to the Godine edition of Doolittle's *Tribute to Freud*, Professor Kenneth Fields writes that Lawrence described the priestess 'in terms that apply very clearly to Hilda Doolittle'.

IVEY, Benjamin Franklin, in Jerome Weidman's *Before You Go* (1960). Such are the similarities between Ivey's career and that of Harry L. Hopkins (1890–1946), the American Special Adviser and Assistant to the President from 1940 to 1945, that Hopkins is thought to be the model.

J

JACK, Esther, in Thomas Wolfe's *The Web and the Rock* (1939). He was twenty-five and unpublished, she forty-four and a successful New York stage designer, when Wolfe met and fell in love with his model for Esther: Aline Bernstein Klein (1880–1955), who was happily married to a well-to-do Wall Street broker. Providing Wolfe with a place where he could work and they could make love, she had an intense affair with him until, six years later, the success of his *Look Homeward, Angel* gave him independence. Now he saw her as an ageing encumbrance: Aline, the mother figure, was no longer needed – until, on his death-bed, he asked for her. But by then she, in turn, had wearied of him.

JACK, Uncle, in Beryl Bainbridge's *The Dressmaker* (1973). Beryl Bainbridge has relatives the way other people have shares . . . and in her novels they have paid good dividends, especially her father, whom she has acknowledged to be Uncle Jack. Richard Bainbridge is a recurring character and inspiration in her writing. A Liverpool commercial traveller, he claimed to have gone to the United States as a sailing ship's cabin-boy, to have introduced safety matches to Berlin and to have been a diamond dealer in Holland. After becoming bankrupt during the Depression, he remained in business, his cheques signed by his wife, born Winifred Baines, educated at a Belgian convent and the French-speaking product of a finishing school, who as the daughter of a director of the Liverpool paint-manufacturers Goodlass Wall felt she had married beneath her. In Bainbridge's *A Quiet Life* (1976) the couple appear as Father and Mother.

JACKSON, in Lord Byron's *Hints from Horace* (written 1811, published 1831), is the English boxer John Jackson (1769–1845), who fought as 'Gentleman Jackson', is credited with investing the sport with scientific principles, and by taking pupils reputedly made more than £1000 a year.

JACKSON, Mr, in E.M. Forster's *The Longest Journey* (1907), is Isaac Smedley (*d.* 1934), the author's classics master at Tonbridge School, Kent, and found by his pupil to be an inspired teacher, though a poor disciplinarian. He subsequently taught at Westminster School.

JACKSON, Sillerton, in Edith Wharton's *The Age of Innocence* (1920), is an amalgam of Egerton Winthrop (*d.* 1916), a cultivated and much-travelled New York lawyer, banker and socialite who introduced the author to Italy; and William R. Travers (1819–87), a Baltimore merchant turned Wall Street broker, a founder of New York's Racquet Club and the New York Athletic Club and a socialite noted for his stutter — encountering him in New York, an old Baltimore acquaintance remarked that he was stuttering more than ever. 'H-h-h-have to', replied Travers. 'B-b-b-b-bigger city!'

JAGO, Paul, in C.P. Snow's *The Light and the Dark* (1947), *The Masters* (1951) and *The Affair* (1960), is Canon Charles Earle Raven (1885–1964), who unlike Jago did become Master — of Christ's College, Cambridge, from 1939 to 1950. The inspiration for *The Masters* was Raven's naive canvassing (in Snow's view) of support for his candidature. In *Stranger and Brother* (1982), Philip Snow tells how in 1939 his novelist brother wrote telling him of Raven's election-morning behaviour — how, when victory seemed assured, Raven was unable to keep the smile from his eyes as he walked round the court time and again. Once installed, he derived obvious pleasure from the eminence of his position, though he was as proud of his college as he was of himself. Regius Professor of Divinity at Cambridge from 1932 to 1950, he was chaplain to three monarchs: George V, George VI and Elizabeth II.

JAMES, Laura, in Thomas Wolfe's *Look Homeward, Angel* (1929), is Clara Paul, of Washington, North Carolina, who at the age of twenty-one took rooms with her ten-year-old brother in Wolfe's parents' home. The author was sixteen at the time, and became infatuated with this visitor. Already engaged, she died in the influenza epidemic of 1918.

JAMES, Miss, in D.H. Lawrence's 'The Last Laugh' (1925; *The Woman Who Rode Away*, 1928), is the Hon. Dorothy Brett. See Mullion, Jenny.

JAMIESON, the Hon. Mrs, in Elizabeth Gaskell's *Cranford* (1851–3). When Lady Jane Stanley provided flagstones for the footpaths of Knutsford, Cheshire – Gaskell's Cranford – they were laid only a single flag wide, for she did not like to see men and women walking arm-in-arm. Her dislike of 'linking' and her gift to the town are mentioned in Gaskell's 'The Last Generation in England' (1849), and – like the Hon. Mrs Jamieson – she lived at Brook House. These factors have prompted her identification with this character. A sister of the Twelfth Earl of Derby, she was so outraged by her brother's marriage to an actress (albeit the celebrated Eliza Farren) that she directed she should not be interred in the family vault, lest the dust of her sister-in-law should mingle with her own.

JANE, in Jack Kerouac's *On the Road* (1957) and *The Subterraneans* (1958), is Joan Vollmer Adams Burroughs. See Dennison, Will.

JANSENIUS, Henrietta, in George Bernard Shaw's *An Unsocial Socialist* (1884), is suggested by the author's biographer, St John Ervine, to be Alice Mary Lockett. See Lindsay, Gertrude.

JARVIS, Henry, in Henry James's *The Aspern Papers* (1888), has two putative prototypes. One is William Graham, an American art critic alleged to have gained admission to the home of Claire Clairmont (see Bordereau, Juliana) with the intention of purloining her Byron/Shelley correspondence. The other, favoured by James's biographer, Leon Edel, is a Boston sea captain named Silsbee, a Shelley enthusiast who so coveted those letters that he became a lodger in the house in which Clairmont was a tenant. When she died, her middle-aged niece offered him the papers on condition that he married her. Considering that 'price' too high, Silsbee departed. Could he, I wonder, have been Captain Edward Augustus Silsbee (*d.* 1904), of Salem, Massachusetts?

JASCHIN, in Thomas Mann's *Death in Venice* (1911), is Janek Fudowski, the sixteen-year-old Polish holiday companion in Venice of Count Władysław Moes (see Tadzio).

JEAN, in Sidonie-Gabrielle Colette's *L'Entrave* (1913), is part-inspired by the author's second husband, Henri Bertrand Léon Robert, Baron de Jouvenel des Ursins (1876–1935), editor-in-chief of *Le Matin*.

JEANNE, in J-K Huysmans's *En ménage* (1881), is Anna Meunier (*d.* 1895), a Paris dressmaker whom the author first met in the early 1870s, when they had a brief affair. The relationship was resumed five years later, and Huysmans's association with her continued until she died, paralysed and insane, after a long illness.

JEEVES, Reginald, in P.G. Wodehouse's Jeeves stories (1917–74). The identification of originals is often bedevilled by vague assertions in writers' memoirs. Typical of such claims is one to be found in *People Worth Talking About* (1933), by Cosmo Hamilton, editor of the *World*, which points to a butler at Brown's Hotel in London as 'probably the model for P.G. Wodehouse's Jeeves'. In the absence of supporting evidence, such statements must be taken with a cellarful of salt. But they cannot be ignored: they might be right. Hamilton's nominee is but one of several candidates. Although Wodehouse denied that he drew his characters from life – 'a real character in one of my books', he once remarked, 'sticks out like a sore thumb' – at least some touches of Jeeves's wisdom and orotund delivery are believed to have been inspired by Wodehouse's butler of the early 1920s, Eugene Robinson. Other butlers suggested as models are those of W.S. Gilbert, Edgar Wallace and J.M. Barrie (Frank Thurston, Barrie's manservant, was a master of the Jeeves shimmering act). Jeeves takes his surname from a Warwickshire county cricketer, Percy Jeeves (*d.* 1916), a fast bowler killed on the Western Front in the First World War. I suspect that, sub-consciously, the name may have commended itself to Wodehouse because of its similarity to 'Jeames', nineteenth-century slang for a flunkey. This, in turn, is possibly derived from Thackeray's *The Diary of Jeames de la Pluche* (1845–6), the story of a footman, James Plush, who upon making a fortune from railway speculation changes his name to Jeames.

JEKYLL, Dr, in Robert Louis Stevenson's *The Strange Case of Dr Jekyll and Mr Hyde* (1886), developed from a dream, which had reached Jekyll's first transformation into Hyde when Stevenson's wife woke him, alarmed by his screams. 'Why did you wake me?' he complained. 'I was dreaming such a fine bogey tale.' It was not his first nightmare with a dual personality theme. In his youth he had been plagued by dreams in which he himself was leading a double life, nightmares disturbing enough to prompt him to see a doctor. The Jekyll dream, however, may have been triggered by the author's play, *Deacon Brodie, or The Double Life* (1880), which he wrote with W.E. Henley, and which chronicled the career of William Brodie (1741–88), deacon of the Incorporation of Edinburgh Wrights and Masons and a Jekyll prototype. Brodie was an Edinburgh councillor and cabinet-maker by day; a thief, picklock and gambler by night. He directed a gang of burglars who were caught raiding the General Excise Office of Scotland. When one of them turned king's evidence Brodie fled to the Continent, was arrested in Amsterdam, and was brought back, tried and hanged. The play was not a success and Stevenson was unhappy in this and other collaborations with Henley, an association from which he strove to break free, feeling it was not allowing him to be himself. Taking all this into account, it is small wonder he had the dream which prompted the Jekyll story.

JELLYBY, Mrs, in Charles Dickens's *Bleak House* (1852–3). 'I do not suppose there was ever such a wrong-headed woman born – such a vain one or such a humbug', said Dickens of the radical feminist writer Harriet Martineau (1802–76). Like Mrs Jellyby, she was petite and pretty, with handsome eyes. Just as Mrs Jellyby was preoccupied with Africa, of which she knew little, so did Martineau pontificate on India, of which she knew nothing. And Mrs Jellyby's dedication to the right of women to sit in Parliament is reflected in Martineau's claim to have 'direct access to the Cabinet' and her conviction that 'nothing is so important than to preach my sermons there'. Like Mrs Jellyby, she devoted herself to the public, whether the public wanted her or not. Didactic, dogmatic and deaf, Martineau lent her earnest pen to innumerable causes. The absurdity of her attempts to persuade Florence Nightingale to align hospital beds with the earth's magnetic field contrasted with her percipience in other matters. Discerning anti-Catholic prejudice in Dickens's *Household Words*, she refused to contribute further to the magazine. Her attachment to mesmerism supposedly contributed to her death, for it was to mesmerism that she attributed her 'cure' of a tumour, which is thought merely to have shifted, later causing her more than twenty-three years of illness which she might have been spared had not her much-publicised claim for the mesmeric 'cure' prevented her from consenting to a medical examination. To the end of her days she held Dickens in high regard, never suspecting that she might be

Mrs Jellyby but expecting to be remembered in other ways. Bequeathing her skull to phrenological research, she had casts made of her head so that posterity would not be deprived should she be lost at sea or crushed in a railway accident.

JEMIMA, in George Bernard Shaw's *The Apple Cart* (1929), is the author's wife, Charlotte (née Payne-Townsend, 1857–1943). Irish and of independent means, she was a patron of the London School of Economics. Before meeting Shaw she fell in love with, but was not encouraged by, the Swedish physician and writer Dr Axel Munthe, author of the best-seller *The Story of San Michele* (1929). Friends described the Shaws as a devoted couple, but their marriage was on Charlotte's insistence unconsummated – although there is evidence that they may have spent a night together eighteen months before their wedding. The celibate nature of their union may not have been as frustrating for Shaw as some biographers have supposed. As a lover, he tended to be all words and no action – hence the affectionate taunt delivered to the vegetarian dramatist by Mrs Patrick Campbell (see Hushabye, Hesione), 'Some day you'll eat a pork chop, Joey, and then God help all women!'

JENKINS, in Ford Madox Ford and Joseph Conrad's *The Inheritors* (1901), is Ford's artist grandfather, Ford Madox Brown (1821–93).

JENKINS, Isobel. See Tolland, Isobel.

JENKINS, Mr 'Lollipop', M.P., in Gerald Berners's *Far From the Madding War* (1941), is Harold Nicolson (see Chilleywater, the Hon. Harold), a National Labour Party MP from 1935 to 1945. 'People began to feel that there was something really rather terrible', remarks Berners, 'about an *enfant terrible* who was growing middle aged and slightly pompous.'

JENKINSON, Dr, in W.H. Mallock's *The New Republic* (1877), is Benjamin Jowett (1817–93), Regius Professor of Greek at Oxford University and Master of Balliol College. Not without arrogance – 'Never regret, never explain, never apologise' – he pledged himself to 'inoculate England' with Balliol men and inspired the verse; 'Here come I, my name is Jowett;/There's no knowledge but I know it;/I am the master of this college;/What I don't know isn't knowledge.'

JENKYNS, Deborah, Mathilda and Peter Marmaduke Arley, in Elizabeth Gaskell's *Cranford* (1851–3). Deborah and Mathilda (Miss Matty) are believed to have been based on the author's cousins, Miss Mary Holland (1793–1877) and Miss Lucy Holland (1800–83), daughters of Dr Peter Holland, the model for *Cranford*'s Dr Hoggins. The sisters lived in Knutsford, Cheshire – Gaskell's Cranford – although Mary had some experience of London society, derived from keeping house for her brother, Sir Henry Holland, Queen Victoria's Physician in Ordinary. Peter is believed to represent the author's brother, John Stevenson (see Hale, Frederick). It was from her Holland cousins that Gaskell obtained much of her *Cranford* material. Thus, in a letter to John Forster (see Podsnap) 'Shall I tell you a Cranfordism? An old lady, a Mrs Frances Wright, said to one of my cousins "I have never been able to spell since I lost my teeth."'

JENNY, in Leigh Hunt's 'Jenny Kissed Me' (1838). This poem was inspired by Hunt's reception when he called on Jane Carlyle (1801–60) after he had been ill. On impulse, she sprang up and kissed him. In the first printing, however, 'Jenny' was 'Nelly', perhaps because Hunt had not sought the original's permission to use her name and did not wish to appear to be taking a liberty; or maybe he thought the verse might upset her husband, Thomas Carlyle (see Anticant, Dr Pessimist).

JENNY, in Dante Gabriel Rossetti's 'Jenny' (1848), has been taken to be the poet's housekeeper-mistress, Fanny Cornforth (née Sarah Cox – she adopted 'Fanny Cornforth' upon a whim). An illiterate cockney, she was Rossetti's model (whom he nicknamed 'Elephant') in many of his later paintings, notably 'Found' and 'Lucretia Borgia'. He began composing the poem, however, before he first met her at, it is believed, London's Argyll Rooms, a resort for ladies of easy virtue. With her second husband, J.B. Schott, whom she married in 1879, she was joint proprietor of the Rose and Crown inn, off Jermyn Street.

JERRY, in Hilda Doolittle's *Palimpsest* (1926), is Havelock Ellis (1859–1939), physician, psychologist and populariser of sex education. He was among Doolittle's companions on a cruise to Greece in 1920. When she saw a vision on the wall of her hotel bedroom in Corfu, he wrote home that she had gone 'right out of her mind'. He also corresponded with Freud about her before she became Freud's pupil, and Richard Aldington's *Death of a Hero* has Elizabeth (Hilda Doolittle) pretending to be uninhibited after reading Havelock Ellis.

JIMMY, in D.H. Lawrence's 'Jimmy and the Desperate Woman' (1924: *The Woman Who Rode Away*, 1928), is John Middleton Murry. See Crich, Gerald.

JIMSON, Gulley, in Joyce Cary's *The Horse's Mouth* (1944), has been popularly identified with the artist Gerald Wilde (?1906–   ), whose work is represented in the Tate Gallery. Noted for his obsession with art and alcohol to the exclusion of everything else, Wilde was reported dead in the 1960s when the body of a tramp resembling him was found near his home in Battersea Park. But Wilde was still alive, and was shortly afterwards given accommodation in the stables of the Sherbourne home of a patron, the philosopher J.G. Bennett. In *Memoirs of the Forties*, however, J. Maclaren-Ross (see Trapnel, Francis X.) claims that Cary did not meet Wilde until several years after the novel's publication.

JOAN, Saint, in George Bernard Shaw's *Saint Joan* (1923). Many liked to call themselves Shaw's inspiration for Saint Joan, but only one was chosen: Mary Hankinson, eldest daughter of John Hankinson, of Alvechurch, Worcestershire. After attending a Swedish physical training college in Kent, she played hockey for England and became a suffragette and a Fabian. One of her sisters married Francis Brett Young (see Knight, Laurence; see also Henneker, Mrs); another was governess to Rudyard Kipling's children. Shaw inscribed a copy of *Saint Joan*: 'To Mary Hankinson, the only woman I know who does not believe she was the model of St. Joan, and also actually the only woman who was.'

JOCELYN, in Rosamond Lehmann's *The Echoing Grove* (1953). When an author produces a novel about a married woman's traumatic rejection by her lover, shortly after she has herself emerged emotionally bruised from such an affair, she should not be surprised if the man in her book is identified with her real-life lover, Cecil Day-Lewis (see MacSpaunday). No wonder her publisher rejected this novel's original title, *Buried Day*. Annoyed, however, by speculation that Day-Lewis was Jocelyn, she said, as Gillian Tindall notes in *Rosamond Lehmann* (1985), that the model — if there were one — would be somebody from much earlier in her life. Tindall also condemns attempts to match real people with fictional characters as 'a vulgar error of considerable magnitude' ...

JOCELYN, Lady, and Rose, in George Meredith's *Evan Harrington* (1861). 'Janet, tie my shoe,' commanded Tennyson while out walking with the sixteen-year-old Janet Duff Gordon. 'No, tie your own shoe,' replied Janet. 'Papa says men should wait on women, not women on men.' Later, recalled Mrs Janet Ross — as Janet Duff Gordon became (see Challoner, Lady Joan) — 'he told my father that I was a clever girl but extremely badly brought up.' It was also as a child that she first met Meredith in 1850. He later fell in love with her, remained a life-long friend and is believed to have used her as Rose in *Evan Harrington*, her mother, Lady Duff Gordon (see Ida, Princess), being the model for Lady Jocelyn.

JOE, in Charles Dickens's *Bleak House* (1852–3), has a possible prototype in George Ruby, who on 8 January 1850 was at the age of fourteen called to give evidence at London's Guildhall in an assault case. He did not know what an oath was, he told the magistrate. He was unable to read, did not know what prayers were and although he had heard of the devil, he did not know him. But he did know how to sweep a crossing.

JOHANNÈS, Dr, in J-K Huysmans's *Là-bas* (1891), is Joseph-Antoine Boullan (1824–93), an unfrocked priest who practised exorcism in Lyons, edited a magazine devoted to the occult and was prosecuted for fraud after he offered to cure clients' diabolic distress, at a price. At a Black Mass in 1860, he sacrificed on the altar a child born to him by a nun who had become his collaborator in diabolism.

JOHANNES THE SEDUCER, in Søren Kierkegaard's *Either/Or* (1843) and *Stages on Life's Road* (1845), is the Danish poet and literary critic P.L. Møller (*b.* 1812), noted, according to Walter Lowrie's *Kierkegaard* (1938), for his free-love philosophy and conquests of serving-maids. While acting editor of a Copenhagen comic periodical, *The Corsair*, he lampooned Kierkegaard and ridiculed him by focusing national attention upon the unequal lengths of his trouser-legs, which became a popular joke.

JOHANSON, Hjalmar, in Hugh Walpole's *Harmer John* (1926), is part-inspired by the author's friend, the Danish operatic tenor Lauritz Melchior (1890–1973). His singing at Bayreuth in 1925,

Walpole noted, moved to tears the man sharing a box with him — Adolf Hitler, whom the author had come to know when the Führer-to-be was leading a fugitive existence. Thinking him 'fearfully ill-educated and quite tenth-rate', both 'silly and brave', Walpole recalled their time together in 'Why didn't I put Poison in his Coffee?' (*John o' London's Weekly*, 11 October 1940): 'I was with Hitler on many occasions, talked, walked and ate with him. I think he rather liked me. I liked him and despised him, both emotions which time has proved I was wrong to indulge. I liked him because he seemed to me a poor fish quite certain to be shortly killed. He was shabby, unkempt, very feminine, very excitable … There was something pathetic about him, I felt. I felt rather maternal towards him!' (It takes a dictator to upstage an opera singer …).

JOHNS, John, in Frederic Carrel's *The Adventures of John Johns* (1897), is Frank Harris (see Parker, Ralph). Wilde found this caricature 'superb', but it is malicious, suggesting that Harris became editor of the London *Evening News* by seducing the proprietor's wife. Despite Harris's track record, this was not the case. An American, Carrel was a contributor to the *Fortnightly Review* during Harris's editorship.

JONES, Blackberry, in Charles Dickens's *Our Mutual Friend* (1864–5), has as probable prototype the Revd Morgan Jones, who in his forty years as curate of Blewbury, in Berkshire, was reputed to have worn but one coat, his only 'new' hat being acquired from a scarecrow.

JONES, Hercules, in Dylan Thomas and John Davenport's *The Death of the King's Canary* (written 1940, published 1976), is Augustus John. See Bidlake, John.

JONES, Judy, in F. Scott Fitzgerald's 'Winter Dreams' (1922; *All the Sad Young Men*, 1926), is Ginevra King (see Borgé, Isabelle), presented as the posed, unattainable yet vulnerable charmer who continued to occupy a pedestal in the author's mind long after they parted.

JONES, Professor, in James Joyce's *Finnegans Wake* (1939), is Wyndham Lewis (see Lypiatt, Casimir), who had earlier attacked Joyce in *Time and Western Man*. Joyce respected Lewis's criticism, although he remarked to a friend that, accepting that all Lewis said was true, was it more than ten per cent of the truth?

JONSEN, Sophus, in C. F. Keary's *The Journalist* (1898). 'Keary's book is very good. He has taken an awful lot of sayings out of my mouth', said the composer Frederick Delius (1862–1934), commenting on his portrayal in Jonsen, an Anglo-Danish dramatist. Keary wrote a number of novels, and the libretto for Delius's opera *Koanga*. More about the composer's fictional role is to be found in *Delius: A Life in Letters 1862–1908*, edited by Lionel Carley (1983).

JORDAN, Robert, in Ernest Hemingway's *For Whom the Bell Tolls* (1940), is part-inspired by Major Robert Merriman, a California professor of economics who served with the Fifteenth International Brigade in the Spanish Civil War. Jordan also has a possible model in the Irredentist Cesare Battisti, who was executed by the Austrians during the First World War.

JORGAN, Silas Jonas, in Charles Dickens's 'A Message from the Sea' (1860), is Captain Elisha Ely Morgan (?1805–64), of Connecticut, master of transatlantic passenger ships including the *Philadelphia* and the *Hendrik Hudson*. Dickens met him in the early 1840s. He subsequently commanded the *Victoria*, the *Devonshire* and the *Southampton* and ended his career as manager of the Black Line in New York. His friends included Thackeray and the artists Turner and Landseer.

JORKINS, in Evelyn Waugh's 'Charles Ryder's Schooldays' (written 1945, published 1982), is Sir Max Mallowan (see Emmott, David), a contemporary of the author at Lancing College, suggests the school's archivist, B.W. Handford, who was also at Lancing with Waugh. Mallowan became Agatha Christie's second husband, and in his memoirs (1977) he recalls, 'Evelyn Waugh was popular among the boys for he was amusing and always ready to lead us into mischief, but he had a way of getting others into trouble and himself invariably escaping. He was courageous, witty and clever but was also an exhibitionist with a cruel nature that cared nothing about humiliating his companions as long as he could expose them to ridicule. Deeply religious, it seemed to me that had he been self-effacing he could have dedicated himself to a monastic life . . .'

JORROCKS, John, in R.S. Surtees's *Jorrocks' Jaunts and Jollities* (serialised 1831–4, published in book form 1838), *Handley Cross* (1843), and *Hillingdon Hall* (1845). 'Of the man upon whom Jorrocks was based we know nothing, for Surtees has left only a few fragmentary and contradictory clues as to his identity', says John Welcome in *The Sporting World of R.S. Surtees* (1982). Had Welcome turned up the *Illustrated Sporting and Dramatic News* of 20 November 1886, he would have found a putative original: a Gloucestershire farmer, Paul Crump of Coombe Hill, who was a master of harriers and hunted the Vale of Severn. Describing him as a 'double Gloucester welter-weight farmer', one who rode with him recalled that a member of his hunt was a Justice of the Peace held by Crump to be a credit to the bench. This was because the magistrate considered that a man who went to hounds could not be thought guilty of any immorality, and as a witness should always be entitled to preferential credence. Although Crump bore a strong likeness to Jorrocks in John Leech's illustrations, the artist's model is believed to have been one Nicholls, a coachman in the service of Lady Louisa Clinton. Or so claims the Christmas 1922 issue of the *Bookman*.

JOYCE, Abner, in Henry Blake Fuller's *Under the Skylights* (1901), is the American novelist Hamlin Garland (1860–1940), who together with Fuller was connected with an 1890s Chicago writers' movement towards regional realism. His work later degenerated into Far West romances.

JUAN, Don. See Don Juan.

JUBB, in Roy Campbell's 'The South African Muse' (*The Wayzgoose*, 1928), is Maurice Webb, English Fabian socialist, vegetarian and business manager of *Voorslag*, a literary magazine launched by Campbell and William Plomer in South Africa. Campbell habitually referred to Webb as 'Polybius Jubb'.

JUDY, in Rudyard Kipling's 'Baa Baa, Black Sheep' (*Wee Willie Winkie*, 1888), is the author's sister, Alice Macdonald ('Trix') Kipling (1868–1948). As infants, the two were sent to a foster home in Southsea – the setting for this story, in which the author is Punch (see also Rosa, Aunt). Trix Kipling wrote two novels and also a volume of verse, in collaboration with her mother. Her marriage in India to John Fleming, of the Queen's Own Borderers, foundered on the rock of her obsessive interest in spiritualism. She later settled in Edinburgh, where after her death she was remembered for her visits to the zoo, during which she addressed the animals in Hindustani.

JULEY, Aunt. See Small, Mrs Septimus.

JULIA, in Lilian Hellman's 'Julia' (*Pentimento*, 1974), is believed to be Muriel Gardiner (?1902–85), an American psychoanalyst who worked, under the code-name 'Mary', in the Austrian Resistance from 1934 to 1938. Reading medicine at Vienna University, she gave refuge to fugitive socialists, many of whom she smuggled out of the country after the Nazi take-over. One of them became her husband. She also had an affair with Stephen Spender (see Elizabeth). Hellman denied this identification, unconvincingly.

JULIA, in George Orwell's *Nineteen Eighty-Four* (1949). Not only was Orwell's second wife, Sonia Brownell (*d.* 1980), painted by Rodrigo Moynihan and William Coldstream; she was also, according to those who knew her, portrayed by the author in Julia. 'It will not do to push the analogy too far', said Hilary Spurling in the *Observer* for 15 January 1984, 'but there are unmistakable traces of Sonia in Julia's courage and confidence, her managing ways, her emphatic dismissal of everything phoney, second-hand or dishonest – "Oh, ghastly rubbish" is Julia's response, as it was Sonia's, to what she considered bad writing – her scorn for the prurience and sexual guilt implanted in adolescents by organisations like the Junior Anti-Sex League . . . ' Recalling his visits to Orwell in hospital, his friend and colleague T.R. Fyvel notes, 'Although Sonia denied it, I felt sure that she had been a partial model at least for the composite figure of the girl Julia in *Nineteen Eighty-four*, who brings unexpected love and warmth to the hapless, middle-aged Orwellian hero, Winston Smith. Whenever she arrived during my visits, bringing literary gossip, she seemed to light up the hospital room in which Orwell lay with her vivacity and laughter' (*George Orwell: a personal memoir*, 1982). Spurling records that, as editorial secretary of Cyril Connolly's *Horizon*, Sonia Brownell accepted Angus Wilson's first story for the magazine, and persuaded Weidenfeld to publish Nigel Dennis, Saul Bellow, Dan Jacobson and Nigel Kneale.

JULIA, in William Wordsworth's *The Prelude* (1799–1805; published 1850), is believed to be Annette Vallon (1766–1841), whom the poet met in Orléans and by whom – in 1792 – he had a daughter.

JULIE, in Jean-Jacques Rousseau's *Julie, ou La nouvelle Héloïse* (1761), is believed to be part-inspired by Élisabeth-Sophie de la Live de Bellegarde, Comtesse d'Houdetot (1730–1813), sister-in-law of the author's patron, Madame d'Épinay, and mistress of his friend, the poet Jean François de Saint-Lambert, to whom she remained faithful, despite the passionate attachment Rousseau formed for her.

JULIP, Uncle John, in H.G. Wells's *The Dream* (1924), is Alfred Williams who, after teaching in the West Indies, in 1880 became head of the village school at Wookey, Somerset. He left in the following year when school inspectors discovered he had forged his teaching credentials. Wells served under him at Wookey as a pupil-teacher.

JUNE, in Jack Kerouac's *Vanity of Duluoz* (1968), is Jane Vollmer Adams Burroughs. See Dennison, Will.

JUNIUS, in Mercy Otis Warren's *The Adulateur* (1773), is Samuel Adams (1722–1803), the American statesman who at the time of the 1770 Boston Massacre led citizens in their successful bid to pressurise the Governor of Massachusetts to remove British troops from the town.

JUNO, Mrs, in George Bernard Shaw's *Overruled* (1912). 'I like wanting you. As long as I have a want, I have a reason for living. Satisfaction is death', Shaw's hero tells Mrs Juno. 'Yes,' she sighs, 'but the impulse to commit suicide is sometimes irresistible.' This farce was written while the author and Mrs Patrick Campbell (see Hushabye, Hesione) were on the brink of an affair. Each sought the advice of a mutual friend, D.D. Lyttelton, who seems to have had their measure – 'You can dance round each other for a long time yet – both pretending a great passion, both knowing perfectly well that you each have a foot firmly caught in the kitchen door', she wrote to Shaw, as Campbell's biographer, Margot Peters, records, identifying Mrs Pat as Mrs Juno.

JUPIEN, in Marcel Proust's *A la recherche du temps perdu* (1913–27), is an amalgam of Albert Le Cuziat (*b.* 1881), a former footman to Prince Constantin Radziwill (see Guermantes, Gilbert, Prince de), who with Proust's assistance in 1917 established a male brothel in Paris; Mineguishi, Japanese valet to Comte Joachim Clary; and Gabriel d'Yturri (1864–1905), manservant/secretary to Comte Robert de Montesquiou-Fezensac (see Charlus, Baron Palamède de), who 'stole' him from Baron Jacques Doasan (see Charlus).

K

K——, in Alexander Pushkin's *Eugene Onegin* (1833–40), has two putative models: Maria Raevsky (see Larin, Tatiana); and Princess Sofia Potocki, a Polish beauty who made her entry into Petersburg society in 1818, at the age of seventeen, and in 1821 married General Pavel Kiselev, subsequently Chief of Staff of the Second Army in southern Russia.

KADIDJA, in Frank Wedekind's *Die Zensur* (1907), is the author's actress wife, Tilly Newes, whom he married in 1906. Their relationship was continually strained, Wedekind's biographer Alan Best, records, and Tilly attempted suicide during their courtship and again shortly before her husband's death in 1918, following the last of their numerous estrangements. Kadidja was the name they gave to their second daughter.

KALITINA, Liza, in Ivan Turgenev's *A Nest of Gentlefolk* (1859; published in Britain as *Liza*). Like Liza, two of the author's acquaintances became nuns after unhappy love affairs. They were Elizaveta Kologriviva, whose home at Oryol resembled the Kalitin residence, and the poet Elizaveta Shakhova, to whom Turgenev was related. Their taking of the veil has prompted their identification with Liza, and another suggested model is Countess Elizaveta Egorovna Lambert (1821–83), daughter of Nicholas I's finance minister, Count Kankrin, and wife of the aide-de-camp to Alexander II. Turgenev corresponded with the countess while writing this novel and her religious aspect has been discerned in his heroine.

KALMAR, Hugo, in Eugene O'Neill's *The Iceman Cometh* (1946), was first identified as Hippolyte Havel, a Hungarian-born political agitator of Greek gipsy descent, by Doris M. Alexander in the Winter 1953 issue of *American Quarterly*. After incarceration in a number of European prisons and an asylum, Havel settled in New York as the cook-cum-lover of Polly Holladay, a Greenwich Village club-owner. Theirs was a tempestuous relationship, during which he repeatedly disappointed her by failing to keep his promises to commit suicide. His friends included the novelist Theodore Dreiser.

KARAMAZOV, Alyosha, Dmitry and Mitya, in Fyodor Dostoevsky's *The Brothers Karamazov* (1879–80). Alyosha is supposedly part-inspired by Vladimir Sergeyevich Solovyov (1853–1900), a poet and philosopher who accompanied the author on his pilgrimage to Optina Pustyn monastery in 1878. Dmitry is primarily a former second lieutenant named Ilynsky, whom the author met at Omsk Penal Settlement. Ten years after being sentenced to twenty years' imprisonment for killing his father for his money, Ilynsky was found to have been the victim of a miscarriage of justice. Dmitry is also believed to be part-inspired by Appolon Aleksandrovich Grigor'yev (1822–64), a critic and poet of irregular, drunken habits, who contributed to the journals published by the Dostoevsky brothers. The prototype of Mitya is Vera Ivanova Zasulich (1849–1919), a revolutionary who was in 1878 acquitted of attempting to kill General F.F. Trepov, Governor of St Petersburg. Her acquittal provoked conservative protests against trial by jury, in which Dostoevsky joined. Forty-one years later, she died of tuberculosis. Biographies by Joseph Frank, Richard Hingley, David Magarshack and Richard Peace put flesh on these bones.

KARENIN, Alexey and Anna, in Leo Tolstoy's *Anna Karenina* (1873–7). Alexey is the author's cousin, Count Dmitri Andreevich Tolstoy (1823–89), Russia's Minister of Education and subsequently Minister of the Interior. His reforms included the creation of 'land commanders' recruited from local aristocracy and empowered to make quick decisions without higher authority. The idea proved to be better in theory than in practice. Anna is supposedly part-inspired by Maria Alexandrovna Hartnung (1832–1919), daughter of Alexander Pushkin (see Khlestakov) – in the novel's first draft, the Karenins were called Pushkins. Also divined in Anna have been attributes of Countess Alexandra Tolstoy (1817–1904), a cousin of Tolstoy's father. The author had a close friendship with her – 'the finest woman I have ever met.'

KARMAZINOV, in Fyodor Dostoevsky's *The Devils* (1871–2), is the Russian novelist Ivan Turgenev (1818–83), whose Berlin-inspired idealism Dostoevsky regarded as anti-Russian. Despite his huge physique, Turgenev was allegedly a physical coward. When a ship on which he was a passenger caught fire, he is reputed to have cried to a sailor, 'Save me, save me! I'm the only son of a rich widow!' The vessel subsequently beached and all were able to wade ashore.

KATE, in Robert Burns's 'Tam o'Shanter' (1788), is Helen Graham (née McTaggart, 1742–98), wife of Douglas Graham (see Tam o' Shanter).

KATE, in Henri-Pierre Roché's *Jules et Jim* (1953), is identified in Charlotte Wolff's *Hindsight* (1980) as Helen Hessel, the Paris fashion correspondent of a Berlin newspaper. In the 1930s she attempted to establish a civilised, non-possessive *ménage à trois* with Roché and her husband, Franz Hessel, a German novelist and translator.

KATERINA IVANOVNA, in Fyodor Dostoevsky's *The Brothers Karamazov* (1879–80). 'To show that her views were advanced, she bobbed her hair and wore dark glasses', said Somerset Maugham of Apollinaria Suslova (see Polina Alexandrovna). Suggesting in *Ten Novels and their Authors* (1954) that she is the model for Dostoevsky's Katerina, he commented, 'The suffering she caused him, the indignities she heaped upon him, were the fillip he needed to satisfy his masochism. He knew that she hated him; he felt sure that she loved him; and so the women who are modelled on her want to dominate and torture the man they love, and at the same time submit to him and suffer at his hands. They are hysterical, spiteful and malevolent because Polina was.'

KATHA, in Richard Aldington's *All Men Are Enemies* (1933), is Brigit Patmore (see Browning, Clariss), according to her *Memoirs* (1968).

KATZ, Mannie and Miriam, in Colin MacInnes's *Absolute Beginners* (1959). The playwright and novelist Bernard Kops (1926–) and his wife, Erica, are identified by Tony Gould (*Inside Outsider: The Life and Times of Colin MacInnes*, 1983) as MacInnes's young Jewish cockney writer, Mannie Katz, and his wife, Miriam. Acknowledging the identification, Kops told Gould that MacInnes was 'the most alone and lonely man we ever met'.

KAY, in Georges Simenon's *Three Beds in Manhattan* (1946), according to his biographer Fenton Bresler, is the author's second wife, Denise Simenon (née Ouimet), a French-Canadian whom he appointed his secretary while on a business visit to New York in 1945, when he was forty-two, she twenty-five. They instantly became lovers; married in 1950; and became estranged and separated in the 1960s, with much recrimination in their books — for she, too, became a writer.

KEAR, Alroy, in W. Somerset Maugham's *Cakes and Ale* (1930), is the novelist Sir Hugh Walpole (1884–1941), transparently disguised as an accomplished golfer, which he was not. One account has it that Walpole began reading *Cakes and Ale* while changing for dinner, the book propped on the mantelpiece of his room in a country house where he was a guest. Within a few pages, he recognised himself. Appalled, he read on, dressing and dinner forgotten. His host, coming to see if anything was amiss, found him still reading at the mantelpiece, still in his shirt-tails, his trousers on the floor around his ankles. The portrait's ridicule — and accuracy — were said to have blighted the last ten years of his life, though he attempted to laugh it off — 'I shan't forgive Willie easily. The beggar had drunk my claret.' When Walpole protested, Maugham denied that any resemblance was intended . . . admitting to it only after his model's death. See also Bertrand, Archie; Hurle, Leverson.

KEELDAR, Shirley, in Charlotte Brontë's *Shirley* (1849). It is no coincidence that many people become fiction's models within a year or two of their death. In many cases, the author will be freed from fear of litigation and other inhibitions; but sometimes a death can centre the writer's thoughts upon a close acquaintance. The latter may be the case with Shirley, for whom the author's sister, Emily Brontë (1818–48), is believed to be the model. Although Charlotte began work on *Shirley* about a year before Emily's death, the novel was written spasmodically and was by no means complete when Emily died. The author of *Wuthering Heights*, Emily was remarkably strong-minded, like Shirley. She was also noted for her dislike of snobbery. She died of consumption exacerbated by a cold caught at the funeral of her brother, Branwell, whom she had often had to extricate from local inns and put to bed.

KEIGHLEY, Mrs Johanna. See von Hebenitz, Johanna.

KEIN, Lionel and Isabel, in Wyndham Lewis's *The Apes of God* (1930), are Sydney Schiff (1868–1944) and his wife, Violet, sister of Ada Leverson (see Sib, the). A member of the Schiff banking family, Sydney was a friend and translator of Proust and a patron of Lewis in the 1920s – he was himself a painter and art-collector, and a novelist under the name Stephen Hudson. Although he had homes in East-bourne and in London's Cambridge Square, his pet subject was the iniquity of income tax which he claimed had reduced him to penury.

KEITH, Eddie, *idem*. Taken at Lewis's face-value, this caricature of the poet Edwin Muir (1887–1959) is difficult to reconcile with the high regard in which Muir was held by others. Lewis appears to have met him only once, in a London café. Muir's wife, Willa, records in *Belonging* (1968) that Lewis 'watched us both suspiciously, but on catching my eye or Edwin's slid his eyes sideways at once. He hardly spoke to me, being, apparently, one of those Englishmen who do not have the habit of talking to women. My invisible antennae conveyed to me that he resented my being there at all, that in his opinion a wife was out of place and that Edwin was a coward for having brought me as protective cover, the only motive he could imagine. We parted with relief on both sides.' Lewis portrays her as Mrs Keith, the one who does all the talking; her husband as a 'very earnest, rather melancholy, freckled little being' who has been 'swallowed' by his patron, Kein (see above). In reality, the poet was always his own man. 'I cannot believe that Edwin Muir ever uttered one disingenuous word in speech', said T.S. Eliot, 'or committed one disingenuous word to print.'

KELLY, Nicole, in F. Scott Fitzgerald's 'One Trip Abroad' (1930; *Afternoon of an Author*, 1957), is Zelda Fitzgerald (see Diver, Nicole). The story mirrors the Fitzgeralds' growing disenchantment with their life in France and their retreat to Switzerland to avoid physical and mental breakdown.

KELNO, Adam, in Leon Uris's *QB VII* (1970), is Dr Wladislaw Dering (d. 1965), who in 1964 sued Uris for libel following the claim in *Exodus* that as a prisoner-doctor in Auschwitz Dering had per-formed 17,000 experimental operations without anaesthetic. Dering was awarded derisory damages of a halfpenny, was ordered to pay costs estimated to be £25,000 and died soon afterwards, aged sixty-two. In *QB VII*, Abe Cady is the Leon Uris figure, sued by Kelno for libel.

KENILWORTH, Lady 'Mouse', in Ouida's *The Massarenes* (1897), is supposedly Frances ('Daisy') Evelyn Greville, Countess of Warwick. See Homartyn, Lady.

KERIM, Darko, in Ian Fleming's *From Russia with Love* (1957). According to Fleming's biographer, John Pearson, Darko Kerim is Nazim Kalkavan, an Oxford-educated ship-owner with whom the author established an immediate rapport when he researched this novel's Istanbul locale.

KERIWAY, Tom, in Saki's *The Unbearable Bassington* (1912), may owe something, suggests the Buchan biographer Janet Adam Smith, to the Hon. Aubrey Herbert (see Arbuthnot, Sandy). Keriway's wanderings through Hungarian horse fairs, hunting on lonely Balkan hillsides and travels in Salonika certainly bring Herbert to mind.

KHLESTAKOV, in Nikolai Gogol's *The Government Inspector* (1836), has a prototype in the Russian poet Alexander Pushkin (1799–1837), in so far that it was Pushkin's experience of being mistaken for a government inspector – during a visit to the military and civil governor of the province of Nizhni Novgorod in 1833 – that inspired Gogol's play.

KHVOSTOV, in Alexander Zinoviev's *The Radiant Future* (1981), is the Nobel prize-winning Russian novelist Mikhail Sholokhov (1905–84), whose authorship of the saga *And Quiet Flows the Don* (1928–40) has been disputed by claims that it was originally the work of Fyodor Kryukov, who died eight years before the first part of the novel was published. Certainly, the novel's sympathy with Cossack opposition to Bolshevism contrasted strangely with Sholokhov's subsequent Party conformity and his attacks on less orthodox authors, such as Pasternak and Solzhenitsyn, whom he described respectively as 'a hermit crab' and 'a Colorado beetle'.

KILBANNOCK, Lord, in Evelyn Waugh's *Sword of Honour* (1965), has a probable model in Lord Kinross (see Balcairn, the Earl of). Like Kilbannock, he was a gossip columnist who later served in the RAF. He was an Oxford contemporary and lifelong friend of the author, and just as in *Sword of Honour* Crouchback and Kilbannock meet in London after enlisting in the Forces, so did Waugh dine with Kinross in London at the same point in their careers.

KINCH, in Oliver St John Gogarty's *Tumbling in the Hay* (1939), is James Joyce (see Ratner, James-julius), who portrayed Gogarty in *Ulysses* (see Mulligan, Buck). Their friendship withered when Joyce began to resent Gogarty's charity, suspecting him of trying to destroy his spirit. Their last meeting, in Dublin in 1909, was bleak. Gogarty, who had pressed Joyce to call on him, has described how his visitor sat for some time, then looked out of the window, asked enigmatically 'Is this your revenge?' and left the house. In Joyce's account of this encounter (in a letter to his brother) he presents himself as the immovable writer, declining offers of refreshment and treating Gogarty's pleas for reconciliation with an icy lack of enthusiasm ('You and I of six years ago are both dead'). But when Gogarty said he did not care what Joyce wrote about him so long as it was literature, Joyce admits to having unbent, consenting to shake hands with him.

KINFOOT, Mrs, in Osbert Sitwell's *At the House of Mrs Kinfoot* (1921), is the London hostess Lady Colefax (née Sibyl Halsey, 1874–1950), whose addiction to name-dropping and story-capping prompted Margot Asquith (see Dodo) to remark that one could not even refer to the birth of Christ without Lady Colefax claiming to have been in the manger. The wife of Sir Arthur Colefax, barrister and patent lawyer, whom she married in 1901, she in 1936 established an outstandingly successful interior-decorating business. 'Although an insatiable appetite for life and a corresponding reluctance to suffer the smallest twinge of boredom might momentarily occlude a great natural kindliness, her gift for creating an atmosphere of intelligent pleasure was among the most eminent of her time', noted her *Times* obituary.

KING, Mr, in Rudyard Kipling's *Stalky and Co.* (1899), is a schoolboy's-eye view of William Carr Crofts, a graduate of Brasenose College, Oxford, who taught Latin and English Literature at the United Services College, Westward Ho, where the author was a pupil. Kipling so valued his judgement that, from India, he sent him his early journalistic efforts for criticism. F.W. Haslam, another Latin master at the school, is also believed to have contributed to King.

KING, the, in Marie Corelli's *Temporal Power* (1902). Miss Corelli, observed one critic, could always be relied upon to act in impeccable bad taste. Upon the publication of *Temporal Power*, newspapers quickly identified the story's king — portrayed as an ineffectual muddler — with Edward VII (1841—1910). As Prince of Wales he had been on friendly terms with the author, the only writer invited to attend his coronation. But after *Temporal Power*, described in one review as a 'tract for the guidance of the King', he 'cut' her.

KING'S FISHER, the, in Cotton Mather's *Political Fables* (*c.* 1692), is Sir William Phips (1651—95), a native of Maine who was knighted for retrieving from the sea-bed West Indian treasure reputedly worth £300,000. It was through the influence of the author's father that Phips in 1692 became Governor of Massachusetts. Subsequently accused of dereliction of duty, he was summoned to London but died before his case was heard.

KINTYRE, the Duke of, in Ford Madox Ford's *The New Humpty Dumpty* (1912; written under the pseudonym Daniel Chaucer), is Arthur Marwood (see Tietjens, Christopher). The author's biographer, Arthur Mizener, suggests that Kintyre's flirting with the novel's Countess Macdonald echoes and is an attempt to justify the attentions paid by Marwood to Ford's estranged wife.

KIRK, Howard, in Malcolm Bradbury's *The History Man* (1975), 'was drawn from quite a variety of people I knew around 1968—72, and a good many sociologists and non-sociologists of his type contributed elements to the portrait', the author tells me. 'It's sometimes said that he was Laurie Taylor, and indeed Taylor has commented on the problems of being identified with him. But in fact I've never met Laurie Taylor, not to this day ... ' Taylor, a popular broadcaster and Professor of Sociology at York University, devoted an article to the fate of being taken for Kirk.

KISTENMAKER, Herr Stephan, in Thomas Mann's *Buddenbrooks* (1901), is Krafft Tesdorpf, administrator of the author's father's estate. He enraged Mann by refusing to allow the heirs to draw on the capital.

KLEBB, Rosa, in Ian Fleming's *From Russia with Love* (1957), has as prototype Madame Rybkin, a Russian colonel in espionage mentioned by Vladimir Petrov after his defection in Australia in 1954.

The author's biographer, John Pearson, notes that shortly after Petrov talked, Fleming wrote on the enigmatic Rybkin in the *Sunday Times*, suggesting her to be the most powerful woman in the world of espionage — 'From the first she seems to have appealed to his sense of the macabre as a sort of potential female Le Chiffre.'

KLESMER, Julius, in George Eliot's *Daniel Deronda* (1876), entered the author's life in 1854 in Weimar, when Franz Liszt (see Conti, Gennaro) introduced her to the Russian composer and pianist Anton Rubinstein (1829–94). Twenty-two years later, Rubinstein became the model for Klesmer, coincidentally lunching with Eliot in London in the year of *Daniel Deronda*'s publication.

KLUG, Armin, in James Gibbons Huneker's 'The Quest of the Elusive' (*Melomaniacs*, 1902), is identified by the author's biographer, Arnold T. Schwab, as the oft-married Polish pianist and composer Theodor Leschetizky (1830–1915), whose pupils included Paderewski and Schnabel.

KNIGHT, David, in Zelda Fitzgerald's *Save Me the Waltz* (1932), is F. Scott Fitzgerald. See Halliday, Manley.

KNIGHT, Laurence and Mrs, in C.P. Snow's *Time of Hope* (1949) and *Homecomings* (1956). Booking in at an Antibes hotel in 1938, the author was told that another English writer and his wife were also staying. So it was that he met and made friends of the novelist Francis Brett Young (1884–1954) and his wife, Jessica (see Henneker, Mrs), later using them as his models for Laurence Knight and his wife. In his preface to Jessica's memoir of her husband (1962), Snow recalled that Brett Young looked like 'a colonial governor slightly down on his luck; not much like the GP he, following his father, had once been. The lids came down sadly over his eyes: but suddenly one was aware, beneath the lid, of a large violet eye, sly and mischievous, missing nothing.'

KNOX, George, in Angela Thirkell's *High Rising* (1933) and *The Demon in the House* (1934), is E.V. Lucas (see Davies, Peter), whose helpful criticism gave Thirkell the confidence to become an author.

KOLLY KIBBER, in Graham Greene's *Brighton Rock* (1938), has as prototype 'Lobby Lud', the 'missing man' of a circulation-raising stunt introduced by the *Westminster Gazette* in 1927, when readers were invited to spot and challenge him in the holiday crowds at Great Yarmouth with the words 'You are Mr Lobby Lud — I claim the *Westminster Gazette* prize' ... which was £50. The original 'Lobby Lud' was William Chinn, who in 1983 was rediscovered, aged ninety-one and living in Cardiff.

KRAMER, Professor Alfred and Louise, in D.H. Lawrence's *Mr Noon* (1984; first portion published as the story 'Mr Noon' in *A Modern Lover*, 1934), are the author's brother-in-law and sister-in-law, Edgar Jaffe (1866—1921), lecturer in political economy at Heidelberg University and the Munich Academy of Commerce, and Elisabeth Frieda Amalie Sophie ('Else') von Richthofen (1874—1973), elder sister of Frieda Lawrence (see Somers, Harriet). Marrying in 1902, the Jaffes divorced after Else left her husband for Alfred Weber (see Sartorius, Professor Ludwig).

KRIEGSMUTH, Baron, in Leo Tolstoy's *Resurrection* (1899). In 1878 the author persuaded Baron Maidel, governor of the Saints Peter and Paul Fortress prison, St Petersburg, to conduct him on a tour of the gaol. Tolstoy was incensed by the harsh treatment of political prisoners and later in a letter described Maidel — his model for Kriegsmuth — as being incapable of recognising his revolutionary inmates as human beings.

KRÖGER, Lebrecht, in Thomas Mann's *Buddenbrooks* (1901), is the author's maternal great-grandfather, Johann Heinrich Marty, a Swiss-born grain merchant who settled in Lübeck, becoming the town's Dutch consul, after a number of years in business in Russia.

KUCHERMAN, Major, in Anthony Powell's *The Military Philosophers* (1968), is identified in the author's memoirs as Major (subsequently Baron) Paul Georges Kronacker (1897—   ), who after escaping from Nazi-occupied Belgium in 1940 was Belgian military attaché in London from 1943 to 1944. A prominent industrialist, research scientist and politician in his country before the war, he was subsequently a post-war Belgian government minister.

KUPRIN, in Maurice Edelman's *A Call on Kuprin* (1959), has as prototype Pyotr Kapitsa (1894—1984), a Russian physicist who assisted Lord Rutherford (see Austin, N.E.) in the splitting of the atom at the Cavendish Laboratory, Cambridge, where in 1924 he became assistant director of magnetic research. Five years later he became the first foreigner for two centuries to be elected to membership of the Royal Society, which in 1933 built the Mond laboratory for him. In the following year he went to Russia to attend a professional conference and was prevented by the Soviet government from returning. He subsequently held a number of research appointments in the USSR and in 1978 he shared the Nobel prize for physics with two American scientists for his contribution to ultra-low-temperature research.

KURAGIN, Anatol, in Leo Tolstoy's *War and Peace* (1865–72), was suggested to the author by the affair of Tatiána Behrs (see Rostóva, Countess Natally) with Anatol Shostak, a St Petersburg libertine. There, however, Shostak's connection with Kuragin ends. Unlike Tolstoy's character, Shostak was a man of considerable affectation, parting his hair from the rear and modelling himself upon his conception of an Englishman.

KURTZ, Mr, in Joseph Conrad's 'Heart of Darkness' (*Youth*, 1902), has three suggested prototypes. The most convincing signpost points to Georges Antoine Klein (*d.* 1890), agent at Stanley Falls, on the Congo, for the Société Anonyme Belge. Succumbing to fever, he was buried at Tchumbiri. Significantly, Kurtz is 'Klein' in the original manuscript, as the Conrad specialist Norman Sherry records. The author may also have been influenced, suggests the Conrad biographer Jerry Allen, by the notorious career of Major Edmund Musgrave Barttelot (1859–88), second son of Sir Walter Barttelot, MP. After Rugby and Sandhurst, he entered the army at nineteen, displaying notable courage – and quickness of temper – in the Egyptian campaign of 1882. In 1887 he commanded the Congo-based rear party of an expedition mounted by the explorer H.M. Stanley, in search of the British administrator Emin Pasha, of whom no news had been received since the 1885 rebellion in the Sudan. More than 200 natives allegedly died under the harshness of Barttelot's regime, which included excessive floggings and the encouragement of cannibalism. Kicking a native woman when she refused to stop singing – her tribe's traditional manner of greeting the dawn – Barttelot was shot and killed by the woman's husband, a native chieftain. A third Conrad biographer, Roger Tennant, puts forward a further, less plausible prototype: A.E.C. Hodister, an enterprising Belgian agent and ivory collector. An outspoken critic of the slave trade, he became a victim of Katanga tribal warfare and was decapitated, his head being displayed on a post.

L

LA CREEVY, Miss, in Charles Dickens's *Nicholas Nickleby* (1838–9), has been taken to be the miniaturist Rose Emma Drummond, who in 1835 painted the author's portrait on ivory. The timing of this commission lends weight to the identification, but it is possible that Dickens had another miniaturist, his aunt, Janet Barrow, in mind.

LA CROASSE, in Lord Brougham's *Albert Lunel, or The Château of Languedoc* (1844), is John Wilson Croker. See Rigby, Mr.

LACY, Delphine, in Doris Grumbach's *The Missing Person* (1981). There was no prize for identifying the model for the heroine of this novel (see Fuller, Franny), and only a passing grade for twigging that Delphine Lacy was a stand-in for Greta Garbo (1905–), remarked Richard Combs in his *Times Literary Supplement* review. Almost as well known for her declared wish for solitude as for her acting, the Swedish film-star suffered when in the 1940s Hollywood attempted to give her a new, all-American-girl image. The result, said one critic, was 'almost as shocking as seeing your mother drunk'.

LADISLAW, Will, in George Eliot's *Middlemarch* (1871–2), has been suggested by Roland Duerksen in the American *Keats-Shelley Journal* to have Percy Bysshe Shelley (see Glowry, Scythrop) as a prototype. The likeness, however, is by no means obvious and the case for perceiving Shelley seems to me to be slight. Duerksen argues that two in-the-same-breath references to Shelley and Ladislaw in *Middlemarch* are of greater significance than the general reader might suppose.

LA FOSCARINA, in Gabriele D'Annunzio's *The Flame of Life* (1900), is the author's lover, the celebrated Italian actress Eleonora

Duse (1859–1924). Born in a railway carriage, she experienced poverty before her talent won her the respect of Shaw and Hofmannsthal for her interpretation of Ibsen heroines – Shaw was particularly impressed by her ability to blush, not through physical exertion, but as 'a genuine effect of the dramatic imagination.' She took leading roles in a number of D'Annunzio's plays. Aware that her love-life with the author was described in *The Flame*, she told her scandalised manager that the portrait had her consent because 'I am forty, and in love.'

LAKE, Diana, in Terence Rattigan's *French without Tears* (1936), is identified by the author's biographers, Michael Darlow and Gillian Hodson, as Irina Basilewich. Leaving the Indian Army officer she had married at sixteen, she returned to England and at twenty-one fell in love with Rattigan's Oxford contemporary, Philip Heimann, becoming his wife. A South African, Heimann was co-author of Rattigan's first play, *First Episode* (1933).

LAMB, Mortimer, in Ivy Compton-Burnett's *Manservant and Maidservant* (1947). In her memoir of the author (1972), Cicely Greig has no doubt that Mortimer Lamb is 'a distant portrait' of Ivy Compton-Burnett's friend and South Kensington neighbour, the actor Ernest Thesiger (1879–1961). Embroidery was among his passions – he was an accomplished needleman and he and the author would sew together. In her account of Compton-Burnett's later years, *Secrets of a Woman's Heart* (1984), Hilary Spurling quotes a Thesiger story from the novelist and critic Francis King. When the actor complained that W. Somerset Maugham wrote nothing for him, Maugham replied 'B-but I am always writing p-parts for you, Ernest. The trouble is that somebody called Gladys Cooper *will* insist on p-playing them!'

LAMIEL, In Stendhal's *Lamiel* (1889). According to Robert Alter and Carol Cosman's *Stendhal* (1980), Lamiel is in part Melanie Guilbert, an actress (under the stage-name Louason) who became the author's mistress. He first met her in 1804, when she was starting her stage career to support herself and her illegitimate five-year-old daughter.

LAMPORT, Percy, in Wyndham Lewis's *Self Condemned* (1954), is the artist-author's patron, Sir Nicholas Waterhouse (1877–1964), senior partner of the London-based chartered accountants, Price

Waterhouse, and one of the few intimates with whom Lewis never quarrelled.

LAMPTON, Joe, in John Braine's *Room at the Top* (1957), evolved from the author's observation (as an Air Raid Precautions warden) of the body of a baby being retrieved from the debris of a Bradford house on which a German bomber had crashed in 1941. Assuming the child had been killed, Braine wondered what would have happened to it had it lived. It was upon this conjecture that he based Joe Lampton. In a broadcast many years later, Braine recalled the manner of Lampton's creation. Listeners included Gareth Boyd, a Yorkshire bus company public relations officer unknown to Braine, who had lost his parents when a Nazi plane crashed on their Bradford home in 1941. Joe Lampton had indeed survived.

LANDAUER, Bernhard, in Christopher Isherwood's *Goodbye to Berlin* (1939), is Wilfrid Israel (1899–1943), an Englishman who in the Berlin of the 1930s assisted in the management of Wertheim's department store, which was owned by his family. Resisting Nazi intimidation and refusing to dismiss Jewish staff, he helped other persecuted Jews to emigrate and did not himself leave Berlin until shortly before the outbreak of the Second World War. In Portugal he assisted young Jewish refugees to emigrate to Palestine, and was killed when the neutral airliner in which he was flying to England was shot down by German fighters over the Bay of Biscay. Other passengers who perished included the actor Leslie Howard.

LANDLESS, Helena, in Charles Dickens's *The Mystery of Edwin Drood* (1870), has been popularly identified with Ellen Lawless Ternan (see Provis, Estella), largely on the strength of Ternan's middle name, which may indeed have suggested 'Landless' to the author. Such identification is purely speculative, however, and may well be a libel on Ternan's true character.

LANGEAIS, the Duchesse de, in Honoré de Balzac's *La Duchesse de Langeais* (1833–4), is the Marquise de Castries, according to the Balzac biographer Félicien Marceau. Separated from her husband, she had a child by the son of Metternich (see Mosca, Count), and although she had been crippled in a riding accident Balzac found her fascinating. After leading him on, first to Aix and then to Geneva, she denied him her bed. This caused him to regard her ever after as heartless, although — once he had recovered from the humiliation — they remained friends.

LANTIER, Claude, in Émile Zola's *Le Ventre de Paris* (1873) and *L'Oeuvre* (1885—6), is believed to be an amalgam of the painters Paul Cézanne (1839—1906), whose friendship with the author the novels terminated; Édouard Manet (1832—83), who painted Zola's portrait; and Claude-Oscar Monet (see Elstir), some of whose paintings correspond closely with Zola's descriptions of works by Lantier.

LANWIN, Margaret, in Christopher Isherwood's *The Memorial* (1932), is Olive Mangeot. See Cheuret, Madame.

LAPIDOTH, Mirah, in George Eliot's *Daniel Deronda* (1876), probably owes her suicide-attempt technique to Mary Wollstone-craft (see Marguerite), who let rain soak her clothes to facilitate sinking before she jumped from Putney Bridge in 1795. Mirah's singing may have been suggested by the example of Sally Shilton (see Sastri, Caterina) or Phoebe 'Hertha' Marks, a protégée of Barbara Bodichon (see Romola).

LARA. See Guishar, Larissa Fyodorovna.

LARIN, Tatiana, in Alexander Pushkin's *Eugene Onegin* (1833—40), supposedly represents three women in the poet's life: Maria Raevsky (probably the primary model), Ekaterina Karamzin, and Countess Eliza Vorontsov. Raevsky was a Russian general's daughter first encountered by Pushkin in 1820, when she was fifteen. In 1825, in accordance with her parents' wishes, she married Prince Sergei Volkonsky, who was seventeen years her senior. When he was sentenced to penal servitude for his revolutionary activities, she left her child and relatives to join him in exile in Siberia. Karamzin (1780—1851) was half-sister of Prince Vyazemsky and wife of the Russian historian Nikolai Mikhailovich Karamzin. Pushkin fell in love with her when he was seventeen, she thirty-six. She treated him with amused, platonic, tolerance, remaining his friend for life, and Pushkin asked her to give him her blessing on his death-bed. Vorontsov (1792—1880), daughter of a Polish count and wife of the Governor-General of southern Russia, is believed to have been Pushkin's mistress for a brief period after their first meeting at Odessa in 1823. The Pushkin biographer Henri Troyat suggests

Raevsky and Vorontsov as Tatiana Larin's models, and to them David Magarshack adds Karamzin as a candidate.

LARIVIÈRE, Dr, in Gustave Flaubert's *Madame Bovary* (1856), is believed to be the author's father, Dr Achille-Cléophas Flaubert (*d.* 1846), director of Rouen hospital. The portrait reflects the author's respect for his father and also his acquaintance with the fallibility of medical men, of which he became painfully aware while being treated by Dr Flaubert. Boiling water spilled by the surgeon on the writer's hand caused a permanent scar and partial paralysis. Traits of Dr Flaubert have also been discerned in Charles Bovary.

LARKINS, Miss (the eldest), in Charles Dickens's *David Copperfield* (1849−50), has a suggested original in Georgina Ross (1803−86), who was claimed by her family to have been Dickens's fiancée. Her brother, Charles Ross (1800−84), was chief parliamentary reporter of *The Times*.

LARTI, in Gabriel de La Rochefoucauld's *L'Amant et le médecin* (1905), is the French novelist Marcel Proust (1871−1922), who is believed to have returned the compliment by using La Rochefoucauld as one of the several models for Robert de Saint-Loup in *A la recherche du temps perdu* (1913−27).

LASPARA, Julius, in Joseph Conrad's *Under Western Eyes* (1911), is based on the Russian revolutionary and assassin Sergei Michaelovich Kravchinsky (1852−95), who worked under the name Sergei Stepniak. He stabbed to death a Russian police chief who had ordered the arrest and flogging of two girl revolutionaries; wrote *The Career of a Nihilist*, a novel concerned with Russian exiles in Geneva; and had as lover Constance Garnett (see Stobhall, Miss). He was killed in London, struck by a train at a railway crossing in Shepherd's Bush.

LAST, Lady Brenda, in Evelyn Waugh's *A Handful of Dust* (1934). When a writer follows his divorce with a novel about the break-up of a marriage, it is inevitable that the story will be to some degree autobiographical. Although Tony Last's background is not that of the author, the nereid-like Lady Brenda resembles the Hon. Evelyn Gardner (*b.* 1903), who was likened by Nancy Mitford to 'a ravishing boy page'. The daughter of the First Baron Burghclere, when Waugh first met her she was sharing a flat with Lady Pansy Pakenham, who married Henry Lamb (see Dodd, Lewis). She married Waugh in 1928, and he divorced her in 1930 when she left him for John Heygate (see Beaver, John). In 1936 she was divorced from Heygate, marrying Ronald Nightingale the following year.

LASTAOLA, Doña Rita de, in Joseph Conrad's *The Arrow of Gold* (1919). Not only did the author use Paula de Somoggy (*d.* 1917) as his model for Doña Rita de Lastaola: he appears also to have employed her in a fantasy which he wove round an unhappy period in his life. She was the mistress of Don Carlos, pretender to the Spanish throne, and Conrad claimed that she involved him in gun-running for the Carlists. In 1877, he said, he narrowly avoided death when he was shot in the chest in a duel over her. Recent research suggests, however, that gun-running for the Carlists at that time would have been impossible, and that Conrad's bullet in the chest was a suicide attempt. In 1887 Somoggy married the Spanish opera singer Angel de Trabadelo, subsequently the Marquis de Trabadelo.

LATHAM, Sir Charles, in Joseph Conrad's *Suspense* (1925), according to the Conrad biographer Thomas C. Moser, is part-inspired by Arthur Marwood (see Tietjens, Christopher).

LATIMER, Darsie, in Sir Walter Scott's *Redgauntlet* (1824), is the author's fellow law-student and lifelong friend, William Clerk, younger son of John Clerk, etcher and naval tactician whose two-volume *An Essay on Naval Tactics, Systematical and Historical* was studied by Nelson and applied at Trafalgar.

LATYMER, Sir Hugo, in Noël Coward's *A Song at Twilight* (1966). Careful though he was to keep his own homosexuality out of the public eye, Coward was not above portraying this proclivity in others. Latymer is an elderly, acerbic and acidic novelist who has spent much of his time concealing his homosexual nature. As *Punch* remarked when the play was first produced, 'the story resonates with the life of Somerset Maugham' (see Bertrand, Archie). A letter Maugham wrote to Coward, lamenting the death of Gerald Haxton (see Sheldon, Perry; see also Flint, Rowley), helped to prompt *A Song at Twilight*. The play also owes something, Coward acknowledged, to a visit paid by the actress Constance Collier to Sir Max Beerbohm. As Carlotta Gray visits Latymer, so did the elderly but still energetic Collier seek to renew her friendship with Beerbohm, whose years weighed more heavily, the visit exhausting him. There was also a parallel between Latymer and Coward, who refused to allow biographical reference to be made to his homosexuality while he was alive lest his royalties should suffer. When he appeared as Latymer in the first production of *A Song at Twilight* he was in a sense playing himself. His biographer, Sheridan Morley, tried to persuade him to consent to his homosexuality being revealed, citing the example of the drama critic T.C. Worsley whose disclosure of his homosexual nature in his memoirs had not shocked the tolerant 1960s. In the prologue to the 1985 reprint of his Coward biography, Morley quotes the playwright's reply: 'There is one essential difference between me and Cuthbert Worsley. The British public at large would not care if Cuthbert Worsley had slept with mice.'

LAUNCE, Mrs, in Hugh Walpole's *Fortitude* (1913), is the novelist Marie Belloc Lowndes (1868–1947), sister of the writer Hilaire Belloc. She first met Walpole in 1910 and was later present when a London hostess attacked him in his absence for leaving the country to avoid the First World War. His visit to Moscow, Mrs Belloc Lowndes protested, had been long arranged and his eyesight would in any case render him unfit for military service. The hostess, however, persisted in her criticism and Mrs Belloc Lowndes later recalled how Henry James took her by the arm, muttering, 'Let you and me who are friends of Walpole leave this house.'

LAUNHART, Alfred, in Frank Wedekind's *Hidalla* (1903), is Albert Langen (1869–1909), publisher of the Munich satirical magazine *Simplicissimus*. Wedekind's exposure as the author of a lampoon in the periodical ridiculing Kaiser Wilhelm prompted his hurried departure for Zurich, Langen also fleeing to Switzerland. Wedekind suspected Langen of engineering this for circulation-raising publicity.

LAURA, in August Strindberg's *The Father* (1887). 'I could see plainly now that I had been in the power of a vampire', said Strindberg after his divorce from his first wife, the actress Siri von Essen (*d.* 1912), who was his model for Laura. When Strindberg first met her she was married to Baron Wangel, an adulterous Guards' officer who divorced her for desertion, her stage aspirations being incompatible with his military and social status. Strindberg married her in 1877 and she bore him three children before their divorce in 1891 on grounds of incompatibility. Suspecting her of being both unfaithful and a lesbian, he refused to share her bed or table and pointedly refrained from referring to her as his wife. But although she arrived drunk for the divorce hearing she was granted custody of the children, the court perhaps recognising the difficulty of living with the dramatist. After two further unsuccessful marriages, he confessed upon hearing of Siri's death that he had loved her more than any other woman.

LAURENT, in George Sand's *Elle et lui* (1858), is the French poet, novelist and playwright Alfred de Musset (1810–57), with whom the author had a traumatic affair which ended in 1835. See also Falconey, Édouard de; Olympe; Pierson, Brigitte.

LAWRENCE, Camilla and Katherine, in Leonard Woolf's *The Wise Virgins* (1914), bear more than a passing resemblance to Virginia Woolf (see Aspasia) and Vanessa Bell (see Ambrose, Helen). Vanessa took exception to the novel, criticising Woolf for using his friends as characters.

LAWSON, in W. Somerset Maugham's *Of Human Bondage* (1915), is the artist Sir Gerald Kelly (1879–1972), President of the Royal Academy from 1949 to 1954. Maugham first met him in France in 1904, when Kelly was living in Paris, and they became lifelong friends. His sister, Rose, married Aleister Crowley (see Haddo, Oliver).

LAWSON, Mildred, in George Moore's 'Mildred Lawson' (*The Celibates*, 1895), is Mrs Pearl Craigie (see Theale, Milly). This story reflects his pique when she rejected him in favour of Lord Curzon (see Derringham, John).

LEA, in *The Inheritors* (1901), by Joseph Conrad and Ford Madox Hueffer (Ford Madox Ford), is the publisher's reader Edward Garnett (1868–1937), 'discoverer' and mentor of writers including Conrad, D.H. Lawrence and John Galsworthy. He was wrong-footed, however, by James Joyce's *A Portrait of the Artist as a Young Man*, which he considered drab, joyless and ugly, advising extensive rewriting. (To rewrite Joyce to suit the publisher's reader, commented Ezra Pound, would be like trying to fit the Venus de Milo into a pisspot.) The narrator of *The Inheritors* says of Lea, 'I had been writing quite as much to satisfy him as to satisfy myself.' Many an author will know the feeling.

LEARNED FRIEND, the, in Thomas Love Peacock's *Crotchet Castle* (1831). After hoaxing the nation in 1839 into believing him to have been killed in a carriage accident, Henry Peter Brougham, Baron Brougham and Vaux (1778–1868), had the mixed pleasure of reading his obituary tributes. Peacock's Learned Friend, he was an outstanding barrister and prominent Parliamentarian and was Lord Chancellor from 1830 to 1834; but his political ability was flawed by vanity, mendacity and irresponsibility.

LEATHERHEAD, Lanthorn, in Ben Jonson's *Bartholomew Fayre* (1614), is supposedly the architect and stage designer Inigo Jones (1573–1652), with whom Jonson often worked in the preparation of masques.

LE CHIFFRE, in Ian Fleming's *Casino Royale* (1953). As a naval intelligence officer, the author in 1941 approached Aleister Crowley (see Haddo, Oliver) for an opinion on what motivated Rudolf Hess, the German deputy Führer who had in that year arrived in Scotland by parachute, and Fleming's biographer, John Pearson, suggests that this led to Crowley's becoming a model for Le Chiffre. He was similar to Le Chiffre in size, ugliness and 'overtones of unmentionable vice', Pearson remarks. 'Both called people "dear boy", and both, like Mussolini, had the whites of their eyes completely visible around the iris.'

LECOQ, in Émile Gaboriau's detective novels, notably *Monsieur Lecoq* (1869). The pioneer police detective François-Eugène Vidocq (see Vautrin) is the prototype for Lecoq, one of the first police investigators in detective fiction. Gaboriau took much of his inspiration from Vidocq's memoirs.

LEE, Annabel, in Edgar Allan Poe's 'Annabel Lee' (1849), is primarily the author's wife, his first cousin Virginia Clemm (1823–47), whom he secretly married when she was thirteen and who died at twenty-four from tuberculosis. In this poem he also, however, supposedly has in mind Mrs Elmira Shelton (née Royster), his fiancée in his University of Virginia youth (1826). Their courtship was aborted by their parents' interception of their correspondence, and at seventeen she married another. Shortly before his death, Poe proposed again to this sweetheart of his student days, now widowed and living in Richmond, Virginia. He was not accepted.

Alice Pleasance Liddell — Alice through Lewis Carroll's camera lens

ABOVE: The octogenarians —
Winston Churchill inspired at
lease four fictional characters,
including H.G. Well's Rupert
Catskill, and Somerset
Maugham no fewer than eight
including Hugh Walpole's
Archie Bertrand. *Jonathan Cape Ltd*

LEFT: 'I am not everybody's cup
of tea, but I am certain people's
liqueur': Gerald Hamilton,
Chistopher Isherwood's
Arthur Norris. *The Times, London*

Model wedding: on the left, John Middleton Murry (see Gerald Crich) is best man to D.H. Lawrence (Mark Rampion) at his marriage to Frieda von Richthofen (Harriet Somers)

Poets Allen Ginsberg (Jack Kerouac's Irwin Garden) and W.H. Auden (Nicholas Blake's Nigel Strangeways). Nicholas Blake is the pseudonym used by another poet, Cecil Day Lewis, for his detective stories. *The Times, London*
BELOW: Rebecca West (H.G. Well's Helen) with George Catlin, the husband of Vera Brittain; 1949. *BBC Hulton Picture Library*

'An elderly wasp in an interesting condition': Mrs Patrick Campbell (George Bernard Shaw's Hesione Hushabye) with Sir Merrick Burrell at Knepp Castle; 1922. *BBC Hulton Picture Library*

Only a flaw of fate, said Edith Sitwell, prevented Vita Sackville-West (Virginia Woolf's *Orlando*) from being one of nature's gentlemen; Ascot 1912.
BBC Hulton Picture Library

LEFT: The Irish physician and writer Oliver St John Gogarty (James Joyce's Buck Mulligan), about to fly from Croydon to Paris with his wife in 1929.
BBC Hulton Picture Library

OPPOSITE PAGE:
ABOVE: Nancy Cunard, Michael Arlen's Iris Storm (also a model for Richard Aldington and Wyndham Lewis), dining with Norman Douglas, D.H. Lawrence's James Argyle.
Ann Chisholm

BELOW: Osbert Sitwell, Aldous Huxley, Graham Greene, D.H. Lawrence . . . all used Lady Ottoline Morrell as a model: see Hermione Roddice.
BBC Hulton Picture Library

  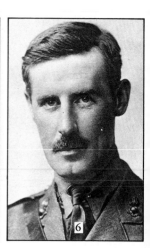

1. Violet Hunt (see 'Norah Nesbit')
2. Gerald Fairlie (see 'Captain Hugh (Bull-Dog) Drummond')
3. Aimée Semple McPherson (see 'Mrs Melrose Ape')
4. Ernest Hemingway (see 'Ahearn')
5. Brian Howard (see 'Ambrose Silk')
6. Herbert Asquith (see 'Maurice Pervin')

Sources: Jonathan Cape Ltd and BBC Hulton Picture Library

LEE, Lorelei, in Anita Loos's *Gentlemen Prefer Blondes* (1925). Crossing the United States by train, the author wondered why 'a golden-haired birdbrain', the actress Mae Davis, was attracting so much attention. While men fell over each other to wait upon the flaxen Davis, the brunette Loos was left to struggle with a heavy suitcase. Davis had already incensed Loos by snatching away her hero, the writer H.L. Mencken; now, as the train journey progressed, it became obvious that Loos's husband, too, was much taken with the 'stupid little blonde'. In her autobiography, *A Girl Like I* (1966), Loos recalled how she pondered the situation. 'Obviously there was some radical difference between that girl and me, but what was it? We were both in pristine years of youth. She was not outstanding as a beauty; we were, in fact, of about the same degree of comeliness; as to our mental acumen, there was nothing to discuss: I was smarter. Then why did that girl so far outdistance me in allure? Why had she attracted one of the keenest minds of our era? Mencken liked me very much indeed, but in the matter of sex he preferred a witless blonde . . . possibly the girl's strength was rooted (like that of Samson) in her hair.' Retiring to another part of the train, Loos drafted *Gentlemen Prefer Blondes*. In her autobiography she recorded that Davis was screen-tested by Charles Chaplin for the role of the *ingénue* in one of his films. She failed to get the part, which went to Paulette Goddard (see Natasha). I presume the film was *Modern Times*.

LEE, Missee, in Arthur Ransome's *Missee Lee* (1941), is Soong Ching-ling (1890–1981). A graduate of the Wesleyan College for Women, Macon, Georgia, she married Sun Yat-sen, founding president of the Chinese Republic, and was sister-in-law of Chiang Kai-shek, China's ruler from 1928 to 1949. Ransome met her when he visited China on behalf of the *Manchester Guardian* in 1926, encountering her again in 1928 in Moscow, where she was among Chinese refugees.

LEE, Old Bull, in Jack Kerouac's *On the Road* (1957), is William S. Burroughs. See Dennison, Will.

LEEDS, Martin, in H.G. Wells's *The Secret Places of the Heart* (1922). This novel was intended to serve in part as a cautionary tale for the author's lover, Rebecca West (see H.G. Wells's Helen), with whom he was becoming disenchanted. As Martin Leeds, she tells the story's Wells figure, 'Your love has never been a steadfast thing. It comes and goes — like the wind. You are an extravagantly imperfect lover.' To this he replies, 'Is *yours* a perfect love, my dear Martin, with its insatiable jealousy, its ruthless criticism? Has the world ever seen a perfect lover yet?' Instead of being piqued or penitent, West found the novel funny. Her mother, who considered West's relationship with Wells to be tragic, was reduced to hopeless laughter, notes Gordon N. Ray in *H.G. Wells and Rebecca West* (1974). Wells was not amused when Rebecca West told him of this reaction.

LEGGATT, in Joseph Conrad's 'The Secret Sharer' ('*Twixt Land and Sea*, 1912), has as prototype Sydney Smith, who as first mate of the barque *Cutty Sark* in 1880 struck and killed a rebellious black seaman. When the vessel arrived at Anjer, in Java, Smith escaped on an American ship, with the connivance of his captain — who afterwards committed suicide. Two years later, Smith was arrested and sentenced in London to seven years' imprisonment for manslaughter.

LEGRAND, William, in Edgar Allan Poe's 'The Gold Bug' (1843; *Tales*, 1845), is supposedly Dr Edmund Ravenel, a naturalist living on Sullivan's Island, South Carolina, in 1827–8, when Poe was stationed there on military service.

LEGRANDIN, in Marcel Proust's *A la recherche du temps perdu* (1913–27), is Dr Henri Cazalis (1840–1909), a minor poet (under the name Jean Lahor) and a social-climbing friend of the poet Stéphane Mallarmé and of Proust's father.

LEIDNER, Louise, in Agatha Christie's *Murder in Mesopotamia* (1936), is Lady Woolley (d. 1945), the despotic wife of the archaeologist Sir Leonard Woolley. Her first husband shot himself at the foot of the Great Pyramid, Sir Max Mallowan (see Emmott, David) recalled in his memoirs (1977), commenting that 'it was only with reluctance that she brought herself to marry Woolley — she needed a man to look after her, but was not intended for the physical side of matrimony ... She had the power of entrancing those associated with her when she was in the mood, or on the contrary of creating a charged poisonous atmosphere; to live with her was to walk on a tightrope.'

LEIGH, Olimpia, in Compton Mackenzie's *Extraordinary Women* (1928), is Romaine Brooks (née Goddard, 1874–1970). An

American heiress, she was assigned by her mother to the role of custodian of her dangerously insane brother. Rebelling against this, she left home to become an artist, living for a time in Capri, where she was briefly married to John Ellingham Brooks (see Hayward). A lesbian, she spent much of her life with Natalie Clifford Barney (see Flossie, Miss). Gabriele D'Annunzio, with whom she lived for a short time, wrote poems in tribute to her. Her intimates also included Maugham (see Bertrand, Archie), Guillaume Apollinaire and Montesquiou (see Charlus, Baron Palamède de).

LEIGH, Romney, in Elizabeth Barrett Browning's *Aurora Leigh* (1856), is in part the author's favourite brother, Edward Barrett Moulton Barrett (*d*. 1840), who drowned in a sailing accident off Torquay, where the Barretts were holidaying.

LEINTWARDINE, Ada, in Anthony Powell's *Books do Furnish a Room* (1971), is Sonia Brownell (see George Orwell's Julia). The critic and Powell specialist, Hilary Spurling, makes the identification.

LEITNER, Felix, in Louis Auchincloss's *The House of the Prophet* (1980), is the New York *Herald Tribune* columnist Walter Lippmann (1889–1974), whose public pronouncements were at times at variance with his private behaviour. After campaigning for military conscription in the First World War, he sought exemption for himself, claiming he could serve his country better in some other way and pleading that his father (who lived a further ten years) was dying. Similarly, his stance as a public moralist was belied by his affair with the wife of his friend Hamilton Fish Armstrong, editor of *Foreign Affairs*.

LEIVERS, Edgar and Miriam, in D.H. Lawrence's *Sons and Lovers* (1913). Had you entered a noisy Nottingham café one day in 1940, you would have chanced upon a reunion of Lawrence originals. Helen Corke (see Verden, Helena) was visiting Nottingham and arranged to meet Jessie Chambers (1887–1944), Lawrence's model for Miriam Leivers, whom she had not seen for thirty years. In a BBC television interview in 1968, Corke recalled how she had hardly recognised her. Once extremely attractive, Chambers had become bent and was so deaf that conversation was almost impossible. Lawrence's first love, she had attended Sunday school with him and they were student-teachers together. She taught at Underwood, Nottinghamshire; and became Mrs John Wood in 1915. Chambers told her story in *D.H. Lawrence: A Personal Record* (1935). Asked if Chambers had really loved Lawrence, Corke said, 'Yes, but it wasn't just a normal ordinary physical affection for a companion. She said to me once, "David is one of the sons of God." She looked upon him as a completely superior being.' Corke felt that Lawrence turned against Jessie Chambers in deference to the wishes of his possessive, dying mother. When he sent Chambers the galley proofs of *Sons and Lovers* she was appalled: 'She had known the manuscript from its beginning . . . But when he sent her the proofs the narrative had been so altered, presenting a completely different picture of herself, that she was not annoyed, she was devastated. That was the end of it. She sent back his letters.' Edgar Leivers is Jessie Chambers's brother, Alan Aubrey Chambers (1882–1946), of Haggs Farm, Eastwood, Nottinghamshire. In 1910 he became the second husband of Alvina Reeve, daughter of the author's paternal uncle, James Lawrence, and emigrated to Canada.

LENEHAN, in James Joyce's *Ulysses* (1922), is Michael Hart, a tipster with *Sport*, an Irish racing paper. A friend of Joyce's father, he had a predilection for speaking French and composing doggerel – he tipped the winners of both the Grand National and the Lincolnshire Handicap in verse, after which his career went into decline. The character's name was taken from Matt Lenehan, an *Irish Times* reporter.

LENNOX, David, in Evelyn Waugh's *Decline and Fall* (1928), is the photographer and designer Sir Cecil Beaton (1904–80), a preparatory schoolfellow of the author, who amused himself by sticking pins into him.

LENNOX, Hamish, in Evelyn Waugh's *A Little Learning* (1964), is the author's Oxford contemporary and lifelong friend, Alastair Graham (1904–58). Leaving university without a degree, he worked in the diplomatic service from 1928 to 1933 (at the British Legation in Athens and Cairo) and subsequently retired to a reclusive existence in Wales. For his mother, see Circumference, Lady.

LENORE, in Edgar Allan Poe's 'The Raven' (1845), is suggested by David Rein (*Edgar Allan Poe: The Inner Pattern*, 1960), to be Mrs Elmira Shelton. See Lee, Annabel.

LENSKY, Lydia, in D.H. Lawrence's *The Rainbow* (1915), according to the Lawrence biographer, Emile Delavenay, is part-inspired by Frieda Lawrence. See Somers, Harriet.

LEONE, Pauline, in Nancy Mitford's *Don't Tell Alfred* (1960), is Lady Diana Cooper (Diana, Viscountess Norwich; see Stitch, Mrs Algernon). With her husband, the British Ambassador in Paris, she lived in a Chantilly château leased to ambassadors by the French Institute at a nominal rent. Her husband was replaced as ambassador in 1948, and died in 1954, but she prolonged her residence at the château into the 1960s, despite the Institute's attempts to dislodge her. Sam White (see Mockbar, Amyas) wondered whether this was Britain's longest occupation of French soil since she abandoned her claim to Calais.

LEONIDOV, Anastasia Alexandrovna, in W. Somerset Maugham's 'Love and Russian Literature' (*Ashenden*, 1928), is Sasha Kropotkin, daughter of the Russian anarchist, writer and geographer Prince Peter Alexeivich Kropotkin (1842–1921). Maugham had a brief affair with her.

LEONIE, in Heinrich Mann's *Actress* (1911), is Carla Mann. See Ende, Ute.

LEONTIEV, Leo Nikolayevich, in Arthur Koestler's *The Age of Longing* (1951), is the Soviet novelist and poet Ilya Ehrenburg (1891–1967), whose gift for survival earned him George Orwell's condemnation as a literary prostitute. Yet he risked the displeasure of Stalin (whose favourite artist he ridiculed), incurred the wrath of Khrushchev and was admired by younger Soviet writers as a liberal.

LEROI, Mme Blanche, in Marcel Proust's *A la recherche du temps perdu* (1913–27), is an amalgam of Mme Laure Baignères (née Boillay), a leading Paris hostess, and the mother of Proust's schoolfriend, Jacques Baignères, whose natural father was reputedly the Orléanist leader Paul de Rémusat; and Mme Gaston Legrand (née Clothilde de Fournès), the wife of a colliery owner.

LEROY, in Jack Kerouac's *The Subterraneans* (1958), is Neal Cassady. See Moriarty, Dean.

LESBIA, in the poems (*c*.61 – 54 BC) of Gaius Valerius Catullus, is Clodia Celer, also a poet, but better known for her beauty and promiscuity. Catullus had a stormy affair with her in Rome, naming her Lesbia after the island home of Sappho, whose verse he much admired. Clodia is believed to have been the sister of the demagogue Publius Clodius Pulcher (*c*.93 – 52 BC), and she was married to Q. Caecilius Metellus Celer. Soon tiring of her lovers, Catullus included, she disposed of one by charging him with trying to poison her.

LESCAUT, Manon, in Abbé Antoine-François Prévost's *Manon Lescaut* (1731), is based on Manon Porcher, who was deported to Louisiana by the French authorities for debauchery and theft. She subsequently married a young aristocrat, Avril de La Varenne.

LESLIE, Lady Emily, in Angela Thirkell's *Wild Strawberries* (1934) and *Love Among the Ruins* (1948). According to Thirkell's biographer, Margot Strickland, Lady Emily is the author's close friend, the Countess of Wemyss (*d.* 1937), wife of the Eleventh Earl and mother of Lady Cynthia Asquith (see Pervin, Isabel).

LESLIE, Kate, in D.H. Lawrence's *The Plumed Serpent* (1926), is part-inspired by Frieda Lawrence. See Somers, Harriet.

LE STRANGE, Walter, in Cyril Connolly's *Enemies of Promise* (1938), is William Le Fanu (1904–   ), an Eton contemporary of the author. He became librarian of the College of Surgeons, married the composer Elizabeth Maconchy and in 1951 published a bibliography of Edward Jenner.

LEVERKÜHN, Adrian, in Thomas Mann's *Doctor Faustus* (1947). 'Instead of accepting my book with a satisfied smile as a piece of contemporary literature that testifies to his tremendous influence upon the musical culture of the era, Schoenberg regards it as an act of rape and insult', the author lamented in the *Saturday Review of Literature*. Much to the annoyance of the composer Arnold Schoenberg (1874 – 1951), his innovatory twelve-note technique of composition was credited to Leverkühn in this novel. In response to Schoenberg's complaints Mann commented, 'It is a sad spectacle to see a man of great worth, whose all-too-understandable hypersensitivity grows out of a life suspended between glorification and neglect, almost wilfully yield to delusions of persecution and of being robbed, and involve himself in rancorous bickering.' Schoen-berg's twelve-note system was only one of the author's borrowings. Leverkühn's collapse at the piano was inspired by that of the Austrian composer Hugo Wolf (1860–1903); and the character is largely inspired by the German philosopher-poet Friedrich Nietzsche (1844–1900), whose syphilitic degeneration culminated in madness.

LEVINSKY, Leon, in Jack Kerouac's *The Town and the City* (1950), is Allen Ginsberg (see Garden, Irwin). Although he was often used by Kerouac in minor roles, he never graduated to a major part. Asked why, Kerouac said: 'Because he's not an interesting character to me. He doesn't do anything but talk.'

LICKFORD, in P.G. Wodehouse's *Love among the Chickens* (1906), is the author's Dulwich schoolfellow, William Townend (1881–1962), a globe-trotting author of numerous books on the sea. Working his passages on tramp-steamers, he followed a variety of occupations — taking a job on a ranch in America, picking lemons near Hollywood, and also living in Brazil and Switzerland. As an artist, he illustrated Wodehouse's *The White Feather* (1907).

LIDA, in Alexander Pushkin's 'Letter to Lida' (1817), is Maria Smith, a Frenchwoman who as a young widow was housekeeper to the headmaster of the Tsarskoye Selo Lycée, in St Petersburg, during Pushkin's time there as a student. Her sudden dismissal suggests that her employer discovered her affair with his pupil.

LILLI, in the lyrics of Johann Wolfgang von Goethe, is Anna Elisabeth Schönemann (1758–1817), the daughter of a Frankfurt banker. Goethe was briefly engaged to her in 1775. In 1778 she married Baron von Türckheim, of Strasbourg.

LINDNER, in Robert Musil's *The Man Without Qualities* (1930–43), is the German educationist, pacifist and professor of philosophy at Munich, Friedrich Wilhelm Foerster (1869–1966).

LINDSAY, Gertrude, in George Bernard Shaw's *An Unsocial Socialist* (1884), is Alice Mary Lockett (1858–1942), a Walthamstow nurse courted by the author in 1882–5. In 1890 she married a London physician, William Salisbury Sharpe, who in 1897 became Shaw's doctor. While others cherished Shaw's correspondence,

Lockett returned one of his letters, writing on the envelope that it was not worth a penny stamp.

LINDSAY, Mrs and Philip, in Christopher Isherwood's *All the Conspirators* (1928), are Kathleen Isherwood (see Vernon, Lily) and (in part) the author's Repton schoolfellow Hector Wintle, who qualified as a doctor at St Thomas's Hospital, London.

LINGARD, Tom, in Joseph Conrad's *Almayer's Folly* (1895), *An Outcast of the Islands* (1896) and *The Rescue* (1920), is Captain William Lingard (?1824—?1896), of Altham, Lancashire, who went to sea in 1843 and within six years was in command of a fleet trading in the East Indies and engaging in occasional battles with pirates. He subsequently became a shipowner, trading from a secret base in Borneo.

LINNET, Kitty, in Samuel Foote's *The Maid of Bath* (1771), is Elizabeth Ann Linley (1754—92), a celebrated soprano born in Bath. In 1773 she married the dramatist Richard Brinsley Sheridan, after a turbulent courtship during which she extricated herself from an engagement to Walter Long (see Flint, Solomon) and Sheridan fought two duels with another unwelcome admirer.

LINSLEY, Philip, in Christopher Isherwood's *Lions and Shadows* (1938), is Hector Wintle. See Lindsay, Philip.

LISIDEIUS, in John Dryden's *Essay of Dramatic Poesy* (1668; revised 1684), is the dramatist and song-writer Sir Charles Sedley (?1639—1701), MP for New Romney, Kent. Wishing to make one of Sedley's daughters his mistress, James II made her Countess of Dorchester. Why, then, Sedley was asked, was he so opposed to the King? 'From a principle of gratitude', he replied. 'For since his majesty has made my daughter a countess, it is fit I should do all I can to make his daughter [Mary, wife of William III] a queen.'

LISTER, the Earl of, in William Douglas-Home's *The Chiltern Hundreds* (1947). 'Dear old man,' said the model for Lister on seeing himself portrayed by A.E. Matthews in this play. 'He knew what's important in life, and what isn't.' This pleased Douglas-Home, for implicit in the comment was an acknowledgement that the portrait had not been false. Lister was based on his father, Charles Cospatrick Archibald Douglas-Home, Thirteenth Earl of Home (1873—1951), a small, red-headed man oblivious to class distinction. It was not unknown to find a housemaid's aunt at dinner, his lordship having encountered her in the grounds and invited her in. After dinner, he would announce that he was going to bed. Seasoned visitors were prepared for the consequences, but others found it unnerving that on retiring for the night the earl would turn the master switch, plunging the building into total darkness. Out shooting, he would miss woodcock on purpose because he liked them, and he treated God as a familiar, nodding acquaintance, often addressing Him upon leaving a room, when it was his habit to pause at the door, pipe in mouth, and say a prayer.

LISTLESS, the Honourable Mr, in Thomas Love Peacock's *Nightmare Abbey* (1818), is Sir Lumley St George Skeffington (1771–1850), dramatist and fop, who created a colour which became known as Skeffington brown. In old age he wore a wig, still rouged his cheeks and declared the secret of a healthy life to be never to step out of doors in the cold, damp winter months, but to live in a suite of rooms enabling one to move constantly from one to another – an allusion to his time spent imprisoned for debt.

LITTLE BILLEE, in George Du Maurier's *Trilby* (1894), has a suggested original in the illustrator Frederick Walker (d. 1875). This identification was refuted by the author, and the character is probably a self-portrait.

LITTLEJOHN, Hugh, in Sir Walter Scott's *Tales of a Grandfather* (1827–8), is the author's grandson, John Hugh Lockhart (d. 1831), elder son of J.G. Lockhart, critic, editor of the *Quarterly Review* and Scott's biographer, who married the author's elder daughter in 1820.

LITTLE MISS MUFFET in the nursery rhyme 'Little Miss Muffet', is supposedly Patience Muffet, daughter of the entomologist Dr Thomas Muffet (1553–1604). An Ipswich and London physician, he was an authority on spiders, for which his admiration was said never to have been surpassed – although it was the silkworm which moved him to verse. Doubt has been cast on this identification because the earliest known printing of the rhyme dates only from 1805, but 'Little Miss Muffet' may well be a considerably older legacy of oral tradition.

LITTLE NELL, in Charles Dickens's *The Old Curiosity Shop* (1841), is part-inspired by Mary Hogarth (see Maylie, Rose). In *Dickens and Women* (1983), Michael Slater argues that 'the difference between Rose Maylie and Little Nell in relation to Mary Hogarth is that in the first instance the longing to bring Mary back to life and 'save' her seems to be the sole *raison d'être* for the fictional character whereas in the second Dickens is exploiting his deliberately recollected experience of intense grief for Mary for the sake of the story. Nell is not a projection of Mary but of Dickens himself.' Little Nell also has a possible prototype in Harriet Lucy Tice, who was born in 1827 at The Old Curiosity Shop, Compton Street, London, and who shared the nomadic life of her father, John Pepperill, a gambler.

LITTLE PHIL, in Aldous Huxley's *Point Counter Point* (1928), owes the manner of his death to Geoffrey Mitchison (*d.* 1927), son of the novelist Naomi Mitchison and G.R. (later Lord) Mitchison. At the age of nine, he died from meningitis. 'I do not now blame Aldous for writing about it', wrote Naomi Mitchison in *You May Well Ask* (1979). 'No doubt in the state I was in I clung on to any friends to tell them, tell them, force them to share.'

LLEWELLYN, Ivor, in P.G. Wodehouse's *The Luck of the Bodkins* (1935). In 1930 Wodehouse was hired by the Hollywood film producer Samuel Goldwyn (1882–1974), who is in part the model for Llewellyn. He was reputed to have given instructions for Shakespeare to be signed up to repolish *Othello*. As Goldwyn himself allegedly remarked of another occasion, this could be summed up in two words: in credible. During the filming of *These Three*, anxiety was expressed about difficulty with the censor, as the characters were lesbians. 'So what's the problem?' said Goldwyn. 'Make them Albanians.'

LLOYD, Ellen, in Richard Henry ('Hengist') Horne's *The Dreamer and the Worker* (1851), is Catherine Clare St George Foggo, whom the author married in 1847. Noted for her beauty, and half Horne's age, she was a friend of Dickens, acting in his amateur theatricals.

LLOYD-JAMES, Somerset, in the early novels of Simon Raven's *Alms for Oblivion* cycle (1964–76), is the author's Charterhouse schoolfellow, Sir William Rees-Mogg (1928–   ). He was editor of *The Times* from 1967 to 1981 and High Sheriff of Somerset in 1978. In 1982 he was appointed chairman of the Arts Council of Great

Britain. Model and character part company, however, in the later novels, Lloyd-James becoming somebody none of the original's acquaintances would recognise.

LOBOV, Alexander, in Fyodor Dostoevsky's *The Eternal Husband* (1870). According to the Dostoevsky biographer, David Magarshack, Lobov is the author's sponging stepson, Pavel Isayev, son of Alexander Isayev (see Marmeladov).

LOEFFLER, in John Buchan's *A Prince of the Captivity* (1933), is part-inspired by Heinrich Brüning (1885–1970), who as Germany's chancellor (1930–2) tried to revitalise the nation's economy, urging his countrymen to accept pay cuts and increase productivity. He subsequently became a refugee in Britain, and then moved to the United States where in 1937 he was appointed a Harvard lecturer. Prior to his retirement in 1955, he was professor of political science at Cologne University.

LOERKE, in D.H. Lawrence's *Women in Love* (1920). Beware of reading too much into a similarity in names. The Lawrence biographer Harry T. Moore says that the artist Mark Gertler (1891–1939) is 'an easily recognizable model for Loerke (even in the sound of his name)'. But Loerke was in the novel's draft before Lawrence met Gertler, so the similar-sounding name can have been no more than coincidence. Lawrence and Gertler became friends, however, shortly after the author began work on what was to become *Women in Love*; and just as Loerke fascinates Gudrun Brangwen, so did Gertler and Katherine Mansfield (the model for Gudrun) make passionate love in an impromptu play that became too realistic for comfort, provoking a shocked Lawrence to intervene and put a stop to the charade. Mansfield, in this home-made drama, was supposed to return to her 'husband', played by her lover John Middleton Murry (the model for Gerald Crich). Instead, she departed from the 'script', refusing to leave Gertler . . . who was drunk and burst into tears upon Lawrence's intervention. 'Fortunately, the next day everybody decided to take it as a joke – the Lawrences were the last to come to this decision, as they were most anxious to weave a real romance out of it', Gertler wrote to the real (but unresponsive) love of his life, Dora Carrington. Gertler was the son of poverty-stricken Jewish immigrants who had settled in London's East End; he became a protégé of Eddie Marsh (see Dean, Mattie). Lytton Strachey complained that, viewed for any length of time, Gertler's 'The

Merry-go-Round' (1916) would give him shell-shock. Lawrence found it 'horrible and terrifying . . . the best *modern* picture I have seen', and put it into *Women in Love* as part of a granite frieze. In 1984 it was bought by the Tate Gallery for an undisclosed sum (believed to be in the region of £150,000). Suffering from tuberculosis and depressed by his unhappy marriage, Gertler committed suicide by gassing himself.

LOGAN, in Gilbert Cannan's *Mendel* (1916), is John Currie (1884–1914), a portrait painter who shot himself after murdering his mistress.

LOIS, in Jean Rhys's *Postures* (1928; later retitled *Quartet*), is Stella Bowen. See Wannop, Valentine.

LOLA, in Heinrich Mann's *Zwischen den Rassen* (1907), is said by the Mann biographer Richard Winston to be part-inspired by the author's fiancée, Ines Schmied, daughter of a German planter in Argentina.

LOMBARD, Ivor, in Aldous Huxley's *Crome Yellow* (1921). A millionaire eccentric, the Hon. Evan Morgan (subsequently the Fourth Baron and Second Viscount Tredegar, 1893–1949) is the primary model for Lombard, in whom there is also a suggestion of S.S. Koteliansky (see Perekatov, Mr). Morgan was an Oxford/Bloomsbury figure, remembered for his penchant for fancy-dress parties (he fancied himself as the explorer Rosita Forbes) and for his affinity with birds. He taught a pet parakeet to climb up inside his trouser leg and peep out through his flies.

LOOT, the, in Evelyn Waugh's *Sword of Honour* trilogy (1952–61), is Stuart Preston, an American art historian who enjoyed remarkable social success while serving as an Army sergeant in London in the Second World War. He appears in James Agate's *Ego* diaries.

LORD JIM, in Joseph Conrad's *Lord Jim* (1900). Two men are known to have gone into the making of Lord Jim. The character displays elements of James Lingard (1862–1921), a Borneo trader known as 'Tuan Jim' and nephew of Captain William Lingard (see Lingard, Tom). But the principal prototype is Augustine Podmore Williams (1852–1916), son of a vicar of Porthleven, Cornwall. In 1880 he was chief mate of the steamship *Jeddah*, which was carrying pilgrims from Penang to Mecca when it got into difficulties. Thinking the vessel would sink, its officers took to the boats, leaving the pilgrims to their fate. But the *Jeddah* was taken in tow by another ship and made port. In the inquiry which followed, Williams said that, fearing for the safety of the captain's wife, he had persuaded her husband to give the order to abandon ship. He was adjudged to have failed to live up to the best traditions of the Service. Becoming a ships' chandler in Singapore, he made and lost a rubber 'boom' fortune, had sixteen children, and through strength of character regained Singapore's respect. In the early 1960s he was identified as Lord Jim's prototype, independently and at much the same time, by the Conrad specialists Norman Sherry and Jerry Allen. Curiously, however, I find that the *New Statesman* in 1932 published a contributor's recollection of a Singapore chandler who was described as Lord Jim's original, was named as 'Andrews' and gave a somewhat different account of the *Jeddah* episode, emerging almost as a hero who managed to bring the ship into port and as a result was offered a job by the Blue Funnel line, which he accepted. If, as I suspect, 'Andrews' was Williams, this would suggest that Williams was partial to reliving the *Jeddah* incident as he wished it had been, rather than as it was.

LORD, Willis, in Doris Grumbach's *The Missing Person* (1981). 'Look out, Jack, your slip's showing!' jeered young cinema-goers when films acquired sound and the voice of the Hollywood actor John ('Jack') Gilbert (John Pringle, 1895–1936) turned out to be too high-pitched for a credible hero. The model for Willis Lord, he was perhaps the best known casualty of the transition from silent movies to talkies, a development which swiftly finished his career. Ironically, despite his voice, he was 'as great a lover off-screen as he was on', said Anita Loos. Greta Garbo (see Lacy, Delphine) was reputed to have been among his conquests, though she denied reports of a romance.

LORRIMER, in Gerald Du Maurier's *Trilby* (1894), is Sir Edward John Poynter (1836–1919), a fellow-student of the author in Paris and subsequently, in London, President of the Royal Academy and Director of the National Gallery.

LORY, the, in Lewis Carroll's *Alice's Adventures in Wonderland* (1865), is the sister of Alice Liddell (see Alice), Lorina Charlotte

Liddell (1849–1930), who in 1874 married William Baillie, of Halyards and Pitlour, Fife, a Fellow of All Souls College, Oxford.

LOUIE, in D.H. Lawrence's 'Kisses in the Train' (*Love Poems and Others*, 1913), is Louie Burrows, to whom Lawrence proposed on impulse during a railway journey from Leicester to Loughborough. See Brangwen, Ursula.

LOUISE, Sister. See Van der Mal, Gabrielle.

LOUKA, in George Bernard Shaw's *Arms and the Man* (1894), according to the Shaw biographer, Margot Peters, is part-inspired by Florence Farr. See Tranfield, Grace.

LOUSTEAU, Étienne, in Honoré de Balzac's *Illusions perdues* (1837–43) and *La Muse du département* (1843), is in part Jules Sandeau (see Sténio), who was for a time Balzac's secretary.

LØVBORG, Eilert, in Henrik Ibsen's *Hedda Gabler* (1890), was taken by the author's rival Nordic playwright, August Strindberg (1849–1912), to be a caricature of himself . . . but Ibsen's portrait of Strindberg was in quite a different form: a painting which Ibsen displayed in his study, remarking that it helped him in his work to have that madman staring down at him. Løvborg's original was Julius Hoffory (1855–97), a Dane living in Berlin who by day was Professor of Scandinavian Philology and Phonetics, but whose dissolute night-life probably contributed to his early demise. He showed his pleasure in having been Ibsen's model by taking 'Løvborg' as his pseudonym. Seven years after a mental breakdown from which he never completely recovered, he died insane. While lamenting his passing, Ibsen was doubtless somewhat relieved: it had become Hoffory's habit to send him old hotel receipts and items of private correspondence, without explanation.

LOVEL, in Charles Lamb's 'On the Old Benchers of the Inner Temple' (1821; *Essays of Elia*, 1823), is the author's father, John Lamb (?1722–99), a servant in the Inner Temple of London's Inns of Court and clerk to the barrister Samuel Salt (*d.* 1792), who bequeathed him £500 worth of South Sea Company stock. In addition to being a South Sea Company director, Salt was a governor of Christ's Hospital and it is believed that it was through his influence that

Charles Lamb and his brother were placed there and obtained positions at East India House and South Sea House respectively.

LOVELACE, Robert, in Samuel Richardson's *Clarissa Harlowe* (1747–8), is suggested by Mark Blackett-Ord's *Hell-Fire Duke* (1983) to be based in part on Philip, First Duke of Wharton (1698–1731), who was noted for his profligacy and changeable politics. Richardson printed the *True Briton*, to which Wharton contributed.

LOWNDES, George, in Hilda Doolittle's *Her* (written 1927, published 1981), is Ezra Pound (see Forbes, Duncan). Doolittle met him in 1901, when she was fifteen. They fell in love and became engaged; but, as with all Doolittle's relationships, it didn't last. As a setter of standards, he was an enduring influence on her poetry; as a man, he was someone Doolittle never quite got out of her system. Her posthumously published memoir, *End To Torment* (1980), suggests that she felt he would have been impossible to live with, but that he was difficult to live without.

LUBIN, Henry Hopkins, in George Bernard Shaw's *Back to Methuselah* (1921). So obvious did Shaw make this caricature that it's a wonder he troubled to change the name. Henry Hopkins Lubin is a Liberal statesman and a deposed wartime prime minister, as was his model, Herbert Henry Asquith (1852–1928), First Earl of Oxford and Asquith and Prime Minister from 1908 to 1916. Just as Lubin admits to playing sixty-six games of bridge on a Sunday to keep his mind off the war, so did rumour have it that Asquith played bridge on a Whit Monday while his Cabinet waited for him to decide who was to succeed Kitchener as War Secretary.

LUCASTA, in Richard Lovelace's *Lucasta* (1649), is supposedly Lucy Sacheverell. See Althea.

LUKE, Mr, in W.H. Mallock's *The New Republic* (1877), is the poet, critic and educationist Matthew Arnold (1822–88), son of Dr Thomas Arnold (see Doctor, the).

LURGAN SAHIB, in Rudyard Kipling's *Kim* (1901). 'No one knew who he was or where he came from', says the Kipling biographer Charles Carrington of the model for Lurgan Sahib: A.M. Jacob (?1836–?1907). Most Kipling chroniclers give him a mention as the inspiration for this character, but few accord him more than a line or two, if that. As he was interesting enough for Kipling to immortalise him, there had to be more to be said . . . and there was, as I found in *The Times* of 17 January 1921. Jacob was a Simla jeweller of Turkish/Armenian-Jewish extraction. He was born near Constantinople, and at the age of ten was sold as a slave to a wealthy pasha who recognised his intelligence and made him a student. Gaining his freedom on the death of his master, Jacob made a pilgrimage to Mecca, worked his passage from Jeddah to Bombay and obtained a clerical post in Hyderabad in the court of the Nizam, on whose behalf he became involved in dealings in precious stones. In 1871 he established his business in Simla, quickly gaining a national reputation not only for his knowledge of jewels but also for his expertise in astrology and the occult — Madame Blavatsky acknowledged his superiority in producing supernatural phenomena at will. He spent his money on possessions rather than on himself and lived — in the words of a viceroy — 'like a skeleton in a jewel room'. In 1891 the cost of protracted litigation over a diamond deal involving the Nizam of Hyderabad virtually bankrupted him, and he spent his declining years as a dealer in old china in Bombay. He was the central character of Francis Marion Crawford's first novel (see Isaacs, Mr) and he appears under his own name in Norman Douglas's *How About Europe?* (1929).

LURIA, Alec, in C.P. Snow's *A Coat of Varnish* (1979). 'When I've been to bed with one woman, I almost immediately want to have another. I don't think that's uncommon', says Luria. But the model for Luria 'never said anything to me like that — it was a general observation', Snow told his oral biographer, John Halperin. In view of the number of women in Snow's life, he should perhaps have said 'personal observation'; it sounds like Snow himself talking. Luria, who 'had a knack of making a scrap of conversation sound like a prophecy', was acknowledged by the author to be based on Philip Rieff (1922—   ), a social psychologist, a University of Pennsylvania professor and ex-husband of the novelist, essayist and film-maker Susan Sontag, from whom he was divorced in 1959.

LUTHIEN, in J.R.R. Tolkien's *The Silmarillion* (1977), is the author's wife, Edith Bratt, an illegitimate orphan three years his senior whom he first met when he was sixteen and both were lodgers in a Birmingham boarding-house. Because she was a Protestant, Tolkien's Catholic guardians enforced three years' separation, but as soon as he was twenty-one he married her. She bore him four children, and upon her death at eighty-two, his biographer, Humphrey Carpenter, records, Tolkien noted how they had rescued each other from the 'dreadful sufferings of our childhoods ... but could not heal wounds that later proved disabling.'

LUTZ, in Philippe Sollers's *Femmes* (1983), is the French Marxist philosopher Louis Althusser (1918–   ), who was in 1980 detained, insane, after his wife had been found strangled in their Paris flat.

LUXEMBOURG, the Princesse de, in Marcel Proust's *A la recherche du temps perdu* (1913–27), is supposedly part-inspired by Marie-Alice Furtado-Heine (1853–1925), who married Armand, Duc de Richelieu (*d.* 1880) and in 1889 became the wife of Prince Albert of Monaco, from whom she separated in 1902. Her daughter, Odile de Richelieu, married Comte Gabriel de La Rochefoucauld (see Saint-Loup, Robert de). The Princesse de Luxembourg is also thought to be modelled in part upon the Princesse de Sagan (née Jeanne-Marguerite Seillière), the daughter of a financier.

LUZ, in Ernest Hemingway's 'A Very Short Story' (*In Our Time*, 1925), is Agnes H. von Kurowski. See Ag; see also Barkley, Catherine.

LUZHIN, Peter, in Fyodor Dostoevsky's *Crime and Punishment* (1866), is supposedly the author's brother-in-law, Pyotr Karepin (see Bykov), who advised Dostoevsky to forget Shakespeare and such 'soap bubbles' and to concentrate on his military career.

LYCIDAS, in John Milton's 'Lycidas' (1637), is Edward King (*d.* 1637), son of the Secretary for Ireland and a contemporary of Milton at Christ's College, Cambridge. Subsequently a Fellow of Christ's, he drowned when his ship – bound from Chester for Dublin – foundered off Parkgate, Cheshire.

LYDGATE, Tertius, in George Eliot's *Middlemarch* (1871–2), was taken to be a portrait of themselves by two of Eliot's friends, Sir T. (Thomas) Clifford Allbutt (1836–1925) and Oscar Browning (1837–1923). Inventor of the short clinical thermometer, Allbutt was Cambridge University's Regius Professor of Physic. As a young doctor he confided his religious and domestic problems to Eliot, who visited his fever hospital in Leeds. Browning, biographer of Eliot (who advised him never to read on trains), was an Eton housemaster who was sacked for his homosexual proclivities and in his retirement wrote an ode to the penis. After his Eton dismissal he resumed his Fellowship at King's, Cambridge, and became the first principal of the Cambridge University Day Training College for teachers. His self-identification with Lydgate was, I suspect, prompted by the colossal ego which caused many to regard him as a buffoon. Lydgate was almost certainly part-inspired by Eliot's brother-in-law, Edward Clarke (1809–52), a physician of Meriden, Warwickshire, who died bankrupt. The fifth son of Robert Clarke, of Brooksby Hall, Leicestershire, he married Eliot's sister, Chrissey, in 1837. He was never able adequately to support his wife and six children by his rural practice, and he received considerable financial assistance from Eliot's father.

LYMPE, Ernest, in Osbert Sitwell's *Triple Fugue* (1924), is the essayist Robert Lynd (1879–1949), who as a critic resisted the temptation to board literary bandwagons in an age susceptible to fashionable but ephemeral reputations. Literary editor of the *News Chronicle* and a regular contributor to the *New Statesman* and *John o' London's Weekly*, he remarked of his partiality for whisky that he was the sort of man his father had warned him against.

LYNCH, in James Joyce's *A Portrait of the Artist as a Young Man* (1916), is Vincent Cosgrave (d. 1927), a University College, Dublin, contemporary and intimate of the author, whose rival he was for the love of Nora Barnacle (see Bloom, Molly). He had the reputation of a wastrel and his death by drowning in the Thames was believed to be suicide.

LYNDON, Barry and Honoria, Countess of, in W.M. Thackeray's *The Luck of Barry Lyndon* (1844; republished as *The Memoirs of Barry Lyndon, Esq.*, 1856), have as prototypes the Irish adventurer Andrew Robinson Stoney, MP for Newcastle-upon-Tyne and High Sheriff of Durham, and Mary Eleanor Bowes, Countess of Strathmore (d. 1800), a rich widow whom Stoney snared in 1777. She divorced him in 1789. Barry Lyndon supposedly owes his craven behaviour in prison to 'Tiger' Roche (b. 1729), an Irish adventurer who ran through the fortunes of two women and was twice tried for murder, being acquitted on both occasions.

LYPIATT, Casimir, in Aldous Huxley's *Antic Hay* (1923). Augustus John once recalled a visit to Huxley's model for Lypiatt: the novelist and Vorticist artist Wyndham Lewis (1881–1957). Lying on Lewis's desk were several drawings of elephants ... with beards. 'Elephants do not, so far as I know, grow beards', John ventured. 'You may be right', Lewis replied brusquely, 'but I happen to *like* beards.' He also liked women, fathering numerous illegitimate children for whom he showed no concern. At the time of *Antic Hay* he was Huxley's rival for the affections of Nancy Cunard (see Viveash, Myra; see also Bucktrout, Baby; Storm, Iris), with whom he made love in his studio while his mistress, returning home from a maternity hospital with Lewis's latest child in her arms, had to wait forlornly on the steps outside. As an artist he was responsible for some of the most arresting portraits of the 1930s; as a polemicist he was disorganised and often self-defeating; as a husband he refused to have children by his wife (see Stamp, Margot), thus avoiding the impediment of offspring he would have to recognise. 'You have more children, I hear', he said to his friend, the poet and critic Geoffrey Grigson. 'Unwise. I have no children, though some, I believe, are attributed to me. I have work to do.' 'The good thing about Lewis', said another friend, Joe Ackerley, 'is that he doesn't care a fart what anyone thinks or feels.'

LYPPIATT, Joanna, in Noël Coward's *Present Laughter* (written 1939, first London production 1943), is the actress Gertrude Lawrence (1898–1952). Coward first met her – 'a vivacious child with ringlets, to whom I took an instant fancy' – when he was twelve, she fourteen, and both appeared at Liverpool Repertory Theatre in a production of Hauptmann's *Hannele*. According to Bernard Levin, her marriage to Robert Aldrich prompted Coward to cable: 'Dear Mrs A hooray, hooray/At last you are deflowered/I love you this and every day/Yours truly, Noël Coward.'

LYRIANE, in Madeleine de Scudéry's *Clélie, histoire romaine* (1656), is Françoise d'Aubigné, Marquise de Maintenon (1635–1719). Born in the prison in which her Huguenot parents were confined, she married the writer Paul Scarron as an alternative to being consigned to a convent. Following his death she became governess to the children of Louis XIV, subsequently secretly marrying him.

LYSIDAS, in Molière's *La Critique de L'École des femmes* (1663), was taken by the dramatist Edmé Boursault (1638–1701) to be a caricature of himself. He replied with *Le Portrait du peintre*, to which Molière responded with *L'Impromptu de Versailles* (1663), in which Boursault is ridiculed.

M

M, in Ian Fleming's James Bond novels (1953−66). A quick glance at his career details and dates in *Who's Who* would tell anyone that Sir Maurice Oldfield (1915−81) could not have been M. Nevertheless, his job as Director-General of Britain's Secret Intelligence Service prompted a number of newspapers to name him as M's model, and once the seeds of such a legend are sown they take some stopping. Disclaiming the M label, Oldfield himself pointed out that he was only 'a minor cog in the organisation out in Singapore' when Fleming was writing his early Bond books. John le Carré, however, may have used some of Oldfield's characteristics for George Smiley. More plausible suggested models for M include the author's exacting mother, Mrs Valentine Fleming (née Evelyn St Croix Rose, 1885−1964), whom Fleming called 'M' during his childhood; Major-General Sir Stewart Menzies (1890−1968), head of MI6 during the Second World War, a candidate put forward by Popov (see Bond, James); and Admiral John Henry Godfrey (1888−1971), the Admiralty's Director of Intelligence from 1939 to 1942. Fleming was personal assistant to Godfrey, who regarded Churchill as a bullying pest and resisted the premier's pressure to exaggerate U-boat sinking statistics. Unable to suffer fools gladly, and continually at odds with colleagues on the Joint Intelligence Committee, Godfrey was relieved of his intelligence duties in 1942, promoted admiral and put in command of the Royal Indian Navy. After the war, when he encountered the rising tide of Indian nationalism, Godfrey suppressed a mutiny at a cost of ten lives. He was promptly retired. Among those with whom he warred in Intelligence was another suggested M original, Henry Maxwell Knight (1900−68), who in 1937 was appointed head of the counter-subversion department of MI5. Best known to the public as a broadcaster on natural history, Maxwell Knight also interested himself in the occult and in conjuring, at which he was an adept. He succeeded in unmasking spies in Woolwich Arsenal, but a number of later misjudgements weakened his credibility in the Intelligence service. His suspicions were dismissed as 'reds under the bed' over-reaction and he took early retirement in 1956. A further putative, though less probable, model for M is Captain Max Despard, a British naval attaché in Belgrade involved in the planning of the 1939—40 project to block the Danube.

MAARTENS, Katy, in Aldous Huxley's *The Genius and the Goddess* (1955), is Frieda Lawrence (see Somers, Harriet), whom Huxley found infuriatingly stupid and yet liked, observing with wonder the strength of the bond between her and her husband, and commenting that D.H. Lawrence seemed physically as dependent upon her 'as one is dependent on the liver in one's belly.'

MACADAM, Effie, in Compton Mackenzie's *Vestal Fire* (1927), is Sophie Graham, a high-spirited member of the English colony in Capri in the 1920s. Inviting friends to join her for hot gin after her husband's funeral, she shocked the writer Archibald Marshall by embracing him passionately. It was the first time, he said, that he had been kissed by a drunken woman.

McALLISTER, Sandy ('The Laird'), in George Du Maurier's *Trilby* (1894), is the Scottish genre water-colourist Thomas Reynolds Lamont (1826—98), according to William Gaunt's *The Aesthetic Adventure* (1945). After ceasing to show at the Royal Academy in 1880, he lived in semi-retirement at St John's Wood, London, and on his Scottish estates.

MACBRIAR, Ephraim, in Sir Walter Scott's *Old Mortality* (1816), has as prototype the Scottish martyr Hugh MacKail (?1640—66), who after attending Edinburgh University was ordained in 1661 and arrested the following year for his preaching. Escaping to Holland, he subsequently joined a covenanters' rising in Scotland and was captured, tortured and hanged in Edinburgh.

McCANN, in James Joyce's *A Portrait of the Artist as a Young Man* (1916) and *Stephen Hero* (1944), is Francis Sheehy-Skeffington (*d.* 1916), a contemporary of the author at University College, Dublin. After his article demanding equal status for women in the university had been rejected by the college magazine, he collaborated with Joyce (author of another rejected article) in publishing the pieces privately. He became University College's first registrar and was later a campaigning freelance journalist, opposing conscription. A pacifist member of the Independent Labour Party, he was shot and killed by a British officer (later found to be insane) while trying to dissuade soldiers from looting. His wife was Hanna Sheehy, daughter of a Dublin MP, David Sheehy, whose family were the inspiration of the Daniels in *Stephen Hero*. See also Clery, Emma.

M'COY, C.P., and Mrs M'Coy, in James Joyce's 'Grace' (*Dubliners*, 1914) and *Ulysses* (1922), are Charles Chance, a Dublin friend of the author's father, and his wife, a soprano who sang at concerts in the 1890s as 'Madame Marie Tallon' (thus, Mrs M'Coy in *Ulysses* sings as 'Madame Marion Tweedy'). Mrs M'Coy is also thought to be part-inspired by Signora Nicolas Santos (see Bloom, Molly).

McCULLOCH, Ferdinand H., in Osbert Sitwell's 'Friendship's Due' (*Triple Fugue*, 1924), is identified by the author's biographer, John Pearson, as Louis McQuilland, a Belfast poetaster and journalist who in a *Daily Express* article in 1920 attacked the work of the Sitwell trio, describing their verse as 'The Asylum School of Poetry'. Sitwell subsequently claimed to have overheard McQuilland assuring two women at a Fleet Street lunch that he 'wouldn't, no, he really couldn't, commit suicide.'

MACDERMOTT, Macdougal, in Mary McCarthy's *The Oasis* (1949), is Dwight MacDonald (1906–82), critic, author and an editor of the *Partisan Review*, for which McCarthy was drama critic. MacDonald was founder-editor of *Politics* (1944–9).

MACDONALD, Countess, in Ford Madox Ford's *The New Humpty-Dumpty* (1912; published under the pseudonym Daniel Chaucer), is the author's wife, Elsie (née Martindale, 1876–1949), whom he left for Violet Hunt (see Nesbitt, Norah). As Elsie Martindale she was a novelist and an essayist for the *English Review*.

McDOUGAL, Ramsy, in H.G. Wells's *The Autocracy of Mr Parham* (1930), is Ramsay MacDonald (see Shand, John), according to J.R. Hammond's *An H.G. Wells Companion* (1979).

MacDOWELL, Gerty, in James Joyce's *Ulysses* (1922). With one pull of a lavatory chain, Marthe Fleischmann unwittingly tugged at the strings of Joyce's heart. Observing this action from the window of his Zurich flat, the author determined to see more of this neighbour, as his biographer, Richard Ellmann, records. So erotic for Joyce was the flushing of that lavatory that I suspect he was at heart a plumber's mate, particularly as this is not the only evidence that women's plumbing arrangements excited him. Fleischmann was the Swiss mistress of an engineer, and lived with him in his apartment. Joyce became infatuated with her, introduced himself by letter and commenced a courtship conducted largely by correspondence. The association ended when, in a moment of stress, she told her lover of Joyce's attentions. In *Ulysses* she is a prototype for Gerty Mac-Dowell. Both walked with a limp.

McGLAND, Gowan, in Peter De Vries's *Reuben, Reuben* (1964), has as prototype the Welsh poet Dylan Thomas (1914–53), who boasted that he had never written a line of verse when the pubs were open. He died in New York during a poetry-reading tour, the victim of a combination of drink, drugs and overwork. The cause of his death, according to the autopsy, was 'insult to the brain'.

McHARG, Lloyd, in Thomas Wolfe's *You Can't Go Home Again* (1940), is the American novelist Sinclair Lewis (1885–1951), according to Lewis's biographer, Mark Schorer. It was Lewis's championing of *Look Homeward, Angel* which led to Wolfe becoming an established author.

MACHIN, Denry (Edward Henry), in Arnold Bennett's *The Card* (1911). Always an opportunist, the model for Denry Machin published in 1936 *The Autobiography of 'The Card'*. After several years in the pottery industry, first as an apprentice and then as a travelling salesman, Harold Keates Hales (1868–1942) entered the motor-car business in Burslem, Staffordshire, in 1897. In 1915 he took part in the Gallipoli landing, and after the war he represented a number of British firms in the Far East, returning in 1929 to establish his own business as a shipper in London. From 1931 to 1935 he was the Conservative MP for Hanley. When he suggested that Bennett, an old school-friend, owed him a share of *The Card*'s royalties, the author replied that the debt had already been settled with the free publicity *The Card* had given him.

MacIVOR, Fergus, in Sir Walter Scott's *Waverley* (1814), has a putative prototype in Donald McDonald, laird of Kinlochmoidart, in the Highlands, and aide-de-camp to Prince Charles Edward, the Young Pretender. After a six-hour trial — quite a marathon by the standards of 1745 — he was sentenced to death for his part in the 'Forty-five' Rebellion, in which the Young Pretender and his followers invaded England. MacIvor may also owe something to Colonel Alexander Ranaldson Macdonell (*d.* 1828), of Glengarry, a friend of the author and a Highland chieftain who never travelled without a full complement of kilted retainers. He died struggling to reach the shore from the wrecked *Stirling Castle*.

MacJONES, Balliol, in Jack Kerouac's *The Subterraneans* (1958), is John Clellon Holmes. See Saybrook, Tom.

MACKENZIE, Alec, in W. Somerset Maugham's *The Explorer* (1907). The author's biographer, Ted Morgan, names as Mackenzie's prototype the journalist Sir Henry Morton Stanley (1841–1904), who explored the course of the Congo and in 1871 located the missing Dr David Livingstone on the eastern shore of Lake Tanganyika.

MACKENZIE, Mrs, in W.M. Thackeray's *The Newcomes* (1853–5), is Mrs Matthew Shawe. See Baynes, Mrs.

MACKENZIE, the Revd, in H. Rider Haggard's *Allan Quatermain* (1887), is the Revd A. Merensky, of the Berlin Missionary Society, who in the 1860s and 1870s ran a fortified mission station at Botsabelo, South Africa.

MACLEAN, Robert, in Rosalind Ashe's *Moths* (1976). Brian Aldiss (1925–) tells me that Rosalind Ashe 'turned me into Robert Maclean, a "notoriously promiscuous" science fiction writer, who disappears on the way to a SF conference in Amsterdam. Leaving his car at Oxford station, what's more.' (Aldiss lives near Oxford.) 'Being of a forgiving nature, I took no offence at what Rosalind had done. She, however, was so alarmed — or conscience-stricken — that she has evaded my company ever since.'

MACLEAN, Lady (Ruby), in Enid Bagnold's *The Loved and the Envied* (1951), is part-inspired by Lady Diana Cooper (see Stitch, Mrs Algernon). Evelyn Waugh makes the identification in a letter to Nancy Mitford.

McLEAR, Patrick, in Jack Kerouac's *Big Sur* (1962) and *Desolation Angels* (1965), is the American poet Michael McClure (1932–   ).

McLEAVY, Hal, in Joe Orton's *Loot* (1966). According to Orton's biographer, John Lahr, Hal McLeavy has as prototype the author's father, William Orton, who was for thirty-five years a gardener for Leicester Corporation.

McLEOD, Donald, in Thomas Keneally's *A Cut-Rate Kingdom* (1980). Reviewing *A Cut-Rate Kingdom* in *The Times Literary Supplement*, Michael Wood wrote: 'The novel is not a *roman-à-clef*, Keneally says, his Australian public figures are not meant to "reflect the character and private life" of historical individuals. But he will forgive us, I imagine, if we see in his American commander, one Donald McLeod, subtly manipulating despatches, inflating statistics, surprising even his enemies by sudden bursts of simplicity, more than a faint shadow of General Douglas MacArthur.' See Haik, General Dewey.

MACMASTER, Vincent, in Ford Madox Ford's *Parade's End* tetralogy (1924–8; principally *Some Do Not*, 1924), is said by Thomas C. Moser (*The Life in the Fiction of Ford Madox Ford*, 1980) to be part-inspired by Joseph Conrad. See Brandetski, Simeon.

MACNAB, John, in John Buchan's *John Macnab* (1925). In his memoirs, *March Past* (1978), Lord Lovat identifies Macnab as Jimmie Dunbar, of Pitgavenny, Elgin, who commanded a squadron of the Second Lovat Scouts in the Boer War.

MacNAIR, Siegmund, in D.H. Lawrence's *The Trespasser* (1912), is H.B. MacCartney. See Verden, Helena.

MACOMBER, Margot, in Ernest Hemingway's 'The Short Happy Life of Francis Macomber' (*The Fifth Column* and *The First Forty-Nine Stories*, 1938), is suggested by the Hemingway biographer Carlos Baker to be Jane Mason. See Bradley, Helene.

McPHAIL, Augusta, in Ford Madox Ford's *Mr Fleight* (1913), is the author's lover, Violet Hunt. See Nesbitt, Norah.

McPHAIL, Rob, in Wyndham Lewis's *Snooty Baronet* (1932). The author apologised to Roy Campbell (see Grovell, Dick) for killing this character, for whom he was the model, says Lewis's biographer Jeffrey Meyers. At the same time, Lewis thanked Campbell for publicly defending *The Apes of God*.

MacQUEDY, Mr, in Thomas Love Peacock's *Crotchet Castle* (1831), is John Ramsay McCulloch (1789–1864), editor of *The Scotsman* from 1818 to 1820, and professor of political economy at University College, London, from 1828 to 1832.

MACREADY, in Maxwell Anderson and Harold Hickerson's *Gods of the Lightning* (1928), has as prototype Nicola Sacco who, with Bartolomeo Vanzetti, was electrocuted in 1927 for the murder of two shoe-company employees killed in 1920 during a wages snatch in South Braintree, Massachusetts. Sacco and Vanzetti – both Italian anarchist immigrants – protested their innocence, and doubt as to their guilt, coupled with legal manoeuvres, delayed their execution for six years. When finally they went to the electric chair riots broke out in Paris, in which Americans were attacked and the United States Embassy had to be protected. The case continued to exercise the public conscience for many years, and in 1977 the Governor of Massachusetts signed a proclamation acknowledging the possibility of a miscarriage of justice.

MacSPAUNDAY, in Roy Campbell's *Talking Bronco* (1946), represents the poets Louis MacNeice (1907–63), Stephen Spender (see Savage, Stephen), W.H. Auden (see Weston, Hugh) and Cecil Day-Lewis (1904–72). The poem expresses Campbell's scorn for these left-wing poets, who he felt should have enlisted to fight for the Nationalists in the Spanish Civil War. Reviewing a biography of Campbell for the *Observer* in 1982, Spender recalled the Mac-Spaunday jibe: 'Incensed by some very anti-semitic remarks directed against me, I wrote him a letter full of hysterical rage. The others took the whole attack with a good-humoured shrug which was probably more infuriating to Campbell than my anger.'

MacTAVISH, Captain. See Trimmer.

MACTAVISH, Newton, in Frederick Rolfe's *The Desire and Pursuit of the Whole* (1934), is Horatio Brown (1854–1926), Venetian scholar and biographer of John Addington Symonds, according to a review by John Raymond in the *New Statesman* (28 September 1957).

M'TURK, in Rudyard Kipling's *Stalky and Co.* (1899), is Major George Charles Beresford (1865–1938), an Irish schoolfellow of the author at the United Services College, Westward Ho, Devon. He later went to India as a civil engineer and subsequently became a photographer and antique dealer in London. With L.C. Dunsterville (see Stalky), he was instrumental in the creation of the Kipling Society, and in 1936 he published *School-days with Kipling*. What did Stalky think of M'Turk? 'Beresford', recalled Dunsterville at the age of eighty, 'was quite the type of stage Irishman who is agin anybody and everybody, and he kept this up till the day of his death.'

MacWALSEY, Professor John, in Ernest Hemingway's *To Have and Have Not* (1937), is said by the author's biographer, Carlos Baker, to be an amalgam of Harry Burns, Professor of English at the University of Washington, Seattle, whom Hemingway first met in 1936, and Arnold Gingrich (1903–76), founder-editor of *Esquire*.

MAD, in Daphne du Maurier's *Rule Britannia* (1972), is primarily the actress Dame Gladys Cooper (1888–1971). Interviewed in the *Illustrated London News* for October 1972, the author said, 'The main character is partly me but really it's an affectionate portrait of Gladys Cooper, who was a great friend and possessed all Mad's strength of character.'

MADDALO, in Percy Bysshe Shelley's *Julian and Maddalo* (1818), is Lord Byron. See Cadurcis, Lord.

MADDEN, Liz, in G.J. Cadbury's *When the Death Penalty Came Back* (1982), has as prototype Myra Hindley (1942–), a shorthand typist of Hyde, ·Cheshire, who in 1966 was sentenced to life imprisonment for the murder of a seventeen-year-old youth and a ten-year-old girl, and to seven years' imprisonment for being an accessory to the murder of a ten-year-old boy. The crime, due to the manner of the victims' burial, became known as the 'Moors Murders'. See also Storrow, Bert. Almost more tantalising is the question of who hid behind the pseudonym G.J. Cadbury, for he, or she, remains unmasked.

MAD HATTER, the, in Lewis Carroll's *Alice's Adventures in Wonderland* (1865), is Theophilus Carter, an Oxford High Street furniture dealer and Christ Church servitor who wore his hat on the back of his head and, like Carroll's Mad Hatter, was preoccupied with Time. At London's Crystal Palace in 1851 he exhibited an Alarm Bed which tipped out its occupant at the desired hour. The term 'mad as a hatter' pre-dates *Alice* and is believed to be derived from an occupational hazard of the craft – absorbed through the skin, mercurious nitrate used in making felt hats could cause St Vitus's Dance. There is a tradition that John Tenniel, illustrator of *Alice*, based his Mad Hatter upon a Lichfield canon named Bradley. My check through a number of editions of *Crockford's Clerical Directory*, however, has failed to discover a contemporary Lichfield canon of that name.

MADWOMAN OF CHAILLOT, the, in the Jean Giraudoux play of that title (1945), is modelled upon an English eccentric in Paris, Madame Leffray, widow of a London coachman, as Blaise Cendrars revealed in a *Paris Review* interview ('Writers at Work': 3). Living in the *rue* Lauriston, she sported a dirty, ostrich-feathered hat, threadbare ermine scarf, outlandish jewellery, lorgnette and a handbag which she trailed on the ground.

MAGGIE, in Arthur Miller's *After the Fall* (1964). A self-destructive victim of showbusiness exploitation: that was Miller's view of the American film actress Marilyn Monroe (1926–62), who became his wife in 1956 and was his model for Maggie. The marriage broke up in 1960, two weeks after the completion of their film *The Misfits*. Like Maggie, Monroe was a naïve sex symbol. Asked by a reporter if on a certain occasion she had anything on, she replied, 'I had the radio on.' After her death, from an overdose of sleeping pills, the suicide verdict was challenged on the ground of lack of medical evidence. There were allegations that she had been murdered to avert a political scandal. She was said to have had associations with President Kennedy (see Baltimore, Scott) and his brother, Robert, the then Attorney General. It was also claimed that she had been killed because she knew of CIA plots to assassinate the Cuban leader, Fidel Castro. Asked why he did not wish to attend her funeral, Miller replied, 'She won't be there.'

MAGGIE, in Tennessee Williams's *Cat on a Hot Tin Roof* (1955). When the Russian-born actress Maria Britneva appeared as an understudy in the first New York production of Williams's *A Streetcar Named Desire*, she gave what he said was the only perfect interpretation he had seen of Blanche Dubois. He invested Maggie with Maria's vitality, tenacity and charm . . . and when she remarked that she could not hear herself saying some of Maggie's lines, he replied that it was her spirit he had borrowed. She it was who coined Maggie's 'no-neck monsters' phrase when in Williams's company at a Rome hotel in 1948, the peace of the swimming pool being continually disturbed by a square, 'neckless' little girl who persistently jumped in and out of the water. In 1956 Britneva became the second wife of Peter George Grenfell, Lord St Just (*d.* 1984).

MAHOUDEAU, in Émile Zola's *L'Oeuvre* (1885–6), is the author's lifelong friend, the sculptor Philippe Solari (1840–1906), according to the Zola biographer F.W.J. Hemmings.

MAID OF ATHENS, the, in Lord Byron's 'The Maid of Athens' (*c.* 1810), is Theresa Macri (*b.* 1797), daughter of Theodore Macri, a vice-consul in Athens. Byron lodged with Macri's widow, becoming fond of Theresa, then aged twelve, whose mother hoped the girl might become the poet's bride. 'But I have better amusements', he wrote to a friend.

MAIGRET, Jules, in Georges Simenon's Maigret detective novels and stories (1928–73), is popularly supposed to have as prototype the French detective Marcel Guillaume, who died in 1963, aged ninety-one. Later that year, however, Simenon said he could not remember where the inspiration for Maigret came from, although he acknowledged that the character of his detective owed something to his father (see Mamelin, Désiré). At the time of the Liberation, Louis Aragon (see Galant, Cyrille), leader of the literary Resistance, put it about Paris that Maigret's original was a well-known Vichy collaborator. But Aragon had an axe to grind: Simenon had not demurred at Maigret films being made during the Occupation.

MAINWROTH, Sir Robert, in Osbert Sitwell's 'The Love-Bird' (*Dumb-Animal*, 1930), is Lord Berners (see Merlin, Lord), who in Sitwell's view 'did more to civilise the wealthy than anyone in England.'

MAISIE, in Rudyard Kipling's *The Light that Failed* (1891). Kipling fell in love with Florence Garrard (*d.* 1902) when he was fourteen, she sixteen, meeting her at the Southsea house where she and his sister boarded. When he left for India he considered himself engaged to her, and although two years later she wrote telling him that their understanding was at an end, she continued to occupy his mind. She later attended the Slade School of Art and when by chance he met her on returning to London, his feelings for her revived . . . but were not reciprocated. She died a spinster.

MAITLAND, Henry, in Morley Roberts's *The Private Life of Henry Maitland* (1912), is the novelist George Gissing (1857–1903), whose early life seemed a determined attempt to outdo fiction. A promising scholar, he was sent by his father – a Wakefield pharmacist – to Owens College, Manchester. There, alone and friendless in an alien city, he fell in love with a young, alcoholic prostitute. To buy her sufficient drink to keep her off the streets, he stole from fellow-students' overcoats; he was discovered, arrested, served a month's imprisonment and then, with the assistance of his friends, went to the United States, where he was reduced to near-starvation. On his return to England he went to Manchester and married his street-walker, in whom he unsuccessfully sought to inculcate a love for classical languages. During their poverty-stricken marriage she continued to drink and returned periodically to prostitution. She died of syphilis.

MALICHO, Lord Michin, in Thomas Love Peacock's *Gryll Grange* (1860–1), is Lord John Russell, First Earl Russell (1792–1878), a British statesman who introduced the Reform Bill of 1832, was twice prime minister, and whose small stature endeared him to political cartoonists. Although, like Peacock, he had supported Roman Catholic emancipation, he was later responsible for the Bill which prevented Catholic bishops from taking English territorial titles, and he came to be regarded as anti-Catholic.

MALIVERT, Octave de, in Stendhal's *Armance* (1827), was admitted by the author to be part-inspired by Lieutenant-Général Comte Philibert Curial (1774–1829), who was noted for his penchant for housemaids and for beating his wife, who was among Stendhal's conquests.

MALLOWS, Henry, in Thomas Wolfe's *You Can't Go Home Again* (1940), is George Bellows (1882–1925), a Greenwich Village artist who had an affair with Isadora Duncan (see Angel, Elise). He is also believed, by the Wolfe biographer Andrew Turnbull, to have had a liaison with Aline Bernstein (see Jack, Esther).

MALMAINS, Eugenia, in Nancy Mitford's *Wigs on the Green* (1935). The author's wayward sister, Unity Valkyrie Mitford (1914–48), was expelled from school three times and was in the habit of attending dances with her pet grass-snake, Enid, coiled about her neck. In the 1930s she became fanatically pro-Nazi, espousing a cause for which her father, Lord Redesdale (see Alconleigh, Lord), also had some sympathy. It is in this role that she appears as Eugenia Malmains. In Munich, she went to the Osteria restaurant, where Adolf Hitler spent his evenings. She caught his eye and became his friend and confidante, despite warnings from his aides that she might be a spy. When Britain declared war on Germany in 1939 she attempted suicide in Munich's English Garden, shooting herself with a pistol which Hitler had given her. The bullet lodged in her brain, and on Hitler's instructions she was treated by some of Germany's most eminent specialists. Visiting her in hospital, he sent her flowers daily, arranged for her dog to be cared for and had her furniture stored at his own expense. As her condition improved, he arranged for her repatriation via Switzerland, ordering a railway carriage to be converted into a hospital ward for her journey to Zurich.

MALONE, Archbishop, in Frank Hardy's *Power without Glory* (1950), is the Most Revd Daniel Mannix (1864–1963), Archbishop of Melbourne from 1917 to 1963. Irish-born, he was an outspoken opponent of conscription in the First World War and was subsequently equally vigorous in his denunciation of Communism.

MALONE, Edward Dunn, in Sir Arthur Conan Doyle's *The Lost World* (1912), is Edmund Dene Morel (1873–1924), a campaigning journalist and secretary of the Congo Reform Association, according to the Doyle biographer, Charles Higham. He was also secretary of the Union of Democratic Control which advocated appeasement in the First World War. His friendship with Doyle – also a Congo campaigner – came to an end when Morel was gaoled for treason after he had sent Union pamphlets to the French novelist Romain Rolland in Switzerland.

MALONE, Professor Eugen, in Harold Nicolson's *Some People* (1927), is said by the author's biographer, James Lees-Milne, to be an amalgam of Dr Emile Joseph Dillon (*d.* 1933), philologist and *Daily Telegraph* correspondent, and Henry Wickham Steed (1871–1956), editor of *The Times* from 1919 to 1922, proprietor-editor of *The*

Review of Reviews from 1923 to 1930 and lecturer in Central European History at King's College, London, from 1925 to 1938.

MALONE, Peter Augustus, in Charlotte Brontë's *Shirley* (1849), is the Revd James William Smith, a curate to the author's father, the vicar of Haworth. Regarding him as an arrogant Irishman, Charlotte Brontë thought him responsible for her father becoming over partial to whisky. She did, however, have hopes that he might marry Ellen Nussey (see Helstone, Caroline) . . . but this came to nothing. Smith later became a curate at Keighley, before leaving Yorkshire and emigrating to Canada. Another cleric in the succession of curates at Haworth, the Revd James Chesterton Bradley, recorded in 1902 his feeling that the *Shirley* caricature had done Smith an injustice, presenting him in a 'false and cruel' way.

MALTBY, Hilary, in Max Beerbohm's 'Maltby and Braxton' (*Seven Men*, 1919), is in part Reggie Temple (*b.* 1868), an Edwardian society figure whose diminutive size thwarted his ambition to become an actor. He was later a member of the English colony in Florence, and appears as Vincy in Ada Leverson's *Tenterhooks* (1912).

MALVOLIO, in William Shakespeare's *Twelfth Night* (*c.* 1601), has a suggested model in William Knollys, First Earl of Banbury (1547–1632). The puritanical treasurer of the household of Elizabeth I, he on one occasion appeared in his nightshirt to reprimand revellers, and conceived a much talked of passion for his ward, Mary Fitton (see Dark Lady, the). His wife was more than forty years his junior, and the paternity of her two sons – neither of whom was mentioned in the Earl's will – became a subject of legal dispute.

MAMELIN, Désiré and Élise, in Georges Simenon's *Pedigree* (1948), are the author's parents, Désiré (*d.* 1921) and Henriette Simenon (née Brull, *d.* 1971, aged ninety-one). The son of a hatter, Désiré was a Liège insurance clerk whose low income compelled his wife to take in lodgers. After his death – in his forties – Henriette married a railway pensioner. The thirteenth child of an alcoholic German property-owner and a Dutch mother, she worked in the Liège branch of a chain store, L'Innovation. Her second marriage was less than happy: before long she and her husband were communicating solely by scribbled notes, each having their own locked larder lest (Georges Simenon suspected) one should poison the other.

MANETTE, Lucie, in Charles Dickens's *A Tale of Two Cities* (1859), is supposedly part-inspired by Ellen Ternan. See Provis, Estella.

MANGAN, Alfred ('Boss'), in George Bernard Shaw's *Heartbreak House* (1917), is a caricature of Hudson Ewbanke Kearley, First Viscount Devonport (1856–1934), chairman of the Port of London Authority from 1909 to 1925 and from 1916 to 1917 the Government food controller. Shaw considered him a 'megalomaniac and a superficial fool'.

MANLEY, Gerontius, in Edmund Martin Geldart's *A Son of Belial* (1882). 'I wish it had another name ... It is an amusing and a sad book', noted the poet Gerard Manley Hopkins (1844–89) after Geldart had lent him a copy of *A Son of Belial*. Hopkins recognised himself as Manley in this disguised autobiography written under the name Nitram Tradleg by Geldart, a Unitarian minister who later resigned his living because his congregation took exception to his socialist views. Gerald Roberts, editor of Hopkins's *Selected Prose*, records that Geldart set out to take a continental holiday in a state of depression and disappeared on the Newhaven-Dieppe boat.

MANN, Charles, in Gilbert Cannan's *Mummery* (1918), is identified by the author's biographer, Diana Farr, as the stage designer Edward Gordon Craig (1872–1966), son of Ellen Terry (see Morrell, Candida) and E. W. Godwin, an architect and theatre-designer. His parents did not marry, and he in turn had by 1906 fathered thirteen illegitimate children – one of the mothers being Isadora Duncan (see Angel, Elise).

MAPPLE, Father, in Herman Melville's *Moby Dick* (1851), is Edward Thompson Taylor (1793–1871), a seaman-turned-preacher who was the first minister of the Boston Seamen's Bethel, established in 1829. Noted for using maritime vernacular in his sermons, he is also to be found in Dickens's *American Notes*, Harriet Martineau's *Retrospect of Western Travel*, Emerson's *Journals* and Dana's *Two Years Before the Mast*.

MARAPPER, Henry, in Brian Aldiss's *Non-Stop* (1958), has a real-life counterpart in Frank Sanders, a well-known Oxford book-seller whose antiquarian book and print shop still stands in The High. 'He was a small, industrious man,' Aldiss has told me, 'his talent running more to making profits than to organisation. He once sold an American dealer a rare, 32-page pamphlet on the American Civil War for £1000.05. After the dealer had written the cheque, he asked Frank, "How come you ask such an odd price?" To which Sanders replied, "I've always wanted to make a clear £1000 profit on a book." Dylan Thomas came into the shop regularly, spinning marvellous, bawdy tales. Under Thomas's magic spell, Sanders would fish a fiver out of the till (this was in the late '40s, when a fiver meant a slap-up dinner for two at the Mitre before it became a Berni Inn) and press it on Thomas. They would then stroll cordially arm-in-arm to the door, laughing and at peace with the world. The moment Thomas had gone, Sanders would clutch his head and curse. "Damn the scoundrel! He's done it to me again. Never more will I have that cheeky blackguard in my shop!" Next week, Thomas would be back. He always got his fiver.' Brian Aldiss wrote *Non-Stop*, his first science-fiction novel, shortly after leaving Frank Sanders's employ. 'Rap' is army slang for a tall tale.

MARCH, Clesant and Lance, in E.M. Forster's 'Arctic Summer' (written *c.* 1912; *Arctic Summer and other fiction*, 1980), are suggested by Forster's editor, Elizabeth Heine, to reflect aspects of Rupert Brooke (see Brookes, Winsome). Lance, says Heine, may represent Brooke as he was before the woman he loved, Ka Cox, displayed such an interest in Henry Lamb (see Dodd, Lewis) that in 1912 Brooke had a nervous breakdown. In portraying Clesant, Forster may have been influenced by Brooke as he later became: anti-feminist and somewhat puritanical. The brothers' mother is dominant, as was Brooke's mother, and their school resembles Brooke's Rugby.

MARCH FAMILY, the, in Louisa May Alcott's *Little Women* (1868−9), is the author's own family. Mr March is her father, Amos Bronson Alcott (1799−1888), a pioneering educational theorist whose ideas, like his farming, did not always succeed in practice. Appointed superintendent of the schools of Concord, Massachusetts, in 1859, he in his later years became largely dependent for income upon the literary endeavours of Louisa . . . who died the day he was buried. Mrs March is the author's mother, Abigail May

Alcott; and Beth, Amy and Meg are the author's sisters, respectively Elizabeth (who died aged twenty-three), May (who illustrated *Little Women*) and Anna. Jo, like the author the second daughter, is a self-portrait.

MARCH, Iris. See Storm, Iris.

MARCH, Nellie, in D.H. Lawrence's 'The Fox' (1922; *The Lady-bird*, 1923), is Violet Monk. See Banford, Jill.

MARCHBANKS, in D. H. Lawrence's 'The Last Laugh' (1925; *The Woman Who Rode Away*, 1928). In 1923, Lawrence's wife and John Middleton Murry (see Crich, Gerald) fell in love, though Murry refused to have an affair out of loyalty to her husband. Did Lawrence suspect? It was during this period that he wrote several stories in which Murry is portrayed unfavourably, often suffering a come-uppance — as he does in the guise of Marchbanks.

MARCHMAIN, Lord, in Evelyn Waugh's *Brideshead Revisited* (1945). The exile of Lord Marchmain echoes that of William Lygon, Seventh Earl Beauchamp (1872–1938), although Beauchamp's was for a different reason: his brother-in-law, the Second Duke of Westminster, got to hear of his homosexuality and hounded him out of the country. Westminster achieved this by having a quiet word with the King, who was appalled to learn that he had made an acknowledged homosexual a Knight of the Garter and asked Beauchamp to retire from public life. A former cabinet minister, he was Chancellor of London University and Lord Lieutenant of Gloucestershire. He relinquished these appointments in 1931, going abroad after his son, Hugh (see Flyte, Lord Sebastian), had talked him out of suicide. The Duke also informed his sister of her husband's nature. This was an uphill task because — as Waugh's biographer, Christopher Sykes, records — she had never heard of homosexuality; and when she did, she had a nervous breakdown which threatened her sanity. Although he failed to persuade his nieces to give evidence against their father, the Duke succeeded in ruining Beauchamp, enlivening his own undistinguished life by getting cheap laughs for referring to the Earl as 'my bugger-in-law'. By persuading the Home Office to take out a warrant for Beauchamp's arrest for homosexual offences, Westminster ensured he would not return — not even for his wife's funeral: the Duke saw to that by applying further pressure where it mattered, and when Beauchamp's boat berthed he was advised not to disembark. He went back to Venice. Within a month the Earl's son, Hugh, died, and again the Duke moved to block Beauchamp's return. But this time the Home Secretary had more sympathy for the Earl than for the vindictive Westminster: Beauchamp was allowed to come back, the warrant for his arrest suspended, then annulled, and he was able not only to attend his son's funeral but also to return to Madresfield, as Marchmain returned to Brideshead.

MARDER, Theophilus, in Klaus Mann's *Mephisto* (1936), is the German satirical dramatist Carl Sternheim (1878—1942), who was divorced from Pamela Wedekind (see Nicoletta).

MAREN, Aunt, in 'The Pearls' (*Winter's Tales*, 1942), by Isak Dinesen (Karen Blixen), is the author's feminist and prominent Unitarian aunt, Mary Bess Westenholz (1857—1947), daughter of a financial adviser to the King of Denmark. Blixen's biographer, Judith Thurman, makes the identification.

MARGUERITE, in the 'Marguerite' poems of Matthew Arnold, is Mary Claude (*d.* 1912, aged ninety-two), a French Protestant born in Berlin, her father being a Liverpool commission merchant. Arnold met her in Cumbria, while she was living with her mother at Ambleside in the late 1840s. A friend of Anne Jemima Clough — founder of Newnham College, Cambridge, and sister of Arthur Hugh Clough — she published a collection of fables, *Twilight Thoughts*, in 1848. She died unmarried.

MARGUERITE, in William Godwin's *St. Leon* (1799), is the author's first wife, Mary Wollstonecraft (1759—97), author of the pioneering *Vindication of the Rights of Woman* (1792). After a difficult and largely unhappy life (when her first husband left her she attempted suicide by jumping into the Thames), she found contentment with Godwin but died giving birth to their daughter, Mary (see Stella), who became the second wife of Percy Bysshe Shelley (see Glowry, Scythrop).

MARIA, in Ernest Hemingway's *For Whom the Bell Tolls* (1940), owes her physical appearance to the author's third wife, the American journalist and travel writer Martha Gellhorn (1908—), daughter of an Austrian-born gynaecologist living in St Louis, Missouri. They married in 1940, and through her activities as a war correspondent in Finland she helped to finance Hemingway during the writing of this novel. But the primary inspiration of Maria is a Spanish nurse, Mariá, who was raped by Fascist soldiers and whom Hemingway met at Mataró hospital, near Barcelona, in 1938.

MARIE ELISABETH, in Ford Madox Ford's *The Marsden Case* (1923), is Violet Hunt. See Nesbit, Norah.

MARIO, in Arthur Koestler's *Scum of the Earth* (1941), is Leo Valiani, a fellow-internee at Le Vernet in 1939. He had previously spent nine years in gaol for his anti-Fascist activities in Italy. Escaping from Le Vernet, he went to Britain and in 1943 was back in Italy with the Resistance movement. He played a principal role in organising the uprising against the Germans in 1945, and in ordering the execution of Mussolini (see Arango, General Tereso). After the war, Valiani abandoned politics for writing, producing works on Benedetto Croce and on the Austro-Hungarian Empire.

MARION, Jervase, in 'Lady Tal' (*Vanitas*, 1893), by Vernon Lee (Violet Paget), is Henry James (see Boon, George), who according to James's biographer, Leon Edel, had offended the author with his cool reception of her *Miss Brown* (1884).

MARIUS, in Walter Pater's *Marius the Epicurean* (1885). Although Thomas Wright's life of the author (1907) is now considered unreliable, it cannot be entirely disregarded in naming as model Richard Charles Jackson (1851 – 1923), who claimed to be the grandson of the Captain Francis Jackson immortalised by Lamb, and to be a friend of Carlyle and Rossetti. A Fellow of the Society of Arts, he was a High Churchman who in his connection with St Austin's Priory, Walworth, was known as the Revd Brother à Becket. He lived in considerable style in Camberwell, although by the time of his death his 8000-volume library, like the rest of his house, had become dirty and neglected. Pater first met him in 1877.

MARJORIE, in Ernest Hemingway's 'The End of Something' and 'The Three-Day Blow' (*In Our Time*, 1925), is Marjorie Bump, of Petoskey, Michigan. The daughter of a hardware dealer, she was seventeen and working as a waitress during vacation from Petoskey High School when Hemingway met her in 1919; they enjoyed a brief romance at Horton Bay, Michigan.

MARKER, Harvey, in Jack Kerouac's *Desolation Angels* (1965), is the American writer Norman Mailer (1923–), whose second wife, Adele Morales, was a girlfriend of Kerouac's.

MARLES, Louise, in J-K Huysmans's *En rade* (1887), is Anna Meunier. See Jeanne.

MARMADUKE, in Allan Monkhouse's *My Daughter Helen* (1922), is Christopher Isherwood (see Pimpernell), whose childhood friends included Monkhouse's son and daughter, Patrick and Rachel.

MARMELADOV and KATERINA IVANOVNA, his wife, in Fyodor Dostoevsky's *Crime and Punishment* (1866), are identified by the author's biographer, Ronald Hingley, as Alexsander Isayev (*d.* 1857), a tubercular, alcoholic schoolteacher-turned-civil servant, and his wife, Maria Dmitriyevna Isayeva, who subsequently married Dostoevsky. She died in Moscow in 1864, of tuberculosis.

MARPLAY, junior, in Henry Fielding's *The Author's Farce* (amended version, 1734), is believed by Austin Dobson in his study of Fielding (1883) to be the actor Theophilus Cibber (1703–58), who was criticised for deserting London's Drury Lane Theatre after his father, Colley Cibber (see Bays), had sold his share in the theatre's patent.

MARPLE, Miss Jane, in Agatha Christie's detective novels, commencing with *Murder at the Vicarage* (1930). '"I shouldn't be surprised if so-and-so isn't going on," my grandmother used to say, nodding her head darkly, and though she had no grounds for these assertions, so-and-so was exactly what *was* going on', recalled Agatha Christie in her autobiography (1977). Mrs Margaret Miller was her father's stepmother, who lived in Ealing and died in 1919, aged ninety-two. 'Miss Marple was not in any way a picture of my grandmother', the author noted. 'She was far more fussy and spinsterish than my grandmother ever was. But one thing she did have in common with her – though a cheerful person, she always expected the worst of everyone and everything, and was, with almost frightening accuracy, usually proved right ... I endowed my Miss Marple with something of Grannie's powers of prophecy.'

MARR, Henrietta, in George Moore's 'Henrietta Marr' (*In Single Strictness*, 1922), according to Sir Rupert Hart-Davis, editor of Moore's *Letters to Lady Cunard* (1957), is Mrs Pearl Craigie. See Theale, Milly; see also Lawson, Mildred.

MARSAC, Count, in Compton Mackenzie's *Vestal Fire* (1927), is Comte Jacques d'Adelsward-Fersen (1879–1923), the son of a steel tycoon. Following a period of imprisonment in Paris for alleged offences against schoolboys, he built a villa on Capri, was banished from the island when his history became known, but was later allowed to return. Becoming an opium addict, he died from a heart attack after what was believed to be an overdose of cocaine.

MARSANTES, Mme de, in Marcel Proust's *A la recherche du temps perdu* (1913–27), is supposedly the Comtesse de Salignac-Fénelon (née Deschamps), mother of Comte Bertrand de Salignac-Fénelon (see Saint-Loup, Robert de).

MARSAY, Henri de, in Honoré de Balzac's *La Fille aux yeux d'or* (1835), *Le Contrat de mariage* (1835), *Autre étude de femme* (1842) and *Illusions perdues* (1837–43), has as probable prototype the French politician Charles Auguste Louis Joseph, Duc de Morny (1811–65), illegitimate son of the Comte de Flahaut and Queen Hortense, half-brother of Napoleon III, and a principal conspirator in the *coup d'état* of December 1851.

MARSHALL, Lewis Ponsonby, in George Moore's *Confessions of a Young Man* (1888) and *Vale* (1914), according to Moore's biographer, Joseph Hone, is Lewis Welden Hawkins (*d.* 1910), a Stuttgart-born artist. Brought up in Brussels, Hawkins was a naturalised Frenchman of English parentage, and Moore first met him in Paris in the early 1870s.

MARSTOCK, J.D., in Harold Nicolson's *Some People* (1927), is an amalgam of the lawyer Sir Harold Handasyde Duncan (1885–1962), Old Etonian and the author's contemporary at Balliol College, Oxford; and John Randal Parsons (1884–1967), grandson of the Third Earl of Rosse, a schoolfellow of the author at Wellington, and from 1926 to 1946 the chairman of Gillett Brothers Discount Co.

MARTIN, Hank, in Adria Locke Langley's *A Lion in the Streets* (1945), has as prototype Huey Long. See Stark, Willie.

MARTIN, Rick, in Dorothy Baker's *Young Man with a Horn* (1938), is the American jazz trumpeter Leon Bismarck ('Bix') Beiderbecke (1903–31).

MARTINEZ, Juan Fernando, in Malcolm Lowry's *Dark as the Grave Wherein my Friend is Laid* (1968), is Juan Fernando Marquez (also known as Fernando Atonalzin). See Cerillo, Juan.

MARX, Carlo, in Jack Kerouac's *On the Road* (1957), is Allen Ginsberg. See Garden, Irwin.

MARY, in Robert Burns's 'Highland Mary' and 'To Mary in Heaven', is Mary Campbell (1763–86), who was born near Dunoon, Strathclyde, and worked as a nursemaid in Mauchline and as a dairymaid in Coilsfield. There is a suspicion that Burns may have wronged her, but that she in turn may well have been as wayward as he. They are believed to have planned to marry and settle in the West Indies, Burns abandoning his proposed emigration when he heard of her sudden death – possibly in childbirth, though he claimed the cause to be fever.

MARY, in Lord Byron's 'The Dream' (1816), is Mary Anne Chaworth, of Annesley Hall, Nottinghamshire, who was under the same guardianship as the poet and to whom he proposed in 1803, when he was still a schoolboy – 'What!' he overheard her say to a friend, 'Me care for that lame boy!' In 1814 she reappeared briefly in his life, expressing dissatisfaction with her marriage to John Musters, from whom she later separated.

MARY, in the nursery rhyme 'Mary had a little lamb'. When Mrs Mary Hughes died in Worthing at the age of ninety, the *Daily Dispatch* reported (10 December 1931) that she was this rhyme's inspiration. Born in Llangollen, north Wales, she was the daughter of John Thomas, of Ty Issa Farm in the Dee valley. 'I was always fond of lambs and if a ewe died in severe weather father would bring the orphan lamb to me', she recalled in 1927. 'Sometimes I had half a dozen lambs under my care and they became so attached to me that they followed me round the farm. Often they would come down the Holyhead road with me to meet the postman. One day when I was eight, Billy, the oldest and most friendly of my pets, created consternation as he followed me down the road to school. He came into the village school and into the classroom, scampered all over the forms and created such fun that the class could not be carried on. In the end the schoolmistress turned him out. A friend took charge of Billy till school was over and then he trotted home behind me for the two miles.' Miss J. Burl, a children's author, visited Ty Issa Farm, heard about Mary's lamb, and promptly wrote the nursery rhyme, according to the *Daily Dispatch*. Inconveniently, 'Mary had a little lamb' was first published in the *Juvenile Miscellany* of September 1830. The author was Sarah Josepha Hale, of Boston, Massachusetts. But why spoil a good story with the facts?

MARY, Mrs, in Ronald Firbank's *Caprice* (1917), is suggested by Brigid Brophy (*Prancing Novelist*, 1973) to be Lillah McCarthy (see Dubedat, Jennifer), whom Firbank had in mind for the title role of *The Princess Zoubaroff* (1920).

MARYLOU, in Jack Kerouac's *On the Road* (1957), is Luanne Henderson, of Denver, Colorado, who in 1945, aged fifteen, married Neal Cassady (see Moriarty, Dean). The marriage broke up in 1947 (see Camille). By 1978, she was a grandmother, living in a San Francisco suburb.

MASHA (Maria Serghyeevna), in Anton Chekhov's *Three Sisters* (1901). 'I do love you, I love your letters, I love the way you act and the way you walk. The only thing I don't love is the way you spend ages at the wash-basin,' Chekhov wrote to his touring actress wife, Olga Knipper (1868–1959), who was in part his inspiration for Masha, and for whom he wrote the role. In *Chekhov's Leading Lady* (1979), Harvey Pitcher tells how they met in 1898 and were married in 1901, Chekhov finally capitulating after a year's prevarication. The delay was caused partly by his anxiety about his tubercular condition and its consequences for her. At last, 'I'll do whatever you say,' he wrote, 'otherwise we shan't live but sip life once an hour by the table-spoon.' He died three years later. Limited though her talents were (she flopped as Gertrude in *Hamlet* and was on another occasion sacked by Stanislavsky), she remained a principal actress of the Moscow Art Theatre for several decades, clinging somewhat pathetically to her successful Chekhov roles when she was well past the characters' age. She made her last appearance on the Art Theatre's stage when she was over ninety.

MASTAKOVICH, Julian, in Fyodor Dostoevsky's 'A Christmas Tree and a Wedding' (1848), is Pyotr Karepin. See Bykov.

MASTER BARBER, the, in James Joyce's *Ulysses* (1922), is Sir Horace Rumbold (1869–1941), who in 1918, as British Minister in Berne, annoyed Joyce by his failure to support the author in his dispute with Henry Carr, an official of the British Consulate, over fees payable following Carr's appearance in a production of Wilde's *The Importance of Being Earnest*, which Joyce had sponsored.

MASTERMAN, in H. G. Wells's *Kipps* (1905), is George Gissing (see Maitland, Henry). A close friend, Wells went to France to nurse Gissing on his death-bed.

MASTERS, Miranda, in John Cournos's *Miranda Masters* (1926), is the American poet Hilda Doolittle (1886–1961). At the time with which this *roman-à-clef* is concerned, she had married Richard Aldington (see Ashton, Rafe) following a broken engagement with Ezra Pound (see Forbes, Duncan). After a miscarriage she wished to avoid further sex and encouraged her husband to take a lover, Dorothy Yorke (see Carter, Bella), thinking this would be of spiritual benefit to her marriage. It wasn't. Aldington left her for Yorke. Doolittle then took up with Cecil Gray (see Sharpe, James), putative father of her daughter, Perdita. According to Janice S. Robinson's *H.D.: The Life and Work of an American Poet* (1982), which claims that Doolittle and Lawrence had an affair, D.H. Lawrence (see Rampion, Mark) is also a runner in the Perdita paternity stakes. Cournos (see Wimsey, Lord Peter) aspired to be Doolittle's lover (*c.* 1916) but his attentions were not encouraged; he was more successful with Yorke.

MATILDA, in Sir Walter Scott's *Rokeby* (1813), is supposedly Williamina Belsches. See Redgauntlet, Lilias.

MATRAVERS, in E.S. Stevens's ' —— *and what happened*', *being an account of some romantic meals* (1916). Should you wish to know what Arthur Ransome (see Pye, Wilfred) was like as a young man, you have the answer in Matravers, a vivid, astringent yet not unsympathetic portrait of Ransome by one who observed him closely, as his biographer Hugh Brogan records. The author of this oddly-titled novel was Stephana Stevens, a literary agent, and she presents Matravers/Ransome as large, shaggy and impecunious, while according to another of her characters, 'He contributes essays to quarterlies, and reviews novels in a literary paper without ever having written one. He is, in print, the most fastidious and meticulous creature. In person he is bombastic, Gargantuan, thunderous, explosive, brutal, and bouncing.' Yet beneath the bounce there was shyness, as Brogan points out.

MATTHESON, Sir Joshua, in D.H. Lawrence's *Women in Love* (1920), is the philosopher Bertrand Russell (Third Earl Russell, 1872–1970), whom Lawrence failed to convert to his view of the way the world should be ordered. Their friendship withered, Russell coming to regard the author as a fascist. When Lawrence was told that Russell had described him as having no mind, he retorted, 'Have you ever seen him in a bathing-dress? Poor Bertie Russell! He is all Disembodied Mind!' Whatever figure he cut in the swimming pool, the philosopher managed to make several conquests, including Lady Ottoline Morrell (see Roddice, Hermione). The surname Mattheson was suggested by that of another of Russell's mistresses, Lady Constance Malleson (the actress Colette O'Neil), daughter of the Fifth Earl Annesley and first wife of Miles Malleson (see Chinnery), from whom she was divorced. See also Orellano, Gregory.

MATTHEW, in D.H. Lawrence's 'Smile' (1926; *The Woman Who Rode Away*, 1928). The death of Katherine Mansfield (see Brangwen, Gudrun) was the inspiration for this story, in which she is Ophelia and her husband, John Middleton Murry (see Crich, Gerald), is Matthew. For Lawrence's possible motive in attacking Murry in this and several other stories, see Marchbanks.

MATTY, Miss. See Jenkyns, Mathilda.

MATURIN, Gray, in W. Somerset Maugham's *The Razor's Edge* (1944), is the author's tribute to his American publisher and friend, Nelson Doubleday (1889–1949), who on his South Carolina estate at Yemassee built Maugham a house and cottage in which to write *The Razor's Edge*, the arrangement being that the novelist would share the cost from royalties.

MAUD, in Alfred, Lord Tennyson's 'Maud' (1855), is supposedly Rosa Baring (?1813–98), with whom the poet was in love in the early 1830s. The daughter of William Baring, a member of the Baring family of London merchant bankers, she is also thought to have been the inspiration of Tennyson's 'The Gardener's Daughter' and 'Rosebud'.

MAUPIN, Camille, in Honoré de Balzac's *Béatrix*. Not only did the French novelist George Sand (1804–76) teach Balzac to smoke Latakia in a hookah; her desertion by Liszt (see Conti, Gennaro) in favour of Marie d'Agoult (see Rochefide, Béatrix de) reputedly inspired this novel. Traces of Mme de Staël (see Ellénore) have also been discovered in Camille.

MAURIAC, the Duc de, in *La Dame aux camélias* (1848), by Alexandre Dumas *fils*, is Count de Stackelberg, the Russian ambassador in Vienna, who is reputed to have paid Marie Duplessis (see Gautier, Marguerite) to give up prostitution because of her resemblance to his deceased daughter. This account appears to be the one accepted by modern biographers, but less charitable versions of the relationship have it that at eighty he showered gifts upon her to persuade her to become his mistress.

MAXIM, Gifford, in Lionel Trilling's *The Middle of the Journey* (1947). Three years after this novel's publication, the man who inspired Gifford Maxim achieved an altogether different distinction. He was Whittaker Chambers (*d.* 1961), an editor of *Time* magazine, who precipitated the 1950 trial of an American State Department lawyer, Alger Hiss, by accusing him of having been a Communist. Sued for libel, Chambers produced evidence that Hiss had passed him State Department secrets. Hiss was tried, convicted and given a five-year prison sentence. Chambers emerged from the investigation as a self-confessed liar, tax-fiddler and ex-Communist courier. He subsequently became a farmer and a recluse.

MAXWELL, Duncan, in Compton Mackenzie's *Vestal Fire* (1927), is Norman Douglas (see Argyle, James), who reacted angrily – not to the portrait, which was affectionate, but to Cyril Connolly's disparaging review of the novel.

MAY, Mr, in D.H. Lawrence's *The Lost Girl* (1920), is Maurice Magnus (1876–1920), one-time business manager of Isadora Duncan (see Angel, Elise) and Edward Gordon Craig (see Mann, Charles), an intimate of Norman Douglas (see Argyle, James), and, briefly, editor of *Roman Review*. An American whose mother claimed to be the illegitimate daughter of William I of Prussia, he deserted from the Foreign Legion and went to Italy. When Italian police sought him for his failure to pay a hotel bill, he fled to Malta. Facing extradition, he committed suicide. Lawrence had lent him money, and prepared his Foreign Legion memoirs for publication, contributing an introduction.

MAYLIE, Rose, in Charles Dickens's *Oliver Twist* (1837–8), is the author's sister-in-law, Mary Hogarth (1819–37). Her death, at seventeen, in his arms so affected him that he had to suspend work on *Pickwick Papers* (when the next instalment failed to appear on time, colourful speculation as to the reason for the delay compelled him to explain the circumstances in an announcement accompanying the fifteenth number). Removing the ring from Mary Hogarth's finger, he wore it for the rest of his life.

MAZLOVA, Katyusha, in Leo Tolstoy's *Resurrection* (1899). It was from a St Petersburg judge that Tolstoy heard the story of Rosalie Oni, the prototype of Katyusha Mazlova. A servant, Oni was banished from the home of her employer when she became pregnant by the son of the house. Poverty forced her to take to prostitution, and when she was charged with stealing from a client the jury which tried her included the young aristocrat who had seduced her and brought about her ruin. Recognising her, he was conscience-stricken and sought to communicate with her in prison, offering to marry her. Before the wedding could take place she died in gaol, of typhus.

MEALY POTATOES, in Charles Dickens's *David Copperfield* (1849–50), is Bob Fagin, a London orphan who lived with his brother-in-law, a waterman. He was employed in the blacking factory where Dickens worked as a child, and where Fagin befriended him.

MEDICI, Lorenzo de, in Thomas Mann's *Fiorenza* (1905), is part-inspired by Heinrich Mann. See Settembrini.

MEEBER, Caroline, in Theodore Dreiser's *Sister Carrie* (1900; unexpurgated, 1981). 'My mind was a blank except for the name. I had no idea who or what she was to be', recalled Dreiser when he described how he began to write this novel. As the story developed, Caroline Meeber turned out to be largely inspired by his sister, Emma Wilhelmina Dreiser (d. 1937). After an affair with a Chicago architect she eloped in 1886 to Toronto with a Chicago saloon manager who confessed to her that he had just stolen several thousand dollars from his employers. Remorse soon prompted him to return most of the money, and the couple settled in New York, as F.O. Matthiessen records in *Theodore Dreiser* (1951). The author lodged with them eight years later and it was on his advice that his sister left her lover, who had become violent.

MEEK, Private Napoleon Alexander Trotsky, in George Bernard Shaw's *Too True to be Good* (1934), is T.E. Lawrence (see Ransom, Michael), who according to Blanche Patch in *Thirty Years with G.B.S.* (1951) was 'pleased as Punch'.

MÈGE, in Émile Zola's *Paris* (1897–8), is identified by the Zola biographer F.W.J. Hemmings as Jules Bazile Guesde (Mathieu Basile, 1845–1922), French socialist, editor of *L'Égalité* and son-in-law of Karl Marx.

MEHTA, Victor, in David Hare's *A Map of the World* (1983), is the West Indian novelist V.S. Naipaul (1932–   ), suggests the literary critic Claire Tomalin – 'It's the first time I've seen a living writer portrayed as the hero of a play' (*Sunday Times*, 6 February 1983).

MEINGAST, in Robert Musil's *The Man without Qualities* (1930–43), is the psychoanalyst Ludwig Klages (1872–1956). Musil was impressed by his exposition on the nature of love, *Vom Kosmogonischen* (1922).

MELL, Mr, in Charles Dickens's *David Copperfield* (1849–50). Was Mr Mell drawn from life or 'lifted' from a friend's book? He has been taken to have been modelled on one Taylor, English master at Wellington House Academy (see Creakle, Mr). But it is possible that Mell was suggested by a biography of Oliver Goldsmith written in 1848 by John Forster (see Podsnap), in which Goldsmith's time as a flute-playing teacher at a school in Peckham is described.

MELLIFONT, Lord, in the Henry James story which gave its name to his collection *The Private Life* (1892), reveals the author as a prophet. Mellifont's original, the artist Frederic Leighton (1830–96), who became President of the Royal Academy in 1878, was just Sir Frederic when the story was written. Nearly four years were to pass before he became Lord Leighton . . . and then he held the title for only twenty-four hours, dying the day after he was gazetted. He lived in somewhat bizarre style in Holland Park Road, Kensington, at what is now Leighton House – built and designed to his requirements, noted for its exotic Arab Hall displaying his collection of Damascus tiles, and quite possibly London's largest single-bedroomed dwelling. Just as James could not have forecast how short-lived the painter's peerage would be, so might he have been surprised to know that — nearly a century later — we still await another. Lord Leighton was both Britain's first artist peer and, so far, the last.

MELMOTTE, Augustus, in Anthony Trollope's *The Way We Live Now* (1875), was created just as the greatest folly of his probable prototype, the company promoter Baron Grant (1830–99), was nearing completion: opposite Kensington Palace, London's largest private mansion was so big that it was never occupied, and in 1883 it was demolished by Grant's creditors. Grant was born Albert Gottheimer, in Dublin, and ennobled by Victor Emmanuel II for promoting Milan's Galleria Vittorio Emmanuele. In the 1860s and 1870s he was twice MP for Kidderminster, and he was a master of the grand gesture — purchasing Leicester Square, he turned it into a public garden and in 1874 presented it to the city. He died comparatively impoverished, after a series of bankruptcy actions.

MELVILLE, Erasmus and Valerie, in D.H. Lawrence's 'Things' (1928; *The Lovely Lady*, 1933), are Earl Henry Brewster (1878–1957) and his wife Achsah Barlow Brewster (1878–1945), American expatriate painters. After meeting them in Capri, Lawrence and his wife stayed at their bungalow near Kandy Lake, Ceylon, in 1922 and in 1927 toured the west coast of Italy with them.

MENALCAS, in Jean de La Bruyère's *Caractères de Théophraste* (1688–94), is identified by Isaac D'Israeli as the absent-minded Comte de Brancas, who was noted for mistaking the Duc de La Rochefoucauld for a beggar. Similarly, Beatrix Potter, whose children's books enabled her to buy a fair slice of the Lake District and present it to the National Trust, was once mistaken for a tramp. The rich can afford to look broke.

MENDEL, in Gilbert Cannan's *Mendel* (1916), is Mark Gertler (see Loerke), a close friend of the author until Cannan's personality began to change, prompting Gertler to describe him in 1918 as a blown-out eggshell. Cannan was becoming insane. See Gunn, Gilbert.

MENELAUS, in Hilda Doolittle's *Helen in Egypt* (1961), represents the author's former fiancé, Ezra Pound. See Forbes, Duncan.

MERCER, in Evelyn Waugh's 'Charles Ryder's Schooldays' (written 1945, published 1982), is Dudley Carew (1903—   ), novelist, and a journalist with *The Times* from 1926 to 1963. A contemporary of Waugh at Lancing College, he subsequently introduced him to Evelyn Gardner (see Last, Brenda). He recalled their schooldays in *A Fragment of Friendship* (1974).

MERDLE, Mr, in Charles Dickens's *Little Dorrit* (1855—7). 'That precious rascality' is how Dickens described the Irish banker and MP, John Sadleir (1814—56), who cut his throat on Hampstead Heath. His suicide followed the Tipperary Joint Stock Bank scandal in which he was implicated as chairman. In addition to his £200,000 fraud on the bank, he swindled the Royal Swedish Railway (of which he was chairman) out of £150,000.

MERE, Jenny, in Max Beerbohm's *The Happy Hypocrite* (1897), is the author's infatuation, committed to paper. Cissie Loftus, actress and mimic, was fifteen when he first saw her, billed as 'The Mimetic Marvel' at London's Tivoli Theatre. Not only did he worship her across the footlights; he also made occasional expeditions to Herne Hill, where she lived with her actress mother, in the hope of seeing her. She died in 1943, aged sixty-six.

MERION, Diana, in George Meredith's *Diana of the Crossways* (1885). Behind the creation of this character lie two scandals: a divorce action allegedly motivated by political malice, and what seems to have been the first newspaper leak to bring down a government. Meredith's model for Diana was Mrs Caroline Elizabeth Sarah Norton (1808—77), poet, celebrated beauty, daughter of a colonial administrator and granddaughter of the dramatist Richard Brinsley Sheridan. Unhappily married, she was living apart from her barrister husband, the Hon. George Chapple Norton, when in 1836 he brought a divorce action in which Lord Melbourne (see Dannisburgh, Lord) was cited as co-respondent. Without leaving the court, the jury dismissed Norton's case, which was believed to have been brought to thwart Melbourne's ambition to become premier. Nine years later, Caroline Norton was suspected of leaking to *The Times* the intention of Sir Robert Peel (see Pecksniff, Mr) to repeal the Corn Laws. Meredith has his Diana, short of money, passing information to a newspaper. But Caroline Norton was innocent: the culprit was Lord Aberdeen. For many years she campaigned for divorce law reform, achieving her own freedom only upon the death of her husband in 1875. Shortly afterwards, in the last year of her life, she married the historian Sir William Stirling Maxwell. Meredith's privately admitted portrait of Caroline outraged her relatives, and it was to mollify them that he added an 'Apology' to later editions: 'A lady of high distinction for wit and beauty, the daughter of an illustrious Irish house, came under the shadow of a calumny. It has latterly been examined and exposed as baseless. The story of *Diana of the Crossways* is to read as fiction.'

MERLIN, Dorothy, in Pamela Hansford Johnson's *The Unspeakable Skipton* (1959), might, the author's friends warned her, be taken to be a caricature of Dame Edith Sitwell (see Whittlebot, Hernia). The novelist's husband wrote to Dame Edith to allay any such suspicion, even though Dorothy Merlin was presented as an Australian housewife with seven children, interested only in her own verse-dramas — in contrast to spinster Dame Edith who was noted for her interest in contemporary writing. Replying that she was currently working on *The Queen and the Hive*, which included a description of Catherine de Medici planning a massacre, Dame Edith said she feared this might be taken as a portrait of Miss Johnson. 'After all, you are not Italian, do not persecute Protestants and are not the mother-in-law of Mary Queen of Scots, so the likeness springs to the eyes!' This is recorded by Elizabeth Salter's *The Last Years of a Rebel* (1967). Objections to *The Unspeakable Skipton* came from quite another quarter — offended Yorkshire readers, who assumed the book was a slur on their town.

MERLIN, Lord, in Nancy Mitford's *The Pursuit of Love* (1945). When it was rumoured that he was to marry Violet Trefusis (see Romanovitch, Princess 'Sasha'), Lord Berners (Mitford's Merlin) notified newspapers' travel columns: 'Lord Berners has left Lesbos for the Isle of Man.' Gerald Hugh Tyrwhitt-Wilson, Fourteenth Baron Berners (1883—1950), was a celebrated joker, even dyeing the pigeons a variety of colours at his home in Faringdon, Oxfordshire. He was also a writer, artist and noted composer of ballet music, his *Triumph of Neptune* (1926) being presented by Diaghilev in London, Paris and Monte Carlo. Built into the rear of his limousine, according to some accounts, was a clavichord, a precaution against inspiration overtaking him on the road. To his hard-pressed fellow-composer William Walton, he gave £50 for the dedication of *Belshazzar's Feast*. Later, when Walton issued an injunction to prevent Berners from caricaturing him in *Count Omega*, he responded with a counter-injunction to prevent Walton attempting to get into his novels.

MERRILIES, Meg, in Sir Walter Scott's *Guy Mannering* (1815), is Jean Gordon (?1670–?1745). A gypsy born at Kirk-Yetholm, on the Roxburgh/Northumberland border, she married Patrick Faa, a member of Scotland's most notable nomad family. All but one of her numerous sons were hanged (three for sheep-stealing); the one who escaped the noose was murdered. Becoming a door-to-door beggar in her old age, she died following a ducking inflicted by Carlisle's Hanoverian supporters after she had loudly proclaimed her support for Prince Charles.

MERRIVALE, Sir Henry, in the detective novels of Carter Dickson (John Dickson Carr), commencing with *The Plague Court Murders* (1935). I am not alone in noting a remarkable similarity between Merrivale and Winston Churchill (see Catskill, Rupert). David Holloway, literary editor of the *Daily Telegraph*, shares my view.

METALLUMAI, Taffimai (Taffy), in Rudyard Kipling's *Just So Stories* (1902), is the author's daughter, Josephine, who died in New York at the age of seven.

METROLAND, Margot, in Evelyn Waugh's *Decline and Fall* (1928), is Nancy Cunard. See Storm, Iris.

MEURSAULT, in *The Outsider* (1942), by Albert Camus. Some originals are born to fictional greatness, others have it thrust upon them and then do their best to live up to it. Which was Pierre Galindo? Largely the inspiration of Meursault, he was an Oran grain exporter whom Camus first met in 1938, in Algiers. Early in the Second World War he sheltered American agents in Algeria and kept the United States consul informed of the movement of German imports of military supplies. A Foreign Legion officer under the Vichy Government which controlled the country, he joined the Resistance and led a successful assault on Oran airport to assist the American invasion of Algeria's coast in 1942. An appointment as a liaison officer with the US Forces followed, and he later worked on

Combat, a daily newspaper edited by Camus. In outlining Galindo's career, Herbert R. Lottmann's *Albert Camus* (1979) presents him as a man of few words but much action. Patrick McCarthy's *Camus* (1982) portrays a more talkative Galindo, a man of bravado who became rather more of Meursault after he recognised himself in the novel than he had been before. The real Galindo is probably to be found somewhere between the two.

MICAWBER, Wilkins and Emma, in Charles Dickens's *David Copperfield* (1849—50). Seeking a loan from his son's bank, John Dickens (1785—1851) wrote of 'a difficulty from which, without some anticipatory pecuniary effort, I cannot extricate myself.' That not only sounds like Micawber; it *is* Micawber. Indeed, John Dickens in full spate could out-Micawber Wilkins himself. The novelist's father was a Navy Pay Office assistant clerk whose tendency to live beyond his means resulted in frequent changes of residence, culminating in his consignment in the early 1820s to a debtors' prison. There he waited for something to turn up, as it duly did, in the form of a legacy which secured his release. He later worked as manager of the reporting staff of the *Daily News*, of which Charles Dickens was the first editor. Also seen in Micawber have been characteristics of Thomas Powell (1809—87), author of *Pictures of the Living Authors of Britain* (1851), who was obsessed with writing letters — even to people in the same room. Suspected of plagiarism, he left England in 1849 to settle in America. Another suggested contributor to Micawber is Richard Chicken, an eccentric and impecunious Leeds elocutionist who worked in the office of an engineer, J.C. Birkinshaw, in whose firm Charles Dickens's brother, Alfred, was a partner. Chicken was also employed for a time by the North Eastern Railway, living at Skeldegate, York. Mrs Micawber, insofar as her loyalty to her wayward, hapless spouse is concerned, is the author's mother. See Nickleby, Mrs.

MICHAELIS, in D.H. Lawrence's *Lady Chatterley's Lover* (1928), is Michael Arlen (Dikran Kouyoumdjian, 1895—1956), Armenian author of *The Green Hat* (1924), which reputedly earned him £120,000. His Rolls-Royce was said to be at least six inches longer than anyone else's, and he is perhaps unique among novelists in having had his trouser buttons torn off by fans in New York. Earlier, from the success of his first novel, *The London Venture*, he lent Noël Coward £250 to enable him to stage *The Vortex*, and he championed Lawrence at a time when Lawrence needed help. Later, he lapsed into obscurity, but he always retained something of the bounce of his heyday when, dapper and fur-coated, he arrived in Chicago and was asked what he thought of himself as an artist. 'Per ardua', he replied, 'ad astrakhan.'

MICHAELIS, Dikran, in Henry Williamson's *The Phoenix Generation* (1965), is Michael Arlen. See Michaelis.

MIDDLETON, Clara and Dr, in George Meredith's *The Egoist* (1879). 'My feet were nourished on her breasts all night', wrote Meredith in his poem 'Modern Love'. Small wonder, if that was indeed his practice, that his first wife left him for another. The inspiration of Clara Middleton, Mary Ellen Nicolls (née Peacock, 1821–61), was the daughter of the novelist Thomas Love Peacock (1785–1866), the model for Dr Middleton. She was a widow of twenty-five, with an infant daughter, when Meredith met her in 1846, and he quickly fell in love with her beauty and impressive intellect. They married three years later, but were sexually maladjusted, Meredith – six years her junior – being more concerned with making his name as a writer than with contenting his wife as a lover. In 1857 they parted, Mary Ellen becoming the mistress of the artist Henry Wallis, for whose 'The Death of Chatterton' Meredith was model. She did not, as Meredith hinted, become insane. She died from dropsy. Meredith's relationship with his father-in-law was an uneasy one. They disliked each other, Meredith the radical unable to abide Peacock's politics, Peacock resenting Meredith's penuriousness, his intrusion on his solitude, his flamboyance . . . and his heavy smoking: the old man loathed tobacco and feared Meredith might set fire to the house.

MIDDLETON, Constance, in W. Somerset Maugham's *The Constant Wife* (1927), is in part the author's wife, Syrie Maugham (1879–1955), daughter of 'Dr' Thomas Barnardo, the celebrated founder of orphanages. She was first married to the pharmaceutical tycoon Henry Wellcome, who was nearly thirty years her senior and in 1916 divorced her for adultery, naming Maugham, whom she married in the following year. In 1929 her second marriage also ended in divorce, her life with Maugham having been rendered intolerable by his homosexuality. An influential interior decorator, she was noted for her pioneering use of white, for which she created a vogue. 'Dear me, how shocking!' exclaimed Lord Berners (see Merlin, Lord), upon hearing that a neighbour's daughter had taken a job in Syrie's shop. 'Fancy selling your daughter to the white furniture traffic!'

MIDLANDER, Sir Orpheus, in George Bernard Shaw's *Geneva* (1938), is suggested by St John Ervine (*Bernard Shaw: His Life, Work and Friends*, 1956) to be an amalgam of the British statesmen Arthur Balfour (see Evesham, Sir Arthur) and Austen Chamberlain (1863—1937), who was Foreign Secretary from 1924 to 1929 and twice Chancellor of the Exchequer. Chamberlain lacked ruthlessness, and his sense of dignity prevented him from lobbying to succeed Balfour. 'Poor man,' said Churchill, 'he always plays the game and never wins it.'

MI-EN-LEH, in Bertolt Brecht's *Me-ti. The Book of Twists and Turns* (1934—50), is Vladimir Ilyich Lenin (1870—1924), founder of modern Russia. When Jean Cocteau was interviewed for the *Paris Review* in 1963 (*Writers at Work:3*, 1967), he recalled that the painter Domergue had at one time employed a 'housemaid' to perform such chores as making the beds and filling the coal-scuttles. 'We all gathered in those days at the Café Rotonde. And a little man with a bulging forehead and black goatee would come there sometimes for a glass, and to hear us talk. And to "look at the painters". This was the "housemaid" of Domergue, out of funds. We asked him once (he said nothing and merely listened) what he did. He said he meant to overthrow the government of Russia. We all laughed, because of course we did, too. That is the kind of time it was! It was Lenin.'

MIGULIN, in Yuri Trifonov's *The Old Man* (1978), is Filipp Kuzmich Mironov (*d.* 1921), a Cossack military commander executed by a Red Guards firing squad after he was falsely denounced as a traitor. Mary Seton-Watson made the identification in a feature entitled 'Are Soviet authors rewriting the history books?' in the *Listener* (19 May 1983).

MILDMAY, Mr, in Anthony Trollope's *Phineas Finn* (1869), *Phineas Redux* (1874) and *The Prime Minister* (1876), is Lord John Russell. See Malicho, Lord Michin.

MILESTONE, Marmaduke, in Thomas Love Peacock's *Headlong Hall* (1816), is Humphrey Repton (1752—1818), pioneer landscape gardener, and the first to describe himself as such.

MILLBANK, Oswald, in Benjamin Disraeli's *Coningsby* (1844). In the wake of *Coningsby*, several 'keys' were issued purporting to identify the novel's originals. The first of these claimed that Millbank was Mark Philips, a noted parliamentary reformer who in 1832 became one of the first two MPs for Manchester, which prior to the Reform Act of 1832 was without representation. In 1837 Philips defeated Gladstone (see Gresham, Mr) at the poll in a sequel to an earlier visit paid by Gladstone to Manchester. He had come to stay with the Philips family at nearby Prestwich, and when his train arrived in Manchester was welcomed by Robert Philips, Mark's father. As their carriage passed through the streets, a cheer went up from bystanders, to which Gladstone responded by leaning out of the window and waving his hat to the crowd. Then, as the cheers subsided, a voice cried, 'Put tha bloody 'ead in – it's Bob Philips we're shoutin'!' A revised 'key' to *Coningsby* identified Gladstone as Millbank. All that can be said with certainty is that Millbank was at least in part modelled upon the Lancashire cotton manufacturer Henry Ashworth (1794–1880), of Eagley Bank, Bolton, whom Disraeli visited and whose paper, *Statistical Illustrations of the Past and Present State of Lancashire* (1842), is the basis of Millbank's lecture to Coningsby on the development of the district of Rossendale.

MILLER, James, in Aldous Huxley's *Eyeless in Gaza* (1936), is in the view of the author's biographer, Sybille Bedford, an amalgam of the celebrated preacher the Very Revd Dick Sheppard (*d.* 1937), successively vicar of London's St Martin's-in-the-Fields, dean of Canterbury and precentor of St Paul's Cathedral; Gerald Heard (see Par, Augustus); F. Matthias Alexander (1869–1955), an Australian actor turned therapist whose pupils included Huxley and Shaw; and J.E.R. McDonagh (1881–1965), surgeon, vegetarian, health food protagonist and founder of the Nature of Disease Institute.

MILLPOND, Miss, in Lord Byron's *Don Juan* (1819–24), is Anna Isabella Milbanke. See Iñez, Donna.

MILLS, in Joseph Conrad's *The Arrow of Gold* (1919), is Arthur Marwood. See Tietjens, Christopher.

MILTON, Mona, in James Gibbons Huneker's *Painted Veils* (1920), is believed to be the author's second wife, the sculptress Clio Huneker (1869–1925). She was the daughter of Howard Hinton, a journalist with the New York *Home Journal*, and Lucy Hinton, also a sculptress, and married Huneker in 1892, divorcing him seven years later for alleged adultery with a number of women. She was subsequently the wife of William Barrie Bracken, a New York lawyer and stock promoter.

MINETTE, in D.H. Lawrence's *Women in Love* (1920), is a composite of Minnie Lucie Channing (see Pussum) and Dora Carrington (see Morrison, Greta), according to Émile Delavenay's *D.H. Lawrence: The Man and His Work* (1972).

MINGOTT, Mrs Manson, in Edith Wharton's *The Age of Innocence* (1920), is an amalgam of the author's aunt, Mason Jones (Mrs Isaac Jones), who on New York's Fifth Avenue, between 57th and 58th Streets, built a spectacular, Parisian-style mansion in which, a victim of obesity, she lived on the ground floor; and a noted New York hostess of the 1880s, Mrs Paran Stevens (née Marietta Reed, *d.* 1895), daughter of a Massachusetts grocer and wife of the hotelier and racehorse-owner Paran Stevens (*d.* 1872). See also Carfry.

MINNS, in H.G. Wells's *The New Machiavelli* (1911), is the poet Sir Henry Newbolt (1862–1938), a member of the Co-efficients, whom Wells joined on leaving the Fabian Society and who in this novel are represented by the Pentagram Circle.

MINTO, Basil, in Dylan Thomas and John Davenport's *The Death of the King's Canary* (written 1940, published 1976), is Cyril Connolly. See Quiggin, J.G.

MIRABEL, Count, in Benjamin Disraeli's *Henrietta Temple* (1837), is Alfred, Count D'Orsay (1801–52), dandy, wit, artist and the novel's dedicatee. Of French extraction, he was adopted by the Earl and Countess of Blessington.

MIRANDA, in James Russell Lowell's *A Fable for Critics* (1848), is Margaret Fuller. See Zenobia.

MIROBOLANT, M Alcide, in W.M. Thackeray's *The History of Pendennis* (1848–50) and 'Little Dinner at Timmins's' (*A Shabby Genteel Story and other Tales*, 1852), is Alexis Benoit Soyer (1809–58), writer on cookery and chef at London's Reform Club from 1837 to 1850. In 1847, at the request of the British Government, he established kitchens in Dublin to alleviate the effects of the famine, and in 1855 he was appointed cookery adviser to the British army in the Crimea.

MISSEE LEE. See Lee, Missee.

MITTY, Walter, in James Thurber's 'The Secret Life of Walter Mitty' (1939; *My World — and Welcome to It*, 1942). Asked by a librarian if Mitty had a model, Thurber replied, 'The original of Walter Mitty is every other man I have ever known. When the story was printed in the *New Yorker* twenty-two years ago, six men from around the country, including a Des Moines dentist, wrote and asked me how I had got to know them so well.' Friends of the author's family, however, discerned in Mitty Thurber's father — Charles Thurber (1867–1939), a clerk in Columbus, Ohio, who declined a job offered by his wealthy father-in-law, preferring to strive for goals which always eluded him. Others took the author's brother, William Thurber (1893–1973), to be the prototype, according to the Thurber biographer Burton Bernstein. William worked for the Ohio Bureau of Weights and Measures, and Bernstein records that James once found him standing in front of a mirror, acting out the arrest of a fraudulent storekeeper. 'I'm taking you in', he informed his reflection. Thurber concluded his reply to the inquiring librarian, 'No writer can ever put his finger on the exact inspiration of any character in fiction that is worthwhile, in my estimation. Even those commonly supposed to be taken from real characters rarely show much similarity in the end . . . '

MNISHEK, Marina, in Alexander Pushkin's *Boris Godunov* (1831), is Yekaterina Raevsky (1797–1885), sister of Maria Raevsky (see Larin, Tatiana). Pushkin first met her in 1820, and in the following year she married General Mikhail Orlov (1788–1842).

MOBERLY, Manfred, in Osbert Sitwell's *Those Were The Days* (1938). Two factors suggest that Sitwell had in mind Ezra Pound (see Forbes, Duncan), for Moberly: the similarity of the surname to that of the poet's *Hugh Selwyn Mauberley*, and Pound's role as a *New Age* music critic.

MOBY DICK, in Herman Melville's novel of that name (1851), has a probable prototype in Mocha Dick, a white bull-whale credited in the mid-nineteenth century with the sinking of a number of ships, the deaths of more than thirty whalers and the accommodation of nineteen harpoons abortively thrust into him. An account of Mocha Dick in the *Knickerbocker Magazine* predates *Moby Dick* by twelve years.

MOCKBAR, Amyas, in Nancy Mitford's *Don't Tell Alfred* (1960). When Sam White, Paris correspondent of the London *Evening Standard*, incensed Mitford by quoting a remark she had made at a cocktail party, she avenged herself by portraying him as Mockbar. The son of a Russian family which fled to Australia from the Ukraine pogroms, White also appears in Frank Hardy's *Power Without Glory* (1950), eloping to England with the daughter of a corrupt business magnate (see West, John), an adventure which had its basis in real life. In the British Press Awards of 1980, he was named Columnist of the Year.

MOFFAT, George, in Ford Madox Ford's *The Benefactor* (1905), is Dr William Martindale (*d.* 1902), co-author of the druggists' hand-book *Extra Pharmacopeia*, a distinguished chemist, and assistant in that role to Lord Lister. In 1894 Ford eloped with and married his seventeen-year-old daughter (see Macdonald, Countess).

MOFFAT, Miss, in Emlyn Williams's *The Corn is Green* (1938). A small-town schoolmistress in north Wales, Sarah Grace Cooke said she could not imagine 'the public being faintly interested in a play about education'. Emlyn Williams thought otherwise and put her into his play as Miss Moffat, a character played on the stage by Sybil Thorndike and Ethel Barrymore and on film by Bette Davis. Miss Cooke came from Bramley, near Leeds. She was thirty-three and teaching at Holywell County School when Emlyn Williams, the son of a local ironworker, arrived as a pupil in 1916. Although she hardly spoke to him for several terms, she quietly observed his progress and decided he had potential. She was responsible for him learning French at the school, she supplied him with footwear and she sent him to France for a term at her own expense, later preparing him for matriculation. She also gave him a bicycle and a typewriter and coached him for his scholarship to Oxford. Her interest in her pupil, however, was unsentimental, her help being given in a breezy, matter-of-fact manner. It was a detached attachment, the teacher remaining 'Miss Cooke' and still signing herself 'S. G. Cooke' on accepting Williams's invitation to be godmother to his first child. 'I've written a play', he wrote to her in 1937; 'it's no good pretending she isn't meant to be you, though all the rest is pretty well dramatic licence. Anything you don't like, I'll change.' She approved the script, wiring back 'No objection', although she wasn't sure that Thorndike was right for the part. In the introduction to his *Collected Plays* (1961), Williams notes: 'As one question about *The Corn is Green* crops up with fair frequency from certain earnest producers, I may as well answer it once and for all. "In spite of everything, you do mean Miss Moffat to be a *bit* in love with the boy, don't you — sort of repressed?" The answer is NO.'

MOHUN, Lord Harry, in W.M. Thackeray's *Henry Esmond* (1852). Charles Mohun, Fourth Baron Mohun (?1675–1712), an inveterate duellist who was twice acquitted of murder, provided Thackeray with a model for Lord Harry's duel scene. Both he and his opponent — James Douglas, Fourth Duke of Hamilton — were killed fighting a duel in Hyde Park over a difference arising from protracted litigation over the estate of the Earl of Macclesfield.

MÖLLN, Kai, in Thomas Mann's *Buddenbrooks* (1901), is the author's boyhood friend, Count Hans Kaspar von Rantzau, according to the Mann biographer, Richard Winston.

MONCKTON, President Richard, in John Ehrlichman's *The Company* (1976), bears more than a chance resemblance to Richard Nixon (1913–), United States President from 1969 to 1974. Ehrlichman was Nixon's Domestic Affairs Adviser, and he was convicted for his part in the Watergate scandal which subsequently forced Nixon's resignation. He wrote this novel while serving his prison sentence.

MOND, Mustapha, in Aldous Huxley's *Brave New World* (1932), is supposedly part-inspired by the British industrialist, financier and statesman Alfred Mond, First Baron Melchett (1868–1930), chairman of Imperial Chemical Industries and Minister of Health from 1921 to 1922.

MONIKA, in Roger McGough's *Summer with Monika* (1967), is Thelma Monaghan, who studied at Liverpool College of Art and then became a fashion designer. In 1965 she established a boutique in Liverpool's Bold Street, trading under the name Monika.

MONMOUTH, Lord, in Benjamin Disraeli's *Coningsby* (1844), is the Third Marquis of Hertford. See Steyne, Lord.

MONOMARK, Lord, in Evelyn Waugh's *Vile Bodies* (1930), is Lord Beaverbrook (see Ottercove, Lord; see also Copper, Lord). Twenty-eight years after he was briefly employed by Beaverbrook on the *Daily Express*, Waugh successfully sued the newspaper twice for libel. The litigation arose from a feud with Nancy Spain, literary critic of the *Daily Express*, who was egged on by Beaverbrook himself.

MONSANTO, Lorenzo, in Jack Kerouac's *Big Sur* (1962), is Lawrence Ferlinghetti. See O'Hara, Larry.

MONSELL, in D.H. Lawrence's *Kangaroo* (1923), is Robert Mountsier (1888–1972), Lawrence's agent in the United States. A graduate of the University of Michigan, he became literary editor of the *New York Sun* in 1910. He served with the Red Cross in the First World War and then rejoined the newspaper, retiring in 1950.

MONTBARBON, Jean-Pierre, in Julian Gloag's *Lost and Found* (1981). When Ian McEwan (1948–   ) published his first novel *The Cement Garden* in 1978 Gloag claimed he could see a resemblance to his own *Our Mother's House*. In *Lost and Found*, a young novelist, Jean-Pierre Montbarbon, wins the Goncourt Prize with a brilliant work . . . by another author. McEwan reacted firmly with a request for Gloag to 'make straight accusations and produce some textual similarities'.

MONTDORE, Lady, in Nancy Mitford's *Don't Tell Alfred* (1960), is in part Violet Trefusis (see Romanovitch, Princess 'Sasha'). She infuriated Mitford by claiming to have had a long affair with Gaston Palewski (see Sauveterre, Fabrice de).

MONTEITH, the Hon. 'Eddy', in Ronald Firbank's *The Flower Beneath the Foot* (1923). This caricature of the Hon. Evan Morgan (see Lombard, Ivor) followed Morgan's refusal to be named in Firbank's dedication to *The Princess Zoubaroff* (1920), a rebuff which delayed publication of the book, since the dedication was already printed and had to be removed. In her biography of Firbank (*Prancing Novelist*, 1973), Brigid Brophy suggests that although the objection appeared to arise from Firbank's antipathy for the Roman

Catholic Church, in reality it was perhaps a shying-away from too close a relationship with Firbank, a homosexual who had formed a particular affection for Morgan.

MONTFORT, Lady (Adèle) de, in Osbert Sitwell's 'Charles and Charlemagne' (*Dumb-Animal*, 1930), is Emerald, Lady Cunard. See Carnal, Lady.

MOORAD, Adam, in Jack Kerouac's *The Subterraneans* (1958), is Allen Ginsberg. See Garden, Irwin.

MOORE, Hortense and Robert Gérard, in Charlotte Brontë's *Shirley* (1849), are Mlle Haussé, a teacher at the Pensionnat Heger in Brussels (see Emmanuel, Paul), and the Brussels-educated son of Joshua Taylor (see Yorke, Hiram), Joe Taylor (*d.* 1857), proprietor of Hunsworth Mills, Cleckheaton.

MOORE, Kathleen, in F. Scott Fitzgerald's *The Last Tycoon* (1941), is part-inspired by the London-born Hollywood gossip columnist Sheilah Graham (née Lily Shiel), with whom Fitzgerald lived intermittently from 1937 until his death in 1940.

MOOREHOUSE, J. Ward, in John Dos Passos's *The Forty-Second Parallel* (1930), is in part the 'founding father' of public relations, Ivy Ledbetter Lee (1877–1934), whose clients included Bethlehem Steel, Pennsylvania Railroad and the philanthropic oil magnate John D. Rockefeller. Dos Passos met Ledbetter while he was writing this novel, in a Moscow hotel.

MOPES, Mr, in Charles Dickens's 'Tom Tiddler's Ground' (1861), is James Lucas (*d.* 1874), son of a West India merchant, who became a recluse on the death of his wife. Known as 'The Hertfordshire Hermit' and living at Red Coats Green, Knebworth, he slept on a bed of ashes and dressed in a blanket fastened with a skewer. Dickens visited him in the summer of the year in which 'Tom Tiddler's Ground' appeared as the Christmas number of *All the Year Round*.

MOREAU, Frédéric, in Gustave Flaubert's *L'Éducation senti-mentale* (1869), is part-inspired by the author's friend, the journalist and novelist Maxime Du Camp (1822–94). Flaubert first met him while reading law in Paris and later travelled with him in the Near East.

MOREL, Charles, in Marcel Proust's *A la recherche du temps perdu* (1913—27), is supposedly a composite of Léon Delafosse (1874—1955), pianist protégé of Comte Robert de Montesquiou-Fezensac (see Charlus, Baron Palamède de), and Henri Rochat (see Simonet, Albertine).

MOREL FAMILY, in D.H. Lawrence's *Sons and Lovers* (1913). The Morels are the Lawrences: the author's own family. Walter Morel is the novelist's father, John Arthur Lawrence (1846—1924), a tailor's son who became a self-employed mining contractor. In 1875 he married 'Gertrude Morel', Lydia Beardsall (1851—1910), daughter of a Sheerness dockyard foreman and great granddaughter of the hymn-writer John Newton. They set up home in Eastwood, Nottinghamshire, and local tradition has it that, far from being the drunkard portrayed in *Sons and Lovers*, Lawrence's father was the victim of a shrew of a wife, driven from his home to spend his evenings in a public house where he would drink no more than a pint. A decade after he wrote the novel, Lawrence confessed he felt it had been unjust to his father and should be rewritten. Why did he portray his father unfairly? Perhaps the answer is provided by Lawrence's admission at his mother's funeral that he had loved her 'like a lover'. Thus, Walter Morel is John Lawrence as seen through his wife's eyes — the view the author himself would see. William Morel is the novelist's brother, William Ernest Lawrence (1878—1901), the child of whom the family expected most. After working locally as a clerk, studying shorthand and typing at night-school and taking correspondence courses in French and German, he obtained a post with a shipping firm in London. He died suddenly, of pneumonia. Annie Morel is Ada Lettice Lawrence (1887—1948), the author's younger sister.

MORELAND, Hugh, in Anthony Powell's *Casanova's Chinese Restaurant* (1960) and subsequent novels in the sequence *A Dance to the Music of Time* (1951—75), is based on the composer and conductor Constant Lambert (1905—51), who at twenty-one became the first British composer to be invited to write a ballet for Diaghilev.

MORENITA, in Arnold Bennett's *Sacred and Profane Love* (1905), is the French Jewish actress Marguerite de Moréno, wife of the critic, short-story writer and translator Marcel Schwob (1867—1905), whom she married in 1900, when he had become an invalid. Schwob considered himself so ugly that he shaved his head and covered the mirror in his apartment lest he should catch sight of himself.

MORGAN, in Hilda Doolittle's *Bid Me to Live* (1960), is Brigit Patmore. See Browning, Clariss.

MORGAUSE, Queen, in T.H. White's *The Once and Future King* (1958), is said by the author's biographer, Sylvia Townsend Warner, to be based on his mother, Constance Edith Southcote White (née Aston, *d.* 1952). The beautiful but temperamental daughter of a judge in India, she was divorced when the author was fourteen. Although he blaméd her for his homosexuality and hated her for what he considered to be extreme selfishness, he supported her financially.

MORIARTY, Dean, in Jack Kerouac's *On the Road* (1957). Claiming to have had his first girl at the age of nine and to have stolen his first car at fourteen, Neal Cassady (*d.* 1968) was both the model for Dean Moriarty and — through his letters — the inspiration for Kerouac's prose style. Brought up in Denver, the son of an alcoholic, he became a reformatory habitué and later worked as a South Pacific railroad brakeman. Kerouac first met him in 1946 and was entranced by his charisma and his uninhibited, 'try anything' lifestyle. A man of unfulfilled literary aspirations, he was also bisexual, his lovers including Allen Ginsberg (see Garden, Irwin) who in 1959 appealed on his behalf to San Quentin Parole Board: Cassady was at the time serving a two-year sentence for possessing marijuana. He died from heart failure attributed to exposure, after being found unconscious beside a railroad near the Mexican town of San Miguel de Allende.

MORIARTY, Professor James, in Sir Arthur Conan Doyle's 'The Final Problem' (*The Memoirs of Sherlock Holmes*, 1893), 'The Adventure of the Empty House' and 'The Adventure of the Missing Three-Quarter' (*The Return of Sherlock Holmes*, 1905), *The Valley of Fear* (1915) and *His Last Bow* (1917). When a London bank was robbed in 1971 by thieves who tunnelled their way to the vaults from premises next door, the exploit was described in court as a re-enactment of Conan Doyle's 'The Adventure of the Red-Headed League' (*The Adventures of Sherlock Holmes*, 1892). Had counsel researched the matter further, they would have found that Conan Doyle's story was in turn inspired by a similar bank-robbery in

Boston, Massachusetts, in 1869. The man behind that, Adam Worth, is supposedly the principal model for Moriarty. Based in London's Piccadilly, he was known in his day as 'the Napoleon of crime' and an account of him is to be found in Charles Higham's *The Adventures of Conan Doyle* (1976). Higham also suggests that, intellectually, Moriarty may owe something to Conan Doyle's astronomer-mathematician acquaintance, Major-General A.W. Drayson, of Southsea, an authority on asteroids (Moriarty's publications included *The Dynamics of an Asteroid*). In appearance, Moriarty's model may have been James Payn (1830–98), editor of *The Cornhill Magazine* and *Chambers's Journal* (Conan Doyle dramatised Payn's novel, *Halves*), while the choice of the name Moriarty may have been inspired by the violent, demonic behaviour in court of an alleged lunatic, George Moriarty, who appeared before Marylebone Magistrates Court in 1874.

MORLAND, Thomas, in Henry Williamson's *The Power of the Dead* (1964), is the novelist and dramatist John Galsworthy (1867–1933), portrayed as a worn-out author of popular but meretricious fiction, whose career has gone into graceful decline.

MORLAND, Tony, in Angela Thirkell's *High Rising* (1933), *The Demon in the House* (1934) and *Summer Half* (1937), is the author's son, Lancelot George Thirkell (1921–). After army service (which included D-Day) and four years as a diplomat, he joined the BBC in 1950 and was at the time of his retirement Controller, Administration, External Broadcasting.

MORRELL, The Revd James Mavor and Candida, in George Bernard Shaw's *Candida* (1895). One of Shaw's declared models for Candida Morrell was Mrs Laura Ormiston Chant (1848–1923), who silenced the music-hall artiste Marie Lloyd in mid-song one evening, crying 'Stop!' A suffragette, preacher, composer and lecturer, Mrs Chant was also the leader of a Purity campaign which objected to the song's line 'She sits among the cabbages and leeks', finding it no great improvement on the original, expurgated 'She sits among the cabbages and peas'. The other models were the artist Dorothy Tennant (*d.* 1926), who married H.M. Stanley (see Mackenzie, Alec) and after his death became the wife of a surgeon, Henry Curtis; and the actress Ellen Terry (1848–1928), who was unhappily married to the artist G.F. Watts and had a son (see Mann, Charles) by the architect and theatre-designer Edward William Godwin, with whom she lived from 1868 to 1874 following the termination of her marriage. Two further putative models for Candida are Lucy Shaw (see Brailsford, Madge), who refused a lover's proposal because she was five years his senior; and the talented but alcoholic and drug-addicted actress Janet Achurch (1864–1916), for whom the part was written. James Morrell has as prototype the Revd Stopford Augustus Brooke (1833–1916), author of works on English literature, theology and church affairs. He wrote *Freedom in the Church of England* in 1871 . . . and left the Church in 1880. Shaw is also thought to have based Morrell in part on Janet Achurch's husband, Charles Charrington (*d*. 1926), an unsuccessful actor-manager who appeared as Morrell (with his wife as Candida) in the play's first provincial production. Although the redoubtable Mrs Chant's contribution to fiction appears to have begun and ended with Candida, she also inspired Winston Churchill (see Catskill, Rupert) to write his first letter to a national newspaper. He was protesting against her campaign in 1894 to erect partitions separating the bars of London's Empire Theatre from promenading ladies of questionable virtue. A Sandhurst cadet at the time, Churchill led an attack in which the partitions were pulled down.

MORRIS, Amanda, in H.G. Wells's *The Research Magnificent* (1915), is Rebecca West (see Helen), portrayed as she was at nineteen, when the author first knew her. The story turned out to be prophetic in its account of the parting of Amanda and her lover, Benham, the novel's Wells figure.

MORRIS, Anna, in Gore Vidal's *The Judgement of Paris* (1952), is Anaïs Nin. See Donegal, Marietta.

MORRIS, Dinah, in George Eliot's *Adam Bede* (1859). 'The character of Dinah grew out of my recollections of my aunt', the author later recalled, 'but Dinah is not at all like my aunt, who was a very small, black-eyed woman, and (as I was told, for I never heard her preach) very vehement in her style of preaching. She had left off preaching when I knew her, being probably 60 years old, and in delicate health; and she had become, as my father told me, much more gentle and subdued than she had been in the days of her active ministry and bodily strength, when she could not rest without exhorting and remonstrating in season and out of season . . . ' It was this aunt, Mrs Samuel Evans (née Elizabeth Tomlinson, 1776–1849), who provided the Hetty Sorrel episode in *Adam Bede*, telling her niece of a journey in a cart to the gallows with a young mother convicted of infanticide. A lace-mender from Nottingham, Elizabeth Evans was converted to Methodism in 1797. Her husband managed a tape-mill in Wirksworth, Derbyshire.

MORRISON, Greta, in Gilbert Cannan's *Mendel* (1916), is the artist Dora Carrington (1893–1932), who discarded her Christian name while studying at the Slade, preferring to be known simply as Carrington. For fifteen years she lived with Lytton Strachey (see Plunkett, Matthew), forming a *ménage à trois* when in 1921 she married Ralph Partridge (*d.* 1960), who in the First World War had commanded a battalion at twenty-three and been awarded the Military Cross. Strachey was in love with Partridge and persuaded him to adopt a literary career which led to his working for the Hogarth Press, reviewing for the *New Statesman* and producing a book on Broadmoor criminal lunatic asylum. Shortly after Strachey's death, Carrington committed suicide.

MORRISON, Peter, in Simon Raven's *Alms for Oblivion* sequence (1964–76), notably *Friends in Low Places* (1965) and *The Survivors* (1976), is based on James Prior (1927–   ), the author's Charterhouse schoolfellow who became a Conservative minister, concluding his government career as Secretary of State for Northern Ireland. Reviewing Raven's memoir, *Shadows on the Grass* (1982), in the *Listener*, D.A.N. Jones noted that 'for readers of his novels there is an especial interest in finding the words and deeds of the fictional characters, "Peter Morrison" and "Somerset Lloyd-James", now attributed to James Prior and William Rees-Mogg.'

MORTON, Jeannie, in Erica Jong's *How to Save Your Own Life* (1977), is the American poet Anne Sexton (1928–74), according to Rosemary Kent, interviewing Jong for the *Observer* (24 April 1977). Writing of the influence of Anne Sexton and Sylvia Plath, the novelist noted, 'They were important because they suddenly made it legitimate to write about being a woman; they gave us the gift of our sexual identity and they gave us the even greater gift of our anger.' (*Observer*, 19 November 1978.)

MORTON, Sir Robert, in Terence Rattigan's *The Winslow Boy* (1946), has as prototype the lawyer Sir Edward (later Baron) Carson (1854–1935), who successfully represented George Archer-Shee (see Winslow, Ronnie) in a *cause célèbre* in 1910. Seven years after this legal battle, in which he trounced the Admiralty, he became its First Lord. He is best remembered for the skilful cross-examination that led to the downfall of Oscar Wilde (see Amarinth, Esme).

MORTON, Wraithly, in Malcolm Muggeridge's *Picture Palace* (1932; withdrawn shortly after publication following a libel action), is Kingsley Martin. See Wilberforce.

MORTSAUF, Mme de, in Honoré de Balzac's *Le Lys dans la vallée* (1835), is Mme de Berny (née Louise-Antoinette-Laure Hinner, 1777–1836), the daughter of a German musician and a lady of Marie Antoinette's bedchamber; Marie-Antoinette was her godmother, and Louis XVI her godfather. She had nine children and was seduced by Balzac when, at twenty-three, he became their tutor. Although more than twenty years his senior, she was the first and most enduring love of his life. She rescued him financially from time to time and he never entirely deserted her, despite his other conquests.

MOSCA, Count, in Stendhal's *La Chartreuse de Parme* (1839), was taken by the author's friend, Honoré de Balzac, to be the Austrian statesman Metternich – Prince Clemens Wenzel Nepomuk Lothar von Metternich-Winneburg (1773–1859).

MOTH, in William Shakespeare's *Love's Labour's Lost* (c. 1595). Could a man in his mid-to-late twenties have been the child page of this comedy? The question is prompted by attempts to identify Moth with the satirical writer and anti-Puritan pamphleteer Thomas Nashe (1567–1601), author of the first English romance, *The Unfortunate Traveller, or The Life of Jacke Wilton* (1594), and of the first known printed reference to Shakespeare. At the time when this play is believed to have been first produced, Nashe would have been twenty-seven or thereabouts – so could he really be Shakespeare's 'child', 'dear imp', 'tender juvenal' or 'well-educated infant', as has been claimed? One of Moth's speeches has a Nashe 'ring' to it, and 'Nashe' suggests 'nesh' meaning tender. 'Juvenal' was perhaps word-play, a reference to Nashe as the Juvenal of English satiric poets. Nashe's education included Cambridge, and he was contemptuous of playwrights lacking a university background; by presenting him as a child, Shakespeare could have been guying this master of invective who may well have been seen as something of a perpetual adolescent, a student who never quite grew up. The evidence is inconclusive, though tempting, and scholars will doubtless long continue to debate it — when they are not pondering the title of the play itself, often given as *Love's Labour Lost*.

MOTTRAM, Rex, in Evelyn Waugh's *Brideshead Revisited* (1945). It was through the influence of Brendan Bracken, Britain's wartime Minister of Information, that Waugh obtained the leave he needed in which to write *Brideshead Revisited*. But if Bracken felt the favour put the novelist under any obligation, he was mistaken: Waugh repaid him with this unflattering caricature. Throughout his life, Bracken was an opportunist. Sedbergh School, in Cumbria, honours the First Viscount Bracken (1901–58) as one of its most distinguished old boys ... though he spent only a term there, and that under false pretences. He approached the headmaster as a nineteen-year-old Australian who had lost both parents in a bush fire but had been left sufficient money to attend an English public school. In reality, his mother was still alive — and she was Irish. Becoming Parliamentary Private Secretary to the Prime Minister in 1940, he created and cultivated a rumour that he was Winston Churchill's illegitimate son. Later, he met Roosevelt, and so complimentary was his description of the President when he addressed a dining club that Randolph Churchill asked if he were proposing to claim him as his father too.

MOUNT, Bella, in George Meredith's *The Ordeal of Richard Feverel* (1859), is Mary Ellen Peacock. See Middleton, Clara.

MOURET, François, in Émile Zola's *La Conquête de Plassans* (1874), is Louis-Auguste Cézanne, father of Paul Cézanne (see Lantier, Claude). A hat merchant and exporter who became an Aix banker, he was appalled by his son's decision to make his career from painting — 'Think of the future: one dies with genius, but one eats with money.' He allowed the artist no more than a subsistence pittance, but left him his fortune.

MOWCHER, Miss, in Charles Dickens's *David Copperfield* (1849–50). 'I have suffered long and much from my personal deformities, but never before at the hands of a man so highly gifted as Charles Dickens, and hitherto considered as a Christian and Friend to his fellow Creatures.' Thus, Mrs Jane Seymour Hill (née Cordery) protested to the author, on recognising herself as Miss Mowcher. A widow, she was a manicurist and chiropodist of 6 York Gate, London, and Dickens encountered her when she attended his wife. Privately referring to her as 'a grotesque little oddity', he portrayed her more favourably in a later instalment of the serialised novel . . . largely as a result of her lawyer's pressure for reparation in the very next episode.

MULLER, Frank, in H. Rider Haggard's *Jess* (1887), is G.H. Buskes, a lawyer first encountered by the author in Pretoria in 1877. Secretary of the Putchefstrom Boer Committee in the Boer War of 1880, he was allegedly responsible for a number of atrocities.

MULLIGAN, Buck, in James Joyce's *Ulysses* (1922). Blamed by Joyce's brother, Stanislaus, for encouraging the author to become a drinker, Oliver St John Gogarty (1878–1957) was in 1904 a medical student renting a Martello tower at Sandycove, Dublin. Eighteen years later he was immortalised as Buck Mulligan. The fort, which Joyce shared rent-free in return for doing the housework, has become the Joyce Memorial Tower. Not that Joyce stayed long – he and Gogarty soon found it impossible to live together, and Joyce moved on . . . with memories that were to make the tower the opening setting of *Ulysses* (see Haines, Celtophile). Gogarty had taken the tower in order to write, and he later achieved a modest success as a poet and playwright. After practising as a doctor in Dublin, where he was also a senator, he left for the United States in 1939 to live by his pen. As a wit, he is remembered for his contribution to an Irish Senate debate on censorship in 1929: 'I think it is high time that the people of this country found some other way of loving God than by hating women.'

MULLIGAN, the, in W.M. Thackeray's 'Mrs Perkins's Ball' (1847; *Christmas Books*, 1857). The Mulligan of Ballymulligan has a probable prototype in Charles James Patrick Mahon (1800–91), an Irish adventurer and politician who was known as the O'Gorman Mahon. He commanded a Chilean fleet against Spain; served as a colonel in Brazil and under Louis Napoleon; held the rank of general in the government army during a Uruguay civil war; and fought in the Union army in the American Civil War. He also served under the Austrian, Russian and Turkish flags and in his later years turned to politics – he was MP for Ennis from 1847 to 1852, for Clare from 1879 to 1885, and for Carlow from 1887 to 1891, winning his last election when he was nearly ninety.

MULLINS, Wyllie, in Roy Bradford's *The Last Ditch* (1982). I would not be so rash as to suggest that Mullins *is* the militant

Protestant priest and Ulster politician, the Revd Ian Paisley
(1926–   ) – but he is surely Mullins's prototype. Had Paisley not
existed it is doubtful if Mullins would have been created in this novel
by a former minister of the Stormont government.

MULLION, Jenny, in Aldous Huxley's *Crome Yellow* (1921). The
last fifty years of the long life of the Hon. Dorothy Brett
(1883–1977) were spent in comparative obscurity, interrupted only
by the occasional knock on her New Mexico door by a visiting
Lawrence researcher. In her earlier years, she had rather more than a
walking-on part in the drama of a colourful period, and she was
Huxley's model for Jenny Mullion. Afflicted by deafness, for which
she carried an ear-trumpet, she was the daughter of the Second
Viscount Esher and was a Slade-trained painter. She shared a house
with Mark Gertler (see Loerke) at Hampstead Heath; helped Maria
Nys (see Quarles, Elinor) to make up her mind about marrying
Huxley; and had an unhappy affair with John Middleton Murry (see
Crich, Gerald). In 1915 she became a follower of D.H. Lawrence (see
Rampion, Mark), trailing after him with a rabbit-like devotion that
soon irritated him. Alone among his disciples, and although she was
already forty, she accompanied him and his wife to begin a new life
in New Mexico ... and stayed there for more than half a century
after the Lawrences left. Her deafness has been variously attributed
to appendicitis and to the shock she experienced when she found
herself alone in a grotto with Lord Harcourt, her father's best friend,
who offered to show her his stalactite and indecently assaulted her.
She remained ignorant of the facts of life until she was in her thirties,
and in her old age told her biographer, Sean Hignett, 'All those
Lawrence scholars want to know is whether I slept with Lawrence
and I'm afraid that's my business.' But, as Hignett records, in a
sealed envelope left to be opened after her death she described how
Lawrence had come to her bed on two successive nights in 1926. The
first time Lawrence found himself to be impotent and left, announcing 'It's no good.' On his second visit the experience was repeated,
but this time he stalked from the room, telling her 'Your pubes are
wrong.' Whereupon he sent her packing and she never saw him
again.

MULLISON, in Sinclair Lewis and Dore Schary's *Storm in the West*
(written 1943, published 1963), is Benito Mussolini. See Arango,
General Tereso.

MUNCHAUSEN, Baron, in Rudolph Erich Raspe's *Baron Munchausen, Narrative of his Marvellous Travels* (1785). Be named in a book's dedication and you risk being identified with its hero. This was the misfortune of the Scottish explorer James Bruce (1730–94), whose accounts of his experiences in Abyssinia were thought to be exaggerated, if not fictitious. Subsequent travellers vindicated his veracity, but meanwhile the publication in 1792 of a sequel to the original *Munchausen*, dedicated to Bruce, prompted readers to assume that he was Munchausen's original. Raspe's model was in fact Baron Karl Friedrich Hieronymus von Münchhausen (1720–97), a German officer engaged to fight with the Russian army against the Turks, and noted for his tall stories.

MUNDUNGUS, in Laurence Sterne's *A Sentimental Journey through France and Italy* (1768), is Dr Samuel Sharp (?1700–78), surgeon to London's Guy's Hospital from 1733 to 1757, and a travel-writer noted for his misanthropy – he was the author of *Letters from Italy* (1766). 'Mundungus' was slang for noisome tobacco.

MURDSTONE, Edward, in Charles Dickens's *David Copperfield* (1849–50). Could the man who encouraged the author's interest in amateur theatricals, a pastime which gave him lifelong pleasure, really be Murdstone, the inhumanly harsh stepfather? It seems unlikely, yet James Lamert, stepson of Dickens's aunt on his mother's side, has been suggested as Murdstone's model, apparently on the strength of his occupation. Lodging with the Dickens family, he managed the London boot-blacking firm for which the author worked as a child. But as a lodger, Lamert built and painted a toy theatre for the young Dickens. Is that the action of a Murdstone?

MURGATROYD, General Mowbray, in Nancy Mitford's *Highland Fling* (1931), at least regarding his sporting proclivities, is the author's father. See Alconleigh, Lord.

MURIEL, in D.H. Lawrence's 'The Fly in the Ointment' (1913; *Young Lorenzo*, 1932), is Jessie Chambers. See Leivers, Miriam.

MURRAY, Alexander, in Colin MacInnes's *June in her Spring* (1952), is the author's father. See Danvers, James.

MURRAY, Mrs and Master Charles, in Anne Brontë's *Agnes Grey* (1847). The danger of identifying originals, even by implication rather than by name, is illustrated by the story behind *Agnes Grey*. Mrs Murray was based upon Lydia Robinson, wife of the Revd Edmund Robinson, of Thorp Green Hall, near York, and Master Charles Murray was their son, Edmund Robinson. Anne Brontë was governess to the family from 1841 to 1845. In 1843 her brother, Branwell (see Huntingdon, Arthur), became Edmund's tutor, and Mrs Robinson is believed to have become his lover. The supposed affair was said to have been terminated by her confession to her husband, who dismissed Branwell, promising to shoot him on sight should he reappear. Seventeen years Branwell's senior, Mrs Robinson was widowed in 1846. To dissuade him from returning, she sent a message saying that her husband's will had a codicil which would disinherit her and deprive her of the custody of her four children should their relationship be resumed. There was no such codicil, and within weeks of Branwell's death in 1848 she married an elderly relative, Sir Edward Dolman Scott. In 1857 Elizabeth Gaskell's *The Life of Charlotte Brontë* was published, and Lady Scott (now widowed again and a hostess in London society) threatened to sue for libel. Although she had not been identified by name, a retraction was published in *The Times* and the *Athenaeum*, and unsold copies of the book were withdrawn, as was the second edition, subsequent printings appearing in expurgated form.

MUSETTE, in Henry Murger's *Scènes de la vie de bohème* (1848), which inspired Puccini's opera *La Bohème*, is suggested by Murger's biographer, Robert Baldick, to be Marie Christine Roux, an artists' model and prostitute in Paris. She was photographed nude, *c.*1855, by Nadar (see Ardan, Michel), and vanished, together with her savings, after boarding a ship for Algiers.

MUSH, Freddy, in H.G. Wells's *Men Like Gods* (1923), is Sir Edward Marsh. See Dean, Mattie.

MUSSET, Evangeline, in Djuna Barnes's *The Ladies' Almanack* (1928), is Natalie Clifford Barney. See Flossie, Miss.

MYERS, Ludovic, in Elizabeth Taylor's *Mrs Palfrey at the Claremont* (1971), is based on the novelist Paul Bailey (1937–   ). When his first novel, *At the Jerusalem*, was published in 1967, *The Times* noted that he was working as an assistant in Harrods. 'A year after publication, I met Elizabeth Taylor at a party', he recalls in his introduction to the 1982 edition of *Mrs Palfrey*. 'She told me how intrigued she had been that a man in his late twenties should have chosen a home for old women as the setting for a novel, and that she had gone to Harrods' magazine department to see what such a curious creature looked like. She went on to say that she had watched me at work for about an hour, from the vantage of a chair in the adjoining lounge.' Ludovic Myers, he notes, is a novelist *manqué*, writing a study of old age and working on his manuscript at Harrods. 'Ludo, like me, is an ex-actor, who has done his stint in a tatty repertory company and has no desire to repeat the experience. In other words, I am flattered to think that I gave Elizabeth Taylor a little bit of inspiration for what is undoubtedly one of her finest books.'

MYFANWY, in John Betjeman's 'Myfanwy' and 'Myfanwy at Oxford' (*Old Lights for New Chancels*, 1940), is Mary Myfanwy Piper (née Evans), wife of the artist John Piper, whom she married in 1935. She wrote the librettos for Benjamin Britten's operas *The Turn of the Screw* (1954), *Owen Wingrave* (1971) and *Death in Venice* (1973).

MYSHKIN, Prince, in Fyodor Dostoevsky's *The Idiot* (1868), in addition to being a Christ-like figure, has a possible model in the author's nephew Alexander Karepin, who was nicknamed 'The Idiot'. The son of Pyotr Karepin (see Bykov), he was talented enough – despite his unworldliness – to have become a professor of medicine by his mid-twenties.

MYSTIC, Mr, in Thomas Love Peacock's *Melincourt* (1817), is Samuel Taylor Coleridge (see Skionar, Mr), whose exposition of metaphysics prompted Byron to wish for an explanation of the explanation.

N

N, Mr, in Richard Henry Dana Jr's *Two Years Before the Mast* (1840). Like a comic character in a film oblivious of pitfall or precipice, Thomas Nuttall (1786–1859) blithely broke numerous appointments with death because he never knew he had made them, and left others to chronicle his narrow escapes, which he was too busy plant-collecting to notice. Not only is he Dana's Mr N; James Fenimore Cooper also used him (see Battius, Obed); he appears in Washington Irving's *Astoria* under his own name; and Emerson extolled him. A Yorkshireman who trained as a printer in Liverpool, he became obsessed by an interest in natural history in general and botany in particular. Emigrating to North America, he found a patron and tutor in Dr Benjamin Barton, professor of natural history at the University of Pennsylvania. In Nuttall, the professor found not only a dedicated pupil but also an innocent prepared to go anywhere, regardless of danger, in search of 'new' plants for his master's collection. So savagely was he attacked by mosquitoes that people thought he must have smallpox and barred him from their homes. So hugely did he swell with another affliction that his trousers had to be cut from him. So acutely did he starve that on his return to civilisation friends failed to recognise him – running out of food, he had sustained himself for a fortnight on the edible parts of an elderly grizzly bear. He also had a genius for getting lost. He tried, but providentially failed, to hire as guide a man who was later arrested as a thieving murderer. Another time, he was narrowly missed by lightning which destroyed a nearby tree. When his companions checked their guns in anticipation of an Indian raid, Nuttall's was found to be jammed solid with dirt: he had been using it as a spade to excavate plants. With the passing of the years he was accepted as the nation's most knowledgeable botanist, and as a pioneering ornithologist he saw his book on the birds of the United States and Canada become a standard work. His reputation was such that when he gave a series of lectures in Boston, there were 12,000 applications for tickets. It was with great reluctance that he retired to the Lancashire estate he had inherited from an uncle. There, the man who had thought nothing of shooting rapids although he couldn't swim finally met his end overstraining himself opening cases of plants. His story is told in Jeanette E. Granstein's *Thomas Nuttall, Naturalist: Explorations in America, 1808—1841* (1967).

NADAB, in W.M. Thackeray's *The Newcomes* (1853—5), is Charles Sloman (1808—70), improvisator at the Cyder Cellars in London's Maiden Lane, near the Adelphi Theatre. Although sufficiently notable to be portrayed in caricature in a theatrical magazine of his day, he died in a London workhouse.

NADDO, in Robert Browning's *Sordello* (1840), according to the Browning biographers William Irvine and Park Honan, is a caricature of John Forster (see Podsnap), with whom Browning had a love-hate relationship.

NAMBY-PAMBY, in Henry Carey's 'Namby-Pamby' (1726). It has been the fate of the poet Ambrose Philips (?1675—1749) to be remembered not for what he wrote, but for the name coined by Carey to describe him. Carey also parodied Philips's verses addressed to the infant daughter of the Earl of Carteret. As a name for Philips, 'Namby-Pamby' appealed to his lifelong enemy, Pope, who guyed him as Namby Pamby in *The Dunciad*. Given this further currency, namby-pamby entered the English language.

NANA, in Émile Zola's *Nana*. See Coupeau, Anna.

NAPOLEON, in George Orwell's *Animal Farm* (1945), represents Joseph Stalin (see Boss). Having difficulty in finding a publisher prepared to accept the novel, Orwell complained of 'the imbecile suggestion' that some animals other than pigs might be made to represent the Bolsheviks. He remarked that Stalin seemed to be acquiring an image of the kind formerly enjoyed by Franco — that of a 'Christian gent' of whom it was not 'done' to be critical.

NAPTHA, in Thomas Mann's *The Magic Mountain* (1924), is the Hungarian critic and philosopher Georg Lukács (1885—1971). A Communist, he was censured by the party after the Second World War for his support of 'bourgeois' novelists including Mann.

NARCISSA, in Alexander Pope's *Moral Essays* (1731–5), is the actress Anne Oldfield (1683–1730), whose career was of such distinction that bearing two children by two different men, to neither of whom she was married, did not prevent her from being buried in Westminster Abbey.

NARCISSA, in Edward Young's *Night Thoughts* (1742–5), is supposedly the poet's stepdaughter, Mrs Elizabeth Temple (*d.* 1736), granddaughter of the Second Earl of Lichfield. She married Henry Temple, son of Lord Palmerston, and died at Lyons of consumption. The assertion of *Night Thoughts* that Narcissa was denied burial as a Protestant gave rise to the erroneous belief that Elizabeth Temple shared this fate and was surreptitiously interred in the Montpelier Botanic Garden, which on the strength of this rumour became a tourist attraction.

NASH, Gabriel, in Henry James's *The Tragic Muse* (1890), is suggested by the author's biographer, Leon Edel, to be part-inspired by Herbert Pratt, a Denver physician and an old friend of James's family. He gave up medicine in 1874 to travel the world for the next forty years. James may also have had in mind Oscar Wilde (see Amarinth, Esme), whose plays he regarded as rivals to his own.

NASSAU, Comte de, in Marcel Proust's *A la recherche du temps perdu* (1913–27), is Comte Pierre de Polignac, who became Prince Pierre de Monaco when he married Princesse Charlotte, heiress of Louis II, crown prince of Monaco. With his wife, he was an influential patron of Diaghilev's ballet company, which changed its name to the Ballets Russes de Monte Carlo because of this connection. His son, Prince Rainier, became Monaco's ruler in 1949.

NASTASYA FILIPOVNA, in Fyodor Dostoevsky's *The Idiot* (1868), is primarily Apollinaria Suslova (see Polina Alexandrovna). Ronald Hingley (*Dostoyevsky: His Life and Work*, 1978) suggests, however, that the character may be part-inspired by Olga Umetskaya, whose parents' violent mistreatment of her prompted her to set fire to their Moscow home four times.

NATALYA PETROVNA, in Ivan Turgenev's *A Month in the Country* (1849). Natalya's relationship with Rakitin in this play is paralleled by Turgenev's association with the famous mezzo-soprano Pauline Viardot (née Garcia, 1821–1910), sister of Maria

Malibran (see Annunziata). Turgenev first met Viardot in Petersburg in 1843, when he was twenty-five. In 1841 she had married her
manager, the art critic Louis Viardot, who was twenty-one years her
senior. Her lifelong friendship with Turgenev was so close,
however, that she adopted a daughter born to him by a serf and
rechristened Paulinette. Making her Paris début in 1838, Viardot
became a prima donna held in high regard by Chopin, Berlioz, Liszt
and Rossini. She was also a talented pianist, was admired as a
composer by Saint-Saëns, and had a knowledge of literature spanning five languages. Turgenev was rumoured to have fathered two
children by her, and for forty years he fluttered like a moth about the
lamp of her brilliance, dying at their joint summer home near Paris in
1883.

NATASHA, in Fyodor Dostoevsky's *The Insulted and the Injured*
(1861), is the author's first wife. See Marmeladov.

NATASHA, in Erich Maria Remarque's *Shadows in Paradise* (1971),
is supposedly the American film actress Paulette Goddard
(1911–), whom the author married in 1958. Her previous husbands were Charles Chaplin and Burgess Meredith.

NATHAN, in Gotthold Ephraim Lessing's *Nathan the Wise* (1779),
is believed to be the author's friend, the Jewish philosopher Moses
Mendelssohn (1729–86), who was known as 'the German Socrates'.

NATTATORINI, Ella, in Carl Van Vechten's *The Tattooed Countess* (1924). Enjoying her popular identification with the outrageous
Countess, Mahala Dutton Benedict Douglas informed the author
that she had been put to considerable expense and pain to acquire the
tattoo necessary for her new image. She was a resident of Van
Vechten's home town in Iowa, Cedar Rapids, and the author was
warned against her by his parents, who considered her altogether too
emancipated. Rescued, with her maid, from the sinking *Titanic* in
which her husband, Walter Douglas, perished, she inherited the
family Quaker Oats fortune.

NAYLOR, Edgar, in Cyril Connolly's *The Rock Pool* (1935), is
part-inspired by Nigel Richards (*d.* 1942). Reputedly the most
handsome man in the England of his day, he was killed in action over
Germany during war service as a pilot. His widow, Betty, a former

Paris mannequin for Chanel and a friend of Violet Trefusis (see Romanovitch, Princess 'Sasha'), married Colonel William Batten.

NEAL, in H.G. Wells's *The New Machiavelli* (1911), is J.L. Garvin (*d.* 1947), editor of the *Observer* from 1908 to 1942.

NELVIL, Lord Oswald, in Mme de Staël's *Corinne* (1807), is Dom Pedro de Souza, Duke of Palmella and sometime prime minister of Portugal. The author had an affair with him when she was thirty-nine, he twenty-four.

NEMO, Captain, in Jules Verne's *Twenty Thousand Leagues Under the Sea* (1870). It has been suggested that Nemo's original is the oceanographer Prince Albert of Monaco (1848–1922), whose second wife was Alice, Dowager Duchess of Richelieu (see Luxembourg, Princesse de). But Albert did not begin to publish the results of his expeditions until 1889. A more probable prototype is the American engineer and inventor Robert Fulton (1765–1815), who in 1800 built the submarine *Nautilus*. He was an idealist, who believed that wars could be rendered impossible by his fearsome submersible, which he offered to Napoleon. The emperor agreed to the submarine's use against the British, at Fulton's expense, the inventor to be rewarded with a fee proportionate to the size of each vessel destroyed. In the summer of 1801 Fulton lurked beneath the surface of the English Channel, his compressed air supply enabling him and his crew to stay submerged for more than four hours at a time. He sank nothing and went unpaid, Napoleon losing interest in his invention. More than 150 years later, Fulton's pioneering was commemorated in the naming of the world's first nuclear submarine, 'Nautilus', launched for the United States' navy in 1954.

NEMOURS, the Duc de, in the Comtesse de La Fayette's *La Princesse de Clèves* (1678), is the French moralistic writer François, Duc de La Rochefoucauld (1613–80), with whom the author had a close relationship. Easily infatuated by members of the opposite sex, and unsuited to the intrigues of the politics of his day, he retired to the company of a small group of intellectuals which included the Comtesse.

NESBIT, Norah, in W. Somerset Maugham's *Of Human Bondage* (1915). When Maugham dedicated his travel book *The Land of the Blessed Virgin* to the novelist Violet Hunt (1862–1942), she was less than pleased, he later noted, because she could not imagine what she would be doing in such a country. When she was forty-one, he twenty-nine, they had a brief affair, and it was partly upon her that he later modelled Nesbit, as his biographer Ted Morgan records. The daughter of Alfred and Margaret Hunt, she was a writer whose feminism earned her the nickname 'Violent' Hunt and whose lovers included Oswald Crawfurd (see Assheton, Ralph) and Ford Madox Ford (Ford Madox Hueffer; see Braddocks, Henry). When she styled herself 'Mrs Hueffer', Ford's wife petitioned for the restitution of conjugal rights. Ordered by the court to return to his wife, Ford refused and was gaoled for contempt. Eight years later, he left Hunt for Stella Bowen (see Wannop, Valentine).

NETTIE, in H.G. Wells's *In the Days of the Comet* (1906), is Isabel Wells. See Ramboat, Marion.

NEWBERRY, Richard, in H.G. Wells's *The Dream* (1924), is Lord Northcliffe (see Tilbury, Lord), with whom the author clashed in 1918 after Northcliffe, as Minister of Propaganda, appointed him Director of Propaganda against Germany. Wells felt Northcliffe's newspaper invective against the enemy was sabotaging his efforts to persuade Germany to surrender, and after a few months the author left the Ministry.

NEWCOME, Colonel Thomas and Ethel, in W.M. Thackeray's *The Newcomes* (1853—5). The romance of Major Henry Carmichael-Smyth (1780—1861) was like a plot for a novel. The author's stepfather, and his model for Colonel Newcome, Carmichael-Smyth was the son of a London physician and as a young subaltern sought the hand of Thackeray's mother, Anne Becher. This was thwarted when the girl's grandmother ended their courtship by telling Anne that Carmichael-Smyth had died of fever, and informing him that Anne had lost interest in him and broken the engagement. When the couple next met, in India, Anne was married to Richard Thackeray, who died three years later. After an interval of eighteen months, in 1817, she married Carmichael-Smyth. Following his overseas service he became governor of Addiscombe, the East India Company's military academy in Surrey. He retired first to Ottery St Mary, in Devon, and then to Paris, where, having lost his fortune in the Calcutta 'crash' of 1833, he sought financial salvation through a number of unsuccessful inventions. Ethel Newcome is part-inspired by Miss Sallie Baxter, daughter of a New York family who were hosts to the author during his first American tour and with whom he corresponded for the rest of his life. She was a lively member of New York society in the early 1850s and her sister, Lucy, later claimed that Thackeray had portrayed Sallie's life-style, not her character.

NEWTON, in D.H. Lawrence's *Sons and Lovers* (1913), is George Henry Neville. See Tempest, Leslie.

NEWTON, Allgood, in W. Somerset Maugham's *Cakes and Ale* (1930), is suggested in Robert Lorin Calder's study of the author (1972) to be Sir Edmund Gosse (see Criscross, Professor James; see also Greene, Sir Nicholas). In 1938 Maugham recalled him as the most interesting and consistently amusing talker he had known.

NICK, in Simon Gray's *The Common Pursuit* (1984), is Kenneth Tynan (1927–80), who was drama critic of the *Observer* from 1954 to 1963. He died from emphysema, as does Nick, and is portrayed smoking himself to death. Giving up smoking doesn't make you live longer, Nick remarks, it only seems longer.

NICKLEBY, Mrs, Kate and Nicholas, in Charles Dickens's *Nicholas Nickleby* (1838–9). See yourself as others see you, and you may not recognise the picture. Thus, Dickens recorded, 'Mrs Nickleby, sitting bodily before me, once asked whether I really believed there ever was such a woman.' She was his mother, Mrs John Dickens (née Elizabeth Barrow, 1789–1863), daughter of a Lambeth music teacher turned Civil Servant, and like Mrs Nickleby an enthusiastic exploiter of 'connections' to further her son's interests. Marrying one of her brother's Civil Service colleagues, she considered her social background to be superior to that of her husband (see Micawber, Wilkins) . . . although her father had fled with £5,689 to the Isle of Man following accusations of embezzlement at the Navy Pay Office. Kate Nickleby is an amalgam of Mary Hogarth (see Maylie, Rose) and the author's sister, Frances ('Fanny') Elizabeth (1810–48), a singer who trained at the Royal Academy of Music, where she taught piano. Fanny's husband, Henry Burnett (1811–93), is supposedly Nicholas Nickleby, although Dickens came to regard him as an imbecile. He was a professional tenor who left the stage when he found it incompatible with his Nonconformist convictions, which were so strong that he never entered a theatre again. Moving to Manchester, he became a teacher of singing and later claimed he had been the artist's model for Nickleby in the novel's original illustrations.

NICOLETTA, in Klaus Mann's *Mephisto* (1936), is the actress Pamela Wedekind, daughter of the dramatist Frank Wedekind and his actress wife, Tilly (see Kadidja). Briefly engaged to Mann, she later married and was divorced from Carl Sternheim (see Marder, Theophilus).

NI-EN, in Bertolt Brecht's *Me-ti. The Book of Twists and Turns* (1934–50), is Joseph Stalin. See Boss.

NIGEL, in Cyril Connolly's *Enemies of Promise* (1938), is Noel Blakiston (1905–84), an Eton contemporary of the author. The son of a Lincolnshire clergyman, he was a King's Scholar at Magdalene College, Cambridge, and from 1928 to 1970 was on the staff of the Cambridge Record Office. In 1975 he published *A Romantic Friendship: The letters of Cyril Connolly to Noel Blakiston.*

NIGHTINGALE, the, in Hans Christian Andersen's 'The Nightingale' (1843), is the Swedish singer Jenny Lind (1820–87). The author fell in love with her on their second meeting, and she returned his attentions with sisterly affection, but no more, marrying the pianist Otto Goldschmidt. 'The Nightingale' was inspired by the conflict between the fashion in Copenhagen for Italian opera and the talent of the then comparatively little known Jenny Lind, who became known as the 'Swedish Nightingale'.

NIMROD, Mr Happerley, in R.S. Surtees's *Jorrocks's Jaunts and Jollities* (1838), is C.J. Apperley. See Ego, Pomponius.

NINA, in Anton Chekhov's *The Seagull* (1896). 'If ever you want my life, come and take it' was the inscription on a watch-chain medallion given to Chekhov by 'Nina' – Lydia Avilov (d. 1942). The line was from one of his stories, and the gift was prompted by her love for the dramatist whom she first met in St Petersburg in 1889. Three years later, when their acquaintance was renewed, she became infatuated with him and declared she wanted to leave her husband and three children for him. Chekhov did not encourage her.

NIXON, Mr, in Ezra Pound's *Hugh Selwyn Mauberley* (1920), is the novelist and literary critic Arnold Bennett (1867–1931), whom Pound considered a philistine, referring to him as 'nickle cash-register Bennett'. 'The mistake of my life was in beginning in London as if publishers were any different from bucket shops', Pound remarked in a letter. 'Arnold Bennett knew his eggs. Whatever his interest in good writing, he never showed the public anything but his AVARICE. Consequently, they adored him.'

NOBLE, Maury, in F. Scott Fitzgerald's *The Beautiful and the Damned* (1922), is the American drama critic George Jean Nathan (1882–1958), joint editor of *The Smart Set*, who recalled Fitzgerald explaining to him that he had tried but could not lionise him in the novel. 'He said that he found himself unable to write a heroic character other than himself and that he had to be the hero of any novel he undertook. So I duly discovered that what he started as heroic me resulted in a wholly minor and subsidiary character not distinguished for any perceptible favorable attribute' (*Esquire*, October 1958).

NOBLE, Mr, in Dorothy Richardson's *March Moonlight* (1967), is the author's husband, Alan Odle (d. 1948), the artist son of a Sittingbourne bank manager. A contributor to the magazine *The Gypsy*, he met Dorothy Richardson while living in the same London boarding-house and they married in 1917. He was fifteen years her junior but died nine years before she did.

NOGGS, Newman, in Charles Dickens's *Nicholas Nickleby* (1838–9), is Newman Knott. Believed to be the ne'er-do-well son of a reputable family, he called weekly to collect an allowance from the offices of the lawyers Ellis and Blackmore in Gray's Inn, where Dickens worked as a clerk in 1827.

NOON, Gilbert, in D.H. Lawrence's 'Mr Noon' (*A Modern Lover*, 1934), is George Henry Neville (see Tempest, Leslie). The story was written in 1920 and was later continued to form a short novel, published posthumously as *Mr Noon* (1984). In the novel's extension of the original story, Noon becomes a Lawrence self-portrait.

NORPOIS, Marquis de, in Marcel Proust's *A la recherche du temps perdu* (1913–27), is a composite of Camille Barrère (1851–1940), French ambassador to Italy from 1897 to 1925, and an ally of the author's father in his campaign against cholera and for international standards of public hygiene; the Comte de Fleury, French ambassador to Russia and lover of Comtesse Sophie de Beaulaincourt (see Villeparisis, Mme de); Anatole France (see Bergotte); Gabriel Hanotaux (1853–1944), the French politician and historian; and Armand Nisard, uncle by marriage of Marie de Bénardaky (see Swann, Gilberte) and French ambassador to the Vatican from 1898 to 1904.

NORRIS, Arthur, in Christopher Isherwood's *Mr Norris Changes Trains* (1935). 'I am not everybody's cup of tea, but I am certain people's liqueur', said Gerald Hamilton (1888–1970). Isherwood, who portrayed him as Norris, later came to regard Hamilton as a rogue laced with poison. To obtain Mexican naturalisation for his German boyfriend who was wanted by the police for draft-evasion, Isherwood sought Hamilton's aid as a 'fixer'. Hamilton took £1,000 which he said would be needed to smooth the way, but failed to deliver the citizenship and was suspected by Isherwood of complicity in his lover's enforced return to Nazi Germany. Nevertheless, the author contributed a foreword to Hamilton's autobiography, *Mr Norris and I* (1956). Hamilton was born to Irish parents in Shanghai and was educated at Rugby, where his contemporaries included Rupert Brooke (see Brookes, Winsome), who 'wore his hair excessively long', Hamilton recalled, 'but no one dared to comment on this.' In the First World War Hamilton was interned because of his pro-German sympathies, and he later worked for *The Times* in Berlin. There, in the 1930s, he met Isherwood, fascinating him with his frank dishonesty. A homosexual gaoled by the British for gross indecency and by the Italians for fraud, he lost his job with *The Times* because of his active Communism. When he set out to attempt to negotiate a peace treaty between Britain and Germany in 1941, he was arrested while trying to make his way to Ireland disguised as a nun and was interned in Brixton prison. His friends included 'Foxy' Ferdinand, ex-King of Bulgaria, who awarded him various decorations which he sold. In his old age he lived in a London flat above the Good Earth restaurant in King's Road, Chelsea. It was better to be above the good earth, he said, than below it. His life had been comfortable enough for him to become an authority on pre-phylloxera clarets, and at seventy-nine he won a *New Statesman* poetry competition for which the subject was 'An Evening at the Vicarage'. His entry began 'Uncle, back from evensong,/Rang for cook and did her wrong.'

NORTH, Abe, in F. Scott Fitzgerald's *Tender is the Night* (1934), is the American journalist and short-story writer Ring Lardner (1885–1933). Fitzgerald tried in vain to persuade an apathetic, self-despising Lardner to develop his talent as a writer.

NORTH, Valentine, in Mary Hayley Bell's *Angel* (1947), has as prototype Constance Kent. See Cuff, Sergeant Richard.

NOVEMALI, Princess, in W. Somerset Maugham's *The Razor's Edge* (1944), is Princess Ottoboni, the American wife of a homosexual Italian nobleman. With her husband, she was a Riviera neighbour of the author. Ted Morgan's *Somerset Maugham* (1980) records the couple's nickname — Pédéraste et Médisance.

NUCIGEN, Baron Frederic de, in Honoré de Balzac's *La Maison Nucigen* (1838), is thought to be part-inspired by Baron James (Jacob) Rothschild. See Gundermann.

O

O, in Claude Simon's *Les Géorgiques* (1981), is George Orwell (see Tait, Basil), in relation to the part he played in the Spanish Civil War. He served in the Republican army, chronicling his experiences in *Homage to Catalonia* (1938).

OAKES, Anselm, in Christopher Isherwood's 'A Visit to Anselm Oakes' (*Exhumations*, 1966), is Aleister Crowley (see Haddo, Oliver), whom Isherwood first met in Berlin in the early 1930s.

O'BRIEN, in W. Somerset Maugham's *The Magician* (1908), is Roderick O'Conor (1860–1940), an artist acquaintance of the author in Paris in the early 1900s. He had been a friend of Gauguin and was responsible for Maugham's interest in that painter (see Strickland, Charles).

O'CARROLL, Miss Marionetta Celestina, in Thomas Love Peacock's *Nightmare Abbey* (1818), is in part Harriet Shelley (née Westbrook, 1795–1816), who eloped with Percy Bysshe Shelley (see Glowry, Scythrop) when she was sixteen and craving release from what she regarded as the imprisonment of school. She bore him two children, but the couple had little in common intellectually and Shelley left her for Mary Wollstonecraft Godwin (see Stella). Two years later, Harriet drowned herself in the Serpentine.

OCHILTREE, Edie, in Sir Walter Scott's *The Antiquary* (1816), is Andrew Gemmels (1687–1793), a celebrated Scots beggar from Old Cumnock, near Ochiltree, Ayrshire. He fought at Fontenoy, and when he died, at Roxburgh Newtown, was reputed to have left a fortune.

O'CONNOR, Dr Matthew, in Djuna Barnes's *Ryder* (1928) and *Nightwood* (1936), is Dan Mahoney, a homosexual American mono-logist whose powdered beard, blued eyelids and persistent voice were a familiar feature of between-the-wars Paris, where he prac-tised as an abortionist.

OCTAVE, in Marcel Proust's *A la recherche du temps perdu* (1913–27), is an amalgam of the poet, essayist, dramatist and film-maker Jean Cocteau (1889–1963); the author's artist acquaint-ance Léonce de Joncières (*b.* 1871); and Marcel Plantevignes, the son of a Paris necktie manufacturer.

OCTAVIA, in Charlotte Barnes's *Octavia Bragaldi* (1837). It was on condition that her husband kill the man who had seduced her that Ann Cook – 'Octavia' – in 1824 married Jeroboam O. Beauchamp, a Kentucky lawyer. The seducer was Colonel Solomon P. Sharp, Kentucky's solicitor-general, and after a number of unsuccessful attempts Beauchamp in 1825 succeeded in his mission. Sentenced to death, he was joined in his cell on the eve of his execution by his wife. Both took poison and, finding they were still alive, then stabbed themselves. She died; he survived and was hanged.

ODDY, Mr, in Hugh Walpole's 'Mr Oddy' (*All Souls' Night*, 1933), is in part Henry James (see Boon, George), with whom Walpole struck up a hero-worshipping friendship, staying with him at weekends and commencing his letters to him, 'My dearest Master ...'.

OGILVIE, Mary, in Henry Williamson's *The Pathway* (1928), is the author's first wife, Ida Loetitia ('Gipsy') Hibbert, daughter of Charles Calvert Hibbert (see Chychester, Uncle Sufford). She bore Williamson six of his seven children, and although they divorced he continued to hold her in high regard.

O'HARA, Larry, in Jack Kerouac's *The Subterraneans* (1958), is part-inspired by the American poet and publisher Lawrence Ferlinghetti (1919–).

O'HARA, Scarlett, in Margaret Mitchell's *Gone with the Wind* (1936), is in part the author's maternal grandmother, Annie Fitzger-ald Stephens (1844–1934), of Atlanta, Georgia. The daughter of a plantation owner from Tipperary, she survived the firing of Atlanta by the Union Army in 1864 and devoted herself to restoring the family farm after it was stripped by Union soldiers. Scarlett O'Hara is also partly an idealised self-portrait of the author, a Southern Belle who drank and told dirty jokes, as her biographer Anne Edwards records. Her life was the reverse of her heroine's: she left a wild man for a tame one. Her first husband (see Butler, Rhett) read *Gone with the Wind* and telephoned to say, 'Now I know you still love me.'

O'KEEFE, Kenneth, in J.P. Donleavy's *The Ginger Man* (1955). 'That stinks', A.K. Donahue would say of whatever he read over Donleavy's shoulder as it emerged from the typewriter. So the author set a snare, copying a classical translation and allowing it, too, to emerge from his machine. It elicited the same comment. Thereafter, Donleavy has claimed, he was freed from all desire for praise. A Harvard classics graduate and O'Keefe's original, Donahue was later a contemporary of the author at Trinity College, Dublin.

OLD GRANITE, in Henry Adams's *Democracy* (1880), has been taken to be Rutherford Birchard Hayes (1822–93), who in 1877 became the nineteenth President of the United States.

OLD STONY PHIZ, in Nathaniel Hawthorne's 'The Great Stone Face' (*The Snow-Image and Other Twice-Told Tales*, 1851), is thought to be the American statesman Daniel Webster (1782–1852).

OLENSKI, Baron, in Edith Wharton's *The Age of Innocence* (1920), is part-inspired by the author's faithless, playboy husband, Edward Robbins Wharton (*d.* 1928), who habitually registered his various lovers as 'Mrs Wharton' at hotels throughout Europe. Married in 1885, the Whartons were divorced in 1913.

OLIVER, Nelly, in Gilbert Cannan's *Mendel* (1916). 'I never recognised myself!' wrote Frieda Lawrence (see Somers, Harriet) on learning that she was portrayed in *Mendel*, which she had read. She supposed that she must be Nelly Oliver, and she was right. She was sorry 'that Gilbert made me quite so horrid – so vulgar'. Her husband noted in a letter that it was a bad book, 'statement without creation – really journalism'.

OLIVIA, Princess, in W.M. Thackeray's *The Memoirs of Barry Lyndon* (1844), has two suggested prototypes. One is Princess Augusta Caroline of Brunswick-Wolfenbüttel (*d.* 1788), first wife of

Frederick II, King of Württemberg, who was allegedly put to death. The other is Princess Sophia Dorothea (1666–1726), wife of George I until 1694, when she was divorced because of her affair with Count Königsmarck and kept prisoner at Ahlden, near Hanover, for the rest of her life.

OLYMPE, in Paul de Musset's *Lui et elle* (1859), is George Sand (see Maupin, Camille), whose *Elle et lui* (1858) had portrayed de Musset's brother, Alfred (see Laurent). See also Falconey, Édouard de.

O'MALLEY, Godfrey, in Charles Lever's *Charles O'Malley, the Irish Dragoon* (1840), is Richard ('Humanity') Martin (1754–1834), an MP for Galway who was noted for duelling and for his campaigning defence of animals.

ONDT, the, in James Joyce's *Finnegans Wake* (1939). The ondt is suggested by Joyce's biographer, Richard Ellmann, to represent in part Wyndham Lewis (see Lypiatt, Casimir), whose criticism of Joyce's *A Portrait of the Artist as a Young Man* had angered the author.

OPALSTEIN, in Robert Louis Stevenson's 'Talk and Talkers' (1882; *Memories and Portraits*, 1887), is the art historian, critic and poet John Addington Symonds (1840–93), whom Stevenson first met at Davos in 1881. Of delicate health, Symonds spent much of his time in Italy, becoming an authority on the Italian Renaissance. One of his sisters married T.H. Green (see Grey, Edward).

OPERA, Signior, in Henry Fielding's *The Author's Farce* (1730), is Senesino (Francesco Bernardi, ?1680–?1750), an Italian castrato singer brought to England by Handel, who went to Dresden especially to engage him. He made his first London appearance in 1720 and is portrayed in Hogarth's *Marriage à la Mode*, iv, 'The Toilette' (1745).

OPHELIA, in D.H. Lawrence's 'Smile' (1926; *The Woman Who Rode Away*, 1928), is Katharine Mansfield. See Brangwen, Gudrun; see also Matthew.

OPHELIA, in William Shakespeare's *Hamlet* (c.1602), may owe something to Katharine Hamlet, of Tiddington, near Stratford-upon-Avon, who drowned in that river in 1579. Although the question of suicide was considered at her inquest, the verdict was accidental death. Similarly, *Hamlet* questions whether Ophelia took her own life or died by accident. Shakespeare probably knew Katharine Hamlet, who lived less than one and a half miles from his home town. He would probably have been aware of her drowning, which was doubtless the talk of Stratford, when he was at the impressionable age of fifteen.

OPISKIN, Foma, in Fyodor Dostoevsky's *The Village of Stepanchikovo and its Inhabitants*, otherwise known as *The Friend of the Family* (1859), is the Russian writer Nikolai Gogol (1809–52), viewed with particular regard to his substandard *Selected Passages from Correspondence with Friends* (1847).

ORANGE, Robert, in *Robert Orange* (1900), by John Oliver Hobbes (Mrs Pearl Craigie), is Benjamin Disraeli (see Daubeny, Mr). The author, who idolised Disraeli, made him a Roman Catholic for the purposes of this Catholic novel. Not that he would have troubled to read it, had he still been alive. 'When I want to read a book,' he said, 'I write one.'

ORATOR, Dr, in Henry Fielding's *The Author's Farce* (1730). To attract an audience, the original of Dr Orator on one occasion promised to reveal a new and rapid way of making shoes. Numerous shoemakers turned up . . . to be told to cut the tops off boots. The speaker was John Henley (1692–1756), a preacher and journalist known as 'Orator Henley'.

ORELLANO, Gregory, in Constance Malleson's *The Coming Back* (1933), is the author's lover, Bertrand Russell. See Mattheson, Sir Joshua.

ORINTHIA, in George Bernard Shaw's *The Apple Cart* (1929). The impossible Mrs Patrick Campbell (see Hushabye, Hesione) was furious at being identified with Orinthia and outraged when Shaw suggested changing the likeness, according to Margot Peters, her biographer. She urged Shaw to tear up the play and write it again, without those passages that she felt vulgarised her relationship with the author, who appears in the guise of King Magnus. Shaw compromised, rewriting only those lines that offended her most.

ORKISH, Lord, in Ronald Firbank's *The Princess Zoubaroff* (1920), is Oscar Wilde (see Amarinth, Esme). Orkish is portrayed living in exile, as did Wilde after his imprisonment, and he uses one of Wilde's witticisms. He is also partnered by an obvious echo of Lord Alfred Douglas (see Quintus, Reggie; see also Hastings, Lord Reggie).

ORLANDO, in Kathleen Hale's *Orlando the Marmalade Cat* books (1938–72), owes his character to the author's husband, Dr Douglas McClean (*d.* 1967), whom she married in 1926. He was 'resourceful, equable, wise and infinitely kind', Kathleen Hale has told me. When she first met him he was pathologist to the Hospital for Sick Children, Great Ormond Street, London. He later worked at the Lister Institute as a biologist. 'Nobody actually influenced my writing', says Miss Hale. 'It was a personal excursion into my own childhood – which had not been a happy one, and which I wanted to substitute for a more "family" one.' The Orlando stories were written for her two sons.

ORLANDO, in Virginia Woolf's *Orlando* (1928). Virginia Woolf would sit at the feet of the woman who had seduced her, knotting pearls about the neck of the Hon. Victoria ('Vita') Sackville-West (1892–1962) – novelist, poet, biographer, creator of the gardens at Sissinghurst Castle in Kent, and Woolf's model for Orlando. Sackville-West was the wife of the Hon. Sir Harold Nicolson (see Chilleywater, the Hon. Harold). Each gave full rein to the other's homosexuality, and Sackville-West's lovers included Violet Trefusis (see Romanovitch, Princess 'Sasha') and Mary Campbell (see Georgiana), as well as her secretary, her BBC producer, and a *Daily Mail* women's editor and her flat-mate ... almost every other woman she met seemed to fall for her. She described herself as 'an honest sensualist' and but for a flaw of fate, Edith Sitwell remarked, she would have been one of nature's gentlemen.

ORME, Lambert, in Harold Nicolson's *Some People* (1927), is the novelist and playwright Ronald Firbank (1886–1926), to whom Nicolson transposed the death circumstances of Rupert Brooke (see Brookes, Winsome).

ORVILLERS, Princesse d', in Marcel Proust's *A la recherche du temps perdu* (1913–27), is the Marquise d'Hervey de Saint-Denis, illegitimate daughter of the last reigning Duke of Parma and the wayward wife of a Chinese scholar. After her husband's death in 1892 she married a nephew of the Comtesse Adhéaume de Chevigné (see Guermantes, Oriane, Duchesse de). Her perpetual youth (her second husband was fifteen years her junior) earned her the sobriquet 'the Demi-Chevreul' (Michel Chevreul, a distinguished chemist, had celebrated his 100th birthday in 1886).

O'SHAY, Ike, in Jack Kerouac's *The Dharma Bums* (1958), is Michael McClure. See McLear, Patrick.

OSMOND, Pansy, in Henry James's *The Portrait of a Lady* (1881), is Elizabeth Boott (1846–88), a friend both of the author and of Minny Temple (see Theale, Milly). Of Bostonian parentage, she spent her youth in Italy with her widowed father, and after studying in France became an unsuccessful artist. She died shortly after her marriage to the American painter Frank Duveneck, leaving a child aged fifteen months.

OTTERCOVE, Lord, in William Gerhardi's *My Sinful Earth* (1928) and *Doom* (originally published as *Jazz and Jasper*, 1929), is the Canadian-born newspaper proprietor Lord Beaverbrook (1879–1964), owner of the London-based *Daily Express* to which he devoted such energy and flair that in 1936 it attained the world's largest circulation for a daily paper. He 'took up' and befriended Gerhardi, who responded by dedicating *Pretty Creatures* (1927) to him 'in the absence of Napoleon Buonaparte'.

OTTILIE, in Johann Wolfgang von Goethe's *The Elective Affinities* (1809), is supposedly Wilhemine Herzlieb (1789–1865), with whom the author fell in love when he was sixty and she eighteen, an orphan living with a Jena bookseller-publisher and his wife. After breaking her engagement to a professor shortly before the wedding was to take place, she married another academic. The physical aspect of sex so horrified her, however, that she suffered a mental breakdown and entered an institution, where she spent the rest of her life.

P, Pier Paolo, in Dominique Fernandez's *Dans la main de l'ange* (1982), is the Italian film director and novelist Pier Paolo Pasolini (1922−75), who was bludgeoned to death by a youth who then used Pasolini's car to drive over him. The youth later claimed that Pasolini had made homosexual advances.

PACCHIAROTTO, Giacomo, in Robert Browning's *Pacchiarotto, and How He Worked in Distemper* (1876), is the poet, critic and editor of the *National Review*, Alfred Austin (1835−1913), who was appointed Poet Laureate in 1895. 'I gave it to him', said Lord Salisbury, 'because no one else applied.' He is believed to have been responsible for the immortal lines on the Prince of Wales (later Edward VII): 'Across the wires the electric message came:/"He is no better, he is much the same."' 'I always thought that Mr Austin's appointment was not a good one,' the King later remarked.

PAGE, Clara, in F. Scott Fitzgerald's *This Side of Paradise* (1920), is the author's cousin, Cecilia Delihant, according to the Fitzgerald biographer, Arthur Mizener. Fitzgerald was a ribbon-holder at her wedding in 1903; he fell in love with her when she was a young widow in Norfolk, Virginia, and he was an undergraduate.

PALACE, Brynhild, in H.G. Wells's *Brynhild* (1937), is believed to be the author's lover, Baroness Marie Budberg (1892−1974), formerly Countess von Benckendorff (née Zakrevskaia), the daughter of a Russian senator. She was widowed in the Russian Revolution and Wells first met her at the Benckendorff family home in St Petersburg in 1914, renewing the acquaintance in 1920 when she was living under the protection of the writer Maxim Gorki, who had rescued her from prison and to whom she was secretary and interpreter. With Gorki's assistance she settled in Estonia, marrying

Baron Budberg. That union was not a happy one and in 1922 she joined Gorki in Berlin, subsequently settling with her children in England. There she remained Wells's close friend for the rest of his life, despite his suspicion that she was a Russian agent 'planted' on him by her masters. Her lovers also included Gorki himself and the author and diplomat Sir Robert Bruce Lockhart, whom she first met in 1918.

PALEY, Susan, in Aldous Huxley's *Point Counter Point* (1928), is Katherine Mansfield (see Brangwen, Gudrun), according to Jerome Meckier's *Aldous Huxley: Satire and Structure* (1969). Her appearance in the novel is posthumous, her husband, John Middleton Murry (see Burlap, Denis; see also Crich, Gerald), being presented as exploiting the reputation of his dead wife.

PALLISER, Plantagenet and Lady Glencora, in Anthony Trollope's *Can You Forgive Her?* (1864), *Phineas Finn* (1869), *The Eustace Diamonds* (1873), *Phineas Redux* (1874), *The Prime Minister* (1876) and *The Duke's Children* (1880). For his patriotic tenacity, honesty and modesty, Palliser is supposedly modelled upon Lord Palmerston (see Brock, Lord). His candour and lack of social graces are believed to come from Lord John Russell (see Malicho, Lord Michin), a poor mixer and of a retiring nature. Something of this stiffness of demeanour is also probably derived from Edward Henry Stanley, Fifteenth Earl of Derby (1826–93). Trollope was a member of the committee of the Royal Literary Fund, over which Stanley presided. The Earl considered him to be incorrigibly middle class and lacking in political acumen. Three celebrated Liberal hostesses have been discerned in Glencora: Lady Palmerston, Lady Russell and Lady Stanley of Alderley. Lady Palmerston (*d.* 1869), widow of the Fifth Earl Cowper, sought to advance Palmerston's career through giving parties. Lady Frances Ann Maria Elliot (*d.* 1898), daughter of the Second Earl of Minto, in 1841 became the second wife of Lord John Russell. She was considerably younger than her husband, and her remark that he would not mind being shoe-black to Lord Aberdeen if it would serve the country is twice echoed by Glencora. Henrietta Maria Dillon (1807–95), daughter of the Thirteenth Viscount Dillon and grandmother of Bertrand Russell (see Mattheson, Sir Joshua), married Edward John Stanley, Second Baron of Alderley, in 1826. She was a founder of Girton College, Cambridge, and of the Girls' Public Day School Company, and her husband's appointment as Postmaster-General led to Trollope — a senior executive of the Post Office — attending a number of her parties. The identification of Trollope's political originals is explored in greater depth in John Halperin's *Trollope and Politics* (1977).

PAMELA, in John Osborne's *Time Present* (1968), has been taken to have as prototype the left-wing actress Vanessa Redgrave (1937—   ), like Pamela the daughter of a famous actor (Sir Michael Redgrave). Osborne denied the identification in an interview with Kenneth Tynan for the *Observer* (30 June 1968). Tynan asked, 'In *Time Present*, when you create the character of an actress who makes pro-Castro speeches, you're not thinking specifically of Vanessa Redgrave?' 'No', Osborne replied. 'Although a character may seem to be identifiable, I hope that I've given something to it, that something has happened in between. There are always people who think it's them when it's nothing like.'

PAN, Peter. See Peter Pan.

PANGLOSS, Dr, in Voltaire's *Candide* (1759). In Pangloss the author lampoons the philosopher Baron Gottfried Wilhelm Leibnitz (1646—1716) and his disciple Johann Christian von Wolff (1679—1754). Although Leibnitz conceded that the interaction of spirit and matter had no explanation, he divined a pre-ordained harmony between them. In Wolff's projection this became a philosophy of optimism in which the creed of Leibnitz was simplified and came to be regarded as a belief in a benign providence controlling the world. Voltaire was opposed to Leibnitz's ideas and even more to their systematic development by Wolff, notes the Voltaire scholar Theodore Besterman. Wolff met Voltaire and described him in his autobiography as 'a truly agreeable man of a jolly disposition in intercourse and very quick in intellectual fancies'. But that was before *Candide*, which appeared after Wolff's death.

PANTOMIME, Monsieur, in Henry Fielding's *The Author's Farce* (1730), is the Covent Garden impresario John Rich (?1682—1761), noted for his pantomimes and, as the first producer of John Gay's *The Beggar's Opera*, said to have 'made Gay rich and Rich gay.'

PANURGE, in François Rabelais's *Pantagruel* (1532/3), has a suggested model in the amoral poet François Villon (1431—?1463). Rabelais related anecdotes about Villon, who had a number of Panurge's characteristics.

PAPERSTAMP, Peter Paypaul, in Thomas Love Peacock's *Melincourt* (1817), is the poet William Wordsworth (1770–1850), who came to be regarded by some of his contemporaries as a two-faced reactionary. Although he inveighed against railways, for instance, he bought shares in them. Peacock's name for him was inspired by Wordsworth's appointment in 1813 as Distributor of Stamps for Westmorland and Cumberland, a sinecure worth about £400 a year.

PAR, Augustus, in Christopher Isherwood's *Down There on a Visit* (1962), is the Irish polymath Gerald Heard (1889–1971), a writer and a prodigious reader reputed to get through 2,000 books a year. He met Aldous Huxley (see Erasmus, William) in 1929, and they became lifelong friends, leaving England together in 1937 to settle in the United States. In 1942 he founded Trabuco College, in California, a monastic establishment which was subsequently acquired by the Vedanta Society. It was from Heard that Harold Nicolson (see Chilleywater, the Hon. Harold) took the notion of the atomic bomb and its implications, which he used in his novel *Public Faces* (1932), thereby in 1945 acquiring a reputation for uncanny prescience. Isherwood was introduced to Heard by W.H. Auden (see Weston, Hugh) in 1932. Seven years later he renewed Heard's acquaintance and through him came to take an interest in Hindu philosophy, which influenced his later work.

PARAMORE, Fred E., in F. Scott Fitzgerald's *The Beautiful and the Damned* (1922), is the Hollywood scriptwriter Ted E. Paramore junior (*d.* 1956), with whom Fitzgerald had a strained relationship when they worked together on the film *Three Comrades*. A friend of the critic Edmund Wilson, Paramore was the author of *The Ballad of Yukon Jake*, a parody of the Klondike verse of Robert W. Service. Films scripted by him include *The Virginian*.

PARAMUZZI, in H.G. Wells's *The Autocracy of Mr Parham* (1930), is Benito Mussolini (see Arango, General Tereso). Wells didn't actually say that Paramuzzi was Mussolini, but then, he didn't need to: the book was illustrated by David Low's lifelike caricatures.

PARIS, in Hilda Doolittle's *Helen in Egypt* (1961), represents the poet's husband, Richard Aldington (see Ashton, Rafe; see also Masters, Miranda), from whom she separated in 1919. They divorced in 1938.

PARKER, Freddy, in Norman Douglas's *South Wind* (1917), is Harold Edward Trower (1853–1941), Capri's British Consular Agent from 1900 to 1916. He incurred the author's displeasure by writing *The Book of Capri*, thereby trespassing upon what Douglas had come to regard as his own literary province. Trower also made official representations to curb Douglas's homosexual activities on the island.

PARKER, Ralph, in Hugh Kingsmill's *The Will to Love* (written under the name Hugh Lunn, 1913). The lubricious autobiographical fantasies of Frank Harris (1856–1931) prompted Rebecca West to remark that he believed he held the sole performing rights in sex. But Harris — Kingsmill's Parker — was rather more than just a legendary lecher. He edited the *Fortnightly Review*, the *Saturday Review* and *Vanity Fair*, and was the author of a number of studies on Shakespeare. He was also unscrupulous and something of a mountebank. 'He has no feelings', said Oscar Wilde. 'It is the secret of his success.' See also Barbara.

PARKINSON, 'Rotter', in Wyndham Lewis's *Self Condemned* (1954), is Hugh Gordon Porteus (1906–), a commercial artist turned critic who wrote *Wyndham Lewis: A Discursive Exposition* (1932). Lewis volunteered to 'ghost' this for him, declaring when the offer was declined, 'When you began to piss against my leg I should have chased you away.'

PARMONT, Mr, in Ford Madox Ford's *The Simple Life Limited* (written under the pseudonym Daniel Chaucer, 1911), is Edward Garnett (see Lea), whose life-style is echoed by the vegetarian members of The Simple Life Ltd. Garnett's vegetarianism, however, was not entirely voluntary. He gathered mushrooms near his home at Limpsfield, Kent, to eke out his family's provisions in hard times. During one summer, according to his son, David, they had mushrooms at every meal.

PARRITT, Don, in Eugene O'Neill's *The Iceman Cometh* (1946), is Louis Holliday (d. 1918). A *habitué* of bars in New York's Greenwich Village, he renounced drink and went West to become a fruit farmer in order to raise sufficient money to marry. When he returned to New York he told friends he had come back to celebrate his saving of the necessary nest-egg, but after a few drinks he confessed that his girl had deserted him for another lover. At his request, Terry Carlin (see Slade, Larry) gave him a lethal amount of heroin, and Holliday committed suicide.

PARSNIP, in Evelyn Waugh's *Put Out More Flags* (1942) and *Love among the Ruins* (1953). Britain's declaration of war on Germany in 1939 found four prominent British intellectuals of military age in the United States. In 1940 they were criticised for having gone to America at such a time, and for having stayed. W.H. Auden (see Weston, Hugh) was one of them, and he is Waugh's Parsnip. With Christopher Isherwood (see Pimpernell), he went to New York in 1939. In the *Spectator*, Harold Nicolson wondered how Americans could be expected to believe in the justice of Britain's cause when 'four of our most liberated intelligences refuse to identify themselves with those who fight.' The others he had in mind were Aldous Huxley and Gerald Heard (see Par, Augustus). The Dean of St Paul's was moved to less than Christian verse: 'This Europe stinks, you cried — swift to desert / Your stricken country in her sore distress. / You may not care, but still I will assert / Since you have left us, here the stink is less.' In Parliament the question was asked, 'Will British citizens of military age, such as Mr W.H. Auden and Mr Christopher Isherwood, who have gone to the United States and expressed their determination not to return to this country until the war is over, be summoned back for registration and calling up in view of the fact that they are seeking refuge abroad?' The *émigré* writers were also criticised by Louis MacNeice (see MacSpaunday) and J.B. Priestley, but E.M. Forster defended them. Others found it hard to imagine what military function the four could have served had they returned. Like that courageous but unsoldierly soldier Waugh himself, they would probably have been as much of an embarrassment as an asset. But for Waugh's Parsnip and Pimpernell, the episode would doubtless have been long since forgotten. *Put Out More Flags* has extended its currency to this day — in 1984, Isherwood was still finding it necessary to defend his Pimpernell role.

PASH, Lady, in Frederick Rolfe's *The Desire and Pursuit of the Whole* (1934), is Lady Layard (née Ada Alexandrina Mortlake), who in 1882 married the Chief Justice of Ceylon. Like Rolfe, she lived in Venice. When she died, he was outraged at not being invited to her funeral, as a fellow member of the British community, and standing outside the church in the vestments of a cardinal, he shouted insults as the coffin arrived.

PASSANT, George, in C.P. Snow's *Strangers and Brothers* (1940; later retitled *George Passant*), *Time of Hope* (1949), *Homecomings* (1956) and *The Sleep of Reason* (1968), is the author's early mentor and lifelong friend, Herbert Edmund Howard (1900–63). In 1922 he was appointed history master at Alderman Newton's Boys' School, Leicester, where Snow was a pupil. He spent his whole career at the school, but was also the author of seven detective novels (under the name R. Philmore) and a regular Midlands representative in BBC radio's *Round Britain Quiz*. In addition to Snow, his protégés at the school included the historian J.H. Plumb. He was best man at Snow's wedding in 1950, but later caused his friend some anguish. Towards the end of his life he had to flee to Holland to escape prosecution after he had seduced a prison warder's son.

PATCH, Gloria, in F. Scott Fitzgerald's *The Beautiful and the Damned* (1922), is Zelda Fitzgerald (see Diver, Nicole). But Gloria, Fitzgerald later wrote to his daughter, 'was a much more trivial and vulgar person than your mother.'

PATHFINDER, in James Fenimore Cooper's *The Pathfinder* (1840), is Daniel Boone. See Bumppo, Natty.

PATIENT B, in William Halse Rivers's *Conflict and Dream* (1923), is Siegfried Sassoon (see Victor, Siegfried). As an army doctor in the First World War, Rivers treated Sassoon for shell-shock.

PAUL, in Christopher Isherwood's *Down There on a Visit* (1962), is Denham Fouts (*d.* 1949), son of the owner of the Safeways grocery chainstores. At sixteen, according to Truman Capote, Fouts eloped from his Florida home with a cosmetics millionaire. They went to Europe, and such was Fouts's bisexual charisma that he was seldom short of rich lovers. When Isherwood met him in 1938 he was enjoying the patronage of Peter Watson, who was also financing the magazine *Horizon*. Fouts was a conscientious objector in the Second World War, in which he became a lumber-camp cook. After the war he moved first to Paris and then to Rome, became addicted to opium, and died following a heart attack.

PAULLE, Lady Queenie, in Arnold Bennett's *The Pretty Lady* (1918). Shortly after the publication of this novel, Bennett dined with Lord Beaverbrook and friends at the Savoy. Among those present was Lady Diana Manners (later Lady Diana Cooper; see

Stitch, Mrs Algernon), who had been popularly identified with Queenie. 'When the conversation turned on Diana being the original of Queen in *The Pretty Lady* my attitude was apparently so harsh that Beaverbrook changed the subject', Bennett noted in his diary. Until that evening, he and Lady Diana had not met. Bennett's biographer, Margaret Drabble, suspects that he used press reports and gossip about Lady Diana as the basis for Queenie, creating a character so close to Lady Diana that she marvelled, she later recorded, at the way he had involved Queenie in incidents similar to those in her own life but of which he could not have known.

PAVIA, Francis Da, in Jack Kerouac's *The Dharma Bums* (1958), is the American poet Philip Lamantia (1927–   ).

PAXTON, Tony, in W. Somerset Maugham's *Our Betters* (1917), is Gerald Haxton (see Flint, Rowley). In Paxton's treatment of the Duchesse de Surennes, Maugham's biographer Ted Morgan sees a reflection of Haxton's relationship with the author.

PEABODY, Dr L.Q.C., in William Faulkner's Yoknapatawpha saga (1929–62), is believed to have as prototype Dr Thomas Dudley Isom, who in the 1830s was one of the founding fathers of Oxford, Mississippi, the author's model for Jefferson, Yoknapatawpha. Isom remained in Oxford as a physician for the greater part of the nineteenth century.

PEACHEY, Ada, in George Gissing's *In the Year of the Jubilee* (1894), is the author's second wife, Edith (née Underwood, *d.* 1917), according to John Halperin's *Gissing: A Life in Books* (1982). The daughter of a Camden Town carpenter, she met Gissing in 1890 at a music hall, when she was twenty-three. They married the following year, separating in 1897. She became insane and spent the last fifteen years of her life in an asylum.

PEACHUM, in John Gay's *The Beggar's Opera* (1728), is Jonathan Wild (?1682–1725), a London buckle-maker turned self-proclaimed 'Thief-taker General of Britain and Ireland' who was suspected of receiving stolen goods in order to claim rewards for their return. Becoming, in effect, the leader of a widespread network of thieves (whom he would 'take' and give evidence against when it suited him), he was eventually exposed and hanged. Gay knew him; Defoe chronicled his career in 1725; and Fielding satirised him in *The Life of Jonathan Wild the Great* (1743).

PECKSNIFF, Mr Seth, in Charles Dickens's *Martin Chuzzlewit* (1843–4), is supposedly Samuel Carter Hall (1800–89), prolific author, editor of the *Literary Observer*, the *Amulet*, the *New Monthly Magazine*, the *Town*, the *Art Union Journal* and *Social Notes*, and a colleague of Dickens's father on the *British Press*. The author's friend, Percy Fitzgerald, having heard Dickens talk of Hall, thought the journalist's identification with Pecksniff not at all far-fetched; and it was as Pecksniff that Hall was hailed when he lectured in America. His wife, Anna Maria Hall, was a noted evangelist and travel writer. It has also been suggested that traces of the architect A.W.N. Pugin (1812–52) are exhibited in Pecksniff. As portrayed by Phiz, however, Pecksniff bore such a resemblance to Sir Robert Peel (1788–1850), 'father' of Britain's police force, that *Punch* guyed Peel as Pecksniff thereafter.

PEEPERKORN, Pieter, in Thomas Mann's *The Magic Mountain* (1924), is part-inspired by the German dramatist, poet and novelist Gerhart Hauptmann (1862–1946), whose skill with the written word deserted him in conversation.

PEGGOTTY, Clara, in Charles Dickens's *David Copperfield* (1849–50), is believed to be modelled in part upon Mary Weller (1805–88), who nursed the author when he was a child. She married a Chatham shipwright, Thomas Gibson.

PEGGY, in Robert Burns's 'Young Peggy', is Margaret Kennedy (1766–95), daughter of Robert Kennedy of Daljarrock, Strathclyde, and niece of Gavin Hamilton, to whom the Kilmarnock edition of Burns's work was dedicated. In the year before her death she gave birth to a daughter. The putative father, Captain Andrew M'Doual, denied both paternity and that he had married her. Lengthy litigation followed, £3,000 in damages being posthumously awarded to Margaret Kennedy in 1798. The episode is believed to have suggested Burns's 'The Banks o' Doon'.

PEHRSEN, in John Paulsen's *The Pehrsen Family* (1882), is the Norwegian dramatist, Henrik Ibsen (1828–1906), who responded to Paulsen's protestation that he had meant no harm by sending him a card bearing a single word: 'Scoundrel'.

PELOUX, Fred (Chéri), in Colette's *Chéri* (1920), is supposedly part-inspired by Auguste Hériot (see Dufferin-Chautel, Max). The author's stepson, Bertrand de Jouvenel, with whom she had a four-year affair, was popularly believed to be the original, but he did not enter her life until after the novel's publication.

PELZ, Benjamin, in Klaus Mann's *Mephisto* (1936), is the German poet Gottfried Benn (1886–1956), who from 1930 to 1936 was the lover of Tilly Wedekind (see Kadidja). His adverse comments on Mann's *Emigranten* prompted this portrayal.

PENDENNIS, Arthur, Helen and Major, in W.M. Thackeray's *The History of Pendennis* (1848–50). Arthur Pendennis is modelled in physical appearance upon Charles Lamb Kenney (?1823–81), second son of the dramatist James Kenney. A journalist on *The Times*, he was also a composer of popular songs and of lyrics for light operas, and secretary to Ferdinand de Lesseps, creator of the Suez Canal. Helen Pendennis is the author's mother, Anne Becher, who was first married to Richard Thackeray and then to Major Henry Carmichael-Smyth (see Newcome, Colonel Thomas). One of the most beautiful English women in India, she lacked humour and was much involved in homeopathy, hydropathy and Evangelical Christianity. She outlived her novelist son (who died in 1863) by a year. Major Pendennis is the author's uncle by marriage, Lieutenant-Colonel Merrick Shawe (*d.* 1843), a lifelong confidant of the Marquis of Wellesley, whom he served as private secretary when Wellesley was Governor-General of India and Lord Lieutenant of Ireland.

PENNILOE, Parson, in R.D. Blackmore's *Perlycross* (1894), according to Blackmore's biographer, Kenneth Budd, is the author's father, the Revd John Blackmore (*d.* 1858), curate of Longworth in Berkshire. In 1825 he lost his wife, daughter, servants and family physician – all victims of a typhus epidemic. Remarrying, he became curate at Culmstock, Devon.

PENNISTONE, David, in Anthony Powell's *The Military Philosophers* (1968), is primarily inspired by Alexander Dru, the Anglo-French brother-in-law of Evelyn Waugh and the son-in-law of the Hon. Aubrey Herbert (see Arbuthnot, Sandy). Translator and editor of the journals of Kierkegaard, he served with Powell in the Second World War as a liaison officer with the Polish army in London.

PEPWORTH-NORTON, the Misses (Virginia and Maimie), in Compton Mackenzie's *Vestal Fire* (1927), are Kate Wolcott and Saidée Perry, American expatriate spinsters who are believed to have been cousins. Settling on the island of Capri, they linked surnames with a hyphen and became known as the Misses Wolcott-Perry.

PERCIVAL, in Christopher Isherwood's *Lions and Shadows* (1938), is the Welsh poet Vernon Watkins (1906–67), a Repton and Cambridge contemporary of the author, whom he annoyed at university by telling a don of a fantasy which Isherwood and Edward Upward (see Chalmers, Allen) were writing together.

PERCIVAL, Jack and Mrs, in Ford Madox Ford's *The Rash Act* (1933), are Ernest Hemingway (see Ahearn) and his early mentor, Gertrude Stein (1874–1946), American novelist, poet and lesbian, whose observation 'A rose is a rose is a rose' drew 'A pose is a pose is a pose' from Violet Trefusis (see Romanovitch, Princess 'Sasha').

PEREKATOV, Mr, in Gilbert Cannan's *Time and Eternity* (1919), is the Russian translator Samuel Solomonovitch Koteliansky (1882–1955). Born in the Ukraine, he arrived in England on a Kiev University research scholarship, and remained in this country. He was a staunch friend of D.H.Lawrence and was credited with persuading H.G. Wells to write his autobiography – not, one might suppose, that Wells needed much persuading. He was infatuated with Katherine Mansfield, who regarded him with amused affection and left him her carved walking-stick in her will.

PERELLI, Tony, in Edgar Wallace's *On the Spot* (1930), has as prototype the Chicago gangster Al Capone (1899–1947), an Italian barber's son who became notorious for his ruthless elimination of rivals. Wallace's play was prompted by a 24-hour tour of Chicago, taking in the gangster's headquarters and the scene of the St Valentine's Day massacre, in which Capone's henchmen (dressed as policemen) machine-gunned to death five members of another gang.

PERRON, Henri, in Simone de Beauvoir's *The Mandarins* (1954), is the French novelist Albert Camus (1913–60), who in 1948 joined with Jean-Paul Sartre (see Dubreuilh, Robert) in launching a new political movement. The two later became political enemies, waging war in open letters, for as Sartre moved further towards Communism, Camus edged away, disillusioned by what he saw as a Russian betrayal of the Revolution.

PERRY, Josephine, in F. Scott Fitzgerald's 'First Blood', 'A Nice Quiet Place' and 'A Woman with a Past' (1930; *Taps at Reveille*, 1935), and 'A Snobbish Story' and 'Emotional Bankruptcy' (1930 and 1931 respectively; *The Basil and Josephine Stories*, 1973), is Ginevra King (see Borgé, Isabelle). In a letter to the Fitzgerald biographer Arthur Mizener in 1947 she confessed, 'I was thoughtless in those days and too much in love with love to think of consequences. These things he has emphasized – and over-emphasized – in the Josephine stories, but it is only fair to say I asked for some of them.'

PERVIN, Maurice and Isabel, in D.H. Lawrence's 'The Blind Man' (1920; *England, My England*, 1922). Two married couples who were friends of the author have been suggested as the models for Maurice and Isabel, and both may have contributed. At the time the story was written, Lady Cynthia Asquith (née Charteris, 1887–1960, daughter of the Eleventh Earl of Wemyss) had become secretary to J.M. Barrie and was much distressed by the shell-shocked state of her war-casualty husband, the Hon. Herbert Asquith (1881–1947), son of the First Earl of Oxford (see Lubin, Henry Hopkins). Similarly situated were the Scottish novelist and biographer, Catherine Carswell (1879–1946), and her second husband. Carswell lost her reviewing post with the *Glasgow Herald* in 1915 after giving Lawrence's *The Rainbow* a favourable notice. In 1918 Lawrence stayed with her and her husband, who had been blinded and disfigured in the war, at their home, Lydbrook Parsonage, in the Forest of Dean.

PETER THE HEADSTRONG, in Washington Irving's *A History of New York* (1809), is Peter Stuyvesant (1592–1672), New York's last Dutch governor.

PETER PAN, in J.M. Barrie's *Peter Pan, or The Boy Who Wouldn't Grow Up* (1904). 'What's in a name?' asked the publisher Peter Llewelyn Davies (1897–1960), who bore the cross of popular identification with Peter Pan. 'My God, what isn't? If that perennially juvenile lead, if that boy so fatally committed to an arrestation of his development, had only been dubbed George, or Jack, or Michael, or Nicholas, what miseries might have been spared me.'

Davies was, in fact, named after another character of fiction: Peter Ibbetson, a creation of his grandfather, George Du Maurier. The identification of Peter Davies with Peter Pan rests solely on the coincidence of his Christian name and his family's association with Barrie (see Darling, Mr and Mrs). The dramatist in fact showed more interest in some of Peter Davies's brothers than in Peter himself, particularly in Michael Llewelyn Davies (1900—21), whose nightmares and sleep-walking were introduced into the play in 1910 and who was the model for Sir George Frampton's statue of Peter Pan in Kensington Gardens. He was drowned in a suspected homosexual suicide pact. In the play's dedication, Barrie acknowledged the influence of the Davies boys: 'I made Peter by rubbing the five of you violently together, as savages with two sticks produce a flame.' But Peter Pan, the boy who wouldn't grow up, was primarily Barrie himself, whose mother had gone into almost permanent mourning for his brother who died aged twelve. Barrie once remarked, 'nothing that happens after we are twelve matters very much'. He was impotent, his marriage unconsummated, his relationships with the three women in his life all of an asexual nature. And Peter Davies, whom the public took to be Peter Pan? He committed suicide by jumping in front of a train at Sloane Square Station. For the man who *was* named after Peter Pan, see Rhayader.

PETERSEN, Harald, in Mary McCarthy's *The Group* (1963), is the author's first husband, Harold Johnsrud, an unsuccessful actor and dramatist. His father was a Minnesota school administrator who became the scapegoat in an academic scandal, as did Petersen's father in *The Group*. McCarthy married Johnsrud in 1933, and they were divorced three years later. He died in a hotel fire during the Second World War.

PETKOFF, Raina, in George Bernard Shaw's *Arms and the Man* (1894), is Mrs Annie Besant (1847—1933), writer, magazine editor and pioneer advocate of birth control. In 1885, Shaw's eloquence converted her to Socialism and Fabianism and he became a contributor to her monthly journal, *Our Corner*. Sixteen years his senior, she fell in love with him, suggesting that she should become his common-law wife and drawing up a contract detailing the terms under which she would live with him. Shaw rejected the arrangement, and the end of the affair was said to have turned her hair grey. In 1889, despite Shaw's pleas that she should think again, she became a leading Theosophist.

PETT, Herbert, in Ford Madox Ford's *The New Humpty-Dumpty* (1912, written under the pseudonym Daniel Chaucer), is H.G. Wells (see Wilson, Hypo), who had briefly been a lover of Ford's mistress, Violet Hunt (see Nesbitt, Norah) and had failed to keep his promise to assist with the editing and financing of Ford's periodical, the *English Review*.

PETULENGRO, Jasper, in George Borrow's *Lavengro* (1851), is the author's friend Ambrose Smith (1804–78), a gypsy of East Anglian stock who attained such celebrity through his identification with Jasper that he was presented to Queen Victoria. The book was written between 1842 and 1851, and it was at Christmas, 1842, that Smith visited Borrow at his Oulton home, complaining of police harassment of gypsies and of residents' meanness towards them. The Borrow biographer W.I. Knapp notes that Jasper appeared as Ambrose in the manuscript of *Lavengro*, the name being altered shortly before the book went to be typeset.

PHILBRICK, Mercy, in Helen Hunt Jackson's *Mercy Philbrick's Choice* (1876), is believed to be the poet Emily Dickinson. See Stanhope, Alison.

PHILLIPS, Jackson, in Ernest Hemingway's *The Green Hills of Africa* (1935), is Philip Percival, a white hunter friend of the author in Kenya.

PICCINO, in Frances Hodgson Burnett's *The Captain's Youngest* (1894; published in the United States as *Piccino*), is Maria Pasqua (1856–1939), the daughter of Italian peasants from the Abruzzi. Becoming an artists' model in Rome in her infancy, she was taken to Paris by her father and was painted by artists including Hébert, Bonnet, Jalabert and de Curzon. For the price of a vineyard, her father sold her to the Comtesse de Noailles (see Aileen, Lady), who adopted her. In 1881 she became the second wife of Philip Shepheard, a retired Norfolk doctor, settling at Abbots Hall, near Aylsham. Her story is told in Magdalen Goffin's *Maria Pasqua* (1979).

PICKLE, Mr, in Charles Dickens's *Pictures from Italy* (1846), is W.B. Le Gros (d. 1850), author of *Fables and Tales, suggested by the Frescoes of Pompeii and Herculaneum* (1835). An English resident of Naples, he acted as a visitors' guide, and it was in that capacity that, leading Dickens down Mount Vesuvius, he slipped, fell a considerable distance and was knocked unconscious.

PICKWICK, Samuel, in Charles Dickens's *The Posthumous Papers of the Pickwick Club* (1836–7). It was the author's publisher, Edward Chapman, who commended his friend John Foster to Dickens as the model for Pickwick. An old-world beau, of Richmond, Surrey, Foster affected drab, old-fashioned tights and black gaiters. Chapman's description of Foster was also the basis of the novel's original illustrations by Robert Seymour, whose first sketches — of a tall, thin man — were rejected. Pickwick's name was taken from Moses Pickwick, coach proprietor, of the White Hart Hotel, Bath, which Dickens observed painted on the door of a Bath coach. Moses Pickwick in turn derived his name from the village of Pickwick, or Pickwick Street, near Bath, where he was found abandoned as an infant and taken to Corsham Workhouse.

PICKWORT, Hedgepinshot Mandeville, in Wyndham Lewis's *The Apes of God* (1930), is the poet, biographer and translator Edgell Rickword (1898–). Lewis's biographer, Jeffrey Meyers, notes how Rickword, in 'The Encounter' (1931; *Collected Poems*, 1947), replied deftly to Lewis's clumsily worded attack.

PIERCE, Hugo, in Emma Tennant's *Woman Beware Woman* (1983). A *cause célèbre* involving the novelist Graham Greene (1904–) led to him becoming a prototype for Hugo Pierce. In 1979 he began a campaign against the municipality of Nice, alleging corruption. His move was prompted by the belief that the daughter of some old friends was being unjustly treated. Though divorced, she was still required to live near her ex-husband. Greene published a pamphlet, *J'Accuse*, claiming his life had been threatened, and in 1983 a Paris court ordered him to pay 30,000 francs in libel damages. The episode was followed with interest by Emma Tennant, and it is echoed, as she admits, in *Woman Beware Woman*. Pierce, a celebrated author, is found murdered after he seeks to defend a local woman against mistreatment by her husband.

PIERCE, Joel, in Thomas Wolfe's *Of Time and the River* (1935), is the author's artist friend, Olin Dows, four years Wolfe's junior, but his contemporary at Harvard. Dows was the son of a wealthy family of Rhinebeck, New York.

PIERSON, Brigitte, in Alfred de Musset's *The Confessions of a Child of the Age* (1836), is George Sand (see Maupin, Camille), with whom the author fell in love in 1832, the two going together to Italy. De Musset later returned alone, following a rift for which he blames himself in this novel. George Sand's reply, after his death, was *Elle et lui*, which also held him culpable. See also Falconey, Édouard de; Laurent; and Olympe.

PILOT, the, in James Fenimore Cooper's *The Pilot* (1823), is believed to represent John Paul Jones (1747–92), a Scottish hero of the American navy. In 1779 he captured the British warship *Serapis*, later serving briefly in the Russian navy before settling in Paris in 1789.

PIMPERNELL, in Evelyn Waugh's *Put Out More Flags* (1942), is the novelist Christopher Isherwood (1904–), who incurred Waugh's contempt by going to New York at the outbreak of the Second World War (see also Parsnip). Questioned about this episode, Isherwood in 1984 said that at the time of the Munich crisis he had volunteered for the War Office. Nothing had come of this, and he was already in the United States when war was declared. He could not have shot a Nazi, anyway – his first-hand observation in 1938 of the Japanese invasion of China and his love for a German (see Norris, Arthur) had made him a pacifist, and in the United States he registered as a conscientious objector.

PINKERTON, in *The Wrecker* (1892), by Robert Louis Stevenson and Lloyd Osbourne, is Samuel Sidney McClure (1857–1949), who in 1884 founded the first newspaper syndicate in the United States and later published *McClure's Magazine* (1893–1929). In 1888, he paid for Stevenson's move to Samoa.

PIPCHIN, Mrs, in Charles Dickens's *Dombey and Son* (1847–8), is part-inspired by Mrs Elizabeth Roylance, with whom the author and his parents lodged in London, at 37 Little College Street, Camden Town. Dickens also lodged with her in Bayham Street, when his parents moved into Marshalsea Prison. Previously, she had boarded children in Brighton.

PIRELLI, Cardinal, in Ronald Firbank's *The Princess Zoubaroff* (1920), is suggested by Firbank's biographer, Brigid Brophy, to be a composite of Oscar Wilde (see Amarinth, Esme) and Firbank himself.

PLAGIARY, Sir Fretful, in Richard Brinsley Sheridan's *The Critic* (1779), is the playwright and translator Richard Cumberland (1732–1811), who is said to have incensed Sheridan with his behaviour at the first night of *The School for Scandal* (1777).

PLANTAGENET, Ruth, in Malcolm Lowry's *Lunar Caustic* (1963), is the author's first wife, Jan Gabrial, according to Lowry's biographer, Douglas Day. They first met when Lowry was staying with Conrad Aiken in Granada in 1933; they were married in Paris in the following year, and divorced in 1938.

PLEYDELL, Paul, in Sir Walter Scott's *Guy Mannering* (1815), owes his sagacity to the author's friend, Adam Rolland (1734–1819), an Edinburgh lawyer who became Deputy Governor of the Bank of Scotland, and his high spirits to Andrew Crosbie (1735–85), an Edinburgh advocate noted for his eloquence and addiction to the tavern. In 1773 Crosbie met Samuel Johnson during the latter's tour of Scotland, and Boswell's *Life* contains a number of references to him.

PLUNKETT, Matthew, in Wyndham Lewis's *The Apes of God* (1930), is identified by the author's biographer, Jeffrey Meyers, as the essayist and biographer Lytton Strachey (1880–1932), who was celebrated for his irreverent *Eminent Victorians* (1918). He was a leading Bloomsbury figure, and a homosexual. His advances were repulsed by a disgusted Mark Gertler (see Loerke), and when he was on the rebound from Duncan Grant (see Forbes, Duncan) he proposed to Virginia Woolf who, to his horror, accepted, whereupon he promptly withdrew the offer. Dora Carrington (see Morrison) worshipped him, and to oblige him married the man he loved, but who loved her, the three setting up home together. Cancer of the stomach killed him. 'If this is dying,' he remarked, 'I don't think much of it.'

PLURABELLE, Anna Livia, in James Joyce's *Finnegans Wake* (1939), is an amalgam of Nora Barnacle (see Bloom, Molly) and Livia Veneziani Schmitz, a handsome woman noted for her magnificent hair. Schmitz was the wife of Italo Svevo (see Bloom, Leopold).

PODD, in Ford Madox Ford's *The Marsden Case* (1923). Disgruntled authors have a novel way of settling scores. Podd is the publisher John Lane (1854–1925), who Ford felt had treated him less than generously in his payment for *The Good Soldier*. Lane, however, claimed the novel had earned the author £67 11s 11d and lost the publisher £54 10s. A former Euston Station railway clerk, Lane was co-founder of the Bodley Head publishing house, and founder, in 1894, of *The Yellow Book*. Those with whom he failed to hit it off included Oscar Wilde, who expressed his opinion of Lane by naming the butler after him in *The Importance of Being Earnest*.

PODSNAP, Mr, in Charles Dickens's *Our Mutual Friend* (1864–5). Dickens's pompous but nevertheless lovable biographer John Forster (1812–76) recognised a few of his mannerisms in Podsnap, though he failed to notice that this 'vulgar, canting' character (his words) relied upon him for more than idiosyncracies – one of his habits was to assume he had rendered the unpalatable non-existent, simply by denying it. The son of a Newcastle butcher and cattle-dealer, he became a barrister and was later editor of the *Examiner*, the *Foreign Quarterly Review* and the *Daily News*. He was also an influential and perceptive critic, with a finger on the pulse of popular taste. He it was who persuaded Tennyson to restore the deleted lines, 'Half a league, half a league/Half a league onward . . .' as the opening of 'The Charge of the Light Brigade'.

POINTET, Odile, in Georges Simenon's *The Disappearance of Odile* (1971), has as prototype the author's daughter, Marie-Jo Simenon (1953–78), who after innumerable love affairs committed suicide in her Paris flat. Written to re-establish communication between father and daughter, the novel was inspired by Marie-Jo's first clandestine flight to Paris from her father's home in Switzerland.

POLEHUE, Mr, in *Gin and Bitters* (1931), by A. Riposte (Elinor Mordaunt), is Hugh Walpole (see Kear, Alroy). *Gin and Bitters* was published as a reply to Somerset Maugham's *Cakes and Ale*, and according to Walpole 'positively bristles with hate'. Walpole was writing to Maugham, attempting to persuade him to seek an injunction; see Hurle, Leverson.

POLINA ALEXANDROVNA, in Fyodor Dostoevsky's *The Gambler* (1866), is Apollinaria Suslova, a factory-owner's daughter who met the author in 1861 when she submitted a story to a magazine he was editing. She was twenty-two at the time. Dostoevsky seduced her and they toured Europe on a gambling spree, but she soon tired of him, departing when they had gambled all their money away. In 1880, at the age of forty, she married the essayist and critic Vasily Rozanov, who was sixteen years her junior and whom she deserted six years later. For seventeen years she refused Rozanov a divorce, despite his acquisition of a common-law wife and two children.

POLITICAL APOTHECARY, the, in Henry Fielding's *The History of Tom Jones, a Foundling* (1749). So insatiable was Thomas Arne's thirst for news and others' opinions on current affairs that he became the model not only for Fielding's Political Apothecary but also for the Political Upholsterer in Joseph Addison and Richard Steele's *Tatler* paper No. 155 and for Quidnunc in Arthur Murphy's *The Upholsterer, or What's New?* (1737). The father of the composer of 'Rule, Britannia' and of the actress Susannah Cibber, Arne was an upholsterer in King Street, Covent Garden.

POLLY, Aunt, in Mark Twain's *The Adventures of Tom Sawyer* (1876), is the author's mother, Jane Lampton, who in 1823 married John Marshall Clemens at Lexington, Kentucky, bringing with her a dowry of two or three Negro slaves. She died in 1890.

P.O.M. (Poor Old Mama), in Ernest Hemingway's *The Green Hills of Africa* (1935), is the author's second wife, Pauline Pfeiffer (1895—1951), the daughter of a landowner of Piggott, Arkansas. At the time of their first meeting she was working for the Paris edition of *Vogue*. They married in 1927 and were divorced thirteen years later.

POMERAY, Cody, in Jack Kerouac's *The Dharma Bums* (1958), *Visions of Cody* (1960), *Book of Dreams* (1961), *Big Sur* (1962) and *Desolation Angels* (1965), is Neal Cassady (see Moriarty, Dean). Barry Gifford and Lawrence Lee's *Jack's Book: Jack Kerouac in the Lives and Words of his Friends* (1979) reveals as much as any reader is likely to want to know about all Kerouac's sources.

POMPOSO, in Charles Churchill's *The Ghost* (1762—3), is Dr Samuel Johnson (1709—84), the essayist, critic, poet and lexicographer, whose forthright manner made him enemies (like Churchill), as well as friends.

PONDEREVO, Edward and George, in H.G. Wells's *Tono-Bungay* (1909). Edward is an amalgam of Samuel Evan Cowap, a Sussex chemist to whom Wells was briefly apprenticed in 1881; Lord Northcliffe (see Tilbury, Lord); and the company promoter Whitaker Wright (1845–1904). Wright emigrated from England to the United States, where he became an assayer and founded his fortune on successful speculation in mining shares. He floated a number of prospecting and mining companies and returned to England to live in conspicuous style at Lea Park in Surrey. There his establishment included a private theatre and observatory and a billiard saloon beneath a lake. He also maintained a London residence, in Park Lane, well-stocked with art treasures. Upon being sentenced to seven years' imprisonment for defrauding shareholders, he committed suicide by taking poison. George Ponderevo owes the manner of his demise to George Gissing (see Maitland, Henry), whose death-bed Wells attended.

PONTIEUX, Professor, in Arthur Koestler's *The Age of Longing* (1951), is the French philosopher Maurice Merleau-Ponty (1908–61), who resisted the concept of absolute freedom embraced by some of his colleagues of the Left, and in *Humanism and Terror* (1947) attacked the ideology of Koestler's *Darkness at Noon*.

PONTIFEX, Alethea and Theobald, in Samuel Butler's *The Way of All Flesh* (1903). Although almost the same age as Butler, the original of Aunt Alethea (in mind but not in body) was also something of an 'aunt' in the author's life: a friend whose judgement he valued and to whom he often turned for advice. He met Eliza Mary Ann Savage (1836–85) when both were art-students in 1870. In appearance she was unprepossessing: plain, lame, short and fat. But she had a lively mind and wit, and on her death Butler recorded, 'I never knew any woman to approach her at once for brilliancy and goodness.' He described his feelings towards her in his poetry. 'I liked, but like and love are far removed; / Hard though I tried to love I tried in vain.' The Revd Theobald Pontifex is the author's tyrannical father, the Revd Thomas Butler (1806–86). The son of a headmaster of Shrewsbury School who became Bishop of Lichfield, he was himself a Shrewsbury master before becoming rector of Langar, Nottinghamshire, and a canon of Lincoln. Perpetually at odds with his son, who felt he could never please him, he accused the author of killing his mother by publishing *Erewhon*.

POOKWORTHY, Anthony, A.B.S., L.L.R., in Stella Gibbons's *Cold Comfort Farm* (1932), is Hugh Walpole (see Kear, Alroy), who was noted for his generous interest in aspiring young writers. The encouragement he gave was thought by some, however, to be not altogether altruistic. Thus, the initials which Gibbons places after Pookworthy's name stand for Associate Back Scratcher and Licensed Log Roller.

POPE JOHN XXIV, in Kingsley Amis's *The Alteration* (1976). Anthony Burgess first suggested that the model for Amis's pope was the novelist John Braine (1922–), and Tom Miller, interviewing Amis for the *Illustrated London News* (September 1978), asked for a confirmation. 'Mr Amis laughed', Miller reported, 'and said that the Pope had started as John Braine, who had been very nice about his appearance in the book.'

PORTER, Alison, in John Osborne's *Look Back in Anger* (1956). The last time I saw John Osborne he was wheeling his bicycle across the pavement to his flat in Derby, where he was an undistinguished, soon-to-be-sacked member of the town's repertory company. That was two years before *Look Back in Anger*, which owes not a little to Derby: Alison Porter is Osborne's first wife, Pamela Lane, who was the leading lady at the Derby Playhouse; and the play's Cliff Lewis was taken by colleagues to be another member of the company. Osborne had met Pamela Lane in repertory in Bridgwater in 1951. Her parents had a drapery business in the town and were dismayed by the prospect of their daughter marrying Osborne. Fearing him to be homosexual (he was being pursued by a fellow actor), they hired a private detective to follow him, as he records in *A Better Class of Person* (1981). I remember Pamela Lane as an actress who was never less than adequate. She had a statuesque figure which inclined to the generous, and she looked rather more mature than her years. In 1954 she left Osborne for a Derby dentist, and the marriage was dissolved in 1957.

PORTER, the Rt Hon. Sir Joseph, KCB, in W.S. Gilbert's libretto for Arthur Sullivan's *HMS Pinafore* (1878). 'You would naturally think', reflected Gilbert, 'that a person who commanded the entire British Navy would be the most accomplished sailor who could be found, but that is not the way in which such things are managed in England.' In 1877 Disraeli had appointed as First Lord of the Admiralty an MP who was best known as a pioneer of railway-station bookstalls: W.H. Smith (1825—91). But in poking fun at the apparent absurdity of having in charge of the navy a civilian who might not know one end of a ship from the other, Gilbert went out of his way to make it clear that nothing personal was intended: it was the office he was lampooning, not the individual. Thus, he wrote to Sullivan, 'the fact that the First Lord in the opera is a radical of the most pronounced type will do away with any suspicion that W.H. Smith is intended.' Nevertheless, Disraeli later referred to his First Lord as 'Pinafore Smith'.

PORTER, Mrs Joseph, in Charles Dickens's 'Mrs Joseph Porter "Over the Way"' (1834; *Sketches by 'Boz'*, 1836), is supposedly Mrs John Porter Leigh, wife of a London corn merchant (see Budden, Octavius) and mother of Marianne Leigh (see Dartle, Rosa).

PORTER, Lola, in Ford Madox Ford's *When the Wicked Man* (1931), is the novelist Jean Rhys (?1890—1979), who had earlier portrayed Ford (see Heidler, Hugh). She had an affair with him while he was living with Stella Bowen (see Wannop, Valentine). In the early 1950s, when nothing had been heard of her for some time, Rhys was thought to be dead. 'Tactless of me to be still alive', she said, on being discovered in Devon.

PORTHOS, in *The Three Musketeers* (1844), by Alexandre Dumas *père*, has as prototype Isaac de Portau, grandson of Abraham de Portau, comptroller of the household of Henry IV. Born in Pau, Isaac became a King's Musketeer in 1643.

PORTMAN, Dr, in W.M. Thackeray's *The History of Pendennis* (1848—50), is the Revd Dr Sidney Cornish, vicar of Ottery St Mary, Devon, where the author spent part of his youth. He has been credited with teaching Thackeray to judge port.

POTT, Mustard, in P.G. Wodehouse's *Uncle Fred in the Springtime* (1939), is supposedly Hugh Cecil Lowther, Fifth Earl of Lonsdale (1857—1944), whose distinctive yellow barouche in London was known as the 'Mustard Pot'. As a penurious young man he was reduced to near-bankruptcy by his taste for high living, but in 1882, upon the premature deaths of those separating him from a fortune, he became the owner of a 50,000-acre estate, with a couple of steam yachts at Cowes, two castles, houses in London and Newmarket ... and an income of nearly £4,000 a week. He was noted for telling tall stories, claiming to have discovered the North Pole (which he swore was pink) and to have met Rasputin in Siberia (though he had never been there). Spending £3,000 a year on cigars, he ran a fleet of twenty-eight cars and instituted boxing's Lonsdale Belt. For this, and several other Wodehouse 'leads', I am obliged to N.T.P. Murphy's *In Search of Blandings* (1981).

POUNCE, Peter, in Henry Fielding's *The History of the Adventures of Joseph Andrews* (1742), is believed to be Peter Walter (?1664—1746), of Stalbridge Park, Dorset. A usurer who left £300,000, he is also supposedly portrayed in Plate I of Hogarth's 'Marriage à la Mode'.

POVEY, Dick, in Arnold Bennett's *The Old Wives' Tale* (1908), is part-inspired by H.K. Hales. See Machin, Denry.

POWLEY, the Revd Rowley, in Lord Byron's *Don Juan* (1818—22), is the Revd George Croly (1780—1860), a prolific Irish poet, novelist, critic and historian who in 1835 became rector of St Stephen's, Walbrook, in London. His poem *Paris in 1815* (1817) was imitative of Byron's *Childe Harold's Pilgrimage*. 'Croly once asked me if I had read a certain book,' another critic recorded. 'I said yes, I had reviewed it. "What!" he exclaimed. "Do you read the books you review?" "Yes, as a rule I do." "That's wrong, it creates a prejudice."'

POYSER, Mrs Rachel, in George Eliot's *Adam Bede* (1859), is the author's mother, Mrs Robert Evans (née Christiana Pearson, 1788—1836). In 1813 she became the second wife of Eliot's widowed father, her family taking the view that she had married beneath her.

POZDNYSHEV, Madame, in Leo Tolstoy's *The Kreutzer Sonata* (1889), is the author's wife, Sofya ('Sonya') Andreyevna Behrs (1844—1919). With monumental insensitivity, he gave her the manuscript of this bitter indictment of their marriage to copy, noting in his diary that she was 'very much affected by it'. They had just celebrated their silver wedding with her latest pregnancy. The daughter of a Moscow doctor, she married Tolstoy when she was eighteen, he thirty-four. She bore him thirteen children and was a martyr to his egotism, his concept of woman's subservience to man, and his sexual inhibitions — a man of many contradictions, he was racked equally by lust and feelings of sexual guilt and self-disgust. In her later years Sonya was plagued by hysteria which has been attributed in part to sexual frustration. Making love with Tolstoy cannot have been pleasant. Getting him to wash, she said, was like pulling teeth — 'I can never get used to the dirt, the bad smell', she noted in her diary. (Each kept a candid journal, showing it to the other: in theory, a laudable notion; in practice, a disaster causing them misery and anger.) He espoused the cause of freeing the peasants by living like one himself, renouncing his title and giving away his money. Sonya saw her security further threatened by his intention to make his friend Vladimir Chertkov his literary executor. Though Tolstoy was by now eighty-two, she accused him of having a homosexual relationship with Chertkov, then in his late sixties. Leaving a note thanking her for 'the forty-eight years of honourable life you spent with me', Tolstoy fled the house. He took a train for nowhere in particular, was taken ill on the journey and died in a stationmaster's cottage. Sonya — who had headed for that railway more than once in unconvincing suicide attempts — pursued him by special train. At his death-bed she sought his forgiveness. He had said it all in *The Kreutzer Sonata*: 'We were two convicts serving life sentences of hard labour welded to the same chain.'

PREMIER, the, in Georges Simenon's *The Premier* (1958), has as prototype the French statesman Georges Clemenceau (1841–1929). Nicknamed 'Le Tigre', he was an authoritarian who, although deaf and in his seventies, became a hero of France when he led his country in the latter part of the First World War. His attempts to ensure post-war security against Germany were less successful, and he retired after his defeat in the 1920 presidential elections.

PRESLEY, in Frank Norris's *The Octopus* (1901), is believed to be the Californian poet Edwin Markham (1852–1940), best known for his blank verse portrayal of a brutalised farmer, *The Man with the Hoe* (1899).

PREST, Mrs, in Henry James's *The Aspern Papers* (1888), is suggested by the author's biographer, Leon Edel, to be Katherine Bronson (née De Kay), an American expatriate whose salon in Venice was frequented by British and American callers, Robert Browning and Henry James among them.

PRESTON, Ned, in W. Somerset Maugham's *Creatures of Circumstance* (1947), is Alan Searle, the author's secretary/lover in his later years. Maugham first met him in 1928, when Searle — the son of a Bermondsey tailor — was twenty-four. Nicknamed 'The Bronzino Boy' by Lytton Strachey, he worked for the Discharged Prisoners' Aid Society, and his prison-visiting recollections provided plots for two of the stories in *Creatures of Circumstance*, 'The Episode' and 'The Kite'. In 1962, obsessed by the suspicion that his daughter might have him certified insane, Maugham sought to foil such a move by adopting Searle as his son.

PRICE, John, in Max Egremont's *The Ladies' Man* (1983), has as prototype the British statesman John Profumo (1915–), who in 1963 confessed that he had lied to the House of Commons about his association with a call-girl, Christine Keeler, and resigned his post as Secretary for War, also giving up his seat in the House. Both the *Sunday Telegraph* and the *Observer* reviews of this novel remarked on the plot's parallel with the Profumo episode, the *Sunday Telegraph* commenting that the story resembled the Profumo affair 'so closely that the reader cannot help identifying characters. Or rather recognising which slots in the tale the novel's characters fit, because all have been much altered.'

PRINGLE, Guy, in Olivia Manning's *The Balkan Trilogy* (1960–5) and *The Levant Trilogy* (1977–80), is the author's husband, Reginald Donald Smith (1914–85). At their wedding, Louis MacNeice (see MacSpaunday) was best man and the poet and novelist Stevie Smith was bridesmaid. At the outbreak of war in 1939 he was in Bucharest, on the staff of the British Council. He was subsequently a BBC drama producer and a professor at the New University of Ulster.

PROFESSOR, the, in Mark Twain's *Tom Sawyer Abroad* (1894), is part-inspired by James W. Paige, the inventor of an automatic typesetting machine in which the author invested — and lost — a fortune. Too sophisticated and temperamental, it comprised some 18,000 individual parts, and bankrupted Twain on a scale from which he took years to recover.

PROKTOPHANTASMIST, in Johann Wolfgang von Goethe's *Faust* (1808–32), is Christoph Friedrich Nicolai (1733–1811), author, bookseller and associate of G.E. Lessing and Moses Mendelssohn (see Nathan). He sought to ridicule Goethe in a parody of *Werther*. Goethe's name for him derives from Nicolai's affliction by visitations from apparitions, of which he was cured by having leeches applied to the base of his spine.

PROSPERO, Duke of Milan, in William Shakespeare's *The Tempest* (*c.* 1611), is supposedly the mathematician and astrologer Dr John Dee (1527–1608), who found it necessary to petition James I in order to have himself officially cleared of allegations that he was a magician. He lived in Mortlake, London, as did Shakespeare's friend and partner Augustine Phillips, and it has been conjectured that the dramatist thus came to know him. Dee's reputation as a 'magician' was such, however, that Shakespeare would almost certainly have known of him anyway.

PROTEUS, in George Bernard Shaw's *The Apple Cart* (1929), is Ramsay MacDonald. See Shand, John.

PROUT, Mr, in Rudyard Kipling's *Stalky and Co.* (1899), is believed to be M.H. Pugh, the author's housemaster at the United Services College, Westward Ho. After leaving the school, Kipling was angered to discover that Pugh had suspected him of being homosexual.

PROVIS, Estella, in Charles Dickens's *Great Expectations* (1860–1), is supposedly the author's alleged mistress, Ellen Lawless Ternan (*d.* 1914), who was an eighteen-year-old actress when Dickens first met her in Manchester in 1857. Her father, an Irish actor, managed the Theatre Royal, Doncaster, and in 1846 committed suicide in an asylum. Her mother, a noted actress in her day, died in 1873. Ellen Ternan retired from the stage in 1859. In 1876, after Dickens's death, she married a Margate schoolmaster-clergyman, George Wharton Robinson, who was twelve years her junior. Her novelist sister, Frances Eleanor, became the second wife of Anthony Trollope's eldest brother. Maria Beadnell (see Spenlow, Dora) has also been suggested as Estella's original, but the timing favours Ternan; she was undoubtedly much in Dickens's mind when he wrote *Great Expectations*.

PRY, Paul, in John Poole's *Paul Pry* (1825), is believed to be Thomas Hill (1760–1840), drysalter, book-collector, gossip, *bon vivant* and part-proprietor of the *Monthly Mirror*. At his cottage in

Sydenham he became a noted host to men of letters, his gatherings being known as 'Sydenham Sundays'. His secretiveness about his age prompted friends to quiz him on the Armada and the Norman Conquest, of which they implied he must have first-hand knowledge.

PRY, Mrs Priscilla, in Charles Lamb's 'Tom Pry's Wife' (1825), is Mary Jane Godwin, grandmother of Lord Byron's daughter, Allegra, and second wife of the political philosopher and novelist William Godwin (1756—1836). Both widowed, they married in 1801.

PRYNNE, Amanda, in Noël Coward's *Private Lives* (1930). 'Edwina and I spent all our married lives getting into other people's beds', said Lord Mountbatten, according to his biographer, Philip Ziegler. This was an exaggeration so far as he was concerned, but Lady (subsequently Countess) Mountbatten (1901—60) was decidedly flighty. The couple were close friends of Coward, who based Amanda Prynne on Edwina. She was the daughter of Lord Mount Temple, granddaughter of the German-Jewish financier Sir Ernest Cassel, and great granddaughter of the Seventh Earl of Shaftesbury. When she married Lord Louis Mountbatten (see Gilpin, Commander Peter), in 1922, she gave him a Rolls-Royce for a wedding present. Her married life was noted for a number of extra-marital relationships — her name was linked with Laddie Sandford, a wealthy American polo player; with Paul Robeson, the American singer; and with Jawaharlal Nehru, the Indian statesman. With the Second World War came a social conscience which prompted her to join the St John Ambulance Brigade, for which she did relief work in Britain during the Blitz. She died, allegedly from exhaustion, touring north Borneo in her role as the Brigade's Superintendent-in-Chief.

PRYNNE, Hester, in Nathaniel Hawthorne's *The Scarlet Letter* (1850), is believed to be part-inspired by the Countess of Somerset who in 1615 was tried for the murder of the poet Sir Thomas Overbury. As Lady Essex, a woman of dubious reputation, she wished to divorce her husband and marry Overbury's close friend, Lord Rochester. Overbury's opposition to the match prompted her to plot to make him appear disrespectful to the King, and Overbury was consequently imprisoned in the Tower of London, where Lady Essex managed to have the governor replaced by her own nominee.

Overbury was poisoned by his gaoler and Lady Essex married Rochester — by now the Earl of Somerset — two months later. When the plot came to light, four of the conspirators involved were tried and hanged. The Countess was spared, although she pleaded guilty. Hawthorne is known to have made a special study of the case.

PSMITH, Ronald Eustace Rupert, in P.G. Wodehouse's Psmith stories (1909—23). The inspiration for Psmith came from the author's cousin's account of his monocled schoolfellow at Winchester, Rupert D'Oyly Carte (1876—1948). The son of Richard D'Oyly Carte, the Gilbert and Sullivan impresario, Rupert became proprietor of the D'Oyly Carte Opera Company and chairman of London's Savoy, Berkeley and New Claridges hotel companies. To that identification, by David A. Jasen's *P.G. Wodehouse: A Portrait of a Master* (1975), Benny Green's *P.G. Wodehouse: A Literary Biography* (1981) adds the suggestion that Psmith's politics may owe something to Henry Mayers Hyndman. See Tanner, John.

PUFFER, Princess, in Charles Dickens's *The Mystery of Edwin Drood* (1870), is believed to be 'Lascar Sal', proprietor of an opium den in New Court, St George's in the East, London. Her establishment was visited by the author on more than one occasion.

PUMPHREY, Mrs, in the 'vet' stories of James Herriot, commencing with *If Only They Could Talk* (1970), is Miss Marjorie Warner (*d.* 1983), of Sowerby, Yorkshire. She was eighty-six when she died, and left the greater part of her £90,000 estate to the old and needy.

PUPICK, Rudolph, who at the age of five months rejects breast-feeding on grounds of immorality in Ben Hecht and Maxwell Bodenheim's *Cutie, a Warm Mamma* (1924), has a probable prototype in John S. Sumner, a campaigner against pornography. In 1925 he brought charges against Bodenheim and his publisher, alleging obscenity in Bodenheim's *Replenishing Jessica*.

PURSEWARDEN, in Lawrence Durrell's *Alexandria Quartet* (1957—60), notably *Clea* (1960). All the characters in the *Quartet* are 'tremendously composite', the author told Peter Adam in a BBC television interview published in the *Listener* (20 April 1978). 'There's no Kodak work in that at all — no happy snaps of live personages.' Pursewarden was his favourite character. Why? 'Well, he's such a bastard!' Was there a lot of Durrell in Pursewarden? asked Adam. 'I'd like to think there was, yes. I think I haven't got his courage.' Some aspects of Pursewarden, however, are modelled on Wyndham Lewis (see Lypiatt, Casimir), according to Lewis's biographer, Jeffrey Meyers. Durrell admired Lewis — 'What a tremendous proser!' — but they never met.

PUSSUM, in D.H. Lawrence's *Women in Love* (1920), is Minnie Lucie Channing (*b.* 1894), who worked in London as an artists' model and was known as 'The Puma', presumably because of her black, shiny hair. Philip Heseltine (Peter Warlock; see Halliday, Julius) presented her with a son and married her although, as he explained to a friend, their relationship had never been other than physical.

PYE, Wilfred, in Malcolm Muggeridge's *Winter in Moscow* (1934), is the writer Arthur Ransome (1884–1967), to whom Muggeridge owed his introduction to professional journalism. In the late 1920s Muggeridge was lecturing at Cairo University. He sent the *Manchester Guardian* some articles on Egyptian politics, upon which Ransome was reporting. Ransome went to see Muggeridge at the newspaper's suggestion, and it was on his recommendation that Muggeridge joined the *Manchester Guardian*. In 1984, Muggeridge recalled how he had been much in awe of Ransome, who had covered the Russian Revolution, played chess with Lenin and married Trotsky's secretary. But after seeing Russia for himself in the 1930s, he no longer took Ransome seriously as a reporter. Ransome's view of Russia was that of a romantic, he concluded, and in the *Observer* for 29 January 1984 he remarked that Ransome 'first went to Russia to collect fairy stories and the big fairy story he collected was his picture of the Soviet regime.'

PYNCHEON, Judge Jaffrey, in Nathaniel Hawthorne's *The House of the Seven Gables* (1851). Conjure up a name like Pyncheon, you might think, and you'll have no trouble. Not so. When this novel appeared the Pyncheons of the world soon let Hawthorne know of their existence. One of them complained that it was monstrous that the virtuous dead could not be allowed to rest quietly in their graves: his grandfather, Judge Pyncheon, a Tory and refugee living in Salem at the time of the Revolution, had been made infamous because of Hawthorne's story and its Salem setting. 'The joke of the matter', Hawthorne told his publisher, 'is that I never heard of his grandfather, nor knew that any Pyncheons had ever lived in Salem, but took the name because it suited the tone of my book and was as much my property for fictitious purposes as that of Smith.' Hawthorne — whose great-grandfather had been a judge at the Salem witch trials — is believed to have had quite another person in mind when he created Pyncheon, Charles Wentworth Upham (1802–75), a Salem Unitarian minister who was a brother-in-law of Oliver Wendell Holmes and who wrote two studies of the Salem trials of 1692. As yet another Pyncheon protested, the author wrote to his publisher, 'I wonder if ever, and how soon, I shall get a just estimate of how many jackasses there are in this ridiculous world.' His latest correspondent estimated the number of Pyncheons to be about twenty. 'I am doubtless to be remonstrated with by each individual. After exchanging shots with each one of them, I shall get you to publish the whole correspondence in a style to match that of my other works, and I anticipate a great run for the volume.'

Q

QUARLES, Elinor, in Aldous Huxley's *Point Counter Point* (1928). As a teenage Belgian refugee, Maria Nys (1898–1955) was taken under the wing of Lady Ottoline Morrell (see Roddice, Hermione) at Garsington, where Huxley first met her in 1916. Three years later they were married. His model for Elinor Quarles, she became the first woman in Italy to hold a driving licence. When the Huxleys ordered a Bugatti, their new car's builder, Ettore Bugatti, was so surprised to learn that a woman was to drive one of his machines that he asked to meet her. In *Aldous Huxley* (1973–4), Sybille Bedford records that, apart from Huxley's brief infatuation with Nancy Cunard (see Storm, Iris), the marriage was a happy one. Maria encouraged her husband in a number of casual affairs, some of which she even helped to engineer. In addition to acting as Huxley's secretary, she typed the manuscript of D.H. Lawrence's *Lady Chatterley's Lover*. As a Belgian, she was unfamiliar with the niceties of the English language, and Lawrence was shocked to hear her using in conversation some of the four-letter words she had typed.

QUATERMAIN, Allan, in the novels of H. Rider Haggard, notably *King Solomon's Mines* (1885) and *Allan Quatermain* (1887), was taken to be the explorer and gold prospector Frederick Courteney Selous (1851–1917). The author denied the identification, although he knew Selous, who had stayed at his Norfolk home. The name Quatermain was taken from a farmer in Garsington, Oxfordshire, where Haggard spent part of his childhood.

QUIGGIN, J.G., in Anthony Powell's *A Dance to the Music of Time* sequence (1951–75), is part-inspired by the author and critic Cyril Connolly (1903–74), founder-editor of *Horizon* (1939) and principal reviewer of books for the *Sunday Times* from 1952 to 1974. Harold Nicolson raised an eloquent eyebrow at his use of a rasher of bacon as a bookmark, and Virginia Woolf called him 'Smarty Boots', a nickname which stuck.

QUILP, Daniel, in Charles Dickens's *The Old Curiosity Shop* (1840–1), is one Prior, a hirer of donkeys for children's rides in Bath, to whom Dickens was introduced in 1840. He reputedly beat his beasts and wife without discrimination.

QUIN, Auberon, in G.K. Chesterton's *The Napoleon of Notting Hill* (1904), was taken to be Sir Max Beerbohm (1872–1956) who, in the words of Malcolm Muggeridge, grew 'ever more famous in literary and intellectual circles with every book he did not write'. An essayist, caricaturist and writer of short stories, he was identified with Quin because, according to Sir Rupert Hart-Davis, editor of Beerbohm's letters, the novel's illustrator, W. Graham Robertson, used him as Quin's model. Beerbohm was not displeased by the identification.

QUINN, Mortimer, in Noël Coward's *Point Valaine* (1935). There are times when the dedication of a work is a way of saying, 'Thanks for letting me borrow you'. *Point Valaine* is dedicated to W. Somerset Maugham (see Bertrand, Archie). Was this Coward's way of disarming Maugham, who has much in common with Mortimer Quinn? The character is presented as a celebrated writer. He has 'a certain dry aloofness in his manner but in spite of his enviable detachment he is quite amiable and polite'. The description is charitable: Maugham could be abominably rude when he wished.

QUINT, Peter, in Henry James's 'The Turn of the Screw' (*The Two Magics*, 1898). Did James have the Irish dramatist George Bernard Shaw (1856–1950) in mind when he created Quint? It seems unlikely . . . until you think about it, as E.A. Sheppard does in *Henry James and 'The Turn of the Screw'* (1974). First, there is the physical likeness. Had James been describing Shaw rather than Quint, he could not have painted a more accurate portrait. Coupled with this Mephistophelean appearance – remember, we are talking about a comparatively young Shaw, before the turn of the century – was the dramatist's reputation as a womanising political agitator. Shaw and Quint also share an unconventional dress sense. Furthermore, Shaw was known to have had a relationship with Mrs Annie Besant (see Petkoff, Raina), just as Quint had an affair with Miss Jessel: not a common name, but where have we heard it before? The judge who in 1879 deprived Mrs Besant of the custody of her daughter was Sir George Jessel.

QUINTUS, Reggie, in Ronald Firbank's *The Princess Zoubaroff* (1920). Given half a chance, Firbank would have been the Lord Alfred Douglas in Oscar Wilde's life, treating Wilde rather better than did Douglas. That is the view of Firbank's biographer, Brigid Brophy, who believes Quintus to be part Firbank and part Lord Alfred Douglas (see Hastings, Lord Reggie). Brophy points to the assonance of the names Reggie Quintus and 'Bosie' Douglas, and to the play's stage directions: 'Enter ... Reggie Quintus. Incredibly young. Incredibly good-looking. No one would suppose him to have figured as hero already in at least one *cause célèbre.*'

QUIXOTE, Don, in Miguel de Cervantes's *Don Quixote* (1605–15), is supposedly part-inspired by Alonso Quixada, an Augustinian friar of Esquivias, near Toledo. The author's great-uncle by marriage, he is reputed to have believed every word of chivalry's romances.

R

R, in W. Somerset Maugham's *Ashenden* (1928), is said by the author's biographer, Ted Morgan, to be Sir John Wallinger (1872–1931). After service with the Imperial Indian Police he became a major with the Imperial General Staff in the First World War, working for British Intelligence in France and Switzerland. In 1915 he recruited Maugham as an agent. From 1919 until his retirement in 1926 he was Deputy Inspector-General of Police.

R, Mlle, in Jean Cocteau's *Le Livre blanc* (1928), is based on Beatrice Hastings (*b.* 1879), a South African partial to outlandish attire – she would dress as an eighteenth-century shepherdess, complete with crook and basket of live ducks. After working in London for the *New Age* – and living with its editor, Alfred Orage – she went to Paris, where she became the mistress of the artist Modigliani and had a brief affair with Raymond Radiguet (see H), although she was more than twice his age.

R, Mrs, in Alexander Solzhenitsyn's *The First Circle* (1955–64). Writing in the *New Humanist* in 1972, W.J. Igoe suggested that Solzhenitsyn's Mrs R is Mrs Eleanor Roosevelt (1884–1962), widow of the United States President, Franklin D. Roosevelt. She visited Russia in 1957 and in her autobiography remarked that the Russians 'never had any freedom, so they do not miss it'.

RABY, Aurora, in Lord Byron's *Don Juan* (1819–24), is Anna Isabella Milbanke (see Iñez, Donna) as she was at the age of twenty, when Byron first met her.

RACHEL, in Marcel Proust's *A la recherche du temps perdu* (1913–27). Like most of Proust's characters, Rachel is a composite. She is supposedly primarily the actress Louisa de Mornand (Louise

Montaud, 1884–1963), mistress of Louis-Joseph Suchet, Duc d'Albufera (see Saint-Loup, Robert de) and so close a friend of Proust that an affair was suspected, despite his homosexuality. Also discerned in Rachel are the courtesan Émilienne d'Alençon, who so infatuated the son of the Dowager Duchesse Anne d'Uzès that he gave her the family jewels and to be cured of the attachment was sent by his mother to Africa, where he died of fever; and the lesbian actress Lantelme (d. 1911), whose death by drowning while yachting with her lover, Alfred Edwards, proprietor of _Le Matin_, attracted speculation.

RADWORTH, Ernest, in Algernon Swinburne's _Love's Cross Currents_ (1905; originally written in 1862 and published in 1877 as _A Year's Letters_), is believed to be the geologist and antiquarian Sir Walter Calverley Trevelyan (1797–1879). Swinburne stayed at Trevelyan's home in Wallington, Northumberland, on a number of occasions, having come to know him as a neighbour of his grandfather. A philanthropic, teetotal eccentric, Sir Walter once found a Balzac novel left on the drawing-room table by his poet guest. Disgusted, he threw the book on the fire. Swinburne, equally outraged, strode from the house.

RAINGO, Lord, in Arnold Bennett's _Lord Raingo_ (1926), is part-inspired by Lord Beaverbrook (see Ottercove, Lord). The fact that Raingo had a mistress, however, prompted Beaverbrook to assume that Lord Rhondda was the original. Three other similarly situated cabinet ministers took Raingo to be themselves.

RAMBOAT, Marion, in H.G. Wells's _Tono-Bungay_ (1909), is the author's first wife, his cousin Isabel Wells (d. 1931), whom he married in 1891. After their divorce in 1895 he continued to be more than fond of her, showing resentment on her remarriage in 1903.

RAMES, Captain, in A.E.W. Mason's _The Turnstile_ (191?), has as prototype the author's friend, the Antarctic explorer Robert Falcon Scott (1868–1912). Scott's death on his South Polar expedition distressed and embarrassed the author. Knowing that Rames's original would be identified, he added a note to his novel explaining that it had been written long before the ill-fated expedition.

RAMINAGROBIS, in François Rabelais's *Pantagruel* (1532/3), is believed to be the poet Guillaume Crétin (*d.* 1525). The *rondeau* ascribed to Raminagrobis is his, and it is suspected that Rabelais felt Crétin had been over-praised, and wished to undermine his reputation.

RAMPION, Mark and Mary, in Aldous Huxley's *Point Counter Point* (1928). 'Rampion is the most boring character in the book — a gas-bag', said the man who inspired him: the novelist D.H. Lawrence (1885–1930). Huxley's biographer, Sybille Bedford, records that to an American friend Huxley confided, 'Rampion is just some of Lawrence's notions on legs. The actual character of the man was incomparably queerer and more complex than that.' In the last four years of his life, Lawrence had become a close friend of Huxley, who was with him when he died and had unsuccessfully helped him in his efforts to find a publisher for *Lady Chatterley's Lover* (see also Quarles, Elinor). He also edited Lawrence's letters, published after his death, and in 1961 remarked, 'He very much disliked the societies he saw round him and he was always hoping to discover some sort of ideal, rather primitive society. But when he did get into the rather primitive societies, he didn't like those very much.' Mary Rampion is Frieda Lawrence (see Somers, Harriet).

RAMSAY, Mr and Mrs, in Virginia Woolf's *To the Lighthouse* (1927), are the author's parents, Sir Leslie Stephen (1832–1904), the first editor of the *Dictionary of National Biography*, and his second wife, Julia (née Jackson, 1846–95), niece of the pioneer photographer Julia Cameron and a model for the artist Edward Burne-Jones. Both Leslie and Julia Stephen had been widowed. By her first marriage, Julia had two children; six more followed her second marriage in 1870. Stephen was first married to Thackeray's younger daughter. A clergyman who resigned his orders and became an agnostic, he was a pioneer mountaineer, and edited the *Alpine Journal* from 1868 to 1871 before assuming the editorship of the *Cornhill Magazine*, which he held from 1871 until he became founder-editor of the *DNB* in 1882, supervising its first twenty-six volumes and writing many of its articles. He was also the author of biographies of Johnson, Pope and Swift. Vanessa Bell (see Ambrose, Helen) was among his children by Julia Stephen, whose death devastated him.

RAMSDEN, Richard, in John Cournos's *Miranda Masters* (1926), is D.H. Lawrence. See Rampion, Mark.

RANDALL, JeriLee, in Harold Robbins's *The Lonely Lady* (1976), is part-inspired by the best-selling American novelist Jacqueline Susann (*d.* 1974). Formerly an unsuccessful actress, she died of cancer at the age of fifty-three.

RANDALL, Merrill, in Jack Kerouac's *Desolation Angels* (1965), is the American poet and novelist James Merrill (1926–   ).

RANDAN, Hermina de, in Compton Mackenzie's *Extraordinary Women* (1928). 'Nothing that has gone before has hurt me like the publication of *Extraordinary Women*', said Marguerite Radclyffe Hall (see Buck-and-Balk, Lady) in a letter to a friend in America. Her biographer, Lovat Dickson, remarks that the similarity between Radclyffe Hall and Hermina de Randan 'may have been accidental, but it may also have been a desire to tease, and how could such a witty young novelist resist a character like Radclyffe Hall, the very caricature of the predatory Lesbian . . .' To her friend in the States she wrote, 'Do you know what would happen in an English court of law were I to be tempted to attack Mackenzie? The case would be given against me at once, because I would not deny being an invert. It would therefore follow that nothing could be too bad to write or to say about me; indeed I do not doubt that Mackenzie would be praised for having been so chaste and so temperate. The result would be that his book would sell thousands, and with every copy a fresh blow would be struck for the persecution of inversion . . . the Government that allows such a book to go free is doing so with a considered intention, and this being so I am done with England. I shake its dust from my spiritual feet.'

RANDOM, Varnum, in Jack Kerouac's *Desolation Angels* (1965), is the American poet Randall Jarrell (1914–65). As poet-in-residence at Washington's Library of Congress, he entertained Kerouac and Gregory Corso (see Gligoric, Yuri) as house guests.

RANSOM, Basil, in Henry James's *The Bostonians* (1886), is part-inspired by the Mississippi senator Lucius Quintus Cincinnatus Lamar (1825–93), United States Secretary of the Interior from 1885 to 1888, and subsequently an associate justice of the Supreme Court. His name, which was identical with that of his father, a Georgia judge, is echoed in the naming of two characters in William Faulkner's Yoknapatawpha saga – Lucius Quintus Carothers McCaslin and Lucius Quintus Carothers McCaslin Beauchamp.

RANSOM, Michael, in *The Ascent of F.6* (1937), by W.H. Auden and Christopher Isherwood. Insofar as the conflict between a contemplative life and personal ambition is concerned, Ransom reflects the complex personality of T.E. Lawrence (1888–1935). An archaeologist, he served as a liaison officer with British Intelligence in the First World War and played a leading role in organising Arab revolt against the Turks. Becoming known as Lawrence of Arabia, he chronicled the Arabian campaign in *Seven Pillars of Wisdom* (1926), which was edited by George Bernard Shaw – 'Confound you and your book, you are no more fit to be trusted with a pen than a child with a torpedo ... you have no rules, and sometimes throw colons about with an unhinged mind ...' Earlier, in 1922, Lawrence had sought to withdraw from the public eye by joining the RAF under an assumed name. He was at first rejected by a suspicious recruiting officer, Captain W.E. Johns, the creator of 'Biggles'. Johns was swiftly overruled by higher authority: the Chief of Air Staff had agreed to Colonel Lawrence's pseudonymous enlistment. When his role as Aircraftman Ross was discovered by the press, Lawrence left the RAF and entered the Tank Corps as Private T.E. Shaw. 'To private Shaw from public Shaw', said the inscription in his copy of *Saint Joan*. In 1935 Henry Williamson asked Lawrence to accompany him to Germany to meet Hitler. Lawrence replied by telegram from his local post office in Dorset, 'Come tomorrow wet or fine'. Minutes later he was killed when he was thrown from his motorcycle, swerving to avoid two cyclists while on his way to his home, 'Clouds Hill', near Bovington. There, over the doorway, he had chiselled a Greek inscription variously translated as 'Nothing matters' and 'I don't care'.

RAPATIO, in Mercy Otis Warren's *The Adulateur* (1773), is Thomas Hutchinson (1711–80), the last royal Governor of Massachusetts. Although he urged the repeal of the Stamp Act, he was obliged to enforce it, and as a result his Boston mansion was sacked by a mob. His policies were also blamed for the Boston Tea Party, after which he settled in England.

RAQUIN, Thérèse, in Émile Zola's *Thérèse Raquin* (1867), has as prototype Fortunée Auphante, a farmer's wife of Gordes, Vaucluse, whose lover shot her husband dead in 1861. The killer – who had been the victim's friend – confessed. Letters were subsequently discovered which revealed that his mistress had urged him to dispose of her husband.

RASCASSE, in Cyril Connolly's *The Rock Pool* (1935), is the Russian-born artist, Grégoire Michonze (1902–   ), whom Connolly met in Paris in the 1920s.

RASTIGNAC, Eugène de, in Honoré de Balzac's *La Comédie humaine*, notably *La Peau de chagrin* (1831), *Le Père Goriot* (1834), *La Maison Nucingen* (1838) and *La Cousine Bette* (1846). The career and love-life of the French statesman and historian Louis Adolphe Thiers (1797–1877) has much in common with that of Rastignac, and Thiers has been taken to be his prototype, although Rastignac lacks Thiers's intellect and industry.

RAT, in Kenneth Grahame's *The Wind in the Willows* (1908), is part-inspired by the sculling enthusiast, philologist and barrister Frederick James Furnivall (1825–1910), president of the National Amateur Rowing Association, joint builder (in 1845) of England's first two narrow sculling boats, and innovator (in 1886–7) of the first sculling-four and sculling-eight races. Founder of the Early English Texts Society, he gave the lie to Max Beerbohm's dismissal of oarsmen – 'Eight men with but a single thought – if that'. Furnivall was also editor of the Philological Society's *New English Dictionary* (subsequently the *Oxford English Dictionary*), and encouraged Grahame's writing, persuading him to join the New Shakespere Society [*sic*].

RATCLIFFE, Senator, in Henry Adams's *Democracy* (1880), is supposedly the American statesman James Gillespie Blaine (1830–93). Allegations that he had a corrupt relationship with a number of railway companies caused him in 1876 to lose his party's nomination for the presidency, but in 1884 he secured it again, and was narrowly beaten by the Democrat candidate.

RATNER, James-Julius, in Wyndham Lewis's *The Apes of God* (1930), is part-inspired by the Irish writer James Joyce (1882–1941), a close associate of Lewis, who has been spotted in Joyce's *Finnegans Wake* (see Ondt). Also present in Ratner is John Rodker, a Jewish publisher, poet, pacifist and translator from London's East End. His Ovid Press in 1919 issued a portfolio of Lewis's drawings.

RAVELSTON, in George Orwell's *Keep the Aspidistra Flying* (1936), is suggested by the author's biographer, Bernard Crick, to be the writer and artist Sir Richard Rees (1900–70), proprietor and editor of the *Adelphi* from 1930 to 1936 and author of *George Orwell: Fugitive from the Camp of Victory* (1961). Orwell named his adopted son after him.

RAYNER, Daniel and Hildegarde, in Compton Mackenzie's *The South Wind of Love* (1942), are D.H. and Frieda Lawrence (see Rampion, Mark; Somers, Harriet). The scenes in which they appear are re-creations of their encounters with Mackenzie (who portrays himself as John Oğilvie) in Chesham, Buckinghamshire.

REBECCA, in Sir Walter Scott's *Ivanhoe* (1819). 'Does the Rebecca I have pictured compare well with the pattern given?' Scott asked Washington Irving, upon sending him a copy of *Ivanhoe*. It was from Irving that Scott had heard the story of Rebecca Gratz (1781–1869), whom the American writer had come to know in 1809 when she nursed his dying fiancée, who was her close friend. Rebecca was the daughter of a Jewish immigrant from Upper Silesia who settled in Philadelphia and prospered as a merchant. Feeling unable to marry the gentile suitor she loved, she remained single, devoting herself to a life of philanthropy and becoming known in Philadelphia as 'the good Jewess'.

REDBURN, Mrs, in D.H. Lawrence's *Kangaroo* (1923), is Dollie Radford (née Maitland, ?1864–1920), poet and dramatist, and wife of the critic and poet Ernest Radford (1857–1919). Lawrence and his wife were befriended by the Radfords, staying with them at their homes in Greatham (Sussex), Hermitage (Berkshire) and Hampstead.

REDGAUNTLET, Hugh, Lilias and Sir Robert, in Sir Walter Scott's *Redgauntlet* (1824). Hugh Redgauntlet is the author's friend, Sir Robert Grierson, Fifth baronet of Lag, who died in 1839 at the age of 106. Lilias is Williamina Wishart Belsches (1775–1810), daughter of Sir John Wishart Belsches, of Edinburgh. Scott declared his love for her in 1795, but a more eligible match came forward: William Forbes, son and heir of Sir William Forbes, a wealthy Edinburgh banker, whose proposal was particularly attractive as Williamina's father was heavily in debt. In 1797 she married Forbes, who in 1806 became the Seventh baronet. Their six children included James David Forbes (1809–68), Professor of Natural Philosophy and Dean of the Faculty of Arts at Edinburgh University, who discovered the polarisation of heat and pioneered the scientific study of glaciers. Sir Robert Redgauntlet has as prototype Sir Robert Grierson (1655–1733), First Baronet of Lag and a much reviled perpetrator of atrocities against Covenanters in Scotland. He was so afflicted by gout on his Dumfries death-bed that a relay of servants was employed to pass buckets of water from the nearest river to cool his burning legs; and had grown so obese that a hole had to be made in the wall to enable his corpse to be removed from the room.

RED QUEEN, the, in Lewis Carroll's *Through the Looking-Glass and What Alice Found There* (1871). When the author heard that Oxford undergraduate gossip suggested he was seeking the hand of the governess to the Liddell children (see Alice), he was disturbed. The rumour was natural enough – the students were not to know that the author was really dancing attendance upon Miss Prickett's charge, Alice. His interest in Miss Prickett took quite a different form: she was his model for the Red Queen, described in early editions as 'one of the thorny kind', an in-joke for the Liddell children who called their governess 'Pricks'. In later editions the allusion was made less obvious, the author replacing it with 'one of the kind that has nine spikes'. Coincidentally, it was in the year of the publication of *Through the Looking-Glass* that student speculation about the author's intentions was ended. At thirty-eight, Miss Prickett became Mrs Charles Foster, wife of the widowed proprietor of Oxford's Mitre Hotel.

REEVES, Anna, in H.G. Wells's *In the Days of the Comet* (1906), is suggested by J.R. Hammond's *An H.G. Wells Companion* (1979) to be Amber Pember Reeves. See Stanley, Ann Veronica.

REGNIER, Guermann, in *Nélida* (1846), by Daniel Stern (Marie d'Agoult), is the author's revenge for what she regarded as her humiliation by Franz Liszt (see Conti, Gennaro), the novel's Regnier. Her association with the composer came to an end through a combination of her failure to become his muse (she showed little or no interest in his work), his long absences touring abroad, and her resentment of reports linking him on his travels with other women, of whom 'Lola Montez' (see Adler, Irene) was the final straw. See also Rochefide, Béatrix de.

REID, Bertie, in D.H. Lawrence's 'The Blind Man' (1920; *England, My England*, 1922), has been taken to be Bertrand Russell (see

Mattheson, Sir Joshua), but Paul Delany's *D.H. Lawrence's Nightmare* (1979) plausibly suggests J.M. Barrie (see Wilson, Murray) as a more likely model.

REID, Sir Malcolm and Hilda, in D.H. Lawrence's *Lady Chatterley's Lover* (1928). in *H.D.: The Life and Work of an American Poet* (1982), Janice S. Robinson suggests that Sir Malcolm is the shipowner Sir John Ellerman (1862–1933); and that Hilda Reid is an amalgam of his daughter, the writer Winifred Ellerman, and her friend Hilda Doolittle (see Masters, Miranda), whom Sir John assisted financially after the birth of her child (a gesture he could afford: he left £40 million). Winifred Ellerman, who died in 1983 aged eighty-eight, wrote historical novels under the pseudonym Bryher. Although twice married, she fell in love with Doolittle.

REINECKER, in Robert Byron's *The Station* (1928), is Gerald Reitlinger (1900–), author, artist and chronicler of the Nazi extermination of the Jews.

REKHELE, in Isaac Bashevis Singer's *Satan in Goray* (1935), is said by the author to be based on his sister, the novelist Esther Kreitman (d. 1954).

REMINGTON, Mr and Mrs Arthur, and Margaret, in H.G. Wells's *The New Machiavelli* (1911), are respectively the author's parents, Joseph Wells (d. 1910), professional cricketer and unsuccessful shopkeeper of Bromley, Kent, and Sarah Wells (d. 1905), unsuccessful housekeeper at Uppark (see Hammerglow, Lady); and the author's second wife, Amy Catherine Robbins. See Stanley, Ann Veronica.

RENATA, in Ernest Hemingway's *Across the River and into the Trees* (1950), is part-inspired by Adriana Ivancich, who was eighteen when she first met the author in Italy in 1948. A member of an old-established Venetian family, she later claimed to have helped Hemingway over a mental block in the writing of the novel, their encounter having given him fresh impetus. She designed a prize-winning dust-jacket for the book – her occupations included writing poetry and painting – and upon her marriage to a German businessman she moved to Milan. Christie's of London in 1967 auctioned sixty-seven letters written to her by Hemingway, who said that Renata was a composite of at least four women.

RENDEZVOUS, Colonel, in H.G. Wells's *Mr Britling Sees It Through* (1916), is Field Marshal Julian Byng, First Viscount Byng (1862–1935), Governor-General of Canada from 1921 to 1926. His wife was the novelist Marie Evelyn.

RENÉ, in Mme d'Épinay's *Mémoires* (1818), is the French philosopher Jean-Jacques Rousseau (1712–78), whom the author first met in 1747. In 1756 she established him in a cottage, where he wrote *Julie, ou La nouvelle Héloïse* (1761). Soon after this they quarrelled.

REUTER, Mlle Zoraide, in Charlotte Brontë's *The Professor* (1857), is part-inspired by Mme Claire Zoé Heger. See Beck, Mme.

RHAYADER, in Paul Gallico's *The Snow Goose* (1941), is the story's illustrator, the artist Sir Peter Scott (1909–   ), chairman of the World Wildlife Fund and honorary director of the Wildfowl Trust. The son of Captain Robert Falcon Scott (see Rames, Captain), and godson of J.M. Barrie (he was named after Peter Pan), Peter Scott was once Gallico's rival for the love of a figure-skating champion.

RHYS, Owen, in D.H. Lawrence's *The Plumed Serpent* (1926), is the American poet Witter Bynner (1881–1968). Lawrence met him at the settlement established by Mabel Dodge Luhan (see Dale, Edith) in Taos.

RICE, Archie and Billy, in John Osborne's *The Entertainer* (1957). Archie Rice has been popularly identified with the music-hall comedian Max Miller (1895–1963), for whom Osborne has declared his veneration. But Rice is not Miller, the author insisted in the *Observer* (19 September 1965), remarking that for cracking a blue joke 'Max got fined £5 and the rest of the world laughed with him. Archie would have got six months and no option.' Miller was billed as 'The Cheekie Chappie' ('Some girls are like flowers – they grow wild in the woods'), and at the peak of his career he earned £1,000 a week at the London Palladium. 'My wife went to see Sir Laurence Olivier after she saw him appear in *The Entertainer*', he told his biographer, John M. East. 'He said he was a great admirer of mine. Never met him myself. I understand he studied me closely before he played the part of this dud comic – to be insulted by Sir Laurence, that's a compliment in my book.' Billy Rice was part-inspired by Osborne's maternal grandfather, William Crawford Grove, says the author in *A Better Class of Person* (1981). A London publican, Grove was licensee of the Marquis of Granby, Peckham Rye, and of the Duncannon, St Martin-in-the-Fields, his clientele including many theatre people. He was a flamboyant figure and a womaniser. Osborne recounts a family tradition that his grandmother, pregnant with his mother, went downstairs at the Duncannon one morning to find the music-hall artiste Marie Lloyd 'reeling around the sawdust-covered bar swearing and shouting. My grandmother drew herself up and ordered the doorman to escort Miss Lloyd out and hailed her a hansom cab. Whereupon, the story continued, Miss Lloyd screamed up the stairs at the young mother-to-be, 'Don't you fucking well talk to me! I've just left your old man after a weekend in Brighton!'''

RICHARD, in Wyndham Lewis's *The Apes of God* (1930), is Edward Wadsworth (1889–1948), Vorticist painter, Royal Academician, heir to a Bradford wool fortune, and a patron of Lewis.

RICHMAN, Danny, in Jack Kerouac's *Visions of Cody* (1960) and *Book of Dreams* (1961), is Lawrence Ferlinghetti. See O'Hara, Larry.

RICHMOND, Marian, in George Meredith's *The Adventures of Harry Richmond* (1871), is the author's first wife, Mary Ellen Peacock. See Middleton, Clara.

RICO, in Hilda Doolittle's *Bid Me to Live* (1960), is D.H. Lawrence (see Rampion, Mark). For the background to Lawrence's appearence in this novel, see Frederick, Elsa; and Masters, Miranda.

RIDD, John, in R.D. Blackmore's *Lorna Doone* (1869). Create 'the biggest man on Exmoor', as Blackmore did with John Ridd, and readers with local knowledge are bound to seek an original. One suggestion is that John Ridd is modelled upon Philip Ridd, a 'giant' who weighed 400 pounds and lived in the Challacombe/Bratton Fleming area. Another candidate is one Lake, from the Torrington district, who was reputed to have lifted a farm wagon from underneath, overturning it, and who became known as Kinglake because of his stature. In 1966, nearly a century after the novel's publication, the identity of Ridd's original was debated in the correspondence column of the *Daily Telegraph*. Such trails never lose their attraction; they are too happy a hunting ground.

RIDGEON, Sir Colenso, in George Bernard Shaw's *The Doctor's Dilemma* (1906), owes his creation to Sir Almoth Wright (1861–1947), Professor of Experimental Pathology at London University and the originator of anti-typhoid inoculation. The author's biographer, St John Ervine, records how the idea for the play came to Shaw when his wife mentioned Wright in conversation. She recalled how the professor, examining a patient at St Mary's Hospital, Paddington, was asked if he could add another to the few he could treat with his new opsonic system. Wright's reply had been, 'Is he worth it?'

RIGAUD, Monsieur, in Charles Dickens's *Little Dorrit* (1855–7). Self-confessed poisoner though he was, the forger Thomas Griffiths Wainewright (see Varney, Gabriel) was ever mindful of caste and the proprieties. Interviewed in Newgate Prison (where Dickens encountered him – see Slinkton, Julius), he declared, 'I have always been a gentleman, always lived like a gentleman, and I am a gentleman still. Yes, sir, even in Newgate, I am a gentleman. The prison regulations are that we should, each in turn, sweep the yard. There are a barber and a sweep here besides myself. They sweep the yard; but, sir, they have never offered me the broom.' This statement prompts the belief that Dickens had Wainewright in mind when he created Rigaud, whose professed determination was to live and die a gentleman.

RIGBY, Mr, in Benjamin Disraeli's *Coningsby* (1844) and W.M. Thackeray's 'Mrs Perkins's Ball' (1847; *Christmas Books*, 1857). 'A man who would go a hundred miles through snow and sleet on the top of a coach to search a parish register and prove a man illegitimate or a woman older than she says she is.' That was the historian Thomas Macaulay's description of John Wilson Croker (1780–1857), who is both Disraeli's and Thackeray's Rigby. If Croker indeed lived up – or down – to Macaulay's view, today's Fleet Street can only lament the man's birth so long before his time. For Croker was not a popular newspaper journalist, outspoken contributor though he was to the *Quarterly Review*, but a Tory politician credited with coining the term 'Conservative' for that party. He was for more than twenty years secretary to the Admiralty, commencing in that office by exposing a colleague's misappropriation of £200,000. He also managed the estates of Lord Hertford (see Steyne, Lord; see also Monmouth, Lord); he appears in Disraeli's *Vivian Grey* (1826–7) as Vivida Vis; and his *Stories for Children from the*

History of England (1817) served as the model for Sir Walter Scott's *Tales of a Grandfather*. He and Macaulay often picked holes in each other's work, Macaulay drawing attention to defects in Croker's editing of Boswell's *Life of Johnson* and declaring that he detested Croker 'more than cold boiled veal'.

RIORDAN, Mrs Dante, in James Joyce's *Ulysses* (1922), is Mrs 'Dante' Hearn Conway, the author's childhood governess. From Cork, she had abandoned her plan to become a nun when she inherited a fortune. She married a member of the Dublin staff of the Bank of Ireland who promptly deserted her, fleeing to South America with her money.

RITCHIE-HOOK, Brigadier Ben, in Evelyn Waugh's *Men at Arms* (1952). Among those who served with the author in the Second World War, opinion is divided as to who was the model for Ritchie-Hook. John St John, author of *To the War with Waugh* (1973), has no doubt that the prototype was Waugh's brigade commander in 1940: Brigadier (later Major-General) Albert Clarence St Clair-Morford (1893–1945). But Lord Lovat (see Trimmer) took Ritchie-Hook to be Lieutenant-General Sir Adrian Carton de Wiart (1880–1963). St Clair-Morford, who had been wounded four times in the First World War, was in 1941 switched from his appointment as commander of the Royal Marine Brigade and sent on loan to the Government of India. He retired in 1943. Carton de Wiart, who was awarded the Victoria Cross in 1916, was wounded nine times in the First World War, losing an eye and a hand. He habitually led his men over the top, walking-stick in one hand and in the other a bag of grenades from which he pulled the pins with his teeth. In the Second World War he led an abortive British expedition to Norway, subsequently served in the Middle East, was captured in 1941, released in 1943 and became special military representative with General Chiang Kai-shek. I suspect that Ritchie-Hook was a composite of the two.

RIVERS, Isabel, in H.G. Wells's *The New Machiavelli* (1911), is Amber Pember Reeves. See Stanley, Ann Veronica.

RIVERS, the Revd St John, in Charlotte Brontë's *Jane Eyre* (1847). Wanting 'that intense attachment which would make me willingly die for him', the author in 1839 declined the marriage proposal of the Revd Henry Nussey, brother of Ellen Nussey (see

Helstone, Caroline). He cannot have been unduly dismayed, since Charlotte was but one name on his list of prospects, ticked off one by one as they failed to come to fruition. Because of that proposal he has been suggested as Rivers's original. But could this cleric, whom Brontë found merely amiable, really have been the forceful clergyman of *Jane Eyre*? A more probable prototype is the Revd Henry Martyn (1781–1812), with whom the author was also associated and who, like Rivers, went to India.

ROARK, Howard, in Ayn Rand's *The Fountainhead* (1943), is the pioneering, uncompromising American architect Frank Lloyd Wright (1869–1959).

ROBERT, in William Cooper's *Scenes from Provincial Life* (1950), *Scenes from Married Life* (1961) and *Scenes from Metropolitan Life* (1982), is part-inspired by the novelist and scientist C.P. Snow (Lord Snow, 1905–80), who first met Cooper (H.S. Hoff) at Christ's College, Cambridge, in the early 1930s, when Snow was Hoff's supervisor in infra-red spectroscopy. It was upon Snow's recommendation that Hoff in 1933 obtained a teaching post at Snow's old school, Alderman Newton's, Leicester.

ROBIN, Christopher. See Christopher Robin.

ROBIN, Paul, in Raymond Radiguet's *Le Bal du comte d'Orgel* (1924), is an amalgam of the French novelist, diplomat and Nazi collaborator Paul Morand (1888–1976) and the French composer Georges Auric (1899–   ).

ROBINSON, R.S., in C.P. Snow's *Homecomings* (1956), is the writer and critic Daniel George (D.G. Bunting, 1890–1967). This is one of many identifications to be found in John Halperin's *C.P. Snow: An Oral Biography* (1983).

ROBTHETILL, Roderick, in Thomas Love Peacock's *Crotchet Castle* (1831), is James Lloyd, a London bank clerk who absconded in 1828, together with his employer.

ROCCO, Mr, in Arnold Bennett's *Imperial Palace* (1930), is the Savoy Hotel chef Jean Baptiste Virlogeux, who returned the compliment after the author's death by concocting the Arnold Bennett Omelette.

ROCH, Thomas, in Jules Verne's *For the Flag* (1896), has as prototype Eugène Turpin (1848–1927), a French chemist who invented the explosive Melinite. In 1885 he was in dispute with the French government over its failure to take up his invention, and he was subsequently imprisoned for disclosing official secrets when he published a pamphlet describing his brain-child. Nine years later, he announced his intention of taking his latest project to Germany. Verne's novel prompted Turpin to sue for libel, an action in which he was unsuccessful.

ROCHECLIFFE, Dr, in Sir Walter Scott's *Woodstock* (1826), has as prototype the Revd Michael Hudson (?1605–48), rector of Uffington, Lincolnshire, who as Royal Chaplain assisted Charles I in his flight from Oxford to Newcastle in 1646. He was arrested, and imprisoned in the Tower of London, but escaped disguised as a pedlar, recruited a troop of Royalists and commandeered Woodcroft House, Northamptonshire. He surrendered when the house was besieged, and sought to escape by dropping from the battlements into the moat. Before he could let go of the parapet his hands were cut off at the wrists, and he was caught and killed as he staggered through the water. A chandler involved in the episode cut out his tongue for display as a trophy.

ROCHEFIDE, Béatrix de, in Honoré de Balzac's *Béatrix* (1844). 'Six inches of snow covering 20 inches of lava' was how a contemporary described Marie de Flavigny, Comtesse d'Agoult (1805–76) and Balzac's Béatrix. She was herself a novelist, under the name Daniel Stern, and left her husband for Franz Liszt (see Conti, Gennaro; see also Regnier, Guermann), bearing him three daughters, one of whom, Cosima, married the composer Richard Wagner.

RODDE, Clarissa, Frau and Inez, in Thomas Mann's *Doctor Faustus* (1947), are respectively Carla Mann (see Ende, Ute); the author's mother (see Buddenbrook, Gerda); and his sister Julia (*b.* 1877), who in 1900 married Josef Löhr, director of the Bavarian Bank of Commerce.

RODDICE, Hermione, in D.H. Lawrence's *Women in Love* (1920). 'Was I really like that?' asked Lady Ottoline Morrell (1872–1938) after Lawrence sent her a copy of the novel in manuscript. She found Hermione, for whom she is the primary model, 'so loathsome one cannot get clean after it'. Later, she recorded, 'For many months the ghastly portrait of myself, written by someone whom I had trusted and liked, haunted my thoughts and horrified me.' Although her friendship with Lawrence could never be quite the same again, she was among those who supported him in 1929 when police seized a number of his paintings when they were on exhibition in London. Mr Justice Mead, refusing to admit the evidence of art experts, ruled that the most splendidly painted picture in the universe could be obscene. Rising from her seat at the back of the court, Lady Ottoline pointed an imperious finger at the judge and announced, 'He ought to be burned.' Half-sister of the Sixth Duke of Portland, she was the daughter of General Arthur Cavendish-Bentinck and Lady Bolsover, his second wife. She married Philip Morrell, a pacifist Liberal MP, and lived with him at Garsington Manor, near Oxford, and at 44 Bedford Square, London, becoming the leading literary hostess of her day. While her husband conceived an unrequited passion for Virginia Woolf, Lady Ottoline fell in love with Axel Munthe (see Jemima). In 1911, with her husband's acquiescence, she had an affair with Bertrand Russell, whose autobiography describes her as 'very tall, with a long thin face like a horse, and very beautiful hair of an unusual colour, more or less like that of marmalade, but rather darker'. She also, Russell recalled, possessed a 'very beautiful, gentle, vibrant voice ... indomitable courage and a will of iron'. Outlandish attire was part of her persona and was frequently mislaid, the Garsington village notice-board announcing: 'Lost. A white bearskin hat, three feet high.' House guests at Garsington found in her a character ready-made, for she was virtually model-in-residence for writers, who in addition to Lawrence included Aldous Huxley (who met his wife at Garsington), Graham Greene and Osbert Sitwell. Hermione Roddice is not Lady Ottoline in appearance, however, but probably Jessie Chambers (see Leivers, Miriam), and she owes something of her ideology to Helen Corke (see Verden, Helena).

RODNEY, Frederick and Jane, in Compton Mackenzie's *The South Wind of Love* (1942). When you can cross a landing to the bedroom of your mistress, why bother to use a ladder? Gilbert Cannan (see Gunn, Gilbert) was a romantic who chose a ladder and was landed in a divorce court. He was in his early twenties when J.M. Barrie (see Wilson, Murray) and his wife, the actress Mary Ansell (d. 1950), befriended him in London. Although Ansell was nearly twice Cannan's age, she became his mistress, and they appear in Mackenzie's novel as the Rodneys. Their story is told by Cannan's biographer, Diana Farr. When his London flat was being redecorated, it was arranged that he should stay at the Barries' country cottage near Tilford, in Surrey. There he was joined by Mrs Barrie, chaperoned by women friends, while her husband remained in London. Instead of going to her door at night, Cannan chose the window. Mrs Barrie told Mackenzie what happened when the time came for Cannan to return to his room. He had failed to take into account the early hour at which the gardener arrived, and found the ladder gone, the gardener not only having removed it but also having mentally filed its implications for future reference. Later, aggrieved by differences with Mrs Barrie, he reported the ladder episode to her husband. Barrie sped back to London and confronted his wife. She refused to give up Cannan, whom she married after her divorce.

ROEHAMPTON, Lord, in Benjamin Disraeli's *Endymion* (1880), is based on Lord Palmerston. See Brock, Lord.

ROGET, Marie, in Edgar Allan Poe's 'The Mystery of Marie Roget' (1842–3; *Tales*, 1845). Poe was a customer of Anderson's tobacco shop at 319 Broadway, New York. Working there was a pretty salesgirl, Mary Cecilia Rogers (1820–41). When she was found murdered, floating in the Hudson River, she inspired Poe's Marie Roget. The crime was never solved, but the alleged suspect – Philip Spencer, a hard-drinking naval officer whose father was Secretary of State for War – was subsequently hanged for participating in a mutiny.

ROMA, Ernesto, in Bertolt Brecht's *The Resistible Rise of Arturo Ui* (written 1941, first performed 1958), is Ernst Röhm (d. 1934), a notorious homosexual who was Chief of Staff of Nazi Germany's storm-troops. When rivalry developed between Röhm and Adolf Hitler (Arturo Ui), the Führer ordered his assassination.

ROMANOVITCH, Princess Marousha Stanislovska Dagmar Natasha Iliana ('Sasha'), in Virginia Woolf's *Orlando* (1928). Remembered for her lesbian relationship with Victoria Sackville-West (see Orlando) rather than for her books, the novelist Violet Trefusis (1894–1972) – Woolf's 'Sasha' – was the daughter of Edward VII's mistress, Alice Keppel (the Hon. Mrs George Keppel). Her father is believed to have been William Beckett, Lord Grimthorpe. In her declining years, Violet Trefusis became socially

impossible, seldom arriving for an engagement at the right time, or
even on the right day. 'Often', Rebecca West recalled, 'she stopped
saying the wrong thing only to do the wrong thing.' Cecil Beaton
noted her 'delightfully insouciant way of putting her cigarette out in
a pat of butter.'

ROMERO, Pedro, in Ernest Hemingway's *The Sun Also Rises*
(1926; published in England as *Fiesta*), is the matador Cayetano
Ordóñez, whose ability in the bullring was much admired by the
author when he first witnessed him at work in 1925.

ROMOLA, in George Eliot's novel of that name (1863), is the
author's close friend, Barbara Bodichon (née Leigh-Smith,
1827–91). An energetic worker for the advancement of women, she
was a founder of Girton College, Cambridge, helped to lead agi-
tation which brought about the Married Women's Property Acts,
and supported the ideal of women's suffrage. In 1857 she married Dr
Eugène Bodichon, who practised in Algiers, wore Arab dress, and
campaigned for the abolition of slavery.

ROSA, Aunt, in Rudyard Kipling's 'Baa Baa, Black Sheep' (*Wee
Willie Winkie*, 1888), is Mrs Harry Holloway, who with her
husband, a retired naval captain, ran the foster home (Lorne Lodge, 4
Campbell Road, Southsea, Hampshire) to which Kipling and his
sisters were sent in their infancy when their parents returned to
India. The Kipling children called the establishment the 'House of
Desolation'.

ROSE, Sir Hector, in C.P. Snow's *The New Men* (1954), *Homecomings* (1956), *Corridors of Power* (1964) and *Last Things* (1970), is the
London theatre impresario Hugh ('Binky') Beaumont (1908–73),
who was managing director of H.M. Tennent Ltd.

ROSE, Mr, in W.H. Mallock's *The New Republic* (1877), is the
essayist Walter Pater (1839–94), whose repressed private life, residing with his two spinster sisters, contrasted with his public image as
an apostle of decadence, with Oscar Wilde among his disciples. 'I am
pleased', he said, 'to be called Mr Rose – the rose being the queen of
flowers.'

ROSEN, Walter, in D.H. Lawrence's *Aaron's Rod* (1922), is Leo
Stein (1872–1947), writer, percipient art collector and brother of
Gertrude Stein (see Percival, Mrs).

ROSMER, John, in Henrik Ibsen's *Rosmersholm* (1886), is the Swedish poet Count Carl Snoilsky (1841–1903). In 1879 he over-came a writing block which had lasted ten years by divorcing his wife, marrying one of her relatives, resigning from his post in the Swedish Foreign Office and taking up residence abroad.

ROSTOV, Counts Ilya and Nikolai and Countesses Vera and Natally (Natasha), in Leo Tolstoy's *War and Peace* (1863–9). Ilya is the author's grandfather, Count Ilya Andreyevich Tolstoy (1757–1820), whose generosity, extravagance and gambling placed the family fortune in jeopardy. Nikolai is the author's father, Count Nikolai Ilyich Tolstoy (1785–1837) who, like Nikolai Rostov, solved the problem of inherited debts by marrying a rich woman. Vera is supposedly the author's elder sister-in-law, Liza Behrs, who helped him to research the historical background of *War and Peace*. Natally is the author's younger sister-in-law, Tatiana Behrs (1846–1925), and, in the epilogue, his wife, Sonya (see Pozdnyshev, Madame).

ROSWALD, Prince Karol de, in George Sand's *Lucrezia Floriani* (1846), is the composer Frédéric François Chopin (1810–49), with whom the author lived intermittently for eight years.

ROTHERHAM, Sir Henry, in Edith Sitwell's *I Live under a Black Sun* (1937). The ruling passion of Sir George Sitwell (1860–1943) was the medieval past, to the virtual exclusion of the present. Thus, he devoted a considerable slice of his life and fortune to restoring a vast Italian castle inhabited by 297 peasants. The author's father, and her model for Sir Henry Rotherham, he refused on principle to pay his spendthrift wife's debts, allowing her to face court action which disgraced the family and resulted in her going to prison. His inventions included a synthetic rectangular egg, a revolver for shooting wasps, and a toothbrush that played 'Annie Laurie'. He was not so dotty, however, as to be duped at a séance. Spotting the outline of corsets under the gown of a 'spirit', he shot out his arm and grabbed her.

ROUGON, Eugène, in Émile Zola's *Son Excellence Eugène Rougon* (1876), was taken by the author's son-in-law and biographer to be the French statesman Eugène Rouher (1814–84), who was twice premier (1849–51 and 1863–9) and who was 'architect' of the national railway system.

ROUMESTAN, Numa, in Alphonse Daudet's *Numa Roumestan* (1881), is believed to be modelled upon Léon Gambetta (1838–82), a Paris barrister-turned-politician noted for his oratory and for his organisation of Paris's resistance to the Prussians in 1870, after the fall of the city, from which he escaped by balloon.

ROUNCEWELL, Mrs, in Charles Dickens's *Bleak House* (1852–3), is the author's grandmother, Elizabeth Ball (*d.* 1824). Formerly housemaid to Lady Blandford, she married William Dickens, a footman who became steward at Crewe Hall, the home of John Crewe, MP for Chester. After her husband's death in 1785, she remained at Crewe Hall as housekeeper for a further thirty-five years.

ROUSSEL, in Arnold Bennett's *The Lion's Share* (1916), is the composer Maurice Ravel (1875–1937). Bennett first made his acquaintance in Paris in 1908, and they became friends for life, the author on one occasion taking Ravel on a conducted tour of Ipswich's antique shops.

ROXTON, Lord John, in Sir Arthur Conan Doyle's *The Lost World* (1912), is believed to have been modelled upon Sir Roger Casement (1864–1916). Doyle greatly admired Casement's work as British Consul in the Congo and South America, Casement having twice distinguished himself by exposing major scandals of labour exploitation. In the First World War, however, Casement espoused the cause of Irish independence. In Germany he attempted to recruit an Irish brigade from prisoner-of-war camps to fight the British in Ireland. He was captured trying to land in Ireland from a German submarine, and was tried for high treason and executed. Doyle campaigned to save Casement's life, and it has been suggested that this may have cost the author a peerage. Support for the campaign faded after well-authenticated rumours let it be known that Casement was homosexual.

ROYCE, Vernon, in C.P. Snow's *The Light and the Dark* (1947) and *The Masters* (1951), is part-inspired by Professor George Stuart Gordon (1881–1942), President of Magdalen College, Oxford, from 1928 to 1942, Vice-Chancellor of the university from 1938 to 1941 and Professor of Poetry there from 1933 to 1938.

ROZANOV, John Robert, in Iris Murdoch's *The Philosopher's Pupil* (1983), is suggested by Mark Amory, writing in the *Tatler* (October 1984), to be Murdoch's version of Sir Isaiah Berlin (1909–   ), Fellow of All Souls College, Oxford, and President of the British Academy from 1974 to 1978.

RUBASHOV, Nikolai Salmanovich, in Arthur Koestler's *Darkness at Noon* (1940), has three prototypes: for his intellect, the Russian Communist leader Nikolai Ivanovich Bukharin (1888–1938), who was tried and executed on suspicion of Trotskyist sympathies; and for his physical appearance, Lev Davidovich Trotsky (see Snowball) and Karl Bernardovich Radek (*b.* 1885), a Russian Communist statesman who was tried for treason, sentenced to ten years' imprisonment, and released after four so that he could devote himself to Party propaganda.

RUBIN, David, in C.P. Snow's *Corridors of Power* (1964), is the nuclear physicist Professor Isidor Rabi (1898–   ). He was awarded the Nobel Prize for physics in 1944 and was Higgins Professor of Physics at Columbia University from 1950 to 1964.

RUBIN, Lev, in Alexander Solzhenitsyn's *The First Circle* (1968), is Lev Zinovievich Kopolev, a Russian writer who was among Solzhenitsyn's fellow-prisoners at a technical design and research unit on Moscow's outskirts in the late 1940s. Released in 1955, Kopolev was expelled from the Communist Party in 1968, from the Writers' Union in 1977 and from the Soviet Union in 1980, when he was deprived of his Soviet citizenship while on a visit to Germany.

RUDIN, in Ivan Turgenev's novel of that name (1856), is the Russian socialist agitator and anarchist Mikhail Bakunin (1814–76), founder of Nihilism – a word Turgenev has been credited with coining. The two became friends, sharing a flat after Turgenev's arrival in Berlin in 1838 as a student of philosophy. At the time of the publication of *Rudin*, Bakunin had been sent to Siberia for his part in a revolt in Dresden, for which he was initially sentenced to death. Five years later he made his way to Switzerland and in 1869 he joined the First International (the International Workingmen's Association), from which he was later expelled after ideological differences with Marx.

RUDOLSTADT, Albert de, in George Sand's *Consuelo* (1842–3), is an amalgam of Frédéric Chopin (see Roswald, Prince Karol de); the French philosopher Pierre Leroux (1797–1871), who in 1843 established an unsuccessful printing business in which he exercised his socialist principles; and the Polish poet Adam Mickiewicz (1798–1855), whose political activities caused him to live in exile in Russia and France.

RUFFORD, Nancy, in Ford Madox Ford's *The Good Soldier* (1915), is an amalgam of Rosamond Fogg Elliott (see Tamville, Lady Dionissia de Egerton de) and Brigit Patmore (see Browning, Clariss).

RUMFOORD, Winston Niles, in Kurt Vonnegut's *The Sirens of Titan* (1959). Interviewed by Joe David Bellamy in *The New Fiction* (1974), Vonnegut acknowledged his model for Rumfoord to be Franklin Delano Roosevelt (1882–1945), President of the United States from 1933 to 1945. Roosevelt had been 'one of the biggest figures of my childhood', said Vonnegut. 'He was elected to the first term when I was ten years old. And he spoke with this aristocratic Hudson Valley accent which nobody had ever heard before, and everybody was charmed.' Like Rumfoord, the author commented, Roosevelt had great hopes for changing things, and childish hopes, too. 'I don't think Roosevelt was an enormous success except as a personality. And maybe that's the only kind of success a president needs to have anyway.'

RUNCIBLE, the Hon. Agatha, in Evelyn Waugh's *Vile Bodies* (1930), is primarily the Hon. Elizabeth Ponsonby (1900–40), daughter of Arthur Ponsonby, First Baron Ponsonby, a pioneer upper-class socialist who was a member of the Labour government in 1924. Prominent among the 'bright young people' of the 1920s, she married a great-grandson of Sir John Pelly, First Bart, in 1929 and was divorced four years later. It was with her brother Matthew, subsequently the Second Baron Ponsonby, that Waugh was arrested in London in 1925 for being drunk and incapable while driving in the Strand. Her cousin, the Hon. Loelia Ponsonby (subsequently the Duchess of Westminster), in 1926 originated the bottle party. Agatha Runcible may also be part-inspired by Elizabeth Ponsonby's cousin, Olivia Plunket Greene (1907–55). Waugh's lifelong friend, she was a granddaughter of the composer Sir Hubert Parry and daughter of the singer Harry Plunket Greene. Her mother's sister married Elizabeth Ponsonby's father. Olivia Plunket Greene's veneer of gay abandon concealed a deep religious faith. In later life she lived with her mother on the Longleat estate in Wiltshire, combining her Catholicism with conversion to Communism, to which she proposed to give what she regarded as her ill-gotten inheritance. Waugh considered her to be part alcoholic, part crackpot and part genius.

RUNNINGBROOK, Tracy, in George Meredith's *Sandra Belloni* (1864; originally published as *Emilia in England*), is the author's friend, the poet Algernon Charles Swinburne (1837–1909), who had in 1862 written a spirited letter to the *Spectator*, denouncing an adverse review of Meredith's *Modern Love*. Swinburne's own notion of modern love was perverse. He was enamoured of the lash (see Dolores) and he enjoyed sex by proxy – in his fantasy 'La Soeur de la Reine', Wordsworth seduces Queen Victoria. Rossetti did his best to set Swinburne on a heterosexual path, giving an actress £10 to seduce him. Swinburne, however, was unable to rise to the occasion, and the actress returned the money.

RUSSELL, Mr, in *Comin' thro' the Rye* (1875), by Helen Mathers (Mrs Henry Reeves), is the Revd John Thomas Richardson Fussell, who from 1852 to 1858 was vicar of Chantry, Somerset, the setting for the early part of this novel. He was a member of the West Country and Midlands Fussell family of agricultural engineers. The identification is made by Anthony Powell, in his memoirs.

RUSTON, Willie, in Anthony Hope's *The God in the Car* (1894), is the British Empire-builder Cecil John Rhodes (1853–1902), who became Prime Minister of Cape Colony in 1902 and after whom Rhodesia was named. His famous 'last' words – 'So little done, so much to do' – in fact preceded the more prosaic final utterance addressed to his secretary: 'Turn me over, Jack'.

RUTHIE, in Christopher Isherwood's *Down There on a Visit* (1962), is Jean Bakewell (*d.* 1950), the first wife of Cyril Connolly (see Quiggin, J.G.), whom she met in Paris in 1929, when she was eighteen. A novelist under the name Barbara Skelton, she was the daughter of the Pittsburgh family that built the city's first eleven-storey skyscraper and the first glass factory in the United States.

RUTHVEN, Lord, in John Polidori's *The Vampyre* (1819), is Lord Byron (see Cadurcis, Lord). Polidori was Byron's personal physician.

RYDAL, Elizabeth, in Christopher Isherwood's *The World in the Evening* (1954). 'Yes, I suppose I *did* have Katherine Mansfield in mind', says Isherwood, in response to my suggestion that she was Elizabeth Rydal's prototype. 'But only in a general way. I never knew her personally but admired her — as a human being rather than as a writer — because of her published letters and diaries. Incidentally, the name "Rydal" was suggested to me by Rydal Water in the Lake District, which has always seemed to me to be very beautiful. Although I never knew Katherine Mansfield personally, I did know Virginia Woolf — she and Leonard Woolf published some of my books — and perhaps there are also memories of Virginia in the character of Rydal.' See also Brangwen, Gudrun.

RYDER, Japhy, in Jack Kerouac's *The Dharma Bums* (1958), is the American poet and 'Japophile' Gary Snyder (1930–   ).

RYLANDS, Cynthia, in H.G. Wells's *Meanwhile* (1927), is part-inspired by the author's second wife, Amy Catherine Robbins. See Stanley, Ann Veronica.

S

SABRECOFF, Anastasia, in Compton Mackenzie's *Extraordinary Women* (1928), is Una, Lady Troubridge (see Tilly-Tweed-in-Blood), according to Lovat Dickson's biography of Marguerite Radclyffe Hall.

SACHARISSA, in the poems of Edmund Waller, is Lady Dorothy Sidney (1617–84), eldest daughter of the Second Earl of Leicester. Waller sought her hand, but she married Robert Spencer, Second Earl of Sunderland, and then Sir Robert Smythe. 'When, Mr Waller, will you write such fine verses upon me again?' she asked, in ravaged old age. 'When your ladyship is as young again', he replied.

SACKBUT, Roderick, in Thomas Love Peacock's *Nightmare Abbey* (1818), is Robert Southey (see Feathernest, Mr), author of *Roderick, the last of the Goths* and, as poet laureate, entitled to the annual emolument of a butt of sack.

SAGNIER, in Émile Zola's *Paris* (1897–8), is Édouard Drumont, editor of *Libre parole*.

ST ALBANS, Father, in Frederick Rolfe's *Hadrian the Seventh* (1904), is the Revd Charles Sidney De Vere Beauclerk (1855–1934), who in 1895, while in charge of St Winifride's well at Holywell, north Wales, engaged Rolfe to paint a set of banners for the shrine in return for his keep. Rolfe then claimed that the Church owed him £1,000 for his paintings and launched a vitriolic attack on Beauclerk in the *Holywell Record*. After leaving Holywell in 1898 Beauclerk was a chaplain to the Forces in Malta and a parish priest in Accrington, Lancashire. He was a descendant of Charles Beauclerk, First Duke of St Albans, the illegitimate son of Charles II by Eleanor Gwynn.

ST BARBE, in Benjamin Disraeli's *Endymion* (1880). Two men who had annoyed Disraeli are his targets in St Barbe. The first model is the novelist William Makepeace Thackeray (1811—63), who had reviewed Disraeli's *Coningsby* derisively, subsequently satirising it in *Codlingsby*. The second is Abraham Hayward (see Flam, Mr) who had revealed the source of an eloquent passage in Disraeli's eulogy on Wellington to be a newspaper translation of Thiers's funeral panegyric on General St Cyr.

ST BUNGAY, the Duke of, in Anthony Trollope's *Can You Forgive Her?* (1864), *Phineas Finn* (1869), *Phineas Redux* (1874), *The Prime Minister* (1876) and *The Duke's Children* (1880), is suggested by R. W. Chapman (*Personal Names in Trollope's Political Novels*, 1948) to be Henry Petty Fitzmaurice, Third Marquess of Lansdowne (1780—1863), who was Britain's Chancellor of the Exchequer and Home Secretary before serving as Lord President of the Council.

ST HILAIRE, Georges de, in Arthur Koestler's *The Age of Longing* (1951), is the French novelist and essayist André Malraux (1901—76), according to Koestler's biographer, Iain Hamilton. While Koestler admired Malraux as a writer, he had the occasional quiet smile at his egocentricity. Malraux was expounding on his support for General de Gaulle when Koestler said, 'What about the General's entourage?' 'L'entourage du Général, c'est moi', Malraux replied. Declaiming on the philosophy of Bergson, Malraux said, 'Je suis le plus grand philosophe du monde'. Was he quoting Bergson or referring to himself? asked Koestler. 'Non, c'est moi qui parle.' Malraux could be forgiven his conceit. A distinguished archaeologist, he made significant discoveries in Mexico, the Far East and Arabia; in the Spanish Civil War he flew as a pilot in the Republican air force; in the Second World War he escaped from his German captors to become a Resistance hero, writing one of his novels while 'on the run'; as Minister of Culture he transformed much of post-war France; and as an expert on the Far East he advised not only de Gaulle but also the United States president, Richard Nixon.

SAINT-LOUP, Robert de, in Marcel Proust's *A la recherche du temps perdu* (1913—27). Not so much a character, more a cricket team — or at least that's the impression created by the number of Proust's acquaintances discerned in Saint-Loup. Prominent among those fielded is Louis-Joseph Suchet, Duc d'Albufera (1877—1953), the lover of Louisa de Mornand (see Rachel). Unable to face the bowling when he recognised himself falling out with Rachel in Proust's pages, he retired hurt, abruptly ending his seven-year friendship with the author. Some stylish strokes are contributed by Comte Boni de Castellane, a colourful batsman — albeit with a walking-stick, with which he attacked his ex-wife's husband. After stealing one of the mistresses of Comte Henri Greffulhe (see Guermantes, Basin, Duc de) and being blackballed at the Jockey Club, he married an American heiress, Anna Gould, in 1895, entering politics as a royalist and living in ostentatious splendour on his wife's money until she divorced him in 1906 and married his cousin, Hélie de Talleyrand-Périgord, Prince de Sagan. This so enraged Castellane, thereafter constrained to support himself by dealing in antiques, that he belaboured the Prince when he met him at a funeral two years later. A scientific element in Saint-Loup is Armand, Duc de Guiche, founder-president of L'Institut d'Optique Théorique, secretary of the Scientific Commission of the Aéro Club of France and author of *The Aviator's Elementary Handbook*. He was the son of Agénor, Duc de Gramont (again, see Guermantes, Basin, Duc de), the half-brother of Élisabeth de Gramont (see Clitoressa, Duchess of Nates-court) and the husband of Elaine Greffulhe, daughter of Comtesse Henri Greffulhe (see Guermantes, Oriane, Duchesse de). A literary element is contributed both by the essayist and novelist Comte Georges-Alfred Lauris (1876—1963), who married Madeleine, daughter of Baronne Aimery Harty de Pierrebourg (see Crécy, Odette de); and by the dramatist Robert Pellevé de la Motte-Ango, Marquis de Flers (1872—1927), who worked for *Le Figaro* and collaborated with Gaston Arman de Caillavet (1869—1915), author of light comedies, who is also seen in Saint-Loup. Completing the team are Comte Gabriel de La Rochefoucauld (son of Comte Aimery de La Rochefoucauld — see Guermantes, Prince de), who married Odile de Richelieu, daughter of Alice Heine (see Luxembourg, Princesse de), after a trip to Constantinople to recover from an affair with a married woman who had committed suicide; Comte Bert-rand de Salignac-Fénelon (1878—1914), a Dreyfusard who first met Proust when he was twenty-three and who served as a diplomat in many parts of the world, volunteered for the Forces in 1914, although exempted from military service, and was killed at Mametz; Jacques d'Uzès (*d.* 1893; see Rachel); and Prince Edmond de Polignac (see Bergotte). Yet that roll-call totals only ten; the eleventh man is lurking in the pavilion, awaiting identification. Scorers to whom I am indebted include the Proust biographer George D. Painter and Mina Curtiss, an editor of Proust's letters.

SALKELD, Cecil Francis, in Flann O'Brien's *At-Swim-Two-Birds* (1939), is the Irish polymath Michael Byrne, who was described by the writer Niall Sheridan as an expert on everything.

SALLUSTE, Don, in Victor Hugo's *Ruy Blas* (1838), is the critic Charles-Augustin Sainte-Beuve (1804–69), who had an affair with Hugo's wife (see Couaën, Mme de).

SALLY, in Patrick Balfour's *The Ruthless Innocent* (1949). 'Poor Patrick has written a novel in praise of Angela', wrote Evelyn Waugh in 1950, in a letter to Nancy Mitford. Balfour (see Balcairn, the Earl of) married Angela Culme-Seymour (*b.* 1912) in 1938 and they were divorced in 1942. She was formerly the wife of John George Spencer-Churchill, whom she married in 1934. He divorced her in 1938. In 1948 she married Comte Réné Guillet de Chatellus.

SALT, Stella, in Wyndham Lewis's *The Roaring Queen* (1936), is Rebecca West (see Helen), who first met the author in 1912. He painted her portrait in 1932, maintaining throughout the sittings the same off-putting silence he preserved when dining out with her, she told his biographer, Jeffrey Meyers.

SALTRAM, in Henry James's 'The Coxon Fund' (1894; *Terminations*, 1895), is Samuel Taylor Coleridge (see Skionar, Mr), whose 'Life' James had read prior to writing his story.

SALVAT, in Émile Zola's *Paris* (1897–8), is Édouard Vaillant (*d.* 1893), who was executed for throwing a bomb into the French Chamber of Deputies.

SAMGRASS, Mr, in Evelyn Waugh's *Brideshead Revisited* (1945). Waugh was annoyed when friends failed to recognise his model for Mr Samgrass, says his biographer, Christopher Sykes. Samgrass is an unattractive version of Sir Maurice Bowra (1898–1971), who became a Fellow of Wadham College, Oxford, in 1922, and Warden in 1938. Sykes says that Bowra was too clever to betray any sign that he was hurt. 'I hope', he would say, 'that you spotted *me*', describing the caricature as the best thing in the book. Waugh was further displeased, Sykes notes, when Bowra's words reached him.

SAMPSON, Abel, in Sir Walter Scott's *Guy Mannering* (1815), is primarily George Thomson (*d.* 1838), who became a licensed preacher in 1816. The son of a Melrose (Borders) clergyman, he was noted for the extreme absent-mindedness which plagued him in the pulpit and for his refusal to succumb to the handicap of a wooden leg — he is reputed to have walked from Edinburgh to Melrose in nine hours, completing his day by climbing to the summit of the Eildons. He was the tutor of Scott's children at Abbotsford and subsequently taught in Edinburgh. Others who are believed to have contributed to 'Dominie Sampson' are the Revd James Sanson (*d.* 1795), minister at Leadhills, Lanarkshire, and tutor to the author's cousins at Crailing, Borders; and Scott's friend, the Revd John Leyden (*d.* 1811), who began his career at Clovenfords, Borders, as a schoolteacher.

SAND, Harold, in Jack Kerouac's *The Subterraneans* (1958), is the American experimental novelist William Gaddis (1922–).

SANDERS, Mr Commissioner, in Edgar Wallace's 'Sanders' stories, commencing in 1909 and including the collection *Sanders of the River* (1911). The legendary reputation of the explorer and colonial administrator Sir Hamilton (Harry) Johnston (1858–1927) is believed to have part-inspired Wallace's Sanders. Johnston, of whom Wallace heard during a visit to the Congo in 1907, was Commissioner of the British Central Africa Protectorate from 1891 to 1897 and wrote numerous books, including one on the River Congo. Tradition in the North Riding police force had it, however, that Sanders was modelled upon the North Riding Chief Constable, Major Sir Robert Lister Bower (1860–1929), a veteran of the Egyptian battles of Kassassin and Tel-el-Kebir and — in West Africa — Political Officer at Jebu Ode from 1892 to 1893 and British resident in Ibadan from 1893 to 1897. Of the two, the former seems to be the more likely model, but one can imagine how the latter, through his previous career, could have inspired a Sanders legend among his men.

SANDORF, Mathias, in Jules Verne's *Mathias Sandorf* (1885), is part-inspired by Louis Salvator. See Antekirtt, Dr.

SANGER, Albert, in Margaret Kennedy's *The Constant Nymph* (1924), has too many of the attributes of Augustus John (see Bidlake, John) for the resemblance to be purely coincidental. Like Augustus John, Albert Sanger has lost a wife in childbirth, has become something of a gypsy and has had many mistresses and numerous illegitimate children. In giving Sanger the talents of a musician rather than those of a painter, the author may have thought she was protecting herself against accusations of using John, a friend of one of her cousins, according to her biographer, Violet Powell. 'She was not perhaps, at that date, sufficiently experienced to know that denials, however indignant, of putting actual portraits into a novel are seldom greeted with anything except scepticism among readers.'

SANSÉVÉRINA, the Duchess of, in Stendhal's *La Chartreuse de Parme* (1839), is an amalgam of Matilde Dembowski (see De la Mole, Mathilde) and Angela Pietragrua, the wife of a clerk in Milan's bureau of weights and measures. She was the mistress of Louis Joinville, Commissioner of War in Milan in 1800, who introduced her to Stendhal, a member of his staff. Ten years later, when she was thirty-four, Stendhal became her lover.

SANT, Jerry, in Frederick Rolfe's *Hadrian the Seventh* (1904), according to Rolfe's biographer, Donald Weeks, is modelled upon James Keir Hardie (1856–1915), founder of the Independent Labour Party.

SANTA SEGUNDA, Magdalena de, in Constance Malleson's *The Coming Back* (1933), is Lady Ottoline Morrell. See Roddice, Hermione.

SANTIAGO, in Ernest Hemingway's *The Old Man and the Sea* (1952), is in part Carlos Gutiérrez (b. 1878), a Cuban fisherman. Hemingway first met him in 1932, hiring him in the following year as the maritime equivalent of a white hunter. It was Gutiérrez who in 1935 told the author the story of an epic battle with a giant marlin.

SAPPHO, in Alexander Pope's 'On the Characters of Women' (*Moral Essays*, 1731–5), is the poet Lady Mary Wortley Montagu (1689–1762), a beauty who became a slut. 'She was always a dirty little thing', Horace Walpole commented. 'This habit has continued with her.' The eldest daughter of the First Duke of Kingston, she was instrumental in the introduction in England of inoculation against smallpox, a practice she had observed in Turkey – her husband was British ambassador to Constantinople. She is said to have turned away Pope's amorous advances by laughing at him, and the two quarrelled over her 'Town Eclogues'.

SARANOFF, Sergius, in George Bernard Shaw's *Arms and the Man* (1894), is R. B. Cunninghame Graham (see Hushabye, Hector), one of whose exchanges in the House of Commons is echoed by Saranoff. Ordered during a Commons debate to withdraw the word 'damn', he replied, 'I never withdraw.'

SARTORIOUS, Blanche, in George Bernard Shaw's *Widowers' Houses* (1892), is Jenny Patterson. See Craven, Julia.

SARTORIS, Colonel, in William Faulkner's *Sartoris* (1929), is the author's great-grandfather, William C. Falkner (1825−89), novelist, lawyer, railroad builder and Colonel of the 2nd Mississippi Regiment. He wrote *The Little Brick Church* (1882) as a reply to *Uncle Tom's Cabin*, and was shot dead by a former friend and railroad associate whom he had defeated in a State Legislature election.

SARTORIUS, Professor Ludwig, in D. H. Lawrence's *Mr Noon* (1984; first portion published as the story 'Mr Noon' in *A Modern Lover*, 1934), is Alfred Weber (1868−1958), Professor of Sociology and Political Science at Heidelberg University, and the lover of Else von Richthofen (see Kramer, Louise).

SASTRI, Caterina, in George Eliot's 'Mr Gilfil's Love Story' (*Scenes of Clerical Life*, 1858), is Mrs Bernard Ebdell (née Sally Shilton, 1774−1824). The daughter of a Warwickshire miner, she was as a child heard singing on a cottage doorstep by Lady Newdigate (see Cheverel, Lady) and thereupon virtually adopted by the Newdigates, living at their family seat, Arbury Hall, Warwickshire, where she was given singing lessons by an Italian master. In 1801 she married the vicar of Chilvers Coton, a model for Mr Gilfil.

SAUNDERS, Mr, in W. H. Mallock's *The New Republic* (1877), is the mathematician and philosopher William Kingdon Clifford (1845−79), Professor of Mathematics at University College, London, and husband of the novelist and dramatist Mrs W. K. Clifford, author of *Mrs Keith's Crime* (1885).

SAUNDERS, Sebastian, in Speed Lamkin's *The Easter-Egg Hunt* (1954), is Christopher Isherwood (see Pimpernell), whom Lamkin first met in 1951, thereafter becoming a firm friend.

SAUVETERRE, Fabrice de, in Nancy Mitford's *The Pursuit of Love* (1945), is the author's lover, Gaston Palewski (1901–84). Born in Paris, of Polish descent, he served as a bomber pilot in 1940 and was head of General de Gaulle's Free French cabinet from 1942 to 1946; French Ambassador to Rome from 1957 to 1962; Minister of State for Scientific Research from 1962 to 1965; and President of the Fifth Republic's Constitutional Council from 1965 to 1974. In 1969 he married the heiress to the American Gould fortune (see Saint-Loup, Robert de), Violette de Talleyrand-Périgord, Duchesse de Sagan.

SAVAGE, Captain, in Frederick Marryat's *Peter Simple* (1834). Some models upstage fiction, and Thomas Cochrane, Tenth Earl of Dundonald (1775–1860), is one of them. He commanded the frigate *Impérieuse*, which the author joined in 1806 as a fourteen-year-old first-class volunteer, and his exploits included capturing a Spanish frigate (with a crew of 319 and 190-pound cannons) when his own crew totalled fifty-four and his heaviest cannons were 28-pounders. In 1809 he played a prominent part in the breaching of a boom set up by the French to protect blockaded ships in the Aix Roads, an action which earned him the Order of the Bath ... withdrawn in 1814 when he was implicated in a stock market scandal and sentenced to a year's imprisonment. Escaping from gaol, he was recaptured attempting to address the House of Commons. Subsequently an admiral in the Greek and Brazilian navies, he returned to England in 1828, was successively appointed rear-admiral and admiral, and in 1841 had his Order of the Bath restored.

SAVAGE, Naomi, in Anthony West's *Heritage* (1955). The author's mother, Rebecca West (see Helen), blocked this novel's publication in Britain, and it is not difficult to see why. In Naomi Savage she is portrayed as a selfish, mendacious monster, and when *Heritage* appeared in Britain after her death her son (by H. G. Wells) prefaced it with the claim that she had been 'minded to do me what hurt she could ... as long as there was breath in her body'. All this and further expressions of his bitterness towards the mother he called paranoid was too much for Victoria Glendinning, Rebecca West's biographer. In a letter to *The Times* (14 April 1984) she cautioned readers to be sceptical, 'in the face of the campaign by the distinguished writer Anthony West to destroy the personal and professional reputation of his late mother, the more distinguished writer, Rebecca West. An obsession with family matters is recognizable at fifty yards. The public expression of it does the sufferer no good. Dame Rebecca herself was not free from it, but the "hostility and aggression" and spitefulness of which he accuses her . . . are as nothing compared with his own unhappy exhibition of these characteristics.'

SAVAGE, Stephen, in Christopher Isherwood's *Lions and Shadows* (1938), is the poet and critic (Sir) Stephen Spender (1909–   ). In a tribute to Isherwood on his eightieth birthday, Spender looked back on their friendship of fifty-five years and wrote in the *Sunday Times*: 'Isherwood has been attacked for lack of invention, a kind of incurable literal-mindedness: the failure to create successfully an entirely self-sufficient fictitious character who does not refer back at all points to some real person known to Christopher. But his peculiar and hypnotic fascination lies, surely, in his eerie ability to transform "real" persons into fictitious characters that seem more real, as though the reality were fictitious, the fictitious real. Sally Bowles took over from Jean Ross. Fans of Gerald Hamilton at the end of his life became so because he himself had become a continuous performance of Mr Norris.'

SAVELYITCH, in Alexander Pushkin's *The Captain's Daughter* (1836), is the author's lifelong valet, Nikita Kozlov, a serf who taught Pushkin to read and write.

SAXTON, Emily and George, in D. H. Lawrence's *The White Peacock* (1911). Emily is Jessie Chambers (see Leivers, Miriam) and George is an amalgam of George Henry Neville (see Tempest, Leslie) and Alan Aubrey Chambers (see Leivers, Edgar).

SAYBROOK, Tom, in Jack Kerouac's *On the Road* (1957), is the American novelist John Clellon Holmes (1926–   ).

SCHLEGEL, Helen and Margaret, in E. M. Forster's *Howards End* (1910), are said by the author's biographer P. N. Furbank to have been suggested by May, Janet and Hester Dickinson, sisters of Forster's friend, the historian and humanist writer Goldsworthy Lowes Dickinson (1862–1932). Of the three, May Dickinson is the most positively perceived, in Margaret Schlegel. Her dedication to intellectual self-improvement prompted her to learn Greek at eighty. The sisters were much involved in social work and staged theatricals at the London Working Men's College in Great Ormond Street.

SCHOOL-MISS ALFRED, in Edward Bulwer Lytton's 'The New Timon' (1846), is the poet Alfred, Lord Tennyson (1809–92), who avenged himself in *Punch* with 'The New Timon and the Poets', in which Bulwer (always something of a dandy) is addressed as 'you band-box'.

SCHROEDER, Fräulein Lina, in Christopher Isherwood's *Mr Norris Changes Trains* (1935) and *Goodbye to Berlin* (1939), is Meta Thurau, the author's Berlin landlady in Nollendorfstrasse in the 1930s. Her only objection to the portrait was that she did not believe she waddled.

SCHWEIK, Josef. See Švejk, Josef.

SCOGAN, Mr, in Aldous Huxley's *Crome Yellow* (1921). In T. S. Eliot's annotated copy of *Crome Yellow*, Mr Scogan is identified as Bertrand Russell (see Mattheson, Sir Joshua). Eliot appears to have been wrong, because when Huxley was interviewed for the *Paris Review* he made no mention of Russell but said there was something of Norman Douglas (see Argyle, James) in Mr Scogan.

SCOT-CRICHTON, Dorian, in Rayner Heppenstall's *The Lesser Infortune* (1953). Anthony Powell could hardly have expected to keep such an eccentric as Julian Maclaren-Ross (see Trapnel, Francis X.) all to himself. At least one other novelist has used him, according to Mark Amory who in the *Tatler* (October 1984) named Dorian Scot-Crichton as Maclaren-Ross in disguise.

SCOTT, Cyril, in D. H. Lawrence's *Aaron's Rod* (1922), is the composer Cecil Gray (see Sharpe, James), appearing under the name of another composer, Cyril Scott, whom Lawrence met in 1917 at a house party. The novel's Cyril Scott suggests that Julia Cunningham should live with him in Dorset, just as in reality Cecil Gray persuaded Hilda Doolittle (the model for Julia) to join him in Cornwall.

SCRAG, Gosling, in the first edition of Tobias Smollett's *Peregrine Pickle* (1751), is the statesman George Lyttelton, First Baron Lyttelton (1709–73). As Smollett forecast, he used his influence to secure the appointment of Justice of the Peace of Westminster for the lawyer-novelist Henry Fielding. Briefly Chancellor of the Exchequer (although, according to a contemporary, he never mastered mathematics sufficiently to know that two and two made four), he also appears as 'another guest' in James Thomson's *The Castle of Indolence* (1748), canto one. Fielding is *Peregrine Pickle*'s Mr Spondy.

SCRATCHERD, Sir Roger, in Anthony Trollope's *Doctor Thorne* (1858), is the landscape gardener and architect Sir Joseph Paxton (1801–65), who was superintendent of the Duke of Devonshire's Chatsworth estate and who designed London's Crystal Palace, a source of great curiosity while it was under construction. So many eminent people attempted to see what was going on behind the hoardings that when the Duke of Devonshire sought permission to visit the site Lord Granville declared, 'If any exception is to be made for him, it can only be as Paxton and Company.'

SCRIASSINE, Victor, in Simone de Beauvoir's *The Mandarins* (1954), is the Hungarian-born novelist and writer on science, Arthur Koestler (1905–83), whose *Darkness at Noon* becomes *The Red Paradise* in *The Mandarins*. A perfectionist to the end, he made four drafts of his suicide note.

SCRIVEN, Mary, in Christopher Isherwood's *The Memorial* (1932), is Olive Mangeot. See Cheuret, Mme.

SEAL, Basil, in Evelyn Waugh's *Black Mischief* (1932), *Put Out More Flags* (1942) and 'Basil Seal Rides Again' (1963). Two of Waugh's Oxford contemporaries are the primary models for Seal: Basil Murray (1902–37) and the Hon. Peter Murray Rennell Rodd (1904–68). Basil Murray, whom Waugh found highly intelligent but flashy and satanic, was the son of Gilbert Murray (see Cusins, Professor Adolphus). A profound disappointment to his father, he took only a Third in Classical Moderations at Oxford, failed to make a success of any career, was continually in debt and thrice unhappily married, and died in Spain during the Civil War. Rodd, the second son of the First Lord Rennell, married the novelist Nancy Mitford in 1933. They were divorced in 1958. His considerable erudition combined oddly with breathtaking irresponsibility and a lust for adventure which found expression in his work with refugees in the Spanish Civil War. In the Second World War he served as a lieutenant-colonel in the Welsh Guards. Two other models have been suggested by Lord Lovat (see Trimmer): Basil Sheridan Hamilton-Temple-Blackwood, Fourth Marquess of Dufferin and Ava (1909—45), and Auberon Herbert (1922—74). The Marquess, who as a house guest would borrow a pound from the butler and then tip him with it, was killed in action in Burma. He was the father of the novelist Caroline Blackwood, and is lamented in Betjeman's 'Friend of my youth, you are dead!' Herbert was the son of the Hon. Aubrey Herbert (see Arbuthnot, Sandy) and the brother-in-law of Waugh, who had such an aversion to him that Herbert could meet his sister only in secret.

SEDLEY, Amelia and Joshua, in W. M. Thackeray's *Vanity Fair* (1847—8). Had Thackeray written this novel ten years earlier, it would probably have lacked the pathos that is one of its character-istics. In 1836 Thackeray had married Isabella Shawe (*d.* 1894), despite opposition from her mother (see Baynes, Mrs). He was becoming established as a writer and his marriage to Isabella — upon whom Amelia is modelled in part — was happy. But in 1840, after the birth of their third child, Isabella became insane, and although she survived throwing herself into the Irish Sea from a cross-channel packet, she remained schizophrenic and spent the rest of her days confined to a home, outliving Thackeray by thirty-one years. One of her daughters became Lady Ritchie (see Hilbery, Mrs Katherine); another was the first wife of Virginia Woolf's father. In the latter part of *Vanity Fair*, Mrs W. H. Brookfield (see Castle-wood, Lady) is also apparent in Amelia. Joshua Sedley is the author's cousin and schoolfellow, George Trant Shakespear (*d.* 1844), a writer in the service of the East India Company. He was an overweight, eccentric, self-centred bachelor of considerable charm and his death in Geneva was believed to be suicide.

SENTIMENT, Mr Popular, in Anthony Trollope's *The Warden* (1855), has as prototype Charles Dickens (1812—70), in his role as a reforming novelist.

SETON, Sally, in Virginia Woolf's *Mrs Dalloway* (1925), is Madge Symonds (1869—1925), daughter of John Addington Symonds (see Opalstein). Woolf had an adolescent infatuation for her, but Symonds married the author's cousin, William Wyamar Vaughan (1865—1938), headmaster of Giggleswick School, in Yorkshire.

SETTEMBRINI, in Thomas Mann's *The Magic Mountain* (1924), is the author's novelist brother, Heinrich Mann (1871–1950), with whom Thomas Mann found himself at odds during the First World War, objecting to his anti-German stance and subsequently satirising his Italian proclivities.

SEYMOUR, Humphrey, in C. P. Snow's *The Conscience of the Rich* (1958), is Claud Cockburn (1904–81), founder-editor of *The Week* from 1933 to 1946, diplomatic and foreign correspondent of the *Daily Worker* from 1935 to 1946, and subsequently a regular contributor to *Punch,* the *New Statesman* and the *Saturday Evening Post* and a columnist of the *Irish Times.* As a foreign news sub-editor with *The Times* in the 1920s he won a competition for the most boring headline: 'Small earthquake in Chile: not many dead.' See also Bowles, Sally.

SEYMOUR, Valerie, in Radclyffe Hall's *The Well of Loneliness* (1928), is Natalie Clifford Barney (see Flossie, Miss), according to her biographer, Jean Chalon.

SHALLOW, Justice, in William Shakespeare's *Henry IV,* Part II (*c.* 1597–8) and *The Merry Wives of Windsor* (*c.* 1600–1). Shakespeare is believed to have left Stratford-upon-Avon in 1585 to avoid prosecution for poaching in the park of Sir Thomas Lucy (1532–1600), of Charlecote, a Stratford Justice of the Peace who was MP for Warwick in 1571 and 1584 and who rebuilt Charlecote as it is today. His identification with Shallow is supported by Shallow's coat of arms which, like Lucy's, displays twelve luces (pike). Interestingly, if less plausibly, Leslie Hotson contends in *Shakespeare versus Shallow* (1931) that the original is William Gardner (1531–97), a London Justice of the Peace who was involved in a dispute with the proprietor of the Swan theatre. Through his marriage into the family of Sir Robert Luce, his coat of arms included three luces. The number of luces, I feel, is the clincher: had Gardner been Shakespeare's target, the dramatist would surely have specified a trio of luces rather than the dozen displayed by Sir Thomas. Furthermore, Shallow's recruitment of bumpkins and his ownership of deer suggests a Charlecote original rather than a London model. Gardner predeceased *The Merry Wives of Windsor,* and perhaps also *Henry IV,* Part II. Would Shakespeare really have troubled to satirise him beyond the grave?

SHAMUS, in John le Carré's *The Naive and Sentimental Lover* (1971), is the novelist James Kennaway (*d.* 1968), with whose wife (see Helen) le Carré (see Fiddes, Dr) had an affair in 1963.

SHAND, John, in J. M. Barrie's *What Every Woman Knows* (1908). A popular novelist and a premier are combined in John Shand. The novelist is A. E. W. Mason (1865–1948), saviour of Barrie's sanity when he was divorced (see Rodney, Frederick and Jane) and author of his entry in the *Dictionary of National Biography*. In 1906 Mason became the Liberal MP for Coventry, Barrie accompanying him during his election campaign and attending the count as one of Mason's tellers. 'He is as big a swell as ever', Barrie wrote of Mason to a mutual friend, 'but his socks don't match and so all is well.' While touches of Mason are apparent in Shand, the primary prototype is Ramsay MacDonald (1866–1937), three times Britain's Prime Minister, as a young man.

SHANDON, Captain Charles, in W. M. Thackeray's *The History of Pendennis* (1848–50), is the Irish journalist William Maginn (1793–1842), who wrote for *Blackwood's Magazine* under the name Ensign O'Doherty. In 1830 he founded *Fraser's Magazine*, to which Thackeray contributed in more ways than one — Maginn cultivated him and touched him for £500. Subsequently imprisoned for debt and declared bankrupt, Maginn jeopardised his journalistic reputation by writing for Tory and Radical journals simultaneously. He died in poverty.

SHANDY, Mrs Elizabeth and Captain Toby, in Laurence Sterne's *The Life and Opinions of Tristram Shandy* (1759–67). Elizabeth is the author's wife, Elizabeth Lumley (1714–73), a clergyman's daughter whom he met in York and married in 1741. She was reputed to be acrimonious and quick to take offence, but life with the profligate Sterne -- something of a rake in cleric's clothing — cannot have been easy. Uncle Toby is the author's father, Roger Sterne (1692–1731), a grandson of Richard Sterne, Archbishop of York, and a lieutenant in the 34th Regiment of Foot (now the King's Own Royal Border Regiment). Like Toby he was much occupied by sieges — he was a veteran of no fewer than four. And just as Toby was wounded in the groin, so was Roger Sterne injured — not in battle, but in a duel with a fellow officer over a goose. He died of fever while serving in Jamaica.

SHANKLAND, Anne, in Terence Rattigan's 'Table by the Window' (*Separate Tables*, 1954), is said by the author's biographers, Michael Darlow and Gillian Hodson, to be part-inspired by Jean Dawnay, a leading London fashion model of the 1950s and a confidante of Rattigan.

SHANTSEE, Mr Rumblesack, in Thomas Love Peacock's *Crotchet Castle* (1831), is Robert Southey. See Feathernest, Mr. For the 'sack' element of the name, see Sackbut, Roderick.

SHARP, Jawster, in Benjamin Disraeli's *Coningsby* (1844), is John Bright (see Turnbull, Mr). He and Disraeli regarded each other with distrust. 'I would give all I ever had to have made that speech you made just now', said Disraeli after one of Bright's feats of oratory. 'Well, you might have made it', replied Bright, 'if you had been honest.'

SHARPE, James, in D. H. Lawrence's *Kangaroo* (1923), is Cecil Gray (1895–1951), an Edinburgh-born musician, composer of operas, writer on musical subjects and lover of Hilda Doolittle (see Masters, Miranda; see also Scott, Cyril). During the First World War he was a neighbour of the author in Cornwall, living at Bosigran Castle. The Lawrences were with him in his cliff-top home one night when security men burst in and accused them of displaying a light in an attempt to signal a German submarine. Lawrence was regarded as a possible spy because of his German wife, a relative of a celebrated German fighter pilot. Gray was fined as a result of this light-showing incident and the Lawrences were given three days to leave Cornwall; as security risks, they were forbidden to live in any other prohibited area. Gray, who told his story in *Musical Chairs* (1948), was fond of recalling the time he answered a knock at his door to be confronted by Lawrence asking, 'Gray, how long have you loved me?'

SHATOV, in Fyodor Dostoevsky's *The Devils* (1871–2), is a revolutionary student named Ivanov, who attended Moscow Agricultural Academy. In 1869, when he declined to pledge unswerving allegiance to Nechayev (see Verkhovensky, Pyotr), he was murdered by fellow members of his cell, on Nechayev's orders.

SHATOV, Michael, in Dorothy Richardson's *Deadlock* (1921). John Rosenberg's *Dorothy Richardson: The Genius They Forgot* (1973) identifies Michael Shatov as Bernard Grad, a Russian Jew whom the author met when she was in lodgings in London, and to whom she was briefly engaged. His marriage to one of her closest friends in 1908 ended in divorce. Interned in France during the Second World War, he later worked in Paris for the European Central Inland Transport Organisation.

SHAUN THE POSTMAN, in James Joyce's *Finnegans Wake* (1939). 'Biography, history, myth, dissolve, heave, and finally solidify into one', wrote John Wain in the *Observer* (4 June 1961), asserting that Shaun is, 'in different facets', the author's brother, Professor Stanislaus Joyce (1884–1955), of Trieste University; Wyndham Lewis (see Lypiatt, Casimir); the Irish-born tenor John McCormack (1884–1945); and T. S. Eliot (see Horty, Mr). The Joyce authority Richard Ellmann, however, names only Stanislaus among Wain's candidates, but adds two more: the Irish statesman Éamon De Valera (1882–1975) and John Ford, a Dublin sandwich-board carrier who was mentally retarded and inarticulate like his brother, James, the two being known in the city as Shem and Shaun. Shaun is generally regarded as being primarily Stanislaus, Shem the penman representing the author.

SHAW, Gordon, in Eugene O'Neill's *Strange Interlude* (1928), has as prototype the American Ivy League athlete 'Hobey' Baker, who was described by F. Scott Fitzgerald as 'an ideal worthy of everything in my enthusiastic admiration'.

SHAW, Harriet Finnian and Lord Osmund Finnian, in Wyndham Lewis's *The Apes of God* (1930), are the author's arch enemies Edith and Osbert Sitwell. See Whittlebot, Hernia and Gob; see also Debingham, Henry, and Esor, Stanley.

SHAWCROSS, Hamer, in Howard Spring's *Fame is the Spur* (1940), has Ramsay MacDonald (see Shand, John) as prototype. Shawcross's increasing wariness and partiality for compromise as his career progresses reflect MacDonald's alienation from his own party upon his formation of a coalition government in 1931, and echo Churchill's description of him as 'a boneless wonder'.

SHCHERBATSKY, Ekaterina (Kitty), in Leo Tolstoy's *Anna Karenina* (1873–7), is the author's wife, Sonya Behrs. See Pozdnyshev, Madame.

SHEARWATER, James, in Aldous Huxley's *Antic Hay* (1923), is Professor J. B. S. Haldane (1892–1964), an outstanding geneticist, populariser of science, brother of the novelist Naomi Mitchison and the author of a children's book which deservedly became an early Puffin: *My Friend Mr Leakey* (1937). A mixture of contradictions, extreme rudeness and kindliness among them, Haldane habitually risked his life by using himself as a guinea-pig in dangerous experiments. While Reader in Biochemistry at Cambridge he became the centre of scandal after the *Daily Express* sent a reporter, Charlotte Burgess, to interview him. Her husband subsequently divorced her, citing Haldane as co-respondent. Sacked for 'gross immorality', Haldane went to court and had his dismissal overruled. Charlotte Burgess (subsequently a novelist and playwright) became his first wife. As a Communist, Haldane was from 1940 to 1949 chairman of the editorial board of the *Daily Worker*. In 1957 he settled in India, returning to England in 1964 for a cancer operation which prompted him to telerecord his own obituary. This was duly broadcast after his death in India, where he claimed to be 'the only Hindu atheist'. As an undergraduate, Huxley lived with the Haldanes at their home, Cherwell Edge; but C. P. Snow condemned his Shearwater as a portrait drawn from the outside without empathy, giving readers who didn't know Haldane no proper impression of the man. Oddly, since most of his colleagues appeared as characters in his novels, Snow seems never to have used Haldane as a model.

SHELDON, Lorraine, in Moss Hart and George S. Kaufman's *The Man Who Came To Dinner* (1939), is Gertrude Lawrence (see Lyppiatt, Joanna), who was 'travestied', in the view of the Kaufman biographer Malcolm Goldstein, as 'a playwright's paradigm of seductiveness and egocentricity'.

SHELDON, Perry, in Noël Coward's *A Song at Twilight* (1966), has Gerald Haxton (see Flint, Rowley) as his prototype, according to Coward's biographer, Sheridan Morley.

SHELMERDINE, Marmaduke Bontrop, in Virginia Woolf's *Orlando* (1928), is Harold Nicolson (see Chilleywater, the Hon. Harold). His fears that his wife's lesbianism might be revealed turned to delight when he read the book, finding it 'one of the strangest and most brilliant evocations ever composed'.

SHIFT, in Samuel Foote's *The Minor* (1760), is the actor-manager Tate Wilkinson (1739–1808), the most celebrated mimic of his day. His speciality was taking-off his fellow actors – including Foote, who was enraged by Wilkinson's imitation.

SHIRIN, in Victoria Sackville-West's *The Dark Island* (1934), is the author's sister-in-law, Gwendolen St Aubyn (*b*. 1896). Daughter of the First Baron Carnock, she married Francis Cecil St Aubyn, Third Baron St Levan (*d*. 1978). He succeeded to the title in 1940, whereupon the family seat, St Michael's Mount, Cornwall, became the couple's home. In later years Lady St Levan became a convert to Roman Catholicism.

SHOBBE, Herr, in Richard Aldington's *Death of a Hero* (1929), is Ford Madox Ford (see Braddocks, Henry) presented as a 'plump, talented snob of German origin' (Ford's father was German) running 'one of those "advanced" reviews beloved by the English, which move rapidly forward with a crab-like motion.'

SHODBUTT, Samuel, in Wyndham Lewis's *The Roaring Queen* (1936). Arnold Bennett (see Nixon, Mr) had been dead for five years when this novel appeared, but that did not deter Lewis from pursuing him. In portraying him as Shodbutt, he was perhaps still smarting from Bennett's remarks in a review written in 1927: 'Wyndham Lewis has considerable gifts, with a slightly amateurish technique. But he is always going and never arriving . . . I would like to be able to state what Mr Wyndham Lewis is mainly "after", but I cannot, because I have not been able to find out. One of his minor purposes is to disembowel his enemies, who are numerous. He would be less tiresome if he were more urbane.' Had he been more urbane, however, he would not have been Wyndham Lewis.

SHORE, Jemima, in Antonia Fraser's *Quiet as a Nun* (1977), *The Wild Island* (1978) and *Cool Repentance* (1982), owes her professionalism, as the author has acknowledged, to Joan Bakewell (1933–   ), broadcaster, writer and television presenter.

SHOTOVER, Captain, in George Bernard Shaw's *Heartbreak House* (1917). 'Sometimes one conceives or observes or hears of a character who insists on being dramatised', remarked Shaw, on being told by the actress Lena Ashwell (Lady Simson, 1872–1957) of her father's career. Commander Charles Ashwell Boteler Pocock,

Shaw's Captain Shotover, was reputed to have become a midshipman at the age of eleven. He took part in the capture of a slave ship, served in the Burmese War, lived in New Zealand, captained a Tyneside ship upon which he quartered his family (complete with nursery and greenhouse) and after taking holy orders settled in Canada as a Church of England clergyman. On his death-bed he refused Communion unless he could have cheese with his consecrated bread. His children also included the explorer Captain Roger Pocock, R.N. (1865–1941). Lena Ashwell, seeing what Shaw had made of her father, said there was no resemblance between 'that quaint old drunkard and my grand old darling with his power of self-control, or self-denial'. There I would have liked to leave Shotover/Pocock, defiantly putting his piece of cheese before his peace with God. In December 1984, however, another candidate emerged. In a BBC World Service programme a BBC pioneer of the 1920s, Cecil Lewis, recalled lunching with Shaw almost every week when the dramatist first became involved in broadcasting. 'I remember on one occasion he was asked if all his characters were invented', said Lewis. 'He replied, "Sometimes they are taken from life". Captain Shotover, for instance, in *Heartbreak House* was moulded on Gordon Craig's father who, on his death-bed, had refused to take the bread of Extreme Unction unless he could have some cheese with it.' Gordon Craig was the illegitimate son of the architect and theatre designer Edward William Godwin (1833–86).

SHYLOCK, in William Shakespeare's *The Merchant of Venice* (*c.* 1596), is supposedly Roderigo Lopez (*d.* 1594), a Jewish doctor at St Bartholomew's Hospital, London. Of Spanish extraction, in 1586 he became principal physician to Elizabeth I. Eight years later he was hanged for conspiring to murder her.

SIB, the, in Wyndham Lewis's *The Apes of God* (1930), is the journalist and novelist Ada Leverson (née Beddington, 1862–1933), for whom Oscar Wilde's pet name was 'the Sphinx'.

SIBLEY, Joe, in George Du Maurier's *Trilby* (1894), is the American artist James Abbott McNeill Whistler (1834–1903), who was incensed by the portrait when *Trilby* first appeared in serial form in *Harper's Magazine*, taking legal advice and threatening violence. Du Maurier consequently toned down the caricature for the novel's appearance in book form.

SID, in Mark Twain's *The Adventures of Tom Sawyer* (1876), is the author's younger brother, Henry Clemens – but Henry, 'although exasperatingly good', was 'a very much finer and better boy than ever Sid was', the author noted in his autobiography. Henry died in 1858 from an overdose of morphine administered while he was recovering from injuries sustained in a boiler explosion on the New Orleans and St Louis packet *Pennsylvania*, on which he was employed as a junior clerk.

SIDNEY, Lord John, in Benjamin Disraeli's *Coningsby* (1844), is Lord John Manners (1818–1906), a founder member of the Young England party of the 1840s, in which Disraeli was a prominent figure. Manners was subsequently a Conservative statesman, and in 1888 he succeeded his brother, becoming the Seventh Duke of Rutland.

SIDROPHEL, in Samuel Butler's *Hudibras* (1663–78), is believed to be the astrologer William Lilly (1602–81), who published an annual almanac from 1644 to 1680. In addition to forecasting the outcome of Civil War battles, he claimed to be able to discover people's birthmarks from their horoscopes. In Butler's 'Heroical Epistle of Hudibras to Sidrophel', however, Sidrophel has been taken to be Sir Paul Neile, an original member of the Royal Society who claimed to have proved that Butler was not the author of *Hudibras*. Neile is also the target of Butler's 'The Elephant in the Moon'.

SILK, Ambrose, in Evelyn Waugh's *Put Out More Flags* (1942). A homosexual exhibitionist with a keen sense of the theatrical, Brian Christian de Claiborne Howard (1905–58) is the principal model for Silk. Of American parentage, he was educated at Eton and at Christ Church, Oxford, and on leaving university acquired a reputation for his stage-management of wild parties, for his physical courage and for his delight in the outrageous – on one occasion he was rescued by the police from the Thames after jumping off Westminster Bridge. He was nicknamed 'Hat' after his successful hoax of 1929, when he staged an exhibition of avant-garde paintings ostensibly by one Bruno Hat but actually by himself. Evelyn Waugh wrote the catalogue; Lytton Strachey was among the buyers. He did some reviewing for the *New Statesman* and his *First Poems* were published by Nancy Cunard in 1931, but he failed to fulfil his early promise. Society's horror of homosexuality in his day left him unabashed –

he even requested the British Consul in Athens to assist him in the prosecution of a local physician who had failed to cure the gonorrhoea he had caught from a Greek sailor. In the Second World War he served as an aircraftman in the RAF. He committed suicide in Nice by taking an overdose of drugs, following the accidental death of his lover.

SILLIVITCH, Countess, in Charles Brooks's *Hints to Pilgrims* (1921). So extravagantly bizarre was Baroness Elsa von Freytag-Loringhoven (*d.* 1927) that it is small wonder most of her writer acquaintances avoided her both in life and in their fiction: nobody would have believed her. A much-married widow whose real name was Ploetz, she lived in poverty in New York's Greenwich Village. She periodically shaved her head and painted it purple, stuck two-cent pink postage stamps on her cheeks in place of rouge and wore black lipstick and yellow face powder. Her hats included a coal scuttle, a cake (complete with lit candles) and a fruit basket. Today's punk youth could have learned much from her. When the poet William Carlos Williams paid her a compliment she took this as a declaration of love and volunteered to give him syphilis to clear his mind for his art. The disease, she explained, had been bequeathed her by her father on his wedding night. Pursuing Williams to Rutherford, New Jersey, she was said to have opened her fur coat, revealing herself naked and announcing, 'Villiam Carlos Villiams, I vant you!' When he failed to co-operate, she attacked him. Hart Crane bought himself another typewriter rather than risk seeing her again by retrieving the one he had lent her; Wallace Stevens also went in fear of her after a traumatic encounter. She worked as an artists' model for painters including George Bellows (see Mallows, Henry), and after following her friend the novelist Djuna Barnes to Paris, she committed suicide. Connoisseurs of eccentrics seeking further information are directed to Andrew Field's *The Formidable Miss Barnes* (1983).

SILVER, Long John, in Robert Louis Stevenson's *Treasure Island* (1883). Few men could claim to have made a more positive impact upon late nineteenth-century popular fiction than the poet, critic and dramatist W. E. Henley (1849–1903). As a publisher's reader, he was largely responsible for the acceptance of Rider Haggard's previously much-rejected *King Solomon's Mines*; and as Stevenson's friend and collaborator (see Jekyll, Dr) he was the model for Long John Silver, who displays the magnetic, vigorous and darker aspects of Henley as well as the shared loss of a leg — Henley's left leg was amputated when he was sixteen, to arrest a tubercular infection. Stevenson acknowledged that Henley's 'maimed masterfulness' was 'the germ from which John Silver grew', and the characterisation was perhaps prophetic. In 1888 the two quarrelled, and towards the end of his life Henley contributed a vitriolic profile of Stevenson to the *Pall Mall Magazine*. Not only did the article scandalise polite literary society: it also tended to vindicate Stevenson's *Treasure Island* portrait.

SILVÈRE, in Émile Zola's *La Fortune des Rougon* (1870–1), is Philippe Solari. See Mahoudeau.

SILVIA, in 'A Silvia', by Giacomo Leopardi (1798–1837), is Teresa Fattorini, daughter of the poet's father's coachman. Leopardi is believed never to have spoken to her — acutely aware of his unprepossessing appearance, he lamented that all that he saw and loved could never be his.

SIMON, in George Sand's *Simon* (1836), is primarily the author's lover, Louis Chrysostome Michel, a Bourges lawyer of peasant parentage, militant republicanism and outstanding oratorical talent. The hero's romance, however, is inspired by the liaison of Franz Liszt (see Conti, Gennaro) and Marie d'Agoult (see Rochefide, Béatrix de).

SIMON, in Émile Zola's *Vérité* (1903), has as prototype Captain Alfred Dreyfus (1859–1935), a Jewish officer in the French War Office who in 1894 was court-martialled for allegedly passing military secrets to the German Embassy in Paris. Convicted and cashiered, he was sentenced to solitary confinement for life on Devil's Island. Two years later, evidence came to light suggesting that Dreyfus had been 'framed' by a French officer in the pay of the Germans. Pressure grew for a retrial, there were allegations of a War Office cover-up, and in 1899 Dreyfus was pardoned. Reinstated with the rank of Major, he served with distinction in the First World War and was awarded the Légion d'honneur. Zola played a leading part in the campaign to secure justice for Dreyfus. Tried for libelling the War Office in his open letter, *J'accuse*, he was convicted, sentenced to imprisonment, and took refuge in England for a year.

SIMONET, Albertine, in Marcel Proust's *A la recherche du temps perdu* (1913–27). Gender was often irrelevant in Proust's confection of a character, and elements of models of both sexes are mingled in Albertine: probably primarily Alfred Agostinelli (1888–1914), a Monégasque of Italian extraction. Proust met him at Cabourg in 1907 and he became the author's secretary and chauffeur. He left to become an aviator, and while taking flying lessons (under the name of Marcel Swann) was killed when his plane crashed into the sea near Antibes. Also perceived in Albertine are Colette d'Alton, daughter of the Vicomte d'Alton and recipient of the gold handbag presented to Albertine in the novel; Marie de Chevilly, whose father owned a *château* at Montjoux, Savoy — Proust flirted with her in 1899, when she was engaged to a journalist; Marie Finaly (1873–1918), with whom Proust fell in love at Trouville in 1892 — the sister of Horace Finaly (see Bloch), she married in 1897 and died in an influenza epidemic; Louisa de Mornand (see Rachel); Albert Nahmias, son of the financial correspondent of *Le Gaulois* and Proust's secretary in 1912; Marie Nördlinger (1876–1981), daughter of a Manchester shipping merchant, cousin of the composer and conductor Reynaldo Hahn and a translator of Ruskin in collaboration with Proust, who commissioned her (as a silversmith) to produce a bronze portrait plaque for his father's grave; and Henri Rochat, a Swiss who was working at the Hôtel Ritz in Paris when Proust first met him and who became the last of the author's secretaries, although his painting was better than his spelling.

SIMONY, Dr, in Samuel Foote's *The Cozeners* (1774), is supposedly Dr William Dodd (1729–77), who was appointed chaplain to the King in 1763 and was executed in London fourteen years later for forging the name of his former pupil, Lord Chesterfield, in relation to a bond for £4,200. Dr Samuel Johnson was among those who appealed against his death sentence.

SIMPLE, Peter, in Frederick Marryat's *Peter Simple* (1834), owes something to Rear-Admiral Donat Henchy O'Brien (1785–1857). Joining the navy in 1796, in 1804 he was captured and taken as a prisoner to Verdun after his ship was wrecked. In 1808 he escaped from Napoleon's fortress at Bitche, north of Strasbourg. At the request of the Governor of Malta he wrote an account of his adventure, for onward transmission to the Admiralty. His narrative was subsequently published, and he became a Rear-Admiral in 1852.

SINCLAIR, Jock, in James Kennaway's *Tunes of Glory* (1956), according to the author's biographer, Trevor Royle, is Captain John ('Jock') Laurie, of the Gordon Highlanders. As a National Serviceman in Germany in 1948, Kennaway observed Laurie's hard drinking and general belligerence.

SINGLETON, Sam, in Henry James's *Roderick Hudson* (1876), is suggested by the author's biographer, Leon Edel, to be an amalgam of Eugene Benson (1839–1908), a landscape painter who James met in Rome and Venice, and John Rollin Tilton (1833–88), another artist encountered by the author in Rome.

SIR, in Ronald Harwood's *The Dresser* (1980), is part-inspired by the actor-manager Sir Donald Wolfit (1902–68), to whom the author was dresser. Wolfit's largely itinerant professional life prompted an uncharitable (and unoriginal) quip from Clement Freud in the House of Commons, comparing him with the actor Sir John Gielgud: one was a *tour de force* while the other was forced to tour. (Who was first with that word-play? Mrs Patrick Campbell, in a message to Eleonora Duse: 'Your performance is a *tour de force*. That is why I am forced to tour.')

SISSON, Aaron, in D. H. Lawrence's *Aaron's Rod* (1922). Although he seems to owe his personality to John Middleton Murry (see Crich, Gerald), in appearance Sisson is suggested by the Lawrence biographers Keith Sagar and Harry T. Moore to be modelled on Thomas Cooper, a talented flautist and teacher turned colliery checkweighman who lived next door to Lawrence in Eastwood, Nottinghamshire, in 1904. Of his five daughters, four died in their twenties of consumption.

SIX, Auburn, in Carl Van Vechten's *Spider Boy* (1928), is the film actress Aileen Pringle (1895–   ), who scandalised lip-readers of one of her silent movies when they observed the swooning heroine say to a man carrying her downstairs, 'If you drop me, you bastard, I'll murder you!'

SIXTINE, in Remy de Gourmont's *Sixtine, Roman de la vie cérébrale* (1890), is Berthe Courrière. See Chantelouve, Mme Hyacinthe.

SKEFFINGTON, Frank, in Edwin O'Connor's *The Last Hurrah* (1956), has as prototype James M. Curley (1874–1958), American statesman and three times mayor of Boston, which he was accused of bringing near to bankruptcy through his lavish expenditure on parks and hospitals. Ruthless to enemies, generous to friends, he spent part of his last mayoralty in gaol for corruption.

SKENE, Hugh, in Eric Linklater's *Magnus Merriman* (1934), is the Scottish poet Hugh MacDiarmid (Christopher Murray Grieve, 1892–1978), who acknowledged the portrait to be himself 'to a T . . . The dirty hands are, of course, due to my going with my hands constantly in pockets full of loose black tobacco.'

SKENE, Ned, in George Bernard Shaw's *Cashel Byron's Profession* (1885–6). In his mid-twenties, Shaw was a keen amateur boxer, coached by Ned Donnelly – his model for Skene – who had a gymnasium in London at 18 Panton Street, Haymarket, and who wrote *Self-Defence, or the Art of Boxing*. He was also Professor of Boxing to the London Athletic Club.

SKI, in Marcel Proust's *A la recherche du temps perdu* (1913–27), is the artist Frédéric ('Coco') de Madrazo (?1878–1938), stepson of the sister of the composer Reynaldo Hahn, Maria.

SKIMPOLE, Harold, in Charles Dickens's *Bleak House* (1852–3). Congratulating himself on this delineation of the poet, critic, essayist and journalist Leigh Hunt (1784–1859), Dickens wrote in a private letter, 'I suppose he [Skimpole] is the most exact portrait that was ever painted in words . . . the likeness is astonishing. I don't think it could be more like the man himself . . . it is an absolute reproduction of a real man.' He sought to mollify Hunt's offended friends by claiming that Skimpole's weaknesses were his own. But in denying that any of Skimpole's less attractive traits had been inspired by Hunt – 'the very soul of truth and honour' – Dickens conveniently ignored the fact that Hunt had shocked society with a less than idealised study of Byron, whose patronage he had been happy to enjoy although he later had reason to feel that Byron had let him down. Doubtless mindful of the possibility of litigation, Dickens made amends by writing a profile of Hunt in *All the Year Round* and by inviting Hunt's son to contribute an article describing his father's true character to *Household Words*. Although Hunt was imprisoned in 1813 for libelling the Prince Regent as 'a violator of his word, a libertine over head and ears in disgrace', he survived to receive a Civil List pension and a gift of £50 from Queen Victoria.

For he had been a pioneer of constructive drama criticism, and was the first to publish Keats, whom he introduced to Shelley. The diary-writing aspect of Skimpole was inspired by Benjamin Robert Haydon (1786–1846), a celebrated historical painter noted for his devotion to biblical subjects long after they had gone out of fashion. He shot himself following prolonged financial difficulties which led to his imprisonment, and Dickens was among those who subscribed to a fund for his dependants after his suicide. See also Father.

SKIONAR, Mr, in Thomas Love Peacock's *Crotchet Castle* (1831), is Samuel Taylor Coleridge (1772–1834), whom Peacock admired as a poet but ridiculed for his commitment to the metaphysical philosophy of Kant and the terminological thicket that went with it.

SKULLION, in Tom Sharpe's *Porterhouse Blue* (1974), is supposedly Albert Jaggard (*d.* 1982), head porter at Corpus Christi, Cambridge, where he was a college servant for more than half a century.

SLADE, Gilgo, in Hamilton Basso's *Sun in Capricorn* (1942), has Huey Long as prototype. See Stark, Willie.

SLADE, Larry, in Eugene O'Neill's *The Iceman Cometh* (1946), is Terry Carlin (né O'Carolan), the son of Irish parents who emigrated to the United States when he was a child. An eloquent, philosophical, anarchistic alcoholic, he eschewed work and lived on his wits in a Cape Cod shack. His mistress, Marie, was the inspiration of O'Neill's Anna Christie, and his acquaintances included Theodore Dreiser and Jack London.

SLAVIN, Joel, in Sinclair Lewis and Dore Schary's *Storm in the West* (written 1943, published 1963), is Joseph Stalin. See Boss.

SLINKTON, Julius, in Charles Dickens's 'Hunted Down' (1859), is Thomas Griffiths Wainewright (see Varney, Gabriel), whom Dickens encountered on a tour of Newgate Prison with the actor William Charles Macready. (See also Rigaud, Monsieur.) Slinkton may also be part-inspired by Palmer the Poisoner – William Palmer (1824–56), of Rugeley, Staffordshire, whose case Dickens studied and wrote about in 'Demeanour of Murderers'. In 1853 Palmer won about £14,000 in the Chester Cup at Chester Races, losing most of it a few weeks later by laying his winnings against the horse West

Australian in the Derby. 'Have you nothing to regret, William?' asked his clergyman brother when, after allegedly killing numerous friends and relations, Palmer arrived at the scaffold. 'I have never ceased to reproach myself', said the poisoner, 'for opposing West Australian.'

SLOP, Dr, in Laurence Sterne's *The Life and Opinions of Tristram Shandy* (1759–67), is Dr John Burton, a York physician whose overtures to Prince Charles Edward at Lancaster in 1745 led to his trial as a suspected Jacobite.

SLOPER, Dr Austin, in Henry James's *Washington Square* (1881), is supposedly part-inspired by the author's elder brother, the psychologist and philosopher William James (1842–1910), who found Henry's success as a novelist difficult to comprehend – just as Sloper cannot believe that anyone could find his daughter attractive.

SLUDGE, Mr, in Robert Browning's 'Mr Sludge "The Medium"' (1864). Expelled from the Roman Catholic Church as a sorcerer, described by Charles Dickens as an impostor and by George Eliot as 'an object of moral disgust', Daniel Dunglas Home (1833–86) is Sludge. An Edinburgh-born American medium and spiritualist, he claimed to be the illegitimate son of the Tenth Earl of Home. He asserted that Browning's poem was written out of pique after the poet attended a seance at which a clematis wreath rose from the table, hovered in the air and moved towards Mrs Browning, whereupon her husband, hoping to be the wreath's recipient, left his seat and stood behind Mrs Browning's chair. But the 'laurels' were not for him: the spirit world deposited them upon Mrs Browning's head. If Home were 'demonstrated a humbug in every microscopic cell of his skin and globule of his blood', said Dickens, 'the disciples would still believe and worship'. They included Napoleon III and Czar Alexander. Trickster he may have been, but some of the effects Home achieved at his seances have never been explained.

SMALL, Mrs Septimus (Aunt Juley), in John Galsworthy's *The Forsyte Saga* (1906–21), is the author's mother, Blanche Galsworthy (née Bartleet, *d.* 1915). After nearly forty years' marriage she accused her husband, then eighty-six, of taking a more than platonic interest in the young governess of one of their grandchildren. She left him in 1903, and he died in the following year.

SMELFUNGUS, in Laurence Sterne's *A Sentimental Journey through France and Italy* (1768), is the novelist and physician Tobias George Smollett (1721−71), who in his *Travels* (1766) had turned an acid eye upon much that he had encountered in Italy.

SMIKE, in Charles Dickens's *Nicholas Nickleby* (1838−9). One Johnson, the proprietor of a toy shop in Bury St Edmunds, was convinced he was Smike's model. He too had been sent to a Yorkshire boarding school kept by a Squeers-like character and had run away. The establishment he attended had been that of a well-known rogue called Clarkson, whose advertising may well have been among that which influenced Dickens in his drafting of Squeers's publicity for Dotheboys Hall, and whose school was 'delightfully situate upon the banks of the Tees', Clarkson − according to his advertisement of 1832 − being 'assisted by teachers of the first eminence'. The inspiration for Smike came when the author saw an inscription on a gravestone pertaining to a youth who had died at Bowes Academy (see Squeers, Wackford). 'I think this ghost put Smike into my head', Dickens later recorded.

SMILEY, George, in John le Carré's *Call for the Dead* (1961), *The Looking-Glass War* (1965), *Tinker Tailor Soldier Spy* (1974), *The Honourable Schoolboy* (1977) and *Smiley's People* (1980). Smiley owes his appearance and many of his mannerisms to a former Civil Service colleague of the author, who has described him as 'the most forgettable man I ever met, who was also very intelligent'. This is John Michael Ward Bingham, Seventh Baron Clanmorris (1908−), a thriller writer who was formerly engaged in Intelligence work in Germany and England. In 1980 *Smiley's Wife*, the autobiography of Lady Clanmorris, was withdrawn prior to publication following Ministry of Defence security objections and a row between her publishers, Hamish Hamilton, and Hodder and Stoughton, publishers of *Smiley's People*, who objected to the title of Lady Clanmorris's memoirs. There was no doubt that her husband was the model for Smiley, she said. 'We knew David Cornwell [John le Carré] very well socially when he first started to write and they often joked about it together.' John le Carré has acknowledged that Smiley is also in part the Revd Vivian Hubert Howard Green (1915−), who in 1983 was appointed Rector of Lincoln College, Oxford. He taught the author at Sherborne School (where he was chaplain from 1942 to 1951) and at Lincoln College. Sir Maurice Oldfield (see M) has been suggested as Smiley's model, although the author has denied this and Oldfield himself thought it unlikely. But le Carré *did* arrange for him to lunch with Sir Alec Guinness when the actor was preparing to play Smiley in a television adaptation of *Tinker Tailor Soldier Spy* . . .

SMITH, Henry Martin, in Ford Madox Ford's *Henry for Hugh* (1934), is part-inspired by the American poet Hart Crane (1899–1932).

SMITH, Hugh Monckton Allard, in Ford Madox Ford's *The Rash Act* (1933) and *Henry for Hugh* (1934), is Arthur Marwood. See Tietjens, Christopher.

SMITH, Mortimer and Martha, in H. G. Wells's *The Dream* (1924), are the author's parents. See Remington, Arthur and Mrs.

SNODGRASS, Sebastian, Lord Simon, Smaragda and Sylvester, in W. J. Turner's *Smaragda's Lover* (1924), are respectively Osbert Sitwell (see Whittlebot, Gob), Sir George Sitwell (see Rotherham, Sir Henry), Edith Sitwell (see Whittlebot, Hernia) and Sacheverell Sitwell (see Whittlebot, Sago).

SNOWBALL, in George Orwell's *Animal Farm* (1945), represents the Soviet politician Lev Davidovich Trotsky (1879–1940), a leader of the Russian Revolution. His subsequent opposition to Stalin (see Napoleon; see also Boss) led to his expulsion from the Communist Party, his banishment from Russia and his assassination in Mexico.

SNUBBIN, Serjeant, in Charles Dickens's *The Posthumous Papers of the Pickwick Club* (1836–7), is supposedly Serjeant William St Julien Arabin, a London lawyer who married into the Meux brewing family.

SOAMES, Enoch, in Max Beerbohm's 'Enoch Soames' (*Seven Men*, 1919), is part-inspired by Theodore Wratislaw, a mini-minor Edwardian poet who wrote a study of Swinburne.

SOLOGDIN, in Alexander Solzhenitsyn's *The First Circle* (1968), is Dimitri Panin (1911–), a Moscow-born engineer who was arrested by the Soviet regime in 1940 and interned for sixteen years. Permitted to return to Moscow in 1956, he was allowed to leave the country in the 1970s and made his home near Paris. He described his internment with Solzhenitsyn in *The Notebooks of Sologdin* (1973).

SOMERS, Harriet, in D. H. Lawrence's *Kangaroo* (1923). Frieda Lawrence appears in these pages more often than anyone else. Not only was she the model for Harriet Somers; she was also the inspiration of at least seven more Lawrence characters, and she served as an original for four other writers. This is attributable to her marriage to Lawrence rather than to her personality, for she was no Lady Ottoline Morrell, no Mrs Patrick Campbell. In line with Shaw's advice ('write about what you know'), novelists write about whom they know, and just about everybody knew the Lawrences. The fact that only four of their writing acquaintances used Frieda, who invariably appears in tandem with Lawrence, never in her own right, puts her into perspective as part of the Lawrence double-act: one of twentieth-century literature's most celebrated love-hate relationships. It was this apparent attraction of opposites, the German aristocrat and the coal-miner's son, their rows, their fights, and their abiding affection and need for each other, that prompted others to write about them. While Aldous Huxley found Frieda obtuse and Katherine Mansfield described her as an 'immense German Christmas pudding', for Lawrence she was both earth mother and an inexhaustible seam which he mined assiduously for his fiction. Uninhibited, she lived the life her husband appeared to preach. Frieda von Richthofen (1879–1956) was the daughter of a German baron and a cousin of the First World War fighter pilot Manfred von Richthofen ('the Red Baron'). She was first married to the philologist Professor Ernest Weekley, of Nottingham University, who was fifteen years her senior and by whom she had three children. 'I've got a genius in my class', Weekley announced to his wife one day. She confirmed his talent-spotting by eloping with the student Lawrence, marrying him two years later, in 1914. This was by no means the first, nor the last, of her infidelities, which included a brief affair with John Middleton Murry (see Crich, Gerald). She was thirty-one when Lawrence spirited her away, and had known him only a few weeks when she abandoned her family and life of comfort to share a precarious future with the impoverished tubercular writer who was five years her junior. Thereafter she sustained Lawrence for the rest of his life, although such was her impracticality that he had to do the housework. On the whole she endured cheerfully their nomadic, penurious life, despite bitter anguish over the children Weekley refused to let her see – children Lawrence selfishly resented as rivals for her love. It was a marriage of two 'impossibles'. In their different ways, both needed looking after. Within two years of Lawrence's death, Frieda settled happily enough with an Italian army officer, Angelo Ravalgi, whom she finally married in 1950.

SONYA, in Leo Tolstoy's *War and Peace* (1863–9), is Tatiana Yergolsky, a ward of the author's grandfather. Following the death of her parents she was adopted by her second cousin, Pelageya Tolstoy, the author's paternal grandmother. Brought up with the author's father (see Rostov, Count Nikolai), she fell in love with him but renounced him to enable him to marry an heiress and save the family fortune. She became the author's 'second mother' after both his parents died during his childhood.

SOREL, Julien, in Stendhal's *Scarlet and Black* (1830), has as prototype Antoine Berthet, a blacksmith's son who in 1827, at the age of twenty-five, was tried and subsequently executed at Grenoble for shooting, in church, the wife of a former employer to whose children he had been tutor until his dismissal — it is supposed that the lady of the house (who survived the shooting) had become his lover. He had later seduced the daughter of another family to which he was tutor. When this came to light and he was sacked, he blamed his previous employers for his misfortune. Adrien Lafargue, of Bagnères-de-Bigorre, is also believed to have contributed to Sorel. In 1829 he was tried for the murder of the mistress who had betrayed and deserted him.

SORREL, Hetty, in George Eliot's *Adam Bede* (1859), has as prototype Mary Voce, who was hanged for child-murder at Nottingham in 1802. See also Morris, Dinah.

SORRELL, Sir William, in Ford Madox Ford's *Ladies Whose Bright Eyes* (1911), is part-inspired by Arthur Marwood. See Tietjens, Christopher.

SOSOSTRIS, Madame, in T. S. Eliot's *The Waste Land* (1922), supposedly represents Bertrand Russell (see Mattheson, Sir Joshua). In Aldous Huxley's *Crome Yellow*, Mr Scogan (whom Eliot took to be Russell) impersonates Sesostris the Sorceress.

SOUTER JOHNIE, in Robert Burns's 'Tam o' Shanter' (1791), is supposedly John Davidson (1732—1806), a shoemaker noted for his wit who lived near Shanter Farm, Ardlochan, Ayrshire.

SOUTH, Squire, in John Arbuthnot's *The History of John Bull* (1712), is Charles VI of Austria (1685—1740).

SOUTHCOTT, Robert, in A. G. Macdonell's *England, Their England* (1933). 'I was one of the characters in *England, Their England*', says Alec Waugh (see Glayde) in his memoirs. He does not say which character. My money is on 'Bobby Southcott, the boy novelist': Alec Waugh's best-selling *The Loom of Youth* was published shortly after he left school.

SPAIN, Ed, in Nancy Mitford's *The Blessing* (1951), is Cyril Connolly (see Quiggin, J. G.). Writing to Mitford when *The Blessing* was published, Evelyn Waugh reported that Connolly had fallen on hard times ('telephone cut off for non-payment and water too by the look of him'). Waugh said that Connolly had told him he intended to become a waiter at a fashionable restaurant in order to embarrass and reproach his friends for their ingratitude. 'He saw a worried look, I suppose, on my face & said: "Ah, I see now I have touched even your cold heart." So I said: "Well no Cyril it isn't quite that. I was thinking of your finger-nails in the soup." '

SPANDRELL, MAURICE, in Aldous Huxley's *Point Counter Point* (1928). The critic Edwin Muir appears to be alone in having seen D. H. Lawrence in Spandrell. Could this be a slip of the pen for Mark Rampion? According to Huxley's biographer, Sybille Bedford, Spandrell's adolescence is based upon that of the French poet and critic Charles Baudelaire (1821—67).

SPELVIN, Rodney, in P. G. Wodehouse's 'Rodney has a Relapse' (*Nothing Serious*, 1950). In a vitriolic letter to *The Times* in 1941, the writer A. A. Milne (1882—1956) attacked Wodehouse for broadcasting for the Germans. Milne's letter was as maladroit as Wodehouse's broadcasts were ill-advised. It also accused the humorist of evading service in the First World War by remaining in America, whereas Wodehouse had in fact volunteered for military service but was found to be unfit. Rodney Spelvin was Wodehouse's mild revenge.

SPENLOW, Dora, in Charles Dickens's *David Copperfield* (1849–50). At seventeen Dickens became infatuated with Maria Sarah Beadnell (1810–86), the daughter of an official of the bank of Smith, Payne and Smith in London's Lombard Street. A year older than Dickens, she alternately encouraged and spurned his advances. He remained besotted with her for two years. In 1845 she married a Finsbury sawmill manager, Henry Louis Winter, who after being declared bankrupt in 1859 became vicar of Alnmouth, Northumberland, and died in 1871. Dora is Dickens's portrait of the Maria of his youth. Twenty years later they met again: see Finching, Flora.

SPINELL, Detlov, in Thomas Mann's 'Tristan' (1900), is the German novelist, journalist and musician Arthur Holitscher (1869–1941), who complained that Mann had furtively examined him through opera glasses in order to present such a detailed portrait.

SPIRE, Jack, in Evelyn Waugh's *Decline and Fall* (1928), is J. C. Squire (see Hodge, William), ridiculed as the editor of the *London Hercules*. Though he attracted Waugh's contempt, his influence on literary journalism in the London of his day was such that his circle was regarded as almost a kind of mafia and was referred to as 'the Squirearchy'.

SPODE, Roderick, in P. G. Wodehouse's *The Code of the Woosters* (1938), is Sir Oswald Mosley (see Webley, Everard). 'The trouble with you, Spode,' says Bertie Wooster, 'is that just because you have succeeded in inducing a handful of half-wits to disfigure the London scene by going about in black shorts, you think you're someone. You hear them shouting "Heil, Spode!" and you imagine it is the Voice of the People. That is where you make your bloomer. What the Voice of the People is saying is: "Look at that frightful ass Spode swanking about in footer bags! Did you ever in your puff see such a perfect perisher?"'

SPORUS, in Alexander Pope's 'Epistle to Dr Arbuthnot' (1735), is John Hervey, First Baron Hervey of Ickworth (1696–1743), co-author of a thinly veiled attack on Pope: *Verses addressed to the Imitator of Horace*. An ally of Lady Mary Wortley Montagu, another of Pope's enemies (see Sappho), Hervey was noted for his effeminate bearing and somewhat fragile appearance. He was epileptic, but that did not stop Pope from labelling him Sporus — the name of an effeminate favourite of the Emperor Nero. See also Fanny, Lord.

SPROTT, Vernon, in William Gerhardi's *Doom* (originally published as *Jazz and Jasper*, 1929), is Arnold Bennett (see Nixon, Mr). A reviewer, like Sprott, he worked in that capacity for the *Evening Standard* and was said by Hugh Walpole to be able to make an author's fortune 'in a night'.

SPRUCE, Everard, in Evelyn Waugh's *Unconditional Surrender* (1961), is Cyril Connolly (see Quiggin, J. G.). Seeking to deny the identification, Waugh wrote to Connolly, 'There are of course asses in London, who don't understand the processes of the imagination, whose hobby it is to treat fiction as a gossip column.'

SQUEERS, Wackford, in Charles Dickens's *Nicholas Nickleby* (1838–9). Upon the publication of this novel, William Shaw (?1783–1850) became the most notorious schoolmaster in English literature. He was headmaster of Bowes Academy at Bowes, near Greta Bridge, North Yorkshire, where his neglect of his pupils became the subject of a court action in 1823. This cost him £300 in damages after two boys in his care lost their sight through lack of medical attention. Remembering the case and recalling press accounts of scandalous conditions at the school at that time, Dickens visited Bowes Academy in the winter of 1837–8, posing as a clockmaker's assistant and accompanied by his illustrator, Phiz (Hablot K. Browne), who is reputed to have made a sketch of Shaw on his thumbnail. *Nicholas Nickleby* ruined Shaw — to the indignation of local residents, who felt he had been disgracefully libelled. After his death, friends installed a stained-glass window at the local church in his memory.

SQUINTUM, Dr, in Samuel Foote's *The Minor* (1760), is the preacher George Whitefield (1714–70), founder of Lady Huntingdon's Connection of Calvinistic Methodists. So highly developed was the modulation of his voice, it was said, that he could make an audience either laugh or cry with his pronunciation of 'Mesopotamia'. He annoyed Foote through his campaigning for the closure of a number of theatres.

STACE, Mrs Sophia, in Ivy Compton-Burnett's *Brothers and Sisters* (1929), is the author's neurotic, tyrannical mother, Katharine

Compton-Burnett (née Rees, 1855—1911), the daughter of a mayor of Dover. Upon her widowed mother's death, the novelist succeeded her in the role of family despot. Two of her sisters rebelled and went to live with the pianist Myra Hess; and two younger sisters were found dead in their room, having apparently poisoned themselves in a suicide pact.

STACKPOLE, Henrietta, in Henry James's *The Portrait of a Lady* (1881). James's biographer, Leon Edel, surmises that this is an American journalist referred to in correspondence as 'Miss Hillard'. She is known to have pursued James with great determination to obtain an interview in 1877. Edel suggests she was Katherine Hillard, who edited an abridgement of Madame Blavatsky's doctrines. Could she, I wonder, have been a relative of the Boston lawyer/journalist George Stillman Hillard (1808—79)?

STAHOV, Elena, in Ivan Turgenev's *On the Eve* (1860), has as prototype Anita Garibaldi (1821—49), the Brazilian wife of the Italian patriot Giuseppe Garibaldi. His inseparable companion, she underwent many rigours in support of her husband's cause and died after taking part in the epic retreat to San Marino.

STAHR, Monroe and Minna, in F. Scott Fitzgerald's *The Last Tycoon* (1941), are the film producer Irving Thalberg (1899—1936) and Zelda Fitzgerald (see Diver, Nicole). The son of a Brooklyn lace merchant, Thalberg left night school at seventeen to take a job as a stenographer with Universal Pictures. He became the company president's private secretary, was at twenty put in charge of Universal's Hollywood studio and at twenty-five was appointed executive producer of the then newly-formed company Metro-Goldwyn-Mayer. His many successful films included *Mutiny on the Bounty* and *The Barretts of Wimpole Street*, but he never allowed his name to appear in the credits. He married Norma Shearer (see Walker, Stella). Monroe Stahr is not, however, solely Thalberg. The character is also in part a self-portrait of the author.

STAINES, Edith, in E. F. Benson's *Dodo* (1893). Now better known for her passionate pursuit of Virginia Woolf than for her music, Benson's Edith Staines is the composer Dame Ethel Smyth (1858—1944). She was briefly engaged to Oscar Wilde's brother, William, a *Daily Telegraph* leader writer, and in 1903 unsuccessfully laid siege to the bisexual Princesse Edmond de Polignac (see Vinaigrette). Benson knew her as the passionate friend of his mother, the wife of the Archbishop of Canterbury. Virginia Woolf noted, 'An old woman of seventy-one has fallen in love with me . . . It is like being caught by a giant crab.' Smyth could be highly entertaining and she beguiled Woolf with 'her vigorous charm', although the writer remarked in a letter, 'The reason why Ethel Smyth is so repulsive is her table manners. She oozes; she chortles; and she half blew her rather red nose in her table napkin . . . I had rather dine with a dog. But you can tell people they are murderers; you cannot tell them that they eat like hogs.' Dame Ethel's death was as bizarre as her life. She literally kicked the bucket, dying when she tripped over the pail she used as a chamber pot.

STALKY, in Rudyard Kipling's *Stalky and Co.* (1899), is Major-General Lionel Charles Dunsterville (1865—1946), the author's schoolfellow at the United Services College, Westward Ho. His autobiographical writings included *Stalky's Reminiscences* (1928) and *Stalky Settles Down* (1932). When, as president, he wrote to apprise Kipling of the formation of the Kipling Society, the author replied, 'How would *you* like to be turned into an anatomical specimen, before you were dead, and shown upon a table, once a quarter?' According to the illustrator Ernest H. Shepard, a Colonel Arthur Corkran also contributed to Stalky. I have been unable to verify this, so there's a furrow for some future Kipling researcher to plough . . .

STAMP, Victor and Margot, in Wyndham Lewis's *The Revenge for Love* (1937), are Roy Campbell (see Grovell, Dick) and Lewis's wife, Gladys Anne Hoskyns (1900—79), who married him in 1930 after working as his model (in his role as artist). She was the daughter of an Okehampton nurseryman who moved from Devon to London, where she was born at Teddington, according to Lewis's biographer, Jeffrey Meyers.

STANHOPE, Alison, in Susan Glaspell's *Alison's House* (1930), has a probable prototype in the reclusive American poet Emily Dickinson (1830—86).

STANHOPE, George, in John P. Marquand's *Wickford Point* (1939), is the American literary agent Carl Brandt (?1888—1957). Brandt's wife, the literary agent Carol Hill, appears as a hard-headed careerist in Katherine Brush's 'Free Women' (1935); Evelyn Waugh described her as 'a secretary raised to the highest power'; and

Alec Waugh referred to her as a prima donna of her profession who expected to be, and was, treated like one.

STANLEY, Ann Veronica, in H. G. Wells's *Ann Veronica* (1909). Two women who flouted convention in their love for the author are combined in Ann Veronica. His second wife, Amy Catherine Robbins (1872–1927), subsequently known as Jane, was one of his students when she eloped with him in 1894, marrying him after his divorce in 1895. For Wells, she proved an ideal partner. Undemanding, she understood and tolerated his many infidelities and became the sheet-anchor of his often turbulent life. He, in turn, resisted all pressure from his highly-charged mistresses to leave her. Jane Wells seems quickly to have come to terms with the fact that while no one woman could own him, he could be retained on a free rein. In their own way, they were devoted. Ann Veronica has a more obvious model, however, in Amber Pember Reeves, eldest daughter of the author's Fabian Society friends, the Hon. William Pember Reeves, New Zealand's High Commissioner in London, and his wife, Maud, head of the Fabians' Women's Section. Like Ann Veronica, Amber – a Cambridge double-first – defied her father, coming and going much as she pleased. Wells, twenty years her senior, was first her mentor, then her lover. In 1909 she bore him a daughter – a child conceived on her own insistence. She later married a former suitor, George Rivers Blanco White, a barrister who was happy to renew his proposal. She never lost touch with Wells, who came to regard their daughter as a niece. Thirty years after their affair, he was heartened by Amber's assurance that she had never regretted their relationship.

STANLEY, Major-General, in W. S. Gilbert's libretto for Arthur Sullivan's *The Pirates of Penzance* (1879). Garnet Wolseley, First Viscount Wolseley (1833–1913), needed no persuading to entertain company by singing 'I am the very model of a modern major-general . . . ' Not only was he an irrepressible egotist; he was also the very model for Gilbert and Sullivan's major-general, a caricature he relished. The celebrated veteran of numerous wars, he later led the abortive expedition to relieve General Gordon at Khartoum. His career was blighted by the Gordon episode, but he soldiered on to become Field Marshal Lord Wolseley, Commander-in-Chief of the British Army.

STARBUCK, General Lucas P., in James Reichley's *Hail to the Chief* (1960), is part-inspired by General Dwight D. Eisenhower (1890–1969), President of the United States from 1953 to 1961.

STARK, Willie, in Robert Penn Warren's *All the King's Men* (1946), has as prototype the Louisiana politician Huey Long (1893–1935). With the slogan 'Every Man a King', he was nicknamed 'Kingfish', became state governor in 1928, a senator in 1932, and had presidential ambitions. He was assassinated in his state capitol by a doctor, believed to have a personal grudge, who was killed by Long's bodyguard.

STARLING, Herbert and Julia, in F. Tennyson Jesse's *A Pin to see the Peepshow* (1934), have as prototypes Percy Thompson, a London shipping clerk, and his wife, Edith, manageress of a London millinery firm. In 1923, aged twenty-eight, Edith Thompson was hanged for the murder of her husband, which had been carried out at her instigation by her lover, Frederick Bywaters (see Carr, Leonard).

STARWICK, Francis, in Thomas Wolfe's *Of Time and the River* (1935), is Kenneth Raisbeck (*d.* 1931) from Moline, Illinois, a Harvard contemporary of the author who went on to become an unfulfilled dramatist. He was homosexual and the circumstances of his death suggested he had been strangled by a male companion.

STAVROGIN, Nikolai, in Fyodor Dostoevsky's *The Devils* (1871–2), is Nikolai Speshnev, leader of the terrorist faction in the quasi-revolutionary Petrachevsky group in St Petersburg. For his connection with this movement, Dostoevsky was first sentenced to death and then imprisoned in Omsk for four years.

STEERFORTH, James, in Charles Dickens's *David Copperfield* (1849–50), is supposedly the author's childhood friend and next-door neighbour, George Stroughill, who lived at 1 Ordnance Terrace, Chatham. His sister, Lucy, was Dickens's childhood sweetheart and is Golden Lucy in his Christmas story 'The Wreck of the Golden Mary' (1856).

STEIN, in Joseph Conrad's *Lord Jim* (1900), is the author's uncle, Tadeusz Bobrowski, of Zmerynka, in the Ukraine. When Conrad was eleven his father died. Bobrowski brought him up and for twenty years financed him.

STEINBERG, Susie, in James Kennaway's *Some Gorgeous Accident* (1967), is Susan Kennaway. See Helen.

STELLA, in Thomas Love Peacock's *Nightmare Abbey* (1818), is Mary Wollstonecraft Godwin (1797–1851), daughter of William and Mary Godwin (see Marguerite; see also Pry, Priscilla) and author of *Frankenstein* (1818). In 1816 she became the second wife of the poet Percy Bysshe Shelley, having eloped with him to the Continent in 1814.

STELLA, in Sir Philip Sidney's *Astrophel and Stella* sonnet sequence (written 1580–4; published 1591), is Penelope Devereux (?1562–1607), daughter of the First Earl of Essex. Sidney first met her when she was a child and he, as a courtier, was accompanying Elizabeth I on a tour which included Penelope's home – her mother was the Queen's cousin. It is thought that marriage to Sidney was mooted by her parents, and that Sidney failed to respond, bitterly regretting this when Penelope became unattainable. Against her will, in 1581 she became the wife of Lord Rich, later Earl of Warwick, who divorced her for adultery when she became the mistress of the Eighth Lord Mountjoy, subsequently Earl of Devon, whom she married in 1605.

STELLA, in Jonathan Swift's *Journal to Stella* (written 1710–13; published 1766–8), is Esther Johnson (1681–1728), supposedly the daughter of the housekeeper of the diplomat and essayist Sir William Temple, to whom Swift was secretary. Swift's duties included educating Esther, a lively and intelligent child aged eight when they first met. It has been suggested that Swift was the illegitimate son of Sir William's father; that Esther was Temple's illegitimate daughter and was thus Swift's niece; and that for this reason Swift could not marry her had he so wished. Another theory has it that he did marry her, secretly. He was buried at her side in St Patrick's Cathedral, Dublin.

STÉNIO, in George Sand's *Lélia* (1833), is an amalgam of the author's lover, the writer Jules Sandeau (1811–83), and Stéphane Ajasson de Grandsagne, atheist son of a former mayor of La Châtre and the putative father of George Sand's daughter.

STENSGAARD, in Henrik Ibsen's *The League of Youth* (1869), has been seen as a portrait of Bjørnstjerne Bjørnson (see Haakonsson, Haakon). Denying that Bjørnson was intended, Ibsen said that Stensgaard was simply a typical Norwegian, himself included.

STEVIE, in Joseph Conrad's *The Secret Agent* (1907), has as prototype the French anarchist Martial Bourdin (*d.* 1894), who was brother-in-law of Henry Samuels, editor of the anarchist journal *Commonweal*. At the age of twenty-six Bourdin was blown to pieces when explosives he was carrying detonated in Greenwich Park, in London.

STEYNE, Lord, in W. M. Thackeray's *Vanity Fair* (1846—8). 'There has been ... no such example of undisguised debauchery exhibited to the world', wrote the diarist Henry William Greville of Steyne's prototype, Francis Charles Seymour-Conway, Third Marquis of Hertford (1777—1842). His mother was a mistress of the Prince Regent, and Seymour-Conway married the illegitimate daughter of Lord Queensberry, kept a French mistress, became a notorious roué and scandalised society both in his lifetime and after, through the revelations of litigation over his will. His London home, Hertford House, now accommodates the Wallace Collection.

STILLINGFLEET, Roger, in Evelyn Waugh's *The Ordeal of Gilbert Pinfold* (1957), as the original himself declared in his biography of Waugh, is the author's friend Christopher Sykes (1907—   ), diplomat turned writer and BBC producer.

STITCH, Mrs Algernon, in Evelyn Waugh's *Scoop* (1933) and *Officers and Gentlemen* (1955). When she caught sight of a friend disappearing underground in Sloane Street, Mrs Stitch followed him in her tiny car and became stuck in the gentlemen's lavatory. How would she cope with the parking restrictions of today? We know the answer, because her model was Lady Diana Cooper, who upon the introduction of traffic wardens became noted for the heart-rending announcements displayed on the windscreen of her illicitly-parked Mini. 'Dear Warden — Taken sad child to cinemar — please forgive', she pleaded in spelling all her own. And again, 'Dearest Warden — Front tooth broken off: look like an 81-year-old pirate, so at dentist 19a. Very old, very lame — no metres. Have mercy!' What warden could fail to be disarmed? None, until she met her match on leaving her car outside Harrods in 1984 with the note, 'Old cripple's car.

Gone for lunch.' She returned to find a parking ticket accompanied by the message, 'Hope you had a good lunch, dear.' At the wheel, however, Lady Diana enjoyed more than sixty-five years' motoring with an unblemished licence, until her Mini bounced off a lorry on the London—Brighton road in 1979 and she was fined £25, after admitting careless driving. Lady Diana Manners was born in 1892, the daughter of the Eighth Duchess of Rutland and, allegedly, Harry Cust (see Tarville, Lord). In 1919 she married Alfred Duff Cooper (later Viscount Norwich). A society beauty, she became an actress noted for her performance in a leading role in Max Reinhardt's *The Miracle*, in which she toured. She met Waugh at a party given by Lady Cunard and the two became lifelong friends. Enid Bagnold, Arnold Bennett, D. H. Lawrence and Nancy Mitford also used her as a model (see Index).

STOBHALL, Miss, in Ford Madox Ford's *The Simple Life Limited* (published under the pseudonym Daniel Chaucer, 1911), is an amalgam of the Russian translator Constance Garnett (1861—1946), wife of Edward Garnett (see Lea), and her sister-in-law, Olive Garnett, who was so affected by the death of Sergei Stepniak (see Laspara, Julius) that she cut off her hair.

STOCKMANN, Dr Thomas, in Henrik Ibsen's *An Enemy of the People* (1882). The last time Ibsen met Bjørnstjerne Bjørnson (see Haakonsson, Haakon), he told him he was the model for Stockmann. Ibsen's biographer, Michael Meyer, suggests three further prototypes: Charles Bradlaugh (1833—91), who was repeatedly elected MP for Northampton but was not admitted to the House of Commons until 1886, it having been held that as an atheist he would not be bound by the oath; Harald Thaulow, a Norwegian chemist who became unpopular in his home town, Christiania (now Oslo), when he attempted to make a speech criticising the local steam kitchens' lack of provision for the poor; and the father of the German poet Alfred Meisner, who in the 1830s had to flee the spa town of Teiplitz, where he was medical officer, after he had ruined the resort's season by disclosing an outbreak of cholera. In his mention of the fugitive doctor's son, I presume Meyer is referring to the Austrian poet Alfred von Meissner (1822—85), who was born at Teplitz.

STOCKTON, Mr, in W. H. Mallock's *The New Republic* (1877), is the populariser of science, John Tyndall (1820—93). A former railway engineer, he became Professor of Natural Philosophy at the Royal Institution, subsequently succeeding Faraday as Superintendent. His research included investigating glaciers with T. H. Huxley (see Storks, Mr).

STOKES, Melian, in Gilbert Cannan's *Pugs and Peacocks* (1921), *Sembal* (1922) and *The House of Prophecy* (1924), is Bertrand Russell. See Mattheson, Sir Joshua.

STONE, Alfred, in J. G. Huneker's *Painted Veils* (1920), is Albert Steinberg (*d.* 1899), music critic of the New York *Herald*. He was noted for his caustic comments and for his addiction to gambling.

STONE, Harvey, in Ernest Hemingway's *The Sun Also Rises* (1926; published in England as *Fiesta*), is the American writer Harold Stearns (1891–1943), a hard-drinking contemporary of Hemingway in Paris in the 1920s.

STORKS, Mr, in W. H. Mallock's *The New Republic* (1877), is the biologist Thomas Henry Huxley (1825–95), President of the Royal Society from 1881 to 1885 and the grandfather of Aldous Huxley.

STORM, Captain Bruno, in Thomas Berger's *Vital Parts* (1970), has as prototype Eldridge Cleaver, one-time leader of the American Black radical group the Black Panthers. Wanted for parole violation and in connection with a shoot-out with police in Oakland, California, in 1975 he gave himself up at the United States Embassy in Paris after seven years' exile. He returned to the United States much mellowed, still radical in outlook but having apparently undergone a political change of heart.

STORM, Iris, in Michael Arlen's *The Green Hat* (1924). Nancy Cunard (1896–1965) seems to have had lovers almost as often as the rest of us have lunch, and such was their variety that one wonders if she even paused to glance at the menu. One was Arlen, and thus she became the model for Iris Storm. She was ostensibly the daughter of Sir Bache Cunard, grandson of the founder of the Cunard steamship line, and his wife Emerald (see Carnal, Lady); but it has been suggested that the novelist George Moore was her natural father. Founding the Hours Press, she published Samuel Beckett long before he was generally recognised, and also issued the first thirty *Cantos* of Ezra Pound. A poet herself, although of no particular distinction, she supported two causes: Spanish republicanism and recognition for Blacks. She covered the Spanish Civil War for the *Manchester Guardian* and organised relief for Spanish refugees; and in addition to taking the black pianist Henry Crowder as lover, she in 1934 published the anthology *Negro*. At twenty-four she had a hysterectomy, telling some friends that this was to obtain sexual freedom, others that it was necessitated by venereal disease. The writers Richard Aldington, Louis Aragon, Aldous Huxley and Wyndham Lewis were also among her lovers. Aragon excepted, they all used her as a model, as did George Moore and Evelyn Waugh (see Index). In her declining years she became an alcoholic near-nymphomaniac. She was certified insane in 1960, was later released, and died in Paris, which had long been her home. At her funeral, the pall-bearers outnumbered the mourners. Iris Storm is also supposedly part-inspired by Iris Tree (*b.* 1897), daughter of the actor Sir Herbert Beerbohm Tree, and Nancy Cunard's flat-mate when the latter was eighteen. A contemporary of Dora Carrington and Dorothy Brett at the Slade, Iris Tree published two collections of verse, in 1919 and 1927.

STORROW, Bert, in G. J. Cadbury's *When the Death Penalty Came Back* (1982), has as prototype Ian Brady, a stock clerk of Hyde, Cheshire, who in 1966, aged twenty-eight was convicted of the murder of two youths, aged seventeen and twelve, and a ten-year-old girl — all buried in moorland graves, from which the crime came to be known as 'the Moors Murders'. Brady and his accomplice (see Madden, Liz) were sentenced to life imprisonment.

STOYTE, Mr, in Aldous Huxley's *After Many a Summer Dies the Swan* (1939), is the American newspaper magnate William Randolph Hearst (1863–1951), who was noted for his obsessive fear of death and for the vast castle which he built for himself on his estate at San Simeon, California.

STRANGEWAYS, Nigel, in the detective novels of Nicholas Blake (Cecil Day-Lewis), commencing with *A Question of Proof* (1935), is part-inspired by the author's friend W. H. Auden (see Weston, Hugh). In a tribute to Day-Lewis upon his death in 1972, Auden wrote, 'In his early days, his detective Nigel Strangeways exhibited certain traits of behaviour which, I am proud to believe, were taken from me.'

STRETT, Sir Luke, in Henry James's *The Wings of the Dove* (1902), is in part Dr W. W. Baldwin, an American physician who practised in Florence. He attended Mark Twain's wife during her final illness.

STRICKLAND, Charles, in W. Somerset Maugham's *The Moon and Sixpence* (1919), was closely modelled on the artist Paul Gauguin (1848—1903), who in 1883 gave up stockbroking for painting, suffered near-starvation and in 1891 settled in Tahiti. His career so fascinated Maugham that he went to the South Sea Islands to see for himself what the artist had seen. In Tahiti he interviewed natives who had known Gauguin, and acquired the artist's last, unfinished, work.

STRIPLING, Tim and Naomi, in Clive James's *Brilliant Creatures* (1983), have been suggested by Mark Amory in the *Tatler* (October 1984) to be the dramatist Tom Stoppard (1937—) and his wife, the writer and broadcaster Dr Miriam Stoppard (1937—). Stripling is portrayed as the author of plays written 'at such an intellectual altitude that only a symbolic logician could follow the plots'.

STRONG, Captain Edward, in W. M. Thackeray's *The History of Pendennis* (1848—50), has a possible prototype in Captain James Glynn (1810—71), an American naval officer who was credited with conducting his country's first successful negotiations with Japan — in 1849 he secured the release of a number of American seamen held captive. He ended his career as an inspector of lighthouses. Strong is known to have been based on a somewhat eccentric Captain Glynn who visited Thackeray in New York in 1855. That was the year in which Captain James Glynn (whose wife was from Geneva, New York) was placed on the retired list. I suspect that Thackeray's visitor and James Glynn were one and the same. American Thackeray scholars are welcome to confirm or torpedo my theory. Doctorates have been won for less!

STRUTHERS, in D. H. Lawrence's *Aaron's Rod* (1922), is Augustus John (see Bidlake, John), portrayed as an artist who discourteously talks during the performance of an opera. John recalls that opera in his memoirs, saying that at the end Lawrence declared 'he would like to howl like a dog'.

STRYVER, Mr, in Charles Dickens's *A Tale of Two Cities* (1859). 'Not bad, I think − especially after only one sitting', replied Dickens upon being complimented for achieving a very good likeness of this character's original. For Stryver was the outcome of a single consultation which Dickens had with a London barrister, Edwin John James (1812−82), four months before the publication of the novel's first instalment. Appointed Recorder of Brighton in 1855, James later became bankrupt and was disbarred in 1861 for unprofessional conduct. This prompted him to go to America, where he practised at the New York Bar and made a number of stage appearances in the period 1861−72. He later returned to England, and died in London.

STUART, in Simon Gray's *The Common Pursuit* (1984), has been taken by critics to owe something to Ian Hamilton (1938−   ), poet and critic, poetry and fiction editor of the *Times Literary Supplement* from 1965 to 1973, and editor of the *New Review* from 1974 to 1979. Somebody has to be elitist, says Stuart, defending the *New Literary Review* which he edits with Arts Council backing . . . until it dries up, leaving him pretending to be the Irish caretaker when a creditor telephones.

STUBBS, Victor in Hugh Kingsmill's 'The Disintegration of a Politician' (*The Dawn's Delay*, 1924), is Herbert Henry Asquith. See Lubin, Henry Hopkins.

STUCLEY, Brian and Lydia, in S. P. B. Mais's *Orange Street* (1926), are Henry and Ida Loetitia Williamson (see Taylor, Stephen, and Ogilvie, Mary), according to Daniel Farson's *Henry: An Appreciation of Henry Williamson* (1982).

SUBTLE, in Ben Jonson's *The Alchemist* (1610), is Dr John Dee. See Prospero, Duke of Milan.

SUDDLECHOP, Dame Ursula, in Sir Walter Scott's *The Fortunes of Nigel* (1822), has a suggested prototype in Mrs Anne Turner (*d.* 1615), the young widow of a doctor. Responsible for introducing to England a starch which dyed cuffs and ruffs bright yellow, she had been the childhood companion of Frances, Countess of Essex (see Prynne, Hester) and subsequently became involved in her friend's adulterous scheming. Lady Essex and her lover, Lord Rochester, are believed to have used Turner's Hammersmith home as a rendezvous, and at Lady Essex's request she assisted as a go-between in the poisoning of Sir Thomas Overbury in the Tower of London in 1613. With her accomplices, she was hanged for murder.

SUMMERSON, Esther, in Charles Dickens's *Bleak House* (1852−3). Three women have been discerned in Esther. The primary model is Esther Elton, eldest daughter of the second marriage of Edward William Elton (1794−1843), an actor who drowned when the ship on which he was returning to London from a theatre engagement in Edinburgh struck a rock and sank near Holy Island. Dickens became chairman of a fund-raising committee formed to assist Elton's seven orphaned children and, holding Esther in the highest regard, took a personal interest in her. She subsequently married, and her son, the Revd James A. Nash, became chaplain of Marylebone Workhouse. Also believed to have contributed to Esther Summerson are Georgina Hogarth (see Wickfield, Agnes) and Sophia Iselin, who in 1847 published *My Dream Book*, a collection of poems.

SUMPH, Captain, in W. M. Thackeray's *The History of Pendennis* (1848−50), is Captain Thomas Medwin (1788−1869), author of *Conversations with Byron* (1824) and a biographer of Shelley.

SURROGATE, Mr, in Graham Greene's *It's a Battlefield* (1934), is part-inspired by the author's impression of John Middleton Murry (see Crich, Gerald), whom Greene did not know personally.

SUTPEN, Thomas, in William Faulkner's Yoknapatawpha saga (1929−62), is believed to have as prototype Alexander H. Pegues, an Oxford (Mississippi) settler. Starting in the 1830s as a poor farmer, he became the owner of 4,000 acres, 150 slaves and a prestigious residence. See Ward L. Miner, *The World of William Faulkner* (1952).

ŠVEJK, Josef, in Jaroslav Hašek's *The Good Soldier Švejk* (1921−3), is part-inspired by a private soldier, Strašlipka, a batman in the Czech 91st Infantry Regiment, in which the author served in 1915.

SVENGALI, in George Du Maurier's *Trilby* (1894). Seeking eye treatment in the late 1850s, the author consulted a specialist in Belgium, staying in Malines. There he came to know Felix Moscheles (1833−1917), his model for Svengali. Moscheles's demonstrations of his prowess as a mesmerist suggested the plot of *Trilby*. Far from being upset by the caricature of himself as the sinister Svengali, Moscheles was pleased to see the potency of mesmerism recognised. He was the son of the pianist and composer Ignaz Moscheles, who was Mendelssohn's teacher and a friend of Beethoven. Felix Moscheles translated and edited his father's correspondence with Mendelssohn and in 1896 he published *In Bohemia with Du Maurier*, which Du Maurier illustrated.

SWALLOWS, the, in Arthur Ransome's *Swallows and Amazons*. See Walker, John, Roger, Susan and Titty.

SWAN, in William Cooper's *Young People* (1958) and in the detective novels (1934–40) of R. Philmore (Herbert Edmund Howard), is C. P. Snow (see Robert). For his friendship with Cooper and Howard, see Robert, and Passant, George.

SWANCOURT, Elfride, in Thomas Hardy's *A Pair of Blue Eyes* (1873). Once they have acquired the spouse of their dreams, some men (and women) quickly lose all interest in their marriage, yearning for a fresh mate who inevitably suffers the same fate as the first. Hardy was such a husband, and Emma Lavinia Gifford (1840–1912) had the misfortune to become his first wife. In Elfride we see her as Hardy saw her during their courtship, his pulse quickened by the thrill of the chase. They first met at St Juliot, Cornwall, in 1871, and they married in 1874. It was not long before the self-centred Hardy was excluding Emma from his life, treating her with an almost studied lack of interest. He also distressed her with his atheism and with his susceptibility to younger, prettier women. One of these he introduced into his household, becoming so besotted with her that he even neglected his wife on her death-bed. Her maid has related that when she rushed to tell Hardy that her mistress was terribly ill, he told her that her collar needed straightening and took his time in accompanying her to Emma's room. Not until he saw Emma, who had only minutes to live, did he show the remorse that was to inspire some of his best poems: unable to love her while she was his wife, he had no difficulty in conceiving a genuine passion for Emma once she was dead. Perhaps his greatest crime, in her eyes, was his failure to hold her in anything remotely approaching the esteem in which she held herself. She was a snob (the niece of an archdeacon, no less), and she was jealous of Hardy's literary success, considering herself to be both his social and his intellectual superior. Although she had plenty to complain about, her keeping of a bitter diary — which she titled 'What I think of my husband' — suggests that she may have come to derive a certain relish from her resentment. See also Driffield, Edward.

SWANN, Charles and Gilberte, in Marcel Proust's *A la recherche de temps perdu* (1913–27). Charles Swann is an amalgam of Charles Haas (1832–1902), the primary model, a hero of the Franco-Prussian war, a connoisseur of Italian art, accomplished womaniser and friend of Edward VII and of the pretender to the French throne, the Comte de Paris; Charles Ephrussi (1848–1905), editor of *La Gazette des Beaux-Arts*; Paul Hervieu (1857–1915), dramatist and novelist; and Émile Straus (1844–1929), prosperous Jewish banker to the Barons Rothschild (of whom he was allegedly a bastard half-brother) and husband of Bizet's widow (see Guermantes, Oriane, Duchesse de). Gilberte Swann is a composite of Proust's childhood sweetheart, Marie de Bénardaky, who in 1898 married Prince Michel Radziwill; Suzette Lemaire, daughter of Madeleine Lemaire (see Verdurin, Mme); and Jeanne Pouquet, who in 1893 married Gaston Arman de Caillavet (see Saint-Loup, Robert de).

SYLVIE, in Lewis Carroll's *Sylvie and Bruno* (1889), is part-inspired by the last of the author's child-friends, Enid Stevens (subsequently Mrs E. G. Shawyer), whom the author first met when she was nine and he called on her parents at their home in Canterbury Road, Oxford. Harry Furniss, the book's illustrator, drew her on several occasions, but she believed his Sylvie was modelled on his own daughter.

T

TABRET, Mrs, in W. Somerset Maugham's *The Sacred Flame* (1928). At the age of twelve the author's nephew, Ormond Maugham, fell while climbing a tree at school and was paralysed for the rest of his short life; he died in 1935, aged twenty-five. His mother's devotion to him gave the author the idea for this play, notes Robin Maugham in *Somerset and all the Maughams* (1966), although the circumstances of the paralysed man and his devoted mother are very different to those of Maugham's nephew and his sister-in-law, Mrs Charles Ormond Maugham, the play's Mrs Tabret. In *The Sacred Flame* Mrs Tabret puts an end to her son's suffering by killing him, and the Bishop of London attacked the drama for condoning euthanasia. Maugham's sister-in-law was the daughter of the artist Heywood Hardy and she produced collages under her nickname, 'Beldy'. Her husband died six months after her son.

TADZIO, in Thomas Mann's 'Death in Venice' (1911; *Stories of a Lifetime*, 1961). In the early 1960s Erika Mann was editing her father's letters when she received a note from Count Władysław Moes, of Warsaw, introducing himself as the model for Tadzio. The Polish translator of 'Death in Venice' was asked to see the count, records the Mann biographer Richard Winston. 'He met a man of sixty-eight who produced undeniable proof, in the form of photos and recollections, that he was indeed the ravishing boy of the story.' As a child he had holidayed with his family at the Hôtel des Bains, Venice, where Mann was also staying at that time. He recalled 'an old man' watching him while he played. The holiday had been cut short, his family leaving because of a cholera epidemic.

TAFFY, in George Du Maurier's *Trilby* (1894), owes his decency and reliability to Thomas Armstrong (1832–1911). The artist son of a Manchester cotton manufacturer, he first met the author in 1856 and became his friend for life. He founded the 'English Group' in Paris and in 1881 became Director of the South Kensington School of Art (subsequently the Royal College). For his physique, Taffy has a suggested model in the Royal Academician and writer of comedies Valentine Cameron Prinsep (1838–1904). Armstrong is also believed to have contributed to *Trilby*'s Little Billee, although this character is primarily a Du Maurier self-portrait.

TAILLANDY, Adolphe, in Sidonie-Gabrielle Colette's *La Vagabonde* (1910), is the author's first husband, Henri ('Willy') Gauthier-Villars (*d.* 1931), a novelist and music critic. He married Colette in 1893 and persuaded her to write provocative novels of schoolgirl life under his name, locking her in her room for four hours at a time so that she would have no distraction. They were divorced in 1910.

TAILOR OF GLOUCESTER, the, in Beatrix Potter's *The Tailor of Gloucester* (1902). When Beatrix Potter visited Gloucestershire in 1894, staying with relations at Harescombe Grange, Stroud, she was intrigued by reports of a local mystery. John Samuel Prichard (*d.* 1934), a Gloucester tailor, had displayed a notice in his shop window: 'Have your suits made by the Tailor of Gloucester, where the work is done by fairies.' Attempting to finish a waistcoat for the Mayor to wear in an annual procession, he had gone home in dejection on finding he was unable to complete the order in time. On returning to his workshop, he had found the garment all but finished, with a note: 'No more twist.' Beatrix Potter called on Prichard to obtain his consent to her using the incident as a basis for her story, saying that she would portray the tailor as an elderly man. Her illustrations of the shop's interior were based on an establishment in Chelsea. The mystery was partly solved a few years later, but a full explanation was not forthcoming until 1979, when Prichard's son, Douglas, about to retire from his air travel business in Bahrain, wrote to Potter's biographer, Margaret Lane. Some of the tailor's workmen, finding themselves the worse for drink on a Saturday night and unable to get home, had taken refuge in their workshop, near the Cathedral. The next morning, rather than venture out unshaven and in their working clothes while local churchgoers paraded in their Sunday best, they had remained on the premises until they could leave unobtrusively at night. They had passed the time by finishing the waistcoats for the Mayor and Corporation, until they had run out of twist. Why did they not 'own up' on the Monday? They did not wish their employer to know they had been inebriated, or that they had a key to the shop.

TAIT, Basil, in Stevie Smith's *The Holiday* (1949), is modelled in part upon the novelist George Orwell (Eric Blair, 1903–50), who is also the part-inspiration of another character in *The Holiday*. 'Splitting George in two', the author later explained, 'seemed likely to lessen the risk of libel.'

TALBOT, Christian, in Nancy Mitford's *The Pursuit of Love* (1945), is the author's husband, Peter Rodd (see Seal, Basil). In *A Little Learning*, Evelyn Waugh recalled him having as a young man 'the sulky, arrogant looks of the young Rimbaud'. In *Nancy Mitford*, Harold Acton described him as 'a very superior con man' whom Mitford disliked. This was challenged by another of her friends, Alastair Forbes, reviewing Acton's book in the *Times Literary Supplement* (12 September 1975). Though Rodd was impossible to live with, Forbes wrote, Mitford did not dislike him as much as Acton suggested. Rodd was 'a highly educated product of Balliol who had insuperable difficulties in adapting his talents to the society into which he was born. He suffered from a sort of galloping mythomania which proved too great even for a Mitford to take in her stride'.

TALBOT, Colonel, in Sir Walter Scott's *Waverley* (1814), has a suggested prototype in Colonel Charles Whitefoord (*d.* 1753), third son of Sir Adam Whitefoord, of Ludlow, Shropshire. As engineer in charge of the English guns in the battle of Prestonpans, he was wounded and captured. He subsequently sought clemency for Alexander Stewart (see Bradwardine, the Baron of).

TAM O'SHANTER, in Robert Burns's poem of that name (1791), is believed to be Douglas Graham (?1738–1811), tenant of Shanter farm, near Maidens, Ayrshire. His boat was called *Tam o'Shanter*, and he was suspected of using it for smuggling.

TAMVILLE, Lady Dionissia de Egerton de, in Ford Madox Ford's *Ladies Whose Bright Eyes* (1911), according to Ford's biographer, Arthur Mizener, is Rosamond Fogg Elliott, who chanced upon the character's improbable name on a tablet in Salisbury Cathedral. A niece of Violet Hunt (see Nesbitt, Norah), she had an adolescent passion for the author.

TANAKA, Tiger, in Ian Fleming's *You Only Live Twice* (1964). It is thanks to John Pearson's *The Life of Ian Fleming* (1966) that we know that Tanaka is based on Torao 'Tiger' Saito, a Japanese war correspondent who later became an architect and an editor. Fleming met him through their mutual friend Richard Hughes (see Henderson, Dikko).

TANNER, John, in George Bernard Shaw's *Man and Superman* (1903), is believed to owe his origin in part to Henry Mayers Hyndman (1842−1921), a pioneer British Marxist who founded the Socialist Democratic Federation. From a wealthy background, he would appear in top hat and frock coat to distribute leaflets or address open-air meetings, at which he would chide his ill-clad audience on their foolishness in providing the money that allowed him to dress so well. As a cricketer, he was a notable Sussex county batsman and it has been suggested that his failure to achieve a Cambridge blue turned him to socialism, to spite society. See Barbara Tuchman, *The Proud Tower* (1966).

TANTAMOUNT, Lucy, in Aldous Huxley's *Point Counter Point* (1928), is Nancy Cunard (see Storm, Iris), who said that sleeping with Huxley was like being crawled over by slugs. Their affair, in 1922−3, was inconsequential to her but obsessional for him, and nearly wrecked his marriage.

TARTUFFE, in Molière's *Le Tartuffe* (1664), is supposedly primarily Louis XIV's confessor, François de La Chaise (1624−1709), a Jesuit priest noted for his addiction to *tartuffes* (truffles). The Paris cemetery of Père-Lachaise (formerly a Jesuit estate which La Chaise was instrumental in developing) was named after him. Tartuffe may also contain elements of the Abbé de Roquette, a toady of Armand, Prince de Conti, once Molière's patron.

TARVRILLE, Lord, in H. G. Wells's *The New Machiavelli* (1911). A mixture of insouciance, flamboyance and insensitivity, Harry Cust (1861−1917) is in part the model for Tarville. Coolness personified, he refused to abandon a dinner party he was holding when fire broke out on a floor above − his guests dutifully ate on, while water from the firemen's hoses dripped from the ceiling. He also repeatedly refused to accept William Waldorf Astor's contributions to the *Pall Mall Gazette*, and this in 1896 cost him his job as editor: Astor was the proprietor. Cust's compulsive womanising produced illegitimate children, allegedly including Lady Diana Cooper (see Stitch, Mrs Algernon), and in 1893 he married Emmeline (Nina) Welby-Gregory, daughter of Sir Glyn Welby-Gregory, of Denton, Lincolnshire. The marriage was one of convenience, and so little did Cust allow it to affect his philandering that several of his subsequent acquaintances assumed he was a bachelor. The more he neglected the wife with whom he was seldom seen, the more was she devoted to him. Outliving Cust by nearly forty years, she sculpted two posthumous figures of her husband, published a collection of his poems (mostly addressed to other women), and more than thirty years after his death dedicated an anthology to him. More about Cust and his milieu is to be found in Jane Abdy and Charlotte Gere's *The Souls* (1984).

TASKERSON, Abraham, in Malcolm Lowry's *Under the Volcano* (1947), is part-inspired by the American poet and novelist Conrad Aiken (1889–1973). In 1929 Lowry went to the United States specifically to become Aiken's disciple and, in turn, himself became Aiken's protégé. See also Hambo.

TAUB, Will, in Mary McCarthy's *The Oasis* (1949), is the critic Philip Rahv (1908–), a founder of the *Partisan Review* in 1934. McCarthy was drama critic of the *Review*, which Rahv co-edited.

TAYLOR, George and Dora, in Dorothy Richardson's *Revolving Lights* (1923), are Charles Daniel and his fiancée, Florence E. Woolland. A London publisher, Daniel was proprietor of *Crank: an Unconventional Magazine*, to which Richardson contributed book reviews, commencing in 1906.

TAYLOR, Stephen, in Frederic Raphael's *The Glittering Prizes* (1976), has three prototypes: the novelist Henry Williamson (1897–1977), noted for *Tarka the Otter* and for his admiration for Adolf Hitler; the architect Frank Lloyd Wright (see Roark, Howard); and the politician Sir Oswald Mosley (see Webley, Everard). When Daniel Farson was writing *Henry. An Appreciation of Henry Williamson* (1982) he asked Raphael whether, as he suspected, Stephen Taylor was based on Williamson. 'Although I had never met the man, Farson was not far wrong', Raphael wrote in the *Sunday Times* (20 June 1982). Replying to Farson, he confirmed the Williamson hunch and added that he had also in mind Frank Lloyd Wright, 'whose organic architecture at one time seemed to be a kind of three-dimensional image of the Good Right. I elected to invent a Williamson/Mosley/Wright compound largely because I wanted to be free of the obligation to be "accurate". I didn't want to get into Mosley's pretentious nonsense but to find an awkward target, for myself and my "hero", a man who held appalling ideas but was not himself appalling or untalented.'

TEBBEN, Richard, in Angela Thirkell's *August Folly* (1936), is Gilbert Welch Barker, author of a biography of Watteau and the youngest son of Colonel F. G. Barker, of Stanlake Park, Twyford, Berkshire. The author first met Barker in the London Library, where he was pursuing his interest in art history. He was for a time her constant escort.

TELLHEIM, Major, in Gotthold Ephraim Lessing's *Minna von Barnhelm* (1767), is the German poet Ewald Christian von Kleist (1715–59). A major in the Prussian army, he was mortally wounded while leading an attack in the battle of Kunersdorf. He had become a close friend of Lessing while stationed at Leipzig the previous year.

TEMPEST, Leslie, in D. H. Lawrence's *The White Peacock* (1911), is George Henry Neville (1886–1959), the son of a self-employed milkman. He attended Ilkeston Teacher Training Centre with Lawrence and in 1912 became a headmaster in Bradnop, Staffordshire. In 1905 he fathered an illegitimate child; another of his children was born in 1912, three months after his marriage. He left teaching to work as a haulier, whisky salesman and accountant. His memoir of Lawrence was published in part in the 1930s and in its entirety in 1982.

TEMPLE, Claire, in Norah Hoult's *There Were No Windows* (1944), is Violet Hunt. See Nesbit, Norah.

TEMPLETON, Elliott, in W. Somerset Maugham's *The Razor's Edge* (1944). In his determination to establish himself in English society, Sir Henry ('Chips') Channon (1897–1958), the son of a Chicago businessman, became more English than the English. Although he was not knighted until 1957, he added aristocratic connections to his wealth in 1933 by marrying Lady Honor Guinness, eldest daughter of the Second Earl of Iveagh, taking up residence in Belgrave Square, next door to the Duke of Kent. In 1935 he succeeded his father-in-law as Conservative MP for Southend-on-Sea. His divorce in 1945 came as no surprise to those acquainted with his homosexuality – his conquests included the dramatist Terence Rattigan, who dedicated *The Winslow Boy* to his son, 'Master Paul Channon', later to become a government minister. A prodigious diarist, in 1944 'Chips' recorded taxing Maugham with portraying him as Templeton. Maugham explained, 'with some embarrassment, that he had split me into three characters, and then written a book about all three'. (See also Darrell, Larry.) Cyril Connolly, however, claimed Templeton's original to be Henry May, 'an old Corniche figure whom I met with Maugham'; and Maugham's biographer, Ted Morgan, has suggested a model for Templeton in the author's international playboy friend, Jerome Zipkin, a Jewish American real-estate heir who bought the manuscript of Maugham's *The Moon and Sixpence* for £2,600 in 1955 – at that time a record figure for a living writer.

TEN PER CENT, Mr, in Viviane Ventura's *April Fool* (1983), is supposedly Adnan Khashoggi (see Al Fay, Baydr), who financed the author's photographic book on Egypt and owned her Chelsea home at the time of *April Fool*'s publication.

TERRIER, Lord de, in Anthony Trollope's *Phineas Finn* (1869) and *Phineas Redux* (1874), is Edward George Geoffrey Smith Stanley, Fourteenth Earl of Derby (1799–1869), three times Britain's Prime Minister, and a translator of the *Iliad*.

TESMAN, Jörgen and Juliane, in Henrik Ibsen's *Hedda Gabler* (1890), are part-inspired by Julius Elias, a German literary historian who made the author's acquaintance in Munich and became co-editor of his posthumously-published work; and Elise Holck, of Trondheim, who met the author in the 1870s while she was tending a dying sister in Dresden, and to whom Ibsen paid tribute in a poem written in 1874.

THEALE, Milly, in Henry James's *The Wings of the Dove* (1902). Two invalids are acknowledged to have been the inspiration for Milly Theale, and to them I would add a third. It is accepted that James based Milly primarily upon his beautiful, vivacious, highly intelligent cousin, Mary ('Minny') Temple (1846–70), who died of tuberculosis in Cambridge, Massachusetts, when the author was hoping she might join him in Rome. Also perceived in Milly by James's biographer Leon Edel is the author's sister, Alice James

(1848–92), a lifelong sufferer from what was believed to be neurasthenia, although she died of cancer. Part of the novel's inspiration, however, was a love affair of the Massachusetts-born novelist John Oliver Hobbes (Mrs Pearl Craigie, 1867–1906), according to Margaret Maison's article 'The Brilliant Mrs Craigie' in the *Listener* (28 August 1969). Mrs Craigie was plagued by a weak heart and, like Milly, was frequently prostrated by exhaustion. She died of heart failure.

THOMAS, Dr Gunther, in Roger L. Simon's *Wild Turkey* (1975), according to David Geherin's *Sons of Sam Spade* (1980), is the American journalist Hunter S. Thompson (1939–   ), national affairs editor of *Rolling Stone* from 1970 to 1975.

THOMAS, Helen, in Gertrude Stein's *Q.E.D.* (1971), is May Bookstaver, with whom the author had a brief lesbian relationship in the early 1900s. In 1906, Bookstaver became Mrs Charles Knoblauch, subsequently acting as Stein's agent in the United States.

THOMPSON, Helen, in Francis King's *Act of Darkness* (1983), has as prototype Constance Kent. See Cuff, Sergeant Richard.

THORNDYKE, Dr John Evelyn, in the detective novels of R. Austin Freeman, commencing with *The Red Thumb Mark* (1907), is identified by Eric Quayle's *The Collector's Book of Detective Fiction* (1972) as Dr Alfred Swayne Taylor, Freeman's tutor at Middlesex Hospital Medical College in the late 1870s.

THORNHILL, Sir William, in Oliver Goldsmith's *The Vicar of Wakefield* (1766), has a suggested original in the Yorkshire MP Sir George Savile (1726–84), whose liberal views prompted him to defend the American colonists and to advocate relief for Roman Catholics and Protestant dissenters. The name Thornhill may have been suggested to Goldsmith by the Thornhill, Yorkshire, connection of the Saviles, Earls of Mexborough.

THORNTON, Helen, in Gertrude Stein's *Fernhurst* (1971), is Carey Thomas. As dean of Bryn Mawr college, Philadelphia, in the 1890s, she became involved in a triangular relationship when her protégée and colleague Mary Gwinn fell in love with another member of the staff, Alfred Hodder, who divorced his wife, married Gwinn and died shortly afterwards.

THORNTON, John, in Elizabeth Gaskell's *North and South* (1854−5), is possibly part-inspired by the author's acquaintance with the Manchester machine-tool engineer James Nasmyth (1808−90), pioneer of assembly lines and inventor (in 1839) of the steam hammer. Ironically, that invention, for which he became famous, was designed to cope with the vast dimensions of a product that was never used: a paddle-shaft for the steamship *Great Britain*, which put to sea with screw propulsion.

THRIFT, Viscount, in Anthony Trollope's *Phineas Finn* (1869), may owe something to the Fourteenth Earl of Derby (see Terrier, Lord de). When he wasn't working as Foreign Secretary, running the country as Prime Minister or decimating the local pheasants, he occupied himself − like Thrift − in translating Homer.

THURGOOD, Red-Ted, in Frank Hardy's *Power without Glory* (1950), is acknowledged by the author to be based on Edward Granville Theodore (1884−1950), the son of a Romanian emigrant and a miner, trade unionist and Federal Labour politician in Australia. He was Premier of Queensland from 1919 to 1925, and served in the Australian government from 1939 to 1945.

THURLOE, Roger, in John Dos Passos's *The Great Days* (1958). In 1968 the author said, in a *Paris Review* interview (see *Writers at Work*, 4th series, 1977), that Thurloe was part-inspired by James Vincent Forrestal (1892−1949), a member of the United States cabinet and First Secretary of the Defense Department. In the Second World War he was responsible for the expansion of the United States navy. He later suffered from depression, and died after throwing himself through a United States Navy hospital window.

TIETJENS, Christopher, Mark and Sylvia, in Ford Madox Ford's *Parade's End* tetralogy (1924−8). Christopher Tietjens is Arthur Marwood (1868−1916), of Busby Hall, Stokesley, Yorkshire, who with Ford founded the *English Review* in 1908. Like his cousin Lewis Carroll he was an accomplished mathematician, and this led him to evolve a social insurance scheme in which he unsuccessfully sought to interest the government. Mark Tietjens is Sir William Marwood (1863−1935), Arthur's brother. He retired in 1923 after a Civil Service career with the General Post Office, the Board of Trade and the Ministry of Transport. Ford described the manner of his death with uncanny prescience, Marwood even uttering Mark Tietjens's last words. Sylvia Tietjens is an amalgam of Violet Hunt (see Nesbit, Norah) and Elsie Martindale (see Macdonald, Countess).

TILBURY, Lord, in P. G. Wodehouse's *Bill the Conqueror* (1924), *Heavy Weather* (1933) and *Frozen Assets* (1964), has a probable prototype in Alfred Harmsworth, First Viscount Northcliffe (1865–1922), founder of the *Daily Mail* and the *Daily Mirror* and proprietor of the *Observer* and *The Times*. In *Bill the Conqueror*, his magazine *Answers* is echoed by *Pyke's Weekly*. The founder of twentieth-century popular journalism in Britain, Northcliffe became insane towards the end of his life, putting a commissionaire at Carmelite House in charge of the advertisement department of the *Daily Mail*.

TILLY-TWEED-IN-BLOOD, in Djuna Barnes's *The Ladies' Almanack* (1928). Although she was the first translator of Colette and the only sculptor to model Nijinsky from the life, it is not as an artist that Una, Lady Troubridge (1887–1963), is remembered. She was the daughter of an impecunious King's Messenger and the wife of Admiral Sir Ernest Troubridge (*d.* 1926), whom she left for Marguerite Radclyffe Hall (see Buck-and-Balk, Lady). Radclyffe Hall dressed as a man, Una Troubridge adopted a monocle, and together they paraded their relationship . . . which was almost as bizarre as their appearance. Richard Ormrod's *Una Troubridge: The Friend of Radclyffe Hall* (1984) tells how Radclyffe Hall's previous lover died during a row over Una, who subsequently had to share Marguerite with the deceased's spirit — they kept in touch through a medium.

TILNEY, Henry, in Jane Austen's *Northanger Abbey* (1818). The critics Lord David Cecil and John Sparrow have both canvassed the case for the Revd Sydney Smith (1771–1845) as Tilney's original. Critic and wit, he declared, 'I never read a book before reviewing it, it prejudices a man so.' On seeing two housewives berating each other from their windows on opposite sides of London's St Paul's Close, he remarked that they would never agree as they were arguing from different premises.

TIN-POT FOREIGN GENERAL, the, in Raymond Briggs's *The Tin-Pot Foreign General and the Old Iron Woman* (1984), is General Leopoldo Fortunato Galtieri, President of Argentina from 1981 to 1982, who in 1982 ordered the invasion of the Falkland Islands.

TOBY, Uncle. See Shandy, Captain Toby.

TOLKACHENKO, in Fyodor Dostoevsky's *The Devils* (1871–2), is the Russian folklorist I. G. Pryzhov, who in 1869 was among revolutionaries involved in the murder of the student Ivanov (see Shatov).

TOLLAND, Isobel, in Anthony Powell's *A Dance to the Music of Time* sequence (1951–75). In his memoirs the author concedes that in Isobel Tolland, 'faint nuances (of which I am myself probably unaware) may to some extent mark her out as my wife . . .', the biographer Lady Violet Powell (1912–   ), third daughter of the Fifth Earl of Longford.

TOLLIVER, Ellen and Hattie, in Louis Bromfield's *The Green Bay Tree* (1924) and *Possession* (1925). According to Bromfield's biographer, Morrison Brown, Ellen and Hattie are respectively the author's musical sister, Ellen Bromfield, a promising pianist who died young; and his mother, Annette Coulter Bromfield, the daughter of a farmer in Richland County, Ohio.

TOM FOOL, in David Stacton's novel of that name (1962), is the American politician and lawyer Wendell Willkie (1892–1944), who was the unsuccessful Republican nominee for the United States presidency in 1940.

TOM, Uncle, in Harriet Beecher Stowe's *Uncle Tom's Cabin* (1851–2), is popularly identified with Josiah Henson (1789–1883), a Negro slave who fled from Maryland to Canada, where he achieved fame as a Methodist preacher and as the founder of an agricultural and educational settlement for Blacks. Part of his life story was used by Mrs Stowe — his dictated autobiography had appeared in 1849 and in the following year she met him at her brother's home in Boston. But the initial inspiration of *Uncle Tom's Cabin* was the husband of a former slave employed as a servant by the author's family. Mrs Stowe wrote letters for this employee to her husband, who was still a slave in Kentucky. Thus the author learned how, although he enjoyed an unusual degree of liberty, he refused to break his pledge of service to his master, trusting that he would in return honour his promise to give him his freedom — an obligation which was from year to year deferred.

TOMS, Joe, in William Hazlitt's 'The Fight' (1822; *Literary Remains*, 1836), is Joseph Parkes (1796–1865), a lawyer who qualified in London and practised in Birmingham, later returning to the capital where in 1847 he became a taxing master in Chancery. In 1824 he married a granddaughter of Joseph Priestley, the discoverer of oxygen, subsequently becoming grandfather of the writer Hilaire Belloc.

TONKA, in Robert Musil's 'Tonka' (*Drei Frauen*, 1924), according to Musil's biographer, David S. Luft, is Herma Dietz (*d. c.* 1907), a Czech working-class girl with whom the author had a prolonged affair, starting in Brno and continuing when Musil moved to Berlin and Dietz followed him. She died in hospital, following an abortion and venereal infection. Musil had earlier been cured of syphilis.

TOOGOOD, Mr, in Thomas Love Peacock's *Crotchet Castle* (1831), is the social reformer Robert Owen (1771–1858), father of English socialism, who in 1817 suggested a plan for self-sufficient communities of about 1,200 residing in one large building around a quadrangle. At New Lanark, where he managed and part-owned a number of cotton mills, he practised many of his ideas for improving workers' conditions.

TOOMEY, Kenneth Marchal, in Anthony Burgess's *Earthly Powers* (1980). Facets of W. Somerset Maugham (see Bertrand, Archie) have been noted in Toomey by critics including Paul Bailey, David Holloway, D. A. N. Jones, Bernard Levin and Jeremy Treglown. They can't all be wrong. Indeed, the Maugham similarities are obvious.

TOUCHES, Félicité des, in Honoré de Balzac's *Illusions perdues* (1837–43), *Honorine* (1843) and *Béatrix* (1844), is George Sand. See Maupin, Camille.

TOWER, Millicent and Willie, in S. N. Behrman's *Jane* (1946), are Syrie Maugham (see Middleton, Constance) and W. Somerset Maugham (see Bertrand, Archie). Ted Morgan, Maugham's biographer, notes that Behrman suggested that the actor playing Willie Tower should study Maugham's portrait and read his autobiography.

TOWN, Max, in Anthony West's *Heritage* (1955), is the author's father, H. G. Wells (see Wilson, Hypo). Reviewing this *roman-à-clef* in the *Sunday Telegraph* (3 June 1984), the Wells biographer Norman Mackenzie remarked that in its pages the author's mother (see Savage, Naomi) could do no right. 'His father, by contrast, can do almost nothing wrong. Mr West gives him the benefit of every doubt, and justifies his ideas and actions so trenchantly, and so much in his father's style, that these pages often read as if the talented but splenetic spirit of H. G. had written them on a planchette.'

TOWNELEY, in Samuel Butler's *The Way of all Flesh* (1903). You won't find him in dictionaries of biography, but the man who was the model for Towneley has a more permanent monument to his endeavour than most of us can hope to achieve. This is the London landmark, Cleopatra's Needle, and it was Charles Paine Pauli who in 1878 organised its passage from Egypt to the Thames embankment. Meeting him in New Zealand in the early 1860s, Butler took Pauli under his wing, brought him back to England and provided him with an income of £200 a year. Pauli appears barely to have tolerated his benefactor, whom he surprised by leaving a tidy sum of money . . . not to Butler, but to a mistress.

TOWN-MOUSE, Johnny, in Beatrix Potter's *The Tale of Johnny Town-mouse* (1918), owes his appearance in the author's illustrations to Dr George Parsons, a Hawkshead friend of Beatrix Potter's solicitor husband. The two men devised their own private golf course, and Johnny Town-mouse's long bag is believed to have been inspired by one used by the doctor to carry his clubs, according to the local historian John Dawson (in the magazine *Lancashire Life*, November 1978).

TOWNSEND, Charlie, in W. Somerset Maugham's *The Painted Veil* (1925), is part-inspired by Charles Hanson Towne (1877—1949), the author's New York agent in the 1920s. A Kentucky-born journalist, novelist and poet, he edited *The Smart Set* and later became a successful actor.

TRADDLES, Thomas, in Charles Dickens's *David Copperfield* (1849—50), is based in part upon the author's friend, Sir Thomas Noon Talfourd (1795—1854), MP, dramatic poet and jurist, who was in 1849 appointed judge of the Court of Common Pleas. His causes included the abolition of the pillory and the promotion of a bill giving writers copyright protection — he was himself the author of a play, *Ion*, in which Macready appeared in 1836, and his habit of attending its performances became a standing joke among acquaintances.

TRAFFORD, Mrs Barton, in W. Somerset Maugham's *Cakes and Ale* (1930). Here is a portrait etched in acid. The sitter is Lady Colvin (*d.* 1924), with whom Robert Louis Stevenson fell in love when he was in his early twenties, she in her mid-thirties. We owe much of our knowledge of the young Stevenson to their correspondence, for after the writer's death his letters were published by Lady Colvin's husband, Sir Sidney Colvin, Keeper of Prints and Drawings at the British Museum and Stevenson's mentor and close friend. Maugham's portrayal of the Colvins is clinical and cynical. Like Lady Colvin, the self-aggrandising Mrs Barton Trafford has had an earlier, unhappy marriage; and she is noted for her association with a now dead, much lamented novelist whose letters to her have been published. Mr Barton Trafford, like Sir Sidney, interests himself in the career and posthumous reputation of the novelist. Trafford writes a Life of the novelist; Colvin was responsible for the Edinburgh edition of Stevenson's works. Maugham's models are unmistakable. Was his judgement jaundiced? An alternative and perhaps corrective view of the Colvins is to be found in James Pope Hennessy's biography of Stevenson.

TRANFIELD, Grace, in George Bernard Shaw's *The Philanderer* (1898), is the actress Florence Farr (1860–1917), who was Shaw's mistress for seven years and was later the mistress of W. B. Yeats. Married to the actor Edward Emery (1861–1938), she had a penchant for the exotic, ranging from mysticism to sage-green drapery which she wore about London, carrying a Celtic harp. Towards the end of her life she became the principal of a Hindu school for girls in Ceylon, where she died of cancer. For her portrait of Shaw, see Travers, George.

TRAPNEL, Francis X., in Anthony Powell's *A Dance to the Music of Time* sequence (1951–75), commencing with *Books do Furnish a Room* (1971). Described by the critic Julian Symons as 'a fascinating bore', the model for Trapnel is the novelist and short-story writer Julian Maclaren-Ross (*d.* 1964). His circle included Martin Jordan, who tells me: 'His wardrobe consisted entirely of fine pearl-coloured suits, silk ties etc. because he liked to dress in these to write, like a priest putting on vestments. Then the rejection slips piled up and he had to take a job as a gardener. Having neither working clothes nor money, he wore the suits on the job, attracting large crowds. Thanks to the impartial effect of the good earth his suits quickly became indistinguishable from working clothes and no one noticed him any more.'

TRAVERS, Dahlia Portarlington, the Aunt Dahlia of P. G. Wodehouse's Bertie Wooster stories (1915–74), is a composite of the author's aunt, Louisa Deane (*d.* 1906), and the Countess of Ilchester (1876–1956). Wodehouse's aunt was the daughter of the Revd John Bathurst Deane, of Cheyne Court, Bath, vicar of St Helen's, Bishopsgate, London. The countess, born Lady Helen Mary Therese Vane-Tempest-Stewart, daughter of the Sixth Marquess of Londonderry, was Wodehouse's house guest in 1923. She was noted as a genial, rubicund, deep-voiced huntswoman with a sense of humour. For this and several other Wodehouse leads I am obliged to David A. Jasen's *P. G. Wodehouse: A Portrait of a Master* (1975).

TRAVERS, George, in Florence Farr's *The Dancing Faun* (1894), is the author's lover, George Bernard Shaw. See Quint, Peter; see also Craven, Julia, and Tranfield, Grace.

TREECE, Professor Stuart, in Malcolm Bradbury's *Eating People is Wrong* (1959). The author tells me that Treece has a double source. He was partly drawn ('the nicer part', says Bradbury) from Professor Arthur Raleigh Humphreys (1911–), Professor of English at Leicester University from 1947 to 1976. 'The other half (the weaker part, so to say) was drawn from myself.' Bradbury took his BA at Leicester University.

TRELAWNEY, Dr, in Anthony Powell's *A Dance to the Music of Time* sequence (1951–75), is 'obviously founded on Aleister Crowley' (see Haddo, Oliver), in the view of the critic Francis King. In his memoirs, Powell recalls Crowley pseudonymously offering Duckworth, the publishers, his mistress's autobiography, *My Hymen*, for an advance of £500 (a lot of money in 1930) and a royalty of fifteen per cent. Although there was much that was absurd about him, Powell notes, 'Crowley was sinister, intensely sinister, both in exterior and manner.'

TRENT, Nell. See Little Nell.

TRESSIDER, Dr. Frederic and Barbara, in D. H. Lawrence's *The Fight for Barbara* (1912), are Professor Ernest Weekley (*d.* 1954), who taught Lawrence French at Nottingham University, and Weekley's wife, Frieda, who left him for the author. See Somers, Harriet.

TRILLO, Mr, in Thomas Love Peacock's *Crochet Castle* (1831), is the Irish poet Thomas Moore (1779–1852).

TRIMMER, in Evelyn Waugh's *Officers and Gentlemen* (1955), is supposedly part-inspired by Brigadier Lord Lovat (Simon Christopher Joseph Fraser, Fifteenth Baron Lovat, 1911–), Scottish land-owner and cattle-breeder and an outstanding Commando leader in the Second World War. Unable to tolerate Waugh's undisciplined behaviour as a soldier, he was involved in moves which led to the author's enforced resignation from the Special Services Brigade in 1943. Thirty-five years later, Lord Lovat's abiding dislike for Waugh found further expression in his memoirs.

TRISSOTIN, in Molière's *Les Femmes savantes* (1672), is Abbé Charles Cotin (1604–82), preacher, writer, councillor and almoner to the King of France, and a savage critic of the plays of Boileau, in which he was satirised.

TROTTER, in George Bernard Shaw's *Fanny's First Play* (1911). A. B. Walkley, (1855–1926), drama critic of the *Star* from 1888 to 1900 and of *The Times* from 1900 to 1926, was so beguiled by the notion of being represented on the stage that he permitted the actor playing Trotter to inspect him at close quarters before deciding on make-up. But when the play was revived in 1915, Walkley advised his readers to stay away. It had been at Walkley's suggestion that Shaw wrote *Man and Superman*.

TROTWOOD, Betsey, in Charles Dickens's *David Copperfield* (1849–50), is Miss Mary Strong, at whose Broadstairs home in Nuttall's Place (subsequently the Dickens House Museum) the author witnessed donkeys being chased off the green.

TRUNK, Thaddeus, in Wyndham Lewis's 'The Doppelgänger' (*Unlucky for Pringle*, 1973), is Ezra Pound (see Forbes, Duncan), presented as a pedagogue preoccupied with the past. Lewis's biographer, Jeffrey Meyers, notes that his last reference to Pound described him as timid beneath his tough veneer, and averse to showdowns.

TRUTH-TELLER, in Alexander Zinoviev's *The Yawning Heights* (1979), is the dissident Russian writer Alexander Solzhenitsyn (1918–   ), who was expelled from the Soviet Union in 1974. 'Truth-teller is a great child-man, who has suffered unjustly, cruelly and senselessly', says another character in the novel. 'He is problem number one of our time. He is something much bigger than ideology, politics and morality. He is the focal point where all the problems are concentrated.' Interviewed by James Fenton in the *Guardian* (20 April 1979), Zinoviev said, 'To a certain extent the dissident movement is convenient to the authorities. You can consider Solzhenitsyn president of the union of anti-Soviet writers, and Sakharov as minister for anti-Soviet affairs. To a certain extent they prevent more extreme forms of resistance. Everyone who plays a positive role plays also a negative role. It is impossible to fight against the Soviet system without in some way helping it.' He admired Solzhenitsyn but thought he did not understand the Soviet system. 'If you had to choose between the present leaders and Solzhenitsyn, you would choose the present leaders.'

TUBBE, Mr Waldo, in Richard Aldington's *Death of a Hero* (1929), is T. S. Eliot (see Horty, Mr), portrayed as an American trying to pass himself off as an Englishman.

TULLIVER, Edward and Tom, in George Eliot's *The Mill on the Floss* (1860), are respectively Thomas Hollick, a farmer and miller of Nuneaton, Warwickshire; and Isaac Pearson Evans (1816–90), the author's elder brother who, like his father, became a land agent for the Newdigate family. Of High Church and subsequently Tractarian inclination, Isaac succeeded in persuading the author to abandon her refusal to attend church – a stand which had upset her father. But when she informed him that she was living, unmarried, with George Henry Lewes, he ceased all communication with her and did not resume contact until she married John Cross twenty-three years later.

TURNBULL, Mr, in Anthony Trollope's *Phineas Finn* (1869), *Ralph the Heir* (1871) and *Phineas Redux* (1874), has as prototype the

Liberal statesman John Bright (1811—89), a prominent agitator against the Corn Law and an outstanding orator who was often at odds with Disraeli (see Sharp, Jawster). Told that he should at least give Disraeli credit for being a self-made man, he is said to have replied, 'And he adores his maker.'

TURTLE, Tom, in William Hazlitt's 'The Fight' (1822; *Literary Remains*, 1836). The year after Hazlitt penned this essay, his model for Turtle became one of the century's most notorious killers. The son of a Norwich alderman, he was John Thurtell (1794—1824), a friend of the boxer Jem Belcher (whom he was given to mimic) and an acquaintance of the actor Edmund Kean. At prize fights in London he acted as a second, and the company he kept led to his undoing. After losing a large sum of money to one William Wheare in a game of billiards, he waylaid Wheare near Elstree, cutting his throat after his bullet was deflected by Wheare's cheekbone. He then thrust his pistol at Wheare's head with such force that it entered his brain. Having pleaded with the court not to distress his pious parents by hanging him, Thurtell went on to meet his execution with cool bravado, asking to see a report of a boxing match shortly before he was despatched. To both public and warders he became a likeable rogue; he is supposedly the unnamed second in Chapter 24 of George Borrow's *Lavengro* (1851) and he also appears as Thornton in Bulwer-Lytton's *Pelham* (1828). His trial was long remembered, not only for its horrific evidence but also because a witness equated respectability with the keeping of a gig, a definition which caught the public's imagination and was echoed twenty-one years later in the correspondence of Tennyson.

TUSHINA, Lizaveta, in Fyodor Dostoevsky's *The Devils* (1871—2), is part-inspired by Apollinaria Suslova (see Polina Alexandrovna). W. Somerset Maugham notes in *Ten Novels and Their Authors* (1954) that some years after his break with Suslova the author met her again in St Petersburg and asked her to marry him. When she refused, Dostoevsky told her she could not forgive him for the fact that she had once given herself to him, and was now avenging herself. 'He could not bring himself to believe that she simply did not like him', Maugham contends, 'and so conceived the idea, to salve, one may suppose, his wounded vanity, that a woman attaches so great an importance to her virginity that she can only hate a man who has taken it without being married to her.'

TWEEDY, Major, in James Joyce's *Ulysses* (1922). The indefatigable Joyce biographer, Richard Ellmann — where would we be without him? — identifies Tweedy as 'Major' Powell, a retired sergeant-major who after serving in the Crimean War and later with the Aldershot Rifles in Australia commuted his pension to buy a farm in Cork. He later moved to Dublin, marrying a property-owner who, wearying of his alcoholic bullying, left him after bearing him five children.

TWIGG, Timothy, in Thomas Hood's *Tylney Hall* (1834), is supposedly Thomas Tegg (1776–1845), a London bookseller and piratical publisher specialising in abridgements of popular works.

TYRONE, James, jun., in Eugene O'Neill's *A Moon for the Misbegotten* (1943), is the author's brother, James O'Neill jun., who drank himself to death before middle age.

TYRONE, Jamie, James and Mary, in Eugene O'Neill's *Long Day's Journey into Night* (1956), are respectively James O'Neill jun. (see Tyrone, James, jun.); the author's father, the actor James O'Neill (1847–1920); and the author's mother, Mary Ellen ('Ella') O'Neill (née Quinlan, 1857–1922). An Irish immigrant, James O'Neill sacrificed his career on the cross of playing the leading role in *The Count of Monte Cristo* more than 5,000 times. 'A chip off the old block, eh?' remarked Eugene on following his father into the theatre. 'Say, rather, a slice off the old ham', replied James. Ella O'Neill, born in New Haven, Connecticut, convent-educated and an accomplished pianist, became a morphine addict after being given the drug to relieve the pain of childbirth.

TYRRELL, Thornton, in Siegfried Sassoon's *Memoirs of an Infantry Officer* (1930), is Bertrand Russell (see Mattheson, Sir Joshua), who encouraged the author to issue his wartime pacifist statement and sought to use him as propaganda for the Non-Conscription movement. After Sassoon had been to see him, Russell wrote to a Non-Conscription colleague: 'He has shown amazing courage in battle, and is now showing still greater courage by his defiance. There is nothing in the faintest degree hysterical or unbalanced in his attitude which is the inevitable development of the thoughts and feelings expressed in his poems.' Russell met his match, however, in Sassoon's fellow officer, the poet Robert Graves, who contrived to have Sassoon placed in a military hospital ostensibly suffering from shell-shock.

U

UBU, in Alfred Jarry's *Ubu Roi* (1896). With a nose which Jarry likened to the upper jaw of a crocodile and a huge paunch fortified with candy from his pockets, Professor Félix Hébert taught physics in Rennes. Jarry was among the students who detested him for what they regarded as his maliciousness towards them. They wrote a puppet play in which Hébert was ridiculed and Jarry later developed it into *Ubu Roi*, with Hébert remaining as the inspiration for Ubu.

UFFENHAM, George, Sixth Viscount, in P. G. Wodehouse's *Money in the Bank* (1946) and *Something Fishy* (1957), is Max Enke (1884–1971), the Manchester-born son of naturalised British parents of German origin. He was running the family business in Belgium, supplying treated rabbit skins to the hat trade, when Germany invaded in 1940 and he became a fellow internee of Wodehouse. After the war he emigrated to Canada, buying a farm on Galiano Island, Vancouver. N. T. P. Murphy's *In Search of Blandings* (1981) quotes Enke's daughter: 'Lord Uffenham was a cruel caricature of my father, who read the book and chuckled ruefully that Wodehouse had caught some of his peculiar ways.'

UI, Arturo, in Bertolt Brecht's *The Resistible Rise of Arturo Ui* (written 1941, first performed 1958), is the Nazi dictator Adolf Hitler (1889–1945). Brecht ignores Hitler's personality, presenting him simply as an opportunist, his rhetoric owing its success to cheap histrionics. The play was written shortly before Brecht arrived in the United States, where he was virtually unknown. This circumstance and the length of the drama (it has seventeen scenes) explain the time-lag between the writing of the play and its first production.

UKRIDGE, Stanley Featherstonehaugh, in P. G. Wodehouse's Ukridge stories (1906–66), was originally inspired by a sponging, calamitously unsuccessful Devon chicken farmer named Carrington Craxton, of whom the author learned from William Townend (see Lickford). Townend himself also lent something to the development of Ukridge. The primary model, however, is Herbert Wotton Westbrook (*d.* 1959), who first met Wodehouse in 1903, at Emsworth House preparatory school in Hampshire, where Westbrook was an assistant master. Wodehouse and Westbrook were joint authors of *Not George Washington* (1907) and together wrote a regular column for the *Globe*. Westbrook's escapades included borrowing Wodehouse's dress suit without telling him, when the author had arranged to dine as a guest at a stately home (an episode echoed in 'First Aid for Dora'), and pawning Wodehouse's banjo without his knowledge, going on to lose the pawn ticket (an incident mirrored in 'Ukridge's Accident Syndicate'). Westbrook eloped with and married Ella King-Hall, sister of the headmaster of Emsworth House. She composed the music for Wodehouse and Westbrook's *The Bandit's Daughter* (1907) and was Wodehouse's literary agent from 1912 until her death in 1932.

UMFRAVILLE, Dicky, in Anthony Powell's *A Dance to the Music of Time* sequence (1951–75), is based on Lieutenant-Colonel Basil Hambrough, of the Welsh Guards, who was attached to a Cossack unit in the First World War and served in the Pioneer Corps in Africa in the Second, after which he settled with his fourth wife in Kenya. A colourful raconteur and chronically unlucky gambler, he lived between the wars at Bosham, Sussex.

UMSLOPOGAAS, in H. Rider Haggard's *King Solomon's Mines* (1885), *Allan Quatermain* (1887), *Nada the Lily* (1892) and *She and Allan* (1921). Asked if he were not proud to be immortalised in Rider Haggard's books, the original of Umslopogaas replied, 'To me it is nothing. Yet I am glad that Indanda [Rider] has set my name in writings that will not be forgotten, so that when my people are no more a people, one of them at least may be remembered.' But when he learned of the stories' success, he hinted that he should perhaps have received a share of the proceeds rather than the author's present of a hunting knife. He was M'hlopekazi (*d.* 1897), otherwise known as Umslopogaas, the warrior son of Mswazi, King of Swaziland, whom he represented as ambassador in Natal. Later he became aide to Sir Theophilus Shepstone, the British government's Secretary for Native Affairs in Natal. Prior to undertaking his diplomatic role, he served in the Nyati Regiment.

UNA, in Rudyard Kipling's *Puck of Pook's Hill* (1906) and *Rewards and Fairies* (1910), is the author's daughter, Mrs George Bambridge (née Elsie Kipling, *d*, 1976). In 1945 she commissioned Lord Birkenhead to write a biography of her father, was displeased with the result and forbade its publication. Birkenhead's book appeared two years after her death.

UNDERSHAFT, Barbara and Lady Britomart, in George Bernard Shaw's *Major Barbara* (1905). Barbara is an amalgam of Lady Mary Henrietta Murray (1865–1956), daughter of the Ninth Earl of Carlisle, wife of Professor Gilbert Murray (see Cusins, Professor Adolphus) and mother of Basil Murray (see Seal, Basil); and the Wigan-born actress, Eleanor Robson (1879–1979), for whom Shaw wrote the part, although contractual difficulties prevented her from playing it. Eleanor Robson retired from the stage in 1910 upon marrying the American banker August Belmont, a promoter of the New York underground railway. She published her correspondence with Shaw in 1957. Lady Britomart is Lady Murray's mother, the Hon. Rosalind Howard, Countess of Carlisle (1845–1921). The youngest daughter of the Second Baron Stanley of Alderley, she in 1864 married the Ninth Earl of Carlisle, from whom she later became estranged over political differences concerning Ireland – he was a Unionist, she supported Home Rule. She had a dominating personality; women's suffrage and temperance were among her causes. She was an aunt of Bertrand Russell (see Mattheson, Sir Joshua).

UNDERWOOD, Julian, in C. P. Snow's *In Their Wisdom* (1974), is the novelist William Gerhardi (1895–1977), whose imagination was so highly developed that having allowed his hand to stray to a girl's knee in an Oxford cinema, he thrilled to sense the return signals, only to discover when the lights went up that the source of his ecstasy was the arm of an empty seat.

UPJOHN, Mr, in Richard Aldington's *Death of a Hero* (1929). In his introduction to the 1984 edition of this novel Christopher Ridgway names Ezra Pound (see Forbes, Duncan) as Upjohn, the story's artist with an American turn of phrase who, 'destitute of any intrinsic and spontaneous originality', invents a new school of painting every season.

URQUHART, Dollie, in D. H. Lawrence's 'The Princess' (*St Mawr*, 1925), is the Hon. Dorothy Brett, portrayed as a middle-aged woman intent on discovering sex by losing her virginity to a mountain guide. The experiment is not a success. Eighteen months after he wrote this story, Lawrence himself attempted intercourse with Brett and, ironically, found himself to be impotent. See Mullion, Jenny.

URSO, Raphael, in Jack Kerouac's *Book of Dreams* (1961) and *Desolation Angels* (1965), is Gregory Corso. See Gligoric, Yuri.

UTHWART, Emerald, in Walter Pater's 'Emerald Uthwart' (1892; *Miscellaneous Studies*, 1895), has been identified by Sir Maurice Bowra (see Samgrass, Mr) as F. F. ('Sligger') Urquhart (1868–1934), Fellow and Tutor of Balliol College, Oxford, from 1896 to 1934 and Dean from 1916 to 1933. Pater's biographers, however, suggest that the character's surname derives from the Uthwatt family of Great Linford, Buckinghamshire, whose early nineteenth-century forebears include an Edolphe and a Eusebius.

UTTERWORD, Lady Ariadne, in George Bernard Shaw's *Heartbreak House* (1917), was inspired by Virginia Woolf (see Aspasia), according to the Shaw biographer Stanley Weintraub. It was while Shaw was writing this play that he met Woolf and was attracted by her.

V

VALE, Emerson, in Arthur Hailey's *Wheels* (1971). A Connecticut lawyer who became a champion of consumer protection, Ralph Nader (1934–) was Emerson Vale's prototype. His *Unsafe at Any Speed* (1965) led to a government-imposed improvement in American automobile safety standards, and he became a national figure after a Congressional inquiry revealed that General Motors had had him tailed by detectives in its efforts to discredit him. In 1966, a *New Yorker* cartoon showed a car salesman telling a prospective customer, 'I happen to know Ralph Nader's mother drives this model.'

VALE, Ron, in Terence Rattigan's *Variation on a Theme* (1958), is the actor Laurence Harvey (1928–73), whose brief marriage to Margaret Leighton (see Fish, Rose) inspired this play. Harvey later married the widow of Harry Cohn (see Brock, Harry). He was noted for his performance as Joe Lampton in the film version of John Braine's *Room at the Top*, and for his flamboyance and egotism – 'I don't say I'm the greatest', he remarked, 'but why be crippled by false modesty?' He died from cancer, commenting after surgeons had removed part of his diseased colon, 'Now I suppose I'm a semi-colon.'

VALENTINE, Brother, in Thomas Berger's *Reinhart's Women* (1981), was inspired by Eldridge Cleaver. See Storm, Captain Bruno.

VALENTINE, Jimmy, in O. Henry's 'A Retrieved Reformation' (*Roads of Destiny*, 1909). At the turn of the century the author was imprisoned at Columbus, Ohio, and it was there that he encountered Valentine's original – Dick Price, who at the age of eleven had been sent to Mansfield Reformatory, Ohio, for stealing a ten-cent box of crackers. Trained in the reformatory as a mechanic, he was later sentenced to life imprisonment for safe-breaking, having developed a technique of filing his nails to the quick, exposing the nerve-ends to make his fingers hypersensitive. At the request of the Governor of Ohio, he was taken under escort from the gaol to open the safe of the bankrupt Press-Post Publishing Co., which was under investigation for fraud. For this assignment — which he executed in twelve seconds — he was promised a pardon, which afterwards was not forthcoming. He died in gaol of tuberculosis, aged thirty-six.

VALHUBERT, Charles Édouard de, in Nancy Mitford's *The Blessing* (1951), is Gaston Palewski (see Sauveterre, Fabrice de). In 1943 Harold Macmillan noted in his diary that though he had known Palewski a long time he could not bring himself to like him. As a bearer of unwelcome communiqués from de Gaulle in wartime London and as the General's 'guard dog', keeping away unwanted callers, Palewski was not popular. His intimates, however, rejoiced in his zest for life, never more evident than when he was in the presence of pretty women, like the girl who was said to have declined a lift home from a ball in his official limousine — 'Thank you, Gaston, I am too tired.'

VALJEAN, Jean, in Victor Hugo's *Les Misérables* (1862), is part-inspired by Pierre François Lacenaire (1800–36), criminal and poet-philosopher, whose imprisonment for theft in 1829 elicited public sympathy. Five years later he murdered an elderly bachelor and his mother for their money, was arrested in the provinces and — to his relief — was tried in Paris. 'It would have been very disagreeable', he remarked, 'to have been executed by a provincial executioner.' To ensure that the accomplices who had informed upon him also received the death penalty, he assumed the role of prosecutor at his trial.

VANBURGH, the Marquess of, in Evelyn Waugh's *Vile Bodies* (1930), has as prototype Edward Arthur Donald St George Hamilton Chichester, Sixth Marquis of Donegall (1903–75), who worked as a newspaper gossip columnist in London and was a war correspondent in the Second World War.

VANCE, Carlotta, in Edna Ferber and George S. Kaufman's *Dinner at Eight* (1932), is the actress Maxine Elliott (née Jessica Dermot, 1871–1940). The daughter of a Liverpool sea captain who made his home at Rockland, Maine, she opened her own theatre in New York in 1908. She was twice married, twice divorced, and upon making her fortune as a skilled investor she retired from the stage and settled in a villa which she built near Cannes.

VANDERHOF, Martin, in George S. Kaufman and Moss Hart's *You Can't Take it With You* (1936), is in part Kaufman's father, Joseph Kaufman (1856–1940), the son of a Pittsburgh trouser manufacturer. After fighting Ute Indians and mining silver in Colorado, Joseph returned to Pennsylvania and established a succession of businesses, losing interest in each one as it began to prosper and lost its challenge. Finally, as the owner of the New York Silk Dyeing Company, he pioneered the introduction of the forty-hour week.

VAN DER MAL, Gabrielle ('Sister Louise'), in Kathryn C. Hulme's *The Nun's Story* (1956). The author was working for the United Nations Relief and Rehabilitation Administration in France in 1945 when she met her model for Sister Louise – a Belgian nurse, Marie Louise Habets. Hulme called her 'the sleeping beauty', such was her tranquillity and her ability to slumber through the noise of a crowded camp dormitory, and decided that she could never cope with the demanding work among refugees which lay ahead. Then Habets was assigned to Hulme's medical team, and gradually the author came to know a little more about her. 'As I picked up bits and parts of her story, I of course did not know that I was getting only the tag ends of a much bigger story I was one day to write', Hulme records in her autobiography, *Undiscovered Country* (1966). 'The tag ends were too bright with bravery and blood to imagine there could be anything more beyond them.' Habets had seen active service in the Belgian underground movement and later in the Ardennes, working among booby-trapped bodies on the battlefield. Three of her colleagues had been killed. Later, in Antwerp, she had toiled amidst the carnage of a bombed theatre in which 600 had died. In Hulme's team she proved to be an outstanding worker, but one night the author found her crying, declaring herself to be a failure. That was nonsense, Hulme remonstrated: to everyone in the camp Habets was a saint. This prompted even more tears. Hulme must never call her that again, Habets cried, disclosing that for seventeen years she had been a nun, working as a nurse for much of that time in the Belgian Congo, until the life had become too much for her and she had left her convent. When Hulme returned to the United States seven years later, Habets went with her. After the success of the author's *The Wild Place*, Habets asked her what she would say when her editor brought up the subject of her next book. 'Oh, I'll think of something', Hulme replied, with little assurance. To her surprise, Habets said, 'Why don't you suggest my story?' Hulme had long dreamed of this, but had never ventured to discuss it. Why, after all those years of guarding her secret, she asked, had Habets had this change of heart? 'Because', she replied, 'I think it might do some good.' The two remained together, Habets becoming Hulme's business partner. When the novelist died in a Hawaii hospital in 1981, at the age of eighty-one, Habets was at her bedside.

VANE, Betty. See Cooke, Betty.

VANESSA, in Jonathan Swift's *Cadenus and Vanessa* (written 1713, published 1726), is Esther Vanhomrigh (?1690–1723), who met Swift in 1708, fell in love with him, and followed him to Ireland in 1714. After their parting (*c.* 1723) she reputedly died of a broken heart. Vanessa was Swift's pet name for her.

VANIO, in Hilda Doolittle's *Bid Me to Live* (1960), is the author's lover, Cecil Gray. See Sharpe, James.

VARAMBON, Mme de, in Marcel Proust's *A la recherche du temps perdu* (1913–27), is Baronne de Galbois, who was celebrated for her conversational gaffes. George D. Painter's definitive *Marcel Proust* (1959–65) notes that when it rained unexpectedly she remarked that anyone would think the barometer had ceased to influence the weather; and when temperatures plummeted she assured her circle that snow was impossible as the pavements had been salted.

VARNEY, Gabriel, in Bulwer-Lytton's *Lucretia, or The Children of the Night* (1847). It was because he found the thickness of her ankles offensive that he poisoned his sister-in-law, said Thomas Griffiths Wainewright (1794–?1852), the original of Varney. He had, however, insured her for £18,000 and she was only one of the relatives he was suspected of poisoning. But it was for forging powers of attorney that he was deported to Tasmania, where he died, allegations of his poisoning activities unproven. A painter who exhibited at the Royal Academy in the 1820s, he was also an art critic and a *London Magazine* essayist, and the grandson and heir of the proprietor of the *Monthly Review*. Charles Lamb was among his friends, Oscar Wilde devoted an essay to him in 1889 and Charles Dickens used him as a model (see Rigaud, Monsieur; Slinkton, Julius). In 1961 he became the subject of Hal Porter's *The Tilted Cross*.

VASSILIOU, Rose, in Margaret Drabble's *The Needle's Eye* (1972), comes from a wealthy background and chooses to live with her three children in a London slum. Small wonder, then, that Mark Amory, presenting an unsubstantiated list of originals in the *Tatler* (October 1984), should equate Vassiliou with the writer Nell Dunn (1936–) . . . who comes from a wealthy background and in the 1960s chose to live with her three children in a London slum. Vassiliou, however, marries a penniless Greek, whereas Nell Dunn was for thirteen years the wife of an Old Etonian. Her affinity with her slum neighbours inspired her two best-known novels, *Up the Junction* (1963) and *Poor Cow* (1967), and was evident again in *Steaming* (1981), with which she made a successful début as a playwright.

VAUGHAN, Gilbert Hereford, in Ada Leverson's *The Limit* (1911), is W. Somerset Maugham (see Bertrand, Archie). Vaughan is besotted with a publican's daughter; Leverson is tilting at her friend Maugham's partiality for using working-class girls in such plays as *Liza of Lambeth*.

VAUTRIN (Jacques Collin), in Honoré de Balzac's *La Comédie humaine*, notably *Le Père Goriot* (1834–5), *La Dernière Incarnation de Vautrin* (1847) and *Le Député d'Arcis* (1847). Balzac is believed to have dined from time to time with François-Eugène Vidocq (1775–1857), thereby gleaning much information on criminal life. He could hardly have consulted a more authoritative source than this poacher-turned-gamekeeper who reputedly became his model for Vautrin. The son of a baker, Vidocq was a thief who three times escaped from imprisonment, became an informer and was in 1812 appointed head of the newly-created Brigade de la Sûreté. In that role he is believed to have been the world's first police detective. His ghost-written, semi-fictitious memoirs were published in 1828–9. After his retirement he lost his fortune attempting to run a factory employing ex-convicts, established what is believed to have been the world's first private detective agency, and died in poverty.

VAWDREY, Clare, in the Henry James short story that lends its title to *The Private Life* (1893), was inspired by Robert Browning (1812–89), who seemed to James to have two personalities: in society he was a bluff, ordinary fellow, the last person anyone would take to be a poet. In 'The Private Life' it is difficult to believe that Vawdrey can be the author of the plays that bear his name. It transpires that he has a double. While Vawdrey socialises, his counterpart remains in his room, writing the dramas.

VENABLES, the Revd Theodore, in Dorothy L. Sayers's *The Nine Tailors* (1934), is the author's father, the Revd Henry Sayers (*d.* 1928). Mildly eccentric, a classical scholar and a musician, he was headmaster of Oxford's Christ Church Cathedral Choir School prior to 1897, when he became rector of Bluntisham, Huntingdonshire, moving to Cambridgeshire twenty years later to become rector of Christchurch, near Wisbech.

VENUS, in Ford Madox Ford's *The Young Lovell* (1913), is Brigit Patmore (see Browning, Clariss), with whom the author fell in love when he was forty.

VERDEN, Helena, in D. H. Lawrence's *The Trespasser* (1912). In 1909 Helen Corke (1882–1978), a schoolteacher colleague of the author in Croydon, told Lawrence of how she had taken a week's holiday on the Isle of Wight with a married man, Herbert Baldwin MacCartney, of the Carl Rosa Opera Company, fourteen years her senior and the father of four children. After five days he had returned home and hanged himself. MacCartney is Siegmund MacNair in *The Trespasser*; Corke, to whom Lawrence proposed unsuccessfully, is Helena Verden. She subsequently wrote *Lawrence and the Apocalypse* (1933); a novel, *Neutral Ground* – see Hamilton, Derrick; and *In Our Infancy* (1975), an account of her friendship with Lawrence.

VERDURIN, M and Mme, in Marcel Proust's *A la recherche du temps perdu* (1913–27). M Verdurin is Albert Arman de Caillavet. Born Albert Arman, he added de Caillavet to his name after his marriage in 1868 – Caillavet was the name of a *château* on his Capian estate. His expertise as a yachtsman led to his appointment as yachting correspondent of *Le Figaro*. Mme Verdurin is a composite of Mme Albert Arman de Caillavet (née Léontine Lippman, ?1847–1910), mother of Gaston Arman de Caillavet (see Saint-

Loup, Robert de) and mistress of Anatole France (see Bergotte); Mme Georges Aubernon (née Lydie de Nerville, *d.* 1899), who regulated conversation at her well-disciplined Paris salon by ringing a handbell; Misia Godebska (see Yourbeletieff, Princess); and Madeleine Lemaire (née Jeanne-Magdeleine Coll, 1845–1928), a hostess noted for her musical evenings and a popular painter of flowers – only God, remarked Dumas *fils*, had created more roses.

VERKHOVENSKY, Pyotr and Stepan Trofimovich, in Fyodor Dostoevsky's *The Devils* (1871–2), are respectively the Russian revolutionary S. G. Nechayev (1847–82) and the Russian historian T. N. Granovsky (1813–55), who was much influenced by Western thinking.

VERLAINE, Maria, in Gore Vidal's *The City and the Pillar* (1948), is Anaïs Nin (see Donegal, Marietta) who in her diary recorded this, the second of Vidal's several portraits of her, as a 'deathblow' to their relationship.

VERNON, John, Lily and Richard, in Christopher Isherwood's *The Memorial* (1932), are respectively the author's grandfather, John Bradshaw-Isherwood, of Marple Hall, Cheshire; his mother, Kathleen Bradshaw-Isherwood (née Machell Smith), a wine merchant's daughter who died in 1960, aged ninety-one; and his father, Colonel Francis Bradshaw-Isherwood, who in 1892, at twenty-three, was commissioned into the York and Lancaster Regiment, was married in 1903, and was killed in 1915 in the second battle of Ypres.

VERNON, Madame de, in Madame de Staël's *Delphine* (1802), is the French diplomat Charles-Maurice de Talleyrand-Périgord (1754–1838). The author was also partial to writing favourable self-portraits; hence Talleyrand's *mot*, 'I understand that we both appear in your new book disguised as women.'

VEROG, Monsieur, in Ezra Pound's *Hugh Selwyn Mauberley* (1920), is Victor Gustave Plarr (1863–1929), author of *Ernest Dowson* (1914), a biography from which Pound's poem derives inspiration.

VIARGUE, M de, in Émile Zola's *Madeleine Férat* (1868), is the author's Italian-born father, Francesco Zola (1795–?1846), a Marseilles civil engineer who endeavoured to promote interest in his plan for enlarging and modernising Marseilles harbour. At the time of his death he was supervising the creation of a reservoir for Aix-en-Provence.

VICKERS, Ann, in Sinclair Lewis's *Ann Vickers* (1933), has as prototype Dorothy Thompson. See Cortwright, Edith.

VICTOR, Prince, in W. M. Thackeray's *The Memoirs of Barry Lyndon* (1844), is Frederick II, King of Württemberg (1754–1816), who reigned from 1797 until his death. His first wife died in suspicious circumstances: see Olivia, Princess.

VICTOR, Siegfried, in Wyndham Lewis's *The Apes of God* (1930), is the poet and autobiographer Siegfried Sassoon (1886–1967). After being awarded the Military Cross, Sassoon publicly rebelled against the horrors of the First World War and was treated for shell-shock, later writing two classic first-hand accounts of trench warfare, *Memoirs of a Fox-Hunting Man* (1928) and *Memoirs of an Infantry Officer* (1930).

VIGIL, Dr Arturo Diaz, in Malcolm Lowry's *Under the Volcano* (1947), is Juan Fernando Márquez (also known as Fernando Atonalzin). See Cerillo, Juan.

VILLEPARISIS, the Marquise de, in Marcel Proust's *A la recherche du temps perdu* (1913–27), is largely inspired by the Comtesse de Beaulaincourt (née Sophie de Castellane, 1818–1904), great-aunt of Comte Boni de Castellane (see Saint-Loup, Robert de). She was the daughter of the Maréchal de Castellane and Cordelia Greffulhe, mistress of Chateaubriand and great-aunt of Comte Henri Greffulhe (see Guermantes, Basin, Duc de). Marrying the Marquise de Contades in 1836, she was also the mistress of the Comte de Fleury (see Norpois, Marquis de) and bore a son by the Comte de Coislin. In 1859 she married the Comte de Beaulaincourt. Her intimates included the Empress Eugénie and Prosper Mérimée, and as age and the pace of her youth destroyed her looks she gave up making love for making artificial flowers. Also perceived in the Marquise de Villeparisis are the Marquise de Chaponay (née de Courval), whose divorce, unusual in her day, diminished her position in society, and Madeleine Lemaire (see Verdurin, Mme).

VILLIERS, Bud, in D. H. Lawrence's *The Plumed Serpent* (1926), is Willard 'Spud' Johnson, poet and editor of a literary magazine, the *Laughing Horse*. When Lawrence met him at Taos, Johnson was secretary to the poet Witter Bynner (see Rhys, Owen).

VINAIGRETTE, in Robert de Montesquiou's 'Vinaigrette' (*Les Quarante Bergères*, 1925), is Winnaretta Eugénie Singer (1865–1943), painter, musician, hostess and an heiress of the Singer sewing-machine fortune, who in 1893 married Prince Edmond de Polignac (see Bergotte). A lesbian, she numbered Violet Trefusis (see Romanovitch, Princess 'Sasha') among her conquests and was herself unsuccessfully pursued by Dame Ethel Smyth (see Staines, Edith). Though her husband — they married when she was twenty-eight, he fifty-nine — jumped over a chair to show he was still young enough for matrimony, this demonstration was hardly necessary: he too was homosexual.

VINTEUIL, in Marcel Proust's *A la recherche du temps perdu* (1913–27), is a composite of the composers Claude Debussy (1862–1918), César-Auguste Franck (1822–90) and Camille Saint-Saëns (1835–1921).

VIOLET, in *Violet: the Story of a Mother* (1910), by Kurt Aram (Hans Fischer), is Elsa Douglas (née FitzGibbon, *d.* 1916), the wife of Norman Douglas (see Argyle, James), who divorced her for adultery. She worked for Fischer as a translator, and died in Germany from burns believed to have been caused by smoking in bed.

VIVEASH, Myra, in Aldous Huxley's *Antic Hay* (1923), is Nancy Cunard. See Storm, Iris; see also Tantamount, Lucy.

VOELKER, Fran, in Sinclair Lewis's *Dodsworth* (1929), is the author's first wife, Grace Livingstone Hegger, who worked for *Vogue* and whom he married in 1914.

VOLKBEIN, Baron Felix, in Djuna Barnes's *Nightwood* (1936), is Guido Bruno (1884–1942), a publisher of poetry in New York's Greenwich Village. In 1915 he issued Barnes's first work, *The Book of Repulsive Women*. He was also the first publisher of Hart Crane, introduced the work of Aubrey Beardsley to the United States and was for a time secretary to Frank Harris (see Parker, Ralph). Village residents regarded him as an undesirable neighbour seeking to cheapen the place by making it a tourist attraction. He was also reputed to sleep with the women whose verse he published — their only way, perhaps, of becoming consummate poets.

VON ASCHENBACH, Gustav, in Thomas Mann's 'Death in Venice' (1911; *Stories of a Lifetime*, 1961), owes his physical attributes to the Austrian composer and conductor Gustav Mahler (1860–1911), although his personality is primarily the author's.

VON GALEN, Adelaide, in Isak Dinesen's 'Copenhagen Season' (*Last Tales*, 1957), is Countess Agnes Frijs, who died of typhoid in Italy in 1871. Two years earlier her cousin, Wilhelm Dinesen (see Angel, Ib), had fallen in love with her.

VON HEBENITZ, Baroness and Johanna, in D. H. Lawrence's *Mr Noon* (1984; first portion published as the story 'Mr Noon' in *A Modern Lover*, 1934), are the author's mother-in-law, Baroness Anna von Richthofen (1851–1930), and Frieda Lawrence (see Somers, Harriet).

VON KEITH, the Marquis, in Frank Wedekind's *Der Marquis von Keith* (1901), is Willy Grétor (*b.* 1868), painter and art forger, for whom the author worked in his youth.

VON RÜDIGER, Clotilde, in George Meredith's *The Tragic Comedians* (1880), is Helene von Dönniges, the daughter of a Bavarian diplomat who locked her in her room when, at twenty, she fell in love with Ferdinand Lassalle (see Alvan). Under pressure, she agreed to marry Count Racowitza of Walachia, who was promptly challenged by Lassalle to a duel in which the latter was killed.

VON STREHLEN, Baron Herbert, in *Violet: the Story of a Mother* (1910), by Kurt Aram (Hans Fischer), is Norman Douglas (see Argyle, James), whose former wife (see Violet) worked for Fischer as a translator.

VORONSKAYA, Nina, in Alexander Pushkin's *Eugene Onegin* (1833–40), has a suggested original in Countess Agrafena Zakrevsky (1799–1879), wife of the Russian Minister of the Interior. She had an affair with Pushkin when she was twenty-nine.

VOSS, Johann Ulrich, in Patrick White's *Voss* (1957), has as prototype the German explorer Friedrich Wilhelm Ludwig Leichardt (1813–48), who disappeared – together with his expedition – while attempting to cross Australia from east to west.

VOTE, Robin, in Djuna Barnes's *Nightwood* (1936), is Thelma Wood (*d.* 1970), an American silverpoint artist and sculptress with whom the author lived for ten years in Paris. She was a lesbian and an alcoholic.

W

WABSTER CHARLIE, in Robert Burns's 'Epistle to James Tennant', is the Scottish scientist Charles Tennant (1768–1838), son of John Tennant (1726–1810), of Glenconner, Ochiltree, Strathclyde, who advised Burns on farming and was factor to the estate of the Countess of Glencairn. Charles Tennant founded a chemical works at St Rollex, Glasgow, which was inherited by his grandson, Sir Charles Tennant, father of Margot Tennant (see Dodo).

WAGG, Mr, in W. M. Thackeray's *Vanity Fair* (1847–8) and *The History of Pendennis* (1848–50). Whatever happened to practical jokers? The question is prompted by the escapades of Theodore Edward Hook (1788–1841), Thackeray's model for Wagg. He halted a production of *Hamlet* by walking on stage in Elizabethan attire during the grave-diggers' scene and handing the Prince a letter. On another occasion he arranged for the Lord Mayor of London, troops of cavalry, the Chancellor of the Exchequer and other notabilities to coincide at the door of a Berners Street address. The son of a writer of popular songs, he edited the Tory journal *John Bull* and was briefly Accountant General in Mauritius, until his recall upon the discovery of a deficiency of £12,000 . . . a matter which he described as a disorder in his chest.

WAGNER, Jarry, in Jack Kerouac's *Desolation Angels* (1965), is Gary Snyder. See Ryder, Japhy.

WAKEM, Philip, in George Eliot's *The Mill on the Floss* (1860), is supposedly part-inspired by the author's Geneva landlord, François D'Albert Durade (1804–86). A hunchback, like Wakem, he painted George Eliot's portrait in 1849 and translated a number of her works into French.

WALDERSHARE, in Benjamin Disraeli's *Endymion* (1880), is the Hon. George Smythe, Seventh Viscount Strangford. See Coningsby, Harry.

WALKER, Clara and Ida, in Sir Arthur Conan Doyle's *Beyond the City* (1892), are the author's sisters, Connie and Lottie, who in their youth were governesses in Portugal. Wooed by Jerome K. Jerome, the author of *Three Men in a Boat*, Connie instead married the writer E. W. Hornung, the creator of 'Raffles'. Lottie went to India as a governess and married Captain Leslie Oldham, of the Royal Engineers, who was killed in the First World War.

WALKER, John, Roger, Susan and Titty, in Arthur Ransome's *Swallows and Amazons* saga (1930–47). Ransome became defensively secretive about the origin of one of the most celebrated families in children's fiction and withheld many of the events leading to the creation of the Swallows — the Walker children — from his *Autobiography*, published posthumously in 1976. In 1903 Ransome went to Coniston, in the English Lake District, hoping the scenery would inspire him to write poetry. His muse eluded him, but instead he struck up a lifelong, close friendship with the Lakeland artist and antiquarian W. G. Collingwood and his family. Collingwood, who had been John Ruskin's secretary, had three daughters and a son who became intimates of Ransome. In 1915 Dora Collingwood married Dr Ernest Altounyan (1888–1962), whose family ran a hospital in Aleppo, Syria. Of Irish-Armenian extraction, he had been a Rugby schoolfellow of her brother. As a poet he was published by Virginia Woolf, and his friends included T. E. Lawrence and E. M. Forster. He brought his children to Coniston Water for a sailing holiday in 1928 and, as Ransome's private papers (now kept at Leeds University) amply reveal, it was upon the young Altounyans that Ransome based the Swallows. In *The Life of Arthur Ransome* (1984), Hugh Brogan sees John Walker primarily as a self-portrait of the author as he wished to be, bearing small resemblance to the eldest of the Altounyan children, a girl named Taqui, who relates her childhood memories of Ransome in her book *In Aleppo Once* (1969). The tomboy of the family, Taqui is to be discerned not in John but in Nancy Blackett (q.v.), according to Christina Hardyment's *Arthur Ransome and Captain Flint's Trunk* (1984). Hardyment quotes a letter written to Ransome by Taqui at the age of fifteen, after she had been teaching some novices to sail and had 'enjoyed giving orders and being thoroughly Captain Nancyish'. She married Robert Stephens who in 1983 retired as Foreign Editor and Diplomatic Correspondent of the *Observer* after thirty-five years with the newspaper. Roger Walker is Dr Roger Altounyan, who still sails 'Mavis' (the original of 'Amazon') on Coniston Water, and now lives in Cheshire. He is noted for his Intal asthma treatment and in 1983 was awarded an honorary medical degree by Southampton University in recognition of his invention of Spincap, a treatment for asthma which projects powder into the lungs by means of a propeller in an inhalation tube. Susan Walker is part-inspired by Susie Altounyan, who lives in Paris and narrowly escaped execution as a suspected British spy during the Nazi occupation of France in the Second World War. Although recognised in her Susan role by her brother, she believes Susan Walker to be 'the image of Aunt Genia', Ransome's second wife, Evgenia (née Shelepina, *d.* 1975; see also Pye, Wilfred). Titty Walker is Mavis Altounyan, whose childhood nickname ('Titty') derived from the nursery tale of Titty Mouse and Tatty Mouse. She studied at the Chelsea School of Art, still paints, and this book's picture of Roger is by her photographer son, Asadour. Like her sister, Brigit (baby Bridget of *Swallows and Amazons*), she lives within a 'ship ahoy' of Coniston Water.

WALKER, Stella, in F. Scott Fitzgerald's 'Crazy Sunday' (1932; *Taps at Reveille*, 1935), is the film actress Norma Shearer (1900–83), who married Irving Thalberg (see Stahr, Monroe).

WALTER, Sir James and Colonel Valentine, in Sir Arthur Conan Doyle's 'The Adventure of the Bruce-Partington Plans' (1908; *His Last Bow*, 1917). In 1907 the Irish crown jewels were stolen, never to be recovered. Doyle's deductive advice was sought by his prototype for Sir James Walter: his mother's second cousin, Sir Arthur Vicars, who as Ulster King of Arms was with his nephew, Peirce Mahony (see West, Cadogan), responsible for the jewels' security. Vicars was murdered in 1921. Also involved in the scandal was Doyle's prototype for Colonel Valentine Walter: Francis Shackleton (*d.* 1925), Dublin Herald, gambler and brother of the explorer Ernest Shackleton. He was believed to have had a homosexual relationship with Vicars and was also associated with King Edward VII's brother-in-law, the Duke of Argyll. This friendship with the duke is thought to have brought the scandal disquietingly close to the throne and to have led to the police investigation being abandoned. The story of the Irish crown jewels affair is told by Charles Higham in *The Adventures of Conan Doyle* (1976).

WALTON, Mrs, in Beryl Bainbridge's *Sweet William* (1975), is the author's mother, Winifred Bainbridge (see Jack, Uncle). 'I have never felt the necessity for invention, life itself being stranger than fiction', the author has remarked.

WANDROUS, Gloria, in John O'Hara's *Butterfield 8* (1935), has as prototype Starr Faithfull (1911–31), a beautiful *habituée* of New York speakeasies who died in mysterious circumstances after attending a shipboard party — her body was found on the shore at Long Beach, Long Island. Alcoholic, promiscuous and suicidal, she had allegedly been sexually molested as a child, her subsequent mental problems stemming from this experience.

WANGEL, Hilde, in Henrik Ibsen's *The Master Builder* (1892), is supposedly part-inspired by Emilie Bardach (see Gabler, Hedda). She has also been erroneously identified as Ibsen's friend, Hildur Andersen (*d.* 1956), to whom he gave the play's manuscript — an odd gesture had she been the model for such a character. Ibsen began *The Master Builder* long before he became interested in Andersen.

WANNOP, Valentine, Gilbert and Mrs, in Ford Madox Ford's *Parade's End* tetralogy (1924–8). The Australian painter Stella Bowen (*d.* 1947) arrived in England in 1914, in order to study at the Westminster School of Art. Four years later she met Ford and became his mistress, living with him for nine years and bearing him a daughter. The primary model for Valentine, she parted from Ford without rancour and twelve years later travelled to Honfleur for a final farewell as he lay on his death-bed. She tells her story in *Drawn from Life* (1940). Also to be seen in Valentine are traits of Dame Margaret Cole (1893–1980), wife of the socialist philosopher G. D. H. Cole, with whom she wrote detective novels, and sister of Raymond Postgate, founder of *The Good Food Guide*. A teacher of Latin at St Paul's Girls' School, London, she became president of the Fabian Society. Gilbert Wannop is Bowen's brother, Tom; Mrs Wannop is Mrs Alfred Hunt, mother of Violet (see Nesbitt, Norah).

WANTAGE, Arthur, in Percival Pollard's *The Imitator* (1901), is the American actor Richard Mansfield (1857–1907), who was first to produce Shaw in the United States and was also responsible for the American *première* of *Peer Gynt*. Pollard adapted a number of plays for him, but received no credit.

WAPSHOT, Alexander, in Desmond Briggs's *The Partners* (1982). 'In my opinion, there are some easily recognisable characters — including one grey-haired self-made pundit called Alexander Wapshot with "a craggy profile" and an inexhaustible knowledge of publishing lore that dates back to Arnold Bennett's days', wrote Eric Hiscock (1900–), reviewing this novel in the *Bookseller* (17 October 1981). The face fits, and so does the background: to whom could Hiscock be referring but himself? The son of a butler at University College, Oxford, he became the influential columnist of *Smith's Trade News* and later of the *Bookseller*, claiming to be able to tell if a work was commercial within ten pages (compared with Arnold Bennett's six). Howard Spring dedicated his first novel, *Shabby Tiger* (1934), to Hiscock, who had persuaded him to write it.

WARING, in Robert Browning's 'Waring' (*Dramatic Romances*, 1842), is the barrister and poet Alfred Domett (1811–87), who left England to settle in New Zealand, where in 1862 he became Prime Minister.

WARMINSTER, the Earl of. See Erridge, Viscount.

WARNER, George Elbert, in John Dos Passos's *Chosen Country* (1951), is Ernest Hemingway (see Ahearn) as youth and young man.

WARREN, Vivie, in George Bernard Shaw's *Mrs Warren's Profession* (1898), is part-inspired by Beatrice Webb (see Bailey, Altiora), who had suggested Shaw should portray a modern young woman of the ruling class.

WARRINGTON, George, in W. M. Thackeray's *The History of Pendennis* (1848–50), is believed to owe his origin to George Stovin Venables (1810–88), barrister and writer, who as a Charterhouse contemporary of the author broke Thackeray's nose in a fight. A regular contributor to the *Saturday Review* (he wrote the first issue's leading article and, later, the Thackeray obituary), he was noted for his charm and his powers of memory. Tennyson was indebted to him for a line in 'The Princess'. Also to be seen in Warrington (according to Thackeray's daughter, Lady Ritchie) is the author's contemporary at Trinity College, Cambridge, the poet and translator Edward Fitzgerald (1809–83).

WARWICK, Diana. See Merion, Diana.

WATERHOUSE, Stephen Fenwick, in Ford Madox Ford's *Parade's End* tetralogy (1924–8), is the British Liberal statesman Charles Masterman (1873–1927), who was in charge of the National Insurance Commission prior to the First World War, in which he directed British propaganda, with Ford among his writers.

WATERLOW, Rosemary, in George Orwell's *Keep the Aspidistra Flying* (1936), is the author's first wife, Eileen O'Shaughnessy (1905–45). The daughter of a Collector of Customs, she took an English degree at Oxford and became a teacher, a journalist and a secretary. She also ran a typing agency – instead of just reproducing one client's thesis, she rewrote it. When she met Orwell in 1935 she was reading for a psychology M.A. at University College, London. They married the following year. She died unexpectedly, under anaesthetic during a minor operation.

WATSON, James, in Jack Kerouac's *Book of Dreams* (1961), is John Clellon Holmes. See Saybrook, Tom.

WATSON, Dr John, in Sir Arthur Conan Doyle's Sherlock Holmes stories (1887–1927). You need to be something of a Holmes to feel the collar of the real Watson, for there is no shortage of candidates. He has been variously identified – primarily, in my view, with a Dr James Watson who was in practice in Portsmouth in Doyle's day and was a fellow-member of the local literary society. It is perhaps significant that Watson was referred to by Doyle as James as well as John – an inconsequential slip of the pen, or an unconscious revelation of the man he really had in mind? Dr Patrick Heron Watson (1832–1907) is another suggested model, on the strength of his surname and the fact that he was a surgeon at Edinburgh Royal Infirmary in Doyle's time. A veteran of the Crimean War, he was president of the Royal College of Surgeons in 1878 and in 1903, when he was also knighted. Ah, yes, but what about Watson's Afghan background? That is supplied by Dr John A. Watson, of Upper Norwood, London, a writer on India who served in the first Afghan War. The author's daughter has said that Watson had no real-life original; but his son has supported the suggestion that Watson may have acquired some of his characteristics from Doyle's secretary, Major Alfred Wood. In Sidney Paget's illustrations, the model for Watson was the artist's architect friend, Alfred Morris Butler.

WAYNFLETE, Lady Cicely, in George Bernard Shaw's *Captain Brassbound's Conversion* (1900), is an amalgam of the author's sister-in-law, Mary Cholmondeley (née Mary Stewart Payne-Townsend, ?1859–1929), whose request for a few notes for her local Women's Institute prompted Shaw to write *The Intelligent Woman's Guide to Socialism and Capitalism*; the explorer Mary Henrietta Kingsley (1862–1900), whose West African expeditions were ended by her death from typhoid fever while nursing wounded soldiers in the Boer War; and Ellen Terry (see Morrell, Candida), for whom the part was written.

WEBLEY, Everard, in Aldous Huxley's *Point Counter Point* (1928). Webley and his British Freemen and Sir Oswald Mosley (1896–1980) and his British Union of Fascists resemble each other so closely that it is small wonder that Mosley has been taken to be the model for Webley. Like Webley, Mosley was an MP until, disillusioned, he resigned from the Labour government and formed his own party. And just as Mosley was an admirer of Mussolini, founding his movement after meeting the Italian dictator, so is Webley referred to by another character as a 'tinpot Mussolini'. QED? No. Standing in the way of this identification is the inconvenient fact that Mosley did not leave parliament until 1931, several years after the publication of *Point Counter Point*. Similarly, it was not until the early 1930s that Mosley founded the British Union of Fascists whose members, much given to strutting about in uniform, were known as Blackshirts, their rallies provoking riots. Two other British Fascist movements, however, were established in 1928 and it was perhaps one of these which inspired Huxley's British Freemen. The Webley/Mosley likeness cannot have been other than a coincidence ... unless Sir Oswald Mosley was impersonating Everard Webley. For a bona fide Mosley identification, see Spode, Roderick.

WEBSTER, Robert Lang, in Margaret Truman's *Murder in the White House* (1980), is supposedly the author's father, Harry S. Truman (1884–1972), President of the United States from 1945 to 1953.

WEIR, Adam. See Hermiston, Lord.

WELCH, Professor, in Kingsley Amis's *Lucky Jim* (1954). Amis himself disclosed, in a radio interview in 1979, that Professor Welch owes his musical aspect in part to Leonard Sidney Bardwell, the folk-dancing father of the author's first wife, Hilary, who later married Lord Kilmarnock. Welch has also been popularly identified with Bonamy Dobrée (1891–1974), Professor of English Literature at Leeds University from 1936 to 1955.

WELDON, Vergil, in Thomas Wolfe's *Look Homeward, Angel*, (1929), is Horace Williams, who as Professor of Philosophy at North Carolina University was a potent influence on the author.

WELLAND, Mrs, in Edith Wharton's *The Age of Innocence* (1920), is the author's mother, Mrs George Frederic Jones (née Lucretia Rhinelander, 1824–1901).

WELLER, Samuel, Mary and Tony, in Charles Dickens's *The Posthumous Papers of the Pickwick Club* (1836–7). The author's illustrator, Marcus Stone, said that Dickens told him that Sam Weller was based on a Chatham market fruiterer; but the character also owes something, it is thought, to the comedian Samuel Vale's ad libbing interpretation of Simon Splatterdash in Samuel Beazley's *The Boarding House*. Mary Weller is supposedly modelled upon her namesake, who was Dickens's childhood nurse (see Peggotty, Clara). Tony Weller is believed to be one Chumley, driver of the Commodore stage coach which conveyed Dickens as a boy from Chatham to the City of London. As a girl, the novelist Eliza Lynn Linton was also among his passengers. She recalled 'Old Chumley' as a 'good-natured, red-faced fellow' who 'came regularly to the door whenever we stopped to change horses or to water them, to ask the little misses if they wanted anything and how they found themselves.'

WELSTED, in Alexander Pope's *The Dunciad* (1728), is Richard Bentley (1662–1742), a critic and scholar remembered for his observation that claret 'would be port if it could'. He took up smoking when he was seventy.

WENDOVER. Squire, in Mrs Humphry Ward's *Robert Elsmere* (1888), is an amalgam of Mark Pattison (see Casaubon, the Revd Edward) and Edward Hartopp Cradock, who was principal of Brasenose College, Oxford, from 1853 until his death in 1886.

WENDY. See Darling.

WENHAM, Mr, in W. M. Thackeray's *Vanity Fair* (1847–8), is John Wilson Croker. See Rigby, Mr.

WERLE, Gregers, in Henrik Ibsen's *The Wild Duck* (1884), is in part the radical Norwegian dramatist, poet and novelist Alexander Kielland (1849–1906).

WERTH, in Philippe Sollers's *Femmes* (1983), is the influential French critic Roland Barthes (1915–80). A key figure in the Structuralist movement, he died after a car accident. In this Parisian *roman-à-clef* – described by John Weightman in the *Observer* as a *Valley of the Dolls* for intellectuals – Barthes is portrayed losing the will to live following the death of his mother.

WEST, Cadogan, in Sir Arthur Conan Doyle's 'The Adventure of the Bruce-Partington Plans' (1908; *His Last Bow*, 1917), has as prototype Peirce Mahony who died in 1914, ostensibly in a wild-fowling shooting accident. Rumour had it that his death was arranged to secure his silence on scandal arising from the theft of the Irish crown jewels in 1907. See Walter, Sir James.

WEST, John, in Frank Hardy's *Power without Glory* (1950). As this novel neared completion, the author became aware that 'West' was perhaps too similar to 'Wren', the name of his original. Faced, however, with hundreds of pages in which the name appeared umpteen times, he baulked at the task of making all those alterations. Imprudently, he left the name unchanged . . . and it was the making of him. When the novel was published he was arrested and charged with criminal libel, his trial and acquittal making the book a *cause célèbre*. For John West was the Australian rags-to-riches financier John Wren (1871–1953), a boxing and horseracing promoter and Brisbane newspaper owner, and also a philanthropist not unconnected with political corruption. Through his wife (who appears in the novel as Nellie West) he sued Hardy, who admitted West to be a 'composite-fictional character based on certain characteristics of the living person, John Wren.'

WESTERLEIGH, Lord, in Hugh Kingsmill's *The Return of William Shakespeare* (1929). What would happen if a scientist managed to restore Shakespeare to life? The bard would spend all his time in hiding, Kingsmill supposes, to escape Lord Beaverbrook (see Ottercove, Lord), this novel's Lord Westerleigh, and a rival newspaper magnate, Viscount Rothermere (see Youngbrother, Lord).

WESTERN, Sophia and Squire, in Henry Fielding's *The History of Tom Jones* (1749). In his youth, Fielding is believed to have wished to elope with a Lyme Regis merchant's daughter, Sarah Andrew, unsuccessfully attempting to carry her off by force while she was on her way to church. Suggestions that Sarah Andrew is Sophia Western have been discredited, however, and it is accepted that the model for Sophia is Charlotte Cradock (see Amelia). Squire Western has two suggested prototypes: Carew Hervey Mildmay and Sir Paulet St John, both Tory landowners of Fielding's acquaintance.

WESTLAKE, David and Rilda, in Carl Van Vechten's *Parties* (1930), are F. Scott Fitzgerald and his wife, Zelda. See Halliday, Manley, and Diver, Nicole.

WESTON, in C. S. Lewis's *Out of the Silent Planet* (1938) and *Perelandra* (1943). Lewis was highly critical of the theology of the science-fiction writer W. Olaf Stapledon (1886–1950), whom he presents as Weston, a scientist possessed by the devil. In *Perelandra* Lewis enters the story himself in the guise of Ransom, who gets the better of Weston in debate. Stapledon, notes his biographer Leslie A. Fiedler, did not respond to this challenge from Lewis, who was not above borrowing Stapledon's ideas when they suited him: the talking Head of Lewis's *That Hideous Strength* owes something to Stapledon's inventive *Last and First Men*.

WESTON, Edward, in Anne Brontë's *Agnes Grey* (1847). Very much a ladies' man, the Revd William Weightman (1814–42) was at the age of twenty-five appointed curate to the author's father at Haworth. Anne Brontë portrayed him as Weston, and her sister Charlotte was attracted by him but resented her role as his confidante in the matter of his flirtations — he even travelled to Bradford to mail separate Valentines to each of the Brontë sisters and to a friend who was staying with them. He died of cholera at Haworth, tended by Branwell Brontë, who idolised him.

WESTON, Hugh, in Christopher Isherwood's *Lions and Shadows* (1938), is the author's prep schoolfellow, lifelong friend and collaborator, the poet Wystan Hugh Auden (1907–73), with whom he travelled to China in 1938. In 1939 they emigrated together to the United States (see Parsnip).

W. H., Mr, the 'onlie begetter' of the dedication of William Shakespeare's *Sonnets* (1609). The enigma of Mr W.H. has done valuable public service in keeping generations of academics off the streets in their quest to identify the man behind the initials. The four principal contenders are: William Hatcliffe (see Friend, the); Sir William Hervey (later Lord Hervey of Kidbrooke), third husband of the mother of the Third Earl of Southampton; William Herbert (1580–1630), who in 1601 succeeded his father as Earl of Pembroke, was Chancellor of Oxford University, Lord Chamberlain of the Household, and in 1604 married the eldest daughter of the Seventh Earl of Shrewsbury; and Shakespeare's patron, Henry Wriothesley, Third Earl of Southampton (1573–1624), the theory being that W.H. is (H)enry (W)riothesley, reversed by the publisher to avoid identification. There is also the suggestion that W.H. is simply a misprint for W.S., a dangerous notion putting the whole W.H. industry at risk.

WHARTON, in Henry Brooks Adams's *Esther* (1884) – written under the pseudonym Frances Snow Compton – is the sculptor Augustus Saint-Gaudens (1848–1907). When Adams's wife died, he commissioned Saint-Gaudens to execute the statue 'The Peace of God' for her grave in Rock Creek Cemetery, Washington, DC. See also Dudley, Esther.

WHEATLEY, in Evelyn Waugh's 'Charles Ryder's Schooldays' (written 1945, published 1982), is the historian and biographer Sir Roger Fulford (1902–83), a contemporary of the author at Lancing College, Sussex.

WHIRLER, Jack, in Samuel Johnson's periodical the *Idler* (1758–60), is the bustling bookseller, publisher and newspaper proprietor John Newbery (1713–67), of St Paul's Churchyard, London, who also appears in Oliver Goldsmith's *The Vicar of Wakefield* (1766) as 'the philanthropic bookseller'. The Newbery Award, offered annually for the most distinguished children's book published in the United States, is named after him in recognition of his particular interest in improving the quality of children's literature. Such was the diligence with which he worked for the *Reading Mercury* that he was left a half interest in the business by the proprietor, whose widow he married, thereupon also inheriting his employer's three children.

WHITBREAD, Hugh, in Virginia Woolf's *Mrs Dalloway* (1925), is part-inspired by Philip Morrell. See Wimbush, Henry; see also Dalloway, Richard.

WHITBY, Martin, in E. M. Forster's 'Arctic Summer' (written *c.* 1912; *Arctic Summer and other fiction*, 1980), is in part the painter and writer on art Roger Fry (1866–1934), a lover of Vanessa Bell (see Ambrose, Helen) and Slade Professor of Fine Art at Cambridge in the last year of his life.

WHITESIDE, Sheridan, in George S. Kaufman and Moss Hart's *The Man Who Came to Dinner* (1939). 'The thing's a terrible insult and I've decided to swallow it', said the New York theatre critic and journalist Alexander Woollcott (1887–1943), who was so taken with this caricature that he went on stage to play Whiteside himself, touring with the comedy in that role. The play stemmed from a traumatic weekend when Hart played host to Woollcott and the visitor criticised the food and wine, accused the servants of being light-fingered and invited his own friends to Sunday dinner. The experience persuaded Hart that the Macbeths had the right idea about house guests. 'Can you imagine', he asked Kaufman the following week, 'what would have happened if the old monster had fractured his hip and had to stay . . . ?'

WHITESTOCK, Frank, in W. M. Thackeray's 'Curate's Walk' (*Sketches and Travels in London*, 1856), is the Revd William Henry Brookfield. See Castlewood, Lady.

WHITFORD, Vernon, in George Meredith's *The Egoist* (1879), is the author's friend, Sir Leslie Stephen (see Ramsay, Mr). In the *Author* of April 1904, Meredith described Stephen in his role as the leader of weekend ramblers known as the Sunday Tramps: 'The chief of the Tramps had a wonderfully calculating eye in the observation of distances and the nature of the land, as he proved by his discovery of untried passes in the higher Alps, and he had no mercy for pursy followers. I have often said of this lifelong student and philosophical head that he had in him the making of a great military captain.'

WHITTINGDON, Dick, in Wyndham Lewis's *The Apes of God* (1930), is Captain Dick Wyndham (1896–1948), nephew of the statesman and man of letters George Wyndham, from whom he inherited in 1913 'Clouds', East Knoyle, Wiltshire. In the 1920s he was a patron-pupil of Lewis, from whom he received painting tuition.

WHITTLEBOT, Gob, Hernia and Sago, in Noël Coward's 'The Swiss Family Whittlebot' (*London Calling!*, 1923). Although she never saw this Coward revue, Dame Edith Sitwell (1887–1964) heard enough about the Whittlebot sketch to persuade herself that it was 'unspeakably obscene'. She promptly retired to bed for six weeks with jaundice believed to have been precipitated by reports of the caricature of herself as Hernia. The sketch was a send-up of her *Façade* poems, which had been declaimed to the music of William Walton, and it caused her to regard Coward as an enemy until almost the end of her life. Gob and Sago are her brothers, Sir Osbert Sitwell (1892–1969), poet, novelist, essayist and autobiographer, and Sir Sacheverell Sitwell (1897–   ), poet and essayist.

WICKFIELD, Agnes, in Charles Dickens's *David Copperfield* (1849–50). Why did Georgina Hogarth (*d.* 1916) deny so vehemently that she was the model for Agnes? She conceded that she might have inspired Dickens's Esther Summerson – but Agnes, never. She was Dickens's sister-in-law and also his companion-housekeeper for thirty years, remaining with him after his wife's departure. She may have feared her identification with Agnes would fuel suspicions that she was Dickens's mistress. In 1984 something happened to lend weight to my theory. *The Times* reported that Dickens's only surviving grandson had been discovered in South Africa. A former Postmaster General of India, Charles Tennyson Dickens (aged eighty-four) claimed that his father was the illegitimate son of Dickens by Georgina, and that he had discreetly been despatched as a child to Australia. This may explain Georgina's aversion to being taken for Agnes, whom Copperfield/Dickens came to love after the death of Dora . . . just as Dickens came to appreciate Georgina and her loyal support after his rift with his wife. The parallel was uncomfortably close to home. In this context, Dickens's wife equates to Dora, although their separation did not take place until eight years after the publication of *David Copperfield* and Catherine Thomson Dickens (1815–79) has been taken to be a model for Agnes. The eldest child of the author's colleague, George Hogarth,

who was music critic of the *Morning Chronicle*, she married Dickens
in 1836. Her sister Mary (see Maylie, Rose) has also been seen in
Agnes, and there is yet another suggested model: the bank heiress
and philanthropist Baroness Burdett Coutts (1814–1906), whose
candidature is canvassed by Edna Healey's *Lady Unknown: the Life of
Angela Burdett Coutts* (1977). Dickens advised her on her charitable
work, in which he acted as her secretary. It was to her emigration
scheme for fallen women that Elizabeth Gaskell successfully applied
for the salvation of the real-life heroine of her novel *Ruth*, whose
surname was Pasley and who was shipped to the Cape in 1850.

WIELD, Inspector, in Charles Dickens's 'Three Detective Anecdotes' (*Reprinted Pieces*, 1858), is Inspector Charles Frederick Field.
See Bucket, Inspector.

WIGGINS, Napoleon Putnam, in W. M. Thackeray's 'Notes on
the North What D'Ye-Callem Election' (1841), is the American poet
and journalist Nathaniel Parker Willis (1806–67), whose communiqués from England to the *New York Mirror* were published as a
collection, *Pencillings by the Way* (1853), annoying those who complained of his indiscretions. From 1839 to 1840 he was editor of the
New York *Corsair*, commissioning Thackeray to write for him.

WIGNALL, Dawson, in Anthony Burgess's *Earthly Powers* (1980),
has as prototype the poet laureate Sir John Betjeman (1906–84),
noted for his attachment to the Edwardian and Victorian eras, for his
flair for capturing the fleeting, contemporary scene, and for his
passionate interest in architecture.

WILBECK, Dolores, in H. G. Wells's *Apropos of Dolores* (1938). 'If
a character in a book should have the luck to seem like a real human
being that is no excuse for imagining an "original"', wrote Wells in
his disingenuous preface. He left too little to the imagination: his
characters were all too recognisable, and he had difficulty in finding a
publisher for this novel. Dolores is Odette Keun (see Campbell,
Clementina), who in 1934, after the termination of her relationship
with the author, wrote a series of *Time and Tide* articles debunking
Wells.

WILBERFORCE, in Malcolm Muggeridge's *In a Valley of this
Restless Mind* (1938), is Kingsley Martin (1897–1969), editor of the

New Statesman from 1930 to 1960. Offered a knighthood after the Second World War, he held out for a peerage, and obtained neither.

WILD, Jonathan, in Henry Fielding's *The Life of Mr Jonathan Wild the Great* (1743), is in part a satirical portrait of Sir Robert Walpole, First Earl of Orford (1676—1745), Britain's first Prime Minister (1721—42), who was notorious for his political sharp practice and for his bribery of the press, and who was gaoled early in his career for corruption.

WILDERNESS, Primrose, in Malcolm Lowry's *Dark as the Grave Wherein my Friend is Laid* (1969), is the author's second wife, the novelist Margerie Bonner Lowry (1905—). As a Hollywood child film-star she played a horse-riding kid sister in Westerns. She shared Lowry's nomadic life, in a waterfront shack in Dollarton, Vancouver, which burned down; and in Mexico, the United States, Sicily, France and England. Her co-editorship of Lowry's *Selected Letters* (1967) prompted Anthony Powell to note in the *Daily Telegraph* that she had 'sustained her husband through hardships, accidents and lack of money. She must be a lady of very considerable courage and endurance.'

WILDFIRE, Nimrod, in J. K. Paulding's *The Lion of the West* (1830), is supposedly part-inspired by the celebrated backwoodsman Davy Crockett (1786—1836), a frontier hero killed in the defence of the Alamo.

WILDSMITH, in Wyndham Lewis's *The Apes of God* (1930), is Arthur Waley (1889—1966), orientalist, poet, translator and skilled skier. Assistant Keeper in the British Museum's Department of Prints and Drawings from 1913 to 1929, he taught himself Chinese and Japanese and became fluent in both — but only on paper, for he spoke neither, just as he never set foot in those countries upon whose literature he became the West's principal expert. 'I expect, Mr Waley', said Ada Leverson, 'you often go to *The Mikado*!'

WILFER, Bella and Mrs Reginald, in Charles Dickens's *Our Mutual Friend* (1864—5). Bella has been popularly identified with Ellen Ternan (see Provis, Estella). I suspect she owes more to the author's daughter, Mrs Kate Perugini (née Kate Macready Dickens, 1839—1929), with whom Dickens enjoyed a happy relationship.

Mrs Reginald Wilfer is supposedly part-inspired by the author's mother. See Nickleby, Mrs.

WILKES, Ashley, in Margaret Mitchell's *Gone with the Wind* (1936), is Clifford West Henry (*d.* 1918), the son of a Connecticut estate agent. He was a poetry-quoting lieutenant recently graduated from Harvard when the author first met him. She was then seventeen, and they became unofficially engaged. He was killed serving with the American army at Saint-Mihiel. The author's story is told in Anne Edwards's *The Road to Tara* (1983).

WILKINSON, in Oliver Goldsmith's *The Vicar of Wakefield* (1766), is supposedly the political agitator John Wilkes (1727–97), founder of the *North Briton*. His abortive attempts to re-enter parliament after his expulsion (he was three times elected, and three times declared ineligible) led to parliamentary reform.

WILKINSON, Peter, in Christopher Isherwood's *Goodbye to Berlin* (1939), is part-inspired by William Robson-Scott. A lecturer at Berlin University in the 1930s, he treated his Nazi students with such disdain that his dismissal was averted only by a colleague telling the authorities that sacking him would provoke an international incident as he was a cousin of the King of England. He resigned when this hoax was exposed.

WILLE, Princess, in Karel Čapek's *Krakatit* (1924: translated as *An Atomic Phantasy*, 1948), is Věra Hruzová (*d.* 1979), the daughter of a Brno professor. She was nineteen and a student when Čapek met her in Prague in 1920. He courted her concurrently with the then eighteen-year-old actress Olga Scheinpflugová, whom he married shortly before his death fifteen years later and who erroneously claimed to be the inspiration of Princess Wille.

WILLEMS, Peter, in Joseph Conrad's *An Outcast of the Islands* (1896). Conrad's Eastern background has been exhaustively researched in Jerry Allen's *The Sea Years of Joseph Conrad* (1965) and Norman Sherry's *Conrad's Eastern World* (1966). Allen supposes Willems to be Carel De Veer (*d.* 1911), an alcoholic Dutch hanger-on at the Borneo trading establishment of W. C. Olmeyer (see Almayer). Rarely speaking, and barely tolerated, he lived in complete subjection to his cake-selling Malay wife, the 'Aïssa' of this story and 'Taminah' in *Almayer's Folly*. Sherry suggests that Willems may be modelled on James Lingard (see *Lord Jim*), who is believed to have lived with a native girl to whom he was much attached.

WILLERSLEY, in H. G. Wells's *The New Machiavelli* (1911), is the political scientist Professor Graham Wallas (1858–1932), a founder member of the Fabian Society. He lectured at the London School of Economics from 1895 to 1923. A friend of Shaw, he assisted Mrs Humphry Ward with information on Socialism for her novel *Marcella* and prompted her creation in 1899 of a school for crippled children in London.

WILLIAM, in Richmal Crompton's stories of the incorrigible schoolboy. See Brown, William.

WILLIAMS, Eric, in F. W. Farrar's *Eric, or Little by Little* (1858), is Cyril Flower, who was a pupil of the author at Harrow. See Dormer, Nick.

WILLIE, in Robert Burns's 'Willie Brew'd a Peck o' Maut', is William Nicol (1744–97), classics master at Edinburgh High School from 1774 to 1795, and a sometimes irascible, sometimes convivial companion of the poet.

WILSON, Hypo and Alma, in Dorothy M. Richardson's *Pilgrimage* cycle of novels (1915–67). A notorious womaniser, the novelist H. G. Wells (1866–1946) quickly added Dorothy Richardson to his conquests, finding her 'most interestingly hairy' and making her pregnant, though he soon tired of her predilection for intellectual conversation. She had a miscarriage and made him her Hypo Wilson. They met when she renewed her acquaintance with Amy Catherine Robbins (see Stanley, Ann Veronica), a school-friend who had become Wells's second wife. Richardson portrayed her as Alma.

WILSON, Murray, in Gilbert Cannan's *Peter Homunculus* (1909). If you are having an adulterous affair and your lover romantically persists in visiting your bedroom via a ladder, stay on the right side of your gardener. Mary Barrie didn't: the gardener told her husband about the ladder, and Cannan was cited by J. M. Barrie in the divorce which followed. Later knighted, the dramatist and novelist Barrie (1860–1937) is Murray Wilson. He should never have married (see Peter Pan); nor should Cannan (see Gunn, Gilbert), who became

Mary Barrie's second husband (see Rodney, Frederick and Jane; see also Dugdale, Mary).

WILSON, Robert, in Ernest Hemingway's 'The Short Happy Life of Francis Macomber' (1936; *The Fifth Column and the First Forty-Nine Stories*, 1938). Here we have two biographers in collision. Hemingway's biographer, Carlos Baker, says Wilson is Philip Percival (see Phillips, Jackson). Judith Thurman, biographer of the writer Isak Dinesen (Karen Blixen), identifies Wilson as Dinesen's womanising husband, Baron Bror von Blixen-Finecke (1886—1946). A white settler in Kenya, he gave her syphilis (it was worth it, she stoically remarked, to become a baroness) and subsequently left her. Both identifications could be partially right, although Hemingway did not as a rule go in for composites.

WILSON, Thomas, in W. Somerset Maugham's 'The Lotus-Eater' (*The Mixture as Before*, 1940), is John Ellingham Brooks. See Hayward.

WILSON, Tom, in Jack Kerouac's *Visions of Cody* (1960), is John Clellon Holmes. See Saybrook, Tom.

WILSON, Will, in Elizabeth Gaskell's *Mary Barton* (1848), is believed to have been suggested by John Stevenson. See Hale, Frederick.

WIMBUSH, Henry and Priscilla, in Aldous Huxley's *Crome Yellow* (1921). The Wimbushs are a blend of the Morrells and the Sitwells: Philip (1870—1943) and Lady Ottoline Morrell (see Roddice, Hermione); and Sir George and Lady Sitwell (see Rotherham, Sir Henry, and Eva, Lady).

WIMSEY, Lord Peter, in Dorothy L. Sayers's detective fiction (1923—73), commencing with *Whose Body?* As attractive to women as Sayers was unattractive to men, Eric Whelpton (1894—1981), schoolmaster and travel writer, is Wimsey's prime prototype. Sayers became infatuated with him when he was invalided from the army in 1918 and she met him at Oxford. While managing to fend off her attentions, he persuaded her in 1919 to accompany him as his secretary to Les Roches, a school near Paris. Less than a year later he left the school, declining the proprietor's offer of a partnership in exchange for marriage to his unprepossessing daughter, and it was at this time that his association with Sayers came to an end. He bore little physical resemblance to Wimsey but displayed the peer's linguistic ability and, like Wimsey, was something of a gourmet. He was also a formative influence on Brendan Bracken (see Mottram, Rex), who became his friend when they were teaching colleagues at Bishop's Stortford, Essex, in 1921. Whelpton himself suggested two other possible models for Wimsey: Sayers's husband (see Fentiman, George) and Charles Crichton, an Old Etonian ex-cavalry officer who for a time lived in the same house as the author and regaled her with stories of Edwardian high life and of his gentleman's gentleman, who had also been his batman. Another influence may have been the Russian-born novelist John Cournos (1881–1966; see also Masters, Miranda), who was a close friend of Sayers during the First World War, when he was employed at the Foreign Office, decoding Russian government messages. Sharing Wimsey's knowledge of music, he ultimately became assistant editor of the *Philadelphia Inquirer*. Professor Maurice Roy Ridley, Fellow and Tutor in English Literature at Balliol College, Oxford, from 1920 to 1945, claimed to be Wimsey's original and bore a close resemblance, but Sayers did not meet him until the mid-1930s.

WINCHESTER, Sir Donald, in Hugh Walpole's *John Cornelius* (1937), is the author's publisher, Sir Frederick Macmillan (1851–1936), of whom Walpole wrote in his diary, 'I love him dearly. I should like hugely to have been his son ... He is the only human I know of in London of whom no one ever speaks a word of ill.'

WINDRIP, Berzelius (Buzz), in Sinclair Lewis's *It Can't Happen Here* (1935), has as prototype Huey Long. See Stark, Willie.

WINGFIELD, Amanda and Laura, in Tennessee Williams's *The Glass Menagerie* (1944), are respectively the author's mother, Edwina Williams (née Dakin), and his schizophrenic sister, Rose Isabel Williams, who in 1937 was confined to a mental hospital and subsequently underwent a leucotomy.

WINIFRED, in D. H. Lawrence's 'England, My England' (1915; *England, My England*, 1922), is Madeline Lucas, wife of Perceval Lucas (see Egbert) and daughter of the writer Wilfred Meynell and the poet Alice Meynell.

WINIFRED, in D. H. Lawrence's 'The Witch à la Mode' (*A Modern Lover*, 1934), is supposedly Helen Corke. See Verden, Helena.

WINNIE, in Francis Carco's *Les Innocents* (1916), is Katherine Mansfield. See Brangwen, Gudrun; see also Duquette, Raoul.

WINSLOW, Ronnie, in Terence Rattigan's *The Winslow Boy* (1946). In 1908, George Archer-Shee, a thirteen-year-old cadet at Osborne Naval College, on the Isle of Wight, was accused of stealing another cadet's postal order and was expelled. He thus became the prototype for Ronnie Winslow. Determined to establish the boy's innocence, his father used a Petition of Right to sue the Crown, bringing the Admiralty to court in what became a *cause célèbre* in 1910, with Sir Edward Carson representing Archer-Shee. Accepting the former cadet's innocence, the Admiralty subsequently paid his father more than £7,000 in compensation. George Archer-Shee returned to his old school, Stonyhurst, and later worked for a New York firm of stockbrokers. He came home to enlist upon the outbreak of the First World War, became a subaltern and was killed in the first Battle of Ypres. Introducing a broadcast version of *The Winslow Boy* in 1957, Rattigan confirmed that he used the facts of the Archer-Shee case for the play. But, he added, 'Ronnie Winslow is *not* George Archer-Shee, Ronnie's father is *not* George's father, and Sir Robert Morton is *not* Sir Edward Carson . . . I wanted to create, not just re-create. The plot was borrowed from life, but if the characters too had been borrowed from life, then I felt the whole play might easily have been dead.'

WINTERBOURNE, Elizabeth, in Richard Aldington's *Death of a Hero* (1929), is the author's first wife, Hilda Doolittle (see Masters, Miranda). Christopher Ridgway comments in his introduction to the 1984 edition of the novel that the plot is 'a grossly unjust representation of Aldington's life with H.D., since the disintegration of the marriage might more justly be blamed on him, and the character of the vain, cynical Elizabeth bears no recognisable relationship to that of H.D.' Well, yes . . . but Doolittle was not the easiest of partners either, and it is perhaps significant that she failed to achieve a stable relationship with any man. Furthermore, *Death of a Hero* at least credits her with rather more depth and subtlety than it accords the woman who supplanted her (see Fanny).

WITCHEM, Sergeant, in Charles Dickens's 'Three Detective Anecdotes' (*Reprinted Pieces*, 1858), is Inspector Jonathan Whicher. See Cuff, Sergeant Richard.

WOLFE, Nero, in Rex Stout's detective fiction (1934—75), commencing with *Fer-de-Lance*, was claimed by Alexander Woollcott (see Whiteside, Sheridan) to have been modelled upon himself. 'I never make up characters', remarked Stout. 'I never contrive them. I know damn well that if I bring someone into a story — I don't care if it's just a man carrying a ladder — unless I'm interested in him then the reader can't be.'

WOLFSHEIM, Meyer, in F. Scott Fitzgerald's *The Great Gatsby* (1925), is Arnold Rothstein, a notorious New York gambler in the 1920s. He was killed by an unidentified gunman in 1928 while leaving an assembly of gangsters and bootleggers at Park Central Hotel.

WONDERFUL OLD SONGSTER OF KEW GREEN, the, in Nancy Mitford's *Pigeon Pie* (1940), is Mark Ogilvie-Grant (1905—69), a homosexual Old Etonian cousin of the Countess of Seafield, noted for his mimicry of Clara Butt singing 'Land of Hope and Glory'. Captured in Italy in the Second World War, he subsequently worked in Athens as an adviser to British Petroleum.

WONHAM, Stephen, in E. M. Forster's *The Longest Journey* (1907), is the Cambridge economist Hugh Owen Meredith (see Ansell). His brand of eccentricity was to call uninvited upon friends, occasionally while they were having breakfast.

WONTSEE, Mr Wilful, in Thomas Love Peacock's *Crotchet Castle* (1831), is William Wordsworth. See Paperstamp, Peter Paypaul.

WOODCOCK, Sir Bussy, in H. G. Wells's *The Autocracy of Mr Parham* (1930), is supposedly Lord Beaverbrook (see Ottercove, Lord). 'The knowing ones say I have been "putting" you "into" my book, *Mr Parham*', Wells wrote to Beaverbrook. 'Don't you believe it. I wanted a man who had made money fast and had an original mind. You seem to be the only one who answers to that description in London. That doesn't make it you.' Like most of Wells's denials, this may be taken with a cellarful of salt.

WOODSEER, Gower, in George Meredith's *The Amazing Marriage* (1895), is the writer Robert Louis Stevenson (1850–94), who found Meredith 'not easy to be with – there is so much of him, and the veracity and the high athletic intellectual humbug are so inter-mixed'. But Meredith swiftly discerned Stevenson's talent, forecast-ing as early as 1878 that 'some day we shall all be proud to have known him'.

WOOSTER, Bertram Wilberforce, in P. G. Wodehouse's Bertie Wooster stories (1917–74), commencing with 'The Man with Two Left Feet' The actor George Grossmith jun. (1874–1935), origi-nator of dude comedy at London's Gaiety Theatre, has been sugges-ted as a model for Wooster. Later in his career, Bertie may have acquired traits from Anthony Bingham Mildmay, Second Baron Mildmay of Flete (1909–50), amateur steeplechase jockey and the author's son-in-law.

WOOTTON, Lord Henry, in Oscar Wilde's *The Picture of Dorian Gray* (1891), is supposedly the sculptor and art critic Lord Ronald Gower (1845–1916), son of the Second Duke of Sutherland. A homosexual whose lovers included Morton Fullerton (see Deering, Vincent), he was a trustee of the National Portrait Gallery and of the Shakespeare Memorial Building, Stratford-upon-Avon, and from 1867 to 1874 MP for Sutherland.

WOULD-BE, Sir Politick, in Ben Jonson's *Volpone* (1606), is supposedly Sir Paul Neile. See Sidrophel.

WREN, Jenny, in Charles Dickens's *Our Mutual Friend* (1864–5), has a possible prototype in the poet and novelist Mary Russell Mitford (1787–1855), who with her writing struggled to support herself and her extravagant, alcoholic father, to whom she referred as her 'bad boy'.

WRENCH, Tom, in Sir Arthur Wing Pinero's *Trelawny of the Wells* (1898), is the actor turned dramatist Thomas William Robertson (1829–71), a pioneer of naturalistic comedies.

WYBROW, Captain Anthony, in George Eliot's 'Mr Gilfil's Love Story' (*Scenes of Clerical Life*, 1858), is supposedly Francis Parker Newdigate II (1774–1862), a boyhood friend of the author's father. Becoming an army officer, he was effectually disinherited by Sir

Roger Newdigate (see Cheverel, Sir Christopher), who gave preference to his favourite nephew, Charles Parker (1756–95), who has also been suggested as the model for Wybrow.

WYKEHAMIST, the, in John Betjeman's 'The Wykehamist' (*Continual Dew*, 1937), is Richard Crossman (1907–74), Labour cabinet minister and editor of the *New Statesman* from 1970 to 1972.

WYLD, Beatrice, in D. H. Lawrence's *Sons and Lovers* (1913) and *A Collier's Friday Night* (1934), is Alice Beatrice Hall. See Gall, Alice.

X

XAVIÈRE, in Simone de Beauvoir's *She Came to Stay* (1943), is Olga Kosakiewicz, a former pupil of the author. She later became part of a triangular relationship with Beauvoir and Jean-Paul Sartre (see Dubreuilh, Robert), which threatened the Beauvoir-Sartre intimacy as Beauvoir began to feel herself excluded. The tension was defused when Kosakiewicz fell in love with a young man, but Beauvoir still felt the need to write the episode out of her system. In *She Came to Stay* (*L'Invitée*), Xavière is murdered by Françoise, the story's Beauvoir figure. The author recorded in *La Force de l'age* that, 'by killing Olga on paper I got rid of the irritation and malice I had felt on her account'.

XENOS, Diogenes Alejandro ('Dax'), in Harold Robbins's *The Adventurers* (1969), is the Dominican playboy diplomat Porfirio Rubirosa (*d.* 1965), who married five times and was described as the world's greatest foreign co-respondent. His wives included the film actress and Woolworth heiress Barbara Hutton. The Dominican dictator, General Rafael Trujillo, was among his fathers-in-law. He died aged fifty-six in a car crash on his way home from a Paris night club.

Y

YEPANCHINA, Aglaya, in Fyodor Dostoevsky's *The Idiot* (1868–9), is the Russian feminist and revolutionary Anna Korvin-Krukovskaya, elder sister of the mathematician and novelist Sofya Kovalevskaya. Dostoevsky first met her in the mid-1860s, when she was twenty-one. His proposal of marriage was unsuccessful.

YORICK, in William Shakespeare's *Hamlet* (*c.* 1603), is supposedly Richard Tarlton (*d.* 1588), a celebrated comic actor from Shropshire who was noted for his audacity as a jester. He joined Queen Elizabeth's players in 1583, but tradition has it that his dissipated life ended in poverty, his play *The Seven Deadly Sins* having been written from experience.

YORKE, Hiram and Rose, in Charlotte Brontë's *Shirley* (1849), are Joshua Taylor (*d.* 1841) and his daughter, Mary (1817–93), who lived at The Red House, Gomersal, Yorkshire. A wool manufacturer whose broad dialect belied his culture, Taylor was an art- and book-collector, widely travelled and fluent in French and Italian, although when the author came to know him he was in reduced circumstances, bankrupted by an army contract. Mary, a lifelong friend of the author from their schooldays, emigrated to New Zealand.

YOUNGBROTHER, Lord, in Hugh Kingsmill's *The Return of William Shakespeare* (1929). News that a scientist has brought Shakespeare back to life launches the newspaper tycoon Lord Youngbrother on a race to find the bard before his rivals. As his name indicates, Youngbrother is a caricature of Harold Sidney Harmsworth, First Viscount Rothermere (1868–1940), a younger brother of Lord Northcliffe (see Tilbury, Lord).

YOURBELETIEFF, Princesse, in Marcel Proust's *A la recherche du temps perdu* (1913−27), is Marie-Sophie-Olga-Zénaïde ('Misia') Godebska (1872−1950), a Polish sculptor's daughter who was successively married to Thadée Natanson, founder-editor of *La Revue blanche*; Alfred Edwards, proprietor of *Le Matin*; and José-Maria Sert, a Spanish painter. A talented pianist, she was a celebrated Parisian hostess of the *belle époque*. After being thrust by her first husband into the arms of her second, who divorced her, as did her third, she became a drug addict and died in comparative obscurity.

YVONNE, in Alain-Fournier's *Le Grand Meaulnes* (1913), is Yvonne de Quièvrecourt, with whom the author fell in love in 1905, when he was nineteen. After first glimpsing her, he followed her through the streets of Paris. This experience and his sole, short conversation with her dominated his life for the next eight years, until this novel's publication . . . which coincided with an affair with an actress.

Z

ZAGREUS, Horace, in Wyndham Lewis's *The Apes of God* (1930), is an amalgam of the writer George Borrow (1803−81) and Horace de Vere Cole, a wealthy Bloomsbury fringe figure of the 1920s. In 1910, Cole and Virginia Woolf, disguised as Abyssinian royalty, perpetrated the 'Dreadnought' hoax when they were ceremonially received on board the warship by the captain.

ZARAH, Queen, in *The Secret History of Queen Zarah and the Zarazians* (1705), attributed to Mary de la Rivière Manley, is Sarah Churchill, Duchess of Marlborough. See Atossa.

ZARETSKY, in Alexander Pushkin's *Eugene Onegin* (1833), is Fyodor Ivanovich Tolstoy (see Dolokhov, Fyodor Ivanovich), who incensed Pushkin by spreading gossip alleging that the poet had been flogged prior to his exile for offending Alexander I. During his banishment Pushkin strove to improve his shooting for a duel with Tolstoy. On his arrival in Moscow in 1826 the poet issued his challenge, but friends interceded and there was a reconciliation. It is as a duellist that Tolstoy appears in *Eugene Onegin*.

ZELLI, Stephan, in Jean Rhys's *Postures* (1928; later retitled *Quartet*), is the author's first husband, Jean Lenglet, songwriter, poet and journalist, whom she married in 1919. When Rhys wrote *Postures* he was imprisoned at Fresnes for an illegal currency transaction. A Resistance hero of the Second World War, he chronicled his marriage and imprisonment in *Barred*.

ZENOBIA, in Nathaniel Hawthorne's *The Blithedale Romance* (1852), is supposedly Margaret Fuller (1810−50), critic and transcendentalist. Like Hawthorne, she took part in the Brook Farm community experiment at West Roxbury, Massachusetts, upon which *The Blithedale Romance* is based. She drowned when the ship which was carrying her back from Europe to America was wrecked in a storm.

ZHIVAGO, Evgraf, Tonya and Dr Yuri, in Boris Pasternak's *Dr Zhivago* (1957). Evgraf, it has been suggested, owes something to the author's brother, Aleksandr Leonidovich Pasternak (1893–1982). As an architect engaged on the construction by slave labour of the Moscow–Volga Canal in 1936 he was employed by the NKVD – the secret police – whose uniform he wore. Tonya is part-inspired by Zinaida Nikolaevna Pasternak and Olga Vsevolodovna Ivinskaya (see Guishar, Larissa Fyodorovna). Although primarily a self-portrait, Yuri is supposedly based also on Dr A. D. Avdeyev, chief physician at Chistopol state hospital in the Ural mountains when Pasternak was among Moscow writers evacuated to the town in the early 1940s. Avdeyev later became a professor of biology in another Soviet provincial town.

ZOÏLUS, in Alexander Pope's *The Dunciad* (1728), is John Dennis. See Appius.

ZOSIMA, Father, in Fyodor Dostoevsky's *The Brothers Kara-mazov* (1879–80). Who would expect a connection between Edith Sitwell and Dostoevsky? One is provided by one of the models for Zosima: Father Amrovsky, Pavel Tchelitchew's father's confessor (see Hare, Jonathan) and Elder of Optina Pustyn monastery near Kozelsk, to which Dostoevsky made a pilgrimage in 1878 following the death of his three-year-old son from an epileptic fit. Zosima is also part-inspired by Tikhon Zadonsky (Timofey Kirilov, 1724–83), who as Bishop of Voronezh was celebrated for his Christian humility and who retired in 1767 to live at Zadonsky monastery.

ZULEIKA, in Lord Byron's *The Bride of Abydos* (1813), echoes Byron's passion for Augusta Leigh (see Astarte). In the initial draft of the poem, Zuleika and her lover, Selim, were brother and sister. Byron later found it prudent to alter the relationship to that of cousins. His alleged affair with his half-sister, who nine months later gave birth to a daughter, coincided with the writing of this poem.

BIBLIOGRAPHY

The following works are among many which have been consulted in the preparation of this book. They are listed here by way of acknowledgement and as suggested further reading.

J. Abdy and C. Gere, *The Souls*, Sidgwick & Jackson, 1984

P. Ackroyd, *T. S. Eliot*, Hamish Hamilton, 1984

H. Acton, *Nancy Mitford: a memoir*, Hamish Hamilton, 1975

A. O. Aldridge, *Voltaire and the Century of Light*, Princeton University Press, 1975

J. Allen, *The Sea Years of Joseph Conrad*, Doubleday, 1965

W. Allen, *George Eliot*, Macmillan, 1964

A. Alpers, *The Life of Katherine Mansfield*, Jonathan Cape, 1980

R. Alter and C. Cosman, *Stendhal: a biography*, Allen & Unwin, 1980

M. Amory (ed.), *The Letters of Evelyn Waugh*, Weidenfeld & Nicolson, 1980

C. G. Anderson, *James Joyce and His World*, Thames & Hudson, 1967

R. Arnold, *The Whiston Matter*, Hart-Davis, 1961

N. Arvin, *Longfellow: his life and work*, Little, Brown, 1963

E. Bagnold, *Enid Bagnold's Autobiography*, Heinemann, 1969

C. Baker, *Ernest Hemingway: a life story*, Scribner's, New York; Collins, London, 1969

R. Baldick, *The First Bohemian: a life of Henry Murger*, Hamish Hamilton, 1961

——, *The Life of J-K. Huysmans*, Oxford University Press, 1955

D. Barker, *John Galsworthy: the man of principle*, Heinemann, 1963

S. Bedford, *Aldous Huxley: a biography*, Collins and Chatto & Windus, 2 vols, 1973–4

Q. Bell, *Virginia Woolf: a biography*, Hogarth Press, 1972

J. D. Bellamy, *The New Fiction*, University of Illinois Press, 1974

B. Bernstein, *Thurber*, Dodd, Mead, New York; Gollancz, London, 1975

A. Best, *Frank Wedekind*, Oswald Wolff, 1975

T. Besterman, *Voltaire Essays*, Oxford University Press, 1962

E. Bigland, *Marie Corelli*, Jarrolds, 1953

L. Blanch, *Pierre Loti*, Collins, 1983

R. Bloom, *Anatomies of Egotism: a reading of the last novels of H. G. Wells*, University of Nebraska Press, 1977

J. L. Blotner, *The Modern American Political Novel, 1900–1960*, University of Texas Press, 1966

L. S. Boas, *Harriet Shelley: five long years*, Oxford University Press, 1962

J. T. Boulton (ed.), *The Letters of D. H. Lawrence*, vol. 1, Cambridge University Press, 1979

——, with A. Robertson (ed.), *The Letters of D. H. Lawrence*, vol. 3, Cambridge University Press, 1985

C. M. Bowra, *Memories*, Weidenfeld & Nicolson, 1966

J. Brabazon, *Dorothy L. Sayers*, Gollancz, 1981

E. Bredsdorff, *Hans Christian Andersen*, Phaidon, 1975

P. Brent, *Lord Byron*, Weidenfeld & Nicolson, 1974

F. Bresler, *The Mystery of Georges Simenon: a biography*, Heinemann/Quixote Press, 1983

C. L. and V. M. Broad, *Dictionary of the Plays and Novels of Bernard Shaw*, A. & C. Black, 1929

H. Brogan, *The Life of Arthur Ransome*, Jonathan Cape, 1984

V. Brome, *H. G. Wells*, Longmans, Green, 1951

B. Brophy, *Prancing Novelist*, Macmillan, 1973

M. Brown, *Louis Bromfield and his Books*, Cassell, 1956

M. J. Bruccoli, *Some Sort of Epic Grandeur: the life of F. Scott Fitzgerald*, Harcourt Brace Jovanovich, 1981

K. Budd, *The Last Victorian: R. D. Blackmore*, Centaur Press, 1960

D. Burg and G. Feifer, *Solzhenitsyn: a biography*, Stein & Day, New York; Hodder & Stoughton, London, 1972

M. Butler, *Peacock Displayed: a satirist in his context*, Routledge, 1979

E. Butscher (ed.), *Sylvia Plath: the woman and the work*, Peter Owen, 1979

W. Byron, *Cervantes: a biography*, Cassell, 1979

R. L. Calder, *W. Somerset Maugham and the Quest for Freedom*, Heinemann, 1972

P. Callow, *Son and Lover: the young Lawrence*, Bodley Head, 1975

L. Carley (ed.), *Delius: a life in letters, 1862–1908*, Scolar Press, 1983

H. Carpenter and M. Prichard, *The Oxford Companion to Children's Literature*, Oxford University Press, 1984

C. Cate, *George Sand: a biography*, Hamish Hamilton, London; Houghton Mifflin, Boston, 1975

D. Cecil, *Max*, Constable, 1964

——, *A Portrait of Jane Austen*, Constable, 1978

S. Chitty, *The Woman who Wrote Black Beauty*, Hodder & Stoughton, 1971

A. Christie, *An Autobiography*, Collins, 1977

A. Clark, *Lewis Carroll: a biography*, Dent, 1979

A. M. Clark, *Sir Walter Scott: the formative years*, William Blackwood, 1969

C. L. Cline (ed.), *The Letters of George Meredith*, Oxford University Press, 1970

M. Collie, *George Borrow, Eccentric*, Cambridge University Press, 1982

R. A. Cordell, *Somerset Maugham: a biographical and critical study*, Heinemann, 1961

M. de Cossart, *The Food of Love: Princesse Edmond de Polignac*, Hamish Hamilton, 1978

P. Costello, *Jules Verne, Inventor of Science Fiction*, Hodder & Stoughton, 1978

W. F. Courtney, *Young Charles Lamb*, Macmillan, 1982

E. Crankshaw, *Tolstoy: the making of a novelist*, Weidenfeld & Nicolson, 1974

B. Crick, *George Orwell: a life*, Secker & Warburg, 1980

W. S. Crockett, *The Scott Originals*, Foulis, 1912

M. Crosland, *Colette*, Peter Owen, 1973

——, *Raymond Radiguet*, Peter Owen, 1976

M. Curtiss (ed.), *Proust's Letters*, Chatto & Windus, 1950

K. Cushman, *D. H. Lawrence at Work*, Harvester Press, 1978

D. Daiches (ed.), *The Penguin Companion to Literature – 1: Britain and the Commonwealth*, Penguin, 1971

M. Darlow and G. Hodson, *Terence Rattigan: the man and his work*, Quartet, 1979

F. J. Harvey Darton, *Vincent Crummles: his theatre and his times*, Wells Gardner Darton, 1926

S. J. Darroch, *Ottoline: the life of Lady Ottoline Morrell*, Chatto & Windus, 1976

M. Davie (ed.), *The Diaries of Evelyn Waugh*, Weidenfeld & Nicolson, 1976

D. Day, *Malcolm Lowry*, Oxford University Press, 1973

L. Deacon and T. Coleman, *Providence and Mr Hardy*, Hutchinson, 1966

P. Delany, *D. H. Lawrence's Nightmare*, Harvester Press, 1979

É. Delavenay, *D. H. Lawrence: the man and his work*, Heinemann, 1972

L. Dickson, *H. G. Wells: his turbulent life and times*, Macmillan, 1969

——, *Radclyffe Hall at the Well of Loneliness*, Collins, 1975

I. D'Israeli, *Curiosities of Literature*, Routledge, 1823

A. Dobson, *Fielding*, Macmillan, 1889

——, *Oliver Goldsmith*, Walter Scott, 1888

M. Drabble, *Arnold Bennett*, Weidenfeld & Nicolson, 1974

W. A. Dutt, *George Borrow in East Anglia*, David Nutt, 1896

A. Easson, *Elizabeth Gaskell*, Routledge & Kegan Paul, 1979

J. M. East, *Max Miller, the Cheeky Chappie*, W. H. Allen, 1977

L. Edel, *Henry James*, Lippincott, Philadelphia; Hart-Davis, London, 5 vols, 1953–72

A. Edwards, *The Road to Tara: the life of Margaret Mitchell*, Ticknor & Fields, New Haven, Conn.; Hodder & Stoughton, 1983

O. D. Edwards, *The Quest for Sherlock Holmes*, Mainstream, 1982

P. B. Ellis, *H. Rider Haggard: a voice from the infinite*, Routledge & Kegan Paul, 1978

——, with P. Williams, *By Jove, Biggles! The Life of Captain W. E. Johns*, W. H. Allen, 1981

R. Ellmann, *James Joyce*, Oxford University Press, 1982 (rev. edn)

M. Elwin, *Thackeray: a personality*, Jonathan Cape, 1932

St J. Ervine, *Bernard Shaw: his life, work and friends*, Constable, 1956

J. J. Espey, *Ezra Pound's Mauberley: a study in composition*, Faber & Faber, 1955

M. Esslin, *Brecht: a choice of evils*, Eyre Methuen, 1959

D. Farr, *Gilbert Cannan: a Georgian prodigy*, Chatto & Windus, 1978

F. Farr, *O'Hara: a biography of John O'Hara*, Little, Brown, 1973

D. Farson, *Henry: an appreciation of Henry Williamson*, Michael Joseph, 1982

F. Felton, *Thomas Love Peacock*, Allen & Unwin, 1973

J. Felstiner, *The Lies of Art: Max Beerbohm's parody and caricature*, Gollancz, 1973

L. A. Fiedler, *Olaf Stapledon: a man divided*, Oxford University Press, 1983

A. Field, *The Formidable Miss Barnes*, Secker & Warburg, 1983

D. Fielding, *The Face on the Sphinx: a portrait of Gladys Deacon*, Hamish Hamilton, 1978

B. Finney, *Christopher Isherwood: a critical biography*, Faber & Faber, 1979

R. B. Fisher, *Syrie Maugham*, Duckworth, 1978

P. Fitzgerald, *The Knox Brothers*, Macmillan, 1977

K. Foss, *Here Lies Richard Brinsley Sheridan*, Martin Secker, 1939

R. Friedenthal, *Goethe: his life and times*, Weidenfeld & Nicolson, 1965

E. I. Fripp, *Shakespeare, Man and Artist*, Oxford University Press, 1938

J. Fryer, *Isherwood: a biography of Christopher Isherwood*, New English Library, 1977

P. N. Furbank, *E. M. Forster: a life*, Secker & Warburg, 2 vols, 1977–8

T. R. Fyvel, *George Orwell: a personal memoir*, Weidenfeld & Nicolson, 1982

D. Garnett, *Great Friends*, Macmillan, 1979

W. Gaunt, *The Aesthetic Adventure*, Jonathan Cape, 1945

D. Geherin, *Sons of Sam Spade*, Frederick Ungar, 1980

A. and B. Gelb, *O'Neill*, Harper, 1962

W. Gérin, *Charlotte Brontë: the evolution of genius*, Oxford University Press, 1967

——, *Emily Brontë*, Oxford University Press, 1971

——, *Elizabeth Gaskell*, Oxford University Press, 1976

B. Gifford and L. Lee, *Jack's Book: Jack Kerouac in the lives and words of his friends*, St Martin's Press, 1978

R. Gittings, *John Keats: the living year*, Heinemann, 1954

——, *Young Thomas Hardy*, Heinemann, 1975

M. Goffin, *Maria Pasqua*, Oxford University Press, 1979

D. Golding, *South Lodge: reminiscences of Violet Hunt, Ford Madox Ford and 'The English Review'*, Constable, 1943

M. Goldstein, *George S. Kaufman: his life, his theater*, Oxford University Press, 1979

C. Gordon, *Beyond the Looking Glass: reflections of Alice and her family*, Hodder & Stoughton, 1982

L. Gordon, *Eliot's Early Years*, Oxford University Press, 1977

——, *Virginia Woolf: a writer's life*, Oxford University Press, 1984

T. Gould, *Inside Outsider: the life and times of Colin MacInnes*, Chatto & Windus, 1983

S. Graham, *The Real Scott Fitzgerald*, Grosset & Dunlap, New York; W. H. Allen, London, 1976

R. Gray, *Brecht the Dramatist*, Cambridge University Press, 1976

S. N. Grebstein, *Sinclair Lewis*, Twayne, 1962

B. Green, *P. G. Wodehouse: a literary biography*, Michael Joseph, 1981

——, *Shaw's Champions*, Elm Tree Books, 1978

R. L. Green, *A. E .W. Mason: the adventures of a storyteller*, Max Parrish, 1952

——, *Tellers of Tales*, Edmund Ward, 1965 (rev. edn)

V. H. H. Green, *Oxford Common Room: a study of Lincoln College and Mark Pattison*, Edward Arnold, 1957

G. Greene, *Ways of Escape*, Bodley Head, 1980

C. Greig, *Ivy Compton-Burnett: a memoir*, Garnstone Press, 1972

F. J. Grover, *Drieu La Rochelle and the Fiction of Testimony*, University of California Press, 1958

D. Grumbach, *The Company She Kept: Mary McCarthy, herself and her writing*, Coward-McCann, New York; Bodley Head, London, 1967

J. Guignet, *Virginia Woolf and her Works*, Hogarth Press, 1965

G. S. Haight, *George Eliot*, Oxford University Press, 1968

J. Halperin, *C. P. Snow: an oral biography*, Harvester Press, 1983

——, *Gissing: a life in books*, Oxford University Press, 1982

——, *Trollope and Politics*, Macmillan, 1977

I. Hamilton, *Koestler: a biography*, Secker & Warburg, 1982

N. Hamilton, *The Brothers Mann*, Secker & Warburg, 1978

J. R. Hammond, *An H. G. Wells Companion*, Macmillan, 1979

F. Hardy, *The Hard Way*, Werner Laurie, 1961

C. Hardyment, *Arthur Ransome and Captain Flint's Trunk*, Jonathan Cape, 1984

J. D. Hart, *The Oxford Companion to American Literature*, Oxford University Press, 1965 (4th edn)

A. Hartcup, *Love and Marriage in the Great Country Houses*, Sidgwick & Jackson, 1984

R. Hart-Davis, *Hugh Walpole*, Macmillan, 1952

——(ed.), *The Letters of Max Beerbohm to Reggie Turner*, Hart-Davis, 1964

——(ed.), *The Letters of Oscar Wilde*, Hart-Davis, 1962

P. Harvey, *The Oxford Companion to English Literature*, Oxford University Press, 1946 (3rd edn)

F. W. J. Hemmings, *Émile Zola*, Oxford University Press, 1953

J. Pope Hennessy, *Robert Louis Stevenson*, Jonathan Cape, 1974

C. Hibbert, *Disraeli and his World*, Thames & Hudson, 1978

D. S. Higgins, *Rider Haggard: the great story teller*, Cassell, 1981

C. Higham, *The Adventures of Conan Doyle*, Hamish Hamilton, 1976

R. Hingley, *Dostoyevsky: his life and work*, Elek, 1978

——, *Pasternak*, Weidenfeld & Nicolson, 1983

J. Hitchman, *Such a Strange Lady: a biography of Dorothy L. Sayers*, New English Library, 1975

J. Hohlenberg, *Søren Kierkegaard*, Routledge & Kegan Paul, 1954

M. Holloway, *Norman Douglas: a biography*, Secker & Warburg, 1976

M. Holroyd, *Hugh Kingsmill*, Heinemann, 1971

——, *Unreceived Opinions*, Heinemann, 1973

H. Holt and H. Pym (ed.), *A Very Private Diary: the diaries, letters and notebooks of Barbara Pym*, Macmillan, 1984

J. Hone, *The Life of George Moore*, Gollancz, 1936

R. Thurston Hopkins, *Rudyard Kipling: a character study*, Simpkin, Marshall, 1921

L. Hotson, *Mr W. H.*, Hart-Davis, 1964

L. Howard, *Herman Melville*, University of California Press, 1951

D. Hudson, *Lewis Carroll: an illustrated biography*, Constable, 1954

K. C. Hulme, *Undiscovered Country*, Little, Brown, 1966

H. J. Hunt, *Balzac's Comédie humaine*, Athlone Press, 1959

P. Hutchins, *James Joyce's World*, Methuen, 1957

H. Montgomery Hyde (ed.), *The Annotated Oscar Wilde*, Orbis, 1982

W. Irvine and P. Honan, *The Book, the Ring and the Poet: a biography of Robert Browning*, Bodley Head, 1975

C. Isherwood, *Christopher and his Kind*, Farrar, Straus & Giroux, 1976

R. R. James (ed.), *Chips: the diaries of Sir Henry Channon*, Weidenfeld & Nicolson, 1967

D. A. Jasen, *P. G. Wodehouse: a portrait of a master*, Mason & Lipscomb, 1974

E. H. Jones, *Mrs Humphry Ward*, Heinemann, 1973

P. Julian and J. Phillips, *Violet Trefusis*, Hamish Hamilton, 1976

J. Kaplan, *Mark Twain and his World*, Simon & Schuster, New York; Michael Joseph, London, 1974

B. Kellner, *Carl Van Vechten and the Irreverent Decades*, University of Oklahoma Press, 1968

J. and S. Kennaway, *The Kennaway Papers*, Jonathan Cape, 1981

J. Killham, *Tennyson and 'The Princess': reflections of an age*, Athlone Press, 1958

C. Klein, *Aline*, Harper & Row, 1979

P. Kolb (ed.), *Marcel Proust: selected letters (1880–1903)*, Collins, 1983

M. M. La Belle, *Alfred Jarry, Nihilism and the Theater of the Absurd*, New York University Press, 1980

C. Lansbury, *Elizabeth Gaskell: the novel of social crisis*, Elek, 1975

M. Laski, *George Eliot and her World*, Thames & Hudson, 1973

A. Latham, *Crazy Sundays: F. Scott Fitzgerald in Hollywood*, Viking Press, 1971

D. H. Laurence (ed.), *Bernard Shaw: collected letters, 1874–97* and *1898–1910*, Max Reinhardt, 2 vols, 1965 and 1972

R. Layman, *Shadow Man: the life of Dashiell Hammett*, Harcourt Brace Jovanovich, New York; Junction Books, London, 1981

J. Lees-Milne, *Harold Nicolson: a biography*, Chatto & Windus, 2 vols, 1980–1

J. Lehmann, *A Nest of Tigers: The Sitwells in their Times*, Macmillan, 1968

C. Lesley, *The Life of Noël Coward*, Jonathan Cape, 1976

M. Levey, *The Case of Walter Pater*, Thames & Hudson, 1978

A. Le Vot, *F. Scott Fitzgerald*, Julliard, 1979

R. W. B. Lewis, *Edith Wharton: a biography*, Constable, 1975

M. Lindsay, *The Burns Encyclopedia*, Hutchinson, 1959

P. Lisca, *John Steinbeck: nature and myth*, Thomas Y. Crowell, 1978

M. Llewelyn, *Jane Austen: a character study*, William Kimber, 1977

W. O. Lofts and D. J. Adley, *The World of Frank Richards*, Howard Baker, 1975

A. Loos, *A Girl Like I*, Viking Press, 1966

——, *Kiss Hollywood Goodbye*, Viking Press, New York; W. H. Allen, London, 1974

C. M. Lorenz, *Lorelei Two: my life with Conrad Aiken*, University of Georgia Press, 1983

H. R. Lottman, *Albert Camus: a biography*, Weidenfeld & Nicolson, 1979

J. T. Low, *Doctors, Devils, Saints and Sinners: a critical study of the major plays of James Bridie*, Ramsay Head Press, 1980

W. Lowrie, *Kierkegaard*, Oxford University Press, 1938

D. S. Luft, *Robert Musil and the Crisis of European Culture, 1880–1942*, University of California Press, 1980

E. C. Mack and W. H. G. Armytage, *Thomas Hughes*, Ernest Benn, 1953

B. McKenzie, *Mary McCarthy*, Twayne, 1966

N. and J. Mackenzie, *The Time Traveller: the life of H. G. Wells*, Weidenfeld & Nicolson, 1973

J. Maclaren-Ross, *Memoirs of the Forties*, Alan Ross, 1965

F. MacShane, *The Life and Work of Ford Madox Ford*, Routledge & Kegan Paul, 1965

D. Magarshack, *Dostoevsky: a life*, Secker & Warburg, 1962

——, *Pushkin*, Chapman & Hall, 1967

G. de Mallac, *Boris Pasternak*, Condor/Souvenir Press/University of Oklahoma Press, 1981

M. Mallowan, *Mallowan's Memoirs: the autobiography of Max Mallowan*, Collins, 1977

W. Mankowitz, *Mazepa: the lives, loves and legends of Adah Isaacs Menken*, Blond & Briggs, 1982

F. Marceau, *Balzac and his World*, W. H. Allen, 1967

R. B. Martin, *Tennyson: the unquiet heart*, Oxford University Press and Faber & Faber, 1983

A. Masters, *Rosa Lewis: an exceptional Edwardian*, Weidenfeld & Nicolson, 1977

B. Masters, *Now Barabbas was a Rotter: the extraordinary life of Marie Corelli*, Hamish Hamilton, 1978

F. O. Matthiessen, *Theodore Dreiser*, Sloane, New York; Methuen, London, 1951

R. Maugham, *Somerset and all the Maughams*, Longmans, Green and Heinemann, 1966

W. Somerset Maugham, *Ten Novels and their Authors*, Heinemann, 1954

A. Maurois, *Victor Hugo*, Jonathan Cape, 1956

K. May, *Aldous Huxley*, Elek, 1972

J. Meckier, *Aldous Huxley: satire and structure*, Chatto & Windus, 1969

M. Meisel, *Shaw and the 19th Century Theatre*, Oxford University Press, 1963

J. R. Mellow, *Charmed Circle: Gertrude Stein and company*, Praeger, New York; Phaidon, London, 1974

L. Melville, *William Makepeace Thackeray*, John Lane, 1909

S. Meredith, *George S. Kaufman*, Doubleday, New York; Allen & Unwin, London, 1974

M. Meyer, *Henrik Ibsen*, Hart-Davis, 3 vols, 1967–71

J. Meyers, *The Enemy: a biography of Wyndham Lewis*, Routledge & Kegan Paul, 1980

W. L. Miner, *The World of William Faulkner*, Duke University Press, 1952

Y. Mitchell, *Colette: a taste of life*, Weidenfeld & Nicolson, 1975

N. Mitchison, *You May Well Ask*, Gollancz, 1979

A. Mizener, *The Far Side of Paradise: a biography of F. Scott Fitzgerald*, Houghton Mifflin, Boston, 1951

——, *The Saddest Story: a biography of Ford Madox Ford*, World Publishing Co., New York; Bodley Head, London, 1971

H. T. Moore, *The Priest of Love: a life of D. H. Lawrence*, Farrar, Straus & Giroux, New York; Heinemann, London, 1974

J. B. Moore, *Maxwell Bodenheim*, Twayne, 1970

J. Morgan, *Agatha Christie: a biography*, Collins, 1984

T. Morgan, *Somerset Maugham*, Simon & Schuster, New York; Jonathan Cape, London, 1980

S. Morley, *A Talent to Amuse: a biography of Noël Coward*, Heinemann, 1969

——, *Tales from the Hollywood Raj*, Weidenfeld & Nicolson, 1983

T. C. Moser, *The Life in the Fiction of Ford Madox Ford*, Princeton University Press, 1980

A. Moss, *Jerome K. Jerome: his life and work*, Selwyn & Blount, 1929

E. Mottram and M. Bradbury (ed.), *The Penguin Companion to Literature – 3: United States*, Penguin, 1971

I. G. Mudge and M. Earl Sears, *A George Eliot Dictionary*, Routledge, 1924

——, *A Thackeray Dictionary*, Routledge, 1910

N. T. P. Murphy, *In Search of Blandings*, Murphy, 1981

G. Murray, *An Unfinished Autobiography*, Allen & Unwin, 1960

J. Northam, *Ibsen: a critical study*, Cambridge University Press, 1973

U. O'Connor, *Oliver St John Gogarty: a poet and his times*, Jonathan Cape, 1964

H. Orel (ed.), *Kipling: interviews and recollections*, Macmillan, 1983

L. Ormond, *George Du Maurier*, Routledge, 1969

R. Ormrod, *Una Troubridge: the friend of Radclyffe Hall*, Jonathan Cape, 1984

C. Osborne, *The Life and Crimes of Agatha Christie*, Collins, 1982

J. Osborne, *A Better Class of Person: an autobiography, 1929–1956*, Faber & Faber, 1981

G. D. Painter, *Marcel Proust: a biography*, Chatto & Windus, London; Little, Brown, Boston, 2 vols, 1959 and 1965

D. Panin, *The Notebooks of Sologdin*, Hutchinson, 1973

B. Patch, *Thirty Years with G.B.S.*, Gollancz, 1951

D. Patmore (ed.), *My Friends When Young: the memoirs of Brigit Patmore*, Heinemann, 1968

R. Peace, *Dostoyevsky*, Cambridge University Press, 1971

J. Pearson, *Façades: Edith, Osbert and Sacheverell Sitwell*, Macmillan, 1978

——, *The Life of Ian Fleming*, Jonathan Cape, 1966

M. Peters, *Bernard Shaw and the Actresses*, Doubleday, 1980

——, *Unquiet Soul: a biography of Charlotte Brontë*, Hodder & Stoughton, 1975

A. J. Philip and W. L. Gadd, *A Dickens Dictionary*, Simpkin Marshall, 1928 (2nd edn)

F. B. Pinion, *A D. H. Lawrence Companion*, Macmillan, 1978

A. Powell, *To Keep the Ball Rolling*, Heinemann, 4 vols, 1976–82

V. Powell, *The Constant Novelist: a study of Margaret Kennedy, 1896–1967*, Heinemann, 1983

C. A. Prance, *A Companion to Charles Lamb*, Mansell, 1983

J. B. Priestley, *Thomas Love Peacock*, Macmillan, 1927

V. S. Pritchett, *Balzac*, Chatto & Windus, 1973

D. Pryce-Jones, *Cyril Connolly*, Collins, 1983

P. Pullar, *Frank Harris*, Hamish Hamilton, 1975

F. Raphael, *Somerset Maugham and his World*, Thames & Hudson, 1976

G. N. Ray, *The Buried Life: a study of the relation between Thackeray's fiction and his personal history*, Royal Society of Literature and Oxford University Press, 1952

——, *H. G. Wells and Rebecca West*, Macmillan, 1974

R. Rees, *George Orwell: fugitive from the camp of victory*, Secker & Warburg, 1961

J. M. H. Reid (ed.), *The Concise Oxford Dictionary of French Literature*, Oxford University Press, 1976

D. Rein, *Edgar Allan Poe: the inner pattern*, Philosophical Library, New York; Peter Owen, London, 1960

M. S. Reynolds, *Hemingway's First War*, Princeton University Press, 1976

P. Richard, *La Bruyère et ses 'Caractères'*, Librairie Nizet, 1965

J. Richardson, *Colette*, Methuen, 1983

——, *Stendhal, a biography*, Gollancz, 1974

——, *Victor Hugo*, Gollancz, 1976

J. S. Robinson, *H. D.: the life and work of an American poet*, Houghton Mifflin, 1982

R. C. Rosen, *John Dos Passos: politics and the writer*, University of Nebraska Press, 1981

J. Rosenberg, *Dorothy Richardson: the genius they forgot*, Duckworth, 1973

T. Royle, *James and Jim: a biography of James Kennaway*, Mainstream, 1983

M. Sadleir, *Trollope: a commentary*, Constable, 1945 (rev. edn)

K. Sagar, *The Life of D. H. Lawrence*, Eyre Methuen, 1980

E. Salter, *The Last Years of a Rebel: a memoir of Edith Sitwell*, Bodley Head, 1967

W. Sansom, *Proust and His World*, Thames & Hudson, 1973

M. Sarde, *Colette*, Michael Joseph, 1981

M. Schorer, *Sinclair Lewis*, University of Minnesota Press, 1963

A. T. Schwab, *James Gibbons Huneker*, Stanford University Press, 1963

D. R. Schwarz, *Disraeli's Fiction*, Macmillan, 1979

M. Secrest, *Between Me and Life: a biography of Romaine Brooks*, Macdonald & Janes, 1976

M. Seymour-Smith, *Robert Graves: his life*, Hutchinson, 1982

J. G. Sharps, *Mrs Gaskell's Observation and Invention*, Linden Press, 1970

L. Sheaffer, *O'Neill, Son and Playwright*, Little, Brown, 1968

E. A. Sheppard, *Henry James and The Turn of the Screw*, Auckland University Press and Oxford University Press, 1974

N. Sherry, *Conrad's Eastern World*, Cambridge University Press, 1966

G. Simenon, *Letters to my Mother*, Hamish Hamilton, 1976

D. Sinclair, *Edgar Allan Poe*, Dent, 1977

E. Simpson, *Poets in their Youth*, Random House, New York; Faber & Faber, London, 1982

M. Slater, *Dickens and Women*, Dent, 1983

C. B. Smith, *Rose Macaulay*, Collins, 1972

J. A. Smith, *John Buchan: a biography*, Hart-Davis, 1965

D. W. Smithers, *Jane Austen in Kent*, Hurtwood, 1981

P. Snow, *Stranger and Brother: a portrait of C. P. Snow*, Macmillan, 1982

R. Soucy, *Fascist Intellectual: Drieu La Rochelle*, University of California Press, 1979

E. Sprigge, *The Life of Ivy Compton-Burnett*, Gollancz, 1973

H. Spurling, *Secrets of a Woman's Heart: the later life of Ivy Compton-Burnett*, Hodder & Stoughton, 1984

F. Steegmuller (ed.), *The letters of Gustave Flaubert, 1857–1880*, Harvard University Press, 1982

N. H. Steiner, *A Closer Look at Ariel: a memory of Sylvia Plath*, Harper's Magazine Press, 1973

M. Strickland, *Angela Thirkell: portrait of a lady novelist*, Duckworth, 1977

I. Strong and L. Osborne, *Memories of Valima*, Scribner's, 1903

D. Stuart, *Dear Duchess: Millicent, Duchess of Sutherland, 1867–1955*, Gollancz, 1982

J. Sutherland, *Best Sellers*, Routledge & Kegan Paul, 1981

C. Sykes, *Evelyn Waugh*, Collins, 1975

J. Symons, *The Tell-Tale Heart: the life and works of Edgar Allan Poe*, Faber & Faber, 1978

T. Tanner, *City of Words: American fiction 1950–1970*, Harper & Row, New York; Jonathan Cape, London, 1971

R. Tennant, *Joseph Conrad*, Sheldon Press, 1981

B. Thomas, *King Cohn: the life and times of Harry Cohn*, Putnam, New York; Barrie & Rockliff, London, 1967

A. Thorlby (ed.), *The Penguin Companion to Literature – 2: European*, Penguin, 1969

J. Thurman, *Isak Dinesen: the life of Karen Blixen*, Weidenfeld & Nicolson, 1982

A. Thwaite, *Edmund Gosse*, Secker & Warburg, 1984

——, *Waiting for the Party: the life of Frances Hodgson Burnett*, Secker & Warburg, 1974

E. W. F. Tomlin (ed.), *Charles Dickens 1812–1870: a centenary volume*, Weidenfeld & Nicolson, 1969

M. Trevor, *The Arnolds: Thomas Arnold and his family*, Bodley Head, 1973

H. Troyat, *Pushkin*, Paris, 1970

——, *Tolstoy*, Fayard, 1967

A. Turnbull, *Scott Fitzgerald*, Scribner's, New York; Bodley Head, London, 1962

——, *Thomas Wolfe*, Scribner's, New York; Bodley Head, London, 1968

H. Van Thal, *Eliza Lynn Linton*, Allen & Unwin, 1979

B. Vesey-Fitzgerald, *Gypsy Borrow*, Dobson, 1953

S. Townsend Warner, *T. H. White: a biography*, Jonathan Cape and Chatto & Windus, 1967

J. Watney, *Mervyn Peake*, Michael Joseph, 1976

F. Watson, *Robert Smith Surtees: a critical study*, Harrap, 1933

C. Watts and L. Davies, *Cunninghame Graham*, Cambridge University Press, 1979

A. Waugh, *My Brother Evelyn and Other Profiles*, Cassell, 1967

——, *The Best Wine Last: an autobiography through the years 1939–1969*, W. H. Allen, 1978

D. Weeks, *Corvo*, Michael Joseph, 1971

S. Weintraub, *Journey to Heartbreak: Bernard Shaw 1914–18*, Routledge & Kegan Paul, 1973

F. West, *Gilbert Murray: a life*, Croom Helm, 1984

A. Whitmarsh, *Simone de Beauvoir and the Limits of Commitment*, Cambridge University Press, 1981

B. Colton Williams, *George Eliot*, Macmillan, 1936

C. B. Williams, *Henry Wadsworth Longfellow*, Twayne, 1964

D. Williams, *Genesis and Exodus: a portrait of the Benson Family*, Hamish Hamilton, 1979

——, *George Meredith: his life and lost love*, Hamish Hamilton, 1977

A. Wilson, *Émile Zola: an introductory study of his novels*, Secker & Warburg, 1952

——, *The Strange Ride of Rudyard Kipling: his life and works*, Secker & Warburg, 1977

R. Winston, *Thomas Mann: the making of an artist, 1875–1911*, Constable, 1982

G. Woodcock, *Dawn and the Darkest Hour: a study of Aldous Huxley*, Faber & Faber, 1972

T. Wright, *The Life of Walter Pater*, Putnam, 1907

J. Brett Young, *Francis Brett Young*, Heinemann, 1963

G. J. Zytaruk and J. T. Boulton, *The Letters of D. H. Lawrence*, vol. 2, Cambridge University Press, 1982

THE CAST: AN INDEX

The following is a list of persons appearing in this book, their names being followed by the entries under which they are to be found. It is *not* a list of identifications, but simply of people mentioned in the text. In a number of instances, the entries make it clear that the persons listed are not the models for the characters with which they have been popularly identified.

THE 'LAST' NAZI

THE LIFE AND TIMES OF

DR JOSEPH MENGELE

GERALD ASTOR

THE ANGEL OF DEATH . . .

Dr Joseph Mengele, the camp doctor at Auschwitz, was personally responsible for the murder of nearly 400,000 people, and for the torture of hundreds more as part of his 'scientific' experiments.

Gerald Astor traces Mengele's roots and looks at the forces that turned him into a mass murderer and torturer. THE 'LAST' NAZI is a towering indictment of Mengele the embodiment of evil and of the system that spawned him.

'Gerald Astor's THE 'LAST' NAZI is at once chastening and engaging. Not because it documents an evil man's freedom from contrition and conscience but because it explains how many "ordinary" people shielded and sustained the monster to the grave and beyond.'
Daily Mail

BIOGRAPHY   0 7221 1296 3   £3.50

The *true* story of the Cannon Film Empire

HOLLYWOOD A GO-GO

ANDREW YULE

Hollywood film moguls Yoram Globus and Menahem Golan of the Cannon Film Group are a phenomenon of 80s enterprise. With next to no capital and by wheeling and dealing their way up the film industry hierarchy, they have established the Cannon Group as a massive, international film empire.

But the downside of this glittering success story is only now being told. The list of films produced by Cannon includes some of the shoddiest fare ever foisted on the public and most have been box-office disasters. Their accounting methods are under investigation and their sources of finance uncertain. How then have they inspired such confidence in the business world?

In this fascinating and hard-hitting account, Andrew Yule blows the lid off the Cannon go-go boys and provides a unique insight into the more buccaneering aspects of modern entrepreneurial practice.

0 7221 9389 0   NON-FICTION   £3.50

As Time Goes By

The Life of Ingrid Bergman

LAURENCE LEAMER

In a career that spanned forty years, Ingrid Bergman brought her astonishing screen presence to star in a string of classics – *Casablanca*, *Joan of Arc*, *For Whom the Bell Tolls*, *Notorious*. She was adored for her transcendent beauty, her devotion to her family, her vulnerability.

Yet, of all Ingrid Bergman's stunning roles, none was as dramatic as her own life. Behind her idealised Hollywood image was a passionate and daring woman who craved excitement and adventure, a woman who had many affairs, a woman who followed her heart into the biggest celebrity scandal in post-war film history.

AS TIME GOES BY is the riveting and sometimes shocking story of a woman of fierce ambition and strong desires, a story of love and lust, of public image and private truth.

'At once chilling and fascinating. No film of Ingrid's will look quite the same again' Sheridan Morley

0 7221 5493 3   BIOGRAPHY £3.95

A selection of bestsellers from SPHERE

FICTION

A TASTE FOR DEATH	P. D. James	£3.50 ☐
THE PRINCESS OF POOR STREET	Emma Blair	£2.99 ☐
WANDERLUST	Danielle Steel	£3.50 ☐
LADY OF HAY	Barbara Erskine	£3.95 ☐
BIRTHRIGHT	Joseph Amiel	£3.50 ☐

FILM AND TV TIE-IN

BLACK FOREST CLINIC	Peter Heim	£2.99 ☐
INTIMATE CONTACT	Jacqueline Osborne	£2.50 ☐
BEST OF BRITISH	Maurice Sellar	£8.95 ☐
SEX WITH PAULA YATES	Paula Yates	£2.95 ☐
RAW DEAL	Walter Wager	£2.50 ☐

NON-FICTION

ALEX THROUGH THE LOOKING GLASS	Alex Higgins with Tony Francis	£2.99 ☐
NEXT TO A LETTER FROM HOME: THE GLENN MILLER STORY	Geoffrey Butcher	£4.99 ☐
AS TIME GOES BY: THE LIFE OF INGRID BERGMAN	Laurence Leamer	£3.95 ☐
BOTHAM	Don Mosey	£3.50 ☐
SOLDIERS	John Keegan & Richard Holmes	£5.95 ☐

All Sphere books are available at your local bookshop or newsagent, or can be ordered direct from the publisher. Just tick the titles you want and fill in the form below.

Name _____

Address _____

_____

Write to Sphere Books, Cash Sales Department, P.O. Box 11, Falmouth, Cornwall TR10 9EN

Please enclose a cheque or postal order to the value of the cover price plus:

UK: 60p for the first book, 25p for the second book and 15p for each additional book ordered to a maximum charge of £1.90.

OVERSEAS & EIRE: £1.25 for the first book, 75p for the second book and 28p for each subsequent title ordered.

BFPO: 60p for the first book, 25p for the second book plus 15p per copy for the next 7 books, thereafter 9p per book.

Sphere Books reserve the right to show new retail prices on covers which may differ from those previously advertised in the text elsewhere, and to increase postal rates in accordance with the P.O.